Schriften des
Zentrum für Europäische Integrationsforschung
Center for European Integration Studies
der Rheinischen Friedrich-Wilhelms-Universität Bonn

Edited by
Prof. Dr. Ludger Kühnhardt

Volume 83

Michael Amoah Awuah

Energy Regionalism in ECOWAS and the EU

A Comparative and Polycentric Governance Study

Nomos

Gedruckt mit der Genehmigung der Philosophischen Fakultät der Rheinischen Friedrich-Wilhelms-Universität Bonn

The Deutsche Nationalbibliothek lists this publication in the Deutsche Nationalbibliografie; detailed bibliographic data are available on the Internet at http://dnb.d-nb.de

a.t..: Bonn, Univ., Diss., 2020

ISBN 978-3-8487-7893-5 (Print)
978-3-7489-2294-0 (ePDF)

British Library Cataloguing-in-Publication Data
A catalogue record for this book is available from the British Library.

ISBN 978-3-8487-7893-5 (Print)
978-3-7489-2294-0 (ePDF)

Library of Congress Cataloging-in-Publication Data
Awuah, Michael Amoah
Energy Regionalism in ECOWAS and the EU
A Comparative and Polycentric Governance Study
Michael Amoah Awuah
534 pp.
Includes bibliographic references.

ISBN 978-3-8487-7893-5 (Print)
978-3-7489-2294-0 (ePDF)

Onlineversion
Nomos eLibrary

1st Edition 2021

To my wise and visionary mother, Joana Juliet Araba Tswinto Adoley Appiah. Your selflessness in nurturing me has made me the man I have become. I am eternally grateful.
To my late father, Joseph Oliver Baffour Awuah, who always encouraged me by saying – "never stop learning".

Preface and Acknowledgements

The Faculty of Philosophy of the Rheinische-Friedrich-Wilhelms-Universität Bonn accepted this thesis as a dissertation in December 2020. It captures regional energy processes that are yet to be rolled out especially by 2021 onwards.

First, I am ultimately grateful to God for giving me life and strengthening me throughout this onerous but inspiring intellectual journey. I proclaim that this work is *For the Greater Glory of God – Ad Maiorem Dei Gloriam (AMDG)*. Secondly, my sincerest and profoundest gratitude go to my *Doktorvater, Prof. Dr. Ludger Kühnhardt*, who took keen interest in me and has guided me since my Master studies. I remember with fond memories all the encounters and stimulating discussions, we had on the research work. They were filled with excellent suggestions and comments. The entire supervision of the thesis was undertaken with competent analytical guidance and diligence. I am also deeply grateful for his patience and all the opportunities he made available to me. I would also like to thank *Prof. Dr. Xuewu Gu* for accepting to be my second supervisor, and the rest of the doctoral committee, *Prof. Dr. Tilman Mayer* (Chair) and *Prof. Dr. Wolfram Hilz*.

My thanks also go to my dear sister *Genevieve*, who painstakingly dedicated herself to look through and edit this work for those things that escaped me during my scientific immersion and for her company. I am indebted to *Maame Afua Senti* for granting me the opportunity to experience first-hand what friendship, solidarity and support really is.

Finally, my greatest thanks go to my mother, *Joana Juliet Appiah* and my siblings *Akos*, *Kwame*, *Gorman* and *Esi Ackom* without their loving backing I could not have come this far.

This doctoral work is offered in thanksgiving to Almighty God and in gratitude for the intercession of Our Lady of Guadalupe, St. Albert the Great, St. Thomas More, St. Pio of Pietrelcina and especially St. Thérèse of Lisieux, whose assistance from her place in heaven made what was impossible, possible. Little Flower pray for us.

Bonn, May 2021 *Michael Amoah Awuah*

Table of Contents

List of Figures

List of Tables

List of Maps

List of Abbreviations

ABN	*Autorité du Bassin du Niger*
ACER	*Agency for the Cooperation of Energy Regulators*
ACP	*Africa, the Caribbean, and Pacific countries*
ADR	*Arbitration and Dispute Resolutions*
AEA	*Association des Etudiants Africains*
AEEP	*Africa-EU Energy Partnership*
AfCFTA	*African Union's Continental Free Trade Area*
AGED	*Association Générale des Etudiants de Dakar*
AOF	*Afrique Occidentale Française*
ARE	*Agência de Regulação Económica*
ASEAN	*Association of Southeast Asian Nations*
AU	*African Union*
BDEW	*German Association of Energy and Water Industries*
BP	*British Petroleum*
BCM	*Billion Cubic Meters of Natural Gas*
CCJA	*Common Court of Justice and Arbitration*
CCUS	*Carbon Capture Utilization and Storage*
CEB	*Communauté Électricité du Benin*
CEE	*Central and Eastern Europe*
CEER	*Council of European Energy Regulators*
CEGB	*Central Electricity Generating Board*
CIE	*Cote d'Ivoire Energies*
CIS	*Combined IAD-SES*
CLSG	*Côte d'Ivoire-Liberia-Sierra Leone-Guinea*
COMELEC	*Comité Maghrébin de l'Electricité*
COP	*Conference of the Parties*
CPR	*Common Pool Resource*
DER	*Distributed Energy Resource*
EAGB	*Guinea-Bissau Electricity and Water Corporation*
EAPP	*East African Power Pool*
EBID	*ECOWAS Bank for Investment and Development*

ECN	*Electricity Corporation of Nigeria*
ECOWAS	*Economic Community of West African States*
ECREEE	*ECOWAS Centre for Renewable Energy and Energy Efficiency*
ECSC	*European Coal and Steel Community*
EDC	*European Defence Community*
EDF	*Electricite de France*
EEC	*European Economic Community*
EEEP	*ECOWAS Energy Efficiency Policy*
EFSI	*European Fund for Strategic Investments*
EFTA	*European Free Trade Association*
EIB	*European Investment Bank*
EITI	*Extractive Industries Transparency Initiative*
ELECTRA	*Empresa de Electricidad e Agua*
ENACOL	*National Fuel Company of Cape Verde*
ENI	*Ente Nazionale Idrocarburi*
ENTSO	*European Network of Transmission System Operators*
ENTSO-E	*European Network of Transmission System Operators-Electricity*
ENTSO-G	*European Network of Transmission System Operators- Gas*
ERCA	*ECOWAS Regional Competition Authority*
EREP	*ECOWAS Regional Policy for Renewable Energy*
ERERA	*ECOWAS Regional Electricity Regulatory Authority*
ERGEG	*European Regulators' Group for Electricity and Gas*
EU	*European Union*
EU DSO	*European Union Distribution System Operators*
EURATOM	*European Atomic Energy Community*
FWA	*French West Africa*
FSRU	*Floating Storage Regasification Unit*
GAEC	*Ghana Atomic Energy Commission*
GATT	*General Agreement on Tariffs and Trade*
GDF	*Gaz de France*
GDP	*Gross domestic product*
GEA	*Global Energy Assessment*
GHG	*Greenhouse Gases*
GIE	*Gas Infrastructure Europe*
GW	*Gigawatts (one billion watts)*

IAD	*Institutional Analysis and Development*
IAEA	*International Atomic Energy Agency*
ICA	*Infrastructure Consortium for Africa*
ICESP	*Integrated Community Energy System Provider*
ICES	*Integrated Community Energy System*
ICSID	*International Centre for the Settlement of Investment Disputes*
IEA	*International Energy Agency*
IIASA	*International Institute for Applied Systems Analysis*
IMF	*International Monetary Fund*
IOT	*internet of things*
IPCC	*Intergovernmental Panel on Climate Change*
IPE	*International Political Economy*
LNG	*Liquefied Natural Gas*
LPG	*Liquefied Petroleum Gas*
MAS	*Mission d'Amenagement du Senegal*
MEND	*Movement for the Emancipation of the Niger-Delta*
MOSOP	*Movement for the Survival of Ogoni People*
MW	*Megawatts (one million watts)*
MTPA	*Million Tonnes Per Annum of LNG*
MMSCFD	*Million Standard Cubic Feet per Day*
NAFTA	*North American Free Trade Agreement*
NCBWA	*National Congress of British West Africa*
NEDECO	*Netherlands Engineering Consultants*
NESCO	*Nigeria Electricity Supply Company*
NGC	*Nigeria Gas Company*
NIASES	*New Institutional Analysis of Social-Ecological Systems*
NIEO	*New International Economic Order*
NNPC	*Nigerian National Petroleum Corporation*
OECD	*Organisation for Economic Coordination and Development*
OEEC	*Organization for European Economic Cooperation*
OHADA	*Organization for the Harmonization of Business Law in African*
OLADE	*Organización Latinoamericana de Energía*
OMVG	*Organisation pour la mise en valeur du fleuve Gambie /Gambia River Basin Organization*
OMVS	*Organisation pour la mise en valeur du fleuve Sénégal/ Senegal River Basin Organization*

OPEC	Organization of the Petroleum Exporting Countries
PAIGC	African Party for the Independence of Guinea-Bissau and Cape Verde
PAICV	African Party for the Independence of Cape Verde
PAYG	Pay-as-you-go
PEAC	Pool Energétique d'Afrique Centrale
PV	Photovoltaic
PWD	Public Works Department
RWE	Rhenish-Westphalian Electric
SAPP	Southern African Power Pool
SES	Socio-Ecological Systems
SETS	Social-Ecological-Technical System
SOMAIR	Société des Mines de l'Aïr
SONICHAR	Société Nigérienne du Charbon Anou Araren
SSA	Sub-Saharan Africa
TAGP	Trans-ASEAN Gas Pipeline
TEN-E	Trans-European Networks for Energy
TFEU	Treaty on the Functioning of the European Union
TOR	Tema Oil Refinery
UCTE	Union for the Coordination of the Transmission of Electricity
UCPTE	Union for the Coordination of Production and Transmission of Electricity
UHEA	Union Hydro-Electrique Africaine
UN	United Nations
UNCITRAL	United Nations Commission of International Trade Law
UNDESA	United Nations Department for Economic and Social Affairs
UNECA/ECA	United Nations Economic Commission for Africa
UNFCCC	United Nations Framework Convention on Climate Change
USAID	United States Agency for International Development
USGS	US Geological Survey
VALCO	Volta Aluminium Company
VRA	Volta River Authority
W-AELG	West African Energy Leaders Group
WAGP	West African Gas Pipeline
WAGPA	West African Gas Pipeline Authority
WAGS	West African Grid System
WAINPG	West African Integrated Nuclear Power Group

WANS	*West African National Secretariat*
WAPP	*West African Power Pool*
WAPCo	*West African Gas Pipeline Company Limited*
WASU	*West African Students' Union*
WATM	*West African Transform Margin*
WERPO	*Wave Electricity Renewable Power Ocean*

Chapter 1

Introduction

Energy is vital for today's modern-day existence. It is the ultimate enabler, without energy access in the twenty-first century and the future, nations and world regions would remain poor and destitute. Access to modern energy anywhere particularly in West Africa[1] is intrinsically linked with improvements in the quality of life. Vaclav Smil expresses the importance of energy in society in a more direct way, "energy is the only universal currency where one of its many forms must be transformed to get anything done."[2] Irrespective of the pivotal status of energy for communities, states and regions, as an agenda prioritised by global institutions, energy and its universal access has only emerged fairly recently.[3]

In the Millennium Development Goals[4] (MDGs) adopted in 2000 during the era of the UN Secretary-General Kofi Annan as a compact between rich and poor countries in an attempt to solve global poverty, disease, education and gender disparities, energy as a priority was clearly omitted. However, in the more inclusive and comprehensive Sustainable Development Goals (SDGs) which replaced the MDGs in September 2015 and is relatively more applicable generally to all the nations of the world, 'access to affordable, reliable, sustainable modern energy services for all' features energy more prominently in its seventh goal.[5] Increasingly, the problem of energy intertwines with the problem of climate change. Many scientists

---

1 Unless stated otherwise, the terms 'West Africa' and 'ECOWAS' will be used interchangeably in the dissertation.

2 Vaclav Smil, *Energy and Civilization : A History* (Cambridge, Massachusetts: The MIT Press, 2017), p. 1.

3 Richard Ponzio and Arunabha Ghosh, *Human Development and Global Institutions: Evolution, Impact, Reform* (London and New York: Routledge, 2016).

4 The Millennium Development Goals were eight goals adopted by the UN. It was perceived as mainly applicable to poor nations however the SDGs an inclusive and comprehensive plan is seen as a means to deal with the many global challenges faced by both rich and poor countries.

5 Francesco Fuso Nerini and others, 'Mapping Synergies and Trade-Offs between Energy and the Sustainable Development Goals', *Nature Energy*, 3.1 (2018), 10–15 <https://doi.org/10.1038/s41560-017-0036-5>; Laurence L. Delina, 'The Politics of Energy and Sustainable Development in Sub-Saharan Africa', in *The Oxford Hand-*

believe that of the many human activities that produce greenhouse gases (GHG), the energy sector contributes the largest share (about 60 %) of anthropogenic emissions.

Efforts to slowdown the pace of global warming has placed the governance of energy systems and its connections to the ecology at the forefront of numerous global initiatives and agreements. The success of the agreement reached at the 21st Conference of the Parties of the UNFCCC (COP 21), held in Paris in December 2015 resulted in skewing energy decisions made at all levels (that is, local, national, regional and international) to be based on the imperative of addressing climate change. Hence, a way forward that affects the global mix of energy supplies and services in addition to its governance at all levels.

In other segments of the global community, institutions with global reach such as some religious organisations have sought to highlight increased attention on the ecology and the detrimental effects of human activity that includes energy use.[6] For instance, Pope Francis in an influential encyclical letter, *Laudato Si – On Care for Our Common Home*[7], published on the eve of COP 21 and not specifically addressed to the Catholic Church alone but to all people more generally, reemphasises cooperation as a potent approach to solving the imminent climate and energy challenges being faced in the world. Furthermore, he emphasises the deficiencies in social justice emanating out of the Western use of energy resulting in the poorest people in the world bearing the brunt of this cost as well as the abuse of the environment. This has literally put the debate on energy governance and the twin issue of the climate change problem into a moral framework making energy use an ethical issue with ripple effects on human (particularly the most vulnerable) and non-human inhabitants (especially our biodiversity) in the world.[8]

---

book of Energy Politics, ed. by Kathleen J. Hancock and Juliann Allison (Oxford and New York: Oxford University Press, 2019), pp. 1–26.

6 Partha Dasgupta and Veerabhadran Ramanathan, 'Pursuit of the Common Good', *Science* (Washington DC, September 2014), 1457–58 <https://doi.org/10.1126/science.1259406>; Jonathan Chaplin, 'The Global Greening of Religion', *Palgrave Communications*, 2 (2016) <https://doi.org/10.1057/palcomms.2016.47>.

7 Pope Francis, 'Laudato Si'- On Care for Our Common Home' (Vatican City: Libreria Editrice Vaticana, 2015).

8 Hilary Marlow, 'Theology of Energy / Laudato Si': Pope Francis' Encyclical on the Environment and Human Ecology' (Cambridge, UK: Energy Transitions Research, University of Cambridge, 2016); Jonathan Chaplin, 'From Inspiration to Implementation: Laudato Si' , Public Theology and the Demands of Energy Policy', in *In Search of Good Energy Policy*, ed. by Marc Ozawa and others (Cambridge:

Today energy governance cannot be separated from climate governance. In fact, analysts claim that getting energy policy right is equal to getting climate policy right since the vast amounts of carbon emissions are linked to energy use.[9] This point further advances the argument that, shifts in sovereignty to larger geographical units, in other words the movement of national sovereignty to supranational organisations across many areas of governance at the regional level is needed to set into motion an effective transformation of the energy space since global energy governance is hard to achieve.[10] This leads to other options beyond the *every state for itself* approach, which seeks to advance conflict and destructive competition in energy matters, rather than a win-win cooperative approach within the context of collective action. A favourable possibility is to consider the (international) regional level as the fulcrum for developing energy policy for effective energy governance.

In this regard, the need for modernised infrastructure and sustainable energy solutions have become key priorities as well in the African Union (AU) Agenda 2063 aimed at transforming the African continent generally (and its constituent parts inclusive of the West African region). This fifty-year action plan seeks to accelerate the provision of energy and infrastructure needs widely across the continent in a series of five ten-year plans.[11] Therefore a possible realisation of the SDGs (especially Goal 7) by the year 2030 would have an overlap with the second (that is, 2023–2033) in the series of the five ten-year plans thereby establishing a linkage between the fulfilment of the AU Agenda 2063 and the UNs SDGs together particularly when the goals are realised.[12]

Cambridge University Press, 2019), pp. 257–72 <https://doi.org/10.1017/9781108639439.018>.

9 Ivan Scrase and Gordon MacKerron, *Energy for the Future: A New Agenda* (Basingstoke: Palgrave Macmillan, 2009), LXVI.

10 Anthony G. Patt, 'Effective Regional Energy Governance-Not Global Environmental Governance-Is What We Need Right Now for Climate Change', *Global Environmental Change*, 20.1 (2010), 33–35 <https://doi.org/10.1016/j.gloenvcha.2009.09.006>.

11 African Union, 'Agenda2063: Infrastructure and Energy Initiatives | African Union', 2019 <https://au.int/en/videos/20190301/agenda2063-infrastructure-and-energy-initiatives> [accessed 25 November 2019].

12 African Union Commission, 'Agenda 2063: The Africa We Want THE VOICES OF THE AFRICAN PEOPLE', *Final Edition*, 2015, 1–24 <http://www.un.org/en/africa/osaa/pdf/au/agenda2063.pdf>; Fuso Nerini and others.

Relatively, regional cooperation among states within a region may be easy compared to across regions.[13] A limited number of countries may partake in a negotiation process; these states may share common historical experiences that may require furtherance or curtailment depending on whether they are good or bad.[14] Conceivably, it fosters economies of scale in the exploitation and development of resources and infrastructure, like that of energy, as well as the strengthening of prior structures of regionalism or regional integration.[15] The scope of regional policy on energy tends to reflect how far a broader system of cooperation is established. Thus, resulting in the function of the readiness or reluctance of states to pool sovereignty.[16]

In the case of West Africa, perhaps the most important developments have taken place in the context of ECOWAS through the West African Power Pool, West African Gas Pipeline, ECOWAS Centre for Renewable Energy and Energy Efficiency and the ECOWAS Regional Electricity Regulatory Authority in a regime that seeks to foster cooperation and integration among the countries of the Western African region. The ECOWAS region has been cooperating on energy policy issues for more than 35 years, building on an initial agreement for sharing power during supply emergencies to a series of agreements to develop regional energy infrastructure namely interconnected grids, pipelines and joint megaprojects as well as foster energy investments in national energy projects. This has been executed through the implementation of a series of ambitious plans to develop an integrated energy infrastructures programme and a common energy market.

1.1 West Africa in the Context of Global Energy

West Africa (and Africa more generally) is not prioritised in global energy discussions but this is gradually changing. The reason behind this dramatic shift in perspective is demographics. If one broadly looks at Africa today, it has a population, which is smaller than China and India, but in the next couple of years, starting from 2023, Africa would have overtaken China to be the most

13 Scrase and MacKerron, LXVI, pp. 27–33.
14 Scrase and MacKerron, LXVI, pp. 27–33.
15 Scrase and MacKerron, LXVI, pp. 27–33.
16 Scrase and MacKerron, LXVI, pp. 27–33.

Figure 1. 1 Africa's Population by 2040

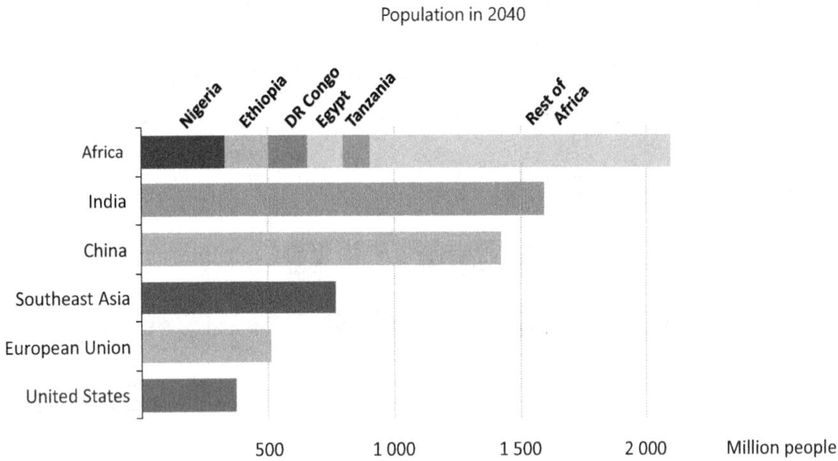

Note: Demographic increases by 800 million making Africa home to 2 billion people. Three quarters of growth will be in cities – the largest urbanisation scale ever.

Source: International Energy Agency (IEA), 'Presentation of the Africa Energy Outlook 2019' (Paris: International Energy Agency, 2019)

populous region in the world (with West Africa accounting for thirty percent of this increasing demography). Since 1950, the population in West Africa has increased from 73 million people to 367 million by 2015 and 395.5 million in 2019 accounting for about a five-fold increase in population making the region the fastest growing of any of the world's regions including those in Africa.[17] By 2040, the total population of Africa will be more than two billion people. About 600 million people from 2019 to 2040 will be born or move to cities in Africa. Simply put this would account for the largest urbanisation process ever witnessed in history. To represent the scalar magnitude of this transitory phenomenon and urbanisation, China during the period of its big economic boom (in the 1990s and by 2010) witnessed about 300 million people being born or moving to

17 UNDESA, 'World Population Prospects: The 2015 Revision' (New York: United Nations, Department of Economic and Social Affairs, Population Division, 2015) <http://esa.un.org/ unpd/wpp/dataquery.>; UNDESA, 'Population of West Africa (2018)' <http://www.worldometers.info/world-population/western-africa-population/>.

cities.[18] Essentially, this rapid urbanisation has implications for everything including politics, the economy and obviously energy.

Figure 1. 2 A Major Shift towards a Modern and Efficient Energy Mix

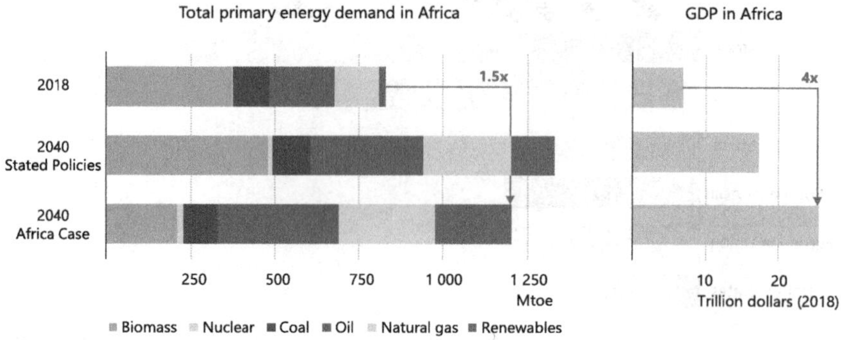

Note: Africa can fuel a continental economy 4-times larger than today with only 50 % more energy, driven by a major shift towards modern energy sources like renewables, nuclear, natural gas and efficiency gains

Source: International Energy Agency (IEA), 'Presentation of the Africa Energy Outlook 2019'

In terms of the growth potential in energy resources, starting with oil demand, the IEA projects that from 2018–2040 after India, Africa would become the second largest growth market.[19] This is based on the following reasons; Beginning with transportation, 15 people out of 1000 persons living on the continent today have a car while most of the cars are inefficient roughly similar to the cars that were being sold in Europe 15 years ago. This means most cars being used in Africa are half as efficient as the cars being used in the EU today. Hence, transportation accounts for a huge growth potential in Africa's oil demand both currently and in the future as it witnesses a growing middle class through rapid economic growth. Additionally, although the Africa region accounts for significant crude oil

18 International Energy Agency (IEA), 'Total Population by Region, China, Africa, India, 2018 and Growth to 2040' (Paris: IEA, 2019) <www.iea.org/data-and-statistics/charts/total-population-by-region-china-africa-india-2018-and-growth-to-2040>.

19 International Energy Agency, *World Energy Outlook 2019* (Paris: OECD Publishing, 2019) <https://doi.org/https://doi.org/10.1787/d87ceb30-en>; International Energy Agency (IEA), 'Africa Energy Outlook 2019', in *World Energy Outlook Special Report* (Paris: OECD Publishing, 2019) <https://doi.org/10.1787/g2120ab250-en>.

exports it underperforms in refining capacity of crude oil, this combined makes the region the world leader in the importation of refined products. In 2018, the continental average utilisation rate of refineries was 58 %, West Africa accounted for 25 % with Nigeria barely accounting for 9 %.[20]

The second growth potential lies in the transition of traditional bioenergy (such as charcoal and firewood use) into electricity generation and advanced biofuels, in addition to, a complete transition from the use of bioenergy to liquefied petroleum gas (LPG) in household cooking. Strictly speaking, most households in Africa still rely on the traditional use of biomass for cooking. In sub-Saharan Africa, bioenergy contributed almost 60 % of primary energy use in 2018. Power generation from bioenergy is generally higher in comparison to gas-fired generation and hydropower. It is estimated that West Africa has the potential to produce 100 Mt per year of agricultural residue useful for conversion into electricity or advanced biofuels that include ethanol and bio-butanol.[21] Through a mix of policy, investment, behavioural change and technology adoption many more people would be relying more on LPG because it is cleaner and safer for women and children who are more exposed to hazardous contaminants in the use of biomass. Much headway has been evident in West Africa especially in Côte d'Ivoire and Ghana that have promoted liquefied petroleum gas (LPG).[22] Across Africa today, 90 million people use LPG with an estimated growth to 400 million people.[23] This explains why growth in African demand will have an impact on global energy trends.

---

20 International Energy Agency (IEA), 'Africa Energy Outlook 2019', p. 69.

21 International Energy Agency (IEA), 'Africa Energy Outlook 2019', p. 74.

22 International Energy Agency (IEA), p. 37.

23 International Energy Agency, 'Energy Access Outlook 2017' (Paris, 2017) <https://doi.org/10.1787/9789264285569-en>.

Figure 1. 3 Africa's Natural Gas Turning Point

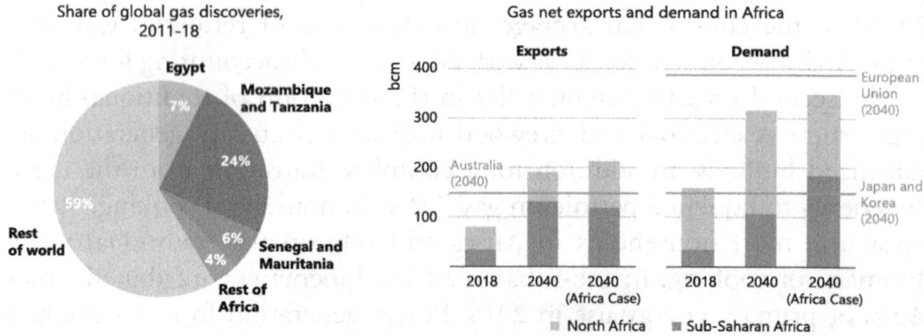

Note: Recent discoveries across Africa fits well with the push towards industrial growth and reliable supply of electricity, however developing infrastructure requires strong policy support

Source: International Energy Agency (IEA), 'Presentation of the Africa Energy Outlook 2019'

In the area of natural gas demand, broadly Africa's role is already patent. Over the past 10 years 40 percent of global natural gas discoveries were in Africa mainly in North Africa (Egypt), West Africa (Senegal and Ghana), East Africa (Tanzania), Southern Africa (Mozambique and South Africa). There is huge expectation that this gas find would be utilised domestically on the continent with limited quantities being exported outside because of these urbanising cities that need to be built using cement, steel and electricity. All these factors of production require energy to feed this economic and developmental growth at the same time it raises a policy challenge which albeit serves as an opportunity.

The renewables sector presents an ultimate growth potential but would take time to materialise. Even though 850 million people globally lack access to electricity, a vast majority reside in Africa particularly in SSA.[24] The situation is getting better but by 2030, about 670 million people would still not have access to electricity globally.[25] To reverse this access deficiency trend, the key lever is renewable energy. To exemplify this fact, as at 2019 the total share of installed solar capacity in Africa was five gigawatts, this is equal to the installed solar capacity in the Netherlands.[26]

24 International Energy Agency, *World Energy Outlook 2019*; IEA, 'World Energy Outlook 2019 Presentation' (Paris, 2019) <www.iea.org>.
25 International Energy Agency, 'Energy Access Outlook 2017'.
26 International Energy Agency (IEA), 'Africa Energy Outlook 2019'.

Africa's solar energy potential as part of the global solar energy market is 40 percent juxtaposed with the current installed capacity in percentage terms of 1 percent when compared to the global average. A potential increase on renewable deployment will have an upside on energy access by using solar, wind and geothermal based on the IEA's 2019 Africa Energy Outlook.

Figure 1. 4 Electricity Access Progress in Sub-Saharan Africa (SSA)

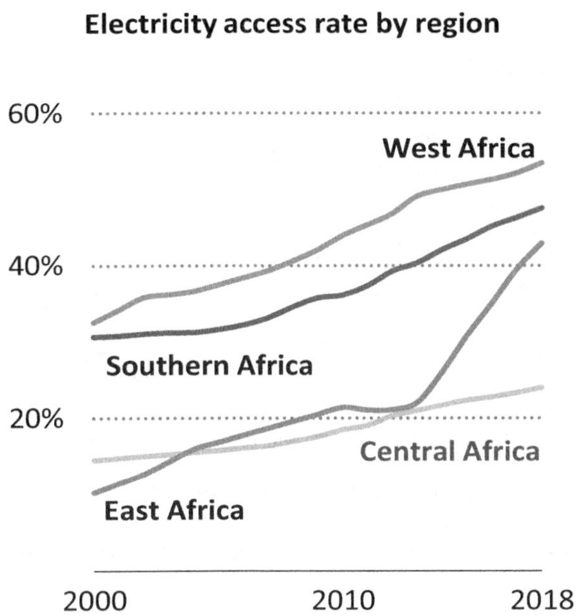

Note: Steady progress in electricity access in West Africa since 2000

Source: International Energy Agency (IEA), "Africa Energy Outlook 2019".

Electricity continues to represent the very core of modern energy security in West Africa. Access to modern and abundant electricity remains the most challenging problem facing the energy sector in the region. To underscore this point using households with electricity based on the most available data in terms of percentages, access in household electricity is 75 percent or higher in only two countries in the ECOWAS region. Three other countries are between less than 75 percent and 50 percent. The ten remaining countries have five of them between the below 50 percent and 25 percent threshold with the bottom five countries under 25 percent energy access. These numbers on household energy consumption in relation to electricity reveals the endemic nature of this access challenge towards modern and abundant energy regardless of income.[27]

Figure 1. 5 Household Electricity Access in ECOWAS (available in percent)

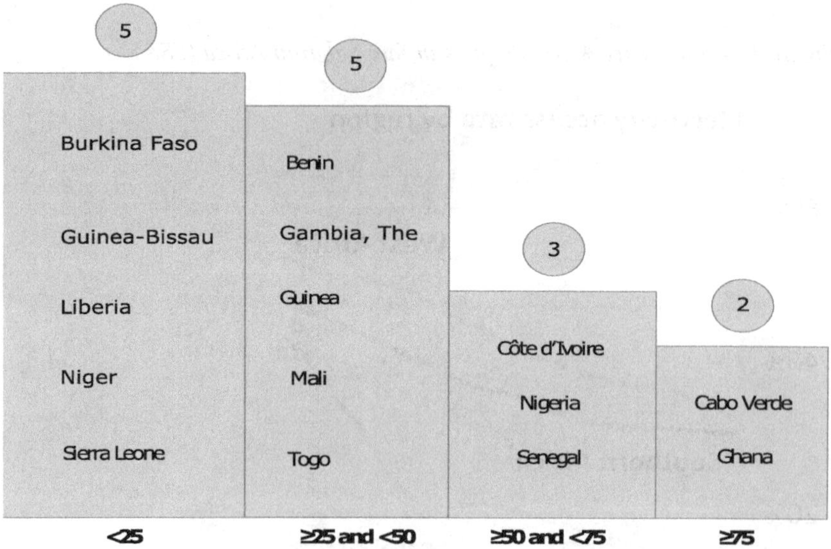

Source: Adapted from Moussa P. Blimpo and Malcom Cosgrove-Davies, *Electricity Access in Sub-Saharan Africa: Uptake, Reliability, and Complementary Factors for Economic Impact. African Development Forum Series*. (Washington, DC: World Bank, 2019)

The next major challenge is the high-cost of the lack and/or overabundance of electricity. This challenge is composed of two dimensions namely excess supply and excess demand. To typify the former, some leading energy hubs in the West African Region like Ghana have surplus power supply resulting in power utilities having to pay producers for energy that is not used. This overcapacity in Ghana's energy sector has arisen due to a sector-specific governance challenge of incoordination thus plunging the sector

27 Moussa P. Blimpo and Malcolm Cosgrove-Davies, *Electricity Access in Sub-Saharan Africa: Uptake, Reliability, and Complementary Factors for Economic Impact, Africa Development Forum Series* (Washington, DC: World Bank, 2019) <https://doi.org/10.1596/978-1-4648-1361-0>.

into avoidable financial difficulty.[28] For the latter, in other countries, like Nigeria, power shortages has resulted in nine hours of power a day and the overdependence on back-up generators. This has led to a significant proportion of the populace relying on generators to ensure regular and steady electricity supply, adding incremental costs to households and businesses. Households expend about 12 billion dollars on self-generated power annually.[29] This binary perspective of underperformance in the regional power sector is due to energy governance challenges, which ultimately gives rise to indebted and unprofitable power companies, resulting in market failure in the regional power sector that results in government bailouts. A rapid shift in the defining nature of this vicious cycle of events in the regional power and electricity sector would change the energy narrative in the region.

To resolve these challenges, one could explore four options; flexibility in the grid, legacy issues, scale and speed as well as stakeholder engagement. In addition, the inclusion of nuclear energy, gas-to-power technologies and renewables (like wind and solar) in power systems could be beneficial in dealing with the variable supply and demand issues. Implementation requires flexibility in the grid (that incorporates both centralised and decentralised systems), power plants, national and international networks as well as demand-side responses. Another addition to this socio-technical system approach would include sufficient investments in the area of energy storage, which may include large-scale batteries as well as effectively deployed energy efficiency strategies.

In West Africa today old energy plants like hydropower and thermal energy (diesel and LPG) power plants leave legacy issues that are solvable with a combination of policy and technology interventions. Crucial investments in retrofitting thermal power plants with carbon capture utilisation and storage (CCUS) would ensure that old thermal energy plants that

28 Moses Mozart Dzawu and Andre Janse Van Vuuren, 'Energy Surplus Leaves Ghana Paying for Unneeded Power - Bloomberg', *Bloomberg*, 2019 <https://www.bloomberg.com/news/articles/2019-11-08/how-having-too-much-energy-creates-a-debt-problem-for-ghana> [accessed 25 November 2019].

29 Anthony Osae-Brown and Ruth Olurounbi, 'Nigeria Runs on Generators and Nine Hours of Power a Day - Bloomberg', *Bloomberg*, 2019 <https://www.bloomberg.com/news/articles/2019-09-23/nigeria-runs-on-generators-and-nine-hours-of-power-a-day> [accessed 25 November 2019]; Dulue Mbachu, 'Nigeria Seeks $3 Billion From World Bank to Tackle Power Crisis - Bloomberg', *Bloomberg*, 2019 <https://www.bloomberg.com/news/articles/2019-11-22/nigeria-seeks-3-billion-from-world-bank-to-tackle-power-crisis> [accessed 25 November 2019].

use oil and gas inefficiently are compatible with climate targets. In the meantime, new diesel- powered thermal fleets could be repurposed to provide the flexibility needed in the grid (which renewables like solar and wind struggle to provide) but would serve the ultimate goal of integrating renewables while reducing CO2 and pollutant emissions. As a result, this would keep the lights on and reduce electricity production from dirty fuels. Another option could also include the early retirements of environmentally hazardous and structurally weak and old hydropower plants as well as old thermal plants.

Scale and speed in the West African energy sector assisted by a host of policies and technologies will be needed across every sector to reach sustainable energy targets, keeping climate targets within reach to pursue the 1.5 degrees Celsius stabilisation (which every nation in the region has signed on to). Working towards these goals would create a robust energy space to deal with energy access in rapidly urbanising and rural regions in West Africa. However, this will entail a massive rollout of technological innovation through increased energy efficiency, increased renewable energy adoption in addition to fuel switching and CCUS technologies among others coupled with understanding and pre-empting clearly the energy policy challenges likely to be encountered so that good decisions could be fashioned.

The pivotal role of all stakeholders cannot be under emphasised. Stakeholder engagement is essential to the realisation of these goals. All stakeholders in the West African energy space have a part to play in ensuring the realisation of the optimistic pathway in West Africa's energy future. The main responsibility rest upon a robust governance model which cuts across all the multiple governance scales and policy areas in the region (such as states, markets and commons) to be able to write the new magnificent chapter in the energy future of West African energy regionalism.

1.2 Problem Definition and Justification

Taking all of the above into consideration, there is a prevailing problem concerning the intractable energy challenges (that is, energy access gap, energy security and climate change) faced in the West African region. To illustrate this dire energy reality in West Africa from a broader Sub-Saharan African (SSA) perspective, an area with the lowest energy access. The then UN under-Secretary-General and first chief executive of the Sustainable Energy for All initiative, Kandeh Yumkella in 2014, described it in this manner, "the energy capacity of 40 sub-Saharan African countries combined is less than that of the 20 million people in New York."[30] SSA accounts for about 560 million people without access to electricity, slightly more than half of the global total.[31] It displays extraordinary diversity in terms of economy, culture, and politics, and as a sum of its parts, it shares the problem of energy poverty. In total about 57 percent of the SSA demographic still lack access to modern, abundant, reliable, sustainable, and affordable energy.[32]

To zero in on West African countries and the region as a whole, low access to modern and abundant energy (that is, energy poverty) is a major challenge. Although incomes are growing per capita in the region with some countries becoming fast economic development growth centres in the world as well as inhabiting countries with some of the fast-growing demographic increases, modern and abundant energy access is still low. The region has been facing epidemic outbreaks like Ebola in Sierra Leone, Guinea and Liberia in 2014 and neglected tropical diseases (NTDs) as well as being vulnerable to exported pandemics to its shores, severe weather conditions resulting in floods and droughts coupled with security insurgencies in Northern Nigeria and its Sahel sub-region limits the ECOWAS region's resilience. So, to deliver affordable and reliable energy is not just about lights in every rural home but energy to power fast growing towns, cities, peri-urban and rural areas that are brimming with young capable people in desperate need for good employment opportunities. This would require significant interconnectivity and economies of scale with a robust and modern energy infrastructure like a central regional grid system as a core piece of any solution.

In the midst of solving this problem the temptation of falling to the allure of the quick fix has been a colossal mistake. Regional energy poverty in ECOWAS exists within a complex socio-economic and political context hence to confront this challenge one cannot ignore governments, markets, community institutions and many other players involved in generating, transporting and using energy at scale. When it comes to the provision of energy in abundance, it is not just about innovating the technology but it

30 Kingsley Ighobor, 'There Is Energy Momentum in Africa', *Africa Renewal* (New York, April 2014) <https://www.un.org/africarenewal/magazine/april-2014/there-energy-momentum-africa>.

31 Delina.

32 See: Sara Fuller, 'The Politics of Energy Justice', in *The Oxford Handbook of Energy Politics*, ed. by Kathleen J. Hancock and Juliann Allison (Oxford and New York: Oxford University Press, 2019).

is about painstakingly working hard to improve institutional governance and broader macro-environment in the regional energy space.

The current West African energy space is predominantly linear, monocentric and static chiefly characterised by a small number of centralised energy producers and utilities at the state level that enter into one-way passive agreements with consumers (be it residential and commercial). Using power interconnections as an example, national grids delivering electricity from suppliers to consumers through on-grid centralised solutions has become the mainstay and feature of the regional electricity system. This phenomenon can be seen in other energy supply systems as well. The dire reality in the use of these energy-governing approaches that are monocentric, linear and static is that they are fraught with huge problems. Among them, include an inefficient supply system, intermittent energy and power supply rationing and cuts, the monopolised structure of power utilities in a given country, heavily subsidized utilities and lastly energy losses and theft resulting from wastage and inefficiencies.

The Energy Access Outlook (2017) published by the International Energy Agency (IEA) gives an account of a promising improvement in closing the energy access gap in Africa, with nearly twenty-six million people being able to access energy annually since 2012. This progress is palpable accounting for a triple increment since 2000; however, the share of the African population without access to electricity continues to grow higher today than in 2000.[33] In its Sustainable Development Scenario[34], the IEA's future projection predicts a rapid increase in population growth and rural-urban migration resulting in the largest urbanisation process witnessed in human history where more than six hundred million people in the region would require access to electricity and modern energy services by 2030.[35] They further project that to meet the goal it would require about $28

33 International Energy Agency, 'Energy Access Outlook 2017'.

34 The Sustainable Development Scenario is a deep decarbonisation scenario tool used by the International Energy Agency in projecting global energy scenarios as of its World Energy Outlook since 2017. It considers the three crucial elements of the Sustainable Development agenda: cleaner air, universal access to energy and climate targets to provide a pathway that achieves them simultaneously, along with providing detailed attention to the security and affordability of energy supply. See:

35 International Energy Agency, 'Energy Access Outlook 2017'; Yaya Keho, 'What Drives Energy Consumption in Developing Countries? The Experience of Selected African Countries', *Energy Policy*, 91.December 2015 (2016), 233–46 <https://doi.org/10.1016/j.enpol.2016.01.010>.

billion investment annually.[36] Currently, Africa is able to attract only 4 percent of total global energy investments, a figure that needs to increase annually to meet the deadline of the SDGs by 2030.[37]

The problem is exacerbated in the West African energy region by two major challenges, the first being the high cost of energy and the second being the jeopardising effects of the high energy access gap on the whole industrialization and transformation agenda in the region.[38] These two factors have everything to do with proper governance of energy policy in the region as a whole. To exemplify the first challenge, in the Sahelian regions and landlocked West African countries like Niger, Mali and Burkina Faso, they pay more for a kilowatt-hour of energy than the rest of the world. This is between 30 and 50 cents for a kilowatt-hour compared to 4 to 17 cents in most countries in the world. To typify the second challenge, in countries like Nigeria, Sierra Leone, Guinea Bissau, Liberia and others every factory or restaurant has a back-up generator adding 20 to 30 percent to their operating cost ultimately preventing these commercial entities from becoming internationally competitive.

These energy problems have negatively affected, for the most part, poor and vulnerable persons and communities in the West African region who are the majority demographic, mainly stripping away the needed resilience due to lack of energy alternatives. For instance, the high maternal mortality among rural women witnessed in hospitals and clinics with intermittent power supply, the increased occurrence of respiratory diseases such as asthma, bronchitis and others due to air pollution caused by the use of firewood and charcoal with women and children being the prime victims. In addition, the collection of firewood and production of charcoal are the chief causes of deforestation a key ingredient of climate change. As an appendage, in fact if climate change continues on the current trajectory as reported by the IPCC, the African continent (inclusive of the West African region) would pay the highest price.[39] The region contributes only less than 3 percent of anthropogenic greenhouse gases but all the worst-case scenarios predict the SSA area in particular would suffer the most

---

36 International Energy Agency, 'Energy Access Outlook 2017'.

37 International Energy Agency, 'Energy Access Outlook 2017'.

38 Ighobor.

39 IPCC, *Climate Change 2007: Impacts, Adaptation and Vulnerability*, ed. by Martin Parry and others, *Contribution of Working Group II to the Fourth Assessment Report of the IPCC* (Cambridge, UK: Cambridge University Press, 2007).

debilitating impact.[40] Mortality and disease prevalence, indoor pollution, desertification and extreme weather conditions are the corollary of the regional energy problems in West Africa. This means issues of regional energy in West Africa are a matter of life and death.

We see, then, that the need to ensure a high energy future for everyone in the region at the same time curbing emissions and ensuring climate stability would require making some complex trade-offs. A high energy future for the ECOWAS region is not mutually exclusive to a low carbon future. And that said it is unjust for the global community to expect West Africa and the entire Sub-Saharan Africa region to remain in energy poverty and vulnerability because of climate change and under the guise of curbing global carbon emissions.

In essence, the facts show that the opposite is true, energy is vital for the region to adapt effectively to climate change and build resilience. Actually, rising temperatures will mean incremental demand for space cooling and cold storage. Declining water tables will mean increased pumped irrigation. Emergent health risks will mean well-resourced health systems. Extreme weather and rising sea levels will require a crucial expansion of reinforcement of the built infrastructure. These are all energy intensive activities. So balancing climate change and the region's need to transition to a high energy future will be tough but doing so is non-negotiable. We will have to find a solvable pathway.

Conceivably, a broad perspective on the energy issues and narratives in West Africa as well as a departure from the limited either/or framing would be extremely favourable to fashioning and shaping better regional energy policy. Moreover, a departure from romanticising solutions that distract from solving the core regional energy challenges is essential. In addition to the awareness that the ECOWAS region is a real place with real people navigating complex challenges and major transitions like any other region in the world would erase the bottlenecks that plague the rollout of real energy solutions.

Since each country and world region has its own social, economic and political distinctions the physics of energy provision are the same everywhere and the energy needs of West African economies are just the same as any other economy. Therefore, it is important to delve into the complex multifarious but reinforcing political economy issues and histori-

40 Ottmar Edenhofer and others, *Climate Change, Justice and Sustainability: Linking Climate and Development Policy* (Dordrecht: Springer, 2012) <https://doi.org/10.1017/CBO9781107415324.004>.

cal antecedents that underpin the function of regional institutions and the governance approaches that support the energy sector to find a workable solution.

In addition to the influence of these factors on the process of charting, a way forward in the provision of modern energy services abundantly and efficiently through good energy governance to everyone in the West African region. The conduct of this research study, investigates the historical emergence and development of energy regionalism in West Africa while drawing on a mirrored or comparative historical view of the European situation. By understanding the transition of governance processes in regional energy spaces, perhaps, I will attempt to tease out the necessary information with a view of contributing to a better understanding of energy governance within a comparative regionalism setting.

This will be done using a cross-case analytical tool (the CIS framework), included in a hybrid research design. The other parts of the hybrid research design are a combination of research methods namely a cross-disciplinary systematic review and qualitative research that uses document analysis for data collection and analysis employing the tools of historical institutionalism and a thematic structure.

1.3 Energy Regionalism and Energy Governance

'Energy' has become one of the central thematic issues in International Studies discussions and gradually has grown in prominence as a topical issue area in Comparative Regionalism. Nevertheless, suffice it to say that, the existing literature and hence policy-relevant knowledge at the intersection of energy studies and regionalism is quite limited in terms of diverse regional perspectives. This work attempts to discuss a potential and possible pathway towards incorporating these different strands of research to understand comparative energy regionalism with particular reference to West Africa and on a lesser note, the EU (since a whole chapter is dedicated to it in this study and used as a cross comparison).

To operationalise *energy regionalism*, Kathleen J. Hancock denotes it as an intersection of resources, regions and energy.[41] The leveraging of regionalism to focus on the role of regional institutions and infrastructure to

41 Kathleen J. Hancock, 'Energy Regionalism : The Intersection of Resources , Regions , and Energy', in *Sustainable Regions* (Centre for the Study of Governance Innovation, University of Pretoria, 2014), pp. 1–5.

facilitate an increase in sustainable energy production and the efficient use of energy is now a new normal.[42] Until recently energy issues were mostly overlooked by research on regionalism – region building led by states and regionalisation – region building by non-state actors.[43] For the purposes of this study, both distinctions would be classified as regionalism in relation to energy. It has been identified that a variety of regional institutions are working on energy issues[44], West Africa (through ECOWAS and other non-state regional efforts) is not an exception in this regard. The regional institutions or bodies are supposedly concerned with the formal and informal regional governance of energy. This regional enquiry pertains to the space between the global and the local[45], hence situating regionalism in terms of states coming together for a number of reasons and issue-areas relating to energy policy and governance.[46] Being specific, energy regionalism includes the "purposive interaction, formal or informal, among state and non-state actors of a given area in pursuit of shared external, domestic and transnational goals"[47]; the given area in this case has to do with the furtherance of energy policy and governance.

This new regionalism/regionalisms approach of studying energy goes beyond formal structures and the role of the state to appraise ideas, policies and goals from different sectors such as the market and commons that transform an area into an identifiable social space.[48] Inter alia, emerging

42 Kathleen J. Hancock, 'The Expanding Horizon of Renewable Energy in Sub-Saharan Africa: Leading Research in the Social Sciences', *Energy Research and Social Science*, 5 (2015), 1–8 <https://doi.org/10.1016/j.erss.2014.12.021>.

43 German Institute for Global Affairs (GIGA), 'Exploring Energy Regionalism', 2015 <https://www.giga-hamburg.de/en/event/exploring-energy-regionalism> [accessed 25 November 2016].

44 Irene Giner-Reichl, 'Renewable Energy in International and Regional Governance: Propelling Development in Africa', *Energy Research and Social Science*, 5 (2015), 116–19 <https://doi.org/10.1016/j.erss.2014.12.008>.

45 IPE focuses on international rather than domestic issues; regionalism used here does not include sub-state regions, such as provinces, as discussed by scholars who study comparative federalism or areas within a state, such as regional studies in local governance or that which pertains to regional policy in the EU.

46 Kathleen J. Hancock and Vlado Vivoda, 'International Political Economy: A Field Born of the OPEC Crisis Returns to Its Energy Roots', *Energy Research and Social Science*, 1 (2014), 206–16 <https://doi.org/10.1016/j.erss.2014.03.017>.

47 Amitav Acharya, 'Comparative Regionalism: A Field Whose Time Has Come?', *International Spectator*, 47.1 (2012), 3–15 <https://doi.org/10.1080/03932729.2012.655004>.

48 Daniel C. Bach, 'New Regionalism as an Alias: Regionalisation through Trans-State Networks.', in *The New Regionalism in Africa*, ed. by A. Grant and F. Söder-

and established literature in this regard have studied: (1) the regional power interconnections that is, electricity grids that rely on resources used to produce energy like water, petroleum, sun, wind among others. (2) Water bodies like rivers used for hydropower that span across state borders thereby creating economic regions. (3) The infrastructure: regional pipelines used to transport oil and natural gas across international boundaries. (4) Regional institutions and trans-state networks dealing with the governance of energy and low-carbon transitions. Overall, these scholars have included regionalism in their analysis of energy.[49]

What is energy governance, and why is it necessary to govern energy? I take a cue in this study from Sovacool and Florini's conceptualisation and Cherp et al.'s issues-based taxonomy of energy governance.[50] As a complex concept, governance is the process of bringing together actors and systems to solve collective action problems in the provision of public goods and

---

baum (Aldershot, UK: Ashgate, 2003), pp. 21–30; Daniel C Bach, *Regionalism in Africa: Genealogies, Institutions and Trans-State Networks*, 1st edn (London: Routledge, 2015) <https://doi.org/10.4324/9781315733180>.

49 Toby Carroll and Benjamin Sovacool, 'Pipelines, Crisis and Capital: Understanding the Contested Regionalism of Southeast Asia', *Pacific Review*, 23.5 (2010), 625–47 <https://doi.org/10.1080/09512748.2010.522248>; Nathaniel Green, Benjamin K. Sovacool, and Kathleen J. Hancock, 'Grand Designs: Assessing the African Energy Security Implications of the Grand Inga Dam', *African Studies Review*, 58.01 (2015), 133–58 <https://doi.org/10.1017/asr.2015.7>; Kathleen J. Hancock, 'Comparative Regionalism and Natural Resources: A Focus on Africa', in *International Studies Association Annual Covention*, 2013, pp. 1–24 <https://doi.org/10.1017/CBO9781107415324.004>; Kathleen J Hancock and Benjamin K Sovacool, 'International Political Economy and Renewable Energy: Hydroelectric Power and the Resource Curse', *International Studies Review*, 2018, 1–18 <https://doi.org/10.1093/isr/vix058>; Kathleen J. Hancock, 'Energy Regionalism and Diffusion in Africa: How Political Actors Created the ECOWAS Center for Renewable Energy and Energy Efficiency', *Energy Research and Social Science*, 5.2015 (2015), 105–15 <https://doi.org/10.1016/j.erss.2014.12.022>; Philip Andrews-Speed, 'Applying Institutional Theory to the Low-Carbon Energy Transition', *Energy Research and Social Science*, 13 (2015), 216–25 <https://doi.org/10.1016/j.erss.2015.12.011>.

50 Benjamin K Sovacool and Ann Florini, 'Examining the Complications of Global Energy Governance', *Journal of Energy and Natural Resource Law*, 30.3 (2012), 235–64 <https://doi.org/10.1080/02646811.2012.11435295>; Aleh Cherp, Jessica Jewell, and Andreas Goldthau, 'Governing Global Energy: Systems, Transitions, Complexity', *Global Policy*, 2.1 (2011), 75–88 <https://doi.org/10.1111/j.1758-5899.2010.00059.x>.

commons[51] while resolving externalities[52] at the same time following a set of agreed rules and norms.

Governance expressed broadly relates to producing "socio-economic order, collective goods or problem solving through purposeful political and social intervention, either by authoritative decisions (hierarchical governance) or by the establishment of self- governing arrangements".[53] Applying governance to energy, it implies an understanding that energy governance involve processes of rulemaking and enforcement that works towards overcoming the collective action problems related to energy supply and use. This entails actors engaged in processes of setting agendas, negotiating, implementing, monitoring and enforcing rules, protocols and agreements related to energy. Actors at the heart of these processes in energy include governments, non-governmental organisations (NGOs), civil society groups, businesses, citizens, public-private partnerships (PPPs) and ordinary consumers. These heterogeneous actors contribute multiple resources and action orientations with respect to their roles in the energy field.[54]

In addition, these governance processes occur at different and multiple governance scales from the micro – individual and household levels; meso – local, community, state, provincial levels; and macro – national, regional, global levels. In sum, energy governance deals with the actors, rules and systems related to energy. Moreover, at the regional level, it refers to a macro governance scale that deals with trans-state and transnational energy interactions that cross national borders in a geopolitical region.

Most energy issues, including electricity access for all and the quest to decrease carbon emissions, are solvable. As already alluded to, this responsibility goes beyond the singular role of states and national governments and incorporates involvement from other actors at multiple governance levels or scales. This in effect emphasises the significance and urgency of

---

51 The term commons is used here to refer to public goods, common pool resources or any area with uncertain property rights. Michael D. McGinnis, *Updated Guide to IAD and the Language of the Ostrom Workshop: A Simplified Overview of a Complex Framework for the Analysis of Institutions and Their Development* (Bloomington, 2016).

52 The term externalities in this instance refers to government failure, market failure and social chaos, unrest or breakdown in the community.

53 Volker Schneider, 'Governance and Complexity', in *The Oxford Handbook of Governance*, ed. by David Levi-Faur (Oxford: Oxford University Press, 2012), pp. 129–42 <https://doi.org/10.1093/oxfordhb/9780199560530.013.0009>.

54 Schneider.

collective action in the energy sector. Meaning asking the question what is the best way to govern energy resources. Two ways have pre-occupied the debates in this area: (1) regional or global governance and (2) formal or informal institutions. A third way is emerging gradually in the debates that underscores (3) monocentric or polycentric governance approaches. The first debate is over whether energy governance is done best at the regional or global levels. Anthony Patt[55] has argued that the most effective way to govern emerging and longstanding energy issues is by resolving collective action problems relating to energy and this could be done most efficiently at the regional level. However, Sovacool and Florini[56] have argued that the ideal way to solve transnational collective action problems in energy could only be done through global governance.

In relation to the second debate, Ostrom and Ostrom et al.[57] show that informal rules can emerge where formal property rights do not attain capable resource use and can be applied in diverse instances. For example, the cases scrutinised in both informal and formal situations have focused on fisheries, water, and forests in different contexts such as sub-state regions like the California Groundwater Basin. However, others have applied formal and informal institutionalisation to a broader context like international energy resource issues. This is demonstrated in the works of Koster and Anderies[58] as well as Shah and Niles[59], who exhibit that formal and informal institutions emerge when practicable in energy governance at both

55 Anthony G. Patt, 'Effective Regional Energy Governance-Not Global Environmental Governance-Is What We Need Right Now for Climate Change', *Global Environmental Change*, 20.1 (2010), 33–35 <https://doi.org/10.1016/j.gloenvcha.2009.09.006>.

56 Ann Florini and Benjamin K Sovacool, 'Who Governs Energy? The Challenges Facing Global Energy Governance', *Energy Policy*, 37.12 (2009), 5239–48 <https://doi.org/10.1016/j.enpol.2009.07.039>; Ann Florini and Benjamin K Sovacool, 'Bridging the Gaps in Global Energy Governance', *Global Governance*, 2011, 57–74 <https://doi.org/10.5555/ggov.2011.17.1.57>; Sovacool and Florini.

57 Elinor Ostrom, Roy Gardner, and James Walker, *Rules, Games and Common-Pool Resources* (Ann Arbor, MI: The University of Michigan Press, 1994); Elinor Ostrom, *Governing the Commons - The Evolution of Institutions for Collective Action* (Cambridge: Cambridge University Press, 1990) <https://doi.org/10.1017/CBO9780511807763>.

58 Auriane Magdalena Koster and John Martin Anderies, 'Institutional Factors That Determine Energy Transitions: A Comparative Case Study Approach', in *Lecture Notes in Energy*, ed. by E Michalena and J.M. Hills, 1st edn (London: Springer-Verlag, 2013), xxiii, 33–61 <https://doi.org/10.1007/978-1-4471-5595-9_3>

59 Kalim U Shah and Keron Niles, 'Energy Policy in the Caribbean Green Economy Context and the Institutional Analysis and Design (IAD) Framework as a

the global and regional levels exemplified by their respective consideration of the global renewable energy regime and the Caribbean region's energy policy.

The third question being posed in debate circles is whether governance is more effective when monocentric or polycentric approaches are in use. For instance, Thijs Van der Graaf plus Sovacool and Van der Graff argue that due to the complexity inherent in solving energy issues at the global level, governance through fragmentation would aid in delivering solutions to collective-action problems in the energy sphere.[60] Since the pervading notion of governing energy systems has been top down and monocentric as the literature has suggested over the period.[61] The promising turn towards a polycentric understanding of energy governance systems at different macro levels will be well suited for this study of energy regionalism in West Africa. Finally, in this regard, in terms of what type of governance is most needed to solve or minimise collective action problems in energy, perhaps an insightful answer provided by Cherp et al.[62] recommend that energy governance arrangements can be best represented when they are:

> "evolving complex systems with their own histories, fluid boundaries, dynamic connections, intricate networks and feedback loops, uncertainties and nonlinearities and that effective governance structures

---

Proposed Tool for Its Development', *Energy Policy*, 98 (2016), 768–77 <https://doi.org/http://dx.doi.org/10.1016/j.enpol.2016.07.045>.

60 Thijs Van de Graaf, 'Fragmentation in Global Energy Governance: Explaining the Creation of IRENA', *Global Environmental Politics*, 13.3 (2013), 14–33 <https://doi.org/10.1162/GLEP_a_00181>; Benjamin K. Sovacool and Thijs Van de Graaf, 'Building or Stumbling Blocks? Assessing the Performance of Polycentric Energy and Climate Governance Networks', *Energy Policy*, 118.March (2018), 317–24 <https://doi.org/10.1016/j.enpol.2018.03.047>.

61 Andreas Goldthau and Jan Martin Witte, 'Back to the Future or Forward to the Past? Strengthening Markets and Rules for Effective Global Energy Governance', *International Affairs*, 85.2 (2009), 373–90 <https://doi.org/10.1111/j.1468-2346.2009.00798.x>; Andreas Goldthau and Jan Martin Witte, *Global Energy Governance : The New Rules of the Game*, ed. by Andreas Goldthau and Jan Martin Witte (Washington, D.C.: Brookings Institution Press, 2010); Florini and Sovacool, 'Who Governs Energy? The Challenges Facing Global Energy Governance'; Neil Gunningham, 'Confronting the Challenge of Energy Governance', *Transnational Environmental Law*, 1.1 (2012), 119–35 <https://doi.org/10.1017/S2047102511000124>.

62 Cherp, Jewell, and Goldthau.

> must 'incorporate diverse institutions and mechanisms arranged in 'nested', 'multilevel' and 'polycentric' systems of governance."[63]

They anchor energy governance further, on three distinct and relatively independent governance arenas: energy security, energy access, and climate change. Moreover, they emphasise that governance in each of the arenas is strengthened, as linkages with the other two arenas are reinforced.[64]

The energy security arena is characterised by limited actor and industry participation however possesses a strong focus on efficiency and exploitation of the existing strengths of the energy space. The climate change arena is mainly a broad space that includes a large array of multiple actors but suffers from inexact effectiveness in the implementation of known solutions or realising tangible progress towards the decarbonisation of the energy space.

The energy access arena is quite exploratory in character; its core task focuses on ensuring flows of financial and technical assistance, which in most cases are insufficient in supporting effective exploitation of known solutions and technologies.

Thus, in terms of the scope of this study, it situates energy regionalism as the starting point. It does this by investigating governance of regional energy and its polycentric governance structures across two supranational regions namely ECOWAS and the EU in order to find and explore variations and consistencies between them to inform a design approach of energy regionalism in West Africa going forward. These observations focus on key concepts like energy, international political economy of energy and institutions. In the end aiding the process of drawing out elements of two unique regionalist perspectives on energy to fashion a more solid and robust governance model for abundant and sustainable energy provision in the West Africa region.

63 Cherp, Jewell, and Goldthau, p. 80.
64 Cherp, Jewell, and Goldthau, p. 81-83.

1.4 Methodology

The methodological approach used in this research study provides the basis for addressing five central questions:

(1) The interaction of energy and comparative regionalism reveal a number of elements. Describe how these elements come together to inform energy governance in a region?

(2) Considering the historical trajectory of energy regionalism and the path taken by institutions of energy governance, what has been the likely evolutionary path taken by ECOWAS and the EU towards a more sustainable energy supply regime using energy, political economy of energy and institutions as the frame?

(3) How has the capacity of the interconnected regional energy institutions in the governance of regional energy been expressed over time to provide energy?

(4) What does this institutional capacity imply for the governance of West Africa's energy regionalism in terms of its potential and obstacles?

And finally (5) how does West Africa design a more robust and effective regional energy governance system?

Energy governance by virtue of institutional responses to the pressing energy challenges in a geopolitical region are deeply rooted in the evolutionary nature of regional governance regimes. In view of that, energy regions emerge almost explicitly as a consequence of processes that maintain a high degree of resolve to deal with collective action problems in a regional energy policy-space. Employing a dynamic comparative lens to help examine the assemblage of institutions that constitute energy regionalism, I contend that the varied landscape of the regional energy space reveals a multiple number of energy governance scales hence the rationale for a polycentric approach to regional energy governance is tenable. Appreciating the historical emergence and evolution of energy regionalism could lead to an understanding of the inherent implications that could inform the design of a more coordinated and effective regional energy governance system.

In this way, my research responds to Kathleen J. Hancock and Vlad Vivoda's call to further advance research in energy social science by including "regionalism in their analysis" and by comparing formal regional energy agreements.[65]

The focal thesis of this dissertation is that the steps taken by a supranational region to ensure good and effective governance in regional energy policy is highly constrained by its history and prevailing institutions of (energy) governance.

---

65 Hancock and Vivoda, p. 211.

The object of this research study is fourfold: first, to explore new research categories like energy regionalism and its relationship with regional energy governance in a comparative regionalism setting. Second, to describe the evolutionary nature of energy regionalism in two world regions (West Africa and Europe) and observe its governance over a specified period of time. Third, to organise and integrate insights from variables and processes for analysis that involves networks of action situations in the regional energy space and serve as a tool for interpretation in understanding the nature, function and governance of energy regionalism, through the use of historical narrative analysis and the CIS framework[66]. The fourth objective is to show that energy regionalism meets the requirements of polycentric energy governance systems and that the underlying intentional design of regional energy governance institutions must bear in mind this polycentric approach in ensuring a robust, sustainable and effective energy governance approach especially in a region like ECOWAS.

Furthermore, the research objectives stated above communicate the intended scholarly contributions of this research study, which Sovacool et al.[67] suggest might occur in three categories, that is, theoretical, methodological or empirical. In this particular research, clear novelty is demonstrated in two categories especially in the empirical and methodological aspects. In the empirical category, the dissertation contributes by the novel application of the theory of polycentrism and the multilevel CIS framework together, to study energy regionalism and regional energy governance relating to the two case studies of regional energy in ECOWAS and the EU.

The primary contribution here is empirical, having observed the descriptive and explanatory longitudinal evidence from historical and archival

66 An analytical tool combining Ostrom's two frameworks: the Institutional Analysis and Development (IAD) Framework and the Social-Ecological Systems (SES) Framework introduced by Dan Cole, Graham Epstein and Michael D. McGinnis based on earlier work by Daniel H Cole, Graham Epstein, and Michael Dean McGinnis, 'Toward a New Institutional Analysis of Social-Ecological Systems (NIASES): Combining Elinor Ostrom's IAD and SES Frameworks', *Maurer School of Law Leg,al Studies Research Paper Series*, 2014, 1–22 <http://ssrn.com/abstract=2490999>. See: Daniel H. Cole, Graham Epstein, and Michael D. McGinnis, 'Combining the IAD and SES Frameworks', *International Journal of the Commons*, 13.1 (2019), 244–75 <https://doi.org/10.18352/ijc.777>.

67 Benjamin K. Sovacool, Jonn Axsen, and Steve Sorrell, 'Promoting Novelty, Rigor, and Style in Energy Social Science: Towards Codes of Practice for Appropriate Methods and Research Design', *Energy Research and Social Science*, 2018, 12–42 <https://doi.org/10.1016/j.erss.2018.07.007>.

sources. It provides improved understanding for the emergence and institutionalism of energy regionalism and energy governance in a comparative research design. This is done using a qualitative research strategy and in this particular instance through a multiple-case study or cross-case study. The use of the polycentricity theory and the CIS framework remedies the theoretical limitation that is associated with empirically novel studies by providing a structure for describing and exploring the grounded data, rather than the unfettered and open approach used for descriptive and exploratory modes that may have been used in such a limitation a point clearly highlighted in Sovacool et al.[68] Moreover this study also tends to be socio-politically relevant by design, seeking to generate insights for the academy, policymakers, and other stakeholders.

Another empirical novelty found in this dissertation includes the collection and analysis of a new type of historical energy data relevant to West Africa, neglected for some other reason thus affecting the drawing of proper inferences particularly when it relates to internal or external energy policy decisions. To illustrate, I identify how energy evolved in the Anglophone, Francophone and Lusophone sub-regions of West Africa that often proves difficult to access in expressing a historical narrative of how modern energy use and governance came into being in the region. This viewpoint provided an important, often missing contribution to the energy social science research literature pertaining to Africa. Revealing that there were variations in the deployment of energy policies in the three colonial polities in West Africa.

Methodologically, applying the CIS framework to regional energy governance and energy regionalism in a comparative sense depicts a clear novelty that the research objectives again intend to contribute to this multilevel framework, which in itself is at a developmental stage and emerging among academics in the field of political science, policy studies and energy research. It reveals the utility and versatility of this framework in conducting comparative policy analysis that relates to the regional level.

The stated research objectives are also communicating the underlying assumption, that is, the paradigm guiding this inquiry about the nature of reality, its interactions and the appropriate methods to use.[69] This research

68 Sovacool, Axsen, and Sorrell, p. 20.

69 Egon G. Guba and Yvonna S. Lincoln, 'Paradigmatic Controversies, Contradictions, and Emerging Confluences', in *The Sage Handbook of Qualitative Research*, ed. by Norman K. Denzin and Yvonna S. Lincoln, Third (Thousand Oaks, 2005) <https://doi.org/10.1108/17465640610666642>.

relies mainly on the interpretivist paradigm, which emphasizes qualitative research methods. Interpretivism, one of the many paradigms in energy social science research is explained using three classifications namely ontology, epistemology and methodology.[70] Relating to the ontology (that is, nature of reality), interpretivism is focused on socially constructed reality and an accommodation of multiple realities as possible. In terms of epistemology, knowledge is generated by the interpretation of subjective meanings and actions of subjects in relation to their own frame of reference. Moreover, there is emphasis on interpretation.

Lastly, as regards methodology it is exploratory and inductive (in certain situations theory generating) with an emphasis on depth rather than generalizability.[71] In this study, to classify the theory and conceptual framework (while acknowledging its analytical emphasis), polycentricity and the multilevel framework is employed as a tool for interpreting the empirical data derived from the energy history of the two regions whiles in chapter two and three a purely historical narrative approach is adopted based on historical institutionalism. It also occupies a hybrid space of bringing together agency, structure and discourse while at the same time emphasising the complex interactions among all three elements. This is exemplified by the basic assumption that at the geopolitical level, regional energy decisions and policies occur across the categories of agency, structure and meaning/discourse based on a hybrid theoretical stance. A key strength of this approach is to provide a tool for identifying, categorising, organising and integrating insights from variable-oriented research and process-oriented research however, it is limited intrinsically in being a tool for inference that is, providing conclusions based on evidence and reasoning.[72]

To reiterate, this study's underlying paradigm has informed the research objectives and determined the choice of research design and type of research methods, analysis and interpretation used in conducting this study. In explicating the research design, the research methods employed in this study were executed to ensure the concepts, theory, approach and multilevel framework used are operationalised, research questions are answered, research objectives are realised and the main working thesis confirmed. To simplify, a research method refers to a technique for gathering or analysing data (in this study a combination of systematic interdisciplinary review,

---

70 John Mingers, *Realising Systems Thinking: Knowledge and Action in Management Science* (New York: Springer Science + Business Media Inc, 2006).

71 Sovacool, Axsen, and Sorrell.

72 Daniel H. Cole, Epstein, and McGinnis.

qualitative research methods and case studies & cross-case comparisons through a historical-comparative approach is used) while a research design is how exactly such a method, or methods, become executed in a particular research.[73] With the ultimate goal of providing enough detail to readers by making the research transparent, accessible in light of the research objectives at the same time facilitating replicability.

To ensure methodological rigor in conducting a systematic interdisciplinary review of the study's literature, I followed the lead of the initially crafted research questions and systematically set out to search the available literature in a number of databases, repositories and online and offline libraries. This research study relies intensively of the use of secondary sources. The online databases and repositories included African Journals Online (AJOL), Google Scholar, Oxford Journals / Oxford Journals Digital Archive, Cambridge Core – the books and journals platform from Cambridge University Press, Nomos eLibrary, Annual Reviews, UN Documentation Centre, JSTOR, OECD iLibrary, Project MUSE, Springer Link and World Bank E-Library Archive. Others included IREON – Fachportal Internationale Beziehungen und Länderkunde, FIND-ER: Library and e-Resources, ElgarOnline, EBSCOhost, ScienceDirect, SSRN, Publications Archive – Oxford Institute for Energy Studies, Taylor & Francis Online, ProQuest EBook Central and Sage Research Methods Online.

I mostly accessed these resources using the online libraries of the University of Bonn LandesBibliothek Datenbanken (DBIS) portal and the University of Ghana Balme Library portal. Subsequent internet searches were conducted for working papers, PowerPoint presentations and other scholarly articles emanating from and allied to the Ostrom Workshop in Indiana University Bloomington. The webpage of Professor Michael Dean McGinnis was an unbelievably helpful resource.

Pertaining to offline documentary material relating to ECOWAS such as reports, magazines and other documents containing the main search terms and keywords that was not found on the internet, a visit to the ECOWAS repository of the Legon Centre for International Affairs (LECIAD) of the University of Ghana, Legon in the summer of 2019 proved immensely helpful. Regular visits to the ZEI/ZEF library facilitated access to books and interlibrary loans of books and copies of journal articles throughout the research phase. Furthermore, the decision to use the developing multi-level (CIS) framework instead of the initially intended IAD framework was based on exposure to this new framework in private discussions whiles on

73 See: Sovacool, Axsen, and Sorrell.

a visit to the School for the Future of Innovation in Society (SFIS), Arizona State University in Tempe, Arizona in 2018.

I used defined search terms and phrases that included: energy, energy as a common / common pool resource, energy as a policy area, IPE of energy, market design and energy, energy sources (oil and gas, renewable energy, nuclear energy etc.), energy in West Africa, energy in the EU, energy regionalism, energy governance. It also included comparative regionalism, regional integration (specific to political science and political economy), institutional analysis and development (IAD) framework, socio-ecological systems (SES) framework and combined IAD-SES (CIS) framework.

I reviewed documents such as policy documents, legislative proposals, legal documents, reports and webpages found on the many organisations, institutions and agencies that have something to do with energy in both ECOWAS and EU. Some of these bodies discussed or mentioned in the dissertation include African Development Bank Energy Portal, UNECA, World Bank, West Africa Power Pool (WAPP), West Africa Gas Pipeline Authority (WAGPA), ECREEE – ECOWAS Centre for Renewable Energy and Energy Efficiency, EU Energy Union, EURATOM among others. I did this to uncover a large body of empirical evidence using mainly internet searches on the webpages, peer reviewed scholarly articles in the databases and reports in the grey literature as an explicit criterion for including and excluding studies. I executed a unique strategy to code these key search terms and phrases by uploading all of my literature (e-books, peer reviewed and grey) into a personal account of the free reference management software, Mendeley. The main purpose of the use of this software was to save and manage all my PDFs, code key search terms and phrases, generate citations and organize references.

In terms of analysing and synthesizing the collected evidence contained in the review a content textual analysis was used, the first part can be seen in Chapter 1 under the heading – Thesis overview and the second part in Chapter 2 under the heading-- Explicating the frame: Energy, Political Economy of Energy and Institutions. All this was done to scour the existing literature (both peer-reviewed and grey) with the ultimate goal of identifying the current state of knowledge.

The second research method used for collecting and analysing empirical evidence was qualitative in nature. B. K. Sovacool et al.[74] defines qualitative research methods within energy social science as a variety of techniques used to obtain empirical evidence regarding the opinions,

74 Sovacool, Axsen, and Sorrell, pp. 17,28-30.

understandings, attitudes, and perceptions of individuals and groups in different contexts. I designed the data collection process for Chapters 3 and 4 because of the second research objective that seeks to explore the emergence and evolution of energy regionalism in the two world regions. Dependence of this research study on disciplines such as history, political science, public policy studies and aspects of science and technology studies contributed to the choice of these qualitative research methods for both data collection and analysis.

On the data collection front, I considered analysis of documents, like reports, websites and news media with the aim of gaining access to historical empirical evidence such as narrative and discourse as presented in these documentary materials. In addition, I sought out scholarly works like dissertations, articles and other grey literature by academics and in some cases by participating stakeholders. These data sources provided insight into the information, frames and storylines presented by different perspectives from actors and observers on the unfolding and construction of regional energy institutions in both West Africa and Europe. Being cognisant of the limitation inherent in using this method of data collection where the evidence produced is limited to the perspectives, agenda and biases of the producers of the documentary materials. I sought to remedy this limitation with two qualitative methods of data analysis chosen to analyse rigorously the obtained historical evidence namely content analysis and historical narrative analyses.

Content analysis was chosen due to research question two, which sought to explore the evolutionary path of energy regionalism in both regions because it possessed a priori analytical categories such as historical institutionalism and regionalism. Bearing in mind this method of analysis required a highly structured framework and a possibility of lacking depth during the process of analysis; it was complemented with the use of the historical narrative analysis in order to access greater depth, explanation and meaning using the historical institutionalism approach.

To highlight this approach briefly, historical institutionalism entails the study of patterns of change and continuity in international institutions.[75]

75 Sven Steinmo and Kathleen Thelen, 'Historical Institutionalism in Comparative Politics', *Structuring Politics: Historical Institutionalism in Comparative Politics*, 1992, pp. 1–32 <https://doi.org/10.1146/annurev.polisci.2.1.369>; Kathleen Thelen, 'Historical Institutionalism in Comparative Politics', *Annual Review of Political Science*, 2.2 (1999), 369–404 <https://doi.org/10.1017/CBO97805118019 38.008>; Ellen M. Immergut, 'Historical-Institutionalism in Political Science and the Problem of Change', *Constellations of Contingency*, 2002, 237–59 <https://doi.o

Generally, in political science but more specifically in comparative regionalism, a component of international studies, historical institutionalism emphasizes types of processes that include legacies of times in history that shape long-term power relations and whether new ideas become consequential particularly occurring in widespread incremental reform resulting in fundamental transformations.[76] In simple terms, historical institutionalism is no longer determining whether history matters, but on when and how historical processes shape political outcomes. Orfeo Fioretos[77] stresses that, although it is not seen as a theory of politics nor a general theory of institutional evolution, it is better typified as a theoretical tradition that focuses on discrete set of themes that are analysed with a distinct mixture of analytical concepts and methods.[78] One distinguishing feature of historical institutionalism is sequencing and temporality of political events. This helps to determine the evolution of constraints and opportunities that occur in the multiple institutions that come together to shape collective action in effect creating different types of political occurrences over time.

A strength displayed by sequence and time in this approach has proven valuable for nested and overlapping regimes by identifying and categorising the conditions under which the strategic context in which states and other polities find themselves in relation to a given policy area. That is to say, timing is crucial for the historical institutionalism approach especially for analytical reasons. Since later events are precipitated by earlier ones and expressed by understanding the stakes of political action in the current setting. It takes stock of some options that may not really exist due to the sequence of prior events. All of this aids in explaining and interpreting diverse and dynamic processes of institutional development over time.[79]

---

rg/10.1177/106591295901200401>; Orfeo Fioretos, 'Historical Institutionalism in International Relations', *International Organization*, 65.02 (2011), 367–99 <https://doi.org/10.1017/S0020818311000002>.

76 Fioretos.

77 Fioretos.

78 Historical institutionalism has contributed to a number of methodological innovation (to exemplify see James Mahoney and Dietrich Rueschemeyer, *Comparative Historical Analysis: Achievements and Agendas*, ed. by James Mahoney and Dietrich Rueschemeyer (Cambridge: Cambridge University Press, 2003) <https://doi.org/10.1017/CBO9780511803963.002>.) but they favour methods like process tracing and comparative case studies.

79 Wolfgang Streeck and Kathleen Thelen, *Beyond Continuity: Institutional Change in Advanced Political Economies* (Oxford and New York: Oxford University Press, 2005) <https://doi.org/10.1093/acprof:oso/9780198701309.003.0010>; James Mahoney and Kathleen Thelen, *Explaining Institutional Change: Ambiguity, Agen-*

To obtain richer analysis, narrative analyses based on the historical institutionalist approach was used to analyse document text with the ultimate aim of ascertaining storylines used in framing unfolding aspects of energy regionalism based on the topics of energy, political economy of energy and institutions. The objective here was empirical, interpretive and explanatory to link causality and effect.

The third research method utilised in this research was case studies. It was to serve the purpose of a cross-case comparison or to conduct comparative case studies. Case studies contain in-depth examination of a phenomenon. In this particular study, it involved an in-depth look into the phenomenon of the variables and processes contained in energy regionalism in the regional bodies of ECOWAS and EU as well as the related contextual conditions inherent in these regions. I based my source of evidence from the qualitative research conducted in Chapters 3 and 4 in addition to using the multilevel CIS framework as my tool of analysis to maintain rigour and replicability. Robert K.Yin recommends case study research for "how and why" questions pertaining to contemporary phenomenon where the research has little to no control over events.[80] However, B.K. Sovacool et al. suggests that case studies are equally appropriate for historical investigations.[81]

The comparative case study conducted in this research captured the decomposable variables and historical processes involved in energy regionalism for ECOWAS and EU with the aim of mirroring their variations over time. Essentially, to look for illustrations that sought an inverse approach, here referring to cases (ECOWAS and EU) where the independent variable (EU) as well as the dependent variable (ECOWAS) co-vary when mirrored together with each other. This variation was done by simply unpacking both regions without making any value judgements but stressing the entirely different times and context of occurrences.

---

cy, and Power (Cambridge and New York: Cambridge University Press, 2009); Paul Pierson, *Politics in Time: History, Institutions, and Social Analysis* (Princeton, NJ: Princeton University Press, 2004) <https://doi.org/10.1515/9781400841080>; Paul Pierson, 'Increasing Returns, Path Dependence, and the Study of Politics', *American Political Science Review*, 94.02 (2006), 251–67 <https://doi.org/10.2307/2586011>.

80 Robert K. Yin, *Case Study Research and Applications: Design and Methods*, Sixth Edition (Los Angeles and London: SAGE Publications, 2018).

81 Sovacool, Axsen, and Sorrell.

I considered a second dimension, where I looked at these cases comparatively. As Sovacool, Axsen and Sorrell[82] would suggest, I sought to confirm the working thesis underpinning the entire dissertation and I realised comparative cases would be good in serving this purpose as well as refuting some of the conjectures that could arise from just looking at a single regional case. This step proved useful in drawing insights and examining causal effects that would otherwise not be gained if I looked at a single instance. Empirically, due to the similarity inherently attended to by the role of regionalising energy, it served as a useful route for meaningful analysis.

The third dimension considered was the requirement of temporal and spatial variation in this cross-case comparison as suggested by John Gerring[83]. In terms of spatial variation, diversity was provided across the two different regions of ECOWAS and the EU moreover the different governance scales for managing regional energy in both regions were varied as well, this challenged the comparability of results but served the purpose of providing a comparative perspective of two energy regions. As indicated by Sovacool et al. temporal variations could permit more natural that is, less artificial boundaries around analysis since it enables researchers to include multiple relevant temporal events as needed.[84] This study was no different, mindful of the need for complex analysis to capture the greater complexity in the data gleaned from the evidence provided in chapters three and four, the CIS framework was immensely useful in teasing out the temporal variations present in the process (of evolution and institutional transition) towards energy regionalisms in ECOWAS and the EU. The combination of the spatial and temporal variations in both regions enhanced the analysis and provided rigorous insights for discussions in Chapter 6.

The conclusive parts of the research design dealt with the results and discussions that were contained in Chapters 6 and 7. It was mainly organised in a thematic format structuring the results and discussions around the themes emerging from the analysis ranging from dimensions like the polycentric nature of regional energy, political, social, economic and financing, legal-regulatory and policy, innovation and technological implications in

---

82 Sovacool, Axsen, and Sorrell.

83 John Gerring, 'What Is a Case Study and What Is It Good For?', *American Political Science Review*, 98.2 (2004), 341–54 <https://doi.org/10.1017/S0003055404001182>; John Gerring, *Case Study Research: Principles and Practices* (Cambridge: Cambridge University Press, 2007).

84 Sovacool, Axsen, and Sorrell.

addition to implications for bi-regional partnerships. To sum up by providing relevance to policymaking, Chapter 7, serving as the conclusion sought to provide policy advice by laying out a principled regional energy policy and governance design approach by using Elinor Ostrom's design principles for robust governance of policy spaces.

In conclusion, the research design for this study was a mixture of the following research methods: a cross-disciplinary systematic review of the energy, comparative regionalism, and institutions literature, a qualitative research approach that entailed analyses of documents (legal, historical, policy, peer reviewed and grey) organised under a historical narrative and thematic structure. Finally, with a cross-case comparison summarising two energy regionalism case studies, I used a spatial and temporal structure to promote novelty and rigour. All of these were captured in a hybrid research design that concluded with a discussion, analysis and policy advice.

1.5 Structure of the Dissertation

The rest of the dissertation is compartmentalised as five fundamental chapters and a conclusion. Chapter 2 is sectionalised in three parts with the purpose of explicating the frame on which this research rests, through the fusion of concepts, theory and a framework. The first section explores the concept of energy and revisits the notions of energy systems, the energy commons and the morphogenetic dimension of energy as a policy area. It shows the multiple aspects of energy as a resource, in its converted state, and as a service. In addition, it closely intertwines this interpretation with the notion of energy infrastructure systems. It does this by teasing out a view on infrastructure and the social-ecological-technical system (SETS) and further explains the normative scope of the energy system in terms of energy types, resources and sectors.

Subsequently, the five unique forms of energy commons are delineated namely, energy resource commons, energy frontiers commons, renewable energy resources, global energy commons and energy infrastructure commons. Lastly, a morphogenetic overview of energy as a policy area is conducted by giving a historical account of the emergence and evolution of the policy making dimension of energy at the international level.

The second section reflects on the International Political Economy (IPE) of Energy by exploring it from the perspective of national energy governance, regional energy governance and energy spaces, an intersectionality of state, market and commons. The third section explores an approach that would be useful for an institutional analysis of energy using the Bloomington School's Combined Institutional Analysis and Development – Social Ecological System (CIS) Framework. It considers the purpose and development of the combined framework and its utility for institutional analysis in the energy space. Finally, a look at the polycentricity theory and the way it characterises energy governance in a polycentric manner is considered.

Chapter 3 presents an overview of energy regionalism in West Africa by illustrating a historical account of the origins and development of energy systems in the region, the evolution of regionalism generally and finalising it with the process of energy regionalism. First, the chapter deals with an account of West African energy history. It focuses on the development of energy systems by the three different colonial regimes present in the region before the independence era and subsequently the construction of national energy systems by the newly independent states in the region. Second, it focuses on the evolution of comparative regionalism in West Africa with particular focus on the coming into being of ECOWAS regionalism. Third, it turns to ECOWAS energy regionalism to reflect on the past milestones, present settings and future prospects on the contributions made towards region building by coalescing around energy policy in the region. Fourth, it deals with the institutions that form the basis of the ECOWAS energy policy regime.

Comparatively, Chapter 4 builds on this historical accounting as it presents a historical overview of energy regionalism in the European Union. It illustrates an account of the path dependence and path creation of energy systems in the region, followed by the evolution of EU regionalism and finally with a focus on how EU energy regionalism has come into being. Initially, the chapter deals with the dimensions of path dependence and path creation by explaining it and goes on further to describe its unravelling in the four geographical zones of the EU. Secondly, it looks at the unfolding of EU regionalism retelling it from the pre-great war years through to the founding of the EU. Thirdly, an account of EU energy regionalism is given to present the past, present and future dimensions of the contributions of energy policy towards region building in the EU region. Fourthly, the institutional foundations that underpin the EU energy policy regime is given attention here.

Building on the historical institutional accounts, Chapter 5 conducts a comparative institutional analysis of the energy regimes in ECOWAS and EU by applying the combined IAD-SES (CIS) framework to the empirical information gleaned from Chapter 3 and Chapter 4. It analyses the two energy regimes by decomposing and unpacking the various institutional components that constitute them. The basic elements of this framework are the network of focal action situations, contextual setting (comprising physical settings that is, resource units and resource systems; attributes of the community that is, primary actors; existing institutional setting that is, governance system) and the temporal dynamic revealed by the snapshots taken of the regional energy governance of both regions when the CIS framework is employed.

After comparatively mirroring the two regional governance architectures, I descend into the specific region of West Africa; Chapter 6 examines implications, that is, potentials and obstacles for regional energy governance of the West African region. In closing, Chapter 7 concludes the research by outlining an intellectual and principled policy agenda for increasing the value of regional energy governance in the ECOWAS region. I argue that the seeds of polycentric energy governance exist in the current energy regionalism being practised in the region, but in order to address energy challenges effectively all the multiple governance scales with its diverse actors would need to be strongly interlinked and focused on commonly shared goals. Policy advice in this regard – towards a more effective, robust and resilient ECOWAS energy governance – is provided using Ostrom's design principles and puts forward some suggestions for future research.

Chapter 2

Explicating the Frame: Energy, Political Economy of Energy and Institutions

2.1 Conceptualising[85] Energy

Energy is a concept which theoretical and experimental physicists over the years have hardly been able to define precisely.[86] Aristotle, the Greek philosopher, formulated the word, ενέργεία *-energeia* – (*actuality in relation to motion*) which he characterised together with *entelecheia* (*potentiality*) in order to elaborate the concept, in his work Metaphysics.[87] This notion according to him, maintained every object's *essence* relating to the object's function. The verb *energeia* thus implied forms of motion, action, work and change.

After Aristotle, the term *energy* was commonly used as a literary, non-technical term by scientists and other scholars alike and used interchangeably with *power* and *force* rendering its usage vague.[88] David Hume confirmed the contemporary use of the term at the time in, *An Enquiry Concerning Human Understanding*, by stating that 'There are no ideas, which occur in metaphysics, more obscure and uncertain, than those of power, force, energy or necessary connexion, of which it is every moment

85 By 'conceptualising' or 'concept/notion' of energy and energy systems I mean ideas, values and approaches about energy as well as the understanding on energy.

86 Ricardo Lopes Coelho, 'On the Concept of Energy: History and Philosophy for Science Teaching', *Procedia - Social and Behavioral Sciences*, 1.1 (2009), 2648–52 <https://doi.org/10.1016/j.sbspro.2009.01.468>.

87 Vaclav Smil, *Energy: A Beg,inner's Guide*, 1st edn (Oxford: Oneworld Publications, 2006).

88 Alessandro Pascolini, 'Historical Aspects in the Development of the Concept of Energy : From Aristotle to Rankine' (Pöllau, 2014), p. 85. A presentation at the 'Energietag 2014' conference in Pöllau, Austria. School textbooks delineate between potential and kinetic energies, and provide examples of its different kinds: electricity, biomass energy, geothermal, fossil fuel, hydropower and ocean energy, nuclear energy, solar energy, wind energy, transportation energy, among others.

necessary for us to treat in all our disquisitions.'[89] Thus, confirming the idea commonly observed that energy means different things to different people and different situations.

In answering the basic question of what energy really is, influential Nobel Physics laureates grappled with this challenge. For instance, Richard Feynman put it this way in volume one of his *Lectures on Physics*[90],

> "It is important to realize that in physics today, we have no knowledge of what energy is. We do not have a picture that energy comes in little blobs of a definite amount. It is not that way. However, there are formulas for calculating some numerical quantity, and when we add it all together it gives "28"—always the same number. It is an abstract thing in that it does not tell us the mechanism or the reasons for the various formulas."

Moreover, Feynman establishes that what is factual is the law that governs all-natural phenomenon, which he characterises as the, *law of energy conservation:*

> "It states that there is a certain quantity, which we call energy that does not change in the manifold changes which nature undergoes. That is a most abstract idea, because it is a mathematical principle; it says that there is a numerical quantity, which does not change when something happens. It is not a description of a mechanism, or anything concrete; it is just a strange fact that we can calculate some number and when we finish watching nature go through her tricks and calculate the number again, it is the same."[91]

The philosopher, Giovanni Frigo, in summarising these debates among the following academics Coelho, Feynman and Smil on the notion of energy, while studying its phenomenon and history opines that they have been clear on pointing out the problem by providing a unified and reliable definition for energy. Further, revealing a pre-existing awareness of

89 David Hume, 'Of the Idea of Necessary Connexion', in *An Enquiry Concerning Human Understanding*, 1748, p. Section VII <https://doi.org/10.4324/9780203802458>.

90 Richard Feynman, Robert B. Leighton, and Matthew Sands, *The Feynman Lectures on Physics, Vol. 1: Mainly Mechanics, Radiation, and Heat, The Feynman Lectures on Physics*, 1st edn (Reading, Massachusetts; Palo Alto, CA; London, UK: Addisson-Wesley Publishing Company, Inc, 1963), I, pp. 4–11 <https://doi.org/10.1119/1.1972241>.

91 Feynman, Leighton, and Sands, I, pp. 4–11.

the epistemological limits of our understanding of energy. He concludes however with the claim that there are implied assumptions in policy and education, which have continued to base their work on what he calls the traditional energy paradigm without recognizing the precautionary advice of these academics.[92]

In this dissertation, bearing in mind the limitations discussed briefly above on the notion of energy, I adopt the approach of the physical concept of energy to assist in the conduct of this research. Physical scientists define *energy* today as the *capacity to do work*. The Dictionary of Energy reveals two perspectives on the definition of energy:

(a) A fundamental physical concept, defined classically as the capacity to do work. Described more generally as the potential ability of a system to influence changes in other systems by imparting either work (forced directional displacement) or heat (chaotic displacement/motion of system microstructure). And (b) the use of this capacity to perform useful functions for humans, such as heating or cooling buildings and enclosures, powering vehicles and machinery, lighting, cooking foods, and so on.[93]

In this regard, human societies, including the earliest, have relied on access to energy endowments that converts into another form of energy for usage as an energy service or product to facilitate work done. Classical and contemporary multi-disciplinary academic reflection on energy studies have sought to characterise energy in three ways, as a resource endowment, converted energy and energy service. An energy resource endowment relates to the type of energy sourced and its location of sourcing. Whereas converted energy deals with a particular sourced energy transformed for use. Moreover, an energy service constitutes the service usage of the sourced energy or converted energy.[94]

---

92 Giovanni Frigo, 'Energy Ethics, Homogenization, and Heg,emony: A Reflection on the Traditional Energy Paradigm', *Energy Research and Social Science*, 30.June (2017), 7–17 <https://doi.org/10.1016/j.erss.2017.06.030>.

93 Cutler J. Cleveland and Christopher G. Morris, *Dictionary of Energy*, ed. by Cutler J. Cleveland and Christopher G. Morris, 2nd edn (Elsevier Ltd., 2015) <https://doi.org/10.1016/B978-0-08-096811-7.50019-6>.

94 See Smil, Energy: A Beginner's Guide; Pascolini; Kathleen J. Hancock, 'Energy Regionalism : The Intersection of Resources, Regions, and Energy', in Sustainable Regions (Centre for the Study of Governance Innovation, University of Pretoria, 2014), pp. 1–5; Andrew Zimmerman Jones, 'Energy – Definition and Examples', About, Inc., 2016 <https://www.thoughtco.com/energy-definition-and-examples-2698976> [accessed 8 April 2017]; Michael James Fell, 'Energy Services: A Conceptual Review', Energy Research & Social Science, 27 (2017), 129–40 <https://doi.org/10.1016/j.erss.2017.02.010>.

Energy as a resource endowment

The term *energy resource endowment* recognises energy as an occurrence, resource and a reserve. Different institutions and organizations use many approaches to clarify an energy resource. This results in the lack of a clear, singular and universally accepted definition of what the term means.[95] However, the Global Energy Assessment (GEA)[96] characterises an energy resource endowment using the *McKelvey Box*[97]. It is used to categorise the nature and attributes of an energy resource. McKelvey proposed a commonly used diagram with a matrix structure for the classification of an energy resource endowment along two dimensions: geological surety and economic viability[98].

This diagram categorises *identified* reserves and resources, *undiscovered* resources and *recoverable and marginal* reserves and resources that rely on a degree of (geological) certainty and economic viability. The schematic is part of the classification used by the United Nations in its global assessment of energy resources.[99] According to this classification, resources are "concentrations of naturally occurring solid, liquid, or gaseous material in or on the Earth's crust in such form that economic extraction is potentially feasible".[100]

---

95 Cleveland and Morris.

96 The Global Energy Assessment (GEA) was launched in 2012. It defined a new global energy policy agenda, one that transforms the way society thinks about, uses, and delivers energy. The International Institute for Applied Systems Analysis (IIASA) coordinated it. Some of the leading energy experts in research, academia, business, industry and policy, representing both the industrialised and the industrialising world, led GEA. GEA was the first ever fully integrated energy assessment that analysed energy challenges, opportunities and strategies, for industrialising, industrialized and emerging economies. Governmental and non-governmental organizations, the United Nations Systems, and the private sector supported it. The Assessment was subjected to rigorous and independent analysis and review. See : http://www.iiasa.ac.at/web/home/research/Flagship-Projects/Global-Energy-Assessment/Home-GEA.en.html

97 The McKelvey resource classification (or simply the McKelvey Box or Diagram) was devised by the then director of the US Geological Survey (USGS), Vincent Ellis McKelvey, which the USGS and the US Bureau of Mines used as a tool to assess resources and reserves in terms of geological certainty and economic viability.

98 V.E. McKelvey, 'Mineral Resource Estimates and Public Policy', *American Scientist*, 60.1 (1972), 32–40 <https://doi.org/10.1021/es401221j>.

99 McKelvey.

100 GEA, *Global Energy Assessment -Toward a Sustainable Future, Cambridge University Press, Cambridge, UK and New York, NY, USA and the International Institute for*

Figure 2. 1 McKelvey Box: Principles of Energy Resource Classification, Illustrating the Definition of the Three Fundamental Concepts: Reserves, Resources, and Occurrences

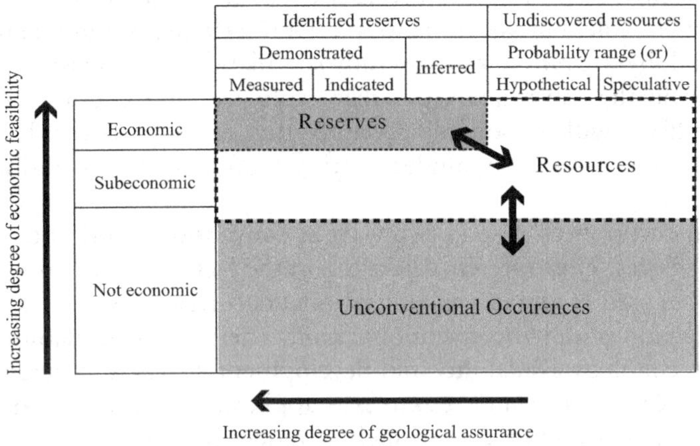

Source:[101]

Geologically, resources are in two forms – the *identified* and the *undiscovered.* The GEA explains that the *identified* are deposits that have a known location, grade, quality, and quantity and estimate from its geological origins[102]. Whereas the *undiscovered* on the other hand are, quantities expected or postulated to exist on materials found in analogous geological conditions.[103] The *identified* resources, based on the diagram, denote reserves. In principle, the entire resource base can become a reserve implying that discovered resources need to be extracted economically to serve as reserves. In order to understand how the frame of the diagram or box works, its usage can interpret the risk of future oil, coal and natural gas accessibility. To conclude on the GEA[104] definition of an energy resource endowment based on the degree of geological certainty and economic profitability, its three main aspects are considered:

Applied Systems Analysis, Laxenburg, Austria. (New York, 2012) <https://doi.org/10.1017/CBO9780511793677>.p.433

101 Adapted from McKelvey, p. 35; GEA, p. 122.

102 GEA, p. 122.

103 GEA, p. 122.

104 GEA. p.434

Occurrences: are hydrocarbons or fissile materials contained in the Earth's crust in some form of recognisable form.[105] Resources: are detected quantities that cannot be profitably recovered with current technology but might be recoverable in the future as well as those quantities that are geologically possible, but yet to be found. Undiscovered resources are what remain and, by definition, one can only speculate on their existence. Reserves: are generally those quantities that geological and engineering information indicate with reasonable certainty that can be recovered in the future from known reservoirs under existing economic and operating conditions.[106]

Hydrocarbon occurrences arise in two ways as conventional and unconventional occurrences. This difference borders on the fact that the technology and processes used in extracting conventional occurrences is not feasible for the extraction of the unconventional kind. Their future availability thus relies on technology availability and development.[107] These different ideas of occurrences, reserves and resources is applicable to varied energy sources even the unconventional ones such as renewable energy sources. Contextually, natural flows of geothermal, hydro, solar and wind energy as well as cultivated biomass can be referred to as renewable occurrences. Resources of renewable energy are harvested by using the concept of *technical potential*, which means the degree of use that is possible within the thermodynamic, geographical, or technological limitations without a full consideration of economic feasibility.[108]

Renewable energy reserves can mean a proportion of the technical potential that could be used cost-effectively with current technology. Since innovation and technology in the future is dynamic, this will lead to expanding the techno-economic frontier further, leading to *reserves* responding based on market conditions, demand and advances in conversion technologies. For example, solar energy's economic potential is largely dependent on the cost effectiveness of photovoltaic or concentrated solar conversion systems, electricity system integration at local, national or regional levels and local market conditions and not the overall amount of solar radiation available.[109]

---

105 WEC, Survey of Energy Resources, 18th Edition, (London: World Energy Council (WEC), 1998).

106 BP, 'Statistical Review of World Energy' (London: BP, 2010), pp. 1–11 <https://doi.org/10.2307/3324639>. p.434

107 GEA. p.434

108 GEA, p. 434.

109 GEA, p. 434.

Energy as converted energy

Another option for deriving energy is through the conversion of resource endowments, by passing it through a conversion system or technology to generate energy. Several innovative inventions in the late 19th century determined this converted energy pathway. Notable amongst them were electricity generation, power transmission systems and internal combustion engines, which led to the transformation of 20th century societies.

Even though their spread was curtailed by WW1 and the economic crises of the 1930s, they flourished during WW2. This was due to the introduction of three ground breaking technological innovations, that is, nuclear fission, gas turbines and rocket propulsion. Following the end of the Second World War, a rapid increase and diffusion of all energy systems was witnessed until the 1960s when the innovation of these systems peaked. Fully developed market systems, unfavourable ecological factors and hikes per unit cost rather than technological innovation were the underlying reasons for this peak.[110]

Energy services and uses

Energy services (or useful energy) is defined as the final use or end use that the addition of fuel makes possible. This understanding of energy services or useful energy concentrates on the supply of the end use and the fulfilment of human needs rather than focusing on the energy source or the conversion of energy (that is, production, diffusion, distribution or transmission technology) being used.[111] As modern economies transform, they shift their patterns of energy consumption.

These shifts focus on an incremental demand for commercial energy at various levels of demand per country be it an advanced or emerging economy. People in these economies require and buy not the commercial energy itself per se, but instead energy services (like mobility, washing, heating, cooking, cooling and lighting) made available by the energy system that converts energy sources and flows from nature into these services.[112]

---

110 Smil, *Energy and Civilization : A History*.

111 ECOWAS/UEMOA, *White Paper for a Regional Policy on Access to Energy Services for People in Rural and Peri-Urban Areas* (Niamey, 2005).

112 Reinhard Haas and others, 'Towards Sustainability of Energy Systems: A Primer on How to Apply the Concept of Energy Services to Identify Necessary Trends and Policies', *Energy Policy*, 36.11 (2008), 4012–21 <https://doi.org/10.1016/j.jpdc.2017.10.001>.

Useful energy is utilised to ensure residential comforts and industrial production. The use and share of energy fluctuate, accounting for the sluggish progression of energy meant for the provision of services. In this vein, useful energy accounts for the production of energy used by households both for essential and discretionary purposes. And ultimately, determines the path associated with increasing household wealth, thus leading to a rise in the share of energy services such as transportation and mobility.[113]

Two key inputs combine to provide energy services namely energy sources and energy technologies. With respect to energy sources, limited access to resource endowments and environmental restrictions constraint the production of these energy services and their availability. Energy technologies on the other hand are constrained by knowledge and expertise, and the limitations can range from being human, physical, natural, capital and institutional.[114] As a result, the provision of energy services can be direct or indirect with examples of direct energy services being lighting, cooling, heating, mobility and transport among others. And that of indirect energy services including communication, food, buildings, and vehicles (see Table 2.1 for a list).

Table 2. 1 Instances of Direct and Indirect Energy Services

Direct energy services		Indirect energy services	
– Lighting	– Cooling	– Food	– Buildings
– Washing	– Transport	– Shoes	– Vehicles
– Heating	– Drilling	– Shirts	– Furniture
– Ironing	– Sawing	– Clothes	– Paper
– Cooking	– Etc.	– Telecommunication and Exchange of information	– Purchasable goods in a market or supermarket
– Mobility			– Etc.

Source:[115]

113 Vaclav Smil, 'Energy in the Twentieth Century: Resources, Conversions, Costs, Uses, and Consequences', *Annu. Rev. Energy Environ.*, 2000, 21–51 <https://doi.org/10.1177/000312240507000602>.

114 Haas and others.

115 Adapted from Haas and others.

Therefore, understanding the concept of energy from the background of early, late and contemporary philosophical thinkers together with contemporary theoretical and experimental physicists provide a basis to contemplate on the aspects of what present-day physical scientists define as our *capacity to do work.* This aids to facilitate our comprehension of the delineated dimensions of the conceptual notion of energy as we know it today namely energy resource endowments, converted energy and energy services. To broaden this conceptual exercise on energy, three other dimensions are unpacked specifically the infrastructure, commons and policy dimensions of the conceptual notion of energy.

2.1.1. Energy Infrastructure Systems Revisited

In conceptualising the notion of energy, its infrastructure systems are essential to its understanding.[116] This is made clear in the idea of infrastructures and its application to the energy system in any geographical area. In appreciating infrastructure systems, one thinks of the notion of large-scale artificially constructed physical resources that enable public consumption. However, there are instances where it may include medium and small-scale fabricated physical resources particularly viewed from a capacious perspective.[117]

2.1.1.1 Infrastructure and Systems

Customary meanings of an *Infrastructure* primarily imply *basic structures and facilities* for the efficient functioning of a system and its *underlying framework*.[118] This requires the need to clarify the attributes of an infrastructure, which is evidenced by the view of Brett Frischmann[119] on the topic. He characterises this process as daunting, and goes on to classify three key features that define an infrastructure:

---

116 Energy infrastructure systems has two other common references, namely energy infrastructure or simply the energy system.

117 Brett M Frischmann, 'An Economic Theory of Infrastructure and Commons Management', *Minesota Law Review*, 89.89 (2005), 917–1030.

118 See in Bryan A. Garner, *Black's Law Dictionary*, ed. by Bryan A. Garner, 8th edn, 2004, p. 2286.

119 Brett M. Frischmann, *Infrastructure : The Social Value of Shared Resources* (New York: Oxford University Press, Inc, 2012).

(i) An *infrastructure* is a rudimentary structure and facility of any kind. For example, power grids and gas pipelines that transmit energy; ecosystems which can deploy mass of any kind; legal systems; healthcare systems; buildings, roads, harbours and bridges; genomes; as well as knowledge and value systems that disseminate information flows.

(ii) Numerous types of infrastructure combine to provide and determine the normative direction of its usage, which ensures efficient functioning. For example, for the purposes of producing services, provisioning products and the flow of information.

(iii) An *infrastructure* serves as the foundational component of any system. That is, the essential requirements needed as a prerequisite to construct a system.

Though few may contest these feature aspects of a traditional infrastructure, they are not adequate in differentiating an *infrastructure* from what is generally known as *capital* within the field of economics. The difference here is a result of the ordinary use of the terms. Where the terms capital or infrastructure implore ideas of commercial and private or shared (partially non-rival) goods, on smaller or larger scales, respectively. Other factors that may differentiate a traditional infrastructure is its ability to provide affordance, considered as an input that produce multiple outputs [analogous to what has been imputed in (ii) and (iii)]. Differences between these terms require careful scrutiny. Since I am more interested in a public, shared and commons managed infrastructure, within the context of energy, and the challenges of producing and maintaining it, the work presented here underscores the foundational aspect of infrastructure in my use of the term.

Similar to Brett Frischmann and John Anderies et al., my interest in infrastructure is motivated by how it functions in structuring social, economic and technical processes regarding energy governance in ways that can be very challenging to observe or quantify.[120] While Frischmann focuses on how managing certain classes of partially non-rivalrous infrastructures as open access will generate positive spillovers that benefit society[121], and Anderies et al. pays attention to how such inherent spillovers affect how

120 Brett M Frischmann; Brett M. Frischmann; John M. Anderies, Marco A. Janssen, and Edella Schlager, 'Institutions and the Performance of Coupled Infrastructure Systems', *International Journal of the Commons*, 10.2 (2016), 495–516 <https://doi.org/10.18352/ijc.651>.

121 Brett M. Frischmann, *Infrastructure: The Social Value of Shared Resources* (New York: Oxford University Press, Inc, 2012). p. 10–60

different classes of infrastructure interact to produce dynamics at the system level.[122]

This interest in how public, shared and commons-managed infrastructure in an energy system could generate positive spillovers that are socially beneficial and at the same time produce dynamics at the *system level* that are efficient, durable and sustainable for its functioning is related to what institutional economists and policy analysts term socio-ecological-technical systems (SETS).

2.1.1.2 Social – Ecological -Technical Systems (SETS)

Artificially constructed technological systems within the energy policy context such as power grids, gas pipelines, and oil refineries inter alia can be conceptualised as socio-ecological-technical systems (SETS). One with a familiarity of the notions of social ecological systems (SES) and social technical systems (STS) will not be wrong in claiming that SETS is a fused notion of both concepts and displays features that are attributable to both.

The distinct domains of socio-technical and socio-ecological systems reflect different objectives, problem frames, development and views of progression.[123] These two parallel and distinct systems emanate from different traditions. Firstly, social-ecological systems are based on biological ecosystems and their interactions with social processes including the appropriation and relationship to biological, physical and other resources. Socio-technical systems on the other hand are based on interactions between social practices and technological artefacts that influence each other.[124] Analysis of socio-technical systems incorporates knowledge, markets, regulation, cultural meaning, infrastructure, maintenance networks and supply networks as well as artefacts and practices.[125] A fusion of the socio-

---

122 John M. Anderies, Marco A. Janssen, and Edella Schlager, 'Institutions and the Performance of Coupled Infrastructure Systems', *International Journal of the Commons*, 10.2 (2016), 495–516 <https://doi.org/10.18352/ijc.651>.

123 Adrian Smith and Andy Stirling, 'The Politics of Social-Ecological Resilience and Sustainable Socio - Technical Transitions', *Ecology and Society*, 15.1 (2010), 11 <https://doi.org/10.5751/ES-03218-150111>.

124 Jennifer Hodbod and W. Neil Adger, 'Integ,rating Social-Ecological Dynamics and Resilience into Energy Systems Research', *Energy Research and Social Science*, 1 (2014), 226–31 <https://doi.org/10.1016/j.erss.2014.03.001>.

125 Frank W. Geels, *Technological Transitions and System Innovations : A Co-Evolutionary and Socio-Technical Analysis* (Edward Elgar, 2005).

ecological and socio- technical systems into a social-ecological-technical system in the energy policy space demonstrates an appreciation of the interactions that take place when social, ecological, economic, political and technological elements of energy systems are combined to identify potential trade-offs and regime shifts.

McGinnis and Ostrom[126] taking a cue from Künneke and Finger[127] outline a number of features that contrasts the new Social-Ecological-Technical-Systems from the conventional Social Ecological Systems. A key feature of socio-ecological technical systems shows in the ways primary users and actors experience their interaction with the system. For example, in contrast to an ordinary SES like a fishery, fish drawn from it can be identified as separate entities, but people reliant on electric power tend to see its delivery more in terms of a continuous service rather than the purchase of separate units.

Another unique variance is the situation where a clear distinction is drawn between people who have the technical expertise to understand the construction and maintenance of social-ecological-technical-systems and those who are merely concerned about their continued access to this resource. They admit a continuing challenge in differentiating between social-ecological-technical-systems (SETS) from social ecological systems (SES).

They also opine that the social side seems the same in both instances, even if the ultimate users of a technical resource do, in most cases, lack any direct knowledge of resource dynamics. They further allude that there is an important distinction between the relatively natural dynamics found in ecological systems and the constructed dynamic process of complex technical systems. But the distinction between the natural ecology and artificial technology is not as clear-cut as it may initially appear. To finish, they emphasise the virtual impossibility in finding an ecological system in the contemporary era, which is entirely free from human interference, nor any SETS in which the continued operation of the relevant technology bears no dependence on a naturally occurring phenomena.

---

126 Michael Dean McGinnis and Elinor Ostrom, 'Social-Ecological System Framework: Initial Changes and Continuing Challenges', *Ecology and Society*, 19.2 (2014) <https://doi.org/10.5751/ES-06387-190230>.

127 Rolf Künneke and Matthias Finger, 'The Governance of Infrastructures as Common Pool Resources', *Fourth Workshop on the Workshop (WOW4), June* 2–7, 2009, 1–24.

In conclusion, infrastructure systems in the energy policy context are social-ecological-technical-systems with multiple interactions, which impacts on the social–ecological systems of land use, food security and household energy consumption in addition to developmental transformation over multiple scales. Hence, for one to engage rigorously with an energy system that is social, ecological and technical in nature, it is crucial to consider the various types, resources and sectors involved in this energy infrastructure system.

2.1.1.3 The Energy System: Types, Resources and Sectors

The energy system encompasses dimensions that relate to generating, distributing and consuming energy. The present energy system incorporates a rather expanded mix of other aspects which includes the longevity of relevant infrastructure, the information technology revolution, population growth, ecological reasons, modern corporate law, sector-specific regulation and even financial issues such as the recent financial crises. Hence this enables one to best describe the energy system into two typical subsystems: the conventional system coupled with energy sources and associated technologies that generate excessive carbon emission problems and an alternative system with energy sources and technologies that do not, that is, decarbonised.

Dangerman and Schellnhuber describe the sources and technologies of this typology of subsystems based on (i) environmental implications (example, air, land, or water pollution; CO2 emissions; nuclear waste generation). (ii) The finiteness of available resources. (iii) The geopolitical stress accompanying their extraction and trading. And (iv) impact on the availability of cropland and food prices especially pertaining to biofuels.[128] Again, another typology of subsystems relates to the centralised and distributed nature of the energy system. The centralised system emphasises a core infrastructure, large scale and a non-end user participation. On the other hand, distributed energy highlights a periphery or edge infrastruc-

---

128 A T C Jérôme Dangerman and Hans Joachim Schellnhuber, 'Energy Systems Transformation', *Proceedings of the National Academy of Sciences*, 110.7 (2013), E549–58 <https://doi.org/10.1073/pnas.1219791110>.

ture, small-scale generation, consumer accessibility and end-user participation.[129]

Now to recap, I present how the various aspects of the introduction on the conceptualisation of energy fit together as components across the energy system value chain. In other words, primary energy resources, energy carriers and end-use applications of energy as typified by the Global Energy Assessment is that which constitutes the energy system.[130] Harnessed primary energy resources convert into energy carriers. These carriers consist of energy vectors such as electricity and fuels such as gasoline. They are further used in end-use application for the provision of energy forms (heat, kinetic energy, light, etc.) required for the delivery of energy services (example, thermal comfort or mobility). The crucial linkage across this energy conversion value chain from the provision of energy services all the way back to the extraction of primary energy resources are energy conversion technologies.

A further look into energy systems reveals two basic sectors: the energy supply sector and the energy end-use sector. The energy supply sector occasions the detailed sequence and process of extracting primary energy resources. This refers to what is known as the upstream activity. It may include, among other processes, oil exploration and production. Converting these into desirable forms of secondary energy is the midstream activity. This includes oil refining and liquefied natural gas transportation and distribution. Then finally, the downstream activity includes delivering energy to places where demand exists. On the other hand, the energy end-use sector delivers energy services such as motive power, cooking, illumination, comfortable indoor climate, refrigerated storage and transportation among others. The purpose of the entire energy system is the fulfilment of demand for energy services in satisfying human necessities.[131]

In conclusion, to characterise the energy infrastructure system, it must be understood to include all the physical resources that are artificially composed in large, medium or small scales that underlie an energy system of a defined geographical space and linked to the extraction, production,

129 George Dafermos and others, 'Transforming the Energy Matrix: Transition Policies for the Development of the Distributed Energy Model', *Journal of Peer Production*, 2015 <http://peerproduction.net/issues/issue-7-policies-for-the-commons/peer-reviewed-papers/transforming-the-energy-matrix/> [accessed 23 November 2018].

130 Global Energy Assessment, *Chapter 1: Energy Primer* (Cambridge: Cambridge University Press, 2012) <https://doi.org/10.1017/CBO9781107415324.004>.

131 Global Energy Assessment.

conversion and utilisation of energy. Energy infrastructure involves the physical infrastructure required for the production, transformation, transmission, distribution and storage of energy. The services it provides electrifies homes and communities, cools and heats residential and commercial buildings, connects producers and consumers in a market, and transports energy carriers of high calorific content across nations and geopolitical regions. An ably functional energy infrastructure system is an imperative in the creation and formation of modern societies. In summary, energy infrastructure is principally pivotal in the progressive functioning of an economy and for the sustainable growth of any society, especially in the transformation of markets and the provision of modern public and social services.

2.1.2. The Energy Commons

According to Professor Michael McGinnis, "the term commons is informally used to refer to public goods, common pool resources, or any area with uncertain property rights...for analytical purposes, it is necessary to be more specific."[132] This section's use of the term *commons* also refers to a resource openly accessible to all users irrespective of their identity or intended use of the resource.[133]

Commons, usually involve communal ownership (common pool resources, community property rights, open access resources, public property rights, joint ownership rights, etc.). This enable members of an applicable community to obtain open access "under rules that may range from 'anything goes' to quite crisply articulated formal rules that are effectively enforced".[134] This also allows for the exclusion of non-members.

---

132 Michael D. McGinnis, *Updated Guide to IAD and the Language of the Ostrom Workshop: A Simplified Overview of a Complex Framework for the Analysis of Institutions and Their Development*.

133 Lawrence Lessig, *The Future of Ideas: The Fate of the Commons in a Connected World, Duke Law Journal*, 2001, LII <https://doi.org/10.1007/s13398-014-0173-7.2>; Elinor Ostrom, *Governing the Commons - The Evolution of Institutions for Collective Action*.

134 Yochai Benkler, 'The Political Economy of Commons', *UPGRADE*, IV.3 (2003), 1–5. Yochai Benkler further explains that, commons are a particular type of institutional arrangement for governing the use and disposition of resources. Their salient characteristic, which defines them in contradistinction to property, is that no single person has exclusive control over the use and disposition of any particular resource. Instead, resources governed by commons may be used

Meanwhile, Elinor Ostrom explains commons as a generalised term, which is used to refer to a wide range of shared resources where it is hard to exclude people from these resources. But once they are involved and engaged with its usage and exploitation, whatever they exploit takes away from others.[135]

Theorising the commons emerged in reaction to arguments that collective action for mutually beneficial goals (including resource governance) is unattainable in large groups[136] without coercion[137] or private property rights[138]. This manner of looking at commons explores a wider set of conditions that can foster collective action.[139] Theoretically and practically a resource may be subject to over exploitation if property rights are not assigned clearly and appropriately. Specifically, this occurs when competing participants benefit entirely from an activity while the costs are spread over to all users of that resource. This is depicted in an activity such as grazing in animal husbandry – in this case all users are the herders.

Garret Hardin coined the famous statement "The Tragedy of the Commons" in order to describe this phenomenon.[140] Hardin's interpretation implied that communal use would lead automatically to sub-optimal management of the commons and that private property rights was the most preferred choice. Elinor Ostrom and her colleagues at the Ostrom Workshop at Indiana University (famously known as the Bloomington School) challenged this assertion by showing that communal rights do not automatically lead to overuse of the commons. They proved this through interdisciplinary research by using designed frameworks and detailed examination

---

or disposed of by anyone among some (more or less well defined) number of persons, under rules that may range from "anything goes" to quite crisply articulated formal rules that are effectively enforced.

135 Elinor Ostrom, 'Common-Pool Resources and Institutions: Toward a Revised Theory', in *Handbook of Agricultural Economics*, ed. by B. Gardner and G. Rausser (Elsevier Science B.V, 2002), II, 1315–39 <https://doi.org/10.1016/S1574-0072(02)10006-5>.

136 Mancur Jr. Olson, *The Logic of Collective Action: Public Goods and the Theory of Groups*, 2nd edn (Cambridge, MA: Harvard University Press, 1965).

137 Garrett Hardin, 'The Tragedy of the Commons', *Science*, 162.3859 (1968), 1243–48.

138 H Scott Gordon, 'The Economic Theory of a Common-Property Resource: The Fishery', *The Journal of Political Economy*, 62.2 (1954), 124–42.

139 Forrest D. Fleischman, Natalie C. Ban, and others, 'Governing Large-Scale Social-Ecological Systems: Lessons from Five Cases', *International Journal of the Commons*, 8.2 (2014), 428–56 <https://doi.org/10.18352/ijc.416>.

140 See Hardin.

of particular cases. They discovered that outcomes are not pre-determined, but rather depend on the attributes of each particular case.[141] In considering very similar situations, it happens that often one community may adopt an excellent governance regime, that is, self-governance, while a neighbouring community may not.

Related to their findings the Ostrom Workshop discovered that externally recommended or imposed solutions, such as individual property rights that replace collective rights, may lead to inferior outcomes.[142] In spite of the apparent variance in both arguments (that is, the argument of enforcement in private property by Garret Hardin and of exchange in the commons by Elinor Ostrom), they both acknowledge that property rights are embedded in a complex institutional frame.

Partha Dasgupta, in his analysis of the commons, shows that the provision of private property rights in this complex setting is an institutional remedy that leads to socially optimal results under certain conditions. He states that;

> "both privatisation of the grazing land and cooperation over the use of that land as a common pool resource (CPR) involve trust. If the allocation defined by equation … is to be realised, the herdsmen have to trust the 'legal system' or rules in use (either written or not) to enforce private property rights in their parcels of land. Similarly, if cooperation over the use of the pasture as a CPR is to be achieved, they

141 Ostrom, Elinor, *Governing the Commons – The Evolution of Institutions for Collective Action* (Cambridge: Cambridge University Press, 1990)

142 Xavier Basurto and Elinor Ostrom, 'Beyond the Tragedy of the Commons', *Economia Delle Fonti Di Energia e Dell'ambiente*, 2009, 35–60 <https://doi.org/10.3280/EFE2009-001004>; Elinor Ostrom, 'A General Framework for Analyzing Sustainability of Social-Ecological Systems', *Science*, 325.5939 (2009), 419–22 <https://doi.org/10.1126/science.1172133>; Elinor Ostrom and others, 'Revisiting the Commons: Local Lessons, Global Challenges Local Lessons, Global Challenges', *Science* (New York, April 1999), 278–82 <https://doi.org/10.1126/science.284.5412.278>; Paul Dragoş. Aligică and Peter J. Boettke, *Challenging Institutional Analysis and Development: The Bloomington School* (Routledge, 2009) <https://www.routledge.com/Challenging-Institutional-Analysis-and-Development-The-Bloomington-School/Aligica-Boettke/p/book/9780415778213> [accessed 20 April 2018]; Bonnie J Mccay and Joan Bennett, 'Elinor Ostrom 1933–2012' (National Academy of Sciences, 2014), p. 9 <http://www.nasonline.org/publications/biographical-memoirs/memoir-pdfs/ostrom-elinor.pdf>.

> have to trust one another to enforce the agreement to limit each herd size..."[143]

The main consideration here is not a focus on ownership and regulation, but on open access (common access and public access). This open access is determined by a resource governance decision that may be obtained privately or publicly, politically or economically, within the context of property rights, regulation, or some hybrid regime.[144]

I deliberately draw on the institutional perspective of property rights, regulations and norms to explain the peculiar institutional function of opening or restricting access. Tying this perspective and function together unveils the fact that access can be made available or restricted through numerous institutional approaches. These approaches could be often mixed (property and regulation, private and communal property, etc.), but it is seldomly observed through one particular model of property rights.[145] This function can arise as an internal governance regime, as a self – governing organization of a market, or because of public policy decision-making.[146]

Eventually, the degree of openness or restrictiveness is contingent on a number of functional political economy considerations. This relates to the nature of the specific resource and the way and manner in which the resource is consumed in terms of value addition, institutional arrangements, and the community setting.[147] The governance of commons in general is 'one of the most difficult tasks facing modern public policy'.[148] To serve the aims of this dissertation, the term 'commons' will refer to a de jure

---

143 Partha Dasgupta, 'Common Property Resources : Economic Analytics', *Economic and Political Weekly*, 40.16 (2005), 1610–22 (p. 1614) <https://doi.org/10.2307/2404396>.

144 Brett Frischmann, 'Privatization and Commercialization of the Internet Infrastructure', *The Columbia Science and Technology Law Review*, 1.1999 (2001) <http://www.law.columbia.edu/stlr> [accessed 23 November 2018].

145 Robert A Heverly, 'The Information Semicommons', *Berkeley Technology Law Journal*, 18.4 (2003), 1127–89 <https://doi.org/10.15779/Z38B69G>.

146 Joseph Farrell and Philip J Weiser, 'Modularity, Vertical Integration, and Open Access Policies: Towards a Convergence of Antitrust and Regulation in the Internet Age', *Harvard Journal of Law & Technology*, 17.1 (2003), 85 <http://scholar.law.colorado.edu/articleshttp://scholar.law.colorado.edu/articles/539.>. Farrell and Weiser term this governance of an open access resource as Modularity.

147 Brett M Frischmann.

148 Ostrom, II.

or de facto governance structure "governing the use and disposition of"[149] an energy resource in a transnational and geopolitical regional community that exhibits a degree of supranationalism. Therefore, an energy region is a *commons*, in this sense, an *energy commons.*

In this regard an understanding of energy, its resources, infrastructures, services and related components as a good is critical. Four types of goods exhibit two primary characteristics of exclusion and subtractability. This defines the nature of goods. Exclusion denotes the degree to which others can preclude non-members from the use of goods.[150] Subtractability refers to the un-shareable nature of the goods, that is, if one person uses the good it subtracts from the pool of available goods.[151]

On occasion where it is easy to exclude others from the use of a good, coupled with a high degree of subtractability, the type of good is likely to be characterized as private goods and are defined by property law and best regulated by the market.[152] Conditionally, when exclusion is difficult and subtractability is low that is, it is difficult to subtract from the good, then the goods are likely considered as public goods and preferably managed by governments.[153] Thirdly, toll goods, are those that exhibit ease of exclusion but low subtractability.[154] Finally, common pool goods are those that have high subtractability and difficulty of exclusion.[155] The two-fold difference along these dimensions is used to create the typology of goods provided in Table 2.2

149 Benkler.p.1 – 5

150 Susan J. Buck, *The Global Commons: An Introduction* (Washington D.C.: Island Press, 1998) <https://doi.org/10.1016/s0962-6298(00)00042-1>.

151 Janine Hiller, Scott Shackelford, and Xiao Ma, *The Firm as Common Pool Resource: Unpacking the Rise of Benefit Corporations*, White Paper Series (Bloomington, 2017).

152 Hiller, Shackelford, and Ma.

153 Daniel H Cole and Michael Dean McGinnis, *Elinor Ostrom and the Bloomington School of Political Economy. Volume 2. Resource Governance : Polycentricity in Public Administration and Political Science, Books by Maurer Faculty*, 2015 <https://www.repository.law.indiana.edu/facbooks/24> [accessed 20 April 2018].

154 Daniel H Cole and McGinnis.

155 Daniel H Cole and McGinnis.

Table 2. 2 Typology of Goods

	Easy exclusion	*Difficult exclusion*
High subtractability	Private goods	Common-pool goods
Low subtractability	Toll goods	Public goods

Source:[156]

The impetus for such a typology is to explore and predict governance challenges and the governance arrangements that might be most effective in managing each type of good. Conventionally, private goods and toll goods are seen as being optimally governed by market rules or private property rights, while public goods and common-pool resources are governed through public property rights and commons management respectively[157].

The justification for this approach is that common-pool resources and public goods create governance challenges commonly referred to as collective-action problems or externalities. These occur when public interests diverge from short-term private interests.[158] In the case of public goods, the creation of public good provision problems occur around the maintenance of energy infrastructure, where participants need to be incentivized in order not to free ride on the efforts of others to provide the public good.[159] On the other hand, common-pool resources produce appropriation challenges, such as the over-exploitation of energy, where participants must be incentivized to manage their consumption of an exhaustible resource.[160]

There are a number of drawbacks inherent in the typology of goods. To begin with, the dimensions of subtractability and excludability alters along a continuum. Here, the distinction between common-pool resources and public goods is not clear. The term 'congestability' describes these differences that exist in relation to subtractability of public goods and common-pool resources.[161] This would then be equivalent to referring to some goods as possessing thresholds of use. There is no more subtractabil-

156 Adapted from Jochen Hinkel and others, 'A Diagnostic Procedure for Applying the Social-Ecological Systems Framework in Diverse Cases', *Ecology and Society*, 20.1 (2015) <http://www.ecologyandsociety.org/vol20/iss1/art32/>.

157 Arild Vatn, *Institutions and the Environment* (Cheltenham, UK: Edward Elgar); David. L Weimer and Aidan. R. Vining, *Policy Analysis : Concepts and Practice*, 5th edn (Upper Saddle River, New Jersey USA: Prentice Hall, 2005).

158 Hinkel and others.

159 Hinkel and others.

160 Hinkel and others.

161 Weimer and Vining.

ity above the threshold while below it, it is less so.[162] An example of this is traffic on highways. It is not different from the subtractability of common-pool resources similar to fishing in a lake: if a fisherman takes a quantity of fish that the fish can replenish, then this usage is not very subtractable.[163] This emphasises an additional weakness of the typology of goods: the attribute of subtractability is tied to a temporal period.

With reference to excludability as well, is also a continuum than a two-fold distinction. Moreover, it is not only an inherent feature of a resource but also a feature of a relationship between the resources and other key aspects such as financial and physical resources or available technologies.[164] The number of issues addressed reveal the difficulty inherent in the use of the typology of goods as a foundation in depicting the governance challenges related to a given good as well as for delineating and recommending the most effective governance structure required.

The energy system and its resources are not inherently commons, in the same way that a banana is not inherently private.[165] However, energy, its infrastructure and (most applicable to this research) its governance at a comparative regionalism level have been referred to as commons or common pool resources (CPRs).[166] Charles Elworthy in characterising energy from the perspective of the commons identified four forms, namely, energy resources as commons, energy frontiers as commons, renewable resources as commons and the global energy commons.[167] Künneke and Finger extended these characterisations by including energy infrastructure

162 Hinkel and others, p. 3.

163 Hinkel and others.

164 Hinkel and others.

165 The focus here is primarily the forms of energy that populate the energy system such as fossil-fuels, particularly oil, and gas and the other alternatives namely coal, nuclear, wind, solar, biofuels, geothermal, hydro and other renewables. Since it may sound as a misnomer to term all of them as "energy" as it may not be their most valuable usage, I will continue to use this convention. The issues of property rights regarding energy in general is interesting to place under this type of consideration.

166 Anders Bäckman, 'The Nordic Electricity System as a Common-Pool Resource.', 2011 <http://www.diva-portal.org/smash/record.jsf?pid=diva2:437865>; Charles Elworthy, 'The Energy Commons: A Governance Framework for Climate Stability and Energy Security', 2011, p. 60 <www.academia.edu>; Künneke and Finger.

167 Elworthy.

within the larger infrastructure commons.[168] Thus, I highlight five unique energy commons worthy of explication.

Energy resource commons refers to fossil fuels, which for the most part is subject to clearly defined property rights. Yet further investigation reveals that in the vast majority of jurisdictions there are complicated private property rights, which provide for the ownership and sale of energy resources comparable to other resources such as land or buildings. Instead, states are predominantly the legal owners of these energy resources, they control extraction directly, either through their own enterprises, or indirectly through the creation of licences to extract under certain conditions. Few countries like the United States that allocate direct ownership rights for energy resources have very extensive legal and regulatory systems which govern multiple dimensions of energy extraction, from financial payments through to technical and environmental provisions.[169]

In relation to energy frontiers as commons, they refer to regions such as the Arctic, where territorial sovereignty is not clearly assigned to particular nation-states.[170] Moreover, energy resources are so highly valuable that where such rights do not exist panaceas tend to be found. Significant progress in the delineation of rights under the Law of the Sea and in areas such as the Arctic and the South China Sea can be attributed to this pressure.[171] Complimentary processes have resulted in the resolution of extractive commons, similar to when several parties had rights to gas resources, which were linked to form one common pool.

The renewable energy resource commons relate to attempts to exploit free available renewable resources such as wind, wave, tidal and solar energy among others. These are open access resources, and with increasing energy harvesting, steadily more adverse spatial externalities among producers could be expected. The establishment of legal frameworks and increased global political attention provides solutions to this characteristic of the energy commons, which includes assigning appropriate property

---

168 Künneke and Finger.

169 Elworthy.

170 Richard C. Powell, 'Configuring an "Arctic Commons"?', *Political Geography*, 27.8 (2008), 827–32 <https://doi.org/10.1016/j.polgeo.2008.08.008>; Oran R. Young, 'Global Commons: The Arctic in World Affairs', *Technology Review*, 93.2 (1990).

171 Myron H Nordquist, John Norton Moore, and Alexander S Skaridov, *International Energy Policy, the Arctic and the Law of the Sea*, *Center for Oceans Law and Policy* (Leiden/Boston: Martinus Nijhoff Publishers, 2005).

rights.[172] To exemplify this phenomenon, distributed energy systems display the features of the renewable energy commons.[173]

The global energy commons, especially those linked to fossil fuels is quite abstract and normative to typify. The international energy system has no clear centralised authority, so that the logic of the fundamental collective action problem is very much alike.[174] Comportment of one country alone, even if large and well intentioned, is doomed to failure unless other countries are similarly cooperative.[175]

In considering the energy infrastructure commons, Künneke and Finger[176], fit the major features of excludability together in a resource system. This includes appropriation problems related to rivalry in the consumption of essential services and the coordination needed to derive system complementarities. In addition, there is also the problem of diffusion of property rights and decision rights with respect to the resource system within the multi-purpose services that contribute to dispersing and conflicting stakeholder interests.

Goldthau's examination of energy infrastructure reaffirms completely the claims by Künneke and Finger. However, he extends the claim of energy infrastructure as a common pool resource by advocating for polycentric governance of these types of infrastructure. He makes this assertion based on the primary characteristics of scale and multiple elements exhibited by the infrastructure. Within the first criterion of scalability, he maintains that energy infrastructure functions on a multi-level scale revealing the features shared with local and global commons. On the second criterion,

---

172 Daniel T Kaffine and Christopher M Worley, 'The Windy Commons?', *Environmental and Resource Economics*, 47.2 (2010), 151–72 <https://doi.org/10.1007/s10640-010-9369-2>.

173 See Maarten Wolsink, 'Distributed Generation of Sustainable Energy as a Common Pool Resource: Social Acceptance in Rural Setting of Smart (Micro-)Grid Configurations', *New Rural Spaces : Towards Renewable Energies, Multifunctional Farming, and Sustainable Tourism*, 2014, 36–47; Maarten Wolsink, 'Non-Hierarchic Polycentric Regimes Facilitating Intelligent Distributed Energy Systems-The CPR Nature of Renewables Conceptualization of Society-Environment Relations View Project Environmental Justice in Environmental Policy Infrastructure View Project N', 2018, p. 6 <https://www.researchgate.net/publication/328916701>.

174 Robert. O. Keohane and Elinor Ostrom, 'Local Commons and Global Interdependence: Heterogeneity and Cooperation in 2 Domains - Introduction', *Journal of Theoretical Politics*, 6.4 (1994), 403–28.

175 Elworthy.

176 Künneke and Finger.

multiple stakeholder groups involved at the various levels, depending on the scale of operation engage in policy processes that advance governance and regulation of these energy systems.[177]

In conclusion, to represent energy as a common pool resource (CPR) or commons is demonstrated by the numerous depictions stated above in various forms. The very nature of energy as a good in terms of the binary references of exclusion and subtractability situates energy clearly as a commons. In that, exclusion from benefiting from an energy system by not obtaining certain energy services among other things is costly and high. An example of this is the consequences of fuel and energy poverty causing deaths in both the developed and developing parts of the world. Moreover, consumption of energy is subtractive, that is, one person's consumption subtracts from the total energy produced even in situations where there is storage capacity involved. Again, this is seen in the emerging renewable energy technologies used for production and storage of energy. Thus, having established that energy is a common (or CPR) it gives rise to a common pool resource type of collective action problems.[178] This is then resolved in energy policy making through a diverse mix of property regimes for the governance of commons (or CPRs) as the subsequent sections in this chapter seeks to address.

2.1.3. Morphogenesis of Energy as a Policy Area

The aim of this next section is to outline energy as a policy area by briefly providing a broad overview of the coming into shape of energy as a vital decision-making area within the public policy space. It sheds light on the emergence and development of energy policy over time. Building on the analyses put forward in the works of Andrew Marquard[179] and Vaclav

177 Andreas Goldthau, 'From the State to the Market and Back: Policy Implications of Changing Energy Paradigms', *Global Policy*, 3.2 (2012), 198–210 <https://doi.org/10.1111/j.1758-5899.2011.00145.x>.

178 Elinor Ostrom, 'How Types of Goods and Property Rights Jointly Affect Collective Action', *Journal of Theoretical Politics*, 15.3 (2003), 239–70 <https://doi.org/10.1177/0951692803015003002>.

179 Andrew Marquard, 'The Origins and Development of South African Energy Policy', 2006, p. 445.

Smil,[180] I distinguish between four major periods in the evolution of what we now call energy policy.

To begin with, the word 'morphogenesis', used here to explain the beginnings of energy policy, is adopted from the work of British sociologist, Margaret Archer. It emanates from the Greek terms *morpho* (shape) and *genesis* (origin). Hence, 'morphogenesis' denotes 'those processes which tend to elaborate or change a system's current form, state, or structure'.[181] Energy policy is the way in which institutions of power decide and allocate resources with regard to energy use and its development. This includes energy generation, distribution and consumption.

The pre-historic foundations of energy use in society expresses its profound importance by how it has shaped the formation of the nature and form of the actors, structures and normative processes involved with the multi-phased evolution of current energy policy making processes. As Andrew Marquard notes, in his *Origins and Development of South African Energy Policy*, that energy policy is a unified policy area that focused on a number of elements. This included, states seeking remedies for security of supply challenges arising out of growing economies, building and rebuilding during pre and post war periods, the rapid progression in regulation of natural resources in mining policy, the promotion of natural resources for energy and the advancement of national industrial programmes. None of this culminated in a cohesive conceptual process in dealing with energy since the centralised focus was the building of networked industries that relied heavily on different sources of energy. Accordingly, energy issues were treated as a secondary infrastructural need. He argues that by the 1970s all nations had adopted the nomenclature 'energy policy' as a state activity.[182]

The Swedish environmentalist Nils Magnus Måns Lönnroth observed that in the Swedish energy policy experience, "...energy as a gestalt is fairly new. It emerged during the 1950s. Earlier Sweden did not have an

---

180 Smil, *Energy: A Beginner's Guide*; Vaclav Smil, *World History and Energy*, ed. by Cutler J. Cleveland, *Concise Encyclopedia of the History of Energy*, 1st edn (San Dieg,o: Elsevier Inc., 2009), i <http://vaclavsmil.com/wp-content/uploads/docs/smil-article-2004world-history-energy.pdf>; Smil, *Energy and Civilization : A History*.

181 Margaret S. Archer, *Realist Social Theory: The Morphogenetic Approach* (Cambridge: Cambridge University Press, 1995), p. 166 <https://doi.org/10.2307/2655684>; Margaret S. Archer, *Social Morphogenesis*, ed. by Margaret S. Archer (Dordrecht: Springer, 2013), p. 2.

182 Marquard, pp. 42–44.

energy policy but an electricity policy, a fuels policy, and so forth".[183] Thus inferring that energy policy came about by combining existing threads of policy relating to energy supply industries and the creation of a policy domain that delineated state intervention in that respect.

In this research study, I enumerate four unique periods in the morphogenetic development of energy planning and policy. One must understand that, a look at these processes is done purely from a uniquely western industrial perspective, which has had spill over effects in other geopolitical regions. This happened due to pre-existing global political dynamics within these periods. Depicting the four stages, I use the following classifications: primary period, secondary period, cyclical period and the energy-climate period.

The primary period of energy policy development started in the late 18th to the 20th centuries. During this era, an initial observation of energy carriers depicts a sequential add-on in their transition from one energy form to the other. In that, when transitioning from the use of fuel wood to coal, carriers do not abandon using the former, instead they add-on coal to the repertoire of energy supply sources. This is similar to when carriers are transitioning from coal to oil. All these supply sources of energy carriers were jointly denoted as 'fuel'. Electricity was categorised separately as 'power' because it relied on motive energy. The merging of these categories as 'energy' was in tandem with the development of the collective term, the 'energy sector'.

All these developments in fuels established the energy supply industries in the energy economy. This period under review set in motion the early innovations of energy production and supply technologies that would later be known as energy carriers. It laid the foundations for the technological developments that underpin today's modern energy systems. This included the heavy energy consuming industries and the modern energy sector technically referred to as *prime movers*.[184]

Notable among the prime movers that were invented in the 1800s were the *steam turbine* by Charles Parsons, which today serves as the technology that underpins electricity power plants. The *internal combustion engine* which was developed for automobiles by the German innovators Daimler, Maybach and Benz as well as the *electric motor* invented by Nikola Tesla.

---

183 M Lönnroth, 'Swedish Energy Policy: Technology in the Political Process', in *The Energy Syndrome: Comparing National Responses to the Energy Crisis*, ed. by LN Lindberg (Lexington: Lexington Books, 1978), pp. 268–69.

184 Smil, *Energy and Civilization : A History*.

Other prime movers invented in the 1800s that formed the pivot on which todays modern energy system was built included the *gas turbine* and the *jet engine*. These were developed in the latter years of the 1800s into the mid-1900s. These new innovations had already been studied. However, two completely independent but simultaneous works brought it to fruition. Hans Joachim Pabst von Ohain, referred to as the father of the gas turbine in Nazi Germany and Sir Frank J. Whittle, the English inventor of the turbo jet aircraft engine concurrently developed these prime movers during this period. The fourth prime mover, the *rocket motor*, a completely different invention in terms of purpose and usage came into being in the 1930s and 1940s. It entirely enabled the launching of objects and sending people into space.[185]

The secondary period of energy policy development was characterised by the coming into being of proper and mature energy policy. This era is demarcated by the consolidation of all the energy carriers as a singular focus of energy public policy making in order to meet energy needs. The temporal foundations of this phase can be situated within the post-World War II period (ca.1950s). This period, depicted by the development of rapid economic growth in the aftermath of the Great War led to a dire need for energy supplies.[186] As a result, it encouraged efforts towards policy harmonisation and integration of the energy carriers and their respective matching sectors that typified this period.

Subsequently, the sectors that arose out of these energy transformations encouraged State participation through the making of public policy decisions on the prime movers as a means for guaranteeing energy supply, mobility and advancing strategic military and space interests. This state-led intervention consequently resulted in the formation of institutions with the aim of legislating, managing, governing and regulating these individual energy supply sectors that inhabited the use of these prime movers for energy supply as a whole. Thus, the coming together of these unique energy sectors led to a new form of state involvement through policy developments and institutional formations that was developed for the whole energy sector as a policy gestalt.

---

185 Smil, 1; Smil, 'Energy in the Twentieth Century: Resources, Conversions, Costs, Uses, and Consequences'; Smil, *Energy and Civilization : A History*.

186 Vaclav Smil, *Energy at the Crossroads - Global Perspectives and Uncertainties*, *Global Science Forum Conference on Scientific Challenges for Energy Research* (Cambridge, Massachusetts: The MIT Press, 2003) <https://doi.org/10.1002/joc.1346>.

The cyclical period of energy policy development denotes the third period, which was characterised by the major world oil crisis in 1973 and 1979. This led to the expansion of energy policymaking particularly in the aftermath of the 1973 oil crisis. Witnessed in this period, was a culminating increase in state involvement and interest in the energy sector. This was coupled with cooperation and collective action of the most affected states in the OECD. The crisis revealed severe shortcomings in the energy policy of these OECD countries. Leading to the creation of an organisation, the International Energy Agency (IEA) that would deal with the energy crisis using a coordinated response.[187]

The early 1990s saw the evolution of a new period of energy policymaking that was linked with narratives connected with the climate. This fourth period of energy policy development is termed as the energy – climate period. The growing concerns of global warming characterises this period. Global warming is the situation where the earth warms up as a result of the increase in carbon and other greenhouse gas emissions into the Earth's atmosphere causing intense atmospheric pressure that upends climatic conditions. It is in part caused by anthropogenic activities (meaning human caused factors) such as energy production through the workings of these prime movers in generating energy and on the other hand by intensive meat production and consumption[188].

This has led to a completely new approach to doing and transforming energy policy with the inclusion of the climate discourse. Another, unique dimension of this period is the nature of the international negotiations that has characterised this thematic issue over the years. This can be seen in conferences and accords such as the Kyoto protocol and Paris climate agreement as well as the Bali, Copenhagen, Durban and Bonn conferences among others that ultimately have had an influence in shaping national, regional and international energy and climate policies.

---

187 Thijs Van de Graaf, *The Politics and Institutions of Global Energy Governance*, 1st edn (London: Palgrave Macmillan, 2013).

188 Vaclav Smil, 'Eating Meat: Constants and Changes', *Global Food Security*, 2014, 1–5 <https://doi.org/10.1016/j.gfs.2014.06.001>; William J Ripple and others, 'Ruminants, Climate Change and Climate Policy', *Nature Climate Change*, 4. January (2014), 2–5 <https://doi.org/10.1038/nclimate2081>.

2.2 International Political Economy (IPE) of Energy: Shaping Energy Policy

It is a clear consideration now that international political economy (IPE) of energy as a section of the scholarly field of IPE should not only be limited to its precursory focus on petroleum or oil but to incorporate other agenda and issues reflective of the entire energy sector.[189] IPE as an interdisciplinary field of study re-emerged within the context of two major historical settings in the 1970s. The first being the end of the fixed exchange rate instituted under the Bretton Woods accords and the second being the global energy crisis triggered by the OPEC oil embargo to Western countries.

In 1971, President Nixon due to pressure from high inflation caused by increasing government expenditure cancelled the fixed dollar exchange rate and the gold standard, which had underpinned the formation of the Bretton Woods institutions namely The World Bank, International Monetary Fund (IMF) and General Agreement on Tariffs and Trade (GATT) (replaced by the World Trade Organisation in 1995). In 1973, the Arab-Israeli War (also known as the *Yom Kippur*) caused oil prices to skyrocket compelling the Arab members of OPEC to suppress oil supplies to western nations. This emphasised to scholars and policy makers the power of commodity exporting states among the newly independent countries. This newfound power by these states encouraged them to call for a new world economic order, which they called the New International Economic Order (NIEO).

Historically, the roots of the IPE field can be traced to classical economists, social change theorists, institutional and welfare economists, anthropologists and international economic relations scholars between the eighteenth through to the first half of the twentieth century.[190] Scholars of IPE in the 1970s leveraged on the intellectual traditions of the political

189 Hancock and Vivoda.

190 Nascent contributions to the founding of the field of IPE leads to the following individuals: Classical economics (e.g., Adam Smith, David Ricardo, and John Stuart Mill), social change theory (e.g., Karl Marx and Emile Durkheim), institutional and welfare economics (e.g., Alfred Marshall, Arthur Cecil Pigou, John Maynard Keynes, Joseph Schumpeter, Karl Polanyi, Thorstein Veblen and Albert Hirschman) and International economic relations scholars (e.g., Jacob Viner, Charles P. Kindleberger and Jagdish Bhagwati)

economy of International Relations.[191] At its core, IPE is the study of the relationship between politics and economics at the international level. Robert Gilpin influenced the definition of IPE to encompass the inquiry of how the State interacts with the market at the global level.[192] Multiple versions of the field of IPE is delineated based on locational origins and theoretical approaches.[193]

Specifically, IPE concerns itself with the interactions between international markets and actors in the allocation of physical and monetary goods and resources. However, IPE recognises that these interactions carry with them certain power dynamics, which cannot be simply consigned to the realm of either politics or economics within the international context. This undertaking is exercised typically with normative aims and methods coupled with a focus on international outcomes. IPE seeks to analyse and explain the interaction between political features and economic outcomes across different systems and across different countries. It also explores the reverse side of economic influence and its impact on political systems. Institutions, ideas and interests are very helpful components for the research of IPE. To sum up on what IPE fundamentally is based on, Laswell's famous question – "who gets what, when and how" depicts the allocation outcomes in the interaction between economic and political processes.[194]

The common principles that underlie this heterogeneous field include the linkage between politics and economics. These undergird the analyses of resource allocation and the interrelated dynamics between the structural

---

191 John Ravenhill, 'International Political Economy', in *The Oxford Handbook of International Relations*, ed. by Christian Reus-Smit Duncan Snidal (Oxford: Oxford University Press, 2008), pp. 539–57 <https://doi.org/10.1093/oxfordhb/9780199219322.003.0031>.

192 Robert Gilpin, *The Political Economy of International Relations* (Princeton,NJ: Princeton University Press, 1987).

193 Mark Blyth, *Routledge Handbook of International Political Economy (IPE)*, ed. by Mark Blyth, *Routledge Handbook of International Political Economy (IPE): IPE as a Global Conversation*, 1st edn (Abingdon, Oxford: Routledge, 2009) <https://doi.org/10.1355/ae26-3j>; Benjamin J. Cohen, *Advanced Introduction to International Political Economy, Elgar Advanced Introductions Series*, 1st edn (Massachusetts: Edward Elgar, 2014) <https://doi.org/10.4337/9781783470600.00011>; Roy H Smith, Imad El-Anis, and Christopher Farrands, *International Political Economy in the 21st Century: Contemporary Issues and Analyses*, ed. by Roy H Smith, Imad El-Anis, and Christopher Farrands, 2nd edn (London and New York: Routledge, 2017).

194 H. D. Lasswell, *Politics: Who Gets What, When, How* (New York: Whittlesey House, 1936).

dimension of global markets and the agency required during political and economic interactions.[195]

Applying IPE to the study of energy reaps immense benefits. It reveals the influence of political structures on energy markets and shape these interactions by consolidating forms of hegemony.[196] It studies the basic dynamics inherently behind deployed energy technologies and policies. Moreover, it reveals who benefits from a programme or policy roll-out and at whose expense. For example, a particular energy transition scheme to non-fossil fuels.[197] The logic of the exchange of energy and its interdisciplinary nature relies heavily on its connectedness with power structures, norms, processes and rules (at the state, regional, international as well as other energy spaces). It results in a clear understanding of the IPE of energy, which aids in comprehending energy governance and the ways to improve it.

Finally, to conclude, it is necessary to clarify that research on the IPE of energy and its analytical approach may reflect three essential aspects that can aid in debates bordering on energy governance and the design of energy policy:

1. IPE of energy identifies the engagement with multiple actors and institutions at the national level.
2. IPE of energy characterises the interconnected and interdependent regional and international influences on policy processes.
3. IPE of energy relies on the intersectionality of the state, market and commons.

2.2.1 National Energy Governance

Traditionally, states have regarded their energy sector as a critical component of national sovereignty despite the rewards derived from internation-

195 Thijs Van De Graaf and others, *The Palgrave Handbook of the International Political Economy of Energy*, ed. by Thijs Van De Graaf and others, 1st edn (London: Palgrave Macmillan, 2016) <https://doi.org/10.1057/978-1-137-55631-8_12>.

196 Van De Graaf and others.

197 Benjamin K. Sovacool, Björn-Ola Linnér, and Michael E. Goodsite, 'The Political Economy of Climate Adaptation', *Nature Climate Change*, 5.7 (2015), 616–18 <https://doi.org/10.1038/nclimate2665>; James Meadowcroft, 'What about the Politics? Sustainable Development, Transition Management, and Long Term Energy Transitions', *Policy Sciences*, 42 (2009), 323–40 <https://doi.org/10.1007/s11077-009-9097-z>.

al cooperation. This illustrates national energy governance as the most dominant domain in comparison to regional or global energy governance. The example of the European Union (EU), by far the most advanced global experiment of regional integration, advances this point. Here, the member states have calculatedly protected their sovereign prerogatives with regard to energy policy. This scenario has resulted in a phenomenon where states with minimal control over energy policy—due to globalised energy markets and its concomitant externalities— remain largely unwilling to act jointly. The resulting picture leads to a "paradox of sovereignty"[198].

Energy markets nationally are shaped by demand and supply. Supply dynamics and demand-pulls are influenced within domestic power structures and processes. These political dynamics that shape energy state-wide occur primarily with a focus on national interests. Although the market and interactions taking place in the energy sector are multilevel and transnational, they are exposed to the vagaries of global price mechanisms and other factors, which ultimately sway national level policy priorities and governance.

National governments play a crucial role in shaping the energy sector generally in spite of the clarion call for the sector's deregulation, liberalization and privatisation. Policy and regulatory frameworks formulated at national levels largely direct the flow of energy investments and consumption choices.[199] Energy decisions of regional institutions reflects the choices, priorities and interests of their constituent members, which in intergovernmental and supranational organizations, are the member states. In as much as there is a growing value of non-state actors, the most essential drivers of energy policy at all levels are still states. Thus, it is critical to pay focused attention to the particularities of national politics around energy on their own terms, in order to understand how they configure and shape particularly regional and global politics of energy in general.

Every country displays a certain kind of politics around energy. This is shaped by natural resource endowments and local institutional histories consistent with the broad trajectory of path dependence undertaken to ensure national energy security. Certain countries share remarkable consistency in the broader patterns of governance such as, opening up their

198 Francis McGowan, 'International Regimes for Energy: Finding the Right Level for Policy', in *Energy for the Future*, ed. by I Scarse and K MacKerron (London: Palgrave Macmillan UK, 2009), pp. 20–34 <https://doi.org/10.1057/9780230235441_2>.

199 Van De Graaf and others.

energy sectors to competition while ensuring private sector involvement. Whereas in others this phenomenon is less pronounced. In effect, new laws are passed dissolving state monopolies and independent regulators are created occurring at varying degrees of success. Nation-states have also concerned themselves with the different energy policy narratives that have defined approaches to their governance. A typical example is the reference of energy policy narratives focused on the move from energy markets to energy security.

These consistent country patterns suggest structures of energy governance that are shaped globally or regionally but mediated by nationally specific factors.[200] Michael Bradshaw[201], the political geographer who has studied energy dilemmas in different regions and countries, provided a practical approach in understanding the energy problems, which occur when governing energy at the national level. *High-income nations* tend to be high-energy societies that wrestle with the balance between decarbonisation, an essential factor in the mitigation of climate-change and the affordability of energy. *Emerging economies* tend to focus on the need to secure abundant and sufficient energy that would fuel economic growth and development to the detriment of greenhouse emissions. Finally, *Low-income nations* tend to prioritise issues related to energy access over the use of clean energy. He further underscored that these different nations could be either energy exporter or importer nations with a unique set of energy dilemmas. He also highlighted a fourth state, *Post-socialist states* which tend to possess divergent future energy paths, and could either become high-income, emerging or low-income economies.

Van de Graaf and Zelli[202] explain the different styles of national energy governance by adapting their explanation on the work of Spencer et al.[203] which deals with the organisational and social differences that outline

---

200 Künneke and Finger; Matthias Finger and Rolf W. Künneke, *International Handbook of Network Industries*, 2011.

201 Michael J. Bradshaw, *Global Energy Dilemmas: Energy Security, Globalization, and Climate Change* (Cambridge: Polity Press, 2014).

202 Thijs Van De Graaf and Fariborz Zelli, 'Actors, Institutions and Frames in Global Energy Politics.', in *The Palgrave Handbook of the International Political Economy of Energy. Palgrave Handbooks in IPE.*, ed. by Thijs Van De Graaf and others (London: Palgrave Macmillan, 2016), pp. 47–71 <https://doi.org/10.1057/978-1-137-55631-8>.

203 Jennifer W. Spencer, Thomas P. Murtha, and Stefanie Ann Lenway, 'How Governments Matter to New Industry Creation', *Academy of Management Review*, 30.2 (2005), 321–37 <https://doi.org/10.5465/AMR.2005.16387889>.

the political structures involved in institutional formation at the national level. They highlight, *state corporatist* countries such as Germany, Japan and Korea that combine a highly centralized public bureaucracy with policy networks that include societal groups recognized and legitimized by the state. *Social-corporatist* countries that include the Nordic states also exhibit interaction among interests formally organized by the state. Yet the state itself plays a less peremptory role. In *liberal-pluralist* countries like the USA, UK and Australia, the state plays a minimalist role, leaving ample space for private interest groups to influence policies. The final group of countries, the *state nations* among them France, Italy and Belgium, include a strong state with close links to business. These groupings reflect variants and varieties of capitalism in high-income capitalist economies. Additional styles exist when non-capitalist, high and low-income economies are factored into the equation.

Differences in governance styles with respect to how national energy governance is organized institutionally and the types of preferred policy instruments adopted plays a unique role in terms of the institutions that are built and developed overtime. For example, five fuel-based ministries control India's energy policy and planning: coal, power, petroleum and natural gas, new and renewable energy, and atomic energy[204]. Conversely, China does not even have an energy ministry responsible for coordinating government policy in the energy arena[205]. The conservative government under Margaret Thatcher in the 1980s, abolished the UK's energy ministry, applying the same set of competition and liberalization rules to energy as it had done for other sectors. However, the government remained profoundly involved in the regulation of the sector[206].

Preferred energy policy instruments and concomitant political effects emerge nationally with reference to the energy sector. This may include taxes, subsidies or regulations that seem to be influenced by distribution-

204 Navroz K. Dubash, 'From Norm Taker to Norm Maker? Indian Energy Governance in Global Context', *Global Policy*, 2.SUPPL.1 (2011), 66–79 <https://doi.org/10.1111/j.1758-5899.2011.00123.x>.

205 Bo Kong, 'Governing China's Energy in the Context of Global Governance', *Global Policy*, 2.SUPPL.1 (2011), 51–65 <https://doi.org/10.1111/j.1758-5899.2011.00124.x>; Philip Andrews-Speed, *The Governance of Energy in China: Transition to a Low-Carbon Economy*, 1st edn (Basingstoke: Palgrave Macmillan, 2012) <https://doi.org/10.1057/9781137284037>.

206 Dieter Helm, 'Energy Policy: Security of Supply, Sustainability and Competition', *Energy Policy*, 30.3 (2002), 173–84 <https://doi.org/10.1016/S0301-4215(01)00141-0>.

al factors in operationalising these respective policies and its impact on important energy-related industries, public sentiment and the institutional capacity of governments[207]. These political effects of a given policy instrument is considered as very important because they "help to explain why governments choose particular instruments over others"[208]. Even though political preferences are crucial in clarifying national energy pathways and policies, national preferences in the IPE of energy are of course also shaped by more structural factors like geography, structure and size of the economy, history and climate inter alia.[209]

In another consideration, nations utilise various types of energy resources in certain specific industries. To exemplify, in the case of extractive industries resources such as coal, oil, gas, and uranium are used, whereas in the manufacturing or services sectors other different provisions of energy resources may be required. Climate factors also influence national energy governance in terms of energy consumption volumes. For example, in temperate zones like the Nordic region and parts of western Europe and Russia, a high heating load contribute to higher per capita consumption of energy, in contrast to that, in the tropics and desert regions like the Gulf region, parts of sub-Saharan Africa and north Africa, a high cooling load contributes similarly to a higher per capita consumption.

In very rare cases do we see energy governance issues propelled to the very top of national debates and the policy agenda of governments. But exceptions to this rule of thumb occur in countries which are major exporters of energy and highly dependent on export revenues to support national budgets. Another exception also occurs in countries who are major energy importers and rely heavily on one major source of energy without diversification. Such that, any adverse impact to these sources becomes a strategic energy supply issue for its economic growth.

However, in most countries, energy supply is mostly taken for granted and does not become a priority issue on the national stage until there is a major energy crisis to be solved. In the meantime, governments give attention to other political economy objectives considered more important. Mostly, impending or apparent energy crisis issues come to the fore of

---

207 Llewelyn Hughes and Johannes Urpelainen, 'Interests, Institutions, and Climate Policy: Explaining the Choice of Policy Instruments for the Energy Sector', *Environmental Science and Policy*, 54 (2015), 52–63 <https://doi.org/10.1016/j.envsci.2015.06.014>.

208 Hughes and Urpelainen, p. 54.

209 Van De Graaf and Zelli.

national debates. Such crises tend to take the form of events or changes in global, regional or national energy trends that results in a threat or contributes to a perceived threat in the national economy. These materialising threats may occur as sudden events or changes and a lessened capability to stem the threat[210]. Mostly, these threats are security of supply, access and climate-change issues that are hurled on to the national agenda. For example, currently almost all the fifty-four countries in Africa are rationing electricity to a certain degree, raising issues pertaining to the energy sector high on every African countries agenda.[211]

The need in emerging and low-income countries to supply citizens with modern and clean energy is high on the agenda. High-income countries have achieved some success in this respect as they transition their energy systems. As a result, the supply of modern energy to all segments of the citizenry is primarily not a major policy concern, although the suitable pricing of this energy remains significant.

The main actors involved in the governance of national energy systems include state and non-state agencies. They are responsible for energy, development planning, research institutions, public enterprises, national treasuries, national energy utilities and national energy champions. National energy champions describe corporations responsible for the following energy sectors: petroleum, electricity, and renewable energy. The non-state actors include energy advocacy NGOs, private energy firms and energy utility companies, among others.[212]

Most governments in developing, emerging and low-income countries have a substantial ownership stake in energy and utility companies compared to the more advanced and developed ones, whether or not they operate using a liberalised approach. Ministries of Finance and Treasury departments play a central role in the sector, as they often influence investment policies and strategies, and exercise oversight of the financial well-being of state-owned enterprises (SOEs) including those in the energy sector. The provision of abundant access to energy and reducing energy and fuel poverty is a stated political priority for many industrialising and

---

210 Dieter Helm, 'The Assessment: The New Energy Paradigm', *Oxford Review of Economic Policy*, 21.1 (2005), 1–18 <https://doi.org/10.1093/oxrep/gri001>.

211 Africa Progress Panel, *Lights Power Action: Electrifying Africa*, 2015; Africa Progress Panel, *Power People Planet Seizing Africa's Energy and Climate Opportunities, Africa Progress Report* (Geneva, 2015) <http://www.africaprogresspanel.org/>.

212 Morgan Bazilian, Smita Nakhooda, and Thijs Van de Graaf, 'Energy Governance and Poverty', *Energy Research & Social Science*, 1.2014 (2014), 217–25 <https://doi.org/10.1016/j.erss.2014.03.006>.

industrialised countries, but the extent to which such policies are implemented by national actors varies substantially.[213]

Another unique national actor is the energy regulator. Most countries have established independent regulators as quasi-governmental intermediaries who provide independent oversight of key actors in the energy sector. This is partly to attract greater private investment, while supporting realisation of energy policy objectives. The role of regulators is pivotal in ensuring that key actors in the energy system act assiduously to address energy and fuel poverty in countries. They do this by addressing key aspects of secure and affordable supply of energy and fuel, prioritising investment in the sector. They are also responsible for regulating entities tasked with dealing with the above stated aspects. Moreover, relevant government agencies and political authorities tend to influence the extent to which different energy services and sources of energy are subsidised by playing the role of setting quality service standards and overseeing compliance with those standards.[214]

Banks and financial institutions play a strategic role in national energy sectors. Public and private banks may usually play an important role in financing and funding programmes that address energy provision. They thereby enable investments that improve access to energy and ensure that vulnerable energy and fuel consumers are able to secure and afford the much-needed available modern energy services. Public and private finance plays a central role in this regard. There is growing emphasis on opportunities that direct private finance to such investments so as to build the needed energy infrastructure, be it centralised core grid systems or decentralised periphery systems.[215]

To conclude, the collaboration between national and regional energy governance is a distinctive aspect of the IPE of energy. This collaborative interaction exists between national governments at the regional level and their subnational actors. The subsequent interactions emerge as complex systems and are characterized by multiple engagements at different levels. It requires good governance that promote shared best practices of energy policymaking among the interacting member states within a transnational energy region.

---

213 Bazilian, Nakhooda, and Van de Graaf.

214 Bazilian, Nakhooda, and Van de Graaf.

215 Georg Inderst, *Private Infrastructure Finance and Investment in Europe*, EIB Working Papers (Luxembourg, 2013) <http://hdl.handle.net/10419/88101>.

2.2.2 Regional Energy Governance

Regional energy governance is the type of energy governance that lies at the intersection between national and global forms of energy governance. The regional organizations and regimes sandwiched between national and global energy initiatives are responsible for this governance.[216] In certain parts of the world, regional agreements pertaining to energy and its infrastructure have made more significant inroads than global agreements.[217] Scholarship in IPE in relation to the political economy of regionalism recognises a number of details that embody the benefits of regional economic agreements over global ones. It facilitates decision making in a closely-knit and sizeable group, which has the capacity to address issues of peculiar interest to regional members.[218] These outcomes are customarily derived from reviewing economic preferential trade agreements and customs unions.[219]

Continuing research on the regional governance of energy is deemed expansive in relation to the entire energy governance field, which began with a focus on the global approach.[220] Broadly, comparative regionalism or regional integration denotes states coming together to work on a number of specialised issues and objectives.[221] Precisely, comparative regionalism includes "purposive interaction, formal or informal, among state and non-state actors of a given area in pursuit of shared external, domestic, and transnational goals".[222] For example, the EU utilises an obvious regional

---

216 Hancock, 'Energy Regionalism : The Intersection of Resources , Regions , and Energy'.

217 Patt.

218 Shaun Breslin, Richard A Higgott, and Ben Rosamond, *Regions in Comparative Perspective, Perspective*, 2002 <https://doi.org/10.4324/9780203361672_chapter_1>; Shaun Breslin and others, *New Regionalisms in the Global Political Economy: Theory and Cases*, ed. by Shaun Breslin and others (London and New York: Routledge, 2002) <https://doi.org/10.4324/9780203361672>.

219 Navroz K. Dubash and Ann Florini, 'Mapping Global Energy Governance', *Global Policy*, 2.SUPPL.1 (2011), 6–18 <https://doi.org/10.1111/j.1758-5899.2011.00119.x>.

220 For a more detail look on the subject see : Hancock and Vivoda.

221 Comparative regionalism or regional integration in this setting does not refer to sub-systems within a nation state such as provinces, regions, districts among others.

222 Acharya.

energy governance approach founded on liberalization, which it also tries to spread to other non-EU regions on the global stage.[223]

The EU Commission's focus on the realisation of an *Energy Union* and placing climate as a priority area emphasises the need for member states to collaborate more effectively and efficiently with shared goals in order to make energy more secure, affordable and sustainable. It has sought to employ four directorates general (DGs) namely for energy, climate action, environment and mobility coupled with transport to deal with all its efforts towards this energy union. On the other hand, the ECOWAS Commission in its quest to advance regional cooperation and integration on matters of energy rely on two directorates, specifically energy and mines. They work together with four other regional agencies[224] to drive the energy integration efforts in this sphere. It is done by prioritising the essential goals of energy provision, abundant access and affordability for citizens in the ECOWAS region.

The multiple number of regional agreements globally, in conjunction with the many bureaucracies and institutions they establish, depend on these governing regional structures to solve some of the world's most precarious energy challenges. Besides the formal agreements which create coherent energy regions, natural resources such as rivers and other water bodies like the River Niger or the Volta River in West Africa, reinforce the linkages that exist in connecting countries within regional economic accords. For instance, albeit the fact that sub-Saharan Africa (SSA) has a plethora of regional economic agreements. Arguably, containing more customs unions and monetary unions perhaps than anywhere globally and coupled with the many transboundary rivers and lakes. Yet it ranks low on electricity access rates even from hydropower.

Regional energy governance provides an opportunity to leverage on the linkage of regional economic agreements and natural resources in a very useful manner to realise abundant energy provision and access.[225] These regional regimes and authorities may be best suited to advance an efficient and workable energy governance agenda instead of the mostly

223 Andreas Goldthau and Nick Sitter, *A Liberal Actor in a Realist World: The European Union Regulatory State and the Global Political Economy of Energy*, 1st edn (Oxford: Oxford University Press, 2015).

224 ECREEE, WAPP, WAGP, ERERA

225 Hancock, 'Energy Regionalism : The Intersection of Resources , Regions , and Energy'.

preferred global initiatives. They also entail fewer states with the ease of decision-making that are less cumbersome and fast paced.

An IPE approach to the dynamics of regional energy governance addresses an extensive range of actors. Requisite for the regional governance of energy, are the norms, values, guiding principles, policy narratives and ideological frameworks. These are exhibited in the growing role of regional science and research organisations in collaboration with national counterparts, international treaties, regulation and law, companies and business lobbies, civil society actors, international organisations and departments of state.[226] The multiplicity of actors within this transnational context enables understanding of energy governance issues in the region.

Bazilian, Nakhooda and Van de Graaf[227] have teased out some of the regional actors, who play an essential role in energy governance. They include, regional development banks such as the European Investment Bank (EIB) and the ECOWAS Bank for Investment and Development (EBID) and ECOBANK. They also involve regional groups and trading blocs such as, the EU, ECOWAS and the Organización Latinoamericana de Energía (OLADE) and NAFTA. Included also are regional regulatory fora, such as the South Asian Forum for Infrastructure Regulation; as well as bilateral cooperation arrangements.

The premise for the IPE of energy within the context of comparative regionalism conceptualises the transnational region as a polycentric political area where decision making on energy is formulated at multiple scales of governance and formally independent of each other. This notion is confirmed by the research which shows that states that work together on a variety of energy issues are more likely to stay true to their agreements and realise necessary regional objectives if they do not entertain parochial interests.[228] Overall, there is ample evidence that solutions to many of the prevailing energy challenges could be remedied at the regional level

---

226 Michael F Keating and others, 'Introduction: Bringing Energy into International Political Economy', in *Dynamics of Energy Governance in Europe and Russia*, ed. by C. Kuzemko and others, 1st edn (Palgrave Macmillan UK, 2012), pp. 1–19 <https://doi.org/10.1057/9780230370944_1>; Van De Graaf and Zelli.

227 Bazilian, Nakhooda, and Van de Graaf.

228 Benjamin K. Sovacool, 'Energy Policy and Cooperation in Southeast Asia: The History, Challenges, and Implications of the Trans-ASEAN Gas Pipeline (TAGP) Network', *Energy Policy*, 37.6 (2009), 2356–67 <https://doi.org/10.1016/j.enpol.2009.02.014>; Carroll and Sovacool.

through the workings of existing regional institutions and the continued participation and engagement of member states and other stakeholders.[229]

2.2.3 Energy Spaces: Intersectionality of the State, Market and Commons

The attributes of energy as a common (or CPR), as well as the rules, regulation and governance that guide its production and distribution affect the diverse incentives that participants encounter. Since energy has high exclusionary costs and its consumption being subtractive, it reinforces an impression that energy sources or services that tend to possess these attributes are produced and distributed through the same type of property regime.

Transnational, national and sub-national polities aside from communal groups, private individuals and corporations, can participate fully in energy commons. Therefore, in situations where energy commons are owned by no one or paradoxically by 'everyone', they are used as open access resources by whomever can gain access[230]. It then raises the question of the most appropriate type of property regime with its different sets of merits and demerits. It raises the question, which type is best suited for the proper design and implementation of operational rules that ultimately influence access, participation and use of the available resource.[231] In such an instance the necessity to consider the governance of energy commons at the intersection of participating governments, communal groups, cooperative voluntary associations, private individuals and corporate firms within the context of transnational regional governance cannot be overstated.

It must be emphasised here that, energy commons and any other form of commons should not be automatically associated with common-property regimes or particularly associated with any one type of property

229 Patt; Hancock, 'The Expanding Horizon of Renewable Energy in Sub-Saharan Africa: Leading Research in the Social Sciences'; Hancock, 'Energy Regionalism and Diffusion in Africa: How Political Actors Created the ECOWAS Center for Renewable Energy and Energy Efficiency'.

230 Elinor Ostrom, 'How Types of Goods and Property Rights Jointly Affect Collective Action', p. 249.

231 David Feeny and others, 'The Tragedy of the Commons: Twenty-Two Years Later', *Human Ecology*, 18.1 (1990), 1–19 <https://doi.org/10.1093/nq/s2-VI.140.189-c>.

regime.[232] Hence, the market design of the entire energy sector with regard to production and distribution networks that occur in the energy marketplace must take into consideration the diverse property right systems that can be utilised. This would have the end goal of catering for the energy aspirations of energy consumers in both the advanced and emerging developmental economies.

In the context of energy commons, there are four types of property rights systems that are extant. McGinnis[233] outlined them as follows: a) *Open Access Property,* refers to systems with no effective restrictions on use of resources. b) *Private Property,* refers to bundles of rights held by and exchanged among individuals; or legally recognized corporate entities typically including full rights of alienation. c) *Public Property,* stands for the bundles of rights held by official agents of some unit of government. d) *Common (or communal) Property,* refers to the bundles of rights held, defined, and exchanged by a communal entity as a whole. Instead of a general conclusion that one kind of property regime is best for all types of energy commons, a hybrid property regime system based on the diversity of resource attributes are preferably adequate when dealing with its governance.

An intersection between governments, firms and communities, in other words state, market and commons, can serve as a starting point for a fresh way of designing the architecture of the energy system. I refer to this intersection of the state, market and commons in the design and structure of the entire energy sector considering the numerous property rights available to this policy and governance process as *energy spaces*.

Governance by multiple actors like public and government authorities, market and private sector entities and also well-defined commons with their specialised agents organised in cooperatives can operate in a properly designed energy *marketplace*. Failures relating to the functioning of energy markets and the role of governments in the energy marketplace reveal an opportunity to rethink governance strategies in the entire energy value chain. A look into the study of markets, marketplaces and the effective design of markets can improve perspectives of avoiding market failures especially in the energy sector.

---

232 Elinor Ostrom, 'How Types of Goods and Property Rights Jointly Affect Collective Action'.

233 Michael D. McGinnis, *Updated Guide to IAD and the Language of the Ostrom Workshop: A Simplified Overview of a Complex Framework for the Analysis of Institutions and Their Development.*

Relying on the ideas of Alvin E. Roth, markets and marketplaces require unique and effective market design to avoid market failure.[234] By implication, for a market to function well enough, the marketplace must design the rules, regulations and governance processes required for the specific market and identify its varied actors in order to function properly. This applies to the many diverse markets found in the energy sector, such as the electricity, gas, oil, and renewable markets, among others. To exemplify this in the West Africa region, a more specific consideration of the regional power sector reveals that, there is presently no standard organization responsible for a liberalized wholesale market of electric power, with the exception of the West Africa Power Pool (WAPP) that attempts to fulfil this end.[235] WAPP does this with a combination of regulations, governance, system management, and markets. A means to bring coherence in the various structures along a single dimension will require focus on degrees of reliance on market or individual sector processes in addition to supervisory preferences.[236]

Professor Roth, a leading proponent of *market design*, which is a nascent field in economics recognises it as an ancient human activity. He argues that markets and marketplaces are human artefacts, like language and just as there are many natural languages, there are many kinds of markets and marketplaces.[237] He alludes further that well-functioning markets depend on detailed rules.[238] Without these rules, markets result in failure. Marketplace design for him goes beyond views expressed by traditional economics, which conceives markets and marketplaces simply as a confluence of supply and demand without considering the relationships and factors that facilitate transactions.[239]

To demonstrate this phenomenon, the supply and demand that drives a regional power pool reflects only a single aspect of the relational contracts which exists between the transacting polities, their representative energy companies and public utilities within the required time period. They also

234 Alvin E Roth, 'Marketplaces and Market Design' (London: London School of Economics, 2017).

235 Pierre Olivier Pineau, 'Electricity Sector Integration in West Africa', *Energy Policy*, 36.1 (2008), 210–23 <https://doi.org/10.1016/j.enpol.2007.09.002>.

236 Robert Wilson, 'Architecture of Power Markets', *Econometrica*, 70.4 (2002), 1299–1340 <https://doi.org/10.1111/1468-0262.00334>.

237 Roth, 'Marketplaces and Market Design'.

238 Alvin E Roth, 'The Art of Designing Markets', *Harvard Business Review*, October 2007, pp. 1–8 <www.hbr.org>.

239 Roth, 'The Art of Designing Markets'.

include the role of other actors like consumers and independent systems operators that are responsible for transmission and distribution. This adds to the exclusive rules and management principles that guide the range of energy sub-sectors covered by the undersigned contracts in the power pool in question.

Lastly, Alvin Roth[240] contends that the principal motive for marketplace design is the need to address market failures and that for markets to work well, marketplaces need to:

1. Provide thickness, that is, they need to attract a sufficient proportion of potential market participants to come together ready to transact with one another;
2. Overcome the congestion that thickness can bring, by providing enough time, or by making transactions fast enough, so that market participants can consider enough alternative possible transactions to arrive at satisfactory ones;
3. Make it safe to participate in the market as simply as possible (a) as opposed to transacting outside the marketplace, or (b) as opposed to engaging in strategic behaviour that reduces overall welfare.
4. Some kinds of transactions are repugnant, and this can be an important constraint on market design.
5. On a methodological note, experiments can play a role, in diagnosing and understanding market failures and successes, in testing new designs, and in communicating results to policy makers.

This notion of the *marketplace* studied by Alvin Roth in his work on market design is akin to the notion of *economic spaces*[241] argued by Francois Perroux in his journal article on the subject published in the Quarterly Journal of Economics[242].The absence of an efficient and effective market design resulting in market failure makes the role of government pivotal

240 Alvin E Roth, 'What Have We Learned from Market Design? (Update)', *Economic Journal*, 118 (2008), 285–310; Nir Vulkan, Alvin E Roth, and Zvika Neeman, *The Handbook of Market Design*, 2013 <https://doi.org/10.1017/CBO9781107415324.004>.

241 They define the economic relations, which exist between economic elements. These economic spaces conveniently reduce to three: (1) economic space as defined by a plan; (2) economic space as a field of forces; and (3) economic space as a homogeneous aggregate. Some of the points Perroux advanced to support his clarification of this concept of economic spaces put forward by August Lösch in his book, Die räumliche Ordnung der Wirtschaft (Jena: G. Fischer, 1944)

242 François Perroux, 'Economic Space: Theory and Applications', *The Quarterly Journal of Economics*, 64.1 (1950), 89–104 <https://doi.org/10.2307/1881960>.

in preventing market failures by considering alternative public policy interventions. On numerous occasions, feasible, low-cost policies have been implemented and that has either eliminated or compensated for market imperfections and barriers. This has enabled markets to operate more efficiently to the benefit of society. Conversely, in other instances, policies may not be feasible; they may not fully eliminate the targeted failure or imperfection. Or they may do so at costs that exceed the benefits resulting then in government failure.[243] The challenges faced in the energy space reveal clear market failures and government failures associated with the energy sector.

In order to minimise or eliminate these defects of market and government failure in the energy sector, an emphasis for the need to introduce a third domain, namely, the commons, becomes a *sine qua non* to balance any defective outcomes when it occurs. This new introduction of the commons sector into this interaction puts forward a new set of actors. Thereby highlighting the significance of actor heterogeneity and the importance of their plural functions[244]. One new set of actors that can be mentioned as having emerged in this wave is the prosumer.[245] They are decentralised private energy producers, mainly citizens or a citizen-action collective, engaged in the coproduction[246] of private and public energy services.

State, market and commons actors organised and structured in a properly designed marketplace or economic space, can minimise or even elimi-

243 M. A. Brown, 'Market Failures and Barriers as a Basis for Clean Energy Policies', *Energy Policy*, 29.14 (2001), 1197–1207 <https://doi.org/10.1016/S0301-4215(01)00067-2>.

244 Robert. O. Keohane and Elinor Ostrom.

245 Yael Parag and Benjamin K. Sovacool, 'Electricity Market Design for the Prosumer Era', *Nature Energy*, 1.4 (2016), 16032 <https://doi.org/10.1038/nenergy.2016.32>.

246 The concept of coproduction is multifarious and it is used in various themes and topics that span public policy and public management studies. Especially concerning public service provision. It emerged as a scientific term during the study of interdependent exchanges between different actors in the delivery and provision of public services. Elinor Ostrom, 'Crossing the Great Divide: Coproduction, Synergy, and Development', *World Development*, 24.6 (1996), 1073–87 <https://doi.org/10.1016/0305-750X(96)00023-X>; Bram Verschuere, Taco Brandsen, and Victor Pestoff, 'Co-Production: The State of the Art in Research and the Future Agenda', *Voluntas*, 23.4 (2012), 1083–1101 <https://doi.org/10.1007/s11266-012-9307-8>; S. Becker, M. Naumann, and T. Moss, 'Between Coproduction and Commons: Understanding Initiatives to Reclaim Urban Energy Provision in Berlin and Hamburg', *Urban Research & Practice*, 0.0 (2016), 1–23 <https://doi.org/10.1080/17535069.2016.1156735>.

nate both market and government failure. They can do so within a given public policy area, like the energy sector, at multiple and overlapping governance scales at the micro, meso and macro levels, and also within a transboundary geopolitical area such as in the context of regional integration.

The relationship of the public, private and commons sectors within a specific economic space or marketplace is impossible to address without talking about the issue that threatens the most vulnerable of the three, the commons. It is also necessary to address, the effect that arises when the commons is sufficiently protected. The imminent threat to the commons sector is imposed by market forces that arise with the commodification and privatisation of the once mutually shared resource.[247] This threat is referred to as enclosures.[248] Commoners are dispossessed by market forces that seize possession of their shared resources. This often occurs with the able and active collaboration of the government. This further contributes in making enclosures inimical to the commons because it substitutes market exchange (mainly executed through the circulation of money) as the primary force of organising society.

Currently, with the prevalence of market enclosures through the support of the state, one might contemplate that markets, states and commons are faded to be eternal enemies. Even though there may be serious tensions between the three in organising production and social life, there are ways to make them co-exist and work together in order to reap the needed benefits. Benefits could still be derived from their respective production systems and their organisations of resource systems. Doing so could be a complicated challenge nonetheless. But an essential prerequisite is the strengthening of the commons sector to be capable of protecting itself from the intervention of state and market intrusion. Just as the state and markets have a mechanism for organising within their contexts, the commons must bolster its mechanisms of law, technology and social organisation to prevent the others from appropriating their shared resources. By obtaining these capacities, it can more safely engage with markets, knowing the daunting power of finance capital and private property on

247 Silke Helfrich and David Bollier, *Commons Als Transformative Kraft*, ed. by Silke Helfrich and Heinrich-Böll-Stiftung, *Commons: Für Eine Neue Politik Jenseits von Markt Und Staat* (Bielefeld,DE: transcript, 2012).

248 David Bollier, *Public Assets, Private Profits. Reclaiming the American Commons in an Age of Market Enclosure* (Washington, DC, 2001) <http://www.bollier.org/pdf/PA_Report.pdf>.

one hand and the power of governments (at whatever governance scale) on the other hand.[249]

Figure 2. 2 Design of Energy Spaces: Nexus of State, Market and Commons

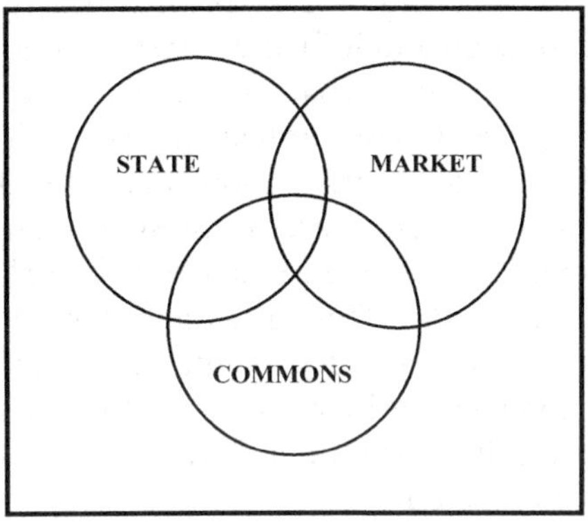

Source:[250]

It is expedient to understand the paradigms that emphasise the design of the energy marketplace and its complimentary networks. Especially, the networks that have dictated the function of the energy marketplace and the transmission and distribution of public energy services[251]. Bevir and Trentmann[252] stated that, "All economic institutions including markets are necessarily established and transformed in the context of political, social, and cultural authorities. All economies have to be governed through com-

249 Silke Helfrich and David Bollier, *Commons Als Transformative Kraft*

250 Author

251 Originating in Ancient Greek's παράδειγμα (paradeigma), – meaning 'pattern' – the contemporary term commonly refers to a 'set of assumptions, concepts, values, and practices that constitutes a way of viewing reality for the community that shares them. See in M. E. Agnes, (ed.) Webster's New World College Dictionary, (2004), fourth edition. Cleveland, OH: Wiley-Blackwell. Thomas Kuhn first presented paradigms to scientific thought by characterising them as 'an accepted model or pattern' for a given discipline. See in Thomas S Kuhn, "The Structure of Scientific Revolutions, and 3rd edition. Chicago: University of Chicago Press, (1996).

252 Mark Bevir and Frank Trentmann, *Markets in Historical Contexts: Ideas and Politics in the Modern World*, ed. by Frank Trentmann and Mark Bevir, 1st edn (Cambridge: cambridge university press), p. 1.

plex patterns of rules that connect and regulate economic actors, organisations and interactions."

The paradigm that shapes the design of marketplace formation and its governance is based on this claim. In clearer terms, the patterns used to articulate the structure and processes of the energy marketplace is heavily dependent on the chosen frame that it rests on and it further prescribes the mode of governance. Andreas Goldthau[253] argues that no other marketplace other than the energy sector has reflected these contextual changes in paradigms over time. It began with the state-led (statist) approach, defined as the public provision and management of energy services by state agencies and companies. Then it was followed by the free market (neo-liberal) paradigm that took over in the 1980s and 1990s. This subsequently made energy production, transmission and distribution dependent on private sector-led provision. Then came the interventionist paradigm which has arisen in the new millennium as a result of sustainability, security of supply issues and energy- and fuel-poverty matters.

A further contribution to the latest paradigm from a critical mixed perspective is by framing an alternative approach where the intersection of the state, market and commons coexist and function together. This intricate reorganisation of the interventionist paradigm can completely shift the way we design and govern energy spaces with the involvement of all actors.

2.3 Institutional Analysis of Energy

This section outlines a broad-based approach to policy analysis that considers institutional design and governance as a need to construct and evaluate effective regional energy governance systems. Studying institutions and their importance in policy and economic development is not novel, and multiple approaches have been used.[254] Three approaches may be recognised: Historical institutionalism that classifies institutions as formal and informal rules and conventions originating from mainly formal political and economic organisations. The second is rational choice institutional-

253 Goldthau, 'From the State to the Market and Back: Policy Implications of Changing Energy Paradigms'.

254 Peter A. Hall and Rosemary C.R. Taylor, 'Political Science and the Three New Institutionalisms', *Political Studies*, 44.5 (1996), 936–57 <https://doi.org/10.1111/j.1467-9248.1996.tb00343.x>.

ism, often denoted as New Institutional Economics, highlights how formal and informal rules and conventions affect economic transaction costs. Third is sociological institutionalism, which employs culture to describe institutions.

Institutions are "enduring regularities of human action in situations structured by rules, norms, and shared strategies, as well as by the physical world. The rules, norms, and shared strategies are constituted and reconstituted by human interaction in frequently occurring or repetitive situations".[255]

Diverse institutional arrangements for governing common-pool resources (CPRs) and public goods at multiple scales, that is, at polycentric levels, contribute to classical political economic theory. This explains phenomena that do not necessarily fall into the binary world of 'the market' and 'the state'. This has led to the development and use of frameworks, theories, and models to understand the diversity of puzzles and problems facing human interactions in an institutional setting.[256]

Institution building is depicted by complex human motivational structures that establish diverse private-for-profit, governmental, and community institutional arrangements that operate at polycentric levels. This is to generate productive and innovative as well as destructive and perverse outcomes.[257] This background on institutions lays out the foundation to consider one of these complex frameworks developed at the Ostrom Workshop at the University of Indiana, Bloomington. This foundation is useful for institutional analysis in general, but extended to analysing institutional formations in energy spaces in this instance. This framework is the *C*ombined *I*nstitutional Analysis and Development – *S*ocial Ecological System (*CIS*) Framework.

The CIS Framework is the combination of the Institutional Analysis and Development (IAD) Framework and the Social Ecological System (SES) Framework. Elinor Ostrom and her colleagues from the Workshop in Po-

---

255 Sue E. S. Crawford and Elinor Ostrom, 'A Grammar of Institutions', *The American Political Science Review*, 89.3 (1995), 582–600 (p. 582).

256 Elinor Ostrom, 'Beyond Markets and States: Polycentric Governance of Complex Economic Systems', *American Economic Review*, 100.3 (2010), 641–72 <https://doi.org/10.1257/aer.100.3.641>.

257 Douglass Cecil North, *Institutions, Institutional Change and Economic Performance* (Cambridge: Cambridge University Press, 1990); Douglass Cecil North, *Understanding the Process of Economic Change* (Princeton, NJ: Princeton University Press, 2005).

litical Theory and Policy Analysis (known as the Bloomington School[258]) developed both frameworks. Even though she was renowned for her empirical studies into common property governance of common pool resources, her reputation in developing analytical frameworks that promoted cross and multi-disciplinary research employing various theories, methods and models has established her influence in the field of institutional analysis.[259] The process towards combining the two frameworks to assist in an all-inclusive institutional analysis was first mooted by her[260]. However, it was actualised in 2013 by the initial work on a new institutional analysis of social-ecological systems (NIASES) by Daniel H. Cole, Graham Epstein

---

258 The Bloomington School is also known as the Bloomington School for Institutional Analysis and Development. Bloomington has cemented its position as one of the predominant centres of the Public Choice and New Institutional Theory movements and become as well one of the most intellectually prolific centres of interdisciplinary social science scholarly research. Its work has touched on varied fields such as political science, economics history, economics, and anthropology among others. Its leading and famous proponents were world-renowned political scientist, Vincent Ostrom and the first woman Nobel laureate in economics, Elinor Ostrom. The Bloomington School emerged from a countermovement to the Metropolitan Governance Reform Movement of the 1970s. The School sought to promote self-governing democracies and its application to self-sustaining social orders. While Metropolitan Reform movement wanted to centralize the administrative structures and units of metropolitan regions, the school campaigned for the preservation of existing, supposedly inefficient redundant structures. To support their thesis, e.g., Vincent Ostrom et al. employed empirical and multi-method methodological ideological approaches to their research. (See: Perroux.

259 Ostrom uses the terms "frameworks," "theories," and "models" as terms of art. "Frameworks" are the "most generalized form of theoretical analysis," providing a general set of variables that comprise a meta-language, which is used for comparative institutional analyses of various "theories" and "models" of social-ecological conditions and interactions. "Theories" (e.g., economic theory or game theory) are comprised of working assumptions and hypothesized specifications of relevant variables (provided by the framework) deemed sufficient to provide adequate explanations or diagnoses of social or social-ecological conditions. "Models" (e.g., the rational actor model or game- theory models) use more "precise assumptions about a limited set of variables and parameters to derive precise predictions about the results of combining these variables using a particular theory." See Ostrom (2011, pp. 8–9). Ostrom and Cox (2010, p. 5) suggest that "frameworks" may best be thought of as "metatheoretical conceptual map[s]."

260 Daniel H Cole, Epstein, and McGinnis.

and Michael D. McGinnis, all of the Bloomington School that sought to combine Elinor Ostrom's IAD and SES Frameworks.[261]

The IAD Framework has been used extensively by social scientists and policy analysts to investigate both distinct cases and institutional change over time.[262] It doubles as one of the innovative frameworks in the policy sciences[263]. The greatest asset of the IAD framework emanates from,

> "its systematic theoretical focus on the impact of rules and norms on individual incentives in complex ecological and economic systems, its empirically oriented focus on outcomes (including the transaction costs of resource governance) and by its accounting for dynamic systemic interactions at multiple tiers of analysis"[264].

Quite simply, the IAD framework identifies the complexity of the world enfolding it; nonetheless, it provides researchers with a means to integrate knowledge by leveraging the strengths of multiple methods.[265]

The SES Framework, on the other hand, was an effort to give attention to the biophysical, ecological and technical foundations of institutional systems. It was fashioned to give equal weight to both the social and ecological sides.[266] It comprises of a large number of factors or variables that researchers identify as being potentially relevant to the dynamic patterns

---

261 Daniel H Cole, Epstein, and McGinnis.

262 See Aligică and Boettke.

263 Elinor Ostrom and Michael Cox, 'Moving beyond Panaceas: A Multi-Tiered Diagnostic Approach for Social-Ecological Analysis', *Environmental Conservation*, 37.4 (2010), 451–63 <https://doi.org/10.1017/S0376892910000834>; E. Ostrom, M. A. Janssen, and J. M. Anderies, 'Going beyond Panaceas', *Proceedings of the National Academy of Sciences*, 104.39 (2007), 15176–78 <https://doi.org/10.1073/pnas.0701886104>; Krister Andersson, 'Understanding Decentralized Forest Governance: An Application of the Institutional Analysis and Development Framework', *Sustainability: Science, Practice and Policy*, 2.1 (2006), 25–35 <https://doi.org/10.1080/15487733.2006.11907975>; Murray A. Rudd, 'An Institutional Framework for Designing and Monitoring Ecosystem-Based Fisheries Management Policy Experiments', *Ecological Economics*, 48.1 (2004), 109–24 <https://doi.org/10.1016/j.ecolecon.2003.10.002>; S.Y. Tang, *Institutions and Collective Action: Self-Governance in Irrigation*, 1992 <http://agris.fao.org/agris-search/search.do?f=1992/US/US92340.xml;US9187212>.

264 Paul A. Sabatier, *Theories of the Policy Process*, ed. by Paul A. Sabatier (Westview Press, 2007), XLII <https://doi.org/10.1081/E-EPAP2-120041405>.p110

265 Rudd.

266 Michael D. McGinnis, 'Connecting Commons and the IAD Framework', in *Routledge Handbook of the Study of the Commons*, ed. by Blake Hudson, Jonathan Rosenbloom, and Dan Cole, 1st edn (London and New York: Routledge, 2018).

of interaction between groups and their environment. These factors or variables are multi-tiered using a set of generic categories with relevance to diverse resource sectors, geophysical regions, political entities and socio-cultural conducts.[267] In effect, the SES framework reflects dynamic iterations of a complex network of inter-related factors or variables that, possibly in any analysis, could be based on the IAD framework.

Paying careful attention to the governance of shared resources, that is, the mode by which political entities at micro, meso and macro levels manage varied resources. This highlights complex collective action problems and reveals an array of complementary solutions. The governance of resources such as, water bodies, forests, encyclopaedic knowledge, software codes, grazing parks, block chain software for cryptocurrencies, national and transnational energy systems (which include power grids, pipelines and the like), reveal these problems and provide clues for resolving them. Tailor-made solutions for socio-ecological, socio-economic and socio-technical contexts, where such collective action problems occur, offer better prospects in resolving these common pool resource problems.

The CIS framework provides an avenue to diagnose and analyse these collective action problems occurring in the use of common pool resources. The first stage in the use of this framework requires a focus on the action situation that is, the policy space where actors interact in a collective action which faces problems or policy issues and requires strategic approaches to produce a shared policy outcome. Taking a cue from Hardin's classic herder problem, in an action situation where people interacted by sharing resources there arose a conflict between what is beneficial to the individual or unit and what is beneficial to the group or community, leading to the "tragedy of the commons".

Suppose a number of herders share a meadow and they each possess a collection of sheep, each individual herder will uniquely benefit from adding an extra sheep and claim the added benefits from this extra sheep. However, the demerit in adding this extra sheep is the burdened reduction of the grass in the meadow, which is being shared by the commune of herders. If the herders will act as rational selfish individuals, they will all place many sheep on the meadow as much as possible, but this will lead to over harvesting of the common resource. In his famous essay, Garret Hardin used this example to show that when people share a common re-

---

267 Michael D. McGinnis, 'An Introduction to IAD and the Language of the Ostrom Workshop: A Simple Guide to a Complex Framework', *Policy Studies Journal*, 39.1 (2011), 169–83 <https://doi.org/10.1111/j.1541-0072.2010.00401.x>.

source in an action situation this would lead to an overuse, an occurrence he termed the *Tragedy of the Commons*.[268]

According to Hardin there are only two possible solutions to resolve this problem. In this action situation; the first is to privatise the resource so that each resource user manages its own property. Whereas, the second solution lied in the bosom of imposing strict external regulation such as permits or licenses from an external local or provincial governmental authority.[269]

However, Elinor Ostrom and her collaborators devised and developed a much sophisticated, useful and superior alternative in addressing and analysing the issues of access and overuse of resources that occur in an action situation, that leads to these collective policy action problems. She published her influential book in 1990, *Governing the Commons*, where she demonstrates self-governance could provide an efficient governance option.[270] In this option, actors in communities under certain circumstances are able to govern their own resources in a sustainable way without external regulation but through a bottom-up or self-regulation. Self-governance may not be appropriate in every situation. However, when it is used it is an effective and efficient modus operandi.

As helpful as the CIS Framework is in the analysis of factors necessary to create a functioning system of polycentric governance to address a given global, regional and national collective-action problem, it is far from perfect and does not serve as a panacea. This Elinor Ostrom admits in her IAD Framework.[271] This CIS framework is now a component of the literature on polycentric governance. Both frameworks, that is, the IAD and SES, attract the most attention in public policy circles given their emphasis on self-understanding beyond classical rational choice.[272] The new combined framework offers an even more comprehensive approach to remedying CPR problems by combining them in a format suited to social-ecological systems, socio-technical systems and other policy settings.[273]

---

268 See Hardin.

269 Hardin.

270 Ostrom, Elinor, Governing the Commons – The Evolution of Institutions for Collective Action (Cambridge: Cambridge University Press, 1990)

271 Elinor Ostrom and others, 'Revisiting the Commons: Local Lessons, Global Challenges.', *Science (New York, N.Y.)*, 284.5412 (1999), 278–82 <https://doi.org/10.1126/science.284.5412.278>.

272 Daniel H Cole and McGinnis.

273 Daniel H. Cole, Epstein, and McGinnis.

2.3.1 Purpose and Development of the Combined IAD-SES (CIS) Framework

To appreciate the purpose and development of the CIS Framework, it is necessary to understand the evolution of its two component frameworks – the IAD and SES Frameworks. The Institutional Analysis and Development (IAD) framework is referred to as "one of the most developed and sophisticated attempts to use institutional and stakeholder assessment in order to link theory and practice, analysis and policy"[274]. An IAD framework analysis examines the "design and performance of an institutional arrangement"[275]. Here, institution is broadly defined to mean both organized bodies (such as supranational and regional organisations) and the particular rules and structures that prevail in those bodies.

Work on the IAD framework started in the 1980s, with Professor Elinor Ostrom and her colleagues at the Workshop in Political Theory and Policy Analysis at the University of Indiana. They leveraged on a number of influences. This started with the influential work of her husband and collaborator for many years, Vincent Ostrom on polycentric theory and systems. Almost all the elements found in the framework can virtually be seen in Vincent Ostrom's work.[276]

Another influential moment in the construction of the framework was Elinor Ostrom's increased interaction with game theory (ca.1981) under the influence of the world-renowned game theorist and Nobel Prize for economic sciences laureate Reinhard Selten, who was then a professor at the University of Bielefeld but later moved to the University of Bonn.

These influences are easily noticeable in the structure of the IAD framework (see Figure 2.3 below): for instance, actors in positions are depicted as entering into social interactions with their own strategies, while ethics and ideas fall under the operation of sets of rules that structure 'the game'. The *action situation* then serves as the de facto *decision node* in an iterated game. Moreover, in the IAD framework, just as in game theory, jointly

274 Daniel H Cole and McGinnis.

275 M T Imperial, 'Institutional Analysis and Ecosystem-Based Management: The Institutional Analysis and Development Framework', *Environmental Management*, 24.4 (1999), 453 <https://doi.org/DOI 10.1007/s002679900246>.

276 Daniel H. Cole, 'Laws, Norms, and the Institutional Analysis and Development Framework', *Journal of Institutional Economics*, 2017, 1–19 <http://dx.doi.org/10.1017/S1744137417000030>.

produced outcomes from social interactions affect the material welfare of the actors.[277]

Elinor Ostrom also promoted the overall framework often as an interdisciplinary research tool that social, political and natural scientists could use to build knowledge that related to the sustainability of social-ecological systems. She also realised that it was not a finished tool but a work in progress that needed further improvement. There were many criticisms and complaints that the IAD framework paid insufficient attention to the great diversity and complexity of natural and built systems and processes. She dealt with the critique through continued revision and refinement of the framework and its elements.[278]

Figure 2. 3 Basic Components of the IAD Framework

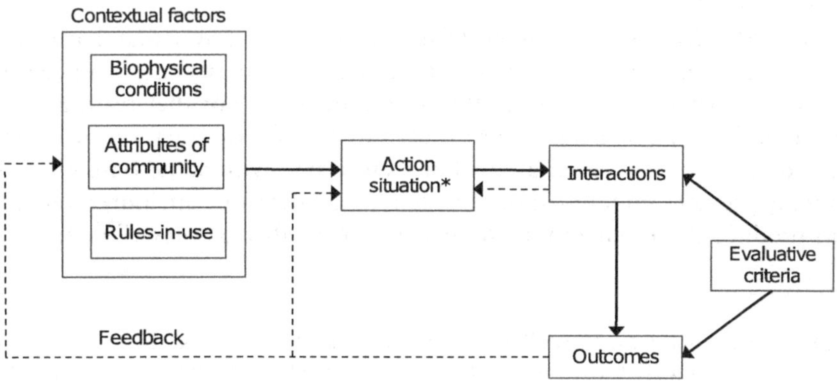

Source: [279]

277 Daniel H. Cole, 'Laws, Norms, and the Institutional Analysis and Development Framework', *Journal of Institutional Economics*, 2017, 1–19 <https://doi.org/10.1017/S1744137417000030>.

278 Ostrom and Cox; Fikret Berkes and Carl Folke, 'Linking Social and Ecological Systems for Resilience and Sustainability', *Linking Social and Ecological Systems*, 1 (1998), 13–20; Oran R Young, 'The Institutional Dimensions of Environmental Change: Fit, Interplay, and Scale', *Organization*, 2002, 221 <http://dx.doi.org/10.1023/A:1024850005580>; Arun Agrawal, 'Sustainable Governance of Common Pool Resources: Context, Methods, and Politics', *Annual Review of Anthropology*, 32.1 (2003), 243–62 <http://dx.doi.org/10.1146/annurev.anthro.32.061002.093112>.

279 Adapted from Daniel H Cole, Epstein, and McGinnis.

Eventually, Ostrom and her colleagues responded with a new framework called the social-ecological system (SES) framework (see Figure 2.4).[280] The SES framework included large, decomposable sets of social and ecological attributes that potentially affect choices and outcomes in social-ecological systems. Although not utilized as widely as the IAD framework[281], the SES framework is said to have played an immense role in understanding and diagnosing policy problems in complex social-ecological systems.[282] Outcomes generated consequent to the interplay of the multiple attributes of the SES framework are in the combination of leadership, social capital and spatial management plans[283]. It also facilitated data coding for purposes of meta-analyses and qualitative and quantitative assessments across a number of cases[284]. Furthermore, it dealt with the insufficiencies of the IAD framework particularly the element of the biophysical or material conditions.[285]

The SES framework inherently harbours certain flaws that have prevented it from replacing the IAD framework. Primarily, the framework lacks the dynamic character of the IAD framework. For that reason, even though the static SES framework is used to classify combinations of social ecological or socio-technical attributes associated with some outcomes, it simply provides no foundation for explaining how those attributes interact to produce those outcomes. Neither does it predict or prescribe changes

280 Ostrom and Cox; Fikret Berkes and Carl Folke, 'Linking Social and Ecological Systems for Resilience and Sustainability', *Linking Social and Ecological Systems*, 1 (1998), 13–20; Oran R Young, 'The Institutional Dimensions of Environmental Change: Fit, Interplay, and Scale', *Organization*, 2002, 221 <https://doi.org/10.1023/A:1024850005580>; Arun Agrawal, 'Sustainable Governance of Common Pool Resources: Context, Methods, and Politics', *Annual Review of Anthropology*, 32.1 (2003), 243–62 <https://doi.org/10.1146/annurev.anthro.32.061002.093112>.

281 Graham Epstein and others, 'Missing Ecology: Integrating Ecological Perspectives with the Social-Ecological System Framework', *International Journal of the Commons*, 7.2 (2013), 432–53 <https://doi.org/10.18352/ijc.371>; Daniel H Cole, Epstein, and McGinnis.

282 See for example, Ostrom and Cox.

283 Nicolás L. Gutiérrez, Ray Hilborn, and Omar Defeo, 'Leadership, Social Capital and Incentives Promote Successful Fisheries', *Nature*, 470.7334 (2011), 386–89 <https://doi.org/10.1038/nature09689>.

284 Ostrom and Cox p. 9 ; Epstein and others.

285 See for example, E. Ostrom, 'A Diagnostic Approach for Going beyond Panaceas', *Proceedings of the National Academy of Sciences*, 104.39 (2007), 15181–87 <https://doi.org/10.1073/pnas.0702288104>; Elinor Ostrom, 'A General Framework for Analyzing Sustainability of Social-Ecological Systems'.

to social-ecological conditions over time.[286] Thus, academics are compelled to choose between the superbly detailed but static SES framework and the dynamic but underspecified IAD framework.[287] Similar to the IAD framework, the SES framework is structured around a central action situation.

The SES framework classifies components and interactions between resource systems (RS), resource units (RU), actors (A), and governance systems (GS) in generating social-ecological outcomes[288]. The SES framework operates just as the IAD framework as a diagnostic policy tool. In that, it proposes a set of second- and third-tier variables (see Table 2.3) for analysis of SESs, and highlights further elements initially appearing in the IAD framework.

Figure 2. 4 Basic Components of the SES Framework

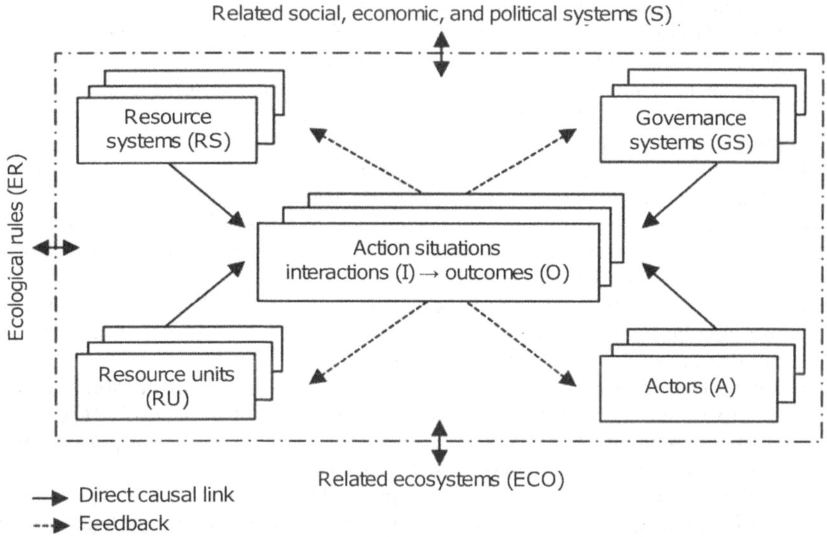

Source:[289]

286 Daniel H Cole, Epstein, and McGinnis.
287 Daniel H Cole, Epstein, and McGinnis.
288 Michael Dean McGinnis and Ostrom.
289 Adapted from Daniel H Cole, Epstein, and McGinnis.

The IAD framework was developed "to study how institutions affect the incentives confronting individuals and their resultant behaviours"[290] in a large mix of empirical setting. Since its development, the IAD framework has been used to interrogate a diverse range of settings. These include international development[291], industrial regulation[292], banking reforms[293], land tenure[294], problems related to the water-energy-food nexus[295], environmental conflicts[296], energy policy[297] and participation analysis[298].

---

290 Elinor Ostrom, *Understanding Institutional Diversity, Public Choice*, 2005, 9 CXXXII <https://doi.org/10.1007/s11127-007-9157-x>.

291 See for example, Gustavo Gordillo and Krister Andersson, 'From Policy Lessons to Policy Actions: Motivation to Take Evaluation Seriously', *Public Administration and Development*, 24.4 (2004), 305–20 <https://doi.org/10.1002/pad.325>.

292 Jeanne Schaaf, 'Governing a Monopoly Market under Sieg,e: Using Institutional Analysis to Understand Competitive Entry into Telecommunications Markets, 1944-1982' (Indiana University, 1989) <https://ostromworkshop.indiana.edu/resources/publications/dissertations.html> [accessed 25 April 2018].

293 Margaret M Polski, *The Invisible Hands of U.S. Commercial Banking Reform: Private Action and Public Guarantees* (Boston, MA: Kluwer, 2003).

294 Esther N. Mwangi, 'Institutional Change and Politics: The Transformation of Property Rights in Kenya's Maasailand' (Indiana University, 2003) <https://doi.org/10.3102/00346543067001043>.

295 Sergio Villamayor-Tomas and others, 'The Water-Energy-Food Security Nexus through the Lenses of the Value Chain and the Institutional Analysis and Development Frameworks', *Water Alternatives*, 8.1 (2015), 735–55.

296 Jampel Dell'Angelo, 'Abusing the Commons? An Integrated Institutional Analysis of Common-Pool Resource Governance in Conflict Situations', *TDX (Tesis Doctorals En Xarxa)* (Universitat Autònoma de Barcelona, 2013) <http://www.tdx.cat/handle/10803/129471> [accessed 25 April 2018].

297 Gary C. Bryner, 'Challenges in Developing a Diverse Domestic Energy Portfolio: Integrating Energy and Climate Policy in the Western United States', *New York University Environmental Law Journal*, 15 (2007) <https://heinonline.org/HOL/Page?handle=hein.journals/nyuev15&id=79&div=8&collection=journals> [accessed 26 April 2018]; Gonzalo Escribano, 'Ecuador's Energy Policy Mix: Development versus Conservation and Nationalism with Chinese Loans', *Energy Policy*, 57 (2013), 152–59 <https://doi.org/10.1016/J.ENPOL.2013.01.022>; Lysianne Reis Amorim, 'Institutional Framework and Sustainable Development: A Case from Electricity Generation in Brazil' (Uppsala University, 2013) <http://www.diva-portal.org/smash/get/diva2:606020/FULLTEXT01.pdf> [accessed 26 April 2018]; Auriane Magdalena Koster, 'An Institutional Approach to Understanding Energy Transitions', *PhD Dissertation* (Arizona State University, 2013) <https://doi.org/10.1017/CBO9781107415324.004>; Shah and Niles.

298 R. P. Bixler and others, 'The Political Ecology of Participatory Conservation: Institutions and Discourse', *Journal of Political Ecology*, 22 (2015), 164–82.

Figure 2. 5 (a) Generic Representation of Combined IAD-SES Framework, and (b) Basic Components of the Combined IAD – SES Framework

(a)

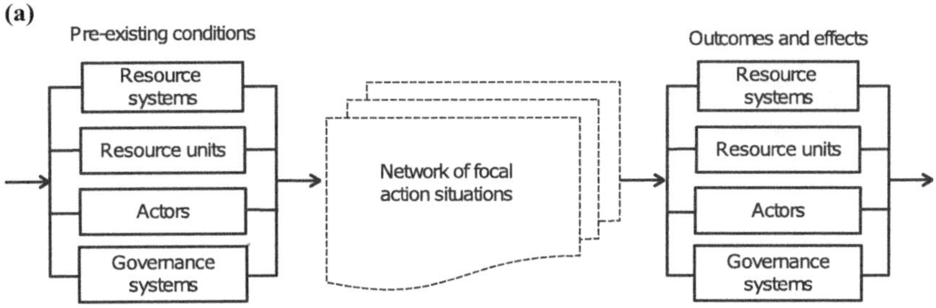

(b)

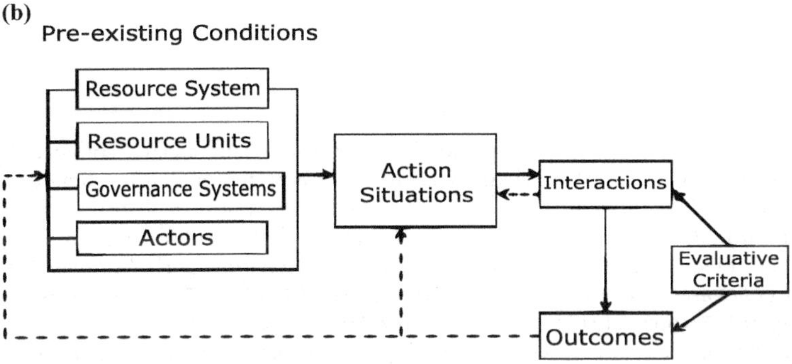

Source:[299]

On the other hand, the SES framework was developed as an attempt to revise the IAD framework. It has been applied to a plethora of social-eco-

299 Adapted from Daniel H Cole, Epstein, and McGinnis.

logical and technical settings, namely fisheries[300], forests[301], water and irrigation[302] and energy and liquefied natural gas developments[303].

300 Xavier Basurto, Stefan Gelcich, and Elinor Ostrom, 'The Social–Ecological System Framework as a Knowledge Classificatory System for Benthic Small-Scale Fisheries', *Global Environmental Change*, 23.6 (2013), 1366–80 <https://doi.org/10.1016/J.GLOENVCHA.2013.08.001>; Joshua E Cinner and others, 'Comanagement of Coral Reef Social-Ecological Systems.', *Proceedings of the National Academy of Sciences of the United States of America*, 109.14 (2012), 5219–22 <https://doi.org/10.1073/pnas.1121215109>; Gutiérrez, Hilborn, and Defeo.

301 Forrest D. Fleischman, Kinga Boenning, and others, 'Disturbance, Response, and Persistence in Self-Organized Forested Communities: Analysis of Robustness and Resilience in Five Communities in Southern Indiana', *Ecology and Society* (Resilience Alliance Inc.) <https://doi.org/10.2307/26268203>.

302 Michael Cox, 'Applying a Social-Ecological System Framework to the Study of the Taos Valley Irrigation System', *Human Ecology*, 42.2 (2014), 311–24 <https://doi.org/10.1007/s10745-014-9651-y>; Róger Madrigal, Francisco Alpízar, and Achim Schlüter, 'Determinants of Performance of Community-Based Drinking Water Organizations', *World Development*, 39.9 (2011), 1663–75 <https://doi.org/10.1016/j.worlddev.2011.02.011>; Elinor Ostrom, 'Reflections on "Some Unsettled Problems of Irrigation"', *American Economic Review*, 101.1 (2011), 49–63 <https://doi.org/10.1257/aer.101.1.49>.

303 Claudia Benham, 'Change, Opportunity and Grief: Understanding the Complex Social-Ecological Impacts of Liquefied Natural Gas Development in the Australian Coastal Zone', *Energy Research and Social Science*, 14 (2016), 61–70 <https://doi.org/10.1016/j.erss.2016.01.006>.

Table 2. 3 Second and Third -Tier Variables for Diagnosing SESs

Resource Systems (RS)	*Resource Units (RU)*	*Governance Systems (GS)*	*Actors (A)*	*Action Situations (AS) Interaction (I) → Outcomes (O)*
RS1 Sector *RS2* Clarity of system boundaries *RS3* Size of resource system *RS4* Infrastructure /Human-constructed facilities *RS5* Productivity of System *RS6* Equilibrium properties a) Recharge dynamics b) Recharge rate c) Number of equilibria d) Feedbacks i) Positive ii) Negative *RS7* Predictability of system dynamics *RS8* Storage features *RS9* Location	*RU1* Resource unit mobility *RU2* Growth or replacement rate *RU3* Interactions among resource units a) Strong to weak b) Predatory or symbiotic *RU4* Economic value *RU5* Number of units *RU6* Distinctive markings *RU7* Spatial and Temporal Distribution a) Spatial heterogeneity b) Temporal heterogeneity	*GS1* Policy Area *GS2* Geographic Scale of Governance System *GS3* Population *GS4* Regime type *GS5* Rulemaking Orgs. a) Public Sector b) Private Sector c) Nongovernmental, non-profit d) Community-based e) Hybrid *GS6* Rules-in-use a) Operational-choice rules b) Collective-choice rules c) Constitutional choice rules d) Mixed *GS7* Property-rights systems *GS8* Repertoire of norms and strategies *GS9* Network structure *GS10* Historical continuity	*A1* Number of relevant actors/users *A2* Socioeconomic attributes of actors a) Economic b) Cultural *A3* History of use / Past experiences *A4* Location *A5* Leadership /entrepreneurship *A6* Norms/social capital *A7* Knowledge of SES/mental models *A8* Importance of resource (dependence) *A9* Technologies used	*AS1* Process a) Monitoring i) Environmental ii) Social b) Sanctioning c) Conflict d) Provision i) Informational ii) Infrastructural e) Appropriation f) Policymaking

Source:[304]

Regardless of the study and use of the IAD and SES frameworks in policy analysis, each have been found to contain apparent weaknesses. The IAD's weakness is its inadequate consideration of natural systems, whilst the SES's shortcoming is its incapacity to offer more than a static list of system components. However, the Bloomington School under Elinor Ostrom envisioned, with limited success, the integration of the much broader SES framework and the initially formulated IAD framework. Eventually, there was a combination of a sort.[305]

Acknowledging these shortcomings and the inceptive limited success, Cole et al[306] formulated the "combined IAD-SES framework[307]," – whose development is still work in progress as at the time of this research. It incorporates the SES variables entirely into the IAD framework. The combined IAD-SES framework, thus, permits the user to employ a multilevel policy analysis tool, which distinguishes the major subsystems of an SES. That is, using the components of the SES framework into a dynamic form where progressive institutional differences are accounted for, by using the components embedded in the IAD framework.[308]

Becoming cognisant of these strengths, this framework appears well suited for detailing the drivers of institutional formation, reform and the outcomes produced through such a reform. A combined IAD-SES framework promises to show dynamism and an ability to include factors such as transaction costs and a broader scope of logical structure into its structural design.[309] Theoretically, applying the combined IAD-SES framework with other relevant literature, such as that of new governance, strives to move international law beyond traditional multilateral treaties. This helps to identify the importance of unilateral, bilateral, and regional measures within the context of comparative regionalism. It further contributes to the conceptual insights in the governance of energy systems in a larger

---

304 Adapted from: Elinor Ostrom, 'A General Framework for Analyzing Sustainability of Social-Ecological Systems'; Ostrom and Cox; Michael Dean McGinnis and Ostrom.

305 Daniel H Cole, Epstein, and McGinnis.

306 Daniel H Cole, Epstein, and McGinnis.

307 Paul McCord and others, 'Polycentric Transformation in Kenyan Water Governance: A Dynamic Analysis of Institutional and Social-Ecological Change', *Policy Studies Journal*, 45.4 (2017), 633–58 <https://doi.org/10.1111/psj.12168>; Scott Shackelford and others, 'When Toasters Attack: A Polycentric Approach to Enhancing the Security of Things', *SSRN Electronic Journal*, 2016, 1–54 <https://doi.org/10.2139/ssrn.2715799>; Daniel H Cole, Epstein, and McGinnis.

308 McCord and others.

309 Daniel H Cole, Epstein, and McGinnis.

trans-boundary and transnational scale. Likewise, it reveals the broad utility of the combined IAD-SES framework in the study of traditional policy issues like energy policy.

2.3.2 Energy and the Combined IAD-SES (CIS) Framework

Using the CIS framework proves to be a beneficial tool for multilevel analysis of regional energy governance systems. It is particularly useful to explore the existing institutional design governing energy systems in energy regions, such as ECOWAS and EU. The ultimate goal for using this analytical tool in such a study is to draw out common attributable elements that can be applied to any geopolitical energy region. This is especially so for the purpose of diagnosing inherent collective action problems and designing further improvements in the governance of regional energy systems through effective policymaking. The purpose of the CIS framework is not to explain outcomes but simply serve as a tool for identifying, categorising and organising variables and processes for analysis.[310]

Modern energy systems are considered as socio-technical commons that are organised and subjected to a constructed market while being governed by constitutional, collective and operational rules, and are designed to be sustainable. The use of the CIS framework can assist in identifying constituent sectors and sub-sectors, categorise actors, users and roles, and organise the varied elemental variables and processes in a coherent and structured manner to ensure a more rigorous analysis of the energy governance field.

The decision to use the CIS framework as the other appropriate tool (alongside the historical approach) in this research study for the analysis of the regional energy spaces of ECOWAS and EU is based on the following reasons. Firstly, this comparative regional energy research expands on the utility of the coupled IAD and SES frameworks as a starting point. The IAD and SES frameworks both independently intend to analyse the basic variable and process components that constitute the set-up of the entire institutional framework that underpins the two energy regions. By doing so it reveals the dynamic and static perspectives that they both contain.

310 Dan Cole, Mike Mcginnis, and Graham Epstein, 'Toward a Combined IAD-SES Framework' (Bloomington,IN, 2013), pp. 1–55 <https://ostromworkshop.indiana.edu/pdf/seriespapers/2013s_c/Cole, McGinnis, Epstein_PowerPoint.pdf>; Daniel H Cole, Epstein, and McGinnis; Daniel H. Cole, Epstein, and McGinnis.

To illustrate, utilising the IAD framework alone, would only capture the dynamics and feedbacks related to the network of action situations under study. But it would fail to fully represent the detailed complexity contained in the biophysical and socioeconomic aspects of the regional energy spaces revealed by the presence of the multiple variables.

The simple representation of this nuanced complexity is what the SES framework seeks to remedy as shown in Figure 2.6 below. The figure shows the interpreted outcomes of policy processes that possibly occur when working parts and associated rules of a focal action situation is connected to adjacent action situations.[311] It further depicts the linkages that exists between a single focal action situation and the series of 'adjacent' or adjoining action situations (the six boxes arrayed around the rectangle in the centre can generate outcomes that define the seven types of rules).

Each of these adjoining action situations occurs alongside the main one and has the effect of influencing the values of one or more of the working parts that ultimately define the main policy action situation. In sum, no single policy action situation can be fully understood without taking cognisance of the policy constellation in which it resides.[312] Therefore, the fusion of both frameworks and its adoption combines; (a) the subsystems of the SES framework with (b) the dynamics of action situations which include interactions, outcomes, and feedbacks.[313] This would be applicable to the entire energy space in the regions under consideration.

Secondly, the interactions taking place in the network of focal policy action situations of the CIS framework produce policy outcomes and effects on regional energy governance. The interactions provide an understanding of the role and function of actors and broader subsystems as they interact to achieve energy policy outcomes that can be observed as potentials and obstacles. It also presents another focus on certain aspects of the regional energy policy system like actor preferences and institutional arrangements. These aspects focus attention on the network of focal action situations that produce patterns of energy policy interactions that lead to energy governance outcomes. These outcomes include provisioning (that is, energy

---

311 Typical of traditional game theory parlance, a similar use of adjacency could be adopted for situations in which the rules governing how a particular game is played are determined by the outcomes of an adjacent game.

312 Daniel H Cole, Epstein, and McGinnis.

313 Dan Cole, Mike Mcginnis, and Graham Epstein, 'Toward a Combined IAD-SES Framework' (Bloomington,IN, 2013), pp. 1–55 <https://ostromworkshop.indiana.edu/pdf/seriespapers/2013s_c/Cole, McGinnis, Epstein_PowerPoint.pdf>; Daniel H Cole, Epstein, and McGinnis; Daniel H. Cole, Epstein, and McGinnis.

access), appropriation (that is, energy security) and monitoring (that is, regulation) action situations among others.

Figure 2. 6 Action Situations Adjacent to a Focal Action Situation

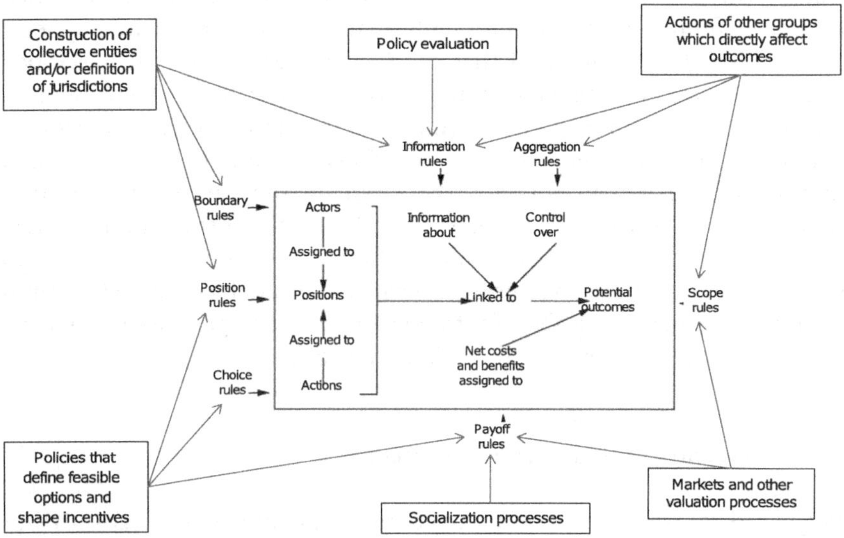

Source:[314]

Thirdly, it is established in energy studies literature that energy systems are complex systems.[315] Hence, the same goes for the complexity demonstrated by the contextual institutional arrangements found in both energy regions under review. Therefore, in this situation the CIS framework is utilised to unpack the elements of these complex energy governance systems found in both energy regions. This is to help understand the prevailing conditions in them. And with this background, it offers grounded evidence-based policy advice on the possible transition to a transformed

314 Daniel H Cole, Epstein, and McGinnis. p.6.

315 Vaclav Smil, *Energy in Nature and Society: General Energetics of Complex Systems* (Boston, MA: Massachusetts Institute of Technology, 2008); Ronan Bolton and Timothy J. Foxon, 'Infrastructure Transformation as a Socio-Technical Process - Implications for the Governance of Energy Distribution Networks in the UK', *Technological Forecasting and Social Change*, 90.PB (2015), 538–50 <https://doi.org/10.1016/j.techfore.2014.02.017>.

energy governance system that would deliver abundant, efficient, affordable and sustainable energy supply services.

The IAD and the SES frameworks has been used to analyse energy governance systems separately.[316] But to my knowledge at the time of concluding this dissertation there was no evidence of the use of the combined multilevel framework to institutionally analyse energy governance systems at any scale. I am convinced that the CIS framework is well developed and well suited for this analytical purpose because it can help identify, categorise and organise the numerous variables and unique processes inherent in the two energy regions of ECOWAS and EU. Even though in and of itself it may not serve as a tool for drawing inferences, it is nonetheless well-matched for the analytical purpose of studying these two energy regions.[317] Furthermore, the application of the CIS framework to energy, integrates these two insights. That is, the variable-oriented research obtained from applying the SES framework and the process–oriented research derived from applying the IAD framework.

2.3.3 Polycentricity and Energy Governance

Polycentricity is a basic notion that connotes a complex set of governance scales and multiple centres of semi-autonomous decision-making with the capability of interacting among themselves competitively and cooperatively. It also possesses a recourse to conflict resolution mechanisms. This set of governance scales possess a certain degree of autonomy when interacting among themselves and it is regarded as a polycentric governance system.[318] Furthermore, this consideration of polycentricity as a system of governance scales that have independent decision-making centres operate under an overarching system of rules, be it rules-in-use or particularly rules-in-form.[319]

Polycentricity is feasible within the context of energy regionalism. Energy governance conceptualised in a broader sense within a comparative regionalism perspective can be considered in terms of a polycentric gov-

---

316 Shah and Niles; Koster; Koster and Anderies, xxiii; Hinkel and others.

317 Daniel H. Cole, Epstein, and McGinnis.

318 Keith Carlisle and Rebecca L. Gruby, 'Polycentric Systems of Governance: A Theoretical Model for the Commons', *Policy Studies Journal*, 00.00 (2017) <https://doi.org/10.1111/psj.12212>.

319 Vlad Tarko, *Elinor Ostrom: An Intellectual Biography* (London, UK and Lanham, Maryland: Rowman & Littlefield International, 2016).

ernance system because it is closely related to the understanding that underpins Ostromian polycentricity. This same approach to governance in regional integration can be seen in the work of Hooghe and Marks[320], who apply this two-fold typology of multi-level governance (MLG) to governance in the EU[321]. It consists of both general-purpose and special-purpose jurisdictions at varying governance scales, and further includes functional overlapping competing jurisdictions (FOCJ)[322].

These types of multi-level governance are not mutually exclusive, but coexist in modern polities like supranational regional organisations such as ECOWAS and the EU. Formal general-purpose institutions of governance, like the Authority of Heads of State and Government, Council of Ministers, ECOWAS Commission, among others, operate alongside, and indeed create, special-purpose bodies. Such bodies are designed to carry out particular tasks that include agencies, partnerships and quangos in specific policy areas like energy, water and financial services.

Polycentricity in the governance of the energy sector represents a multi-level, multi-purpose, multi-functional and multi-sectoral approach to energy governance. Scholars, including Elinor Ostrom and Vincent Ostrom, promoted this approach of polycentric governance in different public policy areas to solve collective action problems.[323] Their understanding underpins regional energy governance as seen in ECOWAS and EU energy regionalism. It challenges convention by exhibiting the benefits of self-organisation and network regulation at multiple scales. Also, it further probes the extent to which political and private control can, in some cases, coexist with communal management.

Michael D. McGinnis defines governance as a "process by which the repertoire of rules, norms, and strategies that guide behaviour within a given realm of policy interactions are formed, applied, interpreted, and

---

320 Liesbet Hooghe and Gary Marks, 'Unraveling the Central States, but How? Types of Multi-Level Governance', *The American Political Science Review*, 97.2 (2003), 233–43 <https://doi.org/10.1017/S0003055403000649>.

321 Liesbet Hooghe and Gary Marks, 'Types of Multi-Level Governance', *European Integration Online Papers (EIoP) N°*, 5.11 (2001) <http://eiop.or.at/eiop/texte/2001-011a.htm>.

322 Reiner Eichenberger and Bruno S. Frey, 'FOCJ: Competitive Governments for Europe', *International Review of Law and Economics*, 16.3 (1996), 315–27; Bruno S. Frey and Reiner. Eichenberger, *The New Democratic Federalism for Europe: Functional, Overlapping, and Competing Jurisdictions* (Edward Elgar, 1999).

323 Elinor Ostrom, *Polycentric Systems as One Approach for Solving Collective - Action Problems*, Working Paper (Bloomington,IN, 2008).

reformed."[324] In essence, it establishes the point, that governance must be considered as a process, and that actors in government and non-governmental spheres play critical roles in that process.[325]

That said, the early 1960s witnessed the foundational developments of polycentricity as an alternative and possible governance approach. Scholars interested in local governance and decentralisation reforms took much interest in this new approach. Then, many provincial areas comprising cities, counties, and suburban authorities, also took interest. Subnational jurisdictions, like regional or federal authorities, who had specialized but limited power in particular policy areas, also took interest in it for guidance to effect reforms. In this case, reforms were initiated because public policy analysts and political science researchers presumed that such overlapping jurisdictions were chaotic and compulsive. And so, they called for consolidation in service provision to improve efficiency in these subnational structures.[326]

Vincent Ostrom, Tiebout, and Warren[327] countered this argument by proposing that consolidating approaches to service provision were likely to be inefficient, because such 'one size fits all' approaches could not account for divergent preferences among different groups of citizens, or differing economies of scale among different public services. Therefore, they confirmed the idea that polycentric systems with varied governance scales of decision making, and formally autonomous to each other, might essentially improve efficiency.[328] Vincent and Elinor Ostrom further opined that governance systems with multiple sub-regional units of varying sizes (polycentric) perform better compared to those with only a small number of large units (monocentric).[329] One of the established principles of the Bloomington School's research led by Elinor and Vincent Ostrom related to metropolitan governance and police districts. They established, that

324 Michael D. McGinnis, 'An Introduction to IAD and the Language of the Ostrom Workshop: A Simple Guide to a Complex Framework', p. 171.

325 Michael D. McGinnis, 'Connecting Commons and the IAD Framework'.

326 Paul D. Aligica and Vlad Tarko, 'Polycentricity: From Polanyi to Ostrom, and Beyond', *Governance*, 25.2 (2012), 237–62 <https://doi.org/10.1111/j.1468-0491.2011.01550.x>; Elinor Ostrom, 'A Long Polycentric Journey', *Annual Review of Political Science*, 13.1 (2010), 1–23 <https://doi.org/10.1146/annurev.polisci.090808.123259>.

327 Ostrom, Tiebout, and Warren.

328 Ostrom, Tiebout, and Warren.

329 Aligica and Tarko.

multiplicity is not necessarily inefficient, and that such complexity should not be interpreted as chaos.[330]

The research pathway on polycentricity, principally the corpus of the Ostroms and the Bloomington School, avoids categorization in favour of any single type of structure. The most commonly known application of polycentric governance to real-world situations remains the work of Elinor Ostrom[331]. She determined that community-based commons management was capable of being sustainable only if its rules were nested within a broader context of polycentric governance that permitted alternative mechanisms of collective decision-making and conflict resolution at all levels of aggregation.

In furtherance to the theoretical and empirical notions of polycentricity and polycentric governance, an increasing number of scholars have dedicated their research careers to consolidate its development in different contexts. Much of the early scholarship focuses on the application of polycentric approaches to the development of natural resource governance. However, there is a burgeoning interest in applying polycentricity to the internet of things (IOT), cybersecurity, internet governance, energy infrastructure and energy resource governance among others.

Political science, political economy and government scholars of the 1960s, including international development scholars in the immediate postcolonial era, leaned towards the inclination that centralised government authority was vital to ensure efficient utility of natural resources. But numerous scholars, famously among them, Elinor Ostrom, have refuted this presumption through the use of empirical research conducted on the management of natural resources where local resource users were able to manage and govern resources effectively.[332] With the significant growth of insight on the concept of polycentric governance, polycentricity has

---

330 Elinor Ostrom, 'A Long Polycentric Journey'.

331 Elinor Ostrom, *Governing the Commons - The Evolution of Institutions for Collective Action*; Elinor Ostrom, 'Beyond Markets and States: Polycentric Governance of Complex Economic Systems'.

332 Arun Agrawal and Clark C. Gibson, 'Enchantment and Disenchantment: The Role of Community in Natural Resource Conservation', *World Development*, 27.4 (1999), 629–49 <https://doi.org/10.1016/S0305-750X(98)00161-2>; Elinor Ostrom, *Governing the Commons - The Evolution of Institutions for Collective Action*; Michael Dean McGinnis, *Polycentric Governance and Development: Readings from the Workshop in Political Theory and Policy Analysis*.

advanced past the original conceptual proposition of V. Ostrom, Tiebout, and Warren.[333]

To comprehend polycentricity and polycentric governance one must begin with its basic components. It primarily consists of action situations, that serve as partially autonomous policy decision centres interconnected at a high level of aggregation to contemplate on the basic attributes of a given policy area. Polycentric governance approaches primarily focus on the processes of provision, production, financing, and evaluation of public goods, in addition to the management of common resources and public infrastructures.[334] This form of governance essentially requires tough decisions that involve trade-offs among alternative goods and resources, many of which could suffice as items of immense importance for different segments of society.

Some kind of authority is critical for solving the problems of free riding seen in polycentric governance. The benefits of enjoying public goods or shared resources cannot be easily appropriated exclusively by the individuals who invest their time and resources in producing or procuring those goods. Usually, authorities need to be able to enforce at least a minimal level of legitimate coercion to gather the resources needed to support public purposes, such as requiring the payment of taxes or altering fees structure to persons seeking access to restricted commons.[335]

As Cole and McGinnis[336] emphasise, in an ideal type of polycentric governance, a diverse array of public and private authorities with overlapping domains of responsibility work together in complex and ever-changing ways. The result of these apparently uncoordinated processes of mutual adjustment, develops a resilient system of social ordering that can support and sustain capacities for self-governance. Generally, early work on polycentricity as associated with polycentric governance of multiple centres of political power and financial expertise serve as overlapping institutional arrangements, weak or unpredictable hierarchical relationships, and nested units and sub-units, with significant autonomy.[337] This autonomy in

---

333 McCord and others.

334 Michael D. McGinnis, 'Connecting Commons and the IAD Framework'.

335 Michael D. McGinnis, 'Connecting Commons and the IAD Framework'.

336 Daniel H. Cole and Michael D. McGinnis, *Elinor Ostrom and the Bloomington School of Political Economy: Volume 1, Polycentricity in Public Administration and Political Science*, ed. by Daniel H. Cole and Michael D. McGinnis (Lexington, Lanham, MD, 2015).

337 Vincent Ostrom, Charles M. Tiebout, and Robert Warren, 'The Organization of Government in Metropolitan Areas: A Theoretical Inquiry', *American Political*

the nodes of power, function in a coherent manner and display steady patterns of interaction that could constitute a *system*.[338] The numerous centres of power and decision making could choose to compete, conclude agreements, or collaborate while making use of conflict resolution mechanisms.[339] Hence, polycentric governance describes an organizational structure where multiple independent actors mutually order their relationships in a coordinated manner with one another under a general system of rules.[340]

A political order is considered polycentric when there are many overlapping nodes of authority and responsibility.[341] The principle is that constructing modern societies encapsulate institutional diversity revealed in multi-level, multi-purpose, multi-sectoral, and multi-functional units of governance.[342] There are numerous approaches employed by scholars to conceptualise polycentricity. But not all of them have a meeting of the minds about what makes a particular governance system *polycentric*, even though studies have been predisposed to converge around a number of key characteristics.

Firstly, polycentric systems permanently involve multiple, independent nodes of decision-making.[343] Polycentricity is differentiated from decentralization. Its difference is depicted through the mechanisms, which in-

---

Science Review, 55.04 (1961), 831–42 <https://doi.org/10.1017/S0003055400125973>.

338 Ostrom, Tiebout, and Warren.p. 831

339 André R. da Silveira and Keith S. Richards, 'The Link Between Polycentrism and Adaptive Capacity in River Basin Governance Systems: Insights from the River Rhine and the Zhujiang (Pearl River) Basin', *Annals of the Association of American Geographers*, 103.2 (2013), 319–29 <https://doi.org/10.1080/00045608.2013.754687>.

340 Vincent Ostrom, 'Polycentricity', *Annual Meeting of the American Political Science Association, Washington Hilton Hotel, Washington, D.C., September 5-9*, 1972, 47 <http://dlc.dlib.indiana.edu/dlc/handle/10535/3763>.

341 Michael Dean McGinnis, *Polycentric Governance and Development: Readings from the Workshop in Political Theory and Policy Analysis*, ed. by Michael Dean McGinnis, 4th edn, 2 (The University of Michigan Press, 1999) <https://doi.org/10.3998/mpub.16052>.

342 Chris Araral, Ed; Hartley, 'Polycentric Governance for a New Environmental Regime : Theoretical Frontiers in Policy Reform and Public Administration', *International Conference on Public Policy, Panel: Polycentric Policy and the Environment*, 2013, 1–31; Shackelford and others.

343 Krister P. Andersson and Elinor Ostrom, 'Analyzing Decentralized Resource Regimes from a Polycentric Perspective', *Policy Sciences*, 41.1 (2008), 71–93 <https://doi.org/10.1007/sl>.

clude shared set of rules for coordination and cooperation between the nodes of decision making, which are fundamental features of polycentric regimes.[344] Polycentric systems also exhibit overlapping jurisdictions that generate, to a degree, redundant institutions.[345] Overlaps may be geographical, possibly in the form of nested decision nodes[346], or may well be functional, where multiple decision nodes have authority in a given policy area.[347]

Furthermore, several scholars of polycentricity have emphasized, either indirectly or directly, that these organisational features trigger good governance outcomes. For example, the presence of multiple autonomous decision nodes is perceived to allow local decision centres to experiment with informal rules that govern resource use and are suggestive of the possibility of innovation and learning.[348] It permits local units to formulate rules, which are responsive and adaptive to domestic conditions. This theoretically makes polycentric systems exhibit resilience to ecological shocks.[349] Since local actors comprehend local needs and conditions better, perhaps they are positioned favourably to construct informal rules, which meet localized needs more efficiently and equitably than government administrators' formal rules.[350]

The coordination of overlapping authorities among these autonomous and independent decision nodes, can enable mutual adjustment among

---

344 Claudia Pahl-Wostl and Christian Knieper, 'The Capacity of Water Governance to Deal with the Climate Change Adaptation Challenge: Using Fuzzy Set Qualitative Comparative Analysis to Distinguish between Polycentric, Fragmented and Centralized Regimes', *Global Environmental Change*, 29 (2014), 139–54 <https://doi.org/10.1016/j.gloenvcha.2014.09.003>.

345 da Silveira and Richards; Michael Dean McGinnis, *Polycentric Governance and Development: Readings from the Workshop in Political Theory and Policy Analysis*.

346 Andersson and Ostrom.

347 Victor Galaz and others, 'Polycentric Systems and Interacting Planetary Boundaries - Emerging Governance of Climate Change-Ocean Acidification-Marine Biodiversity', *Ecological Economics*, 81 (2012), 21–32 <https://doi.org/10.1016/j.ecolecon.2011.11.012>.

348 Andersson and Ostrom.

349 Galaz and others.

350 Carl Folke, Thomas Hahn, and others, 'Adaptive Governance of Social-Ecological Systems', *Annu. Rev. Environ. Resour.*, 30 (2005), 441–473 <https://doi.org/doi : 10.1146/annurev.energy.30.050504.144511>; Jesse C. Ribot, Arun Agrawal, and Anne M. Larson, 'Recentralizing While Decentralizing: How National Governments Reappropriate Forest Resources', *World Development*, 34.11 (2006), 1864–86 <https://doi.org/10.1016/j.worlddev.2005.11.020>.

decision centres[351]. Undeniably, mechanisms for communication and coordination differentiate between polycentric systems and those that are decentralized.[352] Such coordination for instance, could permit local user groups to communicate with national or regional policymakers, making provision for them at the table with regards to policy matters that can help improve outcomes.[353] Coordination can also be essential where multiple local user units are nested within a shared water basin, forestry system, fishery, internet community and energy space. Coordination of overlapping authority allows user groups or units to communicate and modify their use in ways, which are beneficial to the system as a whole. This in essence enables collective action at multiple levels of governance.[354]

It is not conclusive, however, that polycentric governance structures will give rise to the beneficial governance outcomes predicted by theory. That is to say, adopting a polycentric governance approach is not a panacea. Actually, V. Ostrom et al. were careful to argue that independent nodes of decision-making might not predictably give rise to "orderly outcomes"; alternatively, they attribute this to an empirical question.[355] Lately, several studies have published empirical evidence that polycentric governance regimes tend to display high performance[356], particularly when compared with non-polycentric or less-polycentric systems.[357] There has been limited empirical testing, however, of the theoretical propositions that scholars have developed to explain the apparent success of polycentric systems, including experimentation with informal rules and adaptation to local conditions.[358]

Moreover, the analytical frameworks developed by the Ostrom Workshop are genuinely consistent with analysing and understanding polycentric governance. The frameworks are driven by a multitude of decision centres, each with limited ranges of authority typically overlapping with

351 Vincent Ostrom, 'Polycentricity'.

352 Andersson and Ostrom; Pahl-Wostl and Knieper.

353 Andersson and Ostrom.

354 Daniel H Cole, Epstein, and McGinnis.

355 Ostrom, Tiebout, and Warren.p.831

356 Basurto and Ostrom; Elinor Ostrom, 'Coping With Tragedies of the Commons', *Annual Review of Political Science*, 2.1 (1999), 493–535 <https://doi.org/10.1146/annurev.polisci.2.1.493>; Claudia Pahl-Wostl and others, 'From Applying Panaceas to Mastering Complexity: Toward Adaptive Water Governance in River Basins', *Environmental Science and Policy*, 23 (2012), 24–34 <https://doi.org/10.1016/j.envsci.2012.07.014>.

357 da Silveira and Richards; Pahl-Wostl and Knieper.

358 McCord and others.

the jurisdictions of other decision centres. It is required for these authorities to interact with each other to realize shared aspirations, or even to achieve their own goals. Each decision centre typically has jurisdiction over only a few action situations, and the conditions under which one decision centre operates has been shaped by the operation of inter-related decision centres.[359]

The magnitude of the global energy challenge demands a scaling up of efforts to mitigate abundant energy access deficiencies and environmental concerns particularly in low-income regions of the world. The existence of multiple governing authorities in energy governance systems with overlapping jurisdictions offer the possibility of complementary back-up institutions in higher and lower levels. This includes multiple levels that can help offset some of the imperfections of single levels of governance in energy governance. This polycentric approach to energy governance offers the possibility of more substantial outcomes other than only a highly centralized or fully decentralized governance system.[360]

Again, the varied and overlapping levels of governance allows sustainable energy and climate change challenges to be tackled through changes at the energy system level, the firm level, and in the patterns of consumption and behaviour that characterize socio-economic systems.[361] Polycentric policymaking and governing strategies appear to have many unique advantages. This includes complementary back-up institutions at transnational and national levels counterbalancing some of the limitations at any one level. Polycentricity also captures the *flexibility* benefits of local and state action as well as the *uniformity* and *equity* benefits associated with regional and global action. It agrees that multiple jurisdictions with overlapping responsibilities coupled with modes of regulation can offer citizens more choice. Yet it still requires that local actors subscribe to a

---

359 Michael D. McGinnis, 'Connecting Commons and the IAD Framework'.

360 Elinor Ostrom, 'A General Framework for Analyzing Sustainability of Social-Ecological Systems'; Elinor Ostrom, 'Polycentric Systems for Coping with Collective Action and Global Environmental Change', *Global Environmental Change*, 2010 <https://doi.org/10.1016/j.gloenvcha.2010.07.004>; Andersson and Ostrom.

361 Catherine Mitchell, *The Political Economy of Sustainable Energy*, 2nd edn (New York: Palgrave Macmillan, 2010) <https://doi.org/10.1057/9780230279452>.

common set of goals, broad enforcement, minimized 'transaction costs' and the 'dilemmas of collective action'.[362]

When multiple actors at various scales compete in overlapping areas; they often promote innovation, cooperation and increased citizen/consumer involvement. On the other hand, polycentricity also faces several challenges. It requires the coexistence of local, national, and international laws and programs that assess similar energy themes or sectors. Divergent rules and programs can lead to redundancy of regulation, inefficiency, and confusion as people try to figure out which laws apply to them. It may take more time for issues to be resolved because disgruntled parties can always appeal to the other levels of government especially in conflict and dispute resolution but also in the execution of sanctioning regimes. By creating overlapping jurisdictions, regulators and policymakers may blame deficiencies of respective energy governance scales on other levels of government. This may create unfortunate instances to hide behind smokescreens, which help in shirking responsibilities with the intent to mislead disgruntled citizens from intelligently discerning the right authority to precisely vent their rage.

Overall, polycentricity and polycentric governance creates important roles for multiple scales of actors in energy spaces. It reduces the risk of creating an intellectual commons problem by empowering social, political, and intellectual leaders from a variety of places to contribute to the creation of abundant, clean and secure energy systems.[363] As stated by Andreas Goldthau,

> "energy infrastructure systems comprise multiple governing authorities and actors at differing scales. Polycentricity therefore offers a promising lens to rethink the governance of energy infrastructure with a view to facilitating a low carbon future".[364]

Let us look back on the applicability of polycentricity to energy governance. We have seen that among others, polycentricity is an important approach to regional energy governance. It occurs when regional polities

362 Martin J. Pasqualetti and Marilyn A. Brown, 'Ancient Discipline, Modern Concern: Geographers in the Field of Energy and Society', *Energy Research and Social Science*, 1 (2014), 122–33 <https://doi.org/10.1016/j.erss.2014.03.016>.

363 Marilyn A Brown and Benjamin K Sovacool, *Climate Change and Global Energy Security-Technology and Policy Options* (Cambridge, Massachusetts: The MIT Press, 2011).

364 Goldthau, 'Rethinking the Governance of Energy Infrastructure: Scale, Decentralization and Polycentrism p 138'.

inherent within overlapping jurisdictions and centres of authority together with actors interact to determine the conditions under which to act decisively in the provision of better and sustainable energy outcomes. Additionally, in the course of fulfilling this policy action, constraints and obstacles would be faced. This would serve as a direct means of policy feedback or evaluative loop in the strengthening and provision of better and efficient energy policy outcomes in any given energy region.

Also, in polycentric governance settings, energy systems, energy services, monitoring of energy use and appropriation can be well managed. The implementation of polycentric energy governance approaches in a comparative regionalism perspective may include but not limited to a single type of institutional organisation or informal grouping. Moreover, it can be advanced by adopting multi-level units of governance to organise the energy governance scales at the local, provincial, national and regional levels.

Another way is through the adoption of a multi-purpose approach exemplified by the general-purpose nesting of jurisdictions like an energy region bound together by shared commonalities in energy path dependence and path creation. Furthermore, special purpose and cross-jurisdictional political units typified by shared energy infrastructure (such as cross-boundary grid interconnection or shared gas pipeline located in a regional geographical corridor) ensure robust and resilient governance at multiple levels through the implementation of rules and best practices. In essence, a multi-sectoral system with all forms of public, private, voluntary, community-based and hybrid kinds of organisations interlink in an energy region to exhibit attributes of a polycentric energy governance system.

Also, polycentricity and polycentric governance occurs through a multi-functional approach, which incorporates specialised units for energy provision. We can see this through upstream, midstream and downstream energy activity, finance and investments (through public financing and donor support), sector coordination, monitoring, sanctioning, and dispute resolution.

We have seen that the meaning of the word, *polycentric* connotes many nodes or centres of decision making that are formally independent of each other. They either function independently or comprise of an interdependent system of relations. To the extent that, they take each other into account in competitive relationships, enter into various contractual and cooperative undertakings, or have recourse to central mechanisms to resolve conflicts. This may function in a coherent manner with consistent and predictable interactive patterns of behaviour in a particular public policy setting like energy policy in a regional setting. To this extent, they are classified as functioning in a manner resembling a *system*.[365]

It is therefore key to note that one key puzzle in the literature on polycentric governance has to do with the efficiency and measure of productivity of polycentric systems such as regional energy systems. In the end, polycentric energy governance systems have everything to do with the specified governance functions of an energy region. And this entails the manner in which it monitors and governs geographical, temporal, technical and ecological processes involved within the complex energy policy area.[366]

365 Ostrom, Tiebout, and Warren, p. 831.

366 Daniel H. Cole and McGinnis; Daniel A DeCaro and others, 'Legal and Institutional Foundations of Adaptive Environmental Governance', *Ecology and Society*, 22.1 (2017) <https://doi.org/10.5751/ES-09036-220132>.

Chapter 3

Energy Regionalism in West Africa

3.1 Introduction

The Economic Community of West African States (ECOWAS) has been at the forefront in promoting energy regionalism in West Africa since its formation. Using historical institutionalism in international relations generally and more specifically within the broader context of comparative regionalism, I explore the stages behind the origins and development of cooperation, integration, and governance of energy in West Africa through the vehicle of the main regional actor ECOWAS in concert with several other extra-regional, national, private and sub-national actors. Almost all energy policy decisions in the ECOWAS region are made at the country level with a few exceptions made at the regional level especially relating to joint regional projects. This chapter aims to provide an overview of energy regionalism in West Africa particularly with respect to ECOWAS.

The energy access and supply gap in the West Africa region is huge. Home to diverse sources of energy, including petroleum and enormous amounts of untapped renewables, West Africa with over 350 million residents in fifteen nations[367] depend on a consistent energy supply for an increasing population.[368] With geographic and demographic variances coupled with, unique political and socio-economic differences this vast region in terms of land area[369] is expected to be energy sufficient and have abundant supply of energy. But that is not the case. In fact, that raises big

367 Here West Africa is synonymous to ECOWAS. The fifteen member nations of ECOWAS comprise Benin, Burkina Faso, Cape Verde, Gambia, Ghana, Guinea, Guinea-Bissau, Ivory Coast, Liberia, Mali, Niger, Nigeria, Senegal, Sierra Leone and Togo.

368 United States Energy Association, 'The West African Energy Sector: Exploring Current Projects Within the Region and Investment Opportunities' <https://www.usea.org> [accessed 26 March 2019].

369 The geographical land area of the ECOWAS region is estimated at 5,114,162 square kilometres arguably the seventh largest land mass globally by certain estimations. ECOWAS, 'History of the Economic Community of West African States (ECOWAS)' <https://www.ecowas.int> [accessed 12 September 2018].

quantities of oil and natural gas discoveries. The urgency and prioritization by national governments coupled with the workings of ECOWAS in realizing its more than three decades old energy agenda are some contributory factors stimulating this surge in regional energy activity.

Region-building by states and other actors using energy issues as the functional tool within the context of regional relations in West Africa through ECOWAS has been intense and on the rise. Moreover, this interaction focuses on regional energy issues where politics and economics intersect. Looking at the role of a number of actors, member states and external economic partners. In this chapter, the process of exploring the IPE of energy commences with unpacking regional integration history that led to the founding of ECOWAS and follows up with similar processes of exploration of the component elements of ECOWAS energy regionalism temporally.

Furthermore, since ECOWAS energy regionalism is not happening in a vacuum but being spearheaded by institutions such as the legal norms, generalist and specialist regional bodies together with other actors and initiatives. This study seeks to contribute to the limited perspectives on strategic IPE of energy narratives as it pertains to West Africa generally and ECOWAS in particular besides drawing attention to how the study of energy history can highlight these themes.

This chapter is organised as follows. Section 2 presents an overview of West African energy history from the perspective of the three linguistic and colonial sub-groupings that define the region namely Anglophone, Lusophone and Francophone. Furthermore, looking at established colonial energy regimes and the construction of national energy systems after independence. Section 3 examine the historiography of ECOWAS regionalism on its own and Section 4 further discusses the account of ECOWAS energy regionalism under three headings past milestones, present settings and future prospects. Section 5 then looks at the institutional basis that anchors the governance of energy regionalism in ECOWAS. Finally, a recapitulation of the whole chapter serves as the conclusion in Section 6.

Map 3. 1 Economic Community of West African States (ECOWAS)

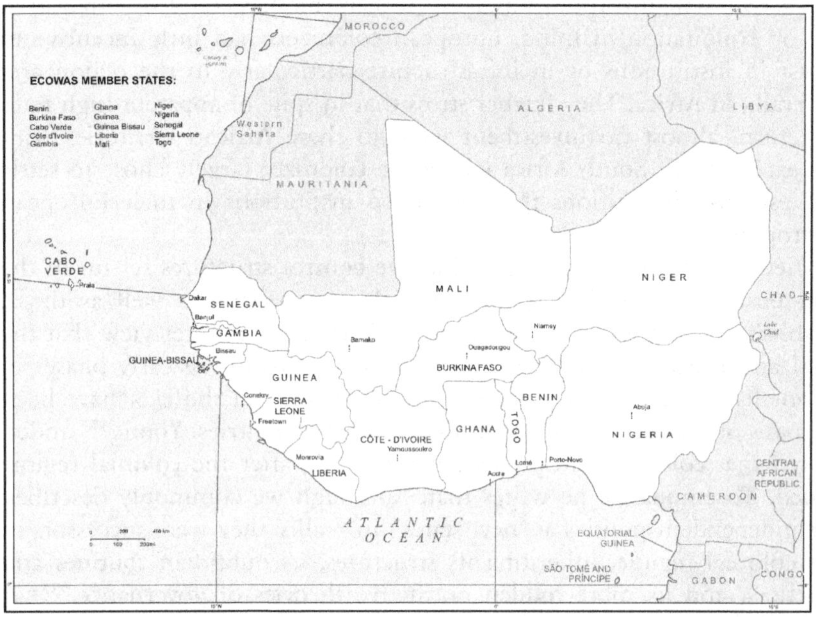

3.2 West African Energy History: Colonial Regime and Construction of National Systems

Deployment and spread of modern energy technologies in West Africa has been directly tied to its recent colonial past. Historically, prior to the decolonization process which began in 1957, availability and provision of energy services was the sole responsibility of the European colonialists in the region. Slightly over sixty years on, the effects of different colonial energy policies, which created varied path dependencies in energy provision in the three linguistically nuanced parts of West Africa that is, Anglophone, Lusophone and Francophone still persist. It has influenced the urgency, investment and transformation from a colonial regional energy economy, which served the needs of the colonizer to an energy economy that seeks to reverse this colonially dependent trend for the benefit of the ever-increasing regional demographic dividend.

Acemoglu, Johnson & Robinson[372] opine that with the set-up of worse (extractive) state institutions in West African colonies coupled with a strategy of exploitation in mind, European colonizers had little incentive to invest in institutions or in infrastructure particularly in the region and generally in Africa. They further stress that in spite of apparent high rates of return, almost no investment went to these African territories with the exception of South Africa where the colonizer largely chose to settle and establish institutions that resembled institutions in their European metropoles.

The established thesis suggest that the control structures set up in the non-settler colonies during the colonial era persisted as well as those, established in settler colonies. Whereas there is no counter view that the legal and private property institutions set up during the early phases of colonialism in Australia, Canada, New Zealand, and the U.S. have been the basis of the current day institutions of these countries. Young[373] underscored that colonial institutions persisted long after the colonial regime ended. To emphasize he writes that, "although we commonly described the independent polities as 'new states', in reality they were successors to the colonial regime, inheriting its structures, its quotidian routines and practices, and its more hidden normative theories of governance."[374] A variety of sources supports this claim on the persistence of institutions set up by colonialists[375] in an occupied territory. And thus, encouraging a dependent path until a reversal through a newly created path is initiated and carried out to its logical conclusion by the newly independent polities.

---

372 Daron Acemoglu, Simon Johnson, and James A. Robinson, *The Colonial Origins of Comparative Development: An Empirical Investigation*, NBER Working Paper (Cambridge, MA, 2000).

373 Crawford Young, *The African Colonial State in Comparative Perspective* (New Haven, CT: Yale University Press, 1994).

374 Crawford Young, p. 283.

375 The claim on the persistence of colonial institutional set up goes back at least to Wittfogel, who argues that the control structures set up by the large "hydraulic" empires like China, Russia, and the Ottoman Empire persisted for more than 500 years to the 20th century. Others also argued that colonial institutions persisted by providing evidence to support the claim. See: Karl A Wittfogel, *Oriental Despotism: A Comparative Study of Total Power* (New Haven, CT: Yale University Press, 1957). Rafael La Porta and others, 'Law and Finance', *Journal of Political Economy*, 106.6 (1998), 1113–55.Rafael La Porta and others, 'The Quality of Government', *The Journal of Law, Economics, & Organization*, 15.1 (1999), 222–79.

Generally, African electricity development emerged from three major reasons: an amenity or symbol of modernity for European settlers, a source of power to drive high productivity for mines and industry[376], and to stimulate industrial development. In most of colonial Africa including West Africa, electricity was not seen as significant to the livelihoods of African and non-urban settlers however, it was the most cost-effective form of power for machinery and railroads since it was no longer profitable to use animal and human labour. The rapid spread of mining and manufacturing centres plus railway development required large-scale electricity plants, prompting grid development.[377]

The historical accounts of energy system pathways in West Africa based on the established thesis of energy developments in Africa occurred in three different ways based on the different colonial strategies adopted. Moreover, the manner in which these energy pathways were deployed has shaped the subsequent path creation of national energy systems in the region and the regional energy economy as a whole. Since the early 1980s after the global energy crises, a move to enable a transitional energy shift from the colonial status quo has shaped the course of action in West Africa albeit increasingly slow with herculean obstacles and bottlenecks. A number of factors has influenced this process these include the reliance of colonial energy plans, adoption of early and latest energy technologies after independence to transform energy systems and the incremental role of policy and governance in the determination of energy pathways in the region.

On the reliance of colonial energy plans, little changes were made in most West African newly independent countries in relation to the energy plans that were devised by the erstwhile colonial leadership. For instance, in Ghana (formerly the Gold Coast), hydropower plans that were drafted during the colonial period served as a launch pad for the construction of a national energy system. To clarify further, in a quest to modernize and set in motion an industrialization agenda as a new state, Ghana implemented the 1925 energy strategy that was published in a British colonial survey by Albert Kitson, a British geologist working for the colonial administration.

376 D. Worth, 'Lighting the Darkness: The Gas Supply Industry in Nineteenth Century Cape Town, and Its Role in the Formation of an Industrial Landscape', in *Proceedings at the Association for Industrial Archaeology Annual Conference, 4–5 September, 1998* (North Abott, Devon, 1998).

377 Kate B Showers, 'Electrifying Africa: An Environmental History with Policy Implications', *Geografiska Annaler, Series B: Human Geography*, 93.3 (2011), 193–221 <https://doi.org/10.1111/j.1468-0467.2011.00373.x>.

This was to boost the utilization and extraction of the Gold Coast's mineral and water resources as well as electrify a railway line to the northern regions of the country by constructing two hydroelectric dams in Akosombo and Bui both on the Volta River.[378]

Adoption of energy technologies by these newly independent states sought to lay the groundwork for an established energy pathway, which was difficult to digress from in favour of another technological pathway. However, on the other hand due to the late adoption of these energy technologies it enabled some of these newly independent West African states to leapfrog quickly and scale up use of these technologies.

In this sense, Grubler and Wilson[379] have argued that first adopters reach a higher market saturation level or develop established dependent paths, whereas later adopters scale more speedily, but less broadly. For example, conventional hydropower dam technology became the obvious option for energy technology diffusion in West Africa. This was due to the presence of a large network of major river bodies which led to the construction of the Kainji, Jebba and Shiroro Dams (Nigeria), Akosombo, Kpong and Bui Dams (Ghana), Ayame I, II and Kossou Dams (Cote d'Ivoire) and the Sélingué and Manantali Dams (Mali) inter alia. The diffusion of large hydropower technology has been scaled relatively speedily but not extensively in the region.

The development of national energy policy and a well-defined energy governance system hinged on day-to-day dealings occurring in these newly emancipated West African societies. These governments were expected to take an active interest in how energy is sourced, accepted and utilized.[380] The usual manner this was done was through divergent viewpoints around market-based approaches contrasted with public-delivery and regulatory approaches. A range of methods thus has defined the way in which these viewpoints could have been dealt with by the newly independent states to ensure an energy transition. These may have included the placement of

---

378 Stephan F. Miescher and Dzodzi Tsikata, 'Hydro-Power and the Promise of Modernity and Development in Ghana: Comparing the Akosombo and Bui Dam Projects', *Ghana Studies, V*, 12.13 (2009), 15–53 <http://www.history.ucsb.edu/wp-content/uploads/1-Miescher_Tsikata.pdf>.

379 Charlie Wilson and Arnulf Grubler, 'Lessons from the History of Technological Change for Clean Energy Scenarios and Policies', *Natural Resources Forum*, 35 (2011), 165–84.

380 Kathleen Araújo, 'The Emerging Field of Energy Transitions: Progress, Challenges, and Opportunities', *Energy Research & Social Science*, 1 (2014), 112–21 <https://doi.org/10.1016/j.erss.2014.03.002>.

employees, bottom-up or societal-led change, leadership, and information or education-led change.

It is significant to underscore that policy tools which have effectively contributed to or enabled an energy transition in one unique colonial sub-region can dramatically differ from those in the others even though they exist in the same West African regional community. That said in evaluating policy tools the lack of consideration of institutions, mechanisms or societal orientation will limit its applicability.[381] To this end, significant contributions of energy policy design and planning centres in the various countries as well as the regional ones cannot be underestimated in the role they play in evaluating the performance of specific policy tools. As well as their capacity to suggest newly defined objectives and options that could transform the regional energy sector in the future.

At best pre-colonial commercial energy history in West Africa has been fragmentary. Coal is reported to have been used in limited quantities in eastern Nigeria for use in the craft industry even though it did not gain widespread popularity as a source of energy. In the case of oil and gas together with the harnessing of river potential, ancient West Africa appears to have done little to exploit its utility as an energy source. Lacking access to what we call today, commercial energy sources, pre-colonial West Africa relied heavily on firewood, dried cow dung, and other agricultural waste as primary energy sources.[382] This *status quo ante* remained even to the early years of colonialism. The conventional energy system only changed slightly in the early 1900s with the development of large-scale production and exploitation of primary commodities for export.

In order to provide the energy input required for upgrading the colonial economic system, authorities resorted to the import of commercial fuels from Europe.[383] Coal was the first commercial fuel to be imported into West African countries in major quantities for use in thermal plants. This began from the 1890s until the 1900s when volumes increased to meet new demand especially for the construction of railway lines which was regarded as vital to economic development in the territories.[384]

Importation of commercial energy and fuels also persisted until attempts were made to prospect for the energy reserves in the territories.

381 Cherp, Jewell, and Goldthau.

382 Joseph A. Sarfoh, *Hydropower Development in West Africa* (New York: Peter Lang, 1990).

383 Sarfoh, *Hydropower Development in West Africa*

384 Sarfoh, *Hydropower Development in West Africa*.

There were limited initial successes for the colonial authorities in Nigeria, Ghana, Benin and Cote d'Ivoire in exploring and eventually exploiting oil and gas, however in the Nigerian case a surprise big find changed the course of energy exploration.[385] Limited amounts of coal deposits were also found in Nigeria but it was not exploited because there was value for money in the import of cheap European coal into West Africa than mining the limited coal deposits that was more expensive and could easily peak.

In terms of their sub-regional groupings colonial authorities did not appear to pursue a vigorous sub-regional energy policy in their respective sub-regions in West Africa as seen in other policy areas such as agriculture and trade.[386] However, they did encourage their proxies – large private companies to investigate possibilities for introducing modern energy and other technologies such as hydroelectricity and rail transport.

It was until the post-independence era that national leaders of these newly founded states set about ambitious goals and embarked on new energy policies seeking to construct national energy systems befitting the status of these newly independent nation-states. In the next sections, I reiterate the energy history of West Africa from the colonial through to the post-independence periods from the perspective of the English-speaking, Portuguese-speaking and French speaking parts of the region.

3.2.1 Anglophone West Africa

3.2.1.1 The Colonial Energy Regime

The unique and differentiated nature of energy as an essential infrastructure, that is, as an energy commons deployed using the means of a tradable public good or service became critical for its widespread distribution during the colonial era. This determined the local provision of energy services via expanded markets and possible energy technologies. It influenced the need to clarify who would provide energy services such as electricity to whom, and for how much.

In British colonial West Africa, small-scale electricity utilities were established as public corporations and was mainly done using nascent railway departments except that they maintained a certain amount of independence under the colonial administration. The existence of these utility cor-

385 Sarfoh, *Hydropower Development in West Africa*.
386 Sarfoh, *Hydropower Development in West Africa*.

porations, did not exclude private sector generation.[387] Public commercial generation of electricity was non-existent. Yet available electricity supply was simply monopolized and used to electrify certain strategic fledgling public sectors particularly mining and railways.

However, in a number of territories the law permitted private enterprise participation in the generation and supply of electricity for lightning and other purposes. To exemplify this, in the Gold Coast (present day Ghana), the Electricity Supply Ordinance of 1920 opened up the supply of electricity to private enterprise involvement in all the three territories that applied the various Ordinances of the Gold Coast Colony, these territories were the Asante, Northern and Gold Coast territories.[388]

The arrival and spread of modern energy like electricity in the colonial era was clearly associated with British commercial interests. Britain claimed four colonies in the West African region. The fifth anglophone territory was independent Liberia with strong ties to the USA. Power grids were most extensive in these British colonies compared to the Portuguese and French territories.[389]

The electrification regime established in these colonies began with isolated, small-scale generators supplying farms and plantations, industries and railway transit systems with power. As well as municipal administration centres electrified for lighting. Most of the turbines generating this electrification were steam-driven and diesel-powered. The small-scale thermal plants were typically fuelled by imported diesel. After its commercial development, run-of-the-river (non-storage) hydroelectric systems would arrive not long in British West Africa to help in the electrification process. Consistent with other parts of the continent modernity expressed in electrification coexisted with conventional power sources.[390]

The colonial energy regime characteristically featured electricity plants, rather than isolated generators and this began to proliferate in the sub-region. In British Nigeria, the Public Works Department (PWD) of the Gov-

---

387 Paul Kuruk, 'Performance of Electric Utilities in Developing Countries : The Ghanaian and Nigerian Experience', *Loyola of Los Angeles International and Comparative Law Review*, 11.3 (1989), 515.

388 Kuruk. Guggisberg, Frederick Gordon, The Gold Coast: A Review of the Events of 1920–1926 and The Prospects of 1927–1928 (Accra, 1927). Wilkinson, W. H., 'West Africa', Journal of Comparative Legislation and International Law, 4.2 and 3 (1922), 151–57 <https://doi.org/10.1017/CBO9781107415324.004>

389 Sarfoh, *Hydropower Development in West Africa*.

390 David. Edgerton, *Shock of the Old: Technology and Global History Since 1900: Technology in Global History Since 1900* (London: Profile Books, 2008).

ernment of Southern Nigeria constructed the first power plant operating two 30-kilowatt generators in 1896 to serve as a source of lighting to the Government House and its environs between the hours of 6 p.m. to 11 p.m.[391]

By 1940, the authorities in charge of the Southern Nigerian government and native administration were providing electricity as a social amenity in very limited quantities in major towns and scattered administrative and commercial centres that inhabited expatriate populations.[392] The African Timber and Plywood Company owned and operated the largest electricity generation plant, and utilized 'wood waste' to fuel a generator that supplied electricity to the sawmills and the adjacent port town of Sapele.[393] With an increasing commercial demand stimulating further public and private thermal plant construction, it was however constrained by the need for more fuel.

The notion of electricity provision as a government-funded public good or service was rare. As Kate Showers discusses in detail, even though electricity supply was considered as a commons for colonial administrative units, urban residential areas as well as serving as a symbol of modernity, it was primarily utilized as a source of power for the extractives and other industries and a means of industrial stimulus. This was exemplified in the electricity supply situation in the British Gold Coast (Ghana).[394]

Electricity production began with diesel powered generation, mainly owned and operated by industrial companies, to be exact mines and factories of fast-moving consumer goods (FMCG) as well as other businesses and municipalities. However, in 1914, the first public electricity supply in the Gold Coast was installed by the colonial administration – owned railway system located at Sekondi in the south-western corner which had a harbour. This public electricity supply system was expanded to Takoradi in 1928. In addition, by 1922, the Public Works Department (PWD) had begun operating a limited direct current supply to Accra (later to be aug-

391 M. N. A. Manafa, *Electricity Development in Nigeria, 1896–1972* (Yaba, Nigeria: Raheem Publishers, 1979); Kuruk.

392 E. S. Simpson, 'Electricity Production in Nigeria', *Economic Geography*, 45.3 (1969), 239–57 <https://doi.org/10.2307/143093>; Kuruk.

393 Simpson.

394 Kate B Showers.

energy policy opportunities and challenges for regional bureaucrats and national governments as well as other actors to deal with.

ECOWAS has advanced an ambitious regional energy agenda, established on the founding ECOWAS Treaty of 1975. The early objectives were to promote cooperation and development in all fields of economic activity, including energy[370]and this is set out to increase the collective energy autonomy of the region.[371] However, 24 years later in 1999 the regional energy agenda and its implementation gradually began to unfold and materialize with the establishment of the West African Power Pool (WAPP) and the ECOWAS Energy Protocol in 2003. These regional efforts have sought to promote a strategic regional energy vision, long-term cooperation, increase complementarity and attract investments to promote regional energy trade in West Africa. The agenda was further expanded with the establishment of the West African Gas Pipeline (WAGP) in 2005 and the ECOWAS Centre for Renewable Energy and Energy Efficiency in 2010.

Amidst all of this, there has been increasing energy activity in the region, in terms of explorations and discoveries of major hydrocarbon finds in the Gulf of Guinea, West African Transform Margin and the Senegal Basin. Literally, there is an intense search for hydrocarbon activity upstream and offshore in the entire coastline of West Africa from the eastern tip of Nigeria to the western threshold of Mauritania. These oil and gas offshore activities has attracted the eye and the resources of some of the major oil companies in the world with particular investments from the known global powers (both emerging and old) ranging from those that are energy sufficient like the US and those seeking to secure supplies such as the EU, China and India.

West Africa has become a hotbed for concentrated energy activity. This activity extends from promoting new energy technologies and renewables to closing the energy access gap in urban, peri-urban and rural electrification programs. This is taking place through the works of new actors such as local energy communities. In addition, enthusiastic state-owned, private and external energy actors are exploring and exploiting commercial

370 ECOWAS, 'Treaty of the Economic Community of West African States (ECOWAS)' (Lagos, Nigeria, 1975), p. 20.

371 ECOWAS, 'A/DEC.3/5/82 Decision of the Authority of Heads of State and Government of the Economic Community of West African States Relating to the ECOWAS Energy Policy', *Official Journal of the ECOWAS*, 4.June (1982), 46–49.

mented with alternating current in 1924) commencing a public electricity supply system in the capital of the Administration.[395]

It seems 1928 was an active electrification year in other British West African territories, a single diesel generator was mounted at Falconbridge, Freetown – Sierra Leone by the colonial government.[396] Generation of electricity spread in British West Africa in the early twentieth century where more supply was directed for commercial and administrative demand than to the residential needs of households.

With the introduction and advancement of hydropower technology to harness river potential major inroads were conducted by the colonial administration. Hydropower surveys were piloted by the British colonial administration after seeing the good work the French had done on the River Niger for its territories. So, in the Gold Coast, Sir Albert Kitson, the territory's first official geologist proposed a scheme to harness the Volta River in an official bulletin to the colonial authorities in 1915 after a rapid survey down the river. The Geological Survey Department that he set up in 1925 recommended hydropower prospects on the Bui River as well.[397]

In Nigeria, the increasingly large and concentrated industrial demand for electricity on the Jos Plateau led to the creation of the Nigeria Electricity Supply Company (NESCO) that took over the existing Kwali station that was installed in 1923 and later built a hydropower system at Kurra in 1929. NESCO became the largest producer of electricity in the whole of Nigeria by 1939. But most was consumed by the tin mines and concentrating plant.[398] After the Second World War and just two years short of independence, the Nigerian colonial government in 1958 and the newly formed Electricity Corporation of Nigeria (ECN) initiated a survey study of the hydroelectric potential of the Niger River to be executed in cooperation with the Netherlands Engineering Consultants (NEDECO). In 1953, they surveyed the Benue and Niger rivers for navigational purposes with British consulting engineers Sir Alan Gibb and Partners, who had initially

---

395 ISSER, *Guide to Electric Power in Ghana* (Accra: Resource Center for Energy Economics and Regulation, Institute of Statistical, Social and Economic Research, University of Ghana, 2005).

396 R. J. Olu-Wright, 'The Physical Growth of Freetown', in *Freetown: A Symposium*, ed. by C. Fyfe and E. Jones (Freetown, Sierra Leone: Sierra Leone University Press, 1968), pp. 24–37.

397 Arthur E. Kitson, *Outline of Mineral and Water-Power Resources of the Gold Coast, British West Africa., Gold Coast Geological Survey Bulletin* (London: C. A. Terry, 1925), I.

398 Simpson.

conducted a dam survey on the Niger River. Added responsibilities included evaluation of river navigation, flood control and irrigation.[399]

In the mid and post war period, the development of the English-speaking region was impacted significantly by the war and its aftermath. Especially, during the immediate post war years, spiralling prices and shortages in supply of essential goods resulted in economic hardship leading to political unrest in all the territories. The British colonial government then became focused increasingly on the socio-economic development of their colonies to quell any unrest a process that took a queue from a similar strategy after World War I.

The most dramatic move was to adopt policies such as the Colonial Development and Welfare Acts of 1940 and 1945, which made Colonial Office funds available for developments in areas like energy and hydropower projects in the territories.[400] For instance, these proactive policies in 1958 encouraged the Colonial administration in Nigeria to effect a comparative cost analysis between the recently proposed hydropower projects for the Niger River and thermal plants fuelled by under-used natural gas from the oil fields. The issued report in 1960, recommended a series of three integrated multi-purpose dams as the cheapest source of energy due to their many predicted benefits. Natural gas would later be used as an added fuel source[401].

Again, the British colonial authorities in West Africa saw the potential in river basin planning thus initiating programs on the Black Volta (Ghana), River Gambia (Gambia), and Niger (Nigeria) among others.[402] Majority of the river basin planning sought to construct dams with a dual purpose for irrigation and potential hydropower generation.[403]

British West Africa's notable oil and gas reserves were concentrated in Nigeria and Ghana with estimates of about 22 billion barrels or 80 percent of the West Africa-wide total. Nigeria was by far the most endowed of the two with about 20 billion barrels of the estimated total. For many years, it was considered uneconomic to develop and invest in new exploration, drilling and production of the oil resources. Another compelling reason was the existing technology, which was incompatible with the conditions

399 For more details see: Simpson.

400 Sarfoh, *Hydropower Development in West Africa*.

401 Simpson.

402 See evidence in : W. M. Adams, *Wasting the Rain: Rivers, People and Planning in Africa* (Minneapolis, MN: University of Minnesota Press, 1992).

403 Kate B Showers.

of the wet and heavy soils in the coastal southern areas of West Africa where the oil was known to exist. It was not until the mid-1950s that a number of major energy companies became interested in intensive exploration and drilling for oil.

These initial efforts made by the companies paid off, particularly in Nigeria, which had produced over 6 million barrels of oil by 1960. The search continued and by late 1982, Ghana was producing oil though not in commercial quantities compared to Nigeria. Elsewhere in the English-speaking sub-region, intensive petroleum prospecting had been carried out in Liberia, and Sierra Leone. Prospects were remarkable for Liberia and Sierra Leone to become crude oil producers. In spite of this, it was not likely to happen soon.[404]

The earliest exploration attempt for oil in Nigeria took place in 1908 based on existing evidence of oil seepages at Araromi, located 200 km from Lagos, colonial authorities in Southern Nigeria granted license to a West German company, the Nigerian Bitumen Corporation. Oil prospecting was halted by the start of World War I, it was until 1937 that an Anglo-Consortium, Shell D'Arcy, later to known as Shell-BP Petroleum Development Company (now Shell Nigeria, the Nigerian operations of Royal Dutch Shell), secured rights under the colonial administration to do further exploratory work.

This second attempt was again stalled at the start of World War II and it was after the war that exploration recommenced. In 1957, the company officially announced the discovery of oil in commercial quantities at Oloibiri, near Port Harcourt in the Niger Delta area. The company had invested over 60 million US dollars in exploratory activity at the time of the announcement. Oil production was confined first at Oloibiri, Afam and Bomu, however two extra wells were discovered at Ebubu and Ugheli that contributed to the production significantly. Oil production volumes increased substantially that Shell-BP found it necessary to build two oil terminals, one at Bonny and one at Forcados to ease evacuation and production facilities consequently more terminals were later to be built.[405]

This energy narrative in British colonial West Africa illustrates vividly the nature of energy developments under the colonial anglophone regime highlighting motivations, interests and results. It also becomes the basis for

---

404 Sarfoh, *Hydropower Development in West Africa*; Phia Steyn, 'Oil Exploration in Colonial Nigeria, C.1903-1958', *The Journal of Imperial and Commonwealth History*, 37.2 (2009), 249–74.

405 Sarfoh, *Hydropower Development in West Africa*; Steyn.

the construction of national energy systems in these former anglophone colonies after more than a hundred years under British colonial rule.

3.2.1.2 Constructing National Energy Systems

Founding political leaders of English-speaking independent West African nations were poised towards an energy abundant future largely embracing principles of modernism and economic models that sought to emphasize industrial development. West Africa's first president of an independent nation, Ghana's Kwame Nkrumah, fully embraced hydropower as an important means for the accelerated development and rapid modernization of this new nation. He endorsed the earlier hydropower surveys conducted by the colonial administration as well as plans for the conversion of local bauxite to aluminium by harnessing the potential energy inherent in the Volta River which had initially been suggested by the 1924 colonial Gold Coast Administration, its commercial viability was assessed in 1938.

Primarily, its bankability was founded on the heightened demand for aluminium in post-World War II Europe thereby leading to the creation of a company, West African Aluminium Limited, to execute these plans. Subsequently, a three-volume report titled 'The Volta River Project' was presented to the colonial authority in the Gold Coast in 1949, which suggested a partnership between a consortium of aluminium companies and the Government to implement the project. The following parts of the project were recommended; a dam and aluminium refining plant at Adjena, an electricity grid, and a second dam at Bui on the Black Volta River.[406] These hydropower and allied projects underpinned Ghana's energy system developments for over forty years until the discovery of oil in commercial quantities. Hydropower developments related to large-scale economic and industrial purposes became a significant feature of newly independent anglophone West African nations.

The bedrock of the constructed national energy systems in anglophone West Africa were the grids, institutions and networks that ensured energy production for these newly independent states. It was characterized by

406 The Volta River Project, *Report of the Preparatory Commission* (London, 1952), VOLUME I; The Volta River Project, *Appendices to the Report of the Preparatory Commission. Appendix I. White Paper on the Volta River Aluminium Scheme* (London, 1956), VOLUME II; The Volta River Project, *Engineering Report to the Preparatory Commission* (London, 1956), VOLUME III; Kuruk.

increased transmission capabilities enabled through the interconnection of power stations and electricity grids. Initially, minor grids which were established served municipalities, mines and industries. The extent of the grid system, institutions and network interconnections was determined largely by industrial and mining demand with less focus on residential and community demand[407].

Sub-regional independence in the majority of anglophone West African states in the 1960s brought about other different approaches in the way in which energy was understood thus changing the way infrastructure systems, institutions and networks were constructed. Energy planning done through the rollout of power grid infrastructure and its implementation using national electricity institutions, was rekindled and influenced by the commodification of electricity in the 1980s. This was an idea internationally inspired by the United Kingdom.[408] As ECOWAS pushed to improve national electricity supplies working in concert with member states especially in the anglophone nations, the idea of sharing electricity regionally emerged. This has necessitated interconnected power grids of which the nationally constructed systems in Anglophone West Africa have played a crucial role.

3.2.2 Lusophone West Africa

3.2.2.1 The Colonial Energy Regime

Portugal's colonial administration of territories in West Africa lasted until 1975. They fought to retain these colonies. This means the energy policy of these territories was determined by Portugal until this period. Before the end of the Portuguese colonial period in West Africa, there was hardly any electricity access outside of the major cities and even in cities there was very limited household access.[409]

Guinea Bissau and Cape Verde Islands relied heavily on biomass and the importation of petroleum products, which was partly used for the

---

407 For a typical discussion such as Nigeria's post World War II colonial grid expansion see Simpson.

408 Kate B. Showers, 'Congo River's Grand Inga Hydroelectricity Scheme: Linking Environmental History, Policy and Impact', *Water History*, 1.1 (2009), 31–58 <https://doi.org/10.1007/s12685-009-0001-8>.

409 Kate B Showers.

generation of thermal energy during the colonial era. Ten years prior to independence, these territories recorded energy per capita values of 75 and 15 kilograms of oil equivalent (kgoe) in Cape Verde and Guinea Bissau respectively. In 1972, per capita consumption of fossil fuels (that is, oil and other energy petroleum products) was comparatively one of the highest in the region.[410] In addition to the thermal energy generated from imported oil, traditional sources of energy, namely, firewood, charcoal, dried dung and agricultural waste dominated the Lusophone energy regime in colonial West Africa.

The over-reliance on biomass during the colonial era, contributed to the excessive exploitation of the forest cover in the Lusophone sub-region particularly that of the Cape Verde Islands. Changes in the land and vegetation cover as well as natural resources of the Cape Verde Islands resulted in the catastrophic degradation of its lands and vegetation. A key cause of this degradation, perhaps indirect but still decisive, could be a political and economic system that tolerated an unspeakably myopic exploitation of the land. The mechanism employed in this exploitative process was perhaps overexploitation of the flora and forest area by people and their animals such as goats, for commercial and domestic purposes.[411]

As Lindskog and Delaite[412] assert, if the Portuguese colonizers had been conscious of the fragility of the ecosystem they came to occupy, they could have persevered particularly the Cape Verdean Islands to profit from the advantages of a dry savanna with a verdant forest cover made up of trees and continuous grass. Contributory causes of deforestation and land degradation in the Cape Verde Islands were surely more complex, they involved both anthropogenic and non-anthropogenic factors. In order to reverse this trend of deforestation and degradation thereof, Lopes de Lima[413] suggested in the 1840s that unless tree planting exercises were done, any attempts to promote agricultural development would possibly end in catastrophic failure. The colonial administrators recognized the

---

410 Sarfoh, *Hydropower Development in West Africa*, pp. 16–18.

411 Per A. Lindskog and Benoit Delaite, 'Degrading Land: An Environmental History Perspective of the Cape Verde Islands', *Environment and History*, 2.3 (1996), 271–90 <https://doi.org/10.3197/096734096779522266>.

412 Lindskog and Delaite.

413 José Joaquim Lopes de Lima, *Ensaios Sobre a Statistica Das Possessoes Portuguezas, Ilhas de Cabo Verde a Suas Dependências.* (Lisbon: Impresa Nacional, 1844), I.

need for reforestation, especially to reverse the trend of desertification and deforestation which was caused by human activity.[414]

In the 1940s, at the end of four years of droughts, Amilcar Cabral published his ideas in some articles in the journal *Cabo Verde: Boletim de Propaganda e Informaçao*. One of them was entitled: 'Some Thoughts on the Rains'[415] with the other four titled: 'In Defence of the Land'[416]. At the time, Cabral, was still an agronomy student. He discussed the reasons for the causation of soil erosion and its function in relation to the devastating evolution of agriculture on the islands. He revealed that the removal of the plant cover made the soils vulnerable to immense erosion. In these scientific articles, there is a hint of Cabral's future political mission. He suggested that the political will necessary to carry out the soil and water conservation works to stall this devastating process must emanate from indigenous Cape Verdeans themselves and not from the colonial power.

It is striking to note that in spite of the pressure upon the Portuguese colonial government, the first soil conservation programs were introduced during the last ten out of the five hundred years of colonial rule.[417] It is sometimes hinted that efforts to reverse the effects of this ecological problem due to over-exploitation inspired the rebellion and liberation struggle against the colonial authorities by Amilcar Cabral who may have been spurned on through his intellectual understanding in agronomy that enabled him to comprehend the situation first-hand.[418]

Guinea-Bissau, similar to the Cape Verde Islands widely adopted low technology extraction fuels like wood, logs, and charcoal for food preparation in households. Kerosene was used for lightning. In rural areas they were almost totally deprived of any electricity supply. In larger cities, such as Bissau electricity supplies were provided in a discontinuous manner, and white settlers and the colonial government agencies tended to oper-

---

414 Laura Bigman, *History and Hunger in West Africa: Food Production and Entitlement in Guinea-Bissau and Cape Verde* (Westport, Connecticut: Greenwood Press, 1993).

415 Amilcar Cabral, 'Algumas Consideraçoes Acêrca Das Chuvas (Some Thoughts on the Rains)', *Cabo Verde: Boletim de Propaganda e Informaçao*, 1.1 (1949), 5–7.

416 Amilcar Cabral, 'Em Defesa Da Terra (In Defence of the Land), 1949-1950', *Cabo Verde: Boletim de Propaganda e Informaçao*, 1–2.2,6,15 (1950), 15-17,19-22,6-8.

417 M. dos Santos Pereira, *Cabo Verde: Duas Tentativas Para a Sua Valorizacao Agropecuária. In Cabo Verde, Guiné, São Tomé e Principe: Curso de Extensao Universitaria Ano Lectivo de 1965-1966* (Lisbon: Instituto Superior de Ciências Sociais e Política Ultramarina. Universidade Técni, 1966).

418 Lindskog and Delaite.

ate their own small thermal generators for lighting, air-conditioning, and food storage. Due to the interlinked relationship between the Lusophone countries during the colonial era and at independence. They shared a number of commonalities especially in the area of energy infrastructure and economy that was beset with a number of extraordinary challenges. For example, In Guinea-Bissau energy served as a major bottleneck, only four percent of the population in the 1980s had access to electricity, and sixty percent of this was in Bissau.[419]

In terms of hydroelectric energy potential, the Corubal and Geba River projects has been under study since the latter days of the colonial period in Guinea-Bissau with its sole objective geared towards bauxite exploration and the improvement of the national baseload. It was estimated that about 184 MW of hydropower could be produced along the rivers of Corubal and Geba.[420] On the other hand, in Cape Verde Islands, there has not been any known economically feasible potential for hydropower generation.[421]

To look into the potential of petroleum deposits, the geological structure of the rocks in Guinea-Bissau consists almost entirely of sedimentary formations, which raises the possibility of hydrocarbon endowments. Again, in an assessment of undiscovered oil and gas in the Guinea-Bissau part of the Senegal Basin, which is in the Casamance sub-basin the potential for hydrocarbon production, has been limited to small oil and gas fields. Actually, in the late-1950s exploration by Exxon gave rise to speculation as to the possible existence of offshore oil and gas however, global prices were too low at that time for development.[422] All these developments have contributed to form the basis on constructing the national energy systems of the erstwhile Portuguese controlled territories of West Africa.

---

419 World Bank, *Guinea-Bissau An Introductory Basic Economic Report* (Washington D.C., 1982), I.

420 World Bank, I.

421 Deutsche Gesellschaft für Technische Zusammenarbeit – GTZ, *Renewable Energies in West Africa* (Frankfurt /Eschborn, 2009).

422 World Bank, I; Michael E. Brownfield and Ronald R. Charpentier, *Assessment of the Undiscovered Oil and Gas of the Senegal Province , Mauritania , Senegal , The Gambia , and Guinea-Bissau , Northwest Africa, U.S. Geological Survey Bulletin 2207–A* (Denver,CO: U.S. Geological Survey, 2003).

3.2.2.2 Constructing National Energy Systems

During the first years after independence which was achieved in 1975, the political landscape of the Lusophone sub-region of West Africa has been dominated by the African Party for the Independence of Guinea-Bissau and Cape Verde (PAIGC). However, this was transformed in 1981, after the split from Guinea Bissau, by the African Party for the Independence of Cape Verde (PAICV) to form a fully independent Cape Verde. Since then attempts have been undertaken to construct national energy systems that would enable the needed energy demand to be met in these two countries.

The late 1970s spurred a move towards reconstruction after the war for independence that required the need to chart a new course for the new nations. This included an energy policy direction that sought to improve the pre-existing energy systems as well as the introduction and inclusion of new energy systems that were non-existent. The PAIGC was committed to the economic reconstruction of Guinea-Bissau and the Cape Verde Islands using an African socialist paradigm. This primarily involved a socio-economic engineering programme focused on rural electrification, mass literacy and agricultural & rural development. The PAIGC consequently tried to carry out the reconstruction programme by utilizing the human and natural resources of Guinea-Bissau and Cape Verde Islands through the injection of overseas development assistance and the diffusion of external technologies.[423]

Aside from the war, colonial neglect rendered Guinea-Bissau and Cape Verde Islands to become one of the poorest and deprived places in the world by the 1980s. This affected the energy provision fortunes of these two countries in terms of the needed energy infrastructure. There was no mining industry but a small manufacturing industry. This was palpably informed by the lack of major energy services available for productive engagement in these two post-independence economies.

Thus, the task for the path creation regarding the rollout of energy infrastructure and the sufficient provision of energy services has been an arduous one for these two nations. Political instability coupled with the separation by Cape Verde Islands in this period did not augur well for energy developments in both countries as well. Among both nations, de-

---

423 Boniface I. Obichere, 'Reconstruction in Guinea Bissau: From Revolutionaries and Guerrillas to Bureaucrats and Politicians', *A Current Bibliography on African Affairs*, 8.3 (1975), 204–19 <https://doi.org/10.1177/001132557500800304>.

mographic and economic features were dissimilar and their energy sector was made up of unique challenges.[424]

At the time, fuel imports remained the main source of external energy. Forests and vegetation covered about 65 percent of Guinea-Bissau whereas Cape Verde was going through a period of land degradation, as intimated above. Yet still the available forest cover and dwindling vegetation of the respective nations met the biomass needs of their populations, which was the major source of residential and household energy.[425] Although, Cape Verde had no hydropower potential, Guinea-Bissau initiated a study into the feasibility of the Corubal and Geba River basin projects for hydroelectricity that could have added 14 MW of power to the baseload. In fact, physical infrastructure was quite limited in the 1980s.[426] For instance, in Guinea-Bissau electricity consumption per capita was among the lowest in developing countries not only in Africa but around the world.

Approximately four percent of the population had electricity for domestic use, and even then, in many cases supply was confined to certain hours of the day or subject to sudden outages. There was virtually no electrification in the rural areas. Total capacity was 12 MW, with roughly 87 percent in the Bissau area. The prevailing energy system was based on about 200 small diesel generators, with the majority in a state of disrepair. In the midst of all this, major energy development projects financed by bilateral donors were being planned to double the pre-existing capacity in order to reinforce the capacity of Bissau and six other cities.

In sum, the 1980s, after centuries of little change, became a period of transition and transformation in political economy terms. In energy, the sectoral priority was rural electrification in addition to diversifying the fuel sources of the thermal generating plants that used petroleum products to alternative sources of energy such as wood, hydropower and biomass.[427]

The 1990s, has witnessed plural segmentation of the energy sectors in both Lusophone nations requiring specific policy action to improve the physical energy infrastructure. The energy sector of Cape Verde is composed of three sub-sectors namely petroleum, electricity with renewable energies and biomass. On the other hand, in Guinea-Bissau, the electricity sub-sector, the petroleum sub-sector and the biomass sub-sector comprise the energy policy space.

---

424 World Bank, I.
425 World Bank, I.
426 World Bank, I.
427 UNEP, 'Energy Profile of Guinea Bissau', 2015, pp. 182–85; World Bank, I.

In Cape Verde the dominant energy source is imported petroleum products whereas in Guinea-Bissau it is biomass particularly fuelwood. The electricity network within this period in Cape Verde covered 25 percent of the country. In addition, it was within this period that efforts to utilize renewable energies were improved. But in Guinea-Bissau due to dysfunctional infrastructure and its insufficient capacity, efforts were started in the 1980s and this process stalled, then proceeded to recede in the 2000s. Again, within this period, electricity prices in Guinea-Bissau were the most expensive in the region.

In the 2000s, Cape Verde and Guinea-Bissau have undertaken divergent paths in their quest towards energy availability and developments. Electricity generation is a joint endeavour between state-owned power producers and Independent Power Producers (IPPs). However, transmission and distribution rights are exclusively the sole responsibility of the national utility company.[428] Guinea-Bissau for its part is entirely dependent on thermal-based diesel power generation.[429] Since 2000, following political turmoil in the country, the power sector has virtually collapsed with no development in the power sector.[430] Institutions falling under the energy sector has been ineffective in data collection and conducting feasibility studies to assess comprehensively community impacts of having access to electricity, economic costs and to analyse alternative energy roadmaps.[431]

As at 2015, Guinea Bissau with a population of 1.75 million, produced from fossil fuels, a total electricity production of about 13 kiloton of oil equivalent (ktoe) with final consumption of electricity in the same year being six ktoe.[432] Hydropower has still not become an important source of energy although plans are far advanced by the Gambia River Basin Organization (OMVG) in the preparation and structuring of a proposed construction of the 20-MW Saltinho run-off-river hydropower plant in

428 Dinesh Surroop and Pravesh Raghoo, 'Renewable Energy to Improve Energy Situation in African Island States', *Renewable and Sustainable Energy Reviews*, 88.July 2017 (2018), 176–83 <https://doi.org/10.1016/j.rser.2018.02.024>.

429 Deutsche Gesellschaft für Technische Zusammenarbeit – GTZ.

430 Deutsche Gesellschaft für Technische Zusammenarbeit – GTZ.

431 Govinda R. Timilsina and Kalim U. Shah, 'Filling the Gaps: Policy Supports and Interventions for Scaling up Renewable Energy Development in Small Island Developing States', *Energy Policy*, 98.March (2016), 653–62 <https://doi.org/10.1016/j.enpol.2016.02.028>.

432 UNEP, *Atlas of Africa Energy Resources* (Nairobi: African Development Bank/The Infrastructure Consortium for Africa, 2017), pp. 182–85.

Guinea-Bissau, on the Corubal River. The project is part of a wider regional grid extension project, the West African Power Pool.[433]

With a commercial viability for tidal energy, a 500 MW tidal energy plant joint venture was announced between the government of Guinea Bissau and the Israeli Wave Electricity Renewable Power Ocean (WERPO).[434] In Guinea Bissau, electricity access stands as one of the most alarming energy issues because electrification levels particularly rural electrification are critically low, with slight progress to expand electricity access made over the last years.[435] The utilization of renewable energies has not been maximized despite its potential. For example, with typical wind speeds ranging from 2.5 to 7 m/s along the coast and some islands there are no plans to exploit this wind energy resource. There is no geothermal energy use in the country and with respect to solar energy use, it is minimal notwithstanding the country receiving over 4.5 kWh of solar radiation and about 3,000 sunshine hours per annum.[436]

The current enabling energy policies, which include renewable energy, energy efficiency, private sector participation and public-private partnership facilitation, are contained in the Master Plan for the Development of the Energy Sector 1980, National Energy Policy 1995 and the Draft Renewable Policy of 2004. The Ministry of Energy and Industry is in charge of both implementing policies in the energy sector and regulating them. The National Electricity and Water Corporation (EAGB) manages the electricity sector in Guinea Bissau. On a regional level, the country is a member of the West African Power Pool.[437]

Cape Verde became almost fully electrified by 2012. However, there are existing issues concerning weak electricity infrastructure for a population of just over half a million people as at 2013.[438] Total electricity produced in 2015 was 31 ktoe, 87 per cent of which was generated from fossil fuels.[439]

---

433 Gregory B. Poindexter, 'Gambia River Basin Organization Seeks to Develop 20-MW Saltinho Hydropower Project in West Africa', *Hydroworld*, 2017 <https://www.hydroworld.com/articles/2017/01/gambia-river-basin-organization-seeks-to-develop-20-mw-saltinho-hydropower-project-in-west-africa.html> [accessed 30 July 2018].

434 UNEP, *Atlas of Africa Energy Resources*, pp. 182–85.

435 Surroop and Raghoo.

436 UNEP, *Atlas of Africa Energy Resources*, pp. 182–85.

437 UNEP, *Atlas of Africa Energy Resources*, pp. 182–85.

438 Surroop and Raghoo.

439 UNEP, *Atlas of Africa Energy Resources*, pp. 122–25.

Total electricity supply in Cape Verde for the period 2010–2014, increased by 22 percent (averaging 6 percent per year).

In 2013, 18 diesel power stations provided 300 GWh, which represented 71 percent of total electricity produced, 26 percent of the total was contributed by wind energy and 3 percent by solar photovoltaic systems. Increasing electricity supply in Cape Verde was realized mostly by renewable energy sources, especially wind where capacity addition added about 24MW and a subsequent 2MW from solar energy sources.[440] Within the period 2006–2013, there was large development in wind energy in the country where electricity generated from wind increased by 91 percent. Having a favourable wind velocity of 5–7 m/s at 50m height.[441] Through the medium of a parastatal agency, the government of Cape Verde with concerted effort from a number of stakeholders have created Cabeólica, tasked with the responsibility for wind energy development in the country. Cabeólica in one year achieved quite an impressive record by supplying Electra enough electricity to make available 21 percent of the electricity demand.[442]

In Cape Verde, there are no possible sites technically and economically viable for the exploitation of hydroelectricity. Its 2008 National Energy Policy indicates that the government will explore the introduction of micro-nuclear plants for electricity generation.[443] The Ministry of Tourism, Industry and Energy (MTIE) is responsible for the Cape Verdean energy sector. The energy regulator is the multisector Economic Regulatory Authority (Agência de Regulação Económica – ARE). ELECTRA (Empresa de Electricidad e Agua) is the national power utility company, the sole generator, transmitter and distributor of electricity. The Renewable Energy Research Group (NER) is responsible for the advancement in research regarding renewable energy adoption in Cape Verde.[444]

On a regional level, the country is headquarters for the ECOWAS Centre for Renewable Energy and Energy Efficiency (ECREEE) a clear indication of its commitment to the promotion of renewable energies internally and externally. The legal framework is provided by the Decree-Law No. 14/2006 (which revises the DL No. 54/99) that sets the foundation for the

440 Surroop and Raghoo.

441 Matteo Ranaboldo and others, 'Renewable Energy Projects to Electrify Rural Communities in Cape Verde', *Applied Energy*, 118 (2014), 280–91 <https://doi.org/10.1016/j.apenergy.2013.12.043>.

442 Surroop and Raghoo.

443 UNEP, *Atlas of Africa Energy Resources*, pp. 122–25.

444 UNEP, *Atlas of Africa Energy Resources*, pp. 122–25.

electricity system in Cape Verde. The main sector policy is the National Energy Policy of 2008. There is also a National Energy Plan for 2003–2012. Cape Verde's National Assembly enacts the laws and provides the statutes under which the governors of the energy sector operate. In the petroleum sector, the National Fuel Company – ENACOL and Shell Cape Verde are responsible for the commercial system of supply for petroleum products.

For the production and the distribution of electric power and water produced by desalination, the Company of Electricity and Water (Electra) is fully in charge. The Ministry of Environment, Rural Development and Marine Resources govern the biomass sector. This ministry also ensures the implementation of the production, the assembly of the wind pumps and the construction of improved stoves.[445] In conclusion, Cape Verde has earmarked an ambitious goal of attaining 100 percent renewable energy by 2025. It has already had tremendous success in integrating wind and solar into its national energy system. Through the adoption of cutting-edge energy technologies and innovative business practices, Cape Verde is equipped to achieve its 100 percent renewable energy goal in a way that is abundant, equitable and cost-effective.[446]

3.2.3 Francophone West Africa

3.2.3.1 The Colonial Energy Regime

Generally speaking, before the 1940s and even into the 1950s, that is, before the Second World War and a little before the spread of independence in the 1960s, the totality of electrification in French West Africa (FWA) was thermal energy. This informed fuel importation into the sub-region and included gas, petroleum, diesel, kerosene and fuel oil. The region had neither discovered coal nor lignite reserves at the time, as opposed to the lignite reserves discovered in Niger. There was an estimated 4 million tons of lignite found in the Agadez region of Niger that would not be exploited and extracted until much later.

---

445 Deutsche Gesellschaft für Technische Zusammenarbeit – GTZ, pp. 52–61; UNEP, *Atlas of Africa Energy Resources*, pp. 122–25.

446 Erik Nordman, 'Cape Verde's Goal Is 100% Renewable Energy by 2025. Why It May Just Do It', *The Conversation*, 2017 <https://theconversation.com/cape-verdes-goal-is-100-renewable-energy-by-2025-why-it-may-just-do-it-85759> [accessed 21 June 2018].

The single domestic fuel used for the operation of machines, locomotive boilers, boats, or vehicles especially gas trucks was wood and charcoal. This enabled the preference for the steam engine for a long period of time to the detriment of electricity generation.[447] In addition, the proliferation of mobile charcoal ovens, quite similar in operation to the ones already used by the local people did not occur without a negative ecological impact on the environment and gradually became an issue of concern in the non-forested areas.

Compared to other parts of French-controlled Africa, like Tunisia, the early use of electricity for public lighting for instance was due to the presence of colonizing settlers such that already in 1872, lightning of the city of Tunis had been contracted to an English company that had installed a certain number of gas nozzles. This was re-acquired by the French Compagnie du Gaz in 1884.[448] In Dakar, the capital of the FWA, electrification of Medina, the local quarters of the city located in the very centre was not planned as an urban settlement until the 1950s.[449]

The post-war period experienced the boom of hydro-electricity. Electricity a major driver of industrialization in other parts of Africa such as South Africa was barely on the agenda on the eve of independence in French West Africa. As Catherine Coquery-Vidrovitch[450] asserts, the post-war transition towards hydroelectric generation deserved a longer incubation period of waiting ready to take effect during the independence era in order to realize the initial large-scale projects. Earlier the existing power plants maintained the use of all sorts of thermal fuels. But to avoid the importation of heavy, expensive and difficult-to-transport fuels such as coal or petroleum, they set out to use local resources like wood and other possible agricultural wastes preferably peanut shells or rice hulls. Moreover, these

---

447 Marie-Therese Francois, *La Production de La Force Motrice Aux Colonies, et plus Particulierement En Afrique Francaise* (Paris: Association Colonies-Sciences, 1937).

448 Catherine Coquery-Vidrovitch, 'Electricity Networks in Africa: A Comparative Study, or How to Write Social History from Economic Sources', in *Sources and Methods in Africa History: Spoken, Written, Unearthed* (Rochester, NY.: University of Rochester Press, 2003), pp. 346–60.

449 Thomas Saupique, 'L'electrification de Dakar Depuis 1945' (Universite Paris-7, 2000); Papa Waly Danfak, 'Equipment Public et Amenagement de La Ville de Dakar, 1930-1957' (Universite Paris-7, 1990).

450 Coquery-Vidrovitch.

were adopted later in a number of Senegalese power plants in Djourbel and Ziguinchor.[451]

Efforts to exploit the use of rivers such as the Niger, Senegal, Bandama and to some extent the Volta was not initially intended towards hydropower production but irrigation. This led in the instance of the River Niger, the French colonial authorities forming the Office du Niger in 1932. One of their key dam projects on the Niger River was the Samsanding Dam project finished in 1947. It was primarily used at the time for the irrigation of farmlands.

Subsequently, concrete attempts made by the colonial authorities in French West Africa focused on the utility of River Senegal. This took effect in 1927 under the leadership of the Governor-General by establishing the Union Hydro-Electrique Africaine (UHEA) in Bordeaux, France with the sole aim of studying the possibilities of both irrigation and electricity generation. In 1935, the Mission d'Etudes du Fleuve Senegal was set up to collect all the needed data. It was later transformed into the Mission d'Amenagement du Senegal (MAS) however in the advent of the Second World War all the efforts initiated was suspended.[452] These two missions were later restarted after the war. The UHEA investigated the hydropower potential of the upper basin of the Senegal River and recommended the construction of a dam. Another investigation was conducted again in 1950, but in 1953 more concrete recommendations were proposed for the construction of the Guira Dam between Kayes in Mali and the mouth of River Senegal.

In the final analysis, it was rejected as being too expensive and a new mission was entrusted to the Commission Consultative des Etudes pour l'Amenagement du fleuve Senegal which commissioned more reports. Within this same period in 1947, the colonial powers in Paris charged the EDF (Electricite de France) to conduct studies of the hydropower potential in French West Africa. Resulting in the submission of a report to the Minister of French Overseas Territories. The EDF report recommended the construction of five dams. These included a dam each on the River Konkoure in Guinea, on the downstream of the River Niger in Mali, on the River Bia in Cote D'Ivoire, on the River Comoe in the Banfora region of Burkina Faso, and the last one on the Felou Falls of the River Senegal.[453]

451 Danfak.
452 Francois.
453 Sarfoh, *Hydropower Development in West Africa*; Joseph A. Sarfoh, *Energy in the Development of West Africa* (Westport, CT: Greenwood Press, 1992); Sophie

In order to implement these projects, a ministerial mission, the Societe d'Energie-AOF was put together to clearly tease out the details of the plans. It was charged with initiating and pursuing the electricity agenda recommended by the EDF for a number of cities in the following countries Cote d'Ivoire, Niger and Burkina Faso their mandate also included Mauritania and Sudan. The agency was unsuccessful in fulfilling the hydropower plans tabled by the EDF. Only one dam was built between 1957 and 1959 in Guinea, to supply the factory of the Great Falls on the River Samou for the production of aluminium, this was completed after the referendum that declared the discontinuance of French colonial rule in the country.[454] Again, all these major deficits and developments in energy construction and provision in French West Africa determines till today the construction of national energy systems in the Francophone sub-region.

3.2.3.2 Constructing National Energy Systems

In effect, post-independence efforts realized the completion of a number of large dams in French West Africa particularly the Kossou in Cote d'Ivoire (1969–1971).[455] It was supported by a mixture of external overseas development assistance, technical assistance and commercial loans from organizations like the European Community, USAID, the World Bank and the West African Development Bank.[456] The significance of these projects became increasingly vital during the 1970s oil crisis, which rendered the countries in Francophone West Africa highly vulnerable because of their high dependence on imported petroleum products from France.

Between 1960 and 1980, the construction of these huge dams changed the landscape of electricity generation in Francophone West Africa. However, the extension of the economic depression, the absence in growth of industrialization and the short-sightedness inherent in the structural adjustment programs that these countries were involved in culminated in the projects becoming idle.[457] This is exemplified in the case of Cote d'Ivoire, at the beginning of the 1980s, hydroelectricity became the dominant ener-

Ardurat, 'L'electrification En AOF Avant 1945' (Universite Paris-1, 1999); Coquery-Vidrovitch.

454 Coquery-Vidrovitch.

455 Sarfoh, *Hydropower Development in West Africa*.

456 Coquery-Vidrovitch.

457 Sarfoh, *Hydropower Development in West Africa*.

gy source providing about 90 percent of needs but the droughts of 1984 -1985 caused 4 out of 5 factories that ensured hydropower production in the country to temporarily shut down with generation percentages falling by 23 percent.[458] Thus, one can conclude that in French West Africa there existed a correlation between industrialization and electricity generation in the colonies.

Due to the lack of willingness in the colonial days and the industrial prospects of the colonial authorities, FWA was plunged into extended delays of realizing major energy developments resulting in time-consuming study missions that gave rise to a number of reports that was not executed. These cycles of repeated project feasibility studies caused this enviable vision of hydropower generation in French West Africa to be slow-paced and redundant.[459] Therefore, at the time of independence, national governments of these new francophone states became preoccupied with domestic energy consumption and provision of energy supplies to highly populated regions especially their cities but rural electrification was not high on the agenda.[460]

This newfound quest encouraged countries like Togo, Benin and Burkina Faso to import electricity from Ghana whereas Niger sought to import electricity from Nigeria in the 1980s and 1990s until today. Cote d'Ivoire has worked to become the energy hub of the francophone sub-region by augmenting its hydropower stations with thermal energy generation after its 1990s energy reforms. In the late and early 2000s, Cote d'Ivoire became a major energy exporter to Ghana revealing that proper and long-term energy planning reaps benefits. This trend reversed during the political instability that occurred in the country in the 2000s.

Most of the independent Francophone West African nations are net importers of petroleum products till today. Only Côte d'Ivoire produces relatively significant quantities of oil, estimated at 2,109 kilotons in 2005. A number of other countries have potential petroleum reserves such as Benin, Mali, Niger, Senegal, and Togo. With the exception of Senegal which has started exploration of its oil and gas reserves the others remain unexplored.

Francophone nations have shown commitment in their participation to regional energy infrastructures such as the regional power pool in West Africa and other institutional arrangements such as ECREEE and the

458 Sarfoh, *Hydropower Development in West Africa*.

459 Coquery-Vidrovitch.

460 Coquery-Vidrovitch.

West African Gas Pipeline which actively involves Benin and Togo. These regional commitments have strengthened the resolve of French-speaking nations in West Africa to increase domestic generation and consumption through a diversified and mixed approach through the use of all available energy options and by liberalizing their energy sectors in order to exchange electricity. This has fostered the development of enabling policy and legal frameworks.[461]

3.3 Evolution of ECOWAS Regionalism

Before I consider the evolution of energy regionalism in West Africa it is important to first unpack the regional integration history in the region. The origins of West African regionalism culminating in the founding of ECOWAS begins after the medieval era through the process of empire and kingdom building. Followed by a wave of Pan-West Africanism and finally supported by decolonisation efforts. Utilising an approach, which is non-linear, I retell the pooling of West African sovereignties and polities in the later 19th century through the 20th century to the current integration project we see today.

This section considers two basic themes. Firstly, with reference to the following factors the narrative of integration history is restated. Recounting the historical pathway resulting in what we now call the Economic Community of West African States (ECOWAS) entwined with the progress made and failures incurred, persons who advanced the idea of regional integration, internal West African political pressures, and external colonial pressures as well as the role of national and regional interests based on ideational beliefs. Secondly, I argue that the process of ECOWAS regionalism has produced a collaborative and consolidated type of a region-building regime.

I argue that this regime was established when the two founding member states began to co-operate in the creation of a regional economic body that would include all the member states in the region from the onset irrespective of linguistic challenges in order to drive the construction of a transnational economy. ECOWAS has since become a unique kind of regional body like no other anywhere, which benefits from collective action by pooling sovereignties through the utilisation of intergovernmental relations and supranational governance processes in dealing with sector

461 UNEP, *Atlas of Africa Energy Resources*.

specific policy issues in the region. This attribute of consolidating regionalism has resulted in furthering extended goals of region building in the larger African integration project.

3.3.1 ECOWAS Regionalism History Reconsidered

West Africa's regional integration has been pursued in various forms under very different circumstances and periods in order to achieve a unified front to contend with the prevailing threat of the day. While some might presume that regionalism was obligated from outside West Africa, this narrative indicates the long historical home-grown processes led by West Africans and supported by foreigners. This narrative further talks about a process that prompted a trajectory which was coupled with a unique ability to harness the best ideas from the African diaspora abroad particularly during the period of colonisation. Also, it establishes the hegemonic expansion in the post medieval era in the region which primarily served as the precursor to this contemporary notion of regional integration in West Africa.

This began with empire and kingdom building, which served as a vehicle for the earliest forms of integration in the region. Earlier military incursions and the creation of alliances were employed to aid the process of unifying peoples and civilisations belonging to the same linguistic groupings and adjoining territories belonging to other smaller ethnic groups. Moreover, over centuries the threat of land degradation of the Sahel also facilitated among other things mobility of large groups of pastoralist peoples and civilisations like the Fulani southwards to parts of present – day Senegal, Guinea, Ghana, and Northern Nigeria.[462] Although in certain respects this has brought about political and cultural friction, it has enabled a furtherance in the integration of the peoples and national polities of West Africa.

Tracing inspiration for contemporary forms of West African Integration in the middle of the nineteenth century, African leaders involved in the

462 G. Wendler and F. Eaton, 'On the Desertification of the Sahel Zone', *Climate Change*, 5.4 (1983), 365–80; Richard A. Kerr, 'The Sahara Is Not Marching Southward', *Science*, July 1998, 633–34 <https://doi.org/10.1126/science.281.5377.633>; Jeremy Swift, 'Sahelian Pastoralists: Underdevelopment, Desertification, and Famine', *Annual Review of Anthropology*, 6.1 (1977), 457–78; A. G. Adebayo, 'Of Man and Cattle: A Reconsideration of the Traditions of Origin of Pastoral Fulani of Nigeria', *History of Africa*, 18 (1991), 1–21.

Pan-African cause were profoundly instrumental in the continent's mission to break free from colonialism, carving out a unique African identity distinct from Europe and promoting African regionalism. From the mid-nineteenth century to the present times, West African regionalism through institutional cooperation has occurred through the agency of non-state actors with a desire to harness economic opportunities, champion a sense of West African nationalism as well as subsuming post-colonial states into a single economic polity.[463]

Possibilities of economic integration, intergovernmental relations and supranational institutions drives this regional collective action. The historiography of West African regionalism would be characterised in four stages, first wave: post-medieval empire and kingdom building, second wave: Pan-West Africanism, third wave: decolonisation and the fourth wave: founding of ECOWAS.

3.3.1.1 First Wave: Post-Medieval Empire and Kingdom Building

West African Regionalism predates the introduction of the Westphalian nation-state partitioning of the region which was prompted by the Berlin General Act at the Berlin West Africa Conference of 1884–1885. This event which sought to partition Africa with the sole purpose to formalise and legalise European Imperialism and colonialism in Africa.[464] I will later address this point when I tackle the nuances of the second wave characterised in this section as Pan-West Africanism.

However, the genesis of West African regionalism could be attributable to homegrown empire building and the amalgamated formation of kingdoms. In the likeness of medieval empires and kingdoms in the West African region such as the Ghana Empire (c. 700 until c. 1240), the third phase of the Jenne-Jeno Kingdom (c. 300 until c. 900) and the Mali Empire (c. 1230–1670) to name but a few. The rise of post-medieval (15th -19th century) West African empires and kingdoms became the means of integrating the many nations, peoples and civilisations of the West African

463 Kofi Oteng Kufuor, 'The Origins and Evolution of Regional Integration in West Africa', in *The Institutional Transformation of the Economic Community of West African States* (Oxford and New York: Routledge, 2016).

464 Matthew Craven, 'Between Law and History: The Berlin Conference of 1884-1885 and the Logic of Free Trade', *London Review of International Law*, 3.1 (2015), 31–59 <https://doi.org/10.1093/lril/lrv002>.

region. Vansina[465] supports this claim by classifying some African empires and kingdoms in the post medieval era as federative particularly in West Africa. These federations were founded on the plural African legal and political systems and the rules and procedures of governance which were established by custom and tradition rather than by written constitutions.

Furthermore, these systems were based on the rule of law, that is, respect for and adherence to customary ways of dispute resolution and upholding the customs, traditions and practices governing political behaviour. Most importantly, customary African laws were subject to full public debate and scrutiny; indeed, kings and their chiefs could not promulgate laws without the consent of the councils.[466] Notable among these federative West African polities was the Asante Empire later diminished to become the Asante Kingdom,[467] the Kingdom of Dahomey, Aro Confederacy,[468] Jollof Confederacy, Mande Empire, Karou Confederacy and the Yoruba Confederacy.[469]

To illustrate, the federative and rules-based nature of these empires and kingdoms formed the early antecedents of modern-day regional integration in West Africa. Vasina further underscores that in the Asante Union, the *Asantehene* (Supreme Overlord of the Asante peoples) ruled over the external affairs of the federation with a council of paramount chiefs that is, overlords of the respective nations and territories that made up the union over which he presided. He served them in this capacity as primus

465 J. Vansina, 'A Comparison of African Kingdoms', *Africa: Journal of the International African Institute*, 32.4 (1962), 324–35.

466 Guy Martin, *African Political Thought* (New York: African Political Thought, 2012).

467 The Asante Empire was at its height in 1701 to 1894. A pre-colonial Akan West African state whose empire stretched from present day central Ghana to present day Togo and Côte d'Ivoire. Asante brought together a vast majority of the Akan States and Kingdoms under its umbrella with a number of notable exceptions among them the Fante States, Akyem Kingdom and the Bono Kingdom. The Dagomba Kingdom to the north and the Kingdom of Dahomey to the east delineated it.

468 The Aro Confederacy also known as Arochukwu (1690–1902) was a political union initiated by the Aro people, an Igbo subgroup, that confederated three heterogeneous ethnic groups, namely, the Igbo, Ibibio, and Akpa. See: Apollos O Nwauwa, 'The Evolution of the Aro Confederacy in Southeastern Nigeria , 1690-1720 . A Theoretical Synthesis of State Formation Process in Africa', *Anthropos*, 90 (1995), 353–64 <http://www.jstor.org/stable/40463184>.

469 B. A. Ogot, *General History of Africa, V: Africa from the Sixteenth to Eighteenth Century*, ed. by B.A. Ogot (Berkeley, Carlifornia: University of California Press, 1992), pp. 262–492.

inter pares. This federative union was determined and strengthened by the superiority of the Asantehene's military might, the consent of the other paramountcies and the degree of pressure from external influences and other factors.[470] The differentiating element of these federations like the Asante Empire from other classifications such as the aristocratic kingdoms and empires is mainly underscored by, "the fact that the members of this type of political structure do view themselves as members of a federation, not of a unitary state".[471]

Another form of regionalism in West Africa, which took inspiration from region building in medieval times, was the influence of Islamic governance. Following from a long heritage of a pacifist tradition in West African Islam that went beyond Jihad.[472] The process of negotiation, adjustment and the formation of alliances with other traditions and cultures formed largely the bedrock of the history of Islamic polities in the post-medieval era in West Africa. Among them included the Kanem-Borno Empire, the Sokoto Caliphate[473], Dagomba and Mossi Kingdoms, Dendi Kingdom, Kong Empire, Wassoulou (Mandinka) Empire, Imamates of Futa Joro and Futa Jallon, and the Segu Tukulor Empire.[474] However to be critical, there is evidence of the military campaigns under the banner of jihad that formed the basis of some of these vast Islamic polities.[475] These Islamic polities welded together in a unified administrative structure the

470 Vansina, pp. 324–335

471 Vansina, p. 333.

472 Lamin Sanneh, *Beyond Jihad: The Pacifist Tradition in West African Islam* (New York: Oxford University Press, 2016).

473 Although the Sokoto Caliphate was started through, a military jihad evidence shows that it was vehemently resisted by the pacifist Islamic scholars of the day as not founded on the precepts of Islam. The Fulani States that were championing this militarised approach against fellow Muslim neighbours were repudiated leading to an end of their conquests and established a peaceful polity that was based on striking alliances. See: Sanneh, pp. 217–37.

474 A.A. Iliasu, 'The Origin of the Mossi-Dagomba States', *African Studies Research Review*, 7.2 (1971), 95–113 <https://doi.org/10.3166/I2M.14.3-4.11-61>; J.F.A. Ajayi, *General History of Africa, VI: Africa in the Nineteenth Century until the 1880s*, ed. by J.F.A. Ajayi (Paris: UNESCO Publishing / Heinemann / University of California Press, 2000), pp. 537–723.

475 Nehemia Levtzion and Randall L. Pouwels, *The History of Islam in Africa* (Athens, Ohio: Ohio University Press, 2000), pp. 63–116; David Robinson, 'The Islamic Revolution of Futa Toro', *The International Journal of African Historical Studies*, 8.2 (1975), 185–221 <https://doi.org/10.2307/216648>; Detlef Gronenborn, 'Kanem-Borno: A Brief Summary of the History and Archeology of an Empire of the Central Bilad Al-Sudan', in *West Africa During the Atlantic Slave*

numerous, hitherto disunited, smaller states of the same ethnic group and sometimes neighbouring states of different ethnicities. This is evidenced in the Sokoto Caliphate where the Hausa states as well as part of Borno, Nupe, and Yorubaland were amalgamated together through an impressively sustained state system based on the precepts of Islam.[476]

3.3.1.2 Second Wave: Pan-West Africanism

Initial ideas and visions for West African regionalism under European colonialism was advanced in the late nineteenth century. At a time when the European incursion into West Africa had reached a crescendo through full-blown colonialism and later given credence among the competing European colonists in the signing of the Berlin General Act of 1885. It obligated the Partition of Africa (otherwise known as the Scramble for Africa), both in theory and in practice, into Westphalian-styled nation states by the end of the 20th century.[477] Pan-West Africanism is a subset of the more elaborate Pan Africanism which was developed in the intellectual works of two major advocates of (West) African Integration, the Liberian, Edward Wilmot Blyden (1832- 1912) and the Sierra Leonean, Africanus Beale Horton (1835- 83) also known as 'the father of modern African political thought'.[478]

Blyden and Horton premised their arguments for regionalism on notions of cultural solidarity and economic expediency rather than political nationalism.[479] Nonetheless, as key contributors to the ideologies of Pan-Africanism and West African nationalism, Blyden advocated as an ultimate objective toward a single West African State with a union of Liberia and Sierra Leone as its fulcrum.[480] Horton, a physician trained at the Forah

---

Trade: Archaeological Perspectives, ed. by Christopher DeCorse, 2nd edn (London and New York: Bloomsbury Academic, 2016), pp. 101–30.

476 Adebayo.

477 A Adu Boahen, *General History of Africa. Vol VII: Africa under Colonial Domination 1880-1935*, ed. by A Adu Boahen (Paris: UNESCO Publishing / Heinemann / University of California Press, 2000), pp. 1–62; Carolyn M. Warner, 'The Rise of the State System in Africa', *Review of International Studies*, 27.05 (2001), 65–89 <https://doi.org/10.1017/s0260210501008038>.

478 Guy Martin, *African Political Thought* (New York: African Political Thought, 2012). pp.47 – 49

479 Martin, *African Political Thought*, pp. 47–49.

480 Hollis R: Lynch, *Edward Wilmot Blyden, Pan-Negro Patriot 1832-1912* (London, Ibadan, New York: Oxford University Press, 1967), pp. 210–11.

Bay College in Sierra Leone and the University of Edinburgh received a commission to serve in the British Army as one of its first African officers posted to the Gold Coast. He advocated persistently for the creation of regional institutions such as establishing a unified University for Western Africa.[481]

The basis for this request in his political writings[482] was to openly campaign for self-government in the whole of British West Africa and champion the cause of what he referred to as an 'African nationality'.[483] Horton supported through writings, African self-government but also took the opportunity to repudiate the dominant Victorian anti-African racism of the time.[484] An experience he had personally lived through during his entire military career.

Horton further developed his ideas, which in 1868 were republished in his most famous book *West African Countries, and People, British and Native with the Requirements Necessary for Establishing that Self-Government recommended by the Committee of the House of Commons, 1865 and a Vindication of the African Race*. In this book, Horton used it to contest the ideas of the anatomist Robert Knox who published a book entitled The Races of Man (1862) in which he had referred to the dangers of a future 'United States of Africa'.[485] The thoughts of these two pan-West African dogmatists, Blyden and Horton, perhaps had a first-hand effect on the drafting of the founding constitution of the Fante Confederation (1868–1874) which Horton believed was working towards the 'self-government of the Gold Coast.'[486]

In the final analysis, these ideas of West African unity remained unattainable ideas without a concrete course of action until the formation of the National Congress of British West Africa (NCBWA) during the colonial era. Influenced by and building on the thoughts and work of

481 Oteng Kufuor.

482 In 1865, Horton began his political writing with the publication of an address to the London-based African Aid Society entitled Political Economy of West Africa – The African's View of the Negro's Place in Nature. His first political writing was prompted by the report of Britain's Parliamentary Select Committee on the West African colonies that recommended ultimate withdrawal from this region by the British government and the creation of conditions that would lead to self-government.

483 Hakim Adi and Marika Sherwood, *Pan-African History: Political Figures from Africa and the African Diaspora since 1787* (London and New York: Routledge, 2003), pp. 85–88.

484 Hakim Adi, *Pan-Africanism : A History* (London: Bloomsbury Academic, 2018).

485 Adi, *Pan-Africanism : A History*, p. 15.

486 Adi, *Pan-Africanism : A History*, pp. 15–16.

James Africanus Horton and Edward Wilmot Blyden, Joseph E. Casely Hayford (1866- 1930) advocated the realisation of racial emancipation through the development of a regional "West African nationality" with a much wider vision for an "African nationality".[487] His advocacy and campaign were not only confined to the assertion of a proud Africa that is a "cradle of civilisation" but sought to mobilise the African peoples all around the globe to modernise African society with its particular African character through education and a sense of a unified nationalism.[488]

Casely Hayford also favoured the creation of a university in West Africa (just as Horton had earlier proposed). This university would serve as a centre of excellence that would provide an Africanized curriculum with the purpose of promoting the ideology of modernisation through the means of an authentic African lens while overcoming Eurocentrism, a characteristic of colonial rule which sought to demean, dehumanise and patronise the African. His efforts were instrumental in the creation of Achimota College in 1927 in the Gold Coast.[489]

The first concrete attempts to put ideas of West African nationalism into practice toward a West African Union led to the creation of the NCBWA in March 1920. This brought together nationalists from Gambia, Nigeria, Ghana and Sierra Leone. Casely Hayford's ideas of a united West Africa had an immense influence on the African students in Britain and served as the guiding philosophy for the creation of the West African Students' Union (WASU) in London in 1925. In addition, it subsequently influenced the formation of the West African National Secretariat in the 1940s by Kwame Nkrumah (later to become first president of independent Ghana). The efforts of the NCBWA were perceived to be essentially elitist because it advocated these political reforms within the context of British colonialism and imperialism. Thus, it failed to enlist the support of the masses and the traditional rulers in the other British colonies.[490]

---

487 Robert W. July, *The Origins of Modern African Thought: Its Development in West Africa during the Nineteeth and Twentieth Centuries*, 2004th edn (Trenton, NJ and Asmara, Eritrea: Africa World Press, Inc., 1967), pp. 433–57.

488 Henry S. Wilson, *Origins of West African Nationalism* (London: Palgrave Macmillan, 1969), pp. 309–80.

489 Wilson, *Origins of West African Nationalism*

490 Norbert C. Brockman, *An African Biographical Dictionary* (Santa Barbara, CA: ABC-CLIO, 1994), pp. 75–76; Adi and Sherwood, pp. 82–85; Martin, *African Political Thought*, pp. 49–50.

3.3.1.3 Third Wave: Decolonisation

The European colonists in West Africa were practicing colonial regionalism[491], somewhat intentionally and unintentionally in their respective colonies. This form of regional integration was done primarily through language and colonial control. It enabled in a way the ideas espoused by Horton, Blyden and Casely Hayford to spread among the peoples under colonial control. With the aid of the common European languages being spoken in the colonial territories among the colonial elite including the local western-educated citizenry.

A radical campaign towards decolonisation ensued at different times and at varying intensities across West Africa. African leaders living on the continent and in the diaspora were at the forefront of the advocacy and movement towards discrediting and defeating colonialism in their linguistically linked colonial sub-regions. Pertaining to West Africa, this is seen in the activities of the youth and student movements that started in Europe and the agitation of the veterans of the colonial armies who fought in World Wars I and II alongside their European counterparts.

In addition to these groups of persons, activities of resident nationalist and local political and social elite, traders and wealthy merchants engaged in mercantile activity with colonial business interests as well as trade and labour unions contributed to this decolonisation struggle which was interconnected with counterparts in all the territories making the decolonisation efforts parallel to the established colonial region. Lastly, rulers and overlords of kingdoms and chieftains as well as other plural traditional polities across the respective colonial sub-regions played consequential roles in the decolonisation effort. These diverse efforts were mostly uncoordinated but among the individual representative groups, they largely functioned using a region-wide approach to combat colonialism mostly through advocacy.

Colonial regionalism started with the realisation of reaping enormous benefits that could be accrued by the colonial authorities through the inte-

---

491 Colonial regionalism is the type of regionalism or regional integration initiated and practiced by colonial powers to collectively group territories under their control mostly in the vein to aid in administering these territories and dominions especially in political, economic and commercial terms. Usually in the forms of a political union, currency union and customs union. Classic examples in Africa were the East African Community, French West Africa federation (Afrique Occidentale Française, or AOF) and the Southern African Customs Union (SACU).

gration of their colonies. This was done by fostering regional integration and entailed strategies that were implemented to steer the process towards this goal in the pre-independence era and it was typified by the establishment of a common currency and some common services. Its approach took a cue from earlier European integration efforts that some of these colonial countries had participated.

In British West Africa, initially headquartered in Sierra Leone, the endeavour to integrate the British territories economically led to the establishment of a common currency, the West African Pound, through the launch of a West African Currency Board in 1912. The Board administered the monetary system, which was effectively an extension of the government of the British Crown: the currency of the territories was visually distinct and was backed by its own reserves, but it was held at parity with and was readily convertible into the currency of the colonial power.

The main function of the regionally integrated colonial banking system, which was also based on the banking system of the metropole, was to enable efficient money supply rather than to increase the volume of money. Bank lending policy was cautious, and advances were limited to the most part to the large expatriate firms. The functions of the Currency Board were mainly of a passive kind, being limited to large-scale money changing activities, to the investment of the reserves of the colonial currency, distribution of the profits derived from these investments and seignorage on coins issued for the region.[492]

Additionally, common agricultural research institutes were set up for cash crop and animal husbandry such as cocoa, oil palm, timber and groundnuts as well as veterinary research. Other common scientific research institutes founded included a regional medical research institute. In addition, the four colonies were connected through the creation of a common airline company, the West African Airways Corporation in 1946. These efforts contributed largely to the economic integration of British West Africa and to a lesser degree political integration.[493]

---

492 G . L . M . Clauson, 'The British Colonial Currency System', *The Economic Journal*, 54.213 (1944), 1–25 <https://www.jstor.org/stable/216483>; A . G . Hopkins, 'The Creation of a Colonial Monetary System : The Origins of the West African Currency Board', *African Historical Studies*, 3.1 (1970), 101–32 <https://www.jstor.org/stable/216483>.

493 Afua Boatemaa Yakohene, 'Overview of Ghana and Regional Integration: Past, Present and Future', in *Ghana in Search of Regional Integration Agenda*, ed. by LECIAD, 1st edn (Accra: Friedrich-Ebert-Stiftung, 2009), pp. 1–22; Johnson Olaosebikan Aremu, 'Administration of British West African Colonies and the

In French West Africa, the colonial administration established a deeper level of political integration by grouping their eight colonies in the region into a French West Africa federation (Afrique Occidentale Française, or AOF) with headquarters in Dakar, Senegal by 1895. This was under the leadership of a governor-general who reported to the Minister of Colonies in Paris, France.[494]

The French federation had a solid political and administrative base; however, it lacked a strong economic foundation with the exception of the establishment of the French West Africa Currency Union in 1945. As a result, post-independence efforts towards economic regionalism in Francophone West Africa was saddled with the task of laying the economic foundations of the French-influenced sub-region. In terms of political regionalism, the AOF gained a reputation for its strategic importance to the France-led Francophone global order. The AOF became a strategic node in various global networks.

People from France and other European countries, aside from French and British colonial territories beyond AOF such as Vietnam and Gambia, used Dakar as a conduit, to build political networks in the global French colonial establishment. This led to the setting up of a rigid colonial surveillance system in interwar French West Africa particularly in Dakar to assist colonial authorities to keep a watchful eye on foreigners, metropolitan Frenchmen and Africans whose behaviour the government saw as morally, socially and politically disruptive to the vision of a stable and static French socio-political order. Colonial Minister Albert Sarraut created this system of surveillance and intelligence in the early 1920s. Information about these disruptive individuals and groups region-wide moved back and forth between the French metropole, AOF, and other French territories. Consequently, it led to a culture of intense fear, silence and paranoia

---

Furtherance of Nigeria-Gold Coast Relations, 1885-1960', *International Journal of Humanities and Cultural Studies*, 1.4 (2015), 54–71 <http://ijhcschiefeditor.wix.com/ijhcs>.

494 The federation was composed of seven territories—Senegal, Côte d'Ivoire, Niger, Dahomey (now Benin), French Sudan (now Mali), French Guinea, and Mauritania—as well as one territory under French mandate by the League of Nations since it was seized from German authority after World War I—Togo. Togo was a territory under a different juridical basis but in close political relation to the Federation of French West Africa.

that assigned a wide range of individuals with the label of 'suspects' who were under constant surveillance.[495]

The reality in Portuguese Guinea which encompassed the Cape Verde Islands and Guinea Bissau under colonial regionalism was not too different except that there was a huge resistance to decolonisation by the imperial power and that resulted in a late realisation of success occasioned by a civil and guerrilla war. Although the Kings of Portugal had laid claim to these territories including parts of Senegal since the 15th century due in part to having built trading posts. They had no influence whatsoever on the peoples of these lands. It took the horrors of a savage war of conquest dubbed as 'pacification' campaigns particularly in Guinea-Bissau to bring these territories under Portuguese control in 1915.[496]

These campaigns by the colonists were met with a long tradition of resistance from the West African peoples of this sub-region. It can be argued that it served as a source of inspiration for the armed liberation struggle waged by Amilcar Cabral and his cohorts for the decolonisation and independence of these territories from Portugal. For Portugal, its territories in West Africa were eventually classified as overseas provinces of the Portuguese state similar to its European provinces thus integrally and intrinsically linking them politically and economically to Portugal.[497]

The Portuguese colonial situation was unlike that of France and Britain. Portugal after World War II was poor in an industrialising Europe. It lacked a democratic tradition which meant it could not give greater freedoms to its populace in the metropole how much more the populace in the colonies (which it rechristened *Overseas Provinces* in the Portuguese revised constitution of 1951) in addition to its woes it did not undergo post-war reconstruction. Moreover, Portugal's poverty made the colonial system more oppressive, brutally exploitative and extractive than the colonial regimes of other European countries in West Africa. Simultaneously, it inhibited the formation of an educated local elite or even a slightly educated mass of the colonial populace that would have advanced the cause of a decolonisation process.[498]

---

495 Daniel Brückenhaus, 'Colonial Suspects: Suspicion, Imperial Rule, and Colonial Society in Interwar French West Africa', *The Journal of Interdisciplinary History*, 49.4 (2019), 699–700 <https://doi.org/https://doi.org/10.1162/jinh_r_01370>.

496 Paul M Whitaker, 'The Revolutions of "Portuguese" Africa', *The Journal of Modern African Studies*, 8.1 (1970), 15–35 <https://doi.org/10.1017/S0022278X00019339>.

497 Whitaker, Paul, M. 'The Revolutions of "Portuguese" Africa'.

498 Whitaker, Paul, M. 'The Revolutions of "Portuguese" Africa'.

The entire approach of colonial regionalism, premised on an extractive ideology, facilitated easy economic activities for the benefit of the colonial metropole at the expense of the colonies. In the West African case, this is confirmed by the lack of infrastructural advancement, which characterised the region, and the path-dependent rigidity put in place when these colonial regionalist efforts collapsed as late as the end of the 1970s.

Decolonisation efforts through radical nationalism or 'radical sub-regionalism'[499] in the colonies were facilitated and fast-tracked through representative groups that acted in a concerted fashion through regional engagement. In order, to make their efforts impactful and effective against the colonial authorities, these representative groups adopted a strategy by forming regional groups in the three colonised sub-regions to advance the cause of decolonisation. These African-led efforts were not the same in the British, French and Portuguese controlled sub-regions. The aftermath of World War I and II became fertile ground for the cause of decolonisation to take root in West Africa.

By drawing inspiration from the Independence of India from colonial Britain in 1947, a strong impetus for self-rule became the strongest proposition for the masses, indigenous rulers, educated elite and veteran soldiers of the colonial armies in West Africa especially that of the Anglophone nations. This movement towards self-rule championed in all the three linguistic sub-regions of West Africa by the local peoples were met with varying degrees of violence and resistance from the purveyors of the European colonial project namely European explorers, geographers, scientists, missionaries, political, business, and military leaders alike.

The scale and degree of violent resistance against decolonisation was influenced by the underpinning governance ideology adopted by each colonial government. The British employed a system of indirect rule and the French adopted a system of assimilation and direct rule.[500] The Portuguese utilised a system of direct rule with the view of seeing these countries as overseas periphery territories to the metropole, similar in theory with

---

499 What I mean by 'radical sub-regionalism' is a form of radical nationalism with a regional character, that is, representing cohesive regionalist interests that are mainly political, economic and cultural.

500 Véronique Dimier, 'Direct or Indirect Rule: Propaganda around a Scientific Controversy', in *Promoting the Colonial Idea : Propaganda and Visions of Empire in France*, ed. by Tony Chafer and Amanda Sackur (London: Palgrave, 2002), pp. 168–83 <https://doi.org/10.1057/9781403919427>.

the policy adopted by the French but different in practice.[501] The colonial governing ideology effectively determined the degree of proximity of the colonies to the metropolitan centre be it Britain, France or Portugal.[502]

In British West Africa, the resistance did not deter these representative regional (and inter-territorial) groups to champion the cause of decolonisation through the formation of institutions and bodies facilitated by the presence of a vigorous African press unlike any other colonially controlled territory in West Africa. This aided the process of converting the call for a unified West Africa from remaining an idealistic dream and turning it into a realistic fact. The earlier bodies to push for this call were the Fante Confederation, a native coastal Akan peoples' rights organisation[503] and the Gold Coast Aborigines' Rights Protection Society in 1897, its advocacy for land rights and equal rights for natives in the colonies particularly the Gold Coast (now Ghana) was trailblazing and forward-looking.[504]

These groups laid the foundation for the formation of other bodies and institutions in the region and in Europe to tread the same path but with broader objectives without losing focus especially on the aim of a united West Africa. These regional bodies championed by various representative groups sprung up in full swing during the post-war years and were at its height during the inter-war years. Notable among them are the already

501 Thomas Henriksen, 'Portugal in Africa: A Noneconomic Interpretation', *African Studies Review*, 16.3 (1973), 405–16.

502 Martin, *African Political Thought*, pp. 44–46.

503 James Sanders, 'The Expansion of the Fante And The Emergence Of Asante In The Eighteenth Century', *The Journal of African History*, 20.3 (1979), 349–64 <https://doi.org/10.1017/S0021853700017357>.

504 Further Reading See: S K B Asante, 'The Neglected Aspects of the Activities of the Gold Coast Aborigines Rights Protection Society', *Phylon (1960-)*, 36.1 (1975), 32–45 <http://www.jstor.org/stable/274843>; Michel R. Doortmont, 'Producing a Received View of Gold Coast Elite Society? C.F. Hutchison's Pen Pictures of Modern Africans and African Celebrities', *History in Africa: An Annual Journal of Method*, 33.May 2015 (2006), 473–93 <https://doi.org/10.2307/20065783>; George Shepperson, 'Abolitionism and African Political Thought', *Transition*, 12.12 (1964), 22–26; Rebecca Shumway, 'From Atlantic Creoles to African Nationalists: Reflections on the Historiography of Nineteenth-Century Fanteland Critical Historiography From Atlantic Creoles to African Nationalists: Reflections on the Historiography of Nineteenth-Century Fanteland', *History in AfricaArticle) History in Africa*, 42.42 (2015), 139–64 <https://muse.jhu.edu/article/583528> [accessed 14 June 2018].

mentioned National Congress of British West Africa – NCBWA (1920)[505], West African Students' Union – WASU founded in London (1925)[506], West African National Secretariat – WANS (1945)[507].

The NCBWA in essence had no expectations of cutting the ties, which bound Britain and its West African territories, it stipulated this in its founding constitution and inter alia, the greater representation of the natives in colonial affairs and administration. In furtherance of these goals, the NCBWA adopted a constitution for a united British West Africa, which effectively would represent its peoples. It was complete with an Executive Council, Legislative Council and a House of Assembly embracing all the four colonies. The NCBWA eventually become extinct by the 1930s. It is believed that its failure to survive was because it did not advocate for the end of colonial rule thus making it a conservative institution to be swept away by the radical nationalism in the sub-region of the post-war era of 1945 that pushed for independence.[508]

In French West Africa, the prelude to the post-war decolonisation process some say was prompted when the Popular Front[509] won the French elections in 1936 giving hopes of emancipation to the colonies.[510] It must be reiterated here that due to the policies of assimilation (or the so-called European civilising mission of the African – in this case – France's imperial and colonial project in Africa) and direct rule, some West Africans in the AOF were represented in the French National Assembly. It began with Blaise Diagne in 1914, who became the first African to serve in the French Parliament. However, it must be emphasised that he represented a tiny portion of West Africans who were referred to as originaires (that is, inhabitants of towns like Dakar, Rufisque, Goree, and Saint Louis that

---

505 For More See: G. I. C. Eluwa, 'Background to the Emergence of the National Congress of British West Africa', *African Studies Review*, 14.2 (1971), 205–218 <https://doi.org/10.2307/523823>; Doortmont.

506 Further See: Philip Garigue, 'The West African Students' Union. A Study in Culture Contact', *Africa: Journal of the International African Institute*, 23.1 (1953), 55–69 <http://www.jstor.org/stable/1156033>; Hakim Adi, 'Pan-Africanism and West African Nationalism in Britain', *African Studies Review*, 43.1 (2000), 69–82.

507 See: Adi, 'Pan-Africanism and West African Nationalism in Britain'.

508 Eluwa; Oteng Kufuor, pp. 19–34.

509 A political movement made up of two parties, the Communists and the Socialists, which espoused anti-colonial views.

510 Ruth Ginio, *French Colonialism Unmasked: The Vichy Years in French West Africa* (Lincoln and London: University of Nebraska Press, 2006).

were granted the right to send representatives to the National Assembly in Paris).[511]

It is however important to note that the regionalist and nationalist movements seen along the lines of the NCBWA or the Nigerian National Democratic Party was not extant in French West Africa during this period. Over the years, the group of West African representatives would be later expanded following the post-war colonial reforms.[512]

On the other hand, the rest of the vast demographic in the AOF were not represented and were subjected to forced labour and to the *indegenal*, a legal system that enabled any French official to inflict limited punishments on Africans extra-judicially. In that same year of winning power in France the Popular Front adopted legislation authorising trade unions. Thus, making the AOF the only French territory on the African continent to allow Africans to join and organise in trade unions although the rules of engagement were restrictive. For instance, in Dakar alone, there were eight thousand union members in forty-two trade unions and sixteen professional associations by 1937.[513]

Although, the advent of the Second World War, eroded the reforms made prior by the Popular Front which included the right to organise in trade unions, it created a new political context after the war in French West Africa. The newly found power by the local peoples in the pre-war and interwar years particularly the fight for empire, led to a deep struggle for emancipation from 1946 -1950 within the context of the policy of assimilation.[514]

Subsequently, in the decade that triggered the crumble of the European colonial project in West Africa in general, that is, in the 1950s due to exhaustion of the colonisers and lack of support from the USA and Russia the two leading superpowers of the time.[515] A rise of political nationalist movements in the form of trade unions, student and youth movements as well AOF-wide political parties sprung up in French West Africa. A good deal of Francophone West African political nationalist movements

---

511 Adu Boahen, pp. 624–47.

512 Adu Boahen, pp. 624–47.

513 Tony Chafer, *The End of Empire in French West Africa: France's Successful Decolonization?*, 1st edn (Oxford: Berg, 2002); Frederick Cooper, *Decolonization and African Society: The Labor Question in French and British Africa* (Cambridge: University of Cambridge, 1996).

514 Cooper; Ginio.

515 Benno J. Ndulu and Stephen A. O'Connell, 'Governance and Growth in Africa', *Journal of Economic Perspectives*, 13.3 (1999), 41–66.

were linked up to radical French political parties and trade unions.[516] By 1950 formal links were diminishing due to the growing challenges it posed for the construction of a cohesive, federation-wide nationalist movement. However, amidst all the challenges of French West African political movements mainly present in the separate constituent territories of the AOF, the first inter-territorial and regionalist party, the RDA, was created in Bamako, Mali (then known as French Sudan) in 1946, which saw a rapid growth within this period. Its constituent parties such as the PCF, BDS and the SFIO that were loosely grouped together had youth wings that fuelled the radical opposition to French colonialism.

Again, with the extension of the right to freedom of association in the colonies post World War II a vast expansion of student and youth movements arose in French West Africa. These groups in their political agitation played a leading role in both mobilising opposition to colonial rule and demanding immediate independence in AOF. Notable among them was the Association des Etudiants Africains (AEA) in Paris and the Association Générale des Etudiants de Dakar (AGED). Lastly, within the period 1956 -1960, nationalist politics in French West Africa had reached a crescendo leading to the division of AOF into smaller recognised territories thus de-regionalising the vast territorial space under French colonial control as the first steps towards political decolonisation.[517]

In Portuguese-controlled West Africa because of late decolonisation in the 1970s, there was a more urgent need for the independence struggle in Guinea Bissau and Cape Verde Islands to be fought together through collective action between the political leaders and citizens in both colonies primarily led by Amilcar Cabral[518].

The setting up of the African Party for the Independence of Guinea and Cape Verde (PAIGC) in 1956 with its sole aim of obtaining independence for the two territories is a clear example of the collective sub-regional decolonisation effort. The defiant holdout against the abdication of imperial power in the 1950s and 1960s in Africa were Portugal's colonies in Africa. Nonetheless, despite the sustained efforts of the Portuguese colonists in Guinea Bissau and Cape Verde Islands to retain these colonies, the destiny

516 Adu Boahen, pp. 624–47; Chafer.

517 Chafer.

518 Amilcar Lopes da Costa Cabral was a native of Guinea-Bissau and Cape Verde. He was a trained agricultural engineer. He led the nationalist movement of Guinea-Bissau and Cape Verde Islands and very instrumental in promoting the independence causes of the then Portuguese colonies. He founded the African Party for the Independence of Guinea and Cape Verde (PAIGC).

to determine the fate of an independent Lusophone West Africa was sustained by the militarised agitation and resistance of the native peoples. This was done in concert with regional and international negotiations besides the normal diplomatic processes which would ultimately render the Portuguese hold indefensible.[519]

The resistance in Portuguese Guinea saw representative groups adopt a militant approach typified by an armed struggle that was fully supported and backed through a civilian organisation. They were inspired by the logic of events happening in Africa as a whole but with specific reference to West Africa. Committed to the economic and political independence, freedom and dignity of the Lusophone sub-region PAIGC executed its goals by soldering a sense of national unity between Guinea-Bissau and Cape Verde. Eventually in 1974, it declared independence after winning the war against Portugal which was internationally recognised. Thus, resulting in a clear example of the creation of a decolonised sub-region in West Africa through radical sub-regionalism which overcame the scourge of an illegitimate colonial political regime by an armed struggle.[520]

After decolonisation in a large number of West African countries, mainly in English-speaking and French-speaking West Africa by the end of the 1960s, political and economic integration in West Africa gained incremental momentum. To be more specific, during the late 1950s when West African countries were gaining independence beginning with Ghana (1957) and followed by Guinea (1958). Concrete efforts towards regionalism in West Africa beyond language barriers led to the formation of the Ghana-Guinea Union, which served as a precursory nucleus to further the integrative process of the decolonising of the West African region.

The union's next step was the accession of Mali when it broke away from the Mali Federation[521]. This led to a name change to the Ghana-Guinea-Mali Union. As West African states began to attain independence,

---

519 Whitaker; Christoph Kohl, 'National Integration in Guinea-Bissau since Independence', *Cadernos de Estudos Africanos*, 2011, 85–109 <https://doi.org/10.4000/cea.155>; Peter Karibe Mendy, 'Amilcar Cabral and the Liberation of Guinea-Bissau: Context, Challenges and Lessons for Effective African Leadership', *African Identities*, 4.1 (2005), 7–21 <https://doi.org/10.1080/14725840500268440>.

520 Whitaker; Kohl; Mendy.

521 The Mali Federation was a union of Senegal and Mali that collapsed a year after its formation because Senegal the more economically prosperous arm of the union could not accept the balance of power in the Federation.

they immediately created numerous cross-national organizations[522]. This form of post-independence regionalist experimentation became the prevailing state of regionalist occurrences in the whole of Africa with West Africa playing a leading role.

3.3.1.4 Fourth Wave: Founding of ECOWAS

The origination of the idea of a united and integrated post-independent West Africa by means of a regional community despite the linguistic disparities emanated from discussions initiated by Nnamdi Azikiwe, then Governor-General of Nigeria, for a West African common market in 1961. This proposal started the intellectual emergence of ECOWAS although no immediate steps was taken to give effect to Azikiwe's proposition. The leaders of Nigeria and Togo, Generals Gowon and Eyadema, would bring it into fruition through the creation of a West Africa-wide economic community after more than a decade later realising concretely post-independent West African regionalism.[523]

This process of uniting West Africa was unveiled in Lagos in 1975 by the member-states of the C.E.A.O.[524] and the M.R.U.[525], together with Nigeria, Ghana, The Gambia, Benin, Togo, Guinea-Bissau, and Cape Verde. This resulted in creating a regional body which overlapped all the linguistic variance in West Africa and also covered a geographical area larger than Western Europe under the founding Treaty of Lagos.[526]

This moment as General Dr. Yakubu Gowon writes,

> "…emerged not as the result of a sudden inspiration, nor as the work of an individual, state or group of states, but as the product of a decade

---

522 Erasmus H. Kloman Jr., 'African Unification Movements', *International Organization*, 16.2 (1962), 387–404.

523 Oteng Kufuor, pp. 19–34.

524 C.E.A.O. was the *La Communauté économique de l'Afrique de l'Ouest also* known as the *Entente Council* was the most established regional body at the time founded in 1973 through the Abidjan Treaty which pooled selected francophone nations; Ivory Coast, Niger, Burkina Faso, Mali, Mauritania and Senegal into an economic community.

525 Mano River Union was also inaugurated in 1973 and primarily made up of Liberia, Sierra Leone and Guinea.

526 Peter Robson, 'Regional Integration and the Crisis in Sub-Saharan Africa', *The Journal of Modern African Studies*, 23.4 (1985), 603–22 <http://www.jstor.org/stable/160681> [accessed 3 July 2018].

and more of patient debate and continuing discussion, in which each state and every leader in the region was, at one time or another, more or less closely involved. In addition to this large body of collective wisdom the West African governments also had the services of their own specialists and advisers...,"[527]

Furthermore, he continues by alluding to the fact that,

"We were fortunate, too, in being able to draw on the recent history of cooperation and integration among the West European nations, whose Common Market stimulated much interest and debate in Africa and in other parts of the developing world. Nearer home, there were valuable lessons to be learnt from the experience of Kenya, Tanzania and Uganda, grouped first in the East African Common Services Organisation (1961) and, after 1967, in the East African Community, a close-knit economic union that survived many vicissitudes until its unfortunate demise in 1977."[528]

Hence, it is significant to note that the steps leading to the formation of ECOWAS found inspiration in part from both the West European project that led to the formation of the EU as well as the example of the East African Community with respect to the binary of successes and failures that relate to regional integration. The agreement that initiated the tangible process of region building in West Africa was signed by nine nations initially, these were, Ghana, Liberia, Mauritania, Niger, Nigeria, Senegal, Sierra Leone, Togo and Upper Volta (now Burkina Faso) in Accra on the 4th of May 1967.

A revised agreement was signed the following year in 1968 in the capital of Liberia, Monrovia. By incentivising the process of conclusively resolving to set up the West African economic community in defiance to all its differences, the cordial diplomatic relationship which had existed between the leaders of Nigeria and Togo particularly during the civil war of the former in the 1960s was leveraged upon. Hence in April 1972, the pre-eminent Nigerian scholar-cum-policy practitioner Adebayo Adedeji[529] noted

527 Yakubu Gowon, *The Economic Community of West African States: A Study in Political and Economic Integration* (Warwick, 1984) pp. 102

528 Gowon.pp.102 – 103

529 Adebayo Adedeji at this time was the then Nigerian Minister for Economic Development and Reconstruction

as the intellectual Father of ECOWAS[530], facilitated the establishment of this Regional Economic Community (REC) during a bilateral meeting between the Generals Yakubu Gowon and Gnassingbé Eyadéma. Adedeji, who later became the longest serving UNECA Executive Secretary, chronicled his description of this partnership as conveying 'a *powerful message*' on the potency of state cooperation in the West African region.[531]

The formation of the M.R.U subsequently by Sierra Leone and Liberia in 1973 would set into motion the establishment of a transnational customs union which would later include Guinea. The MRU sought to cooperate on trade policies that would facilitate and lead to common agriculture and industrialisation. By 1974, member states of the MRU had signed complimentary agreements creating institutions such as a ministerial council, standing and sub-committees, and a secretariat. The sub-committees were tasked with the overarching competences of energy, communication and transportation making it one of the initial moments in regional energy cooperation to be introduced into a regional economic agreement in West Africa this would serve as one of the precursors to ECOWAS energy regionalism.[532]

From the years 1973 to 1974 in the aftermath of bilateral negotiations between the founding proponents and the other founding members towards the formation of ECOWAS, West African economy ministers met and deliberated on the fine details of the founding ECOWAS Treaty. In 1975, the signing of the founding treaties with its subsequent amendments made in 1976 added five new protocols, which further enhanced the organisation. This was done in consultations with the International Monetary Fund (IMF) and UNECA.[533] In effect, the founding of ECOWAS set into motion a new era of regionalism in West Africa with the impetus to conse-

530 Adekeye Adebajo, 'Two Prophets of Regional Integration : Prebisch and Adedeji', in *International Development: Ideas, Experience, and Prospects*, ed. by Bruce Currie-Alder and others, 1st edn (Oxford: Oxford University Press, 2014), pp. 323–38; Adekeye Adebajo, 'A Tale of Three Cassandras: Jean Monnet, Raúl Prebisch, and Adebayo Adedeji', in *Region-Building in Africa: Political and Economic Challenges*, ed. by Daniel H. Levine and Dawn Nagar, 1st edn (New York: Palgrave Macmillan, 2016), pp. 53–70.

531 Adebayo Adedeji, 'ECOWAS: A Retrospective Journey', in *West Africa's Security Challenges: Building Peace in a Troubled Region*, ed. by Adekeye Adebajo and Ismail Rashid (Boulder, CO: Lynne Rienner Publishers, 2004), pp. 28.

532 M.R.U, *Mano River Declaration Establishing the Mano River Union*, *United Nations - Treaty Series* (United Nations - Treaty Series, 1973), pp. 266–75 <https://wits.worldbank.org/GPTAD/PDF/archive/MRU.pdf> [accessed 13 August 2018].

533 Adedeji. Pp. 31–32

quentially influence largely political, economic and socio-cultural cooperation and integration among post-independent West African nation-states. ECOWAS has served as a tool in dealing with major regional issues such as security, trade, energy and transportation, which requires collaboration among states in the region.

To conclude, even though the contributing legacy of colonial regionalism cannot be underestimated the forces for and against it has been in part one of the key, fundamental and distinctive qualities that metamorphosed into a number of the pre and post-independence regional groupings which would finally influence various ideational representations of regionalism in West Africa. Equally, the role of post medieval empire and kingdom building prior to the process of what I call Pan-West Africanism and colonial regionalism cannot be watered-down as a foundational legacy to what has become known today as ECOWAS regionalism or regional integration.

Pan-West African regionalist ideologies that confronted skin colour discrimination and colonialism contributed to the formation of a solid regional identity. This would later shape the identity, ownership, aims and design of ECOWAS as well as the other regional organisations in West Africa that served as forerunners to West African regionalism. The narrative and analyses of such legacies in this manner have been frequently ignored in comparative regionalism literature and when it has been done it is misconstrued.

During the 1960s, much of what integration scholars interpreted as a wave of region building in Africa was actually related to considerations on the deconstruction of policies. These policies had been decided by erstwhile colonial rulers and handed down to their former territories without reference to the capacity and agency of these new nations. Their interpretation also highlighted the pivotal contribution of the peoples of these territories to the creation of the regional institutions that existed before aside from that which would be formed later after independence. A typical example is seen when Joseph Nye considered East African regionalism in the wake of the accession to independence of Kenya, Tanzania and Uganda and celebrated the EAC as unique and unparalleled in Africa.[534]

In doing so, Joseph Nye overlooked the elaborate process of African regionalism and regional integration through his depiction of how this process unfolded and evolved. But this was not in sync to how Ernst B. Haas defines the evolution of regionalism generally. In that, Haas explains

534 Daniel C Bach, pp. 7–8; Joseph Nye, *Pan-Africanism and East African Integration* (Cambridge, MA: Harvard University Press, 1966), p. 131.

that political actors in several distinct national settings are persuaded to shift their loyalties, expectations and political activities towards a new centre, whose institutions possess or demand jurisdiction over the pre-existing national states.[535]

3.3.2 Dual Nature of ECOWAS Regionalism: Collaborative and Consolidative

Ever since the founding of ECOWAS, the unique and significant aspect of West African regionalism since the exit of Mauritania,[536] has been that states have come to appreciate the benefits of collaborative regionalism. This has entailed cooperation among neighbouring and even rival member states in the form of mutual economic transformation, regional policy planning and action instead of parochialism, which has become the best option in consolidating gains for shared prosperity and security.[537]

ECOWAS regionalism features national governments coming together collaboratively to essentially serve as an economically transformative political and security agent. This regional coalescing has been done to tackle some of the most difficult problems that has confronted the region. They include problems such as security challenges caused by civil wars and terrorism; political instability caused by problems of electoral incumbencies and external interference; public health crises caused by the emergence of new viruses; economic and currency bottlenecks caused by its colonial past and neo-colonial hamstrings; as well as dealing with the emergent energy and infrastructure challenges. This collaboration has facilitated a unified approach to face common challenges as they emerge.

When Nigeria and Togo became the nucleus of the West African integration process, it rallied member states in the region from the beginning through skilled diplomacy and cautious engagement despite the political,

535 Ernst B. Haas, *The Uniting of Europe: Political, Social and Economic Forces 1950-1957*, 2nd edn (Stanford, CA: Stanford University Press, 1968), p. 16.

536 Mauritania exited from the main West African regional body, ECOWAS on 26 December 2000 to join the Maghreb union consisting of Libya, Morocco and Algeria.

537 A. J. Jacobs, 'Collaborative Regionalism and Foreign Direct Investment: The Case of the Southeast Automotive Core and the "New Domestics"', *Economic Development Quarterly*, 26.3 (2012), 199–219 <https://doi.org/10.1177/0891242412453481>.

economic, social and linguistic variations that characterised the region.[538] Since the revised treaty in 1993, regional public policy in relation to security and defence became top of the agenda in terms of ECOWAS regionalism although it was not set up to deal with security as its priority. This has defined a new era of collaborative regionalism because ECOWAS, the economic community, began to prioritise the safeguarding of security and democracy by addressing political issues that could threaten the peace and security of the region. This has also contributed to making ECOWAS' collaborative regionalism in areas of defence, security and democratisation a notable mention in the development of a specific security culture gained through region-building. Viewed in retrospect, the security culture of ECOWAS using ECOMOG and the decisions of its security council has proven to be a solid tool for collaborative growth in security regionalism.[539]

ECOWAS regionalism has been consolidative by means of strengthening linkages between national and regional governance aside from the efforts seen in sector specific areas. In order to advance economic transformation and nation-building through the maintenance of peace and the creation of prosperity in the region. Regional integration in West Africa has reinforced the bonds that exist between individual member states and regional institutions through consolidative regional governance.

To illustrate, member states have consolidated gains by being committed to regional goals set by regional institutions in ECOWAS that seek to relay commitments and objectives from wider Pan-African and international organisations like the AU, UNECA and the UN that would promote peace and prosperity.[540] Some of these commitments include the AU Agenda 2063, the UN Climate Accord signed in Paris and the UN Sustainable Development Goals.

Again, this consolidation has also been functional, that is, it has sought to employ sector specific approaches siloed under specific functional commissions and directorates to drive efforts that would cement gains in prior-

---

538 Gowon, pp. 191–98.

539 Osarhieme Benson Osadolor, The Evolution Of Policy On Security And Defence In ECOWAS, 1978 – 2008, *Journal of the Historical Society of Nigeria* 20 (2011), pp. 87–103. Accessed June 14, 2018. www.jstor.org/stable/41857176.

540 Timothy M. Shaw, J. Andrew Grant, and Scarlett Cornelissen, *The Ashgate Research Companion to Regionalisms*, ed. by Timothy M. Shaw, J. Andrew Grant, and Scarlett Cornelissen, *The Ashgate Research Companion to Regionalisms* (Surrey and Burlington,VT: Ashgate Publishing Limited, 2011), pp. 213–40 <https://doi.org/10.4324/9781315613499>; Commission.

ity sectors in order to reap the most benefit for region building. To exemplify this consolidative gain in political and security issues, peacekeeping missions from member states like Ghana, Nigeria and Senegal under ECOMOG to other member states like Liberia, Sierra Leone and recently The Gambia has solidified the region's capacity to deal with regional security threats.

Further, to tighten efforts in terms of regional fiscal and monetary policy engagement, routine meetings every three months by finance and economy ministers in the region are a place to facilitate dialogue and negotiations among member states. These meetings are tasked with the responsibility of removing all bottlenecks, which impede the economic wellbeing of member states as well as to facilitate regional economic activities.

In conclusion, the collaborative regionalism attribute in ECOWAS engenders another distinct attribute that is the consolidation of regionalism in West Africa. These two attributes are not conflictual to the ultimate progress of regionalisation in ECOWAS rather they complement the process in effect generating a formidable process capable of adapting to imminent regional challenges such as peace and security without losing focus on its core purpose of regional economic governance.

3.4 ECOWAS Energy Regionalism: Past, Present and Future

The journey towards the realisation of an ECOWAS energy region has been directed by a number of signposts namely past turning points, present circumstances and future prospects.

The past turning points are characterised as milestones or significant stages in the development of what has become known as ECOWAS energy regionalism. It is defined by early watershed moments that encouraged cooperative solidarity in the sharing of energy among newly independent nations. It envisaged the regional grid system and encouraged convergence around common energy resources in the region.

Again, a number of historic events like the 1970s energy squeeze and the 1980s energy glut transformed the course of regional energy cooperation. It can also be deduced that it is within this same period coupled with the effects of the global energy events that led to the formation of ECOWAS by the founding member nations. The phenomenon of market liberalisation was instigated by the structural adjustment programmes (SAPs) of the 1990s. It opened up national energy markets and influenced the further liberalisation of the regional energy market through the change in ECOWAS Treaty provisions that bordered on energy and other ancillary sectors. A major legacy that can be attributed to this moment was the regional institutional formations in the ECOWAS energy sector.

The present energy circumstances are guided by the quest to integrate the regional energy space. This integration is through the use of regulation and policy practices, the integration of efforts around a number of energy options and the dimension to coalesce together to address a number of pertinent energy issues that are regional in scope, like energy security, energy justice and clean energy transition.

Prospects for the future of energy regionalism in ECOWAS are linked to the governance of cross-border energy networks that are extant in the region such as the current regional energy infrastructure and the effect of how emergent energy governance issues will be addressed.

3.4.1 Past Milestones: Cooperation towards a Common West African Energy Region

The cooperative processes towards the development of energy regionalism in ECOWAS has been denoted by three phases. The earliest significant stage of cooperation towards a common West African energy region began in the 1960s with the process of solidarizing around bilateral energy sharing agreements. This envisioned a regional grid system by intertying national energy grid networks, constructing joint regional infrastructure and lastly, by coalescing around common energy resources.

The 1970s and 1980s, a period which defines the second watershed moment in energy regionalism in ECOWAS. Negative global energy events such as the global energy squeeze of the 1970s and the energy glut of the 1980s increased regional cooperation around energy as a prioritised thematic issue and also around energy resources as never seen before in the region. It can be confidently posited that this period triggered the formation of even the regional community, ECOWAS among other factors.

The third critical point in the determination of regional energy cooperation in ECOWAS occurred in the period between the 1990s and early 2000s with the processes to construct regional energy institutions. This process began with the liberalisation of national energy markets subsequently leading to a liberalised regional energy market that was started by a treaty amendment in the revised ECOWAS Treaty. All this has culminated in the formation of regional energy institutions like the regional power pool – WAPP – the regional power regulator- ERERA – the regional gas pipeline – WAGP – and the regional renewable energy agency – ECREEE.

3.4.1.1 Early Milestones towards ECOWAS Energy Cooperation (1960s)

Collectivising organically around energy in West Africa has been the mainstay in the development of major energy infrastructure in the region since independence. This kind of solidarity, the subject of sharing energy (either bilaterally or through the construction of joint regional infrastructure) has existed and continues since the founding and subsequent evolution of ECOWAS as a regional body.

A certain crop of post-independence countries pursued the construction of energy megaprojects right after independence with technical and financial investment from internal and external sources with examples of the external sources being entities like international companies (example, Kaiser Industries) and banks (example, the World Bank). A number of countries in the region such as Côte d'Ivoire, Liberia, Nigeria, Senegal, Niger and Ghana took an inventory of their hydropower potential leading to the construction of large hydropower dams such as the following, Akosombo in Ghana (1962–64), Kainji in Nigeria (1969), Mt. Coffee in Liberia, and Kossou in Côte d'Ivoire (1969–1971). The result was that hydropower played a significant role in power generation in post-colonial West Africa as well as the basis of ECOWAS energy regionalism.

Hydropower generation aimed at supplying energy to specific heavy industries like mining and the production of aluminium, which meant to drive modernisation and spearhead the industrialisation agenda of these new states. Furthermore, it sought to provide energy to principal ports and harbours, to urban centres in these countries and to supply cross-border interconnections. For example, construction of the Akosombo hydroelectric dam on the Volta River was designed to be a major regional supplier of electricity to neighbouring countries in the region such as Côte d'Ivoire, Togo, Burkina Faso and Benin. At the same time, it was to serve as the main energy provider for the aluminium smelting company, VALCO, the port city of Tema, and the whole of southern Ghana at its inception.[541]

541 Stephan F. Miescher, '"Nkrumah's Baby": The Akosombo Dam and the Dream of Development in Ghana, 1952–1966'. *Water History*, 6. (2014), 341–366 https://doi.org/10.1007/s12685-014-0112-8

Secondly, the building of the Kainji Dam on the Niger River in 1968 in the Niger State of Northern Nigeria established a transmission interconnection between Nigeria and Niger to ensure a constant and affordable power supply to Niamey, the capital of Niger.[542]A major milestone worthy of mention in the 1960s (in terms of the development of large energy projects), was the laying out of a vision to implement a regional grid system that would launch large-scale electrification in the West Africa region.

Even though many countries had limited coverage of electricity supply upon assumption of independence (in terms of generation facilities and power grids among others), their aspiration to modernise after colonialism instigated a systematic process to advance the use of the existing modern energy technology. The rapid adoption of hydropower generation in the production, transmission and distribution of hydroelectric power symbolised, in particular, the speed and leapfrogging ability of the diffusion of modern energy technologies at the time in a region such as West Africa. It also symbolised the ability to roll out energy supplies on a large scale through cross-border interconnections which effected bilateral energy agreements. This is exemplified by the incorporated regional power grid interconnections initiated in the 1960s by the West African Grid System (WAGS). This would serve as a precursor to the mechanism that would underlie energy regionalism in West Africa, especially at the founding of ECOWAS.[543]

WAGS' antecedents originated from the interconnection project between Ghana's Volta River Authority (VRA) and the Communauté Électricité du Benin (CEB) of Togo and Benin with further interconnection plans with Côte d'Ivoire, which eventually saw Ghana transmitting energy via interconnected power lines to Togo, Benin and Côte d'Ivoire.

Another explanation that accounted for the newly found facilitation of regional cooperation in the West African energy sector in the 1960s related to the diversification of energy production sources especially with the introduction and availability of new and more concentrated energy resource developments such as nuclear energy, crude oil, and coal. By the

542 G.V. Eckenfelder, 'Hydro Power Plans in Nigeria. In Energy in the Developing World-The Real Energy Crisis, eds. V. Smil and W.E. Knowland. (Oxford: Oxford University Press, 1980)

543 UNECA, 'Ghana's Experience In Power Interconnections Within The Framework Of ECOWAS' (Addis Ababa: UNECA, 1969) <http://repository.uneca.org/bitstream/handle/123456789/17587/Bib-67662.pdf?sequence=1>.

end of the 1960s eight countries, namely Ghana and Senegal (1960), Mali (1961), Liberia (1962), Côte d'Ivoire (1963), Nigeria (1964), Sierra Leone (1967) and Niger (1969) had become members of the International Atomic Energy Agency (IAEA).[544]

These countries have developed capacity related to non-power applications of nuclear technology in the fields of medical, agricultural and industrial science. In relation to the application of nuclear technology towards power generation Ghana went a step further by acquiring a research reactor from the Soviet Union in 1964 to explore possibilities to generate low-carbon sources of electricity that could diversify and ensure secure supplies of energy. There was very little cooperation on nuclear energy in the 1960s internally in West Africa thus rendering the abundant supply of uranium in Niger to be less leveraged on in the region for commercial and domestic production of electrical power through nuclear energy.

To give a bit of a background relating to the uranium finds in Niger, the French Atomic Energy Commission (C.E.A.) began exploration for uranium in Niger in the mid-1950s before Niger's independence in 1960. Initial discoveries were made in the Arlit area of the Agadez region in 1965. This led to the development and formation of the Société des Mines de l'Aïr (SOMAIR) in 1968 to further exploit uranium for export to France and other parts of Europe.[545] Orano SA, the multinational nuclear fuel cycle company with a majority stake owned by the French State, has controlled SOMAIR since its inception.[546]

One would have thought that with the abundant reserves of uranium in Niger it would have undergone a clean energy transition by now with the support of nuclear power. Niger would have become not only a major exporter of power to the region, while reducing energy security risks but also a leader in region-wide nuclear energy cooperation efforts toward a clean energy transition. Nonetheless this has not been the case for this uranium abundant West African nation.

---

544 IAEA, 'List of Member States', 2019 <https://www.iaea.org/about/governance/list-of-member-states> [accessed 1 January 2019].

545 Guy Martin, 'Uranium : A Case-Study in Franco- African Relations', *The Journal of Modern African Studies*, 27.4 (1989), 625–40 <https://www.jstor.org/stable/161112>; World Nuclear Association, 'Uranium in Niger', *Country Profiles - Niger*, 2019 <https://www.world-nuclear.org/information-library/country-profiles/countries-g-n/niger.aspx> [accessed 1 January 2019].

546 Orano SA, 'Orano Group', 2019 <https://www.orano.group/en> [accessed 1 December 2019].

The early 1960s also witnessed very little regional cooperation in fossil fuel project developments in the West African region. In spite of the abundant crude oil finds in Nigeria since the early 1900s and the coal deposits in Thirozerine, Niger since 1964 which was under the management of Société Nigérienne du Charbon Anou Araren (SONICHAR) which produces electricity for the northern Agadez region including the uranium mines[547] not much regional cooperation occurred in fossil fuel development. In this same vein, Ghana contracted the Italian oil company AGIP to build its first crude oil refinery plant in 1963, thereby establishing the Tema Oil Refinery (TOR), that processed imported and unrefined crude oil to meet Ghana's energy needs and also for export.[548]

One could therefore conclude that in terms of regional energy cooperation in West Africa in the 1960s, the energy generation and distribution sector was principally facilitated by hydropower generation but in terms of other energy sources like nuclear energy and fossil fuel developments the overriding economic priority of the individual member states limited the process towards regional energy cooperation.

3.4.1.2 Global Energy Crisis: Repercussions in West Africa in the 1970s – 1980s

The energy crisis of the 1970s was caused by a number of geopolitical factors such as the OPEC embargo and the Iranian revolution in the Middle East. Its main trigger was the powerful action by the so-called Third World nations who controlled the main portals of crude oil production to hold back energy production sending ripple effects in the global energy sector without excluding the West Africa region.

The ECOWAS region experienced the dire consequences of the OPEC price increases as that resulted in sharp increments in imported petroleum products into the region. In addition, unfavourable corporate decisions by the major international oil companies that were servicing the region through the purchasing, insuring, refining, storing, and delivering of

---

547 Olayinka I. Ogunsola, 'History of Energy Sources and Their Utilization in Nigeria', *Energy Sources*, 12.2 (1990), 181–98 <https://doi.org/10.1080/00908319008960198>; World Nuclear Association.

548 Tom C. McCaskie, 'The United States, Ghana and Oil: Global and Local Perspectives', *African Affairs*, 107.428 (2008), 313–32 <https://doi.org/10.1093/afraf/adn019>.

petroleum and its derivatives, found it appropriately necessary to cut back or to ground their operations completely in the region.

Historically, the pattern of interaction between a purchasing country and the international petroleum trading system ultimately determined the extent to which that country was reliant on petroleum for industry and communication and this became an important consideration in corporate decision making of the petroleum MNCs operating in the region.[549] Moreover, some internal factors and policy decisions also determined the extent to which this energy crisis affected countries especially the national price of petroleum products, this was done in concert with the source and timing of the terrible impact of the energy crisis in the West African region.[550]

These high import prices for energy affected the ECOWAS region gravely. It impacted the international payment accounts of these barely new states throwing them into an ocean of debts and subsequently and abruptly halting energy development plans with the most affected being energy infrastructure projects. This eroded the relatively modest growth rates that the region had experienced during the 1960s with projections of economic stagnation coupled with dismal political consequences in the 1980s. It must be stated however that the impact of the energy crises in the 1970s varied significantly from one country to the other and the different national characteristics as well as energy policy decisions of the affected nations influenced the intensity of the impact of the price increases on individual nations and the region as a whole.[551]

Fortunate for West African states, the energy crisis fostered an increase in regional consumption of crude oil from its sole OPEC member, Nigeria. The regional distribution scheme effected in the 1970s by Nigeria involved the exports of large volumes of petroleum resources to West African states. These petroleum disbursements minimised the crippling effect of the then ongoing financial and energy deprivation of the decade's dramatic petroleum price increases and supply shortages in the region. These efforts by Nigeria improved its regional reputation and enhanced its leadership role in West Africa.[552]

---

549 Willard R. Johnson and Ernest J. Wilson III, 'The "Oil Crises" and African Economies : Oil Wave on a Tidal Flood of Industrial Price Inflation', *Daedalus*, 111.2, Black Africa: A Generation after Independence (1982), 211–41.

550 Johnson and Wilson III.

551 Johnson and Wilson III.

552 Olatunde J B Ojo, *Nigeria and the Formation of ECOWAS, International Organization*, 1980, xxxiv <https://doi.org/10.1017/S0020818300018853>; Johnson

It was around this same period that concrete efforts concerning regional integration was initiated by Nigeria and Togo towards the formation of ECOWAS. One could conclude then that the lasting legacy of the 1970s global energy crises on West Africa was its influencing effects that spearheaded economic regionalism leading to the founding of ECOWAS.

In the 1980s, oil prices collapsed leading to a huge surplus of petroleum the converse of what had happened in the 1970s. A serious drop in demand following from the 1970s energy crisis caused this 'oil glut' as termed by *The New York Times* in describing this phenomenon on June 21st, 1981.[553] The attendant distribution practices following the glut were financially unsustainable for supplier countries due to the lack of financial benefits that was expected to be accrued from sales. Nigeria, the region's largest economy and major commercial crude oil producer aside from being an OPEC member was immensely hit by the price slump.

Though it seemed beneficial for the other smaller economies in the region it did the opposite due to the destructive impact of the 1970s energy squeeze. The energy squeeze left these countries' economies struggling because of huge accruals of debt. Hence, they were unable to take advantage of this unique cheap energy moment to drive the much-needed economic growth that they sought after both nationally and regionally. However, it can be said that, what this moment did was to encourage the adoption of new strategies for energy self-reliance and growth.

Some of the strategies employed included rural electrification, a positive perception and desire to adopt renewable energies generally but solar energy technology in particular and most importantly the commitment towards a regional approach in tackling the existing energy problems collectively. One consequential meeting, which brought the entire region together in dealing with the regional aftershocks of the 1970s energy crisis and the 1980s energy glut worldwide, was the 1981 conference held in Freetown, Sierra Leone under the aegis of ECOWAS under the theme, Energy for Survival.[554] This conference created the opportunity for ECOWAS member states to engage collectively within the context of a regional organisation on energy issues more proactively especially regarding regional

---

and Wilson III; Gilles Carbonnier, *International Development Policy: Energy and Development* (Basingstoke: Palgrave Macmillan, 2011).

553 Robert D. Hershey Jr., 'How the Oil Glut Is Changing Business', *The New York Times*, 1981 <https://www.nytimes.com/1981/06/21/business/how-the-oil-glut-is-changing-business.html?pagewanted=all> [accessed 9 September 2018].

554 Sarfoh, *Energy in the Development of West Africa*.

energy policies, strategies and infrastructures with an outlook on meeting future regional energy needs. The aftermath influenced the drafting of the 1982 ECOWAS energy policy document, the first of its kind, which tabled strategies that sought to deal with the imminent energy insecurity in the region.

As part of this new policy, ECOWAS proposed a natural gas pipeline across West Africa as part of its key regional economic and energy goals. Four countries in the region, Benin, Ghana, Nigeria and Togo later initialled an agreement for the development of the West African Gas Pipeline (WAGP) based on private investment and commercial principles. With the sole purpose of connecting Nigeria's western oil and gas fields to neighbouring Benin, Togo and Ghana.[555]

To summarise, the global energy crises in the 1970s coupled with the 'energy glut' in the 1980s were primarily a call to action by ECOWAS. It emphasised the need to harmonise and coordinate national energy policies among member states. Thus, facilitating energy regionalism through the promotion of programmes, projects, and activities that would increase the collective energy autonomy of the sub-region.[556] This began by building on bilateral connections that led to the ECOWAS energy agenda and priorities first featured in the 1975 ECOWAS Treaty and then in the ECOWAS Energy Policy of 1982 and subsequently in its 1993 revision.[557] This moment ushered in a new era of regional energy policy engagement that had a regional focus and approach. This regional focus and approach sought to utilise cross-border energy interactions like energy production and distribution efforts. These led to processes that encouraged the formation of regional energy institutions in ensuing decades.

555 West African Gas Pipeline Authority, 'WAGPA | West African Gas Pipeline Authority', 2018 <http://www.wagpa.org/about-us/> [accessed 10 October 2018].

556 Karim Karaki, *Understanding ECOWAS Energy Policy From National Interests to Regional Markets and Wider Energy Access?*, PEDRO (Brussels, 2017) <https://ecdpm.org/wp-content/uploads/ECOWAS-Energy-Background-Paper-PEDRO-Political-Economy-Dynamics-Regional-Organisations-Africa-ECDPM-2017.pdf> [accessed 28 December 2017].

557 Karaki.

3.4.1.3 Processes for Constructing Regional Energy Institutions in the 1990s – 2000s

The construction of energy systems in post-independent and regionalising West Africa in the 1990s up until the first decade of the 2000s was determined by many factors. These included among other factors national and external energy challenges, the trend of liberalising the energy sector plus the foundation of bilateral energy sharing. All these have laid a foundation for the construction of regional energy governance bodies that seek to institutionalise the process of regional energy cooperation and further strengthen the integration of energy networks in the region. The process towards energy governance through regional institutions began by laying down a legal framework that designed and constructed an institutional arrangement that comprised bodies that would deal with both conventional and renewal energy separately.

In ECOWAS, most member states began to liberalise their energy sectors to involve private actors particularly in the 1990s as part of the World Bank and IMF's structural adjustment programmes (SAPs) that was being implemented in these countries. Only Cote d'Ivoire and Cabo Verde have been successful to have majority of the players in their power sectors being privately owned companies. However, in a number of other countries such as Burkina Faso, Côte d'Ivoire, Ghana, Nigeria, and Senegal permission is granted to independent power producers to participate in the power sector.[558]

Meanwhile a legal framework underpinned most of the innovations in the regional energy sector. In 1993, the revised ECOWAS Treaty came into being. It legally consolidated the region's energy sector by establishing liberal market principles for building a regional market, which included energy. This was realised by the addition of 93 articles to the amended Treaty.

The new Treaty significantly highlights energy with about 19 mentions to draw attention to its policy importance. Three articles of the 1993 Treaty emphasise the place of energy in the intended and binding integrative agenda of ECOWAS, namely Article 3, Article 22 and Article 28. Article 3 deals with the aims and goals of the regional body, it also calls for

---

558 Pineau. Alfonso Medinilla, Bruce Byiers, and Karim Karaki, *African Power Pools: Regional Energy, National Power*, Political Economy Dynamics of Regional Organisations in Africa (PEDRO) (Maastricht and Brussels, 2019) <www.ecdpm.org/dp244>.

the harmonization and coordination of national policies that promote the integration of programmes, projects, and activities in 19 thematic areas. Energy is a major component of these areas, which is listed as a separate area vis-à-vis other energy related areas such as industry and technology.[559]

Article 22 concerns the institutional composition of ECOWAS along with the eight technical commissions it establishes. The function of energy policy was duly asserted within the responsibilities of the commission for industry, science and technology, and energy. Energy is highlighted and prioritised within the scope of twelve essential sectors. These sectors are singled out for the promotion of collective action that would expedite energy self-reliance and the modernisation of the regional economy.[560]

On the other hand, Article 28 focuses specifically on all aspects of ECOWAS' energy framework. It calls on all member states to ensure an effective development of energy resources and to ensure a steady supply of hydrocarbons. It emphasises the promotion and development of clean and renewable energy within the framework of energy diversification policies with special reference to solar energy. Again, it seeks to harmonise energy infrastructure development plans by prioritising the regional interconnection of national electricity grids.

Additionally, the prospect of coordination in devising a common energy policy through research, exploitation, production and distribution is highlighted. All this is done along with the launching of a mechanism for developing collective solutions geared towards solving the region's varied energy issues such as energy transmission, the shortage of skilled technicians, and the financing of energy projects, which was designated as essential in the legislation.[561]

Along with the revised Treaty provisions, member states signed the ECOWAS Energy Protocol in 2003 whose central vision sought to secure "regionally efficient and reliable supplies of electricity and other forms of energy".[562] Furthermore, the energy protocol encourages cooperation among member states so as to mitigate against disruptions in regional

---

559 ECOWAS, 'Economic Community of West African States (ECOWAS): Revised Treaty', *International Legal Materials*, 1996, 660–97 <http://www.jstor.org/stable/20698567>.

560 Hancock, 'Energy Regionalism and Diffusion in Africa: How Political Actors Created the ECOWAS Center for Renewable Energy and Energy Efficiency'.

561 ECOWAS, 'Economic Community of West African States (ECOWAS): Revised Treaty'.

562 ECOWAS, *ECOWAS Energy Protocol A/P4/1/03* (Abuja, 2003) <http://www.ecowapp.org/sites/default/files/eprotocol.pdf> [accessed 17 August 2018].

energy supplies, modernise energy systems and intertie energy transmission and distribution systems such as high-voltage electricity grids and high-pressure natural gas pipelines. The Energy Protocol enabled ECOWAS and its member states to speed-up prior energy projects by initiating a number of novel energy processes towards realising the much-needed energy cooperation objectives.

In 1999, ECOWAS energy ministers established a regional power pool, the West African Power Pool (WAPP), as part of the laid down five regional power pools in Africa. This sought to promote the integration of power generation, transmission infrastructures, and distribution of electricity through power trades among all 14 of the 15 member states with the exception of Cape Verde. As part of this a regional power regulatory body, the ECOWAS Regional Electricity Regulatory Authority (ERERA) was set up to facilitate the power trade and regulate the exchange of electricity between member states, as well as provide operational support to national regulatory entities through capacity building programmes when WAPP becomes fully functional.[563]

ECOWAS members in line with previous commitments to expand and highlight renewable energy programs also established ECREEE as the region's flagship renewable energy centre in 2008.[564] By 2010, ECREEE was inaugurated and has since generated a number of work programs namely data collection and dissemination, policy coordination in the initiation and enactment of green policies, green energy innovation project financing, capacity building and gender mainstreaming programs like ECOWGEN which ensures that women are active agents in the renewable energy sector. In 2015, ECOWAS substantiated its commitment by enacting the first regional gender and energy policy under the auspices of ECREEE.[565]

The period under review saw also the realisation of the West African Gas Pipeline (WAGP) when four member states of ECOWAS signed the West African Gas Pipeline (WAGP) Treaty in 2003 with the ECOWAS Commission serving as an observer. In terms of implementation, a legal

---

563 ERERA was fully set up in 2008 as the regional power-trading regulator within the framework of the Energy Protocol and the Legislation governing the function of the West African Power Pool.

564 David Vilar and others, *Renewable Energy in West Africa: Status, Experiences and Trends* (Praia, Cape Verde: ECREEE and CASA AFRICA, 2012) <http://www.ecreee.org/sites/default/files/renewable_energy_in_west_africa_0.pdf>.

565 Karin Reiss, 'Developing Renewable Energy Sectors and Technologies in West Africa', *UN Chronicle* (New York, December 2015) <https://unchronicle.un.org/article/developing-renewable-energy-sectors-and-technologies-west-africa>.

vehicle under the treaty was created namely the West African Gas Pipeline Company Limited (WAPCo), a joint international venture that brought together both public and private sector companies from the four signatory member countries.

The Treaty was subsequently ratified in 2005 by the four partner countries. Again in 2005, offshore construction of the West Africa Gas Pipeline commenced it took six later years for it to start operating commercially by delivering natural gas to customers in the partner countries from the gas fields in Nigeria.

As demonstrated, regional energy cooperation in ECOWAS has been denoted by three unique strategic steps. Post independent countries pursuing the construction of essential energy infrastructure to meet national energy demand in the meantime sought to share the produced energy to energy vulnerable neighbouring states. Moreover, the repercussions of the global energy crises served as a conduit to deepen regional cooperation on energy and furthermore contributing even to the founding of the regional economic community. As a result, this has led to the adoption of policy, legal and regulatory frameworks that serves as an impetus and basis for the construction of several regional energy institutions.

3.4.2 Present Settings: Integration of the ECOWAS Energy Region

The integration of the ECOWAS energy region in its current setting has been characterised by three steps as well. Beginning with the use of regulatory processes as a means of consolidation towards regional energy integration. In this case, policy and regulation are sector specific. It targets sectors such as electricity and gas. Moreover, this integration process is also focused on strengthening the sector-specific regulatory institutions.

The second step in integrating ECOWAS energy regionalism further is through efforts aimed around a number of energy options that would provide abundant, secure and sustainable energy access and supply. These options entail transitions towards cleaner energy and the integration of energy efficiency programmes into national energy policies with the support of region-wide programmes.

The third critical step towards the integration of the ECOWAS energy region has been to tackle pertinent thematic issues such as energy security, energy justice and the transitional shift towards clean and low-carbon energy issues collectively as a region.

3.4.2.1 Integration through Regulation of Energy Spaces

The coming together of the fifteen member states in ECOWAS to integrate the energy region has required a significant amount of innovation and motivation despite the challenges. Typically, to integrate an energy space or region it is significant to use regulatory processes as a pre-condition in the context of a robust energy market formation as a vehicle to achieve this objective. This is exemplified by the case of the regionalisation processes in the ECOWAS power sector.

The whole purpose of putting in place an electricity market for the region was to strengthen the energy sharing mechanisms by scaling it from bilateral partnerships to a region-wide process through the assistance of an enabling framework in this case a cooperative market. Ultimately, this can then facilitate the attraction of new investments into the regional power sector in order to alleviate the wide electricity access gap prevalent in the region.

Therefore, the creation of a regional regulatory body with the full powers of a regulator and enforcer of rules to govern the trade in electricity unlike regional regulatory associations found elsewhere in other world regions was quite innovative.[566]

The statutory and quasi-judiciary powers assigned to ERERA enables it to issue regulations and decisions that are binding, directly applicable in the ECOWAS region with its application guaranteed by member states in their various national jurisdictions.[567] The integration of the ECOWAS power sector through the work of the regional regulator, ERERA, has been effected through licensing, passing laws and regulations as well as being tasked with the mandate of establishing a regional electricity market.

By 2016, the fundamental framework for the ECOWAS regional electricity market in the power sector was put in place. This included regional market rules for power trading, the WAPP operational manual, tariff methodology for cross-border electricity tariffs and a dispute resolution mechanism to aid in the resolution of disputes among member states. On

566 A key example in the area of regional regulatory associations is the Agency for the Cooperation of Energy Regulators (ACER), the European Union Agency, created under the Third Energy Package to further push the completion of the internal energy market for both electricity and natural gas.

567 ECOWAS Regional Electricity Regulatory Authority (ERERA), *West African Power Sector Regional Regulation Project. Diagnostic Report on the Institutional and Regulatory Interfaces of the ECOWAS Regional Electricity Regulatory Authority*, 2008 <https://erera.arrec.org/>.

Friday, 29th June 2018, the ECOWAS regional electricity market was fully launched in Cotonou, Benin.[568]

Currently, the global power sector as well as West Africa's electricity sector is experiencing considerable reform. This has included a transition towards smart and clean energy, which has warranted transformations in the standard design of the energy sector including its guiding regulatory frameworks.[569]

Improvements in the electricity sector, which certainly have a profound influence on regional power regulation, include among others the reality that energy consumers are now in a position to produce and distribute energy themselves. We see this happening through the installation and utilisation of renewable energy technologies like solar panels to generate power and then distributing this power using the existing network for transmission thereby turning these onetime consumers into prosumers.[570] This unravels new dimensions of energy market regulation in the regional energy market in ECOWAS. Regulatory changes relating to the progressive transitions and reforms in the national and regional energy markets in the ECOWAS region also includes Mauritania[571] as well as other regional energy bodies.

Efforts to tighten regulatory practices in the ECOWAS gas sector was part of the legal framework put in place at the founding of the West African Gas Pipeline (WAGP). These regulatory practices were to ensure that all the corporate entities including the four founding member states worked towards securing gas supplies in the region. In addition to ensuring the security of gas supplies that is affordable and sustainable it sought to improve the reliability of energy systems in Ghana, Benin, Togo, and Nigeria overall lowering the cost of gas and its advertent effects on power generation.

Furthermore, it sought to do this by significantly reducing gas flaring drastically and eliminating it completely by 2008 in Nigeria. By 2009, the initial legislations and regulations adopted between 2004 and 2005

568 ERERA, 'The ECOWAS Regional Electricity Regulatory Authority (ERERA)', 2016 <https://erera.arrec.org/en/home> [accessed 10 October 2018].

569 Saskia Lavrijssen and Arturo Carrilo, *Radical Innovation in the Energy Sector and the Impact on Regulation*, *TILEC Discussion Paper*, TILEC Discussion Paper (Tilburg, 2017) <https://doi.org/10.2139/ssrn.2979206>.

570 Lavrijssen and Carrilo.

571 Mauritania, although, not a member of ECOWAS has decided to be part of the regional electricity market of ECOWAS because it has signed up to a cooperation agreement in this regard.

by the four member states were amended under the Offshore Damage Prevention Programme Regulation. This was necessitated by attacks on the construction of the pipeline.[572]

Regulation in ECOWAS' regional gas market has developed a regional import and export market for natural gas that prioritises the supply and use of natural gas. Despite the fact that it is mainly a state activity the key example of a collective regional action in the regional natural gas sector has been the activities of WAGP.

Integration in regional energy markets typified by the ECOWAS gas sector is fulfilled through standardizing technical specifications in the sector and following the required regulatory frameworks that further the facilitation of energy exchanges in this case the natural gas trade among member states. It is worth highlighting that aside other sectors such as the regional power sector, the regional gas pipeline has supported immensely the ongoing regional energy integration efforts underway in West Africa.

3.4.2.2 Abundant, Secure and Sustainable Energy Access and Supply

There are a number of energy options under consideration by ECOWAS member states and as a regional community in relation to dealing with the issues of providing abundant energy, and securing sustainable energy supply and access. The options that are under serious consideration are the transitions to cleaner energy such as the adoption of nuclear to power technology and the integration of energy efficiency programmes in government policy especially in the household and industrial sectors.

Nuclear technology for power generation has currently become an option of great interest under serious consideration within ECOWAS to help in the process of energy poverty alleviation and the provision of abundant and secure energy supplies in the region. For instance, in July 2015 an agreement was drafted by several countries for cooperation in the development of an integrated West African regional nuclear power programme, with a three-year action plan. The countries concerned at the Niger meeting were Benin, Burkina Faso, Ghana, Mali, Niger, Nigeria,

572 The West African Gas Pipeline (WAGP), 'Documentation: Documentation Regarding the WAGP Project', *Amendments to WAGP Regulations* <http://www.wagpa.org/project-documentation/> [accessed 1 February 2018]; Reuters, 'Rebel Attacks Swell Nigeria-to-Ghana Pipeline Cost', *Reuters*, 7 December 2009 <https://af.reuters.com/article/nigeriaNews/idAFGEE5B623520091207>.

and Senegal collectively they formed the West African Integrated Nuclear Power Group (WAINPG).

This followed the third African Conference on Energy and Nuclear Power held in April 2015 in Mombasa, Kenya. The work of WAINPG relates to plans underscored by ECOWAS in the full implementation of the regional power pool, WAPP. Where a sizeable amount of regional energy would be produced from nuclear energy.

Individual member states at the forefront of this regional efforts towards the nuclear energy approach is Ghana's nuclear to power programme. In May 2012, Ghana hosted a regional meeting on Co-operation and Networking for Nuclear Power Programme in Africa, organized by the Ghana Atomic Energy Commission (GAEC), this was under the auspices of the IAEA. The GAEC said: "The increasing energy requirements for the socio-economic development of Africa, coupled with the ever-volatile prices of fossil fuels, continue to be a major challenge for a lot of African countries."[573] As a result of this, GAEC under the leadership of the Ministry of Energy are poised to generate 1 gigawatts of power from nuclear energy by 2030. This Ghanaian example reflects the steps that ECOWAS and its member states are taking to produce abundant energy from nuclear to power technologies.

Energy efficiency is one of the many technological innovations in the energy sector which is being considered seriously as one of the available options for the improvement of energy provision in the ECOWAS region. It is seen as a complement to cleaner energy options. This is in view of the fact that the reduction of energy demand through energy efficiency is capable of improving not only the financial feasibility of cleaner energy options like renewables and nuclear but also contribute to lessen energy wastage and emissions of greenhouse gases (GHG). This would thereby ensure sustainable energy access in the region.

While there are common challenges faced by the countries in the region as pertains to the improvement of energy efficiency, those challenges are unique. They include somewhat an insufficient number of locally trained workforce, below par regulatory environment and governance, and inadequate access to financing for energy efficiency programmes. Consuming energy efficiently leads to a number of advantages such as reductions in the price of energy services as well as energy demand. To typify this energy demand especially with respect to household lightning reduces by

573 https://www.world-nuclear.org/information-library/country-profiles/others/emerging-nuclear-energy-countries.aspx

replacing incandescent bulbs with compact fluorescent lamps (CFLs) and light-emitting diode bulbs (LED).

As Worrell et al have emphasised, energy efficiency proponents do not only focus on household energy use, but also lately have increased attention on the industry sector particularly the energy intensive industries such as chemicals, iron and steel, minerals, and petroleum refining that contribute a larger share of GHG emissions as well as waste energy.[574] They further stress that energy efficiency requires a shift in approach in gaining access to and using advanced technology that tends to use less energy in the employed sectors like households and industrial sectors.[575]

It is against this background that regional energy policy discussions have in recent years increased focus on integrating energy efficiency more proactively and aggressively in government policy as a mechanism for social development, economic growth and resilience in addition to reducing emissions of carbon dioxide (CO2) and other pollutants. With the enhancement of efficiency programmes added to the use of emergent energy efficiency technologies in the ECOWAS region, many of the countries are at varying degrees in successfully implementing energy efficiency policies. Some immediate benefits have been in the creation of new jobs in the construction and energy sectors, resilience in existing energy systems, energy security and available access of energy. This has contributed to doing away with the characteristic feature inherent in the region of utilising inefficient technologies in the building and industrial sectors.

An example of this proactive approach to support governments and firms in ECOWAS towards a successful implementation of energy efficiency policies and programmes in order to draw on their benefits is a project under the aegis of ECREEE called the Supporting Energy Efficiency Access in West Africa (SEEA-WA) Project. The project aims to overcome the technical, financial, legal, institutional, social, gender and capacity related barriers that hinder the implementation of cost-effective energy efficiency measures and processes.[576]

---

574 Ernst Worrell and others, 'Industrial Energy Efficiency and Climate Change Mitigation', *Energy Efficiency*, 2.2 (2009), 109–23 <https://doi.org/10.1007/s12053-008-9032-8>.

575 Worrell and others.

576 ECREEE, 'Supporting Energy Efficiency Access in West Africa (SEEA-WA) Project Funded by the European Union' <http://www.ecreee.org/page/supporting-energy-efficiency-access-west-africa-seea-wa-project-funded-european-union> [accessed 7 June 2018].

Many other examples in several ECOWAS countries have been the implementation of different energy efficiency projects and programmes that include national compact fluorescent lamp (CFL) replacement programmes, solar water heating, standardisation and labelling, sensitisation programmes among energy audits in the industrial and building sectors. Ghana recently unveiled a programme for labelling appliances. This is targeted at revealing to the consumers the energy consumption and efficiency of products. These efforts together with the country's energy efficiency regulatory framework have led to an estimated peak energy savings of over 120 megawatts (MW). Furthermore, the programme has saved the country USD 105 million in generation investment and reducing emissions by over 11,000 tons annually.[577]

3.4.2.3 Energy Security, Energy Justice and Clean Energy Transition Issues

One can argue that the three serious issues that faces ECOWAS energy systems occur along the lines of energy security, energy justice and a low carbon transition. Although most aspects of these issues are well documented, in the following I only briefly lay out certain pertinent aspects of these issues in order to explicate their dynamics.

Energy security can be defined as the way of equitably providing available, abundant, affordable, reliable, efficient, environmentally benign, proactively governed, and socially acceptable energy services to end-users. It has been more prominent in modern-day energy policy circles. Energy security entails supply-side and demand-side components.[578] A pertinent aspect of energy security as it applies to the ECOWAS region is its interface with a particular energy market model. Energy market models include mixed models such as the liberal market model, which in certain situations is currently under stress, in addition to other alternative energy market models that are based on active state intervention.[579]

577 USAID, 'Examining Energy Efficiency Issues in Sub-Saharan Africa' <https://www.usaid.gov/powerafrica/newsletter/dec2014/smarter-power-in-africa> [accessed 7 June 2018].

578 Andreas Goldthau and Benjamin K Sovacool, 'The Uniqueness of the Energy Security, Justice, and Governance Problem', *Energy Policy*, 41 (2012), 232–40 <https://doi.org/10.1016/j.enpol.2011.10.042>.

579 Goldthau, 'From the State to the Market and Back: Policy Implications of Changing Energy Paradigms'.

Therefore, energy supply security in the ECOWAS region, deals with making available abundant energy resources for regional consumers in a world characterized by old (OECD) and new rapidly emerging (mostly Asian) consumers seeking energy resources to fuel economic growth. This process of securing energy supply brings about mercantilist approaches to play towards energy resource access in the ECOWAS region.

A second related aspect to energy security in ECOWAS is the incidence of rapidly aging energy infrastructure. Critical energy infrastructure includes infrastructure associated with electricity transmission and distribution, petroleum production and pipeline systems, liquefied natural gas facilities, coal-fired transport trains and management technology such as advanced electricity metering and distribution systems, in addition to modern power plant control systems and smart building technologies.[580]

Most of the aging infrastructure was installed in the early post-independent era of the 1960s and during the global energy crisis period of the 1970s. However, insufficient investments in upgrading these installations with efficient modern technology has resulted in frequent blackouts and engineering inefficiencies. From 2006 to 2017, major hydropower dams in the region have undergone series of retrofitting to become more efficient even in situations of drought as was witnessed in the drought crisis that hit many countries in the region between 2005 and 2010. For instance, among the many hydropower dams, the Manantali dam in Mali and the Kpong dam in Ghana have undergone retrofitting to become more efficient.[581]

In terms of energy justice, which is primarily on the demand-side, West Africa's energy system is unbelievably unjust, access to energy services is often unequal, with energy and fuel poverty often a contested issue. This has left millions of people without access to electricity and in most cases dependent on highly polluting traditional fuels for cooking and heating. Moreover, while energy supply in the region is predominantly insufficient it is very costly. Energy consumers in West Africa are paying among some of the highest prices for unreliable energy supply compared to people in industrialised countries.[582] But the worst affected are low-income house-

---

580 Victoria R. Nalule, *Energy Poverty and Access Challenges in Sub-Saharan Africa: The Role of Regionalism, Energy Poverty and Access Challenges in Sub-Saharan Africa* (Cham: Palgrave Macmillan, 2019), p. 144 <https://doi.org/10.1007/978-3-319-95402-8>.

581 Andritz Hydro, 'Hydropower in West Africa', 2016, pp. 24–25 <https://www.andritz.com/hydronews-africa-14-west-africa-data.pdf>.

582 ECREEE, 'Supporting Energy Efficiency Access in West Africa (SEEA-WA) Project Funded by the European Union'.

holds who pay proportionally more for energy services. This has hindered their ability to accumulate the needed capital necessary for savings and investments in order to escape poverty.[583]

Furthermore, thousands of West Africans die every year by air pollution caused by the use of firewood and charcoal for cooking. Women and children are the primary victims. Such grim energy and fuel inequality and poverty intersects with other pressing complications, such as gender inequity, social injustice, and environmental degradation. Devoid of access to modern energy carriers, rural women and children are normally compelled to a large part of their day searching for firewood as well as burning wood, dung and charcoal indoors for cooking and the preparation of meals.

Poor rural and peri-urban households pay out a larger percentage of their daily income on energy services despite using less energy than wealthy and middle-income urban household use. For these rural and peri-urban households the availability, access and sustainability of clean and modern forms of energy is of supreme importance in order to foster rural economic development and improve social welfare.

Another crucial issue worthy of addressing in the energy space in West Africa is the transition towards clean and low carbon energy. Even though a clean energy transition typifies a fundamental change in the quantity, quality, and structure of energy production and energy use, the term has now been normatively ascribed within the context of climate change.[584] Firewood collection and charcoal production are part of the main causes of deforestation in West Africa and this has had major ecological ramifications.

Albeit that the region contributes less emissions towards climate change. Alongside the entire African continent, the highest price is paid for the region's inability to avert the debilitating effects of this global climate catastrophe.[585] A clean and low carbon energy future would go a long way as an authentic shift from insufficient and unsustainable forms of energy to abundant, affordable and sustainable energy. This transitional future for abundant, clean and sustainable regional energy cannot happen without the inclusion of renewable energy sources, improved nuclear to power technology and cleaner options of fossil-based energy systems.

583 Goldthau and Sovacool.

584 Cleveland and Morris; Goldthau and Sovacool.

585 Africa Progress Panel, *Lights Power Action: Electrifying Africa*.

In West Africa, one of the major projects being undertaken in this regard by ECOWAS Centre for Renewable Energy and Energy Efficiency (ECREEE) is the Regional Off-Grid Electrification Project (ROGEP) that seeks to promote standalone solar systems across the region. The ECOWAS region is abundant in solar energy, ROGEP primarily supports the harmonisation of the regional energy market by providing incentives for the proliferation of stand-alone solar equipment (example, solar lanterns, solar home systems, solar water pumps, solar milling equipment, etc.) for households and enterprises in rural and peri-urban communities that are without access to the centralised grid infrastructure. ROGEP has an entrenched gender strategy as an essential component to aid gender mainstreaming in all project implementation activities.[586]

3.4.3 Future Prospects: Governance of Cross-Border Energy Networks

The development of regional energy infrastructure unveils the governance outlook of cross-border energy networks. Though this section focuses mostly on on-grid electricity interconnection, it highlights the rise in off-grid electricity interconnections mainly solar and wind energy, which ECOWAS countries are adopting in an endeavour to close the energy access gap.

Additionally, petroleum production and gas pipelines have also attracted a lot of attention mostly due to the rise in hydrocarbon discoveries in the West African Transform Margin (WATM) that is, the new geopolitical centre of active oil and gas exploration in Africa. The petroleum production and gas pipeline developments alongside the electricity interconnections are the various aspects of the existing regional energy infrastructure.

The governance of these cross-border energy networks determines and highlights the future prospects of regional energy whether from the perspective of the regional grid interconnection and how that interacts with the dynamic of the centralised versus decentralised systems. As well as the governance of challenges around the regional gas pipeline. And lastly dealing with the overarching prospective regional energy governance issues of reliability and expansion of these regional energy systems.

---

586 ECREEE, 'ROGEP - Regional Off-Grid Electrification Project', 2018 <http://www.ecreee.org/node/87265> [accessed 15 February 2018].

3.4.3.1 Regional Power Pool

With considerable investment financing largely from the Member States, World Bank, European Union and International development agencies, ECOWAS created a regional power pool. This is a regional power grid interconnection with various corridors that has a transnational goal to trade, exchange and share power. The regional power pool is known as the West African Power Pool (WAPP). The regional power pool in West Africa was created two decades ago in 1999.

This power pool is part of a grand scheme to link up the other regional power pools on the entire African continent. These regional power pools are the Southern African Power Pool (SAPP), East African Power Pool (EAPP), Central African Power Pool (PEAC-Pool Energétique d'Afrique Centrale) and the Comité Maghrébin de l'Electricité (COMELEC) of Northern Africa. They would constitute a continent-wide or mega-regional electricity grid system.[587]

West Africa's power pool has been designed to lower electricity prices and expand access through competition thus encouraging trade and investment in electricity. The idea for the formation of WAPP resulted from two situations, the first being the success of the West African Grid System (WAGS) in the 1960s. As well as the feasibility studies conducted by Purdue University that demonstrated the region would benefit immensely from regional electricity integration and trade. This persuaded eventually the 15 member states of ECOWAS to sign up for it.[588]

The West African power pool does not exist in a geographical or sectoral vacuum because there are older initiatives aimed at promoting energy integration at the regional level. This includes River Basin Organisations (RBOs), which are key drivers of regional hydropower cooperation. Cooperation countries are not hesitant to utilise and develop these other existing options whenever necessary to advance their national energy interests. In this context, aside from WAPP, these options include the Organisation pour la mise en valeur du fleuve Gambie (OMVG), Organisation pour la mise en valeur du fleuve Sénégal (OMVS) and the Autorité du Bassin

587 Kathleen J. Hancock, 'Comparative Regionalism and Natural Resources: A Focus on Africa.' *Paper presented at the International Studies Association Annual Convention*. (2013)

588 UNECA, 'Ghana's Experience In Power Interconnections Within The Framework Of ECOWAS'. Frederick T. Sparrow et al. 'Electricity trade and capacity expansion options in West Africa', *Purdue University, West Lafayette, IN* (2002).

du Niger (ABN). These River Basin Projects have been transformed into constituent components of the implementation of the WAPP Infrastructure Programme fundamentally based on realising distinct but mutually reinforcing infrastructure project initiatives.[589]

Practically, the decision-making, commercial and investment agreements all take place in separate sub-regional structures made up of the very same governments, their utilities and private partners involved in the regional power pool (WAPP). The key goal in the medium term is to expand power trading and exchange among the members of the OMVS and OMVG and at the same time integrate these two sub-regional energy organisations fully into the wider WAPP system. Another component of this interlinkage would entail interconnections not only among themselves but with the Côte d'Ivoire-Liberia-Sierra Leone-Guinea (CLSG) power interconnection project as well. One critical aspect in the ongoing institutionalisation of the regional power pool in West Africa is the process of developing a well-resourced energy information sharing capability. The WAPP and OMVS for instance share relevant data, information and coordinate in the preparation of annual reports.[590]

The OMVS is a particularly interesting case, it manages power interconnectivity between four countries namely Senegal, Mali, Mauritania and Guinea. It centrally manages the exchange of electricity from a growing number of hydropower dams in the Senegal basin. It does so on the basis of a fixed, negotiated country allocation of regionally operated dams and rates energy exchanges that are far below regional market value. This dynamic inherent in the RBO approach exemplified by the OMVS and its functional role complements the goals of the West African power pool.[591]

In sum, the complete implementation of the interlinkages of the priority sub-regional power interconnections would fully realise and operationalise the prospect of West Africa's regional power pool. These priority sub-regional power interconnections include the two transnational river basin organisations enumerated above that is, the OMVG and the OMVS power system development programme. Aside from the other earmarked power interconnections of the coastal transmission backbone programme,

---

589 World Bank, *West African Power Pool (WAPP) - Côte d'Ivoire, Sierra Leone, Liberia, and Guinea Power Interconnection Project WAPP. WAPP Integration and Technical Assistance Project.* (Washington, D.C., 2012) <http://documents.worldbank.org/curated/en/116431468006606003/pdf/672960PAD0P1130Official0Use0Only090.pdf> [accessed 1 May 2018].

590 Medinilla, Byiers, and Karaki.

591 Medinilla, Byiers, and Karaki.

inter-zonal transmission hub programme, north-core transmission programme and CLSG power system re-development programme.

3.4.3.2 Regional Petroleum Production and Gas Pipelines

Petroleum production and gas pipelines are beginning to play a critical role in West African energy regionalism. The existence of these unique critical regional energy infrastructures seek to enhance the utilisation of fossil fuels particularly that of natural gas. West Africa's regional pipeline is the 678 km West Africa Gas Pipeline (WAGP), which connects Benin, Ghana, Nigeria, and Togo. The Gas pipeline ties into a larger pipeline in Nigeria. Besides, the four states, the other shareholders include Chevron-Texaco, Shell, NNPC, VRA, Bengaz and Sotogaz. Under the auspices of ECOWAS, negotiations began in 1982 and after a long and arduous process, finally an agreement in 2003 was brokered for the construction of a 600 km pipeline to transport natural gas across the four member countries. First receipts of transported natural gas flowed-in by 2008, but commercial supplies were not available until March 2011.

It must be stated here that the West African region is one of the leading hydrocarbon resource-rich regions in Africa. Particularly in the Gulf of Guinea starting from the Bight of Benin that is, off the coast of Nigeria and across the entire West African Transform Margin (WATM). The WATM, a 1500 kilometre stretch mostly along the coast of Ghana, Côte d'Ivoire, Liberia, and Sierra Leone, as well as parts of the Guinea coastline is the new site for oil accumulation, exploration and extraction. In addition, the coasts of The Gambia and Senegal have witnessed successful exploration with subsequent deals signed with major multi-national energy corporations to begin exploitation.[592]

The regional gas pipeline is a fuel – switching project with the prospect to immensely reduce the overall production costs of power generation through the use of natural gas. The thermal power plants existing in the catchment area of the pipeline run on crude oil, that is a very expensive way to generate power but switching to natural gas the price is set up to be less expensive compared to crude oil. This accounts for about 40 to

592 Authority; Franklin Obeng-Odoom, 'Oil in the West African Transform Margin: Dangers and Possibilities', *International Critical Thought*, 6.1 (2016), 101–18 <https://doi.org/10.1080/21598282.2016.1142385>; ECREEE, 'ROGEP - Regional Off-Grid Electrification Project'.

50 percent price decrease compared to the price of crude oil at its peak price. Therefore, the regional gas pipeline is expected to improve energy access and reduce gas flaring in the Niger Delta region of Nigeria, which is associated with environmental pollution and emissions of greenhouse gases (GHG).

The main associated risk related to the regional gas pipeline that has the potential to affect its future prospects has to do with the gas flow supply risk. Until the reverse side of the pipeline is completed to enable gas supplies from Ghana's western gas fields to feed into the regional gas pipeline. The only source is the Niger Delta which is a volatile area. Gas supply has been interrupted a number of times over the years and this has affected the delivery of gas flows causing delays and major disruptions.

A key observation on this regional effort is that it is mostly spearheaded by the participating states and corporate firms that are directly involved with the pipeline infrastructure. A specialised authority of the regional pipeline is responsible for the regulation of the activities of participating actors. However, it must be emphasised that this major regional energy project is under the aegis of ECOWAS. Therefore, it can be argued that WAGP is a singular initiative of partner states and companies with the intention to benefit from such a regional project and at the same time it takes the form of a priority regional energy institutional project with the aim of meeting the much needed regional energy goals of ECOWAS.

3.4.3.3 Regional Energy Governance Issues

A rapid increase in energy demand is expected in West Africa mainly due to demographic indicators and economic growth. The twin issues of reliability and scalability/expansion of energy supply would critically inform discussions on the governance of energy provision in the region. Whether it is executed through a continued extension of the regional energy infrastructures that is, generation sources, power grid interconnections and hydrocarbon pipelines or through a disruptive energy technology adoption such as the use of small-scale solar and battery storage systems that operate in the periphery of the centralised grid system. It is without doubt that energy supply must and should expand at a rapidly exponential rate as approximately 170 million people (1 out of 3 persons) in West Africa would have an urgent and emergent need to be connected to reliable, abundant, modern and affordable energy services.[593]

The current West African energy system is characterised by available fossil and non-fossil fuel resources, cash-strapped energy utilities and a weak regulatory framework. All these pose enormous energy governance challenges. To remedy most of these challenges going forward would be to implement governance strategies that would leverage the use of centralised and decentralised energy supply systems to meet the ever-growing regional energy demand in terms of reliability and expansion.

Centralised and decentralised energy supply systems have their merits and demerits. A lot of reasons have been adduced in global energy policy circles about how developing and emerging economies like those found in West Africa can leapfrog by pursuing aggressively decentralized energy systems. That is, energy systems built from scratch and wholly dependent on mainly periphery disruptive energy technologies such as off-grid solutions. This narrative is inspired by Silicon Valley.

The argument is further advanced, that by doing so, West Africa can side-step the need for centralised transmission and distribution infrastructure together with the use of the present inefficient energy utilities that is currently operational in the region. It can be said that in terms of ownership most of these energy utilities are nationalised and monopolised. Often cited as a basis to push this claim is the use of the anecdotal evidence of the mobile telephony revolution in Africa that leapfrogged the lack of telephone lines.[594]

However, the huge energy deficit in the region does require a dominant role for centralised energy infrastructure that caters also for decentralised distributed generation as well. Definitely, there is a role for distributed energy systems such as smart grids, better conductors, cheaper transmission alternatives, small natural gas-fuelled generators, combined heat and power plants, electricity storage, solar photovoltaics (PV) and distributed

593 ECOWAS, *Ecowas Energy Efficiency Policy* (Praia, Cape Verde, 2015) <http://www.ecreee.org> [accessed 17 August 2016].

594 Ben Leo, Jared Kalow, and Todd Moss, 'What Can We Learn about Energy Access and Demand from Mobile-Phone Surveys? Nine Findings from Twelve African Countries', *CGD Policy Paper*, 120. February (2018) <https://www.cgdev.org/publication/what-can-we-learn-about-energy-access-and-demand-mobile-phone-surveys>.

energy resources (DERs)[595] in the region's overall energy system. But to be able to reap the full benefits of abundant energy provision rapidly both systems have to be deployed in a complementary manner. This raises the stakes for energy systems governance especially in the areas of the reliability and scalability of an integrated energy systems infrastructure that brings together both centralised and decentralised systems.

Another aspect that requires attention in relation to these twin governance issues in the future is the role of emerging actors such as prosumers. Prosumers are leading actors fronting the energy innovation charge with respect to decentralised energy systems. The issues that would be of necessity is to deal with governance dynamics bordering on the role of prosumers. This would encompass their usage of technological improvements like DERs; the provision of policy incentives; consumer choices in terms of the available specific energy technologies and services provided by them; the regulatory framework needed to guide their operations in an ever-expanding regional energy economy; and the reliability of such a participation in the regional energy economy.

A particular focus on the key technological innovation and its role highlights the nature of the energy governance issues of reliability and scalability/expansion that needs to be addressed in the future regional energy space of West Africa. One major energy innovation is the introduction of DERs, which fall under distributed energy systems as opposed to a centralised grid network and this is likely to become transformative in the future energy prospects of the region. This is expected to influence aspects of the polycentric governance of the regional energy system.

The Electric Power Research Institute (EPRI), an independent energy think tank, in its integrated grid programme that was initiated in 2014 emphasises the importance and significance of DERs on the centralised grid system in the future.[596] This assertion raises the issue of the successful integration of DERs into the existing centralised power grid. Further, it highlights ways of improving energy system design particularly at country level in order to accommodate the penetration of DERs while at the same

595 Distributed Energy Resources (DERs) are decentralised energy systems that include small-scale renewables, storage and make provision for demand response and management.

596 EPRI, *The Integrated Grid: Realizing the Full Value of Central and Distributed Energy Resources* (Palo Alto, CA, 2014) <https://www.epri.com/#/pages/product/3002002733/?lang=en-us>.

time maintaining the levels of quality and reliability in the operations of an integrated grid system.

At both country and regional levels transitioning to an integrated grid equipped with distributed energy resources (DERs) and complemented with periphery off-grid solutions is feasible but at the same time not inexpensive. It stands to raise serious energy governance concerns especially in relation to the management of the combined and integrated energy system and its attendant effects on the reliability of the energy infrastructure. Moreover, the expansion of such a system also highlights the issues of cost-effectiveness in the introduction of these integrated systems, affordability of the energy produced and the overall usefulness of such a system in the long term for economic development in a region that is already paying high-energy bills for unreliable energy supply.

That said the verdict on the suitability of centralised and decentralised energy systems in the ECOWAS region reveal a number of options in the governance of regional energy systems. Local communities and individuals at country level with low levels of energy access, what the World Bank refers to as *Tier One* access, would benefit somewhat from stand-alone decentralised energy systems that have seen a sharp decline in costs.[597]

In order for low-income communities in the region to meet set targets in the SE4ALL by 2030, emphasis on decentralised stand-alone systems to deliver household energy and improve economic and social welfare benefits is well placed and essential. In certain places, the use of off-grid solar systems will help people climb the so-called energy ladder. However, excluding these decentralised alternatives will literally render the attainment of the 2030 target of universal access an impossible feet.

On the other hand, the importance to extend the centralized grid network, that is, the core critical energy infrastructure cannot be emphasised enough on its usefulness in the expansion of universal energy access beyond the current estimates in the ECOWAS region. The power grid interconnections in the region need to be extended to unreached corners to deliver much needed electricity that would power fast growing cities, spur economic growth and create the much-needed jobs. The value gained from this goes beyond provisioning basic rural household energy services like lights but facilitating solid economic activity consequently transforming the way of life of low-income communities and their inhabitants who cannot afford energy in the region.

597 Mikul Bhatia and Niki Angelou, 'Beyond Connections: Energy Access Redefined', *ESMAP Technical Report*, 008/15, (World Bank, Washington, DC: 2015)

The expansion and scaling of large centralised grid infrastructure plays a pivotal role in the energy fortunes of the region. This is because a central grid system has been tried and tested. This massive and absolutely essential grid is the existing system that underpins all the periphery technological disruptions such as off-grid solar and the like that occur in the energy sector and this should not be taken for granted. In addition, this core grid infrastructure exists within a proven governance framework. It is essential to note here that there is no advanced economy with an all periphery energy infrastructure without a centred scale.[598] Therefore, country-level grid interconnections and the grid networks at the regional level in West Africa that deliver electricity cannot afford to function in its current form without a massive scalable expansion.

The governance issues of reliability and scalability/expansion that are likely to shape the West African energy space in the coming decades would rely on two key things namely the construction and modernisation of a large-scale centralised grid infrastructure and distributed off-grid infrastructure. These two system infrastructures will be incrementally deployed and their respective system technologies will play a greater role in the future governance of regional energy systems both at country and region-wide levels.[599]

Ultimately, no approach (be it centralised or distributed and renewable or fossil-based) can singularly solve the surfacing energy governance issues that relate to energy poverty without finding a way to deliver energy in West Africa. Reliable and affordable energy supply ought to be more accessible to the regions emerging industrial and commercial sectors as well as its low-income households. Again, this holistic approach and the governance of emerging actors such as prosumers serve as an opportunity to set out a roadmap for governments, energy sector markets and communities in the region to work together at multiple levels to improve energy system productivity and performance to spur economic growth and prosperity.

---

598 Rose M. Mutiso, 'How to bring affordable, sustainable electricity to Africa',(July, 2019) [Video file]. Retrieved from https://www.ted.com/talks/rose_m_mutiso_how_to_bring_affordable_sustainable_electricity_to_africa

599 Samuel Oguah and Debabrata Chattopadhyay, 'A Pro-Grid Middle Path for Africa: Sub-Saharan Region Electricity Upgrades', *IEEE Power and Energy Magazine*, 17.2 (2019), 61–68 <https://doi.org/10.1109/MPE.2018.2884114>.

3.5 Institutional Foundations of ECOWAS Energy Regionalism

The inclusion of ECOWAS energy regionalism as a legal and regional priority was from the onset part of the founding of the organisation under the 1975 ECOWAS Treaty. It was framed as a policy objective with the introduction of the ECOWAS Energy Policy of 1982. In the revised ECOWAS Treaty of 1993, energy issues became very evident in Community rules and featured the building of bilateral and trilateral energy partnerships alongside establishing an institutional framework that would govern the regional energy sector.

These legal and policy documents highlighted the need for harmonisation and coordination of national energy policies among member states. This would lead to promoting regional energy integration programmes, projects, and activities. It would eventually enable collective energy autonomy and sufficiency in the region. The creation of a West African energy region that is open and fosters a competitive regional energy sector requires the presence of an appropriate institutional and regulatory framework. This includes country level legislations as well as harmonized technical and commercial standards and rules for the promotion and protection of investments.

In line with this the Energy Protocol came into force in 2003 to add to the gamut of legal and institutional documentation that would advance the energy space in ECOWAS. The protocol served as the general outline for the adoption of the different national energy legislations required for the development of regional energy institutions like the West African Power Pool (WAPP) inter alia.

3.5.1 The Legal Framework of ECOWAS Energy: ECOWAS Treaty and Energy Protocol

3.5.1.1 ECOWAS Revised Treaty

Legal provisions under Articles 3, 22, 26, 28, and 55 of the ECOWAS Revised Treaty of 1993 provides the basic tenets for the promotion, cooperation, integration and development of the regional energy sector at both country and regional levels. Even though ECOWAS Heads of State and Government by Decision A/DEC.3/5/82 had adopted a regional energy policy seeking to harmonize member states' energy policies and increase collective energy autonomy.[600] The Revised Treaty enshrined this policy objective as a legal principle in Community law.

The Revised ECOWAS Treaty of 1993 consolidated the idea of building the regional energy sector as a standard legal normative in ECOWAS jurisprudence. The legal process was realised by the addition of 93 different articles to the amended Treaty. Among these new articles the energy sector was significantly stressed with about 19 mentions to draw attention to its policy significance and importance to region building. Five of the articles strongly emphasise the place of energy in the region building (that is, the binding and integrative) agenda of ECOWAS. These are Article 3, 22, 26, 28 and Article 55.

Article 3 deals with the aims and goals of ECOWAS. It calls for harmonizing and coordinating country level policies and promoting programmes, projects, and activities that would integrate the region under 19 thematic areas. Among them energy is listed as a one of the priority areas vis-à-vis other energy related areas such as industry and technology.[601]

Article 22 is concerned with the institutional composition of the organisation plus the eight technical commissions that constitute the regional body. In here, the function of energy policy is duly asserted within the responsibilities of the commission in charge of industry, science and technology, and energy. Energy is considered in 12 essential sectors earmarked as vehicles for the promotion of regional collective action to enable competitiveness and modernisation of the regional economy.[602]

Article 26 seeks to create a solid base for industrialisation that would promote collective self-reliance. It permits the promotion of priority sectors. This includes joint industrial projects and the creation of multinational enterprises in the natural resources and energy sectors.[603]

Article 28 focuses specifically on all aspects of the energy policy framework of ECOWAS. It calls on member states to ensure effective develop-

600 ECOWAS, 'A/DEC.3/5/82 Decision Of The Authority Of Heads Of State And Government Of The Economic Community Of West African States Relating To The ECOWAS Energy Policy'.

601 ECOWAS, 'Economic Community of West African States (ECOWAS): Revised Treaty'.pp.5 – 6

602 Hancock, 'Energy Regionalism and Diffusion in Africa: How Political Actors Created the ECOWAS Center for Renewable Energy and Energy Efficiency'. ECOWAS, 'Economic Community of West African States (ECOWAS): Revised Treaty'.p.15

603 ECOWAS, 'Economic Community of West African States (ECOWAS): Revised Treaty'.pp.17 – 19

ment of energy resources. It also calls on them to cooperate on ensuring a steady supply of hydrocarbons, and promote the development and use of clean and renewable energy technologies within the frame of their energy diversification policies. In this case it makes particular reference to utilising the vast solar energy resources in the region.

Again, it encourages the harmonization of the various national energy development plans for instance by prioritising the regional inter-connectivity of electricity grids. Additionally, it advocates for coordination in devising a common energy policy for research, exploitation, production and distribution as well as institute a mechanism for unearthing collective solutions for the many energy issues faced in the region among them are energy transmission issues, the shortage of skilled technicians, and the financing of energy projects.[604]

Article 55 enumerates the principle for the completion of the economic and monetary union of ECOWAS. As part of the completion of the ECOWAS economic union, the adoption of a common policy on energy alongside five other areas is a prerequisite.[605]

3.5.1.2 ECOWAS Energy Protocol

In addition to the revised treaty provisions, Heads of State in 2003 adopted and signed the ECOWAS Energy Protocol. This came into force after ratification from at least nine member states. The Protocol has enabled ECOWAS and member states to speed-up prior energy projects and initiate a number of novel major energy processes. This has culminated into major regional initiatives with specialised institutions that serve as a foundation for constructing a strong ECOWAS energy regionalism alongside the main regional institutions in ECOWAS. Notable among these specialised institutions are the West Africa Power Pool (WAPP), ECOWAS Regional Electricity Regulatory Authority (ERERA), West African Gas Pipeline (WAGP), West African Gas Pipeline Authority (WAGPA), and the ECOWAS Centre for Renewable Energy and Energy Efficiency (ECREEE).

According to Article 2 of this Protocol, energy cooperation was determined by complementarity and mutual benefit with a view to augment

---

604 ECOWAS, 'Economic Community of West African States (ECOWAS): Revised Treaty'.pp. 20–21

605 ECOWAS, 'Economic Community of West African States (ECOWAS): Revised Treaty'.pp. 34–35

investment into the energy sector as well as develop the trade of energy within the ECOWAS region. It also encourages cooperation among states in the mitigation of energy supply disruptions, modernisation and interconnection of transmission infrastructure which includes high-voltage power grids and high-pressure natural gas pipelines.[606]

Articles 6, 7 and 18 of the Protocol relate respectively to competition, wheeling, and access to resources hence having a direct influence on the operation of the regional energy space especially relating to electricity and gas markets. These energy markets are arranged according to the legal principles enshrined in the articles although member states require agreement on implementation timelines. In one option, member states are obligated to contest market distortions and obstacles to competition in relation to energy market activities by adopting the necessary legal provisions in their domestic law.[607]

As an alternative, member states have committed themselves to ensure open and non-discriminatory access to energy generation sources and transmission equipment situated in their respective territories. Granted authorisations, licences and other contractual documents will facilitate access to energy resources and enable exploitation of these resources in a transparent and non-discriminatory manner. Also, member states have committed to facilitate free-wheeling of energy flows on their territories by treating them in the same or in a more favourable manner than their own products and by cooperating in the establishment of new wheeling arrangements.[608]

Finally, the ECOWAS Energy Protocol encourages dispute resolution through arbitration among parties. It makes provision for arbitration between contracting parties or between them and their investors in cases of a dispute under the three following options namely an appeal to national jurisdictions, an appeal to the agreed proceedings foreseen in contracts, an appeal to international arbitration and conciliation proceedings. The arbitration and conciliation proceedings are guided by norms put forward by a number of international organisations. The international organisations include the International Centre for the Settlement of Investment Disputes (ICSID), the arbitration settlement of the United Nations Commission of International Trade Law (UNCITRAL), the Institute of Arbitration of the Stockholm Chamber of Commerce and the arbitration proceedings of the

606 ECOWAS, *ECOWAS Energy Protocol A/P4/1/03*.
607 ECOWAS, *ECOWAS Energy Protocol A/P4/1/03*.
608 ECOWAS, *ECOWAS Energy Protocol A/P4/1/03*.

Organization for the Harmonization of Business Law in Africa (OHADA) which is maintained by the Common Court of Justice and Arbitration (CCJA).[609]

3.5.2 General Institutions

The establishing Treaty of ECOWAS specifies the composition of various organs and agencies that compliment other institutions in the Community and is responsible for the functioning and performance of the regional body including sector-specific developments in the region such as energy. Both institutions of ECOWAS, general and specialised, are creations of community law and are established to achieve defined ends, in this case economic regionalism or integration.

ECOWAS, under its establishing Treaty, infers on these organs and institutions, general competence that ensure a proper functioning of the energy sector. These consist of the Authority of Heads of State and Government, the Council of Ministers, the Community Parliament, the Community Court of Justice, and the ECOWAS Commission. It is important to note that on its website, ECOWAS does not represent the Authority of Heads of State and Government and the Council of Ministers as institutions of ECOWAS. However, it will be considered here as an institution based on the contents of its founding and amended Treaties. In addition to the general institutions and the legal framework that brings it into being, ECOWAS is instrumental in the development of major regional energy infrastructures. It does so by obtaining funds for feasibility studies of the selected regional infrastructure, which in turn is used to attract investments for the particular regional energy project.

3.5.2.1 Authority of Heads of State and Government

Simply known as the Authority, it was established under Article 7 of the revised ECOWAS Treaty it is the highest institution in the hierarchy with the sole responsibility of giving general direction and providing incentive to the development and achievement of the aims and objectives of the Community. At the helm of this superior executive body of ECOWAS is the Chairman of the Authority of Heads of State and Government. The

609 ECOWAS, *ECOWAS Energy Protocol A/P4/1/03*.

Chairman is the current Head of State and Government appointed by the other fifteen Heads of State and Government to oversee the affairs for a period of one year. The general responsibility of the Authority is to initiate, direct and oversee the strategy of ECOWAS which includes its overall energy strategy. Article 7 continues to empower the Authority to refer abuse of power by any institution to the Community Court this includes energy bodies and agencies.[610]

In terms of its functions, the Authority is empowered to execute a number of them. The functions include (a) to determine the general policy guidelines of the Community, by giving directives, harmonising and co-ordinating economic, scientific, technical, cultural and social policies of Member States; (b) to oversee the functioning of Community institutions and follow up the implementation of Community objectives; (c) to prepare and adopt rules of procedure; (d) to appoint the President of the ECOWAS Commission in accordance with the provisions of community law (e) to appoint external auditors as recommended by the Council; (f) to delegate to the Council responsibility to take decisions under Article 9 of the Treaty; and (g) to refer any matter to the Community Court of Justice when it confirms that a Member State or institution of the Community has failed to honour and comply with any of its obligations. It also refers to instances where an institution of the Community has acted beyond the limits of its authority or has abused the powers conferred on it by the provisions of the Revised Treaty, by a decision of the Authority or a Regulation of the Council.[611]

It limits the power of referral relating to incidences of abuse to institutions specified by provisions in the Revised Treaty, decisions of the Authority or a regulation of the Council. The Authority holds two kinds of meetings. The first is the ordinary session, which is held at least once in a year. However, by virtue of the amendment of certain portions of the Revised Treaty contained in supplementary legislation, the ordinary session is held at least twice a year.[612]

The second group of meetings recognised under treaty law for the Authority is the extraordinary session. This is often convened at the behest of the Chairman of the Authority. Considering the Acts of the Authority,

---

610 ECOWAS, 'Economic Community of West African States (ECOWAS): Revised Treaty'.

611 Jerry Ukaigwe, *ECOWAS Law*, *ECOWAS Law*, 2016, pp. 56–57 <https://doi.org/10.1007/978-3-319-26233-8>.

612 Ukaigwe, pp. 57–59.

as provided by the Revised Treaty, the Authority shall act by decisions. All member states and institutions of the Community are bound by these decisions. The Authority adopts its decisions by unanimity, consensus or a two-thirds majority of the member states and the employment of any of these voting systems will depend on the subject matter under consideration. The Revised Treaty provides that a protocol will be made which shall set out a system that will be used in respect of any measure, but until that protocol is made, the Authority is limited to adopting its decision by consensus. It is common knowledge that the Treaty is *traité cadre.* Thus, it is not expected to provide in detail everything that the Authority puts in place only the outline is required.[613] This applies to matters relating to regional energy issues.

3.5.2.2 Council of Ministers

The Council is responsible for the functioning and development of the Community and for making policy decisions relating to the efficient and harmonious functioning of the Community. The Council effectuates the functions and decisions of the Authority as well as its own regulations that are binding on member states. The Minister in charge of ECOWAS affairs, held by the foreign minister of the chairing country of the Authority, automatically becomes the Chairman of the Council of Ministers. He/she presides over all other ECOWAS statutory annual meetings at ministerial and senior governmental levels such as the technical committees which include energy and infrastructure.[614]

In terms of responsibilities and functions, the Council of Ministers sees to it that the Community develops and functions properly. These specific functions among others include (a) making recommendations to the Authority on any action aimed at attaining the objectives of the Community; (b) appointing all statutory appointees other than the President of the Commission; (c) issuing directives on matters concerning co-ordination and harmonisation of economic integration policies—where the Authority delegates to it the appropriate power to do so; and (d) making recommendations to the Authority on the appointment of the external auditors.[615]

---

613 Ukaigwe, pp. 57–59.
614 Ukaigwe, pp. 59–61.
615 Ukaigwe, pp. 59–61.

The Council holds two kinds of meetings, ordinary sessions and extraordinary sessions. The ordinary sessions take place at least twice in a year and extraordinary sessions occur at the request of the Chairman who has the power to convene these meetings. However, a member can as well request for such a meeting provided a simple majority of the member states support the request. The Revised Treaty provides that the Council shall act by regulation.[616] The Council adopts regulation, depending on the subject matter under consideration. Regional energy issues decided by the Council are effected by issuing energy regulations.

This is done by unanimity, consensus or a two-thirds majority of member states. Similar to the provision in Article 9 (2) and (3) of the Revised Treaty, a protocol ought to be made for defining at what point or in what circumstances, should any voting system be employed. However, the Council is empowered to adopt its regulation through consensus until the protocol is adopted and made enforceable. Notably, the binding nature of a regulation differs from that of a decision. Regulations of the community binds all institutions under the purview of the Council. Consequently, regulations made by the Council will not have binding effect on the Authority of Heads of State because it is not an institution under the Council. Regulations will be binding only on member states after approval from the Authority. It is significant to note that the Council may, on delegated powers, issue directives and can make recommendations in certain circumstances. Hence, regulations are not the only Acts issued by the Council of Ministers.[617]

3.5.2.3 ECOWAS Commission

The Commission is the main institution essentially responsible for the implementation of the decisions and policies of the governing bodies of the Community. At the helm of this Executive arm of the Community is the President of the ECOWAS Commission appointed by the Authority for a non-renewable period of four years. A Vice President and 13 Commissioners assist him. In general, the Commission oversees the promotion of regional development projects and programmes, organising ministerial meetings for various sectors to examine the sectoral issues, which con-

616 Ukaigwe, pp. 59–61.
617 Ukaigwe, pp. 59–61.

tribute to the realisation of the objectives of the Community and prepares draft laws and work programmes.[618]

For these purposes, the powers conferred on it by the Supplementary Protocol A/SP.1/06/06 of 14th June 2006 notably include: The powers to 1) make proposals to the Authority of Heads of State and Government and the Council of Ministers to enable them to declare their rulings on the main direction of the policies pertaining to member states and the Community as well as formulate recommendations and opinions; and 2) issue regulations to implement the laws of the Community, collect useful information and engage in consultations with Community institutions and bodies.[619]

The Commission is therefore involved in the development of draft laws submitted for adoption to the Authority of Heads of State, or the Council of Ministers whose meetings it is also responsible for organising. Under Community law, a regional competition body embedded under the scope of work of the Commission is responsible for overseeing commercial activities in the community market with a view to ascertain practices and prevent behaviour that may distort the efficient functioning of the market and may have adverse effects on the interest of consumers.[620]

The ECOWAS Regional Competition Authority (ERCA) was launched in May 2019 although compliance rules in relation to Community Competition Rules were adopted in 2008. It is headquartered in Banjul, The Gambia. This competition agency is tasked with the responsibility to maintain the application of competition rules in the regional bloc and to prevent market abuse, dominance and anti-trust practices.[621] The agency's coming into force is part of the processes to complete the economic union of the bloc. Of which the energy sector is a major priority sector. This major step in institutionalising ECOWAS competition policy with oversight from the Commission through the establishment of the authority refocuses its purpose back to the regional economy. For an organisation that has mainly been engrossed in security matters the shift to re-engage in its original mission of establishing and completing a common market is laudable.

---

618 Ukaigwe, p. 68.

619 Ukaigwe, p. 68.

620 Ukaigwe, p. 68.

621 ECOWAS, 'Adopting Community Competition Rules and the Modalities of their Application within ECOWAS', *Supplementary Act A/SA.1/12/08*, (Abuja, Nigeria : 2008); ECOWAS, 'On the Establishment, Functions And Operation of the Regional Competition Authority for ECOWAS', *Supplementary Act A/SA.2/12/08*, (Abuja, Nigeria : 2008)

The competition authority would have a significant impact on regional energy market activities and the work of regional energy bodies especially on issues bordering on anti-trust practices in the energy sector. Its general objective is to facilitate regional investments as well as preserve and stimulate regional competitiveness through the prohibition of dominant and anti-trust behaviour. It is also endowed with broad powers including to issue injunctions against anti-trust practices ranging from the prohibition against entering into agreements to their cancellation, as well as to sanction and authorise mergers and acquisitions.[622]

Another unique aspect of the ECOWAS Commission's structure is its technical committees. These special Technical Commissions are provided for as institutions of the Community under Article 22 of the revised Treaty however, they have been renamed as committees. It is clear from the provision that new technical committees (commissions) were included to the committees created by the original Treaty. The Authority whenever it deems appropriate can restructure the existing committees and even establish new ones. In addition, each technical committee shall comprise of representatives of the member states.

Within the confines of community law, every committee within its field of competence shall prepare Community projects and programmes and submits them for consideration at the Council. The functions of the technical committees also entail the harmonisation and co-ordination of projects and programmes of the Community. As well as monitoring and facilitating the application of Revised Treaty provisions and related protocols that pertain to its area of responsibility. Finally, it carries out any other functions assigned to it provided under the Revised Treaty.[623]

3.5.2.4 Community Parliament

The Protocol relating to the Parliament was signed in Abuja on 6th August, 1994 and entered into force on 14th March 2002. It provides for the structure, composition, competence and other matters relating to the Parliament. Also known as the ECOWAS Parliament, the Community

---

622 ECOWAS, 'Adopting Community Competition Rules and the Modalities of their Application within ECOWAS', *Supplementary Act A/SA.1/12/08.*; ECOWAS, 'On the Establishment, Functions and Operation of the Regional Competition Authority for ECOWAS', *Supplementary Act A/SA.2/12/08.*

623 Ukaigwe, p. 68.

Parliament, is a forum for dialogue, consultation and consensus for representatives of the people of West Africa with the aim of promoting regional integration. It was established under Article 6 and 13 of the ECOWAS Revised Treaty of 1993.[624]

The structure of the Parliament is divided into two arms namely the political and administrative arms. The political arm is composed of the plenary, the bureau and the conference of bureaux. Serving as an advisory Parliament, the plenary section is the highest body of the Parliament and its decisions are binding on other structures. In addition, it adopts all resolutions of Parliament, which are to be forwarded to the decision – making bodies of the Community. The Bureau is the governing organ of the Parliament and it consists of the Speaker and all the Deputy Speakers of the Parliament. They determine the draft agenda and all programmes or business of sessions amid various other functions.[625]

The Conference of Bureaux consists of the Speaker, Chairmen or Deputy Chairmen and the Rapporteur of each of the Standing Committees. They work with the bureau of the Parliament to prepare the draft annual work-plan taking into account the priority Community programs including other functions. They collaborate closely with country and AU level Parliaments. The Parliament's composition is made up of 115 seats with members coming from the 15 members states. States have a guaranteed minimum of five seats. The remaining seats are shared based on population sizes of the member states. In this regard, Nigeria has 35 seats, Ghana 8 seats, Cote d'Ivoire 7 seats, while Burkina Faso, Guinea, Mali, Niger and Senegal have six seats each. The others are Benin, Cape Verde, The Gambia, Guinea Bissau, Liberia, Sierra Leone and Togo each have five seats.[626]

In terms of competencies, the Parliament is empowered to consider issues concerning human rights and fundamental freedoms of citizens; interconnection of energy networks; interconnection of communication links between member states; interconnection of telecommunications systems; increased cooperation in the area of radio, television and other intra and inter-Community media links; as well as development of national communication systems.[627]

---

624 Ukaigwe, pp. 61–63.
625 Ukaigwe, pp. 61–63.
626 Ukaigwe, pp. 61–63.
627 Ukaigwe, pp. 61–63.

The Parliament is consulted on matters relating to public health policies and issues including those caused by energy related matters such as air pollution, oil spills etc. It can also be consulted for issues relating to common educational policy such as harmonising existing systems and specialisation of existing universities. Other areas they can be consulted is fine-tuning of educational standards within the Community to meet international standards, matters relating to youth and sports, scientific and technological research as well as environment policy. Lastly, they consider any other issues affecting the Community, especially relating to the review of the ECOWAS Treaty, citizenship and social integration. On these issues, the Parliament may make recommendations to the appropriate institutions and organs of the Community.[628]

3.5.2.5 ECOWAS Court of Justice

ECOWAS Court of Justice, otherwise known as the ECOWAS Court, was established under Article 15 of the Revised Treaty. It is governed by the initial 1991 Protocol, which was subsequently amended by supplementary Protocols 2005, and 2006 respectively.[629] It is mandated to ensure the observance of the law and the principles of equity in the interpretation and application of the provisions of the Revised Treaty and all other subsidiary legal instruments adopted by the Community.

The ECOWAS Court is the only Community body with appellate jurisdiction for decisions taken by institutions of the Community including specialised energy agencies such as ERERA, WAPP etc. Remarkably, the Court possesses wide-ranging authority over disputes originating from the application and interpretation of laws, acts and decisions of the Community or breaches by member states in terms of obligations obtained under these laws.[630]

628 ECOWAS Parliament, 'Parlement de La CEDEAO / ECOWAS Parliament', *About Us*, 2018 <http://parl.ecowas.int/en/about-us/> [accessed 12 June 2018].

629 ECOWAS Community Court of Justice, 'Protocol A/P.l/7/91 On the Community Court Of Justice' (Abuja: ECOWAS, 1991); ECOWAS Community Court of Justice, 'Supplememtary Protocol A/Sp.1/01/05 Amending the Preamble and Articles 1, 2, 9 and 30 of Protocol A/P.1/7/91 Relating to the Community Court of Justice and Article 4 Paragraph 1 of the English Version of the said Protocol' (Abuja: ECOWAS, 2005).

630 Ukaigwe, pp. 70–100.

The Community Court's authority extends to all issues including energy matters determined in any agreement among member states, or with ECOWAS and those that give it jurisdiction. In addition, it has reach on any other matter entrusted to it by Protocols and Decisions of the Community. Additionally, the Authority of Heads of State and Government refers cases to the ECOWAS Court on any dispute or matter of contention other than those cited in the Protocols of which the Court of Justice has jurisdiction.[631]

As a final point, the Court, which is empowered to hear cases on human rights violations in any member state can receive cases from individuals or any legal entity. It also exercises its appellate jurisdiction by hearing appeals on the judgement and legality of any Act of the Community that may cause a grievance. The ECOWAS Court also exercises advisory and arbitral competencies. It plays that role by providing legal opinion and acting as an arbitrator until the Arbitration Tribunal of the Community is put in place.[632]

3.5.3 Specialised Institutions

ECOWAS has restructured itself by creating specialised institutions to deal with region specific energy infrastructural projects and other energy issues such as regulation, governance, policy research and formulation. They include institutions like West African Power Pool (WAPP), ECOWAS Regional Electricity Regulatory Authority (ERERA), ECOWAS Centre for Renewable Energy and Energy Efficiency (ECREEE) as well as the West African Gas Pipeline (WAGP) of which it maintains an observer status because of its vital significance to the regional energy priorities and architecture.

3.5.3.1 West Africa Power Pool (WAPP)

WAPP is composed of national electricity utility companies and multinational electricity operators. They make up the principal participants of this regional body responsible for cross-border electricity trade and exchanges in the ECOWAS region. The main purpose of WAPP is to facilitate

631 Ukaigwe, pp. 70–100.
632 Ukaigwe, pp. 70–100.

the cross-border trade of electricity. It does so primarily by developing, building and maintaining cross-border power infrastructure, securing investment for national energy generation, transmission and interconnection when needed as well as governing by an operational framework the interconnected regional energy infrastructure to facilitate smooth exchanges of electricity in the region.

WAPP issues rules and acts that are the outcome of agreements between its participating members. These acts are only applicable between the signatory members as it operates the regional electricity infrastructure. It applies rules and acts and these have binding effect on member states. Other responsibilities it undertakes are operational planning for the expansion and scaling of the regional grid interconnections as well as investment promotion into the regional power sector complementing national efforts.

WAPP exercises its operational planning by recommending planning criteria and proposals on electricity infrastructural development through the preparation of strategic regional power master plans for endorsement by the ECOWAS Commission. Concerning the governance of the ECOWAS electricity trade exchanges and market, it develops technical rules applicable to the respective participating national power utilities. It also has specific committees made up of representatives of the national power operators that serves as fora for tackling issues that confront the regional power pool. The technical rules of operation and access to the regional electricity transmission network are submitted to the regional power regulatory body, ERERA for approval.[633]

3.5.3.2 ECOWAS Regional Electricity Regulatory Authority (ERERA)

ERERA is responsible for regulating the cross-border electricity market in ECOWAS. Regionally, ERERA is to WAPP what the national regulators are to national electricity operators. Additionally, with reference to the community judicial system to which they both belong, it is important to recall that the legal nature of the acts and decisions of the two institutions differ. The regulatory authority issues regulations and decisions that are binding and directly applicable in the ECOWAS zone and their application is guaranteed by member states in their territory. All these regulations and decisions of ERERA are subject to appeal before the ECOWAS Court of Justice, which intervenes in the process as an appellate jurisdiction. ER-

633 ECOWAS Regional Electricity Regulatory Authority (ERERA).

ERA participates fully in all the activities of WAPP, including the General Assembly meetings with the same rights as the operators but it has no right to vote in proceedings.[634]

On the subject of transmission tariffs and ancillary services, it is necessary that this is done by means of dialogue on the definition and implementation of the methodology of transmission tariffs and commercial rules in the regional power market. This is in spite of the fact that ERERA will determine or revise the cost accounting rules and the tariff structure, approve tariff proposals submitted by operators, publish applicable tariffs and control their application,

ERERA organises a system for the collection and management of information on power exchanges and the performance of participants in the power sector. It does this in collaboration with national regulators, WAPP, transmission network managers, market operators and other sub-regional and regional institutions. One of the main tasks assigned to ERERA by its governing document is to caution and sanction anti-trust practices, abuse of dominant positions and high-risk situations, which could affect negatively the proper functioning of the regional power market. Moreover, ERERA works in concert with national power regulators and their respective authorities. In some countries there are two categories of national authorities that may act on the same matters arising from discrepancies occurring in the power trade exchanges these are administrative authorities and judicial authorities.[635]

The constitutive laws of ERERA confer on it the responsibility to establish and implement efficient procedures for the resolution of disputes between participants of the regional market and supervise the proper application of these procedures. ERERA is empowered with the authority to resolve disputes between all public or private participants provided the dispute relates to the application and interpretation of any regulation relating to the regional electricity market. It also resolves issues where the facts or behaviours of participants affect the smooth operation of cross-border electricity exchanges. In the exercise of its dispute and conflict resolution function ERERA acts on its own instance or any natural or legal person

634 Article 23 of the Convention on the organisation and operation of WAPP

635 ECOWAS Regional Electricity Regulatory Authority (ERERA); Ibrahima Thiam, *Regulatory Issues of the Regional Power Market: West Africa Case* (Abuja,Nigeria, 2011) <https://pubs.naruc.org> [accessed 3 January 2018].

with a stake in the matter may refer to it cases. It takes decisions on mediation, conciliation and sanctions of breaches or violations observed.[636]

ERERA's governing rules require it to inform the ECOWAS Commission, WAPP, national regulators and any other person with legitimate interest in the disputes under review. Its decisions are obligatory and binding as well as being subject to appeals before the ECOWAS Court of Justice. The Court of Justice issues its decision with respect to the legality and application of Community law.[637]

In each member state, the decisions of ERERA are implemented according to the rules of proceedings issued by ERERA. The signatory countries guarantee the application of ERERA's decisions in their jurisdictions. In the case where a country fails to take necessary measures to ensure the implementation of the decisions taken by ERERA. A referral is made to the ECOWAS Commission to implement the provisions of the ECOWAS Treaty that relates to the applicable sanctions on the failure to respect the necessary obligations.[638]

3.5.3.3 West African Gas Pipeline (WAGP)

The WAGP was suggested by ECOWAS in 1982 as a regional energy infrastructure project that would harness the vast natural gas potential in the region. It was completed in 2007 with the goal of using flare gas in Nigeria to feed power stations in neighbouring countries. WAGP was fully established leveraging on private financial capital and using competitive market rules. The vehicle for executing WAGP is the West African Gas Pipeline Company Limited (WAPCo). WAPCo owns and controls the pipeline, a consortium between public and private sector stakeholders and the governments of the partner nations namely Benin, Ghana, Nigeria and Togo together with other commercial shareholders[639].

---

636 Article 16 to 18 and 26 to 21 of Regulation C/REG.27/12/07 on the composition, organisation, responsibilities and operation of ERERA

637 Honoré Bogler, 'Overview of Recent Regulatory Developments - ERERA', in *(Fourth High-Level Meeting of Regional Associations of Emerging Markets)* (Milan,Italy: ERERA, 2016); ECOWAS Regional Electricity Regulatory Authority (ERERA).

638 Article 77 of the Revised Treaty of 24 July 1993

639 These include Chevron (36.9 %), Nigerian National Petroleum Corporation (NNPC) (24.9 %), Shell (17.9 %), Takoradi Power Company Limited (16.3 %), Société Togolaise de Gaz (2 %), and Société BenGaz (2 %)

A regulatory authority was set up to regulate the gas market activity under the treaty that established WAGP. The West African Gas Pipeline Authority (WAGPA), was then established in pursuance of the WAGP Treaty.[640] It appears to be the only properly constituted regional gas regulatory body in Sub-Saharan Africa. An International Project Agreement between the governments of Nigeria, Benin, Togo and Ghana together with the pipeline company defines this process. It provides for each country to incorporate in their domestic legislation the West African Gas Pipeline Acts, which established WAGPA as the regulatory body with the relevant powers to regulate all aspects of operating the pipeline.[641]

As already mentioned above, the pipeline is 678 km long and connects into the existing Escravos-Lagos pipeline at the Nigeria Gas Company's (NGC) Itoki Natural Gas Export Terminal and then proceeds to a beachhead in Lagos. From there it moves offshore to Takoradi, in Ghana, with gas delivery laterals from the main line extending to Cotonou (Benin), Lomé (Togo), and Tema (Ghana). The pipeline was initially supposed to carry a volume of 160 mmscfd and peak over time at a capacity of 470 mmscfd. The project was based on a foundation contract of 133.6 mmscfd, of which 123.2 mmscfd was destined to be transported to Ghana and 5.2 mmscfd each to Benin and Togo.

From its commencement, WAGP has been encountering some internal and external challenges that has affected its productivity and competitiveness. Nigeria's inconsistent supply of gas under the terms of the contract has been a bane to the proper functioning of the pipeline. This has been in part due to vandalism in blowing up the NGC pipelines, partly because of gas supply issues, as well as unmet domestic gas demand in Nigeria resulting in the diversion of the gas meant for WAGP to be used in domestic power plants. Again, a pipeline breach in August 2012 occurred when pirates hijacked a tanker and dragged an anchor over the pipeline, resulting in long delays while the pipeline was under repair. As a result of these issues, the contracts have been operating under force majeure effectively since the start date of 2011, with none of the parties concerned showing much willingness to try to enforce the contractual terms.[642]

---

640 WAGP, 'Treaty on the West African Gas Pipeline Project', 1995 <http://www.wagpa.org/Treaty_on_WAGP_Project.pdf> [accessed 10 October 2018].

641 Authority.

642 Mike Fulwood and Thierry Bros, 'Future Prospects for LNG Demand in Ghana', *Oxford Energy Insight*, 2018, 1–15.

In August 2014, the VRA, the sole purchaser of gas in Ghana, stopped paying for the gas as it was not receiving payment from the electricity distributors, who in turn were not being paid by most of their customers, principally the Government of Ghana.[643] VRA resumed paying current bills in the third quarter of 2016, and the large accumulated debt is gradually being paid. Further ongoing developments to the pipeline seeks to create an entry point at Takoradi to receive gas from the Ghana pipeline system for onward delivery to Tema. This project will also increase the Tema offtake capacity to 240 mmscfd and was ready in time for the start-up of gas from the Sankofa gas field in the third quarter of 2018. Ghana's production volumes is coming from the Jubilee and TEN fields whereas the Sankofa project is just starting up.

Fulwood and Bros[644] confirm that with the domestic production growth and imports from Nigeria, LNG imports would not be required until 2021 at the earliest, even if gas completely displaced oil in power generation in the ECOWAS region. Other tie-in projects have been tabled to ensure productivity of the WAGP. This is in respect to the offshore Aje field in Nigeria, which has a close proximity to the regional pipeline located near the Benin border. A future connection to the regional pipeline and exporting volumes of natural gas through it is a viable option. Benin's proposed Floating Storage Regasification Unit (FSRU) with Gasol for the production of LNG, seeks to import gas into Benin and then re-export any surplus LNG via the regional gas pipeline offshore especially targeting the Ghana market. Togo has signed an MOU with Equatorial Guinea to study the feasibility of LNG imports.[645]

The regional gas pipeline's operation and the changing face of electrification in West Africa in addition to the expanding gas-to-power option of electricity generation has given prominence to the utility of natural gas and the need to produce and import LNG in the ECOWAS region. Highlighted above, in addition to domestic production in Ghana and pipeline imports from Nigeria, proposals for a number of LNG projects have been tabled. After 2020, LNG is likely to be a critical energy alternative in the ECOWAS energy space especially when we consider that Ghana's electricity demand is surging and seeks increasingly to displace oil powered

---

643 It should be noted that Benin and Togo customers have continued paying.

644 Fulwood and Bros.

645 Mike Fulwood, 'Opportunities for Gas in Sub-Saharan Africa', *Oxford Energy Insight*, 2019 <https://www.oxfordenergy.org>.

thermal generation plants with gas. Again, this same trend is happening in Togo, Benin and Nigeria.[646]

Additionally, in Cote d'Ivoire power generation is dominated by the use of domestic gas at a rate of about eighty-three percent in 2016. Although domestic gas production has plateaued at just over two bcm/year due to growing power demand. The country is turning to gas imports to supplement demand thus increasing future regional demand for natural gas and LNG for electricity production. When the WAGP was being planned, there was some discussion of extending the pipeline to Cote d'Ivoire, but it is yet to be seen whether the pipeline will be extended in the near future. However, a Total-led consortium is close to securing a deal on three mtpa FSRU, but this is awaiting final government approval.[647]

The West Africa Gas Pipeline has initiated a process of constructing a common regional infrastructure for the transport, storage, exchange and trade of natural gas in the region. Alongside, it has unearthed potential in the entirety of the regional gas sector such as the developments being seen in the LNG space. The regional pipeline is further exploring interests in the regional natural gas sector by scaling infrastructure systems like transmission systems, storage systems and LNG terminals. Its expansion to other jurisdictions in the region is essential for the energy future of ECOWAS.

3.5.3.4 ECOWAS Centre for Renewable Energy and Energy Efficiency (ECREEE)

ECOWAS member states in line with earlier commitments to expand and highlight the use of renewable energy established ECREEE as the region's flagship renewable energy centre in 2007.[648] In 2010, ECREEE was inaugurated and has since generated a number of work programs namely data collection and dissemination, policy coordination in the initiation and enactment of green energy policies, green energy innovation project financing, capacity building and gender mainstreaming programs like ECOW-GEN which ensures that women are active agents in the re-

646 Fulwood.
647 Fulwood.
648 Vilar and others.

newable energy sector. In 2015, ECOWAS demonstrated its commitment by enacting the first regional gender and energy policy in the world.[649]

Since its inception, ECREEE has developed the ECOWAS Regional Policy for Renewable Energy (EREP) and the ECOWAS Energy Efficiency Policy (EEEP). These policies were adopted by the ECOWAS Energy Ministers in 2012 and sanctioned by the 43rd Ordinary Session of the ECOWAS Authority of Heads of State and Government, in Abuja, Nigeria, on 18 July 2013.[650] These energy policies, EREP and EEEP are aligned with ECREEE's overall objective, which seeks to contribute to the sustainable economic, social and environmental development of West Africa. They seek to do this by improving access to modern, reliable and affordable energy services, energy security and reduction of energy related externalities such as green-house gases (GHG) and air pollution as well as promoting women participation.[651]

Current research shows that the creation of ECREEE has fostered an increase in renewable energy policymaking at country and regional levels on the deployment and use of renewable energy. It has also put energy efficiency on the regional energy agenda.[652]All these have deepened regional integration on matters relating to renewable energy that is renewable energy regionalism in ECOWAS.

3.5.4 Other Actors and Initiatives

The Vision 2020 agenda of ECOWAS geared towards a democratic and prosperous economic community envisions a bright energy future in West Africa. The quoted statement captures the energy vision clearly. It is as follows, "… advances made in energy augur well for the achievement of a dynamic regional energy market, based on both traditional and renewable

649 Reiss.

650 ECOWAS Centre for Renewable Energy and Energy Efficiency, 'ECOWAS Renewable Energy Policy (EREP)' (Praia, Cape Verde: ECREEE, 2013); ECOWAS, *ECOWAS Energy Efficiency Policy*.

651 Monica Maduekwe and others, 'Gender Equity and Mainstreaming in Renewable Energy Policies—Empowering Women in the Energy Value Chain in the Economic Community of West African States (ECOWAS)', *Current Sustainable/Renewable Energy Reports*, 6.1 (2019), 13–21 <https://doi.org/10.1007/s40518-019-00127-2>.

652 Hancock, 'The Expanding Horizon of Renewable Energy in Sub-Saharan Africa: Leading Research in the Social Sciences'.

sources of energy, which is envisioned as part of the 2020 competitive West African economy..."[653]. Furthermore, the agenda anticipates that the regional power pool, WAPP, would be well positioned by the end of 2020 to guarantee efficient regional energy production, transmission and distribution across the region.[654] Numerous ECOWAS wide energy initiatives has pooled together people, capital and political will in governments, businesses, civil society and the international development spheres to help realise the energy goals in the region.

These initiatives have been championed in an array of conferences and forums. Notable among them are the UN programme on Sustainable Energy for All (SE4ALL) initiative, West African Energy Leaders Group (W-AELG), Power Africa and the Electrification Financing Initiative (ElectriFI). Since, ECOWAS energy regionalism is undergoing a second major energy transformation since the immediate post-independence era, the region is beginning to see real momentum for change and development in its energy sector.

3.5.4.1 Sustainable Energy for All (SE4ALL)

The United Nations launched the SE4ALL programme in 2011. Its General Assembly in 2012 declared the period 2014–2024 as the Decade for Sustainable Energy for All.[655] The programme is currently an independent organisation which maintains a close partnership with the UN, through a relationship agreement. It also partners with UN agencies with its CEO acting as the UN Secretary-General's Special Representative for Sustainable Energy for All and Co-Chair of UN-Energy. It seeks to drive action toward achieving the Sustainable Development Goal 7 (SDG 7), which calls for universal access to sustainable energy by 2030, and the Paris Agreement, which calls for reducing greenhouse gas emissions to limit climate warming to below 2° Celsius.[656]

---

653 ECOWAS Commission, 'ECOWAS Vision 2020' (ABUJA: ECOWAS Commission, 2011), pp. 14–15 <http://www.spu.ecowas.int/wp-content/uploads/2010/03/ECOWAS-Vision-2020-Thematic-Pamphlets-in-English.pdf>.

654 ECOWAS Commission.

655 Irene Giner-Reichl, 'Renewable energy in international and regional governance: Propelling development in Africa', *Energy Research & Social Science* 5 (2015), pp. 116–119.

656 SEFORALL, 'Who we are', 2018 < https://www.seforall.org/who-we-are > [accessed 17 June 2018].

The SE4ALL coordinates efforts that seeks to address energy issues around the world. In developing and emerging countries, it seeks to support the tackling of energy and fuel poverty, affordability plus the provision of sustainable energy. SE4ALL catalyses a strong push by global institutions to create an energy revolution. It has sought to marshal public sector, private sector, and civil society activity as well as mobilise private capital and involvement into all aspects of the energy value chain in these places tackling energy vulnerability. Sub-Saharan Africa (SSA) which includes the ECOWAS region is one of the many priority regions of this global organisation.[657]

3.5.4.2 West African Energy Leaders Group (W-AELG)

The W-AELG was launched in Abidjan on 30 June 2015 under the broader African Energy Leaders Group (AELG) framework. The AELG was established at the January 2015 World Economic Forum in Davos, Switzerland. It serves as a vehicle used by the SE4All Africa Hub housed by the African Development Bank (AfDB) to execute the objective of provisioning sustainable, affordable and clean energy in Africa.

W-AELG brings together political, economic and civic leaders at the highest level in the region to drive the reforms and investment needed to end energy and fuel poverty. It serves as a coordination platform between governments, private and civil society sectors in the West African region on energy matters. One main objective of its existence is to fashion out concrete plans to speed up energy reforms and pipeline bankable investment projects for abundant and sustainable energy access that would ultimately facilitate the rapid economic transformation of the region through the services sector and industry.[658]

---

657 Antonio Castellano and others, 'Brighter Africa', *McKinsey & Company Monthly Journal*, 2015, 4–8 <http://www.mckinsey.com/~/media/mckinsey/dotcom/insights/energy resources materials/powering africa/brighter_africa_the_growth_potential_of_the_sub-saharan_electricity_sector.ashx>.

658 Afdb, 'Launch of the West African Energy Leaders Group Hotel Ivoire , Abidjan , 30 June 2015', 2015, pp. 1–6 <http://www.afdb.org/fileadmin/uploads/afdb/Documents/Generic-Documents/Summary_of_the_launch_event_of_the_WAELG.pdf> [accessed 29 September 2016].

3.5.4.3 Energy Partnerships with the EU and US

Other energy actors championing initiatives actively in the ECOWAS region are the external partners from the EU, US and other countries. A discourse on all the external energy actors and their activities within the context of international energy investments would suffice for another voluminous study. But due to the focus of this study I would only address but a few namely partnerships with the EU and US.

Electrification Financing Initiative (ElectriFI):

The EU has committed to provide support to developing and emerging countries to leapfrog carbon intensive energy infrastructure. A commitment made as part of the negotiations to reduce climate warming under the aegis of the UN Framework Convention on Climate Change UNFCCC. Therefore, through a multiplicity of initiatives such as the Electrification Financing Initiative (ElectriFI) among many others has been launched since.

ElectriFI was launched during COP 21 after the signing of the Paris Agreement. It seeks to provide investments into the electricity sector particularly rural electrification projects with the aim of offering new and improved power infrastructure that is scalable to rural and peri-urban communities.[659] ElectriFI uses different approaches to realise its goals. This is in terms of the energy business models, utilities and mini-grids in use.[660] The EU and its member states efforts in the African energy space, in the case of electricity, has been fragmented and plural and in some cases has been counterproductive.[661]

---

659 Simone Tagliapietra, 'Financing the European Energy Infrastructure of the Future', 2013, 1–13 <www.feem.it> [accessed 11 December 2018]; Simone Tagliapietra, *Electrifying Africa: How to Make Europe's Contribution Count, Bruegel Policy Contribution*, Bruegel Policy Contribution (Brussels, 2017) <https://ideas.repec.org/p/bre/polcon/20882.html>.

660 African Development Bank, *The New Deal on Energy for Africa* (Abidjan, 2016).

661 Simone Tagliapietra and Morgan Bazilian, 'The Role of International Institutions in Fostering Sub-Saharan Africa's Electrification', *The Electricity Journal*, 32.2 (2019), 13–20<https://doi.org/10.1016/j.tej.2019.01.016>.

Power Africa

Power Africa is the United States' initiative on electrification targeted at boosting power generation and access on the African continent.[662] The initiative launched by President Barak Obama in June 2013 as an attempt to enlist the American private sector in an effort to generate enthusiasm about energy in Africa. It is a multi-agency initiative with broad bipartisan support and codified into law through the Electrify Africa Act of 2016.[663] In keeping with the aims of the initiative, Power Africa is working currently in eleven ECOWAS countries and Mauritania the largest involvement in any regional bloc in Africa.[664] It also works with over 140 private sector partners, as well as the World Bank and African Development Bank.

Power Africa has built an assorted energy portfolio and embraces a range of technologies that includes natural gas. Its main objective is to add more than 30,000 megawatts of generation capacity to the African energy sector. The initiative envisages to scale energy solutions and construct power generation, transmission, and distribution infrastructure across where it works.

If implemented smartly, Power Africa would create electricity access through 60 million new connections that would be available for 300 million people and commercial entities. Through the improvement of energy management capabilities of utilities and enabling partner countries to meet critical energy needs by achieving sustainable and long-term energy security for these partner countries by 2030.[665] The major challenge confronting Power Africa is its susceptibility to bureaucratic dynamics and conflicting agendas from the State Department. This is because its coordinator is based inside USAID and is expected to work with multiple agencies. Therefore, to overcome these challenges Power Africa must deal

662 USAID, *Leveraging Partnerships To Increase Access To Power In Sub-Saharan Africa* <www.usaid.gov/powerafrica.>.

663 U.S. House of Representatives, 'Electrify Africa Act of 2016', *S. 2152*. https://www.gpo.gov/fdsys/pkg/BILLS114s2152rfh/pdf/BILLS-114s2152rfh.pdf.

664 The ECOWAS countries include Benin, Burkina Faso, Cote d'Ivoire, Gambia, Ghana, Guinea, Liberia, Mali, Nigeria, Senegal and Sierra Leone. Although Mauritania is not a member of ECOWAS, it exited from the economic community in 2000, it participates in ECOWAS energy regionalism especially in the regional power pool.

665 USAID, *Leveraging Partnerships To Increase Access To Power In Sub-Saharan Africa.*

with the political and institutional hurdles that threaten its continued success and perhaps its very survival.[666]

3.6 Recapitulation

An account of the origins and development of regionalism and its interaction with energy in the West African region is borne out of the conceptual relationship between energy, international political economy of energy (IPE of energy), and institutions. As such, it creates a new understanding of energy regionalism and its governance especially with regard to the historical evolution of the ECOWAS region. Key issues raised in this chapter have been the following:

1. The trajectory of West African energy history in the three linguistic sub-regions namely the Anglophone, Lusophone and Francophone sub-regions. It has been hinged on two paradigms, beginning with the pre-existing colonial energy regime, which locked-in an energy path-dependency and the subsequent post-colonial construction of national energy systems that began a path-creative energy pathway.
2. To reiterate the evolution of ECOWAS regionalism, four historical stages were identified, that is, the first wave: post-medieval empire and kingdom building, second wave: pan-West Africanism, third wave: decolonisation and the fourth wave: founding of ECOWAS. In addition to these, two distinctive features, which characterise it namely its collaborative and consolidative nature, were outlined.
3. ECOWAS energy regionalism was categorised under three temporal narrative frames to draw out its past milestones, which involved cooperation towards a common energy region, present settings, which highlighted the integration of the ECOWAS energy region, and its future prospects that outlined the governance of West Africa's cross-border energy networks and systems.
4. Finally, to understand the institutional foundations upon which ECOWAS energy regionalism is pivoted, I considered the legal framework of current ECOWAS energy policy, general institutions as well as other actors and initiatives that operate in the region on matters regarding regional energy policy.

666 Todd Moss and Morgan Bazilian, 'Signalling, governance, and goals: Reorienting the United States Power Africa initiative', *Energy Research & Social Science*, 39 (2018), 74–77

This historical institutionalist approach of recounting West Africa's (that is, ECOWAS) energy regionalism can be summed up under a singular proposition. To espouse this proposition, West African countries and their peoples have surmounted major energy bottlenecks irrespective of their linguistic and colonial energy past. This setback has been translated into a major opportunity to upend the inherited negative energy fortunes of the past.

The region was challenged to meet their energy needs by adopting a more modern international political economy of energy approach through the means of comparative energy regionalism. This has been possible by developing institutions around regional energy through the adoption of legal norms, general institutional formation in addition to the involvement of other external actors and initiatives. The ultimate aim in this regional energy institutionalisation process is to improve energy autonomy and self-reliance. It is done in order to provide abundant, sustainable and affordable energy services at both country and regional levels so as to eliminate the energy access and supply gap in the region.

Chapter 4

Energy Regionalism in the European Union

4.1 Introduction

The EU is a net importer of energy. Until being overtaken by China, it was the world's largest importer of fossil fuels.[667] The path to regional integration in Europe after World War 2 was founded on the need to cooperate and integrate major energy – related resources and production commodities (coal, steel and atomic energy) which had a potential to stem the conflict and facilitate cooperation. It reached a pinnacle in the 1950s with the establishment of the European Coal and Steel Community (ECSC) and European Atomic Energy Community (EURATOM). This has subsequently led to the pursuit of an EU Energy Union by 2020, having prompted a long process towards European energy cooperation, integration and governance.

Energy policy focus in the EU was revitalised under the Juncker Commission, which adopted the energy union strategy (2015). The start of the energy union seeks to improve the functioning of the single energy market, strengthening security of supply in electricity and natural gas, and adopting legislation to deliver on the goals of the 2030 EU climate and energy framework. The strategy contains five key compatible dimensions: energy security, solidarity and trust; a fully integrated European energy market; energy efficiency geared towards moderating energy demand; decarbonisation; research, innovation and competitiveness. It augments a regularly updated roadmap that lists the actions to be executed by the Commission during its official term.[668]

---

667 Kacper Szulecki, *Energy Security in Europe : Divergent Perceptions and Policy Challenges*, ed. by Kacper Szulecki (Cham: Palgrave Macmillan, 2018).

668 Alex Benjamin Wilson and Alina Dobreva, 'EU Policies-Delivering for Citizens : Energy Supply and Security' (Strasbourg: EPRS | European Parliamentary Research Service, 2018) <http://www.europarl.europa.eu> [accessed 6 December 2018].

Most energy policy in the EU is still made at the national level.[669] A range of policy domains such as economic policy, security policy, external policy and environmental policy affects EU energy policy, vice versa, by its very nature, it does same.[670] The gradual pace of an emerging coherent and harmonised EU energy policy has aided the evolution of energy regionalism in the EU from its beginnings to the progressive realisation of an internal energy market and the prospective creation of an energy union.

Using historical institutionalism within the context of international relations generally and more specifically within the broader context of comparative regionalism in this case EU studies. I trace the stages inherent in the evolution of energy regionalism in the EU by focusing on the cooperation, integration, and governance of energy in the European Union. Region building with a focus on energy issues has been a key means towards stronger European integration.

In this consideration, I highlight the process of energy path dependency and path creation in the EU. Using a historical perspective, I look at the role played by a variety of region-wide actors and member states to explore the IPE of energy in the context of the European Union. The study in this chapter seeks to contribute to perspectives on strategic IPE of energy narratives concerning the EU while focusing on aspects of EU energy history.

I start with an overview of the EU's energy path dependency and path creation in its four geographical sub-regions highlighting unique dimensions exhibited by each (Section 2). In Section 3, I retell the history of EU regionalism focusing on the pre, mid and post war years to the founding of the EU. I also present a short discourse on the dual character of the EU.

Furthermore, I unpack EU energy regionalism in terms of its past, present and future prospects in Section 4, and then summarize the institutional foundations of EU energy regionalism (Section 5), before concluding in Section 6 by recapitulating the major issues emphasised in the entire chapter.

---

669 Haaland Janne Matlary, *Energy Policy in the European Union*, 1st edn (London: Macmillan Press Ltd, 1997).

670 David Buchan, 'Energy Policy: Sharp Challenges and Rising Ambitions', in *Policy-Making in the European Union*, ed. by Helen Wallace, Mark A. Pollack, and Alasdair R. Young, 7th edn (Oxford: Oxford University Press, 2015), p. 570 <https://doi.org/10.1177/0010414013516917>.

Map 4. 1 European Union (2020)

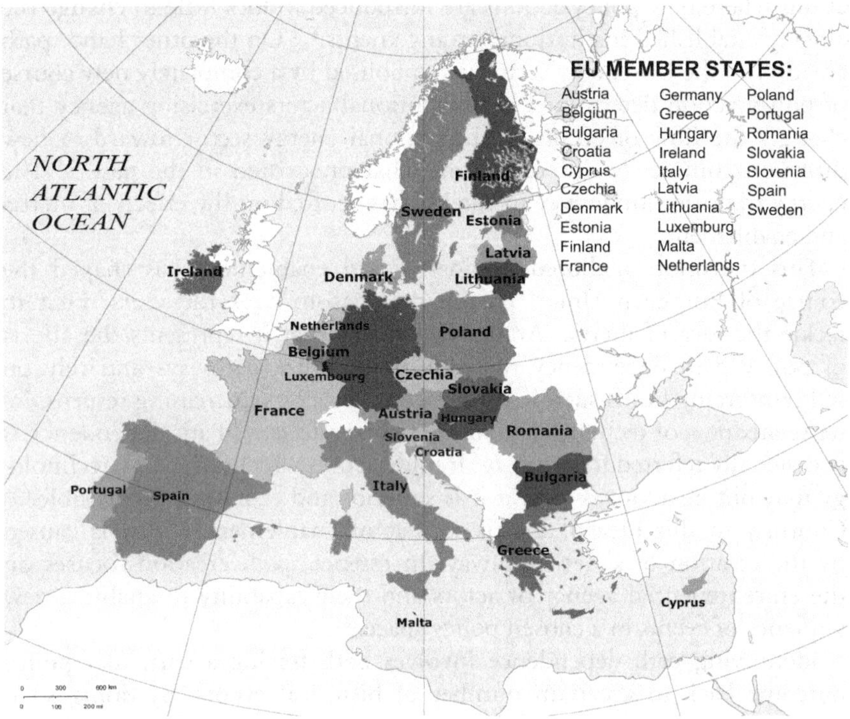

4.2 The European Union's Energy Path Dependence and Path Creation

A historical institutionalist perspective highlights the importance of the development of energy policy and demonstrate the influence of path dependency and path creation on the trajectory of the European Union's energy sector. This perspective explores further how values and norms in the EU energy policy space entrench and change within the EU's institutional setting.[671]

Path dependence in the EU energy sector typify the progress of institutional arrangements in the regional energy sector that is determined by

671 Tomas Maltby, 'European Union Energy Policy Integration: A Case of European Commission Policy Entrepreneurship and Increasing Supranationalism', *Energy Policy*, 55 (2013), 435–44 <https://doi.org/10.1016/j.enpol.2012.12.031>.

historical events and based on pre-existing policy actions. And even in situations where new policy actions are introduced it does little to change the already established institutional arrangements.[672] On the other hand, path creation in the EU energy sector is symbolised by a completely new course of policy action determined by institutional actors exercising agency that changes the flow of events in the regional energy sector towards a new direction completely different from what pre-existed in the past.[673] The energy transition underway in the EU has centred on the effects of inertia and enablement.

This transition anchored on inertia and enablement has shaped the course of European Union energy regionalism over the years. First to tackle the idea of inertia, Araujo[674] explains that it represents the effects of policy path dependency that constrain future pathways and rely on self-reinforcing limits such as sunk investment costs, increasing returns, inter-relatedness of technologies and network effects.[675] Path dependency is occasionally referred to as *lock-in*. It underscores why new energy technology may not be adopted even if it is superior and economically feasible.[676] Contrary to this idea of inertia is that of enablement which is caused by the creation of a new pathway. In essence, path creation focuses on the entrepreneurial agency of actors and their capability to enable a new sequence of events in a chosen policy space.[677]

Identifying path dependence involves both tracing a particular policy outcome back to a certain number of historical events. By doing so it demonstrates the inability of these contingent events to be explained with

---

672 James Mahoney, 'Path Dependence in Historical Sociology', *Theory and Society*, 29.4 (2000), 507–48.

673 Raghu Garud and Peter Karnøe, *Path Dependence and Creation.*, ed. by Raghu Garud and Peter Karnøe (Mahwah, New Jersey: Lawrence Erlbaum Associates Inc, Publishers, 2001).

674 Araújo.

675 W Brian Arthur, 'Competing Technologies, Increasing Returns, and Lock-In by Historical Events', *The Economic Journal*, 99.394 (1989), 116–31 <https://doi.org/10.2307/2234208>; Paul A. David, 'Clio and the Economics of QWERTY', *American Economic Review*, 75.2 (1985), 332–37.

676 Robin Cowan, 'Nuclear Power Reactors: A Study in Technological Lock-In', *The Journal of Economic History*, 50.3 (1990), 541–67 <https://doi.org/10.1017/S0022050700037153>; Gregory C. Unruh, 'Understanding Carbon Lock-In', *Energy Policy*, 28 (2000), 817–30; G Unruh, 'Escaping the Carbon Lock-In', *Energy Policy*, 30 (2002), 317–25 <https://doi.org/10.1016/S0301-4215(01)00098-2>.

677 Raghu Garud, Arun Kumaraswamy, and Peter Karnøe, 'Path Dependence or Path Creation?', *Journal of Management Studies*, 47.4 (2010), 760–74 <https://doi.org/10.1111/j.1467-6486.2009.00914.x>.

other earlier historical or initial conditions.[678] We can describe a process as path dependent when initial moves in a particular direction occasion further moves in that same direction. Suffice also to say that the order in which things occur affects how they happen. The course of change up to a certain point constrains the trajectory after that point.[679]

Path dependence in developing energy pathways rely on a number of factors. Among them includes the cost of long-lasting capital vital for deploying energy systems and technologies. A policy regime that facilitates change but this change is quite rare due to its disruptive nature. As well as the realisation that prior policy choices forms the bedrock of later paths because of interactions on the path.[680]

On the other hand, path creation occurs in a chosen policy area when actors and institutions decide on policy processes that determine a new policy cycle shaped and influenced by evolving processes in real-time. Here creating a new path connects all the three notions of time namely past, present and future. The coupling of the terms path and creation represents this. In sum, actors mobilise the past to generate new future options.[681] In this sense relating path creation to energy policy, it is sufficient to say that past and present energy decisions shape and transform future ones.

Path dependence and path creation has been applicable to energy policy development in the four sub-regional settings in the European Union. With respect to path dependency, the initial conditions (that is, the resource endowments, price, etc.) and the historical paths taken has led to diverse energy arrangements and processes. This has resulted in differences in the structure of the EU's energy economy. The reliance on initial conditions and the development pathways taken explains the differences among the established and pre-existing energy systems.[682] Path dependence in EU energy regionalism entails substantial inertia especially in relation to altering chosen energy development pathways even as conditions prevailing at

---

678 Jack A. Goldstone, 'Initial Conditions, General Laws, Path Dependence, and Explanation in Historical Sociology', *American Journal of Sociology*, 104.3 (2002), 829–45 <https://doi.org/10.1086/210088>.

679 Adrian Kay, 'A Critique of the Use of Path Dependency in Policy Studies', *Public Administration*, 83.3 (2005), 553–72.

680 R. Schmalensee, 'Lecture 5: Path Dependence in Energy Systems' (Cambridge, MA: Sloan School of Management, MIT, 2012) <https://ocw.mit.edu>.

681 Garud, Kumaraswamy, and Karnøe.

682 Arthur, 'Competing Technologies, Increasing Returns, and Lock-In by Historical Events'.

specific moments in history change. This has created a *lock-in effect* in the regional energy economy of the EU.[683]

Again, path dependency and the lock-in effect in the EU's energy systems show persistent differences in initial conditions such as, available energy resource endowments among other geographical, climatic, economic, social, and institutional factors. There are further drivers like structural policy and regulatory factors that affect differences in infrastructures, spatial structures and consumption patterns. All these influence the levels and types of technologies adopted by energy consumers within the EU's energy sector. Mostly, these adopted technologies are difficult to change quickly due to high sunk investment costs, causing a *technological lock-in* in the European Union's energy sector.[684] The existence of path dependency and technological lock-in in EU energy regionalism explains the differences in energy consumption patterns across countries and sub-regions even for those at similar income levels, particularly when they are devoid of obvious signs of convergence.[685]

With respect to path creation in the EU energy sector, the different entrepreneurial actors, be it at country level or region-wide, create new energy and technological pathways. They do so by navigating occurrences or events affecting the European Union's energy space. These occurrences or events happen in 'real time' and seek to initiate the movement of new energy policy processes to carefully depart from the normal state of the regional energy sector.[686] This explanation of understanding how energy pathways are created, underpins what is known as energy path creation.[687] To recap path dependency and path creativity in relation to EU energy regionalism, it is important to understand that path dependence originates from the general premise that early events have a substantial effect on later ones.[688] On the other hand, path creation follows from the premise that

683 W Brian Arthur, *Increasing Returns and Path Dependence in the Economy* (University of Michigan Press, 1994).

684 Arnulf Grubler, 'Transitions in Energy Use', *Encyclopedia of Energy*, 6 (2004), 163–77 <https://doi.org/http://dx.doi.org/10.1016/B0-12-176480-X/00023-1>.

685 Grubler.

686 Garud and Karnøe, p. 2.

687 James Simmie, 'Path Dependence and New Technological Path Creation in the Danish Wind Power Industry', *European Planning Studies*, 20.5 (2012), 753–72 <https://doi.org/10.1080/09654313.2012.667924>.

688 Sebastian Mayer, 'Path Dependence and Commission Activism in the Evolution of the European Union's External Energy Policy', *Journal of International Relations and Development*, 11.3 (2008), 251–78 <https://doi.org/10.1057/jird.2008.12>.

actors acting innovatively can shift the course of a path dependent policy and technological adoption in a new direction, in effect causing change.[689]

In conclusion, we have explored the European Union's energy regionalism which has been determined through the adoption of old and new energy technologies, as well as guided by an ever-evolving policy framework. It is essential to appreciate how path dependent and path creative pathways have occurred in the evolution and furtherance of energy institutions in the EU. Subsequently, over the years the supranational institutions that make up the European Union have developed tools that have influenced the course of regional energy. In effect they have guided the processes towards energy policy making at country levels and in the overall region. However, it is crucial to state that this has been expressed differently in the four sub-regions of the European Union namely, Northern Europe, Central and Eastern Europe, Western Europe and Southern Europe.

4.2.1 Northern Europe

The countries in the Nordic region of Europe are, Denmark, Sweden, Finland, Iceland and Norway (the latter two are not part of the EU). Their energy history development reflects the two dimensions of path dependence and path creation. The northern European sub-region of the EU has a common feature in the use of traditional energy carriers for its energy consumption. Concurrently, the development of new energy carriers is also contributing to the share of total energy input in the sub-region.

To illustrate these two dimensions of path dependence and path creation in Nordic European energy history, I try to go as far back as I possibly can, to reflect the use of both old and new energy carriers. From the very beginning, food for men and fodder for working animals, firewood, wind, water and peat have served as traditional energy carriers. The evidence provides that until the late 1920s, total energy input became less than 50 percent in Sweden and by extension in the entire Nordic region.[690]

689 Simmie; Peter Karnøe and Raghu Garud, 'Path Creation : Co-Creation of Heterogeneous Resources in the Emergence of the Danish Wind Turbine Cluster Path Creation : Co-Creation of Heterogeneous Resources in the Emergence of the Danish Wind Turbine Cluster', 4313 (2012) <https://doi.org/10.1080/09654313.2012.667923>.

690 Ben Gales and others, 'North versus South: Energy Transition and Energy Intensity in Europe over 200 Years', *European Review of Economic History*, 11.2 (2007), 219–53 <https://doi.org/10.1017/S1361491607001967>.

During the first industrial revolution, the dominant energy source in this region was firewood, contributing about 75 per cent of energy until 1850, whilst food and fodder made up the remaining part. A common phenomenon, particularly in Sweden, was the use of hot wastewater from industrial processes for direct household heating. In addition, the waste from pulp manufacturing, that is, spent pulping liquor, was used as fuel in the pulp industry.[691] Over a long period, energy use in the Nordics was stable and somewhat modestly incremental, specifically, during the agrarian period. But the last 100 years witnessed an unusual exponential growth particularly during the 1950s -1970s period and from 2000 -2010. During the first half of the twentieth century, the growth witnessed was higher than in the preceding centuries with the exception of the Second World War hiatus.[692]

The initial conditions prevalent in the Nordics energy sector are quite similar at country level in terms of the sub-region's energy path dependence. This is especially visible looking at their adopted energy technologies. However, these similarities exist with only slight differences. Due to the high energy demand because of the sub-region's very cold climate, it has always sought to prioritise affordable, sustainable and reliable energy.

Hydropower has been an essential source of generating energy, that is, electricity, in the sub-region. The main hydropower producers are Sweden and Norway whereas Finland and Denmark have sought to import hydropower since they produce it minimally. Sweden's share of hydropower to its energy mix, contributes about 50 percent to its energy economy. It accounts for over 1000 hydropower plants since its first set up in 1906. For Norway, hydropower contributes about 95 percent of its electricity mix.[693]

The sub-region is also a producer of oil and natural gas, which is mainly found in Norway and Denmark. There is a growing danger of creating technological lock-ins regarding natural gas particularly in Norway. A sizeable share of the Nordic sub-region's energy is also contributed by nuclear

---

691 Gales and others.

692 Bent Sorensen, 'Can We Learn from History?', *European Review*, 22.1 (2014), 92–96 <https://doi.org/10.1017/S1062798713000653>.

693 All the energy data under this part of the section is from the Nordic Energy Research, International Energy Agency (IEA), and Nordic Center for Spatial Development. See: International Energy Agency and Nordic Energy Research, 'Nordic Energy Technology Perspectives 2013', (Paris: OECD, 2013). Available at www.iea.org/etp/nordic; International Energy Agency and Nordic Energy Research, 'Nordic Energy Technology Perspectives 2016', (Paris: OECD, 2016). Available at www.iea.org/etp/nordic

energy, usually found in Sweden and Finland. This type of energy accounts for about 18 percent of their respective national energy needs.[694]

The Nordics have shown progress in the creation of an internal energy market especially for power transmission and distribution whether it is from hydropower or fossil fuel generation.[695] This has been a characteristic feature in the recent energy history of the Nordics to minimise the energy deficiencies at the various country levels within the region. In sum, an energy mix based on largely hydropower, fossil fuels (coal, crude oil and natural gas and wood-based biofuels) besides nuclear energy typify the initial conditions of energy path-dependency in the Nordics.

New pathways of energy use are being created in Nordic countries as well. This is based on the niches that have existed in each nation due to prior energy infrastructure and a fundamental shift to adopt new energy technology. It has been done by establishing processes to achieve a critical mass and overcoming barriers to create new energy pathways.[696] For instance, there has been a vast deployment of renewable technology pathways, above the 10 percent EU target, across all the member states in the region.

Over one-third of the region's energy supply originates from renewable sources. The vast quantities are biomass and waste, which are used in the generation of electricity, heat and transport fuels. Wind is emerging, with a growing share in electricity production, although its contribution fluctuates. Altogether, the Nordic sub-region of the EU register targets above the EU-28 average, Norway, a non-EU member state, accounts for almost 100 percent renewable electricity consumption with portions of it transmitted through the Nordic regional grid interconnection.[697]

Another element of Nordic energy path creation can be seen in policy formulation at different levels that seeks to address uncertainties, learn

---

694 Jörgen Sjödin and Stefan Grönkvist, 'Emissions accounting for use and supply of electricity in the Nordic market,' *Energy policy* 32.13 (2004): 1555–1564.

695 Jorma Ollila and Jens Skov-Spilling, 'Nordic Energy Co-operation: Strong today–Stronger tomorrow', *Nordic Council of Ministers*, Vol. 2017732. (2017); Eirik S. Amundsen and Lars Bergman, 'Why has the Nordic electricity market worked so well?', *Utilities policy*, 14.3 (2006): 148–157.

696 Teis Hansen and others, 'Path Creation in Nordic Energy and Road Transport Systems – The Role of Technological Characteristics', *Renewable and Sustainable Energy Reviews*, 70. August 2015 (2017), 551–62 <https://doi.org/10.1016/j.rser.2016.11.131>.

697 Benjamin K. Sovacool, 'Contestation, Contingency, and Justice in the Nordic low-carbon energy transition,' *Energy Policy*, 102 (2017), 569–582.

from mistakes and avoid new lock-ins in new paths. These policy changes are supporting system innovations and infrastructure changes as well as institutional change.[698] A case in point is the development of specific policy instruments to increase renewable energy production. This is highlighted by the carbon taxes in Norway, feed-in tariffs in Denmark, investment grants in Finland and electricity certificates in Sweden.[699]

To conclude, the energy sector in the Nordic sub-region of the European Union has depended on already established pathways and has created new pathways to address its energy needs over the years. They have chalked remarkable progress especially in energy path creation through the use of renewable energy sources over the last two decades. This has been a means to shift from pre-existing energy infrastructure lock-ins that are not clean, to a cleaner and more resilient energy future. The Northern part of the EU is focused on creating a significant share of its electricity from renewable sources. Yet, there are considerable differences on how this is executed among the countries due to the available natural resources and the political will to do this has been significant.

4.2.2 Central and Eastern Europe

Historically, the Central and Eastern European (CEE) sub-region (comprising of Estonia, Latvia, Lithuania, Czech Republic, Slovakia, Poland, Hungary, Slovenia, Romania, Bulgaria, and Croatia) has relied primarily on lignite and hard coal for electricity generation. This has been supplemented with nuclear energy and energy imports. Energy imports consist of natural gas and oil from Russia and some gas reserves in Croatia. However, overall, coal resources have sustained CEE sub-regional electricity generation for decades.

The energy choices made in the sub-region has resulted in an over reliance on coal-fired power plants. This has established a path dependent lock-in on the use of coal technology. This technology for some time has

698 Antje Klitkou and others, 'Path Creation in Nordic Energy and Road Transport Systems', *Renewable Energy Research Conference (RERC) 2014 Oslo, June 16-18 2014* (Oslo, Norway, 2014), pp. 1–17 <https://doi.org/10.1016/j.rser.2016.11.131 >.

699 Manuchehr Irandoust, 'The Renewable Energy-Growth Nexus with Carbon Emissions and Technological Innovation: Evidence from the Nordic Countries', *Ecological Indicators*, 69 (2016), 118–25 <https://doi.org/10.1016/j.ecolind.2016.03 .051>.

been beset with the inability of retrofitting, which in certain instances has caused major air pollution resulting in the flying of ash waste into the atmosphere. Due to its huge dependence on particular energy sources during the socialist period, energy supply data does not reveal a lot of variance, in comparison to other EU regions. In the past, coal powered energy was the largest emitter of pollutants in the CEE sub-region until the climax of the socialist period.

The so-called 'Black Triangle' that is, the heavy industry and mining areas of East Germany, Poland and Hungary experienced acid rains. As a result, hectares of forests were turned into wasteland due to the energy intensive use of coal. Around 80 million tonnes of lignite coal were used annually in this sub-region, contributing to about 3 million tonnes of sulphur dioxide (SO2) and 1 million tonnes of nitrogen dioxide (NO2) emissions. In addition, these countries' carbon dioxide (CO2) emissions were among the highest globally and surpassed the OECD average for emissions.[700]

Countries in the CEE sub-region in the past have exhibited little diversity in terms of the energy policy choices they have made to deal with their energy needs. In 2000, Poland relied on coal for about 62 percent of its primary energy and 97 percent of its electricity supply. As at year 2002, Lithuania, Bulgaria, Slovakia and Hungary relied mostly on nuclear energy for their electricity supply and primary energy. Production levels in each country were as follows: 82.7 percent, 51.5 percent, 55.5 percent, 39.7 percent respectively. This shows that at country level the CEE sub-region of the EU was locked in on a number of energy technologies put in place in the past, making it difficult to transition to other cleaner more efficient energy sources.[701]

Another attribute that has defined the energy path of the CEE sub-region has been its dependence on Russian energy supplies. Huge quantities of natural gas, electricity, oil, nuclear power and other primary energy carriers shapes the basis of CEE energy supply. Energy represents one of the linkages Russia has used to maintain influence on its neighbours, such as the countries of the CEE sub-region in the EU. Russian energy imports

700 Ürge-Vorsatz, Miladinova, and Paizs; Milena Novy, *International Actions to Combat Pollution in the Black Triangle and Katowice Regions*, Working Papers (Laxenburg , Austria, 1996).

701 Diana Ürge-Vorsatz, Gergana Miladinova, and László Paizs, 'Energy in Transition: From the Iron Curtain to the European Union', *Energy Policy*, 34.15 (2006), 2279–97 <https://doi.org/10.1016/j.enpol.2005.03.007>.

(mainly natural gas) has gained a high share in the energy mix of the CEE sub-region. This has ensured the establishment of relatively well-developed natural gas infrastructure such as pipelines, that are interconnected from Russia throughout the sub-region.

Since, Russia is blessed with some of the world's largest natural gas reserves, reliance on its energy exports has created energy dependence and technological lock-ins for these CEE nations. This is championed by its state-owned energy companies.[702]

To exemplify this, Gazprom, Russia's natural gas monopoly, has developed an extensive pipeline network to provide the Baltic States in most of Central Europe with natural gas, making it the sole supplier. This has created a relatively high dependency on Russian natural gas in countries such as Estonia, Latvia, Lithuania and Slovakia. It is also responsible for 91 percent of Hungary's natural gas imports, 79 percent of Poland's and about 70 percent of the Czech Republic's gas imports.[703] This in effect has made natural gas an essential energy source in the CEE sub-region.

The energy path dependence of the CEE sub-region has contributed to the socio-economic legacy of a region which once were centrally planned economies that recorded high and systemic levels of energy poverty, the highest in Europe.[704] The populations in the sub-region were vulnerable to poor thermal insulation in their residential facilities. Again, this was exacerbated by the historically low energy prices and the prevalence of an unsustainable energy supply mix.

In the 1990s, the market economy transition worsened these issues through the upward readjustment of energy tariffs without the provision of adequate social welfare and energy-efficiency mechanisms. Institutional inertia intensified the recurring difficulties facing countries in the region,

---

702 Pierre Noël, 'A Market between us: reducing the political cost of Europe's dependence on Russian gas,' *Electricity Policy Research Group (EPRG)*, University of Cambridge, EPRG Working Paper 916 (2009); Martin Jirušek et al., ' Energy security in Central and Eastern Europe and the operations of Russian State-Owned Energy Enterprises', (Brno: Masaryk University, 2015).

703 Filip Černoch, 'Natural Gas Market of the European Union and Its Impact on the Position of Gazprom in Europe', *Energy Security in Central and Eastern Europe and the Operations of Russian State-Owned Energy Enterprises*, (Brno: Masaryk University, 2015) pp. 377–399.

704 Stefan Bouzarovski and Sergio Tirado Herrero, 'The Energy Divide: Integrating Energy Transitions, Regional Inequalities and Poverty Trends in the European Union', *European Urban and Regional Studies*, 24.1 (2017), 69–86 <https://doi.org/10.1177/0969776415596449>; Ürge-Vorsatz, Miladinova, and Paizs.

along with attendant infrastructural lock-ins in addition to the over reliance on Russian energy supplies.[705]

In terms of path creation, strategies being implemented in the CEE sub-region has been the quest to upgrade the centralized grid system to accommodate any new electricity generation from cleaner energy sources. This has, however, been prompted by EU legislation. Smart grid technology advancement, comprising of supervisory control and data acquisition (SCADA) systems, flexible AC transmission systems (FACTS) devices, smart inverters, and other energy efficiency technology are being pursued to transform the sub-regional power system. This is particularly being done in the electricity supply system. Also, the pursuance of periphery renewable energy technology is in the transitioning energy mix.

These changes in energy policies by the CEE countries have been prompted by ambitious EU energy and climate policies. Meanwhile, these CEE countries have often objected to EU legislation on energy and climate, although without a common voting front and position. Thus, they have finally ended up succumbing to EU energy and climate positions.[706] Another aspect of the CEE sub-regional energy path creation is the impact of the governance of the EU energy union. That is, the impact of the EU's internal energy market which seeks to enhance energy security and climate policies. The key energy policy priority of all the CEE countries is to diversify energy imports and fuels, in order to increase national sovereignty, energy security and energy solidarity in the EU.

The sub-region has become pivotal to the long-term energy infrastructure plans of the EU. The development of new interconnecting gas pipelines seeks to be the essence of energy path creation in the CEE sub-region. Three energy development plans have been outlined for natural gas imports from other sources. With the exception of the Brotherhood (Testvériség) pipeline, they include, the expansion of the Austrian-Hungarian gas interconnector (Baumgarten/Moson) and the construction of the Slovakian-Hungarian gas interconnector. It is estimated that their total capacity would suffice for all imports and would provide a connection to the Western European market.

705 Stefan Bouzarovski and Sergio Tirado Herrero; Ürge-Vorsatz, Miladinova, and Paizs.

706 Stefan Ćetković, and Aron Buzogány, 'The political economy of EU climate and energy policies in Central and Eastern Europe revisited: Shifting coalitions and prospects for clean energy transitions,' *Politics and Governance* 7.1 (2019): 124.

The North-South gas interconnector is another project that incorporates the Slovakia-Hungary and Croatia-Hungary connections as well as the Adriatic oil pipeline. This would enable access to the Polish, Croatian, Slovenian and Italian LNG terminals. Upon completion, the Polish shale gas production would ultimately also feed into this gas interconnection.[707] A shift towards natural gas from other sources other than Russia's, reduces the energy security risk to the sub-region and EU as a whole.

4.2.3 Western Europe

Some western European members of the EU (consisting of, Austria, Germany, France, UK, Ireland, Belgium, Netherlands and Luxembourg) have influenced global energy history for many centuries. It has in turn, been impacted significantly by transformations and shifts in the global energy arena. A brief account of these interactions around energy in the past reveal that, energy consumption of Western Europe was characterised by shifts from one primary energy source to the next. Being the fulcrum of modern era global hegemony for many centuries, Western Europe has led the way in the discovery of various technological expertise to extract newly found primary energy sources.

Again, this sub-region has been the main driver of European integration, with most of it having been driven by occurrences in the field of energy. The make-up of the modern energy system in western Europe was initiated by the first industrial revolution, which sought to employ mechanisation to reduce reliance on human labour and facilitate production efficiency.[708] An unprecedented rise in energy consumption in the early nineteenth century based on the so-called *British model* took effect in this sub-region. For instance, Britain and The Netherlands developed energy systems dependent on new fuels such as, coal and peat. This resulted in a seven-fold increase in per capita terms and a twenty-one to twenty-two-fold increase

707 Janos Szlavik and Maria Csete, 'Climate and Energy Policy in Hungary', *Energies*, 5.2 (2012), 494–517 <https://doi.org/10.3390/en5020494>.

708 Astrid Kander, Paolo Malanima, and Paul Warde, *Power to the People: Energy in Europe over the Last Five Centuries*, ed. by Astrid Kander, Paolo Malanima, and Paul Warde, *Power to the People: Energy in Europe over the Last Five Centuries* (Princeton and Oxford: Princeton University Press, 2014), p. 225 <https://doi.org/10.2307/j.ctt4cgb93>.

in general economic terms, simply by using these new fuels to power production.[709]

All the key transformations in the energy system of this sub-region was fuelled largely by coal consumption. By 1820, about one-third of energy consumption in Western Europe was coal.[710] This share of energy from coal increased to about four-fifths by the First World War. This provided abundant and cheap energy for urban dwellers, but with destructive health effects on them due to sulphur dioxide emissions and vitamin deficiencies from the lack of sunlight. It also caused serious lung ailments among the populace. The effects were so devastating that it got to a breaking point prompting scientific scholars to deduce that coal usage and large CO2 emissions would raise the Earth's temperature therefore causing global warming.[711]

Coal was king during this period in the western European sub-region, but it did not mean traditional energy carriers (such as food, fodder, water and wind) were excluded. Although they may have diminished in relative importance, their consumption, however, rose exponentially.[712] Through to the 2000s, coal remained vital to the energy economy of Germany and Britain.

The second and third industrial revolutions in the western European sub-region made it the epicentre for the incubation of an energy transition. This happened with the rise of oil and electricity, and its global ripple effect in the twentieth century. This energy transition again did not imply that traditional energy was being phased-out. What it actually did was to increase the total energy consumption. Over the period from 1870–2000 covering the long twentieth century, the use of energy in western Europe grew seven-fold while the population only grew two-fold. In simpler terms, it means that in year 2000, an average person had slightly more than three times the energy he or she needed in comparison to an average person in 1870.

There were clear disparities in energy distribution here again. For instance, in western Europe, Britain led the process in terms of the expansion and consumption of energy, followed by the second largest energy con-

709 Kander, Malanima, and Warde, p. 131.

710 Kander, Malanima, and Warde, p. 131.

711 Svante Arrhenius, 'On the Influence of Carbonic Acid in the Air upon the Temperature of the Ground', *Philosophical Magazine and Journal of Science*, 41.5 (1896), 237–76 <https://doi.org/10.1002/cta.4490080404>.

712 Kander, Malanima, and Warde, p. 144.

sumer, Germany, who consumed a quarter of what Britain consumed. This same trend applied to Dutch and French energy consumption.[713] By 1870, the western European had established a path dependence on heavy energy use equalled only by the United States and Canada who consumed more energy per capita. This level of consumption was unparalleled anywhere else in the world.[714]

The energy history of the western European sub-region of the EU in the nineteenth century was based on coal. That of the twentieth century was based on oil and electricity. Transforming and building the capital equipment and infrastructure for these new technologies of oil and electricity involved a huge cost. In the case of heavily dependent coal-fired power generation countries, huge capital investments were sunk into coal-powered technology, which continued to maintain its competitiveness as a relatively cheap and affordable fuel source. This discouraged a swift and major shift to oil.[715] This energy path dependence and rigid infrastructure (that is, lock-in) related to energy systems development defined the western European sub-region for quite some time.

The oil transition in western Europe was abrupt, due to a slow shift in transitioning from coal infrastructure. This was alongside an increasing dependence on oil use and imports. For almost a century, the share of oil increased gradually. Then, it rapidly jumped during the 1950s and 1960s when cheap oil flowed into the European energy commodities market, during which it witnessed a rise from ten percent to fifty percent. Electricity remained the second major energy carrier that saw an incremental growth in terms of contribution to the energy mix over the 1870–2005 period. This share of electricity was produced by mainly non-thermal sources, that is, hydropower (water-turbines) and nuclear power. In the 1970s, natural gas, another major energy carrier grew in terms of its share of the energy mix. Natural gas consumption did not generally apply to the whole of Europe. It was mainly used in Britain and The Netherlands where large natural gas reserves were discovered offshore. Nevertheless,

713 Kander, Malanima, and Warde, p. 254.

714 Sofia Teives Henriques, *Energy Transitions, Economic Growth and Structural Change: Portugal in a Long-Run Comparative Perspective*, *Lund Studies in Economic History 54* (Lund: Lund University Press, 2011).

715 Kander, Malanima, and Warde, p. 256.

this switch from oil to natural gas was huge enough to determine the entire European energy landscape.[716]

The western European sub-region of the EU, today is facing another energy shift under the so-called fourth industrial revolution. This is characterised by the digitisation of spaces and industry which enables individuals to navigate online and offline reality for productive purposes.[717] New paths are being created despite the lock-in effects arising from previous adopted energy carriers. This is being done partly through research and development (R&D), together with changes in national and EU energy policy.

This is illustrated in the environmental policy processes that is affecting coal generation. Another illustration is the pioneering work of innovators and inventors of new renewable energy technologies such as wind power – through niches developed in prior path dependent technological innovations, contemporary wind power technologies and infrastructure have emerged and are in use in countries like Germany, Denmark, The Netherlands and Britain. This has been done through a mix of R&D and investments (particularly in Britain) as well as commercialisation policy (especially in Germany).[718]

One of the problems associated with this path creation process is the usual chicken-and-egg challenges that do happen when new energy systems are being rolled out. A typical case is being able to use a fuel cell vehicle only when there are charging stations dotted across a city.

---

716 Harold Lubell, 'Security of Supply and Energy Policy in Western Europe', *World Politics*, 13.03 (2006), 400–422 <https://doi.org/10.2307/2009482>; Kander, Malanima, and Warde, pp. 256–57.

717 For more on the fourth industrial revolution see: Min Xu, Jeanne M. David, and Suk Hi Kim, 'The Fourth Industrial Revolution: Opportunities and Challenges', *International Journal of Financial Research*, 9.2 (2018), 90 <https://doi.org/10.5430/ijfr.v9n2p90>; World Economic Forum, 'Fostering Effective Energy Transition. A Fact-Based Framework to Support Decision-Making', *McKinsey & Company*, 2018, p. 40 <http://www3.weforum.org/docs/WEF_Fostering_Effective_Energy_Transition_report_2018.pdf>.

718 James Simmie, Rolf Sternberg, and Juliet Carpenter, 'New Technological Path Creation: Evidence from the British and German Wind Energy Industries', *Journal of Evolutionary Economics*, 24.4 (2014), 875–904 <https://doi.org/10.1007/s00191-014-0354-8>.

4.2.4 Southern Europe

The southern European sub-region of the EU (made up of Spain, Portugal, Italy, Greece, Cyprus and Malta) mainly located in the Mediterranean, have experienced a long trajectory of reliance on traditional energy carriers (food, fodder, etc.) and a move to modern energy carriers. Due to their warm climate, much energy is not needed for heating houses though, on the contrary, cooling has required a sizeable share of energy recently. This in one way has contributed to their total energy composition that was defined by a relatively small amount of firewood and coal, and a relatively large part of feed for animals and food for people in terms of traditional energy. Before the transition from traditional energy to modern energy especially in the period before the twentieth century, traditional energy carriers represented between seventy to eighty percent of the total energy consumed in southern Europe.[719]

During the period when coal was the predominant energy source, Italy did not possess any indigenous coal deposits or reserves and had to rely on imports for all of its consumption. Hence, the coal transition was never as profound as exhibited by the coal economies of the CEE and western sub-regions of the EU. Coal peaked in Italy when it became 35 percent of its energy mix in the first half of the twentieth century. Oil became the dominant energy source in southern Europe in the decades after the Second World War, and it was characterised by variations, with Spain and Portugal closely following Italy. Electric power generation and industrial heat processes were based on the oil transition.[720].

Reserves of energy carriers like oil and natural gas do not exist in substantial quantities within the sub-region. Until recently, the oil and natural gas exploration in the sub-region got a major boost from the significant finds of natural gas in Cyprus.[721] For a long period, the region has entirely been dependent on external fossil fuel supplies.

The total installed capacity of hydroelectricity in the sub-region is about 50 GW, with Italy and Spain being the top hydropower producing coun-

719 Silvana Bartoletto and Maria del Mar Rubio Varas, 'Energy Transition and CO2 Emissions in Southern Europe: Italy and Spain (1861–2000)', *Global Environment*, 2 (2008), 47–81.

720 Kander, Malanima, and Warde, p. 275.

721 Constantinos Taliotis and others, 'Natural Gas in Cyprus: The Need for Consolidated Planning', *Energy Policy*, 107. April 2017 (2017), 197–209 <https://doi.org/10.1016/j.enpol.2017.04.047>.

tries in the sub-region.[722] Hydropower contributes a limited amount of southern Europe's energy supply. But it is subject to the unpredictability of an irregular hydrological year, with severe dry summers sometimes.

Economically, the region was a late comer to the industrialization process. To a degree, the countries in the region share similarities that have resulted in parallel energy trajectories, albeit with some nuanced difference.

Nuclear power generation in the region for electricity began in the early 1960s with Italy, and later Spain. But in 2011, the Italian people voted to completely phase-out and decommission all nuclear power plants in the country.[723] The sub-region's major strength in the European Union's energy regionalism has been its contribution to the Liquefied Natural Gas (LNG) market originally developed in the 1970s-1980s in the Mediterranean Basin. France, Italy and Spain have been the main LNG importing countries taking deliveries from Algeria and Libya who were their main export countries.

LNG development in southern Europe employed the method of partner states and triangular diplomacy.[724] National Energy Champions from the region namely Gaz de France (GDF) in France, Ente Nazionale Idrocarburi (ENI)-Snam in Italy, and Enagas in Spain have been the main promoters and developers of these sub-regional gas megaprojects. They have also negotiated contractual deals with their producer counterparts – Sonatrach of Algeria and National Oil Company of Libya – supported by state diplomacy in Madrid, Rome and Paris.[725]

A major consequence of the energy path of the region has been higher levels of energy poverty. Although the winters are milder, the region has reported higher percentages of people who cannot keep their homes

---

722 World Energy Council, 'Europe : Hydropower', *World Energy Resources*, 2016 <https://www.worldenergy.org/data/resources/region/europe/hydropower/> [accessed 1 March 2019].

723 Bartoletto and Varas; Sonia Brondi and others, 'Parliamentary and Press Discourses on Sustainable Energy in Italy: No More Hard Paths, Not yet Soft Paths', *Energy Research and Social Science*, 2 (2014), 38–48 <https://doi.org/10.1016/j.erss.2014.04.011>.

724 Andrea Prontera, 'The New Politics of Energy Security and the Rise of the Catalytic State in Southern Europe', *Journal of Public Policy*, 38.4 (2018), 511–51 <https://doi.org/10.1017/S0143814X1700006X>.

725 Francis Ghilès, 'España y El Gas Argelino', *Política Exterior*, 9.44 (1995), 169–76; Phillip C. Naylor, *France and Algeria: A History of Decolonization and Transformation, Canadian Journal of African Studies / Revue Canadienne Des Études Africaines* (Gainesville: University Press of Florida, 2008), xxxvi <https://doi.org/10.2307/4107416>.

warm.[726] For example, the evidence shows that higher levels of indoor thermal discomfort were discovered in southern Europe in the 2000s.[727]

In an attempt to help address the effect of energy and fuel poverty, southern European members of the EU have been an attractive destination for Chinese energy investments. They offer their expertise and investments to southern European countries to attain energy supply security and to construct the energy infrastructure they require. Four countries have been the primary beneficiaries, namely, Italy, Spain Portugal and Greece; with impressive Chinese acquisitions situated in the Italian and Portuguese energy markets. Conversely, Chinese presence in the Greek and Spanish energy markets have been a bit discrete.

More specifically, in the area of renewable energy investments among the four countries, Chinese investments in solar-related projects have been more prominent in Italy and Spain, than in Greece and Portugal. Whereas, Greece and Spain have benefitted more in funding operations in wind-related projects than the others have. Overall, some experts see these Chinese energy investments in modern conventional energy sources and renewables in southern Europe as a mix bag of opportunities and challenges.[728]

The development of new energy pathways in the southern European sub-region (as a result of the adopted and implemented energy policies at country level since the 1990s), is contributing to an improvement in energy supply diversity. This has been executed by the initiation of the transition toward a more sustainable energy system. However, the debilitating effects of the financial crisis in the region minimised their attractiveness to imported resources predominantly in the transport sector. Yet, it has also increased the role of renewable energy sources, requiring adequate and sufficient financial capital to drive this transition.[729]

---

726 Bouzarovski and Tirado Herrero.

727 Harriet Thomson and Carolyn Snell, 'Quantifying the Prevalence of Fuel Poverty across the European Union', *Energy Policy*, 52.2013 (2013), 563–72 <https://doi.org/10.1016/j.enpol.2012.10.009>.

728 Pablo Pareja-Alcaraz, 'Chinese Investments in Southern Europe's Energy Sectors: Similarities and Divergences in China's Strategies in Greece, Italy, Portugal and Spain', *Energy Policy*, 101 (2017), 700–710 <https://doi.org/10.1016/j.enpol.2016.09.034>.

729 Konstantinos J. Chalvatzis and Alexis Ioannidis, 'Energy Supply Security in Southern Europe and Ireland', *Energy Procedia*, 105.2006 (2017), 2916–22 <https://doi.org/10.1016/j.eg,ypro.2017.03.660>.

The southern European sub-region of the European Union has undergone energy path dependence through the use of hydropower and thermal powered generation of electricity. On the other hand, it is undergoing path creation through the development of LNG terminals and renewable energy technologies. Since this energy path creation requires major investments, positioning itself to attract both internal EU investments and external Chinese investments, has been noted as being crucial for the sub-region in this process.

4.3 Evolution of EU Regionalism

Before considering the evolution of energy regionalism in the European Union, it is essential to explore European integration history. The origins of EU regionalism, which resulted in the founding of the EU, began way before 1945. This falls within the period I call the Pre-Great War Years, which was followed by the Mid – War Years and then the Post War Years.

The origins of European integration occurred way before the turbulence of the post-1930 era and it evolved over time. Some of the most authoritative accounts of European integration by political historians and social scientists stop short of telling an integration narrative that goes way before the commencement of World War 1.[730] Using a non-linear approach, I recap the pooling of European sovereignties a little before 1800 until it climaxed into the reliable regional integration project we know today.

This section considers two basic themes. Firstly, with reference to the following factors the narrative of integration history is retold. I weave a historical narrative that follows a path which leads up to what we now call the European Union. It is laced with the main successes and failures, key elites that championed this process of integration, internal European political pressures, and external global pressures as well as the role of national and European interests based on their ideational beliefs. Secondly, I argue that EU regionalism is a process that has produced a distinctive and

730 Martin Dedman, *The Origins and Development of the European Union 1945-2008: A History of European Integration*, 2nd edn (London and New York: Routledge, 2010); Desmond Dinan, *Europe Recast: A History of European Union*, 2nd edn (Basingstoke, UK: Palgrave Macmillan, 2014); Ludger Kühnhardt, *European Union–the Second Founding: The Changing Rationale of European Integration*, 2nd edn (Baden-Baden: Nomos, 2010); Giuliano Garavini, *After Empires: European Integration, Decolonization, and the Challenge from the Global South 1957-1986*, 1st edn (Oxford: Oxford University Press, 2012).

cohesive political system. I argue that this political system was established when the six founding member states began to co-operate in the production of coal and steel, which then became the key industrial drivers of the European economy.

EU regionalism has since developed into a peculiar kind of political system, which benefits from collective action by pooling sovereignties through the use of intergovernmental relations and supranational governance processes. The processes inherent in EU regionalism has created an entity capable of representing its member states with a unified front not only to express its interests with one voice on the global stage, but also to coalesce around common policy areas such as energy.

4.3.1 EU Regionalism History Retold

A Europe united in peace and prosperity has been the aim of numerous European political and intellectual leaders throughout the ages. Despite Europe's diverse demography, the essence of European unity was promoted and aided by the proximate nature of its geography and interconnectedness present among its peoples. Pursuant to the realisation of this course for unity, earlier attempts were achieved using violent approaches. Exemplifying this narrative are the actions of the Holy Roman Emperors, Napoleon, Hitler, among others who sought regional unity employing monarchical or canonical alliances, ethnic cohesion, ideology or raw power.[731]

Since the emergence of the modern state in the mid-seventeenth century, a united Europe has been imagined to help assuage a myopic national view composed of territorial interests.[732] States that signed the various treaties leading to the formation of the European communities (ECSC, EURATOM, European Economic Community inter alia) which eventually resulted in the creation of the EU, decided to limit but not eliminate their sovereignty, the key ingredient of the modern nation-state.[733] It made it possible for them to benefit from collective action in relation to economic integration, supranational governance and intergovernmental relations.

731 Dinan, *Europe Recast: A History of European Union*.

732 Dinan, *Europe Recast: A History of European Union*.

733 Alan S. Milward, *The European Rescue of the Nation-State*, ed. by Alan S.Milward, George Brennan, and Federico Romero, 2nd edn (London and New York: Routledge, 2000); Kühnhardt.

Milestones in the historiography of European regionalism can be characterised in four stages. These include, the first wave: pre-Great War years, second wave: mid-war years, third wave: post-war years and the fourth wave: founding of the EU.

4.3.1.1 First Wave: Pre-Great War Years

One can confidently assert that the notion of European integration appeared long before 1945. Earlier attempts to unify Europe preceded the First World War going back centuries even into the eighteenth century.[734] However, it intensified after the destructive effects of the second global conflict instigated by an allure to consolidate German hegemony that pulled in other powerful European nation-states. The end of the Napoleonic wars of 1793–1815 in Europe sealed with the Vienna settlement spurred the victors, the United Kingdom, Prussia, Austria and Russia to reconstruct the devastated continent. The triumphant powers promised each other mutual assistance in case of internal commotion and external threats.[735]

In fact, this major reconstruction was occurring at the same time the first industrial revolution (1760–1840) got underway. This facilitated an extraordinary level of international trade through the quest and search for raw materials and labour (that is, slavery and indentured workers from and to colonised territories). Subsequently, the face of the geopolitical landscape globally began to change through colonialism and international trade. This led to the many formations of customs unions and the signing of a number of trade treaties. It often included bilateral agreements on military support between the greater powers in Europe. In addition, it prompted ideas on cross-national cooperation, and this could be interpreted as early attempts of setting-up a Pan-European integration agenda.[736]

---

734 For a wide-ranging background see Michael Gehler, *EUROPA* (Frankfurt am Main: Fischer Taschenbuch Verlag, 2002), pp. 3–27; Michael. Gehler, *Europa : Ideen - Institutionen - Vereinigung* (Munich: Olzog, 2010), pp. 67–100; Peter Krüger, *Das Unberechenbare Europa : Epochen Des Integrationsprozesses Vom Späten 18. Jahrhundert Bis Zur Europäischen Union* (Stuttgart: Kohlhammer, 2006), pp. 19–34.

735 Eric J. Hobsbawm, *Nations and Nationalism since 1780 : Programme, Myth, Reality*, 2nd edn (Cambridge,UK: Cambridge University Press, 1992).

736 Peter M.R. Stirk, *A History of European Integration since 1914*, 2nd edn (London and New York: Continuum, 2001).

Yet, little came of it and instead, 'nationalism' and the rise of constitutional liberalism, catalysed the political events within European countries until the start of the Great War in 1914.[737]

At the Vienna Congress of 1814 -1815, the main objective was to provide a long-term peace plan for Europe. This was to be achieved by settling issues arising out of the French Revolutionary wars and the Napoleonic wars. One key dynamic of the Vienna Settlement was to reorder, geographically and politically, the central European region (*Mitteleuropa*). This redistribution included the reconstitution of Germany as a confederacy made up of 39 states.[738]

The setting-up of the German Confederation in 1815 proved to be successful and beneficial for its constituents and neighbours alike. First, it led to the establishment of a customs union, *Zollverein*, in 1834 guaranteeing rapid economic growth for members of the confederation and laying the foundations for unification under Prussia. Second, the sovereign princes who made up the confederacy hoped to secure the gains made under this new political order from radical nationalist tendencies and actors. Third, the redistribution of territory and power between the two major powers (Prussia and Austria) and a host of some minor powers sought to curtail the threat that Germany posed.[739] The *Zollverein* served as an effective tool for the unification of Germany in 1871, an important *prototype* that exemplified how European economic integration could be done. This obvious success story exerted an enduring influence on the debates that characterised European regionalism in the twentieth century.[740]

A careful look at Mahant and De Vanssay's[741] account of the *Zollverein* reveals a much more nuanced representation of its setup and its contributions to the origins of free trade areas and customs unions in Europe. Thirty states constituted the customs union dominated by Prussia, which contributed fifty-four percent of the union's population. The second largest was Bavaria with thirteen percent. There were a series of three customs unions, each one identified by the same name, *Zollverein*. The first customs

737 Hans Keman, 'It's a Long Way to Europe : The Post War Process of Integration' (Chengdu, 2007).

738 Harold Nicolson, *The Congress of Vienna : A Study in Allied Unity, 1812-1822* (New York: Grove Press, 1946).

739 Stirk.

740 Stirk.

741 Edelgard Mahant and Xavier De Vanssay, 'The Origins of Customs Unions and Free Trade Areas', *Journal of European Integration*, 17.2–3 (1994), 181–210 <https://doi.org/10.1080/07036339408429004>.

union was formed in 1818 between the various geographical territories that constituted post-1815 Prussia. This Zollverein was fundamentally an internal Prussian affair. With the conclusion of the border alterations sanctioned by the Congress of Vienna, the second Zollverein was created progressively ending the adoption of a general treaty on January 1, 1834. In this case as well, Prussia controlled the most influence over the constituent states mostly the south and central (excluding the north) German states.

The Habsburg customs union by Austria was established as a counter balance to undermine the Prussian-led Zollverein. This instigated further tensions between Prussia and Austria who were both trying to gain dominant influence over the shared confederated states they both were engaging in. After the Prussian victory in the Austro-Prussian war, the third Zollverein of 1867 was instituted. Here it included most of the German states with the exception of Austria and the North Sea ports.

The motivation of Prussia to create the *Zollverein* was definitely not a long-term strategic move to expand its hegemonic powers in continental Europe but rather to set up a scheme to unify Germany.[742] The Prussian elite then were aware that economic integration set into motion a virtuous cycle of economic growth and national political enhancement. The *Zollverein* immensely enhanced free trade, drawing protectionist France into a Franco-Prussian Treaty, which Prussia compelled other members of the union to abide by as a condition for renewal.[743] Prussia employed the Zollverein as a political tool when it realised Austria had alternate plans to undermine its ultimate unification agenda. But this tool was the means to hedge its place in the power politics of the European landscape of the time, especially, in opposition to Austria and France.

Overall, the innovation of the Zollvereins as an instrument by Prussia, did not only serve the purpose of expansionism and unification. Nevertheless, it was useful in fuelling economic growth and cooperation. It also predicted the political successes that an integrated region could benefit from as was witnessed with that of Prussia and the confederacy states. The threats posed was that the increasing national power of German unification made its neighbours, that is, Austria and France, militarily insecure.

Around Europe, the desire for peaceful coexistence and economic prosperity was at its peak and being advocated for by key European elite. The French political and economic theorist Henri de Saint-Simon in 1814, advocated for European integration through social-economic homogeneity,

742 Mahant and De Vanssay.
743 Stirk.

using a federation which has common interests independent of the constituent states, as the vehicle. He published his ideas just around the period of the Vienna Congress.[744] Von Gentz, the prominent architect of the Vienna settlement drew up institutional provisions of periodic conferences that would engage the great powers, which he called the Congress system. Other notable figures in that era who were working and pushing for integration of a sort were the proponents of the Austrian customs union, which was going to constitute their share of the German confederacy.

Ludwig Von Bruck, then Commerce Minister, and his political senior, Minister-President Prince Felix zu Schwarzenberg, promoted a vision of a central Europe composed of three federations namely, the new Austrian led Zollverein, Swiss federation and the Italian federation. This idea was updated many years later by the academic proposal from the Frenchman Guido de Molinari, on the establishment of a central European customs union, drawing heavily from the Zollverein innovation. Thus, in 1879 it suggested its composition should be France, Belgium, Holland, Germany, Denmark, Austria and Switzerland.[745]

Another notable personality was Victor Hugo, the Italian leader of the Congress of the Friends of Peace (1849) gathering in Paris. He assembled the leading philosophers and politicians of the day including Charles Gilpin and Richard Cobden. Whilst in this meeting he promoted his idea of the United States of Europe. In this idea, Europe would be composed of parliamentary systems that would eventually unite in the course of time. However, intellectual disciples of Giuseppe Mazzini opposed these ideas vehemently.[746]

Considering the political pressures that defined these processes, one point arises in this setting: whether or not economic progress of the underdeveloped was supported or rather obstructed by their relationship with the economically advanced. Again, another consideration of whether or not free trade or protection presented the best opportunities or risks for growth, as well as, whether integration symbolised by the novel custom unions were the advantageous options needed.

As the University of Durham political historian, Peter Stirk looks at it, the discussion transpired in independent states like Romania and transna-

744 Saint-Simon Claude-Henri, *De La Réorganisation de La Société Européenne* (Paris: Adrian Égron, 1814).

745 Guido de Molinari, 'L'union Douanière de l'Europe Centrale', *Journal Des Économistes*, 5 (1879), 309–18.

746 Stirk.

tional territories like the Habsburg Empire.[747] For instance, the Habsburg customs union produced an enabling atmosphere for economic growth.

These free trade and custom union (Zollverein) trends, pointed themselves towards greater European integration and unity. The Prussian-led *Zollvereins,* the Habsburg Empire's "federal solution"[748] and the numerous arguments by the political and intellectual elite of Europe in the pre-great war years for a unified Europe of a sort (either a Europe-wide union, federation, customs union or a loose-knit confederacy) were the prevailing ideas that sowed the seeds for EU regionalism as we know it.

4.3.1.2 Second Wave: Mid-War Years

Early advocates of European Regionalism in the twentieth-century consisted of authoritarians and nationalists focused on revising borders established at Versailles, and ideologues (communists and agrarian radicals). The model of European unity and their political ideology was the main dividing factor. They contested principally two main points. That is, the membership composition of any union of Europe and whether or not Britain would be interested to be part. Many recognised the need for Franco-German alliance and the role of Britain to maintain that balance between these two great trouble-causing powers in the region.

World War One ended the nineteenth century European order and introduced an attempt to reconfigure Europe in the mould of a German-dominated *Mitteleuropa* which was flawed from within.[749] At the core of this defect stood an alliance between the two great powers, the German Reich and the Habsburg Empire with divergent ambitions. The Habsburg Empire made up of multiple nationalities sought to use the benefits of victory to minimise the tensions existing between its constituent nations. Meanwhile, the German Reich was leaning more towards Germanic hegemony with expansive colonial influence all the way into Russia. Mitteleuropa failed not as a result of its domestic political pressures but because it was overcome by the superior might of its opponents, most notably the United States. As Peter Stirk asserts, the indifference or active intervention

747 Stirk.
748 Stirk, p. 13.
749 Stirk, p. 18.

war saw a decline by both western and eastern European states towards increased integration.

Reconstruction efforts were conducted based on a universalist approach through the League of Nations. Even though Article 21 of its Charter provided for the maintenance of valid international engagements such as regional and arbitration treaties such as the Monroe Doctrine. Woodrow Wilson who was the architect of the League envisioned an international, not a regionalist, project. The main critics of this global vision insisting on a European federation was Giovanni Agnelli, the founder of the automaker FIAT, and his compatriot Attilio Cabiati, an economist. They called for a European federation modelled after the United States of America and contended that "any other milder version is but a delusion"[754].

The Austrian aristocrat, Richard Coudenhove-Karlergi, founder of the Pan-European Union and his vision of a *Pan-Europa* captured the imagination of both political and intellectual elite of Europe for some time in the 1920s. Coudenhove-Karlergi published his influential book Pan-Europa in 1923, and called for a federal union of European states pivoted by Germany and France but with the exclusion of the Soviet Union and Britain due to communism and their imperialist tendencies respectively.[755] A competitor on this Federalist Europa idea, in the person of Wilhelm Heile (the chairman of the Verband für europäische Verständigung as well as the vice-President of the Österreichisch-Deutschen Volksbund whose agenda was Austro-German Anschluss) opposed the exclusion of Russia and Britain on the basis that Britain could temper the perceived understanding of a union that will prop up German hegemony.[756] The first person he approached with his ideas was the fascist leader of Italy, Benito Mussolini. However, the idea, which originally was not a democratic vision, was rejected. Based on this upset, and on the swelling public support for the idea, Heile transformed the vision to be more representative and democratic.[757]

By the time the Treaty of Locarno was signed in 1925 the Pan-European union vision was the most prevailing idea for European integration. This was justified by the plethora of journals and publications dedicated to this movement. This was confirmed in the two speeches delivered by the French Prime Minister Edouard Herriot in 1924 and 1925 anticipating the realisation of the United States of Europe. Moreover, the positive response

754 Quoted from Stirk, p. 23.

755 Stirk, pp. 26–27.

756 Stirk, p. 28.

757 Stirk, p. 26; Dinan, *Europe Recast: A History of European Union*, pp. 2–3.

in 1925 by the German Foreign Minister (and one-time Chancellor) Gustav Stresemann in support for a United States of Europe, was seen as a step in the right direction for European regionalism by a section of the European media.[758]

A plan devised by the French Prime Minister Aristide Briand in 1930 for an association of European states subordinated to the League of Nations with the aim of coordinating economic policies and the promotion of a political union would influence subsequent developments for European integration. Briand's famous memo did not recommend any loss of sovereignty to the constituent states. The League established the Committee of Enquiry on the European Union to look further into Briand's memorandum. This Briand plan entailed three parts. The first part composed of the introductory and foundational dimension of the pact. The second part focused on the institutional mechanism necessary for the establishment of the union. This was shaped by the example of the institutional structure of the League of Nations. The third part indicated the subordination of the economic problem to the political. This was the most contentious of all the proposals inherent in Briand's memorandum. Because it sought to suggest a reversal of the order of priorities, which had been set out previously.[759]

The mid-war years were characterised by a unique set of bold ideas, interests, initiatives and persons geared towards European integration. It would be incomplete to consider the process of EU regionalism without taking into account the contributions of this consequential era that led to the post-war efforts to reunite Europe.

4.3.1.3 Third Wave: Post-War Years

The war between European states from 1931 to 1941 reached a climax into what became known as the Second World War. It decimated Europe's power tremendously, leading to the loss of its colonial strongholds. A renewal of interests in federalism began to surge to counter the rise of fascist regimes that were springing up across the European continent prior to and during the war. In Britain this saw the thriving of federalist ideas, notable among the intellectual leaders who championed this cause

758 Stirk, pp. 28–29.
759 Stirk, pp. 28–35.

were Lionel Curtis, Lord Lothain and Harold Laski. They established the Federal Union in 1938 to serve as a conduit for the cause.

The Federal Union adopted a goal in September 1944, of an "immediate aim for the promotion of a democratic federation of Europe as part of the post-war settlement."[760] In addition to the British federalists was the Italian federalist movement that was brewing in the prisons of the island of Ventotene. Notable among its leaders was the democratic socialist, Altiero Spinelli. In July 1941, they sneaked out their Manifesto for a Free and United Europe during the Nazi occupation of Rome.[761] The so-called Ventotene Manifesto was modelled after nineteenth century Italian federalism calling for a post-war federation of Europe which included Germany in order to preserve the peace. This enthused the Italian federalists after conferring with other resistance movements across Nazi-occupied Europe. They secretly circulated the International Federalist Declaration after an underground conference held in Geneva in 1944.[762]

While the Nazis malevolently integrated Europe with coercive force, Albert Speer, Hitler's architect and the Third Reich's minister of arms tinkered with the idea of a possibly voluntary and collectively-shared post-war economic community in Europe. Based on accounts from his military liaison officer, Speer was convinced of a collective economic sovereignty: "He was certain that the only way towards a better and peaceful future, not only for Germany but for all of Europe, was if Germany could eventually be part of an economic European entity."[763] Decades later, Speer confirmed this assertion by claiming that together with the French minister of production Jean Bichelonne, they agreed to avoid the errors of the Great War era by finding a path for economic integration in Europe.[764]

Winston Churchill, the British Prime Minister (in 1940–45 and 1951–55) became a dynamic campaigner for an integrated Europe. In 1946, Churchill delivered a legendary speech, at the University of Zurich, in which he promoted the idea of a 'United States of Europe', urging Europeans to renounce the horrors, hatreds and injuries of the past and look forward as a European family to forge a common peaceful and prosperous

760 Michael Burgess, *The British Tradition of Federalism* (London: Leicester University Press, 1995), p. 146.; Stirk, pp. 30–40

761 Charles F. Delzell, 'The European Federalist Movement in Italy: The First Phase, 1918-1947', *The Journal of Modern History*, 23.3 (1960), 241–50.

762 Dinan, *Europe Recast: A History of European Union*.

763 Quoted in Gitta. Sereny, *Albert Speer : His Battle With Truth* (New York: Vintage Books, 1996), p. 554.

764 Sereny, pp. 385–90.

future. As a strategic response to his Zurich speech, Churchill advocated as a first step to European integration the founding of the Council of Europe project. On 5 May 1949, the organisation was created, and in attendance was Churchill himself to witness such a ground-breaking occasion.[765]

An external political pressure, which supported European integration after the Second World War, was the central influence of the United States of America. Even though the US did not overtly recommend the federation of European states, it reinforced its commitment for economic integration in the interest of guaranteed peace in Europe.[766] However, though the USA subsidised the reconstruction efforts of the European states through the 1947 Marshall Plan, and demanded that the recipient states should co-operate in its implementation, it did not insist on a formation of a United States of Europe because it was opposed by the UK and France, the two most powerful western European states at the time.[767] In effect, the Marshall Plan was the most history altering response to combat the crisis of economic disintegration, the threats of Soviet communism being debated in Europe and the devastating failure of political existence that threatened western Europe's relevance.[768]

This idealism, together with the pragmatism of the post-war years for deeper European integration, were strong driving forces that would mould modern European Regionalism. Within this era the key players behind this movement responded aptly to the prevailing circumstances leading eventually to the processes that triggered the creation of today's European Union.

---

765 Max Beloff, 'Churchill and Europe', in *Churchill* (Oxford: Oxford University Press, 1996), pp. 443–56 <https://doi.org/10.1093/acprof:oso/9780198206262.003.0026>.

766 Desmond Dinan, *Ever Closer Union : An Introduction to European Integration*, 4th edn (London: Lynne Rienner Publishers, Inc, 2010), pp. 13–15.

767 Eric J. Hobsbawm, *The Age of Extremes : A History of the World, 1914-1991* (London: Vintage Books, 1996).

768 Michael Gehler, 'Challenges and Opportunities: Surmounting Integration Crises in Historical Context', in *Crises in European Integration: Challenges and Responses, 1945-2005*, ed. by Ludger Kühnhardt, Challenges and Responses, 1945-2005 (New York and Oxford: Berghahn Books, 2011), pp. 109–30 (p. 113).

4.3.1.4 Fourth Wave: Founding of the EU

Reflecting on the founding of the EU brings to mind the need to mention the two foremost economic philosophies that shaped the process of European integration after the post-war years. That is, the philosophy of Friedrich von Hayek, the liberal theoreticians of the Freiburg School and the pragmatic and interventionist ideas of Jean Monnet, the towering figure considered by many as one of the founding fathers of European unity. This would consequently make his ideas pivotal to the construction of European integration.[769]

The idea that the removal of marketplace distortions in favour of competition will fuel growth and result in integration was a prevalent view that influenced EU regionalism. Hayek and the Freiburg School were those most closely linked with this philosophical approach. In a pioneering article on the eve of the Second World War, Hayek postulated that, formerly diverse populations could come together in an interstate federation, through the removal of trade blockades. Thus, averting identification of special economic interests between states, and minimising prospects for market-distorting policies. The spontaneous nature of the market could thus play out without any distractions. Furthermore, he suggested that the competition principle, if allowed to function in the process, sets in motion a reciprocally reinforcing mutual process in which the market and government together reduce interstate conflict and promote economic growth. This liberal logic underlined Hayek's understanding of the process for integration in Europe.[770]

After the collapse of the Bretton Woods system, Ludwig Erhard, the man who turned West Germany into the engine and model of European economic growth and his economic team, introduced Hayekian approaches into the integration process.[771] Another proponent of Hayekian ideas, Margaret Thatcher, the liberal conservative UK Prime Minister became a

769 Christopher Chivvis, 'A Liberal History of European Integration', *International Affairs*, 79.5 (2003), 1065–69.

770 John R Gillingham, 'A Theoretical Vacuum: European Integration and Historical Research Today', *Journal of European Integration History*, 14.1995 (2008), 27–34 <http://www.eu-historians.eu/uploads/Dateien/jeih-27-2008_1.pdf>.

771 Gillingham, 'A Theoretical Vacuum: European Integration and Historical Research Today'.

driving force behind the relaunch of European integration in the 1980s with the coming into force of the Single European Act.[772]

Now, the question was the direction to take in achieving European integration. This was between negative integration and positive integration. *Negative integration* stands for the application of stipulated rules to guide economic activity whereas *Positive integration* stands for the establishment of newly created institutions to overcome *market failure*. These two integration approaches took precedence on how the integration process could be achieved. Overtime, the pragmatic and interventionist adherents of positive integration like Jean Monnet and Jacques Delors occupied centre stage in the integration dialogue but liberal market thinkers of the Hayekian persuasion were more productive. This is depicted by the EU success stories such as the generation of new wealth, stimulation of ideas in the midst of crises and chaos, and vigorous social change.[773]

Robert Schuman, then French Foreign Minister, on 9 May 1950 issued a declaration, which was inspired and drafted by Jean Monnet, the head of the French department of economic planning, Commisariate de Plan. The Schuman Declaration would lead to the pooling of the heavy industries of his nation France and that of Germany as well as other neighboring states. This pooling of coal and steel would lead to the creation of what would later be called the European Coal and Steel Community (ECSC). According to the declaration,

> "The French Government proposes that Franco-German production of coal and steel as a whole be placed under a common High Authority, within the framework of an organisation open to the participation of other countries of Europe. The pooling of coal and steel production should immediately provide for the setting up of common foundations for economic development as a first step in the federation of Europe..."[774]

With subsequent negotiations, 'the Six', that is the six founding nations of the community namely France, Germany, Belgium, The Netherlands, Luxembourg and Italy on 19th March 1951 would sign the Paris Treaty setting up a High Authority to serve as the executive organ of the ECSC. Jean

772 John R Gillingham, *European Integration, 1950-2003: Superstate or New Market Economy?* (Cambridge,UK: Cambridge University Press, 2003).

773 Gillingham, *European Integration, 1950-2003: Superstate or New Market Economy?*

774 Robert Schuman, 'Declaration of 9th May 1950 Delivered by Robert Schuman', *European Issue*, 2011, 1–3.

Monnet became the first president of the High Authority until 1955. Monnet's greatest accomplishment was the founding of the ECSC. It set off the process that changed Europe from a continent traditionally divided by nationalism into an emergent civilization formed by collective economic institutions and animated by a common political spirit.[775] The founding documents established the ECSC as a supranational body. This led to the creation of a common market for coal, steel, coke, iron ore and scrap between the six founding member states. Britain refused to participate in the talks from the beginning. States that participated and agreed to join the predecessor of the EU, the ECSC, did so principally as a means to secure the national interest rather than out of federalist zeal.[776]

One of the successes of the ECSC was that it substituted for a peace plan with Germany and did not only serve as an economic and industrial benefit. It again served as a political foundation for a more thorough international settlement premised on the recognition that unlimited national sovereignty has become a costly historical hindrance. Monnet understood this basic and authoritative truth during World War I. The ECSC however came to a disappointing halt when it was beset with overwhelming challenges that it could not surmount chief among them included, the failure to reform big business rather it restored it.

In addition, the High Authority was unable either to govern in a supranational manner or create a genuine common market. Amidst all these failures that had the potential to obscure the significant aspects of Jean Monnet's work, he had a vision, a plan and the capability to execute this visionary future, which his critics were unable to achieve. Nor can one readily envisage a more boldly imagined and implemented diplomatic initiative than the one undertaken based on the Schuman Plan. Short of the amazing strength of Monnet's Washington networks in the end, it would have been impossible to assure the Germans equality while in the meantime guaranteeing French security. Even though the coal and steel collective was imperfect, it was not a failure. The ECSC would ultimately become a forerunner to a stronger and more permanent union. Jean Mon-

775 John R Gillingham, *Coal, Steel, and the Rebirth of Europe, 1945—1955: The Germans and French from Ruhr Conflict to Economic Community* (Cambridge,UK: Cambridge University Press, 1991).

776 Milward.

net's vision and proactive execution enabled Europeans to reshape again their own destiny.[777]

Again, in the 1950s two Treaties of Rome were signed into being, creating the European Economic Community (EEC) and the European Atomic Energy Community (EURATOM) in 1957. The link established between the devised European common market and cooperation in the area of nuclear energy was vital in the beginning. Nuclear energy was perceived as the energy fuel source of the future. It was believed generally that any country that did not adopt this novel energy technology would soon become impoverished. In France, there was consensus for the development of an atomic energy industry that was vital to serve as a critical fuel source and facilitate technical and scientific advancement.[778]

Another important factor in these considerations was the role of Germany, even though Germany trailed France in the area of nuclear energy, it possessed immense scientific capability with thriving expertise in the chemical industry, which it could rapidly deploy to enhance concrete cooperation in this area.[779] Moreover, this strategic coupling between the EEC and EURATOM was essential in initially persuading and ultimately convincing France, which was sceptical, to fully participate in European integration after the debacle concerning the 'European Army'. In effect, this tactical pairing served as a strategic political move. Eventually becoming the vehicle for relaunching European integration after the miscarriage of the European Defence Community (EDC).

Thus, the origins of the revitalisation of European integration through EURATOM and the EEC are closely intertwined with that of the ECSC and EDC failures. Finally, EURATOM was to be overshadowed by the common market. However, earlier discussions in many quarters in 1955 and early 1956 widely believed otherwise.[780] A less well-known fact differ-

---

777 John R Gillingham, 'Jean Monnet and the European Coal and Steel Community: A Preliminary Appraisal', in *Jean Monnet: The Path to European Unity* (New York: St. Martin's Press, 1991), pp. 129–62 <https://doi.org/10.1007/978-1-137-12050-2>.

778 Documents Diplomatiques Français, 'Memorandum of End April/Beginning of May : Document 239', 1955.

779 Christian Deubner, 'The Expansion of West German Capital and the Founding of Euratom', *International Organization*, 33.2 (1979), 203–28 <https://doi.org/10.1017/S0020818300032148>.

780 Mervyn O'Driscoll, 'The Origins and Early History of Euratom, 1955-1968', in *The European Parliament and the Euratom Treaty: Past, Present and Future* (Luxembourg: European Parliament, 2002), pp. 1–44 <http://www.europarl.eu.int/studies.> [accessed 1 March 2018].

ent from traditional analyses was that, the Atomic Community was neither an irrelevant fringe concern seconded to common market deliberations, nor was it simply a vehicle to realise the EEC. Quite the reverse, the idea and consultations toward EURATOM became indispensable stepping-stones to the realisation and development of the common market.[781] In this vein, this strategic connection regarding the common market and nuclear energy cooperation contributed a generous service to the European project.

The EEC developed gradually throughout the mid-1950s and 1960 but in the 1970s its evolution rapidly began to take effect. The 'old guard' of integration pioneers began to give way to the 'new guard' this transformed the pace of integration. A key characteristic was the strengthening and consolidation of the European Commission. In a Community enlarged to nine members, very different from what was witnessed in the earlier years of a six-member group with France blocking the accession of the UK under Charles de Gaulle, the EEC sought to be the preferred nucleus of European integration. The British decided to form a separate free trade association with the members of the Organization for European Economic Cooperation (OEEC) that were non-members of the six member EEC. This led to the formation of the European Free Trade Association (EFTA) by the Macmillan government. The main motivating factor was the expectation that the Six would be more ready to negotiate once they were faced with the prospect of a determined competing trade alliance. However, the British strategy lost steam almost immediately. In the 1959 session of the European Parliament, President Hallstein of the EEC Commission put forward five key recommendations—on quota liberalization, tariff reduction, assistance to underdeveloped countries, institutionalization of Atlantic consultations, and accelerated implementation of the Common Market. These thematic issues were of direct concern to the United Kingdom since it was a reason for their decision to form the EFTA.[782]

The last proposal in the declaration had the most far-reaching effects. The EEC Treaty became effective in 1961 in a bid to give new impetus to the Community and to undermine the EFTA. This led to an important decision by the British that same year to apply for membership to the Common Market. An accelerating and booming EEC economy were ma-

---

781 Deubner.

782 Walter Yondorf, 'Monnet and the Action Committee: The Formative Period of the European Communities', *International Organization*, 19.4 (1965), 885–912 <https://doi.org/10.1017/S0020818300012650>.

of the United States became pivotal to the prospects of European integration.[750]

Horst Möller[751] views the finality of the Great War as a dual transformative event that involved both the internal and external modernisation of the nation-state and with this a redefinition of regional integration. The demise of the Vienna system concurrently saw the collapse of European monarchies and their evolution into democratic-republican political regimes which encouraged a vibrant European civic culture. It is sufficient to say that by 1923 the apparent failure to build a stable and prosperous order in Europe had prompted notable people to return to the idea of European integration. They did so within the newly founded political phenomena that had evolved with the reinvention of the nation-state.

First, although the customs union had been the most favoured approach to build European integration (especially with the success of the *Zollverein* in the nineteenth century), it was not the only prevailing idea. By the 1920s, the model transnational role of Europe's industrialists was providing a transformational alternative by which integration in Europe could be executed. However, integration, be it political or economic could only be possible with the policy involvement of the states.

Second, the key figures within this period that pushed around ideas pertaining to a European union notably included the German theologian and politician, Friedrich Naumann who advocated for a united Europe around the notion of Mitteleuropa. He supported German nationalistic ideals intertwined with militaristic, annexionist and condescending standards. This he expressed through his book Mitteleuropa (1915) advocating for German leadership of the geopolitics of Central Europe.[752] Naumann commented on the need for an economic union but gave little consideration on the modus and ramifications of regional economic integration in his idea of Mitteleuropa.

However, by 1916 the leading *Verein für Sozialpolitik*, that is, the German Economic Association in considering the pros and cons of the concept of Mitteleuropa concluded that it was not viable economically unless it was employed as a wartime strategy.[753] The aftermath of the Great

---

750 Stirk, pp. 18–46.

751 Horst Möller, *Europa Zwischen Den Weltkriegen*, Oldenbourg Grundriss Der Geschichte (München: R. Oldenbourg Verlag, 1998), xxi.

752 Friedrich Naumann, *Mitteleuropa* (Berlin: Georg Reimer, 1915) <https://archive.org>.

753 Henry Cord Meyer, *Mitteleuropa: In German Thought and Action 1815–1945* (The Hague: Martinus Nijhoff, 1955).

jor drivers in inducing the United Kingdom and the other EFTA members to apply for membership to the Common Market less than a year later. The UK and the other EFTA's members accession to the common market was a definitive turn in the fortunes of European Integration. In order to court the support of the United States in European integration efforts on which the solidarity of the nine-member common market depended, the Monnet-Hallstein team recognised the need and it acted accordingly.[783]

The creation of other institutions such as the European Council in 1974 provided more avenues for more politicised public debates on European issues. Furthermore, it created a discursive platform for the Franco-German alliance. With increase in institutions, more tools were formulated such as new spending programmes notably the European Regional Development Fund, consolidation of microeconomic and sectoral policies, new policy areas particularly in the area of environment and policy experimentation in seemingly intergovernmental fields, notably monetary policy and foreign policy. Essentially, inter-institutional interactions within the Community began to transform significantly.

The European Parliament benefited from enhanced powers and status because of treaty changes in 1970, 1975 and 1978, however this received little to no public commentary. This period was also marked by failures in the communication of institutional and policy successes thus causing gains in modest policy advances to be ignored and witnessing an era of negative publicity. One major headline touted, *Eurosclerosis*. The incremental advances chalked in the implemented policy areas were not accompanied by a roadmap of new emblematic visions. Within this same time, distributional issues were often discussed partly instigated by the United Kingdom who were mainly concerned with issues of budgetary equity.[784]

The late 1970s witnessed a period of mounting discontent with European integration. In his Florence speech in 1977, Roy Jenkins, president of the Commission, bemoaned the gradualist approach of European integration as being *politique des petits pas* and advocated for an ambitious advance towards building a unified Europe. This new leap was triggered by monetary integration an initiative of the Franco-German alliance. In 1978, German Chancellor Helmut Schmidt and French President Giscard d'Estaing inaugurated the new European Monetary System to serve as a

783 Yondorf.

784 David Phinnemore and Alex Warleigh-Lack, *Reflections on European Integration*, ed. by David Phinnemore and Alex Warleigh-Lack, 1st edn (Basingstoke, UK: Palgrave Macmillan, 2009), pp. 11–21 <https://doi.org/10.1057/9780230232839>.

launch pad for a monetary union. Again, this period saw the decline of US influence on global political economy, the world economy was threatened by crippling volatility from unstable energy and raw materials prices and external trade imbalances. Unfortunately, Europe did not have much to offer to assume global leadership.[785] The persuasive reason for establishing the EMU was the global financial turmoil of the late 1960s, which concluded in 1971 in the formal collapse of the Bretton Woods system.[786] In dealing with concomitant challenges and threats such as the two oil crises in the decade, economic recession, and a threatened Community model tied with strained economic relations with the United States.

The 1970s saw a remarkable international initiative that gave the EEC some positive public relations. This was the negotiation of the Lomé Convention, a trade and development assistance agreement between the EEC and 46 developing countries in Africa, the Caribbean, and the Pacific (ACP) regions. These were past colonies of some member states in the European Community. As a substitute for renegotiation an existing relationship in the Yaoundé Convention with the ACP countries, the EEC sought a new pathway in accordance with global concerns about the growing North–South divide.

The first Lomé Convention gained positive feedback in development circles and enhanced the EEC's profile although it was later criticized for being post-colonial and exploitative. It was however regarded by the Americans at the time as a threat to US foreign trade interests.[787] Throughout the 1970s, the fault lines of European integration were tested and it prevailed. Seeing to the emergence of another enlargement process in the 1980s of Greece, Portugal and Spain as possible members of the union.

Europe was relaunched in the 1980s. This period was widely seen as an impressive revival in the European integration process. A new set of political actors joined the process of integration by contributing an added momentum to the European project. One such group were the policy en-

785 Jürgen von Hagen, 'Through Crises to EMU: Perspectives for Fiscal Union and Political Union', in *Crises in European Integration*, ed. by Ludger Kühnhardt, Challenges and Responses, 1945-2005, NED-New (Berghahn Books, 2009), pp. 61–78 <http://www.jstor.org/stable/j.ctt9qcpnp.8>.

786 Desmond Dinan, 'European Integration: From the Common Market to the Single Market', in *A Companion to Europe since 1945*, ed. by Klaus Larres, 1st edn (Chichester, West Sussex: Wiley-Blackwell, 2009), pp. 133–50 <https://doi.org/10.1002/9781444308600.ch21>.

787 Dinan, 'European Integration: From the Common Market to the Single Market'.

trepreneurs, those employed within the European institutions particularly in the European Commission to steer affairs with technocratic precision by working on specific policy initiatives.

A remarkable example of this group included Jacques Delors and Arthur Cockfield in relation to the execution of the European Single Market (a programme that served as a jumpstart for deeper dynamic advances in unifying Europe[788]). Other persons championed the agenda in other policy domains. Another group was the corporate sector that was congregating in Brussels to influence the policy processes that could affect them. They were not alone; lobbyists and consultants joined them.

Their presence transformed substantially the formulation and execution of policy in the integration process. The members and staffers of the European Parliament that constituted the third group of new political actors became more active. With growing powers, their presence grew in prominence from Luxembourg to Brussels. Thus, enhancing the policy making process by encouraging plural and diverse voices and using process tracing as a more effective approach for both policy makers and analysts.[789]

This period again was marked by the expansion of EU legislative politics, which curbed the explicit exploitation of qualified majority voting in the Council as a tool of majoritarian decision-making. Again, this period was characterised by the emergence of a new approach to realise sustained integration goals through linkages between policy development and treaty reform culminating in the Single European Act of 1986, and in the preparation of what became the Treaty on European Union that is, the Maastricht Treaty.

A striking feature in the 1980s was the branding and global competitiveness of European integration. EEC logos and a flag were designed, Schiller's Ode to Joy with the music of Beethoven was put together as an anthem for the union. On the wider global stage, the triangular forces of international economic competition among the EEC, the United States and Japan marked the period. These competition pressures in the world economy with the Japanese advancing in technology and the United States promoting security and defence caused the Europeans to adjust their focus

788 For more on this see: Gilles Grin, *Battle Of Single European Market: Achievements and Economics 1945-2000* (New York: Columbia University Press, 2003); David Howarth and Tal Sadeh, 'The Ever Incomplete Single Market: Differentiation and the Evolving Frontier of Integration', *Journal of European Public Policy*, 17.7 (2010), 922–35 <https://doi.org/10.1080/13501763.2010.499220>.

789 Phinnemore and Warleigh-Lack, pp. 11–21.

on market liberalisation and emphasise the move towards the free market by using the tool of monetary integration. To intensify supranationalism the issue of a monetary union dominated the agenda in the 1990s. Having witnessed the success and dominance of the Deutschmark in unified Germany and the single market coupled with the experimentation of currency unions by France in Francophone West and Central Africa including the Pacific region, a potent and credible motive had been discovered for integration in this area.[790]

In this decade, a rechristening from *European Community* to the *European Union* took effect literally bringing to life in a name the phrase "ever closer union"[791] reiterating the founding aim of European integration in deeper and stronger solidarity. This decade, saw difficult referenda for incumbents like Denmark, France and Ireland on treaty reform for the Maastricht Treaty and the Treaty of Nice as well as for several other Nordic countries like Finland, Norway and Sweden who were seeking to join the EU. These contests reignited the tussle between Europhiles and Europhobes across these nations in a way putting pressure on the idea of the way forward for European integration. Although others may argue these contestations were beneficial in strengthening the process for a unified Europe.

The other definitive European story of the decade was the untangling of Central and Eastern Europe from the grip of the Soviet Union. This was due to the collapse of the Soviet Union in 1991. It was followed by the rapid transformation of these Central and Eastern European nations

790 Phinnemore and Warleigh-Lack, pp. 11–22; Stirk, p. 203; Jeffrey Cavanaugh, 'FOREX Africa: The CFA Franc Aka The African Euro', 2014 <http://afkinsider.com/41946/forex-africa-african-euro/#sthash.bAiuUVxB.dpuf> [accessed 3 February 2019].

791 "Ever closer union" is the central aim of the EU and is enshrined in the EU Treaties. The 1957 Treaty of Rome first stated the phrase. Subsequently, the Solemn Declaration on European Union of June 1983 and the 1986 Single European Act state it with further qualifications to add emphasis. The Preamble to the 1992 Treaty on European Union (Maastricht Treaty) and the 1997 Amsterdam Treaty also added new qualifications to highlight the meaning of the phrase. However, in the Nice Treaty it did not add or change any qualification added to the previous one made in Amsterdam. Since the Lisbon Treaty (2009), the EU Treaties have contained three references to "ever closer union". Finally, at the EU Court of Justice in four cases, "ever closer union" occurred in a footnote in the ruling, referring to a landmark case relating to judicial cooperation (in the Punino Case C – 105/03). For further simplified reading on the subject see: Vaughne Miller, '"Ever Closer Union" in the EU Treaties and Court of Justice Case Law' (London: House of Commons Library, 2015).

who were eventually roped into the European Union. The end of the Cold War and complete annihilation of Soviet power caused rapid integration in Western Europe and disintegration in Central and Eastern Europe. Culminating in the application and accession of ten new states joining the European Union in the new millennium, the biggest membership drive ever seen since its founding in 1957. With this large-scale membership increase, an attendant challenge of varying socio-economic conditions and national policy needed to be resolved. In effect the EU have developed a plethora of approaches to meet this challenge.[792]

EU Regionalism in the new millennium is being fashioned by ongoing internal crises and external threats with its attendant responses. The first fifteen years of the twenty-first century has witnessed prolonged and tense debates over how to adapt the EU framework to new times, new circumstances and new members, against a backdrop of waning public confidence. The uncompleted journey of enlargement to south-eastern Europe, which started in 2004 and the rancour around the European Constitution in the early part of this period remain a challenge for the integration process. Some are of the opinion that the signing of the document in 2004 and its subsequent ratification in 2007 by a majority of EU member states has fast-tracked the pace of the EU towards a constitutional polity with constitution-like attributes.[793]

The Eurozone debt crises that started by the end of the first decade of this period undermined gravely the principle of solidarity that underpins European integration.[794] This pitched so-called periphery countries in the EU against countries at the core such as Germany and France. The uncompleted issue of Brexit[795] with its effects on the disintegration of the EU is a looming threat. The UK's affiliation with the EU has been characterised

792 Desmond Dinan, *Origins and Evolution of the European Union*, ed. by Desmond Dinan, 2nd edn (Oxford: Oxford University Press, 2014), pp. 254–301.

793 Ludger. Kuhnhardt, *Crises in European Integration : Challenges and Responses, 1945-2005.* (Berghahn Books, Inc, 2008) <http://www.jstor.org/stable/j.ctt9qcpnp> [accessed 15 June 2017]; Kühnhardt; Dinan, *Origins and Evolution of the European Union*, pp. 327–42.

794 Vestert Borger, 'How the Debt Crisis Exposes the Development of Solidarity in the Euro Area', *European Constitutional Law Review*, 9.1 (2013), 7–36 <https://doi.org/10.1017/S1574019612001022>.

795 Brexit is the nomenclature denoting the outcome of the British referendum on European Union (EU) membership on the 24 June 2016. For an early introduction to the Brexit phenomenon see: Sara B. Hobolt, 'The Brexit Vote: A Divided Nation, a Divided Continent', *Journal of European Public Policy*, 23.9 (2016), 1259–77 <https://doi.org/10.1080/13501763.2016.1225785>.

by difficulties, compromises and proactivity. However, it is still uncertain if by the climax of the second decade of this period whether or not the UK and EU negotiations on Brexit would be successful. If the story concludes abysmally, it would set a precedent for EU disintegration. Elevating to the fore the current of Eurosceptic tendencies prevalent among the peoples and nations of the European Union.

4.3.2 Dual Character of EU Regionalism: Distinctive and Cohesive

In the seminal work of Ernst Haas, *Uniting of Europe*[796] an exclusive focus on the cooperation of six founding members of the ECSC (the predecessor to the EU) in the production of coal and steel alongside the development of the common market highlights energy as the *locus classicus* of modern European regionalism. This distinct attribute sets the EU apart from other regionalism experiments around the globe. The pooling of energy resources and other production elements for heavy industry within western Europe establishes a unique dynamic.

In the beginnings of the political economy of regional integration. Although this cooperation on energy was done primarily as a means of securing national interest rather than for the need of a federalist zeal.[797] It culminated into an enduring work in progress made up of a mixture of institutions that are largely supranational and intergovernmental in nature to deal with the regionalism or regional integration process based on a differentiated frame.[798] Its proponents perceived this method of integrating energy resources as a means by which similar cooperation around other policy areas could occur. Jean Monnet conceived this method of integration. Two implications essential to understand this line of reasoning are that, first and foremost, it was perhaps the only option available to guar-

796 Haas.

797 Milward.

798 Wayne Sandholtz and Alec Stone Sweet, 'Neo-Functionalism and Supranational Governance', in *The Oxford Handbook of the European Union*, ed. by Erik Jones, Anand Menon, and Stephen Weatherill, 1st edn (Oxford: Oxford University Press, 2012), pp. 18–33; Andrew Moravscik, 'Liberal Intergovernmentalism and Integration: A Rejoinder', *JCMS: Journal of Common Market Studies*, 33.4 (1995), 611–28 <https://doi.org/10.1111/j.1468-5965.1995.tb00554.x>; Dirk Leuffen, Berthold Rittberger, and Frank Schimmelfennig, *Differentiated Integration: Explaining Variation in the European Union* (Basingstoke, UK: Palgrave Macmillan, 2013), XII.

antee economic development and propel rapid growth through *resource* regionalism after decades of devastation. And second, it had provided not only distinctive opportunities to the EU but it had contributed to its challenges and crises.

The institutional rationalism that underpinned the Monnet Method was that member states would prefer to capitalize on the gains they received from pooling sovereignties by permitting it to proceed from one area of policy to another, despite their national autonomy. This presumption has proven to be incorrect in spite of the fact that the EU chalked remarkable gains since the 1950s, its progress has been determined by the member states and public opinion in these states. Since the Monnet method sought to engineer an EU steered by elites rather than a fully democratic, organisation. As Bellamy and Warleigh[799] opine, the method should share part of the blame for the 'democratic deficit' in the EU.

Cohesive Europe as articulated in a study by Best et al.[800] typifies the presence of a competitive European market and social security combined with the attendant threats it faces in its quest to achieve these goals. For those in favour of competition the threats include socio-economic disparities held by EU member states, ill effects of globalisation on welfare and the EU's transatlantic relations with the US. Conversely for those in favour of social security the likely threats posed are from EU enlargement further east and the heightening of immigration. In recent years, the narrative of immigration has triggered a new kind of angst between both adherents of competitive markets and social security respectively. The two sides perceive immigration as a threat to cohesive Europe however not on the same magnitude.

Free market adherents are concerned with their political fortunes even though they do not see immigrants as contradictory to the free movement principles. They are more concerned with the perception from their opponents who caricature them to be lacking toughness in addressing migration policy issues. On the contrary, social security adherents consider

799 Richard Bellamy and Alex Warleigh, 'From an Ethics of Integration to an Ethics of Participation: Citizenship and the Future of the European Union', *Millennium: Journal of International Studies*, 27.3 (1998), 447–68 <https://doi.org/10.1177/03058298980270030801>.

800 Heinrich Best, György Lengyel, and Luca Verzichelli, *The Europe of Elites: A Study into the Europeanness of Europe's Political and Economic Elites*, ed. by Heinrich Best, György Lengyel, and Luca Verzichelli, 1st edn (New York: Oxford University Press Inc., 2012).

that scapegoating the influx of immigrants with warped narratives and dehumanising optics will curb the trend and preserve a cohesive Europe.

Again, the divide between supranationalism and intergovernmentalism has a key influence on the idea of a cohesive Europe. Proponents of supranationalism perceive increasing nationalism and the deterioration of transatlantic relations with the US under President Donald Trump as major threats whereas proponents of intergovernmentalism perceive EU enlargement and non-EU states immigration as debilitating threats to a cohesive Europe.

4.4 EU Energy Regionalism: Past, Present and Future

The evolution of energy, its path dependence and collective action within the context of regionalism in Europe is synonymous with the genesis of the EU by certain historical accounts as the narrative above tries to demonstrate. In simple terms, it can be alluded that EU energy regionalism initiated the process of post-war European integration.

When the ECSC was set up in 1952, coal accounted for more than 80 percent of the energy consumed in the original six Member States (Germany, France, Benelux countries and Italy), oil consumption in distant second was 10 percent with most analysts predicting that coal would remain the most important fuel well into the future. As the treaty establishing the ECSC came into force it created a common market in coal (as well as steel) almost immediately. This collective action came with minimal exceptions required namely to eliminate almost proximately any restrictions on trade, which included import and export duties, quantitative restrictions (quotas), discriminatory prices along with transport and delivery rates, including state subsidies. In order to ensure the proper functioning of the common market, the community with unprecedented supranational powers mandated a High Authority. It had the power to dissolve cartels, restrict output, and distribute supplies, levy fines, guarantee loans, influence investments, and, in rare settings, fix prices.[801]

This initial process of collective institutionalisation around resources and energy within a region like western Europe set the tone for regional energy policymaking and governance in what will later become the EU. The rest of this section elaborates on the past milestones of energy

801 William Diebold, *The Schuman Plan: A Study in Economic Cooperation 1950-1959* (New York : Frederick A. Praeg,er, 1959).

regionalism from its fruitful beginnings to its present and ambitious future prospects. It further explains the progress towards an integrated European energy region by considering the pathways taken to develop a regional energy governance system through cooperation, integration and governance.

4.4.1 Past Milestones: Cooperation towards a Common European Energy Region

The early phase of cooperation regarding energy in European regionalism occurs in the attempt to reconstruct Europe's industrial base in the aftermath of the Second World War and to meet the energy supply needs of consumers in search of affordable energy. This process sustained the most rapid economic growth and development in Europe during the post war years. This period was dominated by the cooperative dynamics of member states who were working towards European integration.

In addition, the two major external energy shocks namely the oil crises in 1973 and 1979 coupled with the nuclear disaster in Chernobyl (1986) influenced the early years of collectivising efforts on energy. In view of integrating European energy processes and exchange in the 1990s, an adoption of *deregulation* in the sector, due to the liberalisation agenda that heavily characterised the EU economy brought gains. We also witness the rise of the European Commission within this period in its role to drive the European energy sector more coherently and in a harmonised fashion despite the internal and external challenges it faces and also emphasising the aim of the common market.

4.4.1.1 Early Milestones in EU Energy Cooperation

By way of introduction, it is important to reiterate that energy has always been at the forefront of the reconstruction agenda of post-war European regionalism. The 1950s and 1960s underscores the tremendous achievement in early energy cooperation. The Treaty establishing the European Coal and Steel Community (ESCS) in 1951 initiated by Robert Schuman was reliant on a type of political and economic cooperation, which involved placing coal and steel production in the Ruhr area under a common supranational regime.

With the establishment of the ECSC, a common customs union was set up to allow for free trade and to charge the same import duties. Steel was needed for the reconstruction of machinery that would spur the industrial sector whereas coal as stated above constituted almost entirely the energy production output. Therefore, both were extremely vital in accelerating the economies of the member states in times of peace in order to prevent war.[802] The quest to control collectively these two commodities was to prevent the possibility of another war and to maintain the peace and prosperity of Europe through an energy and commodity production community.

Subsequently, the founding of the EEC under the Rome Treaty of 1957 focused on economic cooperation. In that same year, the European Atomic Energy Community came into being based on the Euratom Treaty. This highlighted the critical importance of viable cooperation of innovative energy sources and technologies such as coal and nuclear energy at the time on the overall process of European regionalism. Issues pertaining to energy have therefore constituted a pivotal part of the integration process of Europe from its very foundations.[803]

The Coal and Steel Community Treaty and the Atomic Energy Treaty were the two Treaties concerned with energy out of the three foundational Treaties. A legal case before the European Court of Justice relating to electricity, *Costa v Enel*, indicated clearly from the beginning that the EEC Treaty would regulate the energy sector. It was against this backdrop that energy as a political issue was closely knit with national sovereignty for European level regulation to be possible.[804] Albeit European transnational coordination of electricity interconnections via the Union for the Coordination of the Transmission of Electricity (UCTE)[805] commenced in 1951 laying the foundation for the pooling of electricity among European countries way before the other forms of energy was collectivised in the European region.[806]

---

802 Susanne Langsdorf, 'EU Energy Policy: From the ECSC to the Energy Roadmap 2050' <https://doi.org/10.1038/179559a0>.

803 Kim Talus, *Introduction to EU Energy Law* (Oxford: Oxford University Press, 2016).

804 Talus, *Introduction to EU Energy Law*.

805 Formerly the Union for the Coordination of Production and Transmission of Electricity (UCPTE) changed its name to UCTE in 1999 Union for the Coordination of Transmission of Electricity (UCTE), *UCPTE/UCTE: The 50 Year Success Story – Evolution of a European Interconnected Grid* (Brussels: Secretariat of UCTE, 2009).

806 Paul Adrianus Van Baal and Matthias Finger, 'The Effect of European Integration on Swiss Energy Policy and Governance', *Politics and Governance*, 7.1 (2019), 6 <https://doi.org/10.17645/pag.v7i1.1780>.

Economically, the ECSC did not successfully realise all its aims resulting in its demise. The inaction of the High Authority to enforce treaty violations by France and Germany who practiced protectionism in the winter of 1958/59 when large coal surpluses led to a decline in consumption was a huge test to this initial energy cooperation. Petroleum overtook coal as the fuel of choice by asserting rapidly its place in the market. It was obvious that the European coal industry could not compete. The strategic significance of heavy industry was also in decline and with the rise of nuclear technology through atomic capability. It shifted economic priorities relating to energy in favour of the integration process.[807] Accordingly, the ECSC Council of Ministers and the High Authority tabled a call for a coordinated energy policy at a Special Council of Ministers meeting in 1957.[808]

When Jean Monnet proposed the need for an atomic energy community to drive the next stage of industrialisation after coal was dethroned as king. Entangled with the failure of the EDC and Political Community, the leaders of Benelux countries signed the Benelux Memorandum as the next step for European energy regionalism. Its main aim was to secure cheap energy to offset the rising demand and eventually limit expensive oil imports. There were suspicions in the implementation of the atomic community by some states so Monnet suggested it to be linked to an economic community.

However, the events of 5th and 6th November 1956, which led to the Suez Crisis, exposed the dependence of European countries like France and Britain on external geopolitical activity to prop up dominance. This transformed eventually the view of those states who opposed the atomic community. A boost in France's determination to forge ahead and construct a Europe with nuclear potential was strongly championed. Finally, by early 1957 the negotiating European states had come to an agreement and it resulted in the signing of the Rome Treaties scheduled to take effect on the 1st of January 1958.

This created the European Economic Community (EEC) and the European Atomic Community (EAC) that is, EURATOM on the 25th of March 1957. This secured a place for the teething integration process within the

---

807 Gillingham, *Coal, Steel, and the Rebirth of Europe, 1945—1955 : The Germans and French from Ruhr Conflict to Economic Community*.

808 Samuel R. Schubert, Johannes Pollack, and Maren Kreutler, *Energy Policy of the European Union* (London: Palgrave, 2016), p. 95.

context of an emerging global *pax atomica*[809]. Overall, EURATOM initiated a *relance* and was considered the most plausible vehicle for furthering European regionalism by Monnet, Spaak, France, USA and the Action Committee.[810] Regardless of the fact that the ECSC, EURATOM, and EEC single-handedly on their own terms addressed energy-related policy issues, which affected members numerous impediments barred the early creation of a community-wide energy policy.[811]

In the early decades of European integration particularly in the 1960s, the competence of the community institutions to act with one voice on energy was limited. The main attribute of energy regionalism was a focus on the national level. Much of the European energy sector at the time was composed of at least national systems, and indeed in many cases characterised by local and sub-national systems. In the early, post-war years, a shift from local to national electricity and municipality gas systems was in progress.

A nationalised central grid was the most dominant feature, France and Britain were the best examples of this phenomenon however, local and provincial authorities showed reluctance in offloading interests in public utilities. Closely associated with focused national energy policies was the rise of national energy champions, among them were, Rhenish-Westphalian Electric power company (RWE), Electricité de France (EDF) and the Central Electricity Generating Board (CEGB). An energy sector highly concentrated in a few hands and with close corporatist relationships to provincial and national governments was the feature of time. Most countries encouraged monopolies by providing statutory reliefs for proscribed competition.[812]

---

809 *Pax Atomica,* a term that denotes a world order guaranteed by the nuclear superpowers. For more see: Ralph Dietl, 'Suez 1956: A European Intervention?', *Journal of Contemporary History*, 43.2 (2008), 259–78 <https://doi.org/10.1177/0022009408089032>.

810 O'Driscoll.

811 Schubert, Pollack, and Kreutler.

812 Dieter Helm, 'European Energy Policy', in *The Oxford Handbook of the European Union*, ed. by Erik Jones, Anand Menon, and Stephen Weatherill, 1st edn (Oxford: Oxford University Press, 2012), pp. 556–69 <https://doi.org/10.1093/oxfordhb/9780199546282.013.0039>.

4.4.1.2 External Energy Crises: Middle Eastern Oil and Chernobyl Nuclear Crises in the 1970s – 1980s

The 1970s enlargement of the EEC, EURATOM and ECSC by members of the EFTA strategically introduced into the fold countries that made huge discoveries of oil and gas finds in the North Sea in the 1960s. As a result, this enabled the first imports of North Sea oil into the enlarged European energy market in 1975. This led to diminishing reliance on Middle Eastern oil imports.

When the first oil crises hit Europe in the autumn of 1973 repercussions were felt even into the ensuing years. The decisive response adopted was deeper regional integration to quell the effects of the global energy crises. The oil crisis occurred in the wake of the Israeli invasion of Egypt and Syria. Western powers, Europe and USA, as allies supported Israel. In reaction to this the Arab members of the Organisation of Petroleum Exporting Countries (OPEC), retaliated with the issuance of an oil embargo meaning they cut off oil production to the barest minimum resulting in diminished energy exports.[813]

The EEC at the time imported a large quantity of its petroleum needs which was about 95 percent. It could not adjust immediately from the energy shock because of the limited supplies it received. This caused energy prices to soar through the roof within 1973 and 1974. A negative effect of the crisis was the impact it had on European solidarity as some states decide to enter bilateral deals with certain Arab supplier nations.[814]

In contrast, the positive consequence was the establishment of the International Energy Agency (IEA) of the Organisation for Economic Coordination and Development (OECD) under the auspices of the USA during the time of President Richard Nixon. Nixon's Secretary of State, Henry Kissinger, championed this process. A mechanism to act collectively by sharing oil in times of emergency was signed among sixteen countries (that is, all EEC member states with the exception of France) under the *Agreement on an International Energy Programme*. This served as an introduction for community-wide approaches on oil sharing in the EEC. By 1977,

---

813 Frank Bösch and Rüdiger Graf, 'Reacting to anticipations: Energy crises and energy policy in the 1970s. An introduction,' *Historical Social Research/Historische Sozialforschung*, (2014): 7–21.

814 Garavini Giuliano, 'Western Europe and the Long Energy Crisis of the 1970s,' *Europe in a Globalising World*, (Nomos Verlagsgesellschaft GmbH & Co. KG : 2014)

EEC member states agreed to allow the Commission to make inputs on Community-wide reduction of oil consumption in times of emergency. However, because the terms of the agreement were not clear and with obvious preference on the part of EEC members for national options rather than Europe-wide approaches, an opportunity was missed to cooperate effectively on regional energy policy with respect to petroleum.[815]

The second oil crises in 1979 was because of the Iranian revolution which was further intensified with the Iraq-Iran war in 1980. A rapidly escalating price hike brought about by this situation and the ongoing Saudi Arabian led OPEC oil embargo resulted in a global energy market that was in much need of oil supplies in the 1970s and early 1980s. Despite these petroleum shortages, a boom in coal surpluses within the period helped to offset the energy supply deficits. Europe's response was only limited to a general strategy of adopting energy efficiency mechanisms and ensuring secure energy supplies. In a resolution, reflecting its opinion on the state of community-wide energy cooperation the European Parliament expressed its regret on the persistent inability of the Council of Energy Ministers to implement European Council decisions on a common energy policy.[816]

The Chernobyl Nuclear Power Complex located in Ukraine, formerly part of the Soviet Union, on 26th April 1986, saw its flawed Nuclear Reactor 4 explode. This created what has been described as the worst nuclear disaster ever witnessed.[817] The disaster caused the most lethal uncontrolled dose of radiation ever recorded to be released into the atmosphere from any civilian nuclear facility. An enormous amount of radioactive material was released into the air for more than a week. Large quantities of the released substances were deposited close by as debris. However, dust and other materials were carried airborne over Ukraine, Belarus, Russia, and extended over parts of Northern, Central and Western Europe.[818]

---

815 Garavini Giuliano, 'Western Europe and the Long Energy Crisis of the 1970s,'

816 Council of the European Communities, *Resolution Embodying the Opinion of the European Parliament on the Communication from the Commission of the European Communities to the Council on the Energy Objectives of the Community for 1990 and Convergence of Policies of the Member States on Nuclear Energy and Energy Policy, Official Journal of the European Communities* (C, 1980), pp. 41–44 <https://eur-lex.europa.eu/> [accessed 20 May 2018].

817 IAEA, 'The International Chernobyl Project: Technical Report, Assessment of Radiological Consequences and Evaluation of Protective Measures' (Vienna: International Atomic Energy Agency, 1991), p. 640.

818 IAEA, 'The International Chernobyl Project: Technical Report, Assessment of Radiological Consequences and Evaluation of Protective Measures'.

The aftermath of the Chernobyl accident marked a transformational moment in the public opinion of Europeans in relation to nuclear energy. Nuclear energy became highly controversial causing Germany to decide to phase out nuclear energy by 2020 and it also caused the temporary closure of two Belgian reactors which had cracks.[819] The optimism of the early 1970s for energy-related nuclear technology as the solution for Europe's energy problems was gravely dimmed. Regulatory reforms after Chernobyl were issued to ensure proper safety measures around nuclear plants.

Also, measures were undertaken based on the issuance of directives from the EEC and EURATOM to protect life and property of citizens in Europe. This related to the maximum permissible limits of radiation contamination allowed in foodstuffs and animal feeds after a nuclear accident as well as the encouragement of imports of agricultural produce emanating from third countries. In addition, a decision was passed in favour of speeding the spread of information between member states and the Commission in the event of a radiological crisis caused by an accident or the detection of abnormal levels of radiation either within or outside the territory of a member state.[820] Chernobyl exposed the European community's lack of preparedness on internal or external nuclear accidents due to its inefficient early warning systems and public safety measures.[821]

4.4.1.3 Deregulation of the Energy Sector in the 1990s

The coming into being of the Single European Act (SEA) in 1986 placed two key themes essential for the construction of a single energy market on the table – that is, deregulation and liberalisation. European energy markets were right in the centre of the process which resulted in the realisation of SEA. In order to harmonise and liberalise the EU's internal energy market, measures were adopted in 1996 to deal with market access, transparency and regulation, consumer protection, support for energy infrastructure interconnection and preservation of adequate levels of energy supply.

---

819 Frédéric Gouardères, 'Nuclear Energy' (Strasbourg: EPRS, 2018).

820 Martin O'Connor and Sybille Van den Hove, 'Prospects for Public Participation on Nuclear Risks and Policy Options: Innovations in Governance Practices for Sustainable Development in the European Union', *Journal of Hazardous Materials*, 86.1–3 (2001), 77–99 <https://doi.org/10.1016/S0304-3894(01)00256-4>.

821 Schubert, Pollack, and Kreutler.

The broader measures under SEA were aimed at the completion of the EU's internal market which required the removal of numerous obstacles and trade barriers, the approximation of tax and pricing policies and measures regarding norms and standards and finally, environmental and safety regulations. Its legal basis came from Article 194 and Article 114 of the Treaty on the Functioning of the European Union (TFEU) whose central objective was to ensure a functioning market with fair market access and a high level of consumer protection.[822]

In the 1990s, while a majority of national electricity and natural gas markets were still monopolies, the European Union and its member states resolved to open these markets gradually to competition. The first liberalisation directives (that is, the First Energy Package) were adopted in 1996 to focus on electricity and 1998 to focus on gas. This was later expected to be transposed into the legal systems of member states by 1998 for electricity and 2000 for gas. By 2003, the Second Energy Package was adopted. Its directives were also to be transposed into national legislation by the member states in 2004, while certain provisions were entered into force in 2007.

Commercial and household consumers now had options to choose freely their own gas and electricity suppliers from a broader range of competitors. The Third Energy Package then took effect on April 2009 seeking to liberalise further the internal electricity and gas markets as adopted. This led to an amendment of the second package and provided the basis for the implementation and completion of the internal energy market.[823]

4.4.2 Present Settings: Integration of the European Energy Region

The integration of the energy sector in the EU was chiefly implemented through the internal energy market in the EU. It was put in place using the three market liberalisation packages adopted in the 1990s, 2003 and 2009. This provided for the 'unbundling' of energy production and supply that is, electricity and gas from energy-transmission networks as well as provide third-party access to gas storage facilities, strengthened consumer protection, and reinforced regulatory scrutiny. The EU Commission is

822 Stephen Padgett, 'The single European energy market: The politics of realization,' *Journal of Common Market Studies,* 30 (1992) 53.

823 Burkard Eberlein, 'The making of the European energy market: The interplay of governance and government,' *Journal of Public Policy* (2008): 73–92.

presently monitoring and implementing the 'third energy package' across the member states, which should have transposed all the provisions into domestic law by 2011.

The present state of EU energy has chalked tremendous successes such as energy market regulation, security of supply for electricity, natural gas and oil, including the maintenance of the trans-European networks for energy (TEN-E). However, it is concerned with major challenges that continue to affect the process of energy integration. These include but not limited to energy security issues, energy justice issues and environmental sustainability. In addition, to the overall completion of the internal energy market which is high on the agenda.

4.4.2.1 Regulation: A Means of Integration for Energy Markets

The European Agency for the Cooperation of Energy Regulators (ACER) an organisation that has been functional since March 2011 based on Regulation (EC) No 713/2009, is charged with the responsibility for promoting cooperation between national regulatory authorities at sub-national and European levels. It fulfils its mandate by monitoring progress of the network and the internal electricity and gas markets. It exercises investigative competencies in cases of market abuse and dominance in addition to coordinating the application of appropriate penalties with the member states. However, the obligation for applying sanctions applicable to violations rests in the purview of member states.[824]

Furthermore, with the adoption of two regulations establishing structures of cooperation for European Network Transmission Systems Operators (ENTSOs). That is one for electricity (Regulation (EC) No 714/2009) and the other for gas (Regulation (EC) No 715/2009) as amended by Commission Decision 2010/685/EU. ACER together with the ENTSOs, have helped construct detailed network access rules and technical codes, which ensure the coordination of grid operation through the exchange of operational information and the advancement of common safety and emergency standards and procedures. ENTSOs have been responsible for the design of a decade long network investment plan biennially, which is subject to the review processes of ACER.

---

824 Peter Cameron, 'Legal aspects of EU energy regulation,' *Implementing the New Directives on Electricity and Gas Across Europe* (2005)

A further step in energy market integration in the EU is seen in Directive 2008/92/EC that seeks to develop transparency and openness in setting gas and electricity prices charged to commercial and industrial end-users by obliging member states to ensure that these prices and the pricing systems employed are communicated to Eurostat biannually.[825]

The EU adopted Regulation (EU) No 1227/2011 in October 2011, which was responsible for wholesale energy market integrity and transparency (REMIT). The goal for the REMIT regulation was to maintain fair trading practices in the European energy markets. The European Commission on 30 November 2016 suggested a new regulation (COM (2016) 0863) aimed at further reforms of ACER. It was meant to reorganize legal provisions pertaining to ACER and to reinforce its main role as a coordinator of the activity of national regulators. Its main focus was on areas where fragmented national policy existed on issues related to cross-border aspects that could pose problems or discrepancies for the internal energy market.[826]

Subsequently an updated list of tasks is now included in ACER's new duties in the field of wholesale market supervision and the governance of cross-border energy infrastructure. It has provided ACER with a wider scope of responsibility in clarifying and submitting the final proposal for a network code to the Commission. In addition to, exercising influence on the review process of the regional electricity market's bidding process which has been formulated and enforced in the recast of the Electricity Regulation (COM (2016) 0861).[827]

4.4.2.2 Security of Energy Supplies

The EU legislation on security of energy supplies focuses on natural gas and electricity markets. It is also associated with other EU energy-related goals such as the consolidation of the internal energy market, improving

---

825 M. Kanellakis, G. Martinopoulos, and T. Zachariadis, 'European Energy Policy-A Review', *Energy Policy*, 62 (2013), 1020–30 <https://doi.org/10.1016/j.enpol.2013.08.008>.

826 Siddharth Fresa, 'Multilevel EU governance in energy infrastructure development: A new role for ACER,' (DIW Working Paper: 2015). Retrieved from http://www. diw. de/documents/dokumentenarchiv/17/diw_01. c. 508434. de/fresa.

827 Frédéric Gouardères, *Internal Energy Market* (Strasbourg, 2018) <http://www.europarl.europa.eu/RegData/etudes/fiches_techniques/2017/N54579/en.pdf> [accessed 11 February 2018].

energy efficiency, promoting renewable energy sources to aid in the decarbonization of the economy and the full realization of the objectives of the Paris Agreement.

A strength of the internal energy market has been to ensure the security of energy supplies like electricity, natural gas and oil. Directive 2005/89/EC, which establishes the mechanisms that underpin the internal energy market is aimed at safeguarding the security of electricity supply, ensuring the proper functioning of the internal market for electricity, establishing an adequate level of interconnectivity between member states, providing an adequate level of generation capacity, and ensuring a balance between energy supply and demand. In response to counter future occurrences similar to the Russian-Ukrainian gas crisis during the winter of 2008–2009. The European Union placed critical importance on gas as a component of the overall mix of the EU's energy supply and put into effect in 2010 Regulation (EU) No 994/2010 focused on measures to safeguard the security of gas supply. The regulation sought to reinforce prevention and crisis response mechanisms.[828]

In dealing with the secure supply of oil a directive, Directive 2009/119/EC, was put in place which required member states to ensure minimum oil stocks, that corresponded with a 90 days average of daily net imports or a 61 days average of daily inland consumption. The choice of policy by the member states focused on whichever option would ensure the most abundant secure supplies. With respect to the issue raised in relation to Russian gas deliveries via Ukraine through the gas interconnections, the Commission released an Energy Security Strategy on May 2014 (COM (2014) 0330). The strategy focused on the availability of a stable and abundant supply of gas for the European economy and its citizen. These strategic measures sought to ensure energy sufficiency, domestic energy production and the completion of alternative gas infrastructure linkages that would support the redirection of energy distribution in instances of a gas supply crisis.[829]

---

828 Per Ove Eikeland, 'The Third Internal Energy Market Package: New Power Relations among Member States, EU Institutions and Non-State Actors?', *Journal of Common Market Studies*, 49.2 (2011), 243–63 <https://doi.org/10.1111/j.1468-5965.2010.02140.x>; Ole Gunnar Austvik, 'The Energy Union and Security-of-Gas Supply', *Energy Policy*, 96 (2016), 372–82 <https://doi.org/10.1016/j.enpol.2016.06.013>; Gouardères, *Internal Energy Market*.

829 Per Ove Eikeland, 'The Third Internal Energy Market Package: New Power Relations among Member States, EU Institutions and Non-State Actors?.' ; Ole

In order to avoid distortions in the internal energy market, the European Commission again on 8th November 2017, adopted a new legislative proposal targeted at revising the 2009 natural gas directive (COM (2017) 0660). This also proffered key provisions of the gas directive immediately applicable to cross-border gas pipelines with third countries, especially in parts of the pipeline infrastructure that fell within the territorial scope of the EU. This sought to guarantee security of supply and prevent market distortions in the midst of current, planned and future gas infrastructure projects between EU member states and a third country like Russia.[830]

4.4.2.3 Cross-Border Energy Networks: Trans-European Networks for Energy (TEN-E)

The guidelines for the trans-European energy networks, which identify projects of common interest (PCI) as well as priority projects among cross-border European electricity and gas networks were stipulated in Regulation (EU) No 347/2013. These projects of common interest had priority status with regards to obtaining investments and financial aid provided for under Regulation (EC) No 2236/95. Budgetary allocations made to the TEN-E were intended for only financing feasibility studies. Moreover, it made provision for other financial instruments that enabled investments into TEN-E projects. A typical example is the European Structural and Investment Funds or the European Fund for Strategic Investments (EFSI) which serve as possible funding sources to make investments into PCIs.[831]

Additionally, the European Parliament and its counterpart the Council in Regulation (EU) No 256/2014 of 26 February 2014 sent a notification to the Commission on the investment of energy infrastructure projects within the European Union. This regulation required member states to notify the Commission on any investments in their energy infrastructure projects.[832]

Again, in the communication titled 'A Budget for Europe 2020' (COM (2011) 0500), the European Commission tabled a new mechanism, the Connecting Europe Facility (CEF), which is meant for funding priority

---

Gunnar Austvik, 'The Energy Union and Security-of-Gas Supply'.; Gouardères, *Internal Energy Market*.

830 Gouardères, *Internal Energy Market*.

831 Gouardères, *Internal Energy Market*.

832 Gouardères, *Internal Energy Market*.

projects in the field of energy, transport and critical digital infrastructure from 2014 to 2020.

Parliament endorsed this and a deal was reached with the Council relating to the budget for the CEF on November 2013. An amount of EUR 5.12 billion is earmarked for the development of trans-European energy infrastructure network through specialized projects. Several other projects of common interest were selected for EU support based on energy infrastructure guidelines endorsed in March 2013 by the Council and Parliament.[833] This is testament to the maturation of Community-wide energy integration that relate to financing and the construction of the energy infrastructure networks in the European Union.

4.4.2.4 Energy Security Issues

The EU's place as a major global energy importer is undisputed. Singularly, the EU is not a collective buyer of energy commodities. Individual member states purchase their own energy supplies based on their respective energy needs. However, an aggregate measure of energy supplies to the region offers analysts and observers a composite view of energy imports, demand and consumption. Cumulatively, by 2004, the EU's total energy imports accounted for 50 percent of its energy needs. This was influenced by falling indigenous production coupled with an improvement in energy efficiency. By 2014, the mix of imported energy accounting for 53.5 percent of the EU-28's gross internal energy consumption constituted 45.64 percent of solid fuels, 94.01 percent of crude oil and petroleum products and 67.4 percent of natural gas. With the drop of energy production by Denmark in the North Sea by 2013, all member states had become net importers of energy.[834]

Issues that have to do with energy security within the EU mostly depend on the ease with which European citizens gain access to reliable flows of energy supplies and its attendant variants such as natural gas or oil and the corresponding price tag that is, energy affordability. Conventionally, energy security has been the weakest of the three energy policy strands of

833 Gouardères, *Internal Energy Market*.

834 Jakub M. Godzimirski and Zuzanna Nowak, 'EU Gas Supply Security: The Power of the Importer', in *Energy Security in Europe* (Cham: Springer International Publishing, 2018), pp. 221–49 <https://doi.org/10.1007/978-3-319-64964-1_9>.

the EU. Enlargement of EU regionalism in 2004 and 2007 raised the need for strengthening this aspect of the EU's energy objectives.[835]

Member states from Central and Eastern Europe are keen on an EU energy-security policy that would support them to avoid over-dependence on Russian energy, whereas member states predominantly from western Europe such as Germany and Italy generally prefer bilateral energy deals with Russia and other third countries. Previously, authorities in the EU have exercised limited influence in securing energy supply but all this changed with the introduction of the Treaty of Lisbon, which guaranteed formal competence in ensuring security of energy supply.[836]

In the context of the EU's energy-security, issues discussed have habitually been about gas supplies particularly through pipelines that locks customer states into a fixed dependency on suppliers, rather than on a focus on oil, where supply can originate from the broad international oil market. The whole idea of dependency on gas pipelines has raised significant interest including an amount of discord between EU member states on the issue of a possible revival of a European indigenous gas industry by replicating the US shale gas revolution or hydraulic fracturing simply known as fracking.

When considering the political economy of EU energy security there is a disconnection between potential that is, what EU members could execute together and performance that is, what they actually do together to ensure regional energy security.[837] In relation to nuclear energy, perspectives on it as a source of energy security has been quite contentious in the EU. This is because of a number of factors that include risk perceptions, value of sunk investment and the fact that corporations likely to champion commercial activity in the sector are going bankrupt because of lack of numerous investment options.

While some experts predicted a renaissance in nuclear energy appeal due to its capacity to secure energy supply particularly electricity for residential and production purposes.[838] The Fukushima Daiichi disaster in 2011 have halted efforts to revive the sector's appeal presently and seemingly in the

835 Kacper Szulecki, ed., '*Energy security in Europe: Divergent perceptions and policy challenges*,' (Springer, 2017)

836 Kacper Szulecki, ed., '*Energy security in Europe: Divergent perceptions and policy challenges*.

837 Buchan, 'Energy Policy : Sharp Challenges and Rising Ambitions', pp. 355–59.

838 Robin W. Grimes and William J. Nuttall, 'Generating the Option of a Two-Stage Nuclear Renaissance', *Science*, 329.5993 (2010), 799–803 <https://doi.org/10.1126/science.1188928>.

near future. This caused European politicians and the general public to reconsider their support for new nuclear power plants. A classic example is Germany that has opted for a nuclear phase-out.

On the subject of the value of financial investments, the sector is witnessing high costs of investments making it unattractive and reducing its bankability. The British government in a 2016 report suggested that the lifespan cost of Hinkley Point C would cost about 37 billion GBP.[839] Lastly, a bankruptcy in Westinghouse and a lifeline for Areva (both nuclear energy generation companies) is making the nuclear power generation sector a domain left only for largely state-led entities like Russia's Rosatom and France's EDF to dominate.[840]

The implication for these issues in relation to the EU's energy security which considers nuclear energy as an option is uncertain.[841] Because there is a split in general European public opinion with instances like that of Germany taking a stand against nuclear energy generation while the UK, France and the countries of Central and Eastern Europe are on the opposite side. However, there are projected estimates of increased production and supply of nuclear energy in the EU due to new nuclear facility projects which have been underway since 2012 in countries like Lithuania, Hungary, Poland and Czech Republic. The split European public opinion on the nuclear energy option has in a way caused even limited progress on these projects which are mainly in CEE countries as at 2017.[842]

---

839 UK Government, 'DECC Government Major Projects Portfolio Data 2016 - GOV.UK', 2016 <https://www.gov.uk/government/publications/decc-government-major-projects-portfolio-data-2016> [accessed 12 February 2019].

840 Benjamin Mallet, 'France's EDF Throws Areva a Lifeline with Reactor Deal | Reuters', *Reuters*, 2016 <https://www.reuters.com/article/us-france-edf-areva/frances-edf-throws-areva-a-lifeline-with-reactor-deal-idUSKBN13B0TG> [accessed 12 February 2018]; Tom Hals, 'Westinghouse Reaches Deal for $800 Million U.S. Bankruptcy Loan', *Reuters*, 2017 <https://www.reuters.com/article/us-toshiba-accounting-westinghouse/westinghouse-reaches-deal-for-800-million-u-s-bankruptcy-loan-idUSKBN18J2M2> [accessed 12 February 2018].

841 Kacper Szulecki and Kirsten Westphal, 'Taking Security Seriously in EU Energy Governance: Crimean Shock and the Energy Union', in *Energy Security in Europe. Energy, Climate and the Environment.*, ed. by Kacper Szulecki (Cham: Springer International Publishing, 2018), pp. 177–202 <https://doi.org/10.1007/978-3-319-64964-1>.

842 Szulecki and Westphal.

4.4.2.5 Energy Justice Issues

Issues pertaining to energy justice in the European Union are gradually emerging in EU energy discourse.[843] Energy justice is a newly conceptualised area in the broader field of energy studies that encourages discussions relating to how the EU can be just and equitable with its dealings of energy and fuel access for its citizens. Questions relating to the sustainable access and affordability of energy have been the focus of these energy justice issues which are under discussion between a gradually increasing number of policy makers and academics alike. These issues have emerged because the present energy system that exists is already unjust.[844] And with its effect in the European Union, a differentiated energy system exists in the four geographical sub-regions.

In trying to address these energy justice issues, the EU mentions energy poverty as highlighted in the Third Energy Package as the inadequate access to energy fuels and the issues related to domestic energy deprivation. Moreover, EU member states (namely Germany, Belgium, Greece, Spain, Poland, Slovakia, France and UK) describe the precarious nature of an increasing section of their populations being exposed to the inequities in energy distribution. This is happening because of high and rising energy prices as well as inefficient buildings that waste available energy. This results in a lack of energy services in the home in addition to long and short-term mental and physical health implications of the affected energy poor population.[845]

Relying on 2011 data across the EU, domestic energy deprivation was captured as being unevenly distributed spatially with proportions of energy poverty varying greatly among countries. High levels were recorded especially in CEE and Southern European countries.[846] The use of data

---

843 Energy justice, as defined by Benjamin Sovacool, is a concept that refers to an energy system that fairly disseminates both the benefits and costs of energy services, and one that has representative and impartial energy decision-making. For more see: Benjamin K. Sovacool, *Energy & Ethics: Justice and the Global Energy Challenge* (London: Palgrave Macmillan, 2013), xci.

844 Goldthau and Sovacool; Benjamin K. Sovacool and Michael H. Dworkin, 'Energy Justice: Conceptual Insights and Practical Applications', *Applied Energy*, 142 (2015), 435–44 <https://doi.org/10.1016/j.apenergy.2015.01.002>.

845 Stefan Bouzarovski and Saska Petrova, 'A Global Perspective on Domestic Energy Deprivation: Overcoming the Energy Poverty–Fuel Poverty Binary', *Energy Research & Social Science*, 10 (2015), 31–40 <https://doi.org/10.1016/j.erss.2015.06.007>.

846 Thomson and Snell.

on excessive winter deaths (EWD) which is mostly used as a synonym for fuel poverty established that EWDs are higher in the UK than in Scandinavian countries irrespective of the fact that the latter has a colder climate.[847] However, a lack of recognition and stigmatisation persists in some European political circles on the issues of domestic energy deprivation, which has debilitating implications for households that has further created inequalities in energy distribution policies across the EU.[848]

4.4.2.6 Environmental Sustainability Issues

The European Council authorised the EU climate and energy framework for 2030 in October 2014. This framework sets out targets on GHG emission reductions, improved utilisation of renewable energy, and a boost in energy efficiency by 2030. Its execution is presently part of the EU participation of the Paris Climate Agreement, which aims at a transition towards a sustainable low-carbon energy future.[849] The way the EU's energy policy was conceptualised by the Commission did not exclude environmental sustainability issues as an important component.[850] A 2006 Green Paper issued by the Commission references sustainability as a key objective of the EU energy strategy, and this dimension has proven to become the EU energy policy's particular strength.[851]

Dieter Helm notes that the European Community's biggest success in designing its energy policies and moving it towards sustainability was

---

847 Vanessa Burholt and Gill Windle, 'Keeping Warm? Self-Reported Housing and Home Energy Efficiency Factors Impacting on Older People Heating Homes in North Wales', *Energy Policy*, 34 (2006), 1198–1208 <https://doi.org/10.1016/j.enpol.2004.09.009>.

848 Stefan Bouzarovski and Neil Simcock, 'Spatializing Energy Justice', *Energy Policy*, 107.October 2016 (2017), 640–48 <https://doi.org/10.1016/j.enpol.2017.03.064>.

849 Wilson and Dobreva.

850 Israel Solorio Sandoval and Francesc Morata, 'Introduction: The Re-Evolution of Energy Policy in Europe', in *European Energy Policy: An Environmental Approach*, ed. by Israel Solorio Sandoval and Francesc Morata (Cheltenham: Edward Elgar Publishing, 2012), pp. 1–22 <https://doi.org/10.4337/9780857939203.00008>.

851 Kirsten Westphal, 'Energy Policy between Multilateral Governance and Geopolitics: Whither Europe?', *Internationale Politik Und Gesellschaft*, 4 (2006), 44–62.

pivoted on the Climate and Energy Package.[852] Indeed for a long period of time, EU energy policy has aimed at establishing and completing the internal energy market for gas and electricity, in an energy union, the essence of the package was a set of short-term objectives targeted at reducing energy prices. As well as promoting energy security through the advancement of a gradual integration of the domestic energy markets.[853]

This has enabled a recalibration of the energy and climate strategy of the EU. Renewable energy has been included in the mix, as a major alternative source of sustainable energy. Its expansion within the novel energy and climate regime in place coupled with falling prices of renewable energy and improving efficiency, is expected to lead to a significant reduction in hydrocarbon demand. Moreover, affecting price decreases in energy making it unreliable to pursue new fossil fuel sources.[854]

The fusion of climate and energy policies have become a solid base to influence energy governance region-wide across the EU. It also contributes to a process that serves as a remedy for climate change concerns.[855] Finally, environmental sustainability through climate measures, energy efficiency and adoption of renewables remains the strategic options for the EU as it debates and implements its regional energy policy in a uniquely pragmatic way.[856] In addition the connection between energy and climate policies have steadily altered the entire EU energy policymaking process.[857]

4.4.3 Future Prospects: Governance of the Energy Union

The future towards a completely created internal energy market in the EU seems a bit distant but it is steadily progressing. To realise this vision a

---

852 Dieter Helm, 'The European Framework for Energy and Climate Policies', *Energy Policy*, 64 (2014), 29–35 <https://doi.org/10.1016/j.enpol.2013.05.063>.

853 Rafael Leal-Arcas, Juan Alemany Rios, and Costantino Grasso, 'The European Union and Its Energy Security Challenges', *Journal of World Energy Law and Business*, 8.4 (2015), 291–336 <https://doi.org/10.1093/jwelb/jwv020>.

854 Szulecki and Westphal.

855 Ute Collier, 'EU Energy Policy in a Changing Climate', in *Environmental Policy Integration: Greening Sectoral Policies in Europe*, ed. by Andrea Lenschow (London: Earthscan Publications, 2002), pp. 175–92.

856 Andris Piebalgs, *How the European Union Is Preparing the" Third Industrial Revolution" with an Innovative Energy Policy, EUI Working Paper RSCAS*, RSCAS 2009/11 (Florence, 2009), xɪ <www.euthat is,u>.

857 David Buchan, *Energy and Climate Change: Europe at the Crossroads* (Oxford: Oxford University Press, 2009).

revolutionary undertaking of an EU Energy Union has been introduced which is making progress. The origins of this idea can be traced to the former European Parliament president Jerzy Buzek and erstwhile European Commission president Jacques Delors who tabled in a joint declaration a concept for a new European Energy Community in 2010 under the aegis of a policy proposal submitted by the think tank Notre Europe.[858]

Four years later in the wake of the Ukrainian crisis, the then Polish Prime Minister, Donald Tusk, the President of the European Council proposed the notion of an *Energy Union* where he presented six pillars based on geopolitical concerns about Russia's weaponization of energy and the way forward. The proposal called for a) joint negotiations by EU member states on energy particularly on gas supply contracts with external suppliers; b) strengthen the solidarity mechanisms between member states in relation to gas supply interruptions; c) an expansion of strategic and cross-border energy infrastructure, comprising pipelines, storage facilities and LNG terminals; d) the full appropriation of indigenous European fossil fuels, like coal and shale gas, extracted in a sustainable way; e) diversifying oil and gas supplies through, example, shipping liquefied gas from the United States or Australia; f) the promotion of energy security in the EU neighbourhood by strengthening the energy community with Balkan states, Moldova and Ukraine.[859]

In a Financial Times op-ed Tusk underscored a possible European stance to "confront Russia's monopolistic position with a single European body charged with buying gas" in a determined attempt by "breaking up the Russian gas monopoly and restoring free market competition" cautioning further that "excessive dependence on Russian energy makes Europe weak".[860] Subsequently, the opening address in the European Parliament by the new European Commission Chief, Jean Claude Junker in July 2014

858 Jerzy Buzek and Jacques Delors, *Towards a New European Energy Community* (Brussels, 2010) <http://institutdelors.eu/wp-content/uploads/2018/01/en_buzek-delors_declaration.pdf> [accessed 13 February 2017]; Sami Andoura, Leigh Hancher, and Marc Van der Woude, *Towards a European Energy Community: A Policy Proposal*, *Notre Europe* (Paris and Berlin, 2010) <http://www.notre-europe.eu>.

859 Kacper Szulecki and others, *Giving Shape to the Energy Union: Evolution, National Expectations and Implications for EU Energy and Climate Governance*, *SSRN*, 2015 <https://doi.org/10.2139/ssrn.2623892>.

860 Donald Tusk, 'A United Europe Can End Russia's Energy Stranglehold', *FT.com* (London, 2014), pp. 4–5 <http://www.ft.com/cms/s/0/91508464-c661-11e3-ba0e-00144feabdc0.html#axzz30viqhrqv> [accessed 13 February 2018].

featured 10 key priorities that would serve as the starting point of his mandate.[861] It included the reform and reorganisation of Europe's energy policy into a new resilient European Energy Union with a bold climate change policy as one of its priorities.

On 25 February 2015, the EU Commission launched a blueprint through its Energy Union Package to chart a course for the new union focused on "secure, affordable, and climate-friendly energy for citizens and businesses".[862] To actualise these legislative and non-legislative objectives contained in the package, the EU Commission appointed Maroš Šefčovič as the first ever vice-president for the Energy Union and Miguel Arias Cañete as commissioner for Climate Action and Energy. The assigned duties among others of the novel vice presidency was the absolute priority of bringing to pass the Energy Union.[863] The Commission publicises its proposals for the energy union as a new era of progress. Šefčovič called it the biggest leap forward in European energy policy since the European Coal and Steel Community treaty that formed the basis for the European Union's subsequent formation.[864]

Indeed, the five basic dimensions of the EU's Energy Union strategy seeks to bring about effective energy security, sustainability and competitiveness in a range of policy areas including but not limited to competitiveness of the single market, climate change, transportation and mobility, industry, research, the digital economy, and agriculture[865]. The dimensions of the energy union package included the security of energy supplies, improvement of the internal energy market, energy efficiency, carbon emis-

---

861 Jean-Claude Juncker, *A New Start for Europe: My Agenda for Jobs, Growth, Fairness and Democratic Change.*, *Political Guidelines for the next European Commission* (Strasbourg, 2014) <https://ec.europa.eu> [accessed 13 February 2018].

862 European Commission, 'Energy Union Package - A Framework Strategy for a Resilient Energy Union with a Forward-Looking Climate Change Policy COM(2015) 80 Final', 2015, pp. 1–21 <https://doi.org/10.1017/CBO9781107415324.004>.

863 Jean-Claude Juncker, 'Mission Letter - Vice-President for Energy Union' (Brussels: European Commission, 2014), pp. 1–6 <https://ec.europa.eu/commission/sites/cwt/files/commissioner_mission_letters/sefcovic_en.pdf>.

864 David Buchan and Malcolm Keay, 'Europe's "Energy Union" Plan: A Reasonable Start to a Long Journey', *Oxford Energy Comment*, 2015, p. 2 <https://www.oxfordenergy.org/wpcms/wp-content/uploads/2015/03/Europes-Energy-Union-plan-a-reasonable-start-to-a-long-journey.pdf> [accessed 30 June 2018].

865 European Commission, 'Energy Union Package - A Framework Strategy for a Resilient Energy Union with a Forward-Looking Climate Change Policy COM(2015) 80 Final'.

sions reduction and the enhancement of energy research and innovation. The aspect of security of energy supplies seeks to reduce dependency on energy supplies from third parties outside the EU.

Moreover, it encourages this be done by means of the efficient use of domestic energy sources and diversification through the adoption of other energy sources and supplies. The proposal emphasises a solidarity clause that assures reducing dependency on single energy suppliers and fully relying on neighbours, particularly on occasions when confronted with energy supply disruptions. The aspect that deals with improving the internal energy market contends that energy should flow freely across the EU without any technical or regulatory barriers and in effect be like a fifth freedom. This literally guarantees a new freedom in the single market, that is, the free movement of energy supplies. It encourages present rules to be strictly enforced mainly in the areas of energy infrastructure unbundling. It also encourages the independence of energy regulators to take legal action where necessary.

The third aspect that borders on increasing energy efficiency seeks to promote energy efficiency as an alternative energy source in its own right. It also advocates that energy efficiency would reduce energy consumption which in effect would reduce pollution, preserve domestic energy sources and reduce the need for external energy imports. The next aspect on reducing carbon emissions have sought to fulfil emission targets of at least 40 percent of greenhouse gases by 2030 is a first step. With the next step being to renew the European emissions trading scheme (EMTS) while investing more in the development of renewable energy sources as a potent and viable energy alternative.

The last aspect of the energy union package is committed to enhance competitiveness through research and innovation. It seeks to spearhead the innovation of renewable energy technologies in the next generation which would reduce energy consumption and create export and industrial opportunities that would boost growth and jobs.[866]

Governance reforms undergirding the process of establishing concretely the energy union is unfolding and expected to be in place before the new EU Commission takes over in December of 2019.

To finalise a clear energy governance pathway that would guide the energy union, a systematic legislative process is underway. This process has

---

866 European Commission, 'Energy Union Package - A Framework Strategy for a Resilient Energy Union with a Forward-Looking Climate Change Policy COM(2015) 80 Final'.

raised issues related to the governance of the energy union as well as put focus on the prevailing energy issues that the energy union package seeks to consider. I will give a brief overview of the legislative process that has undergirded the realization of the energy union. On 30th of November 2016, the EU Commission as part of its Clean Energy package proposed a regulation on the governance of the energy union.[867]

This proposal's objective was to streamline the process of monitoring progress and support in the implementation of the aims of the EU energy union. In particular, to fulfil the 2030 EU targets on greenhouse gas emissions, renewable energy adoption and energy efficiency. One salient feature connected to the proposal is the preparation of national energy and climate plans for the 2021–2030 period that would be followed up by progress reports to measure and monitor progress in the implementation of objectives at the national level. The Commission will provide inputs into both national plans and progress reports and that will be binding on member states. The contents of the EU energy union regulation envision national and EU registries and inventories on greenhouse gas emissions for the post-2020 period. And it will serve as a framework for assessing progress in realising the goals of the Paris Agreement.

On February 2018, Trilogue negotiations between the Parliament, Council and Commission started and concluded with a provisional agreement on 20th June 2018. It was published in the Official Journal of the European Parliament on 21st December 2018 and subsequently came into force on 24 December 2018. This was possible because the European Parliament and Council of Ministers formally adopted the final text on 3rd November 2018 and 4th December 2018 respectively.[868]

4.4.3.1 Current Legal and Situational Context

The existing legal context of the EU energy union regulation is Articles 191, 192 and 194 of the Treaty on the Functioning of the European Union (TFEU). Whereas Articles 191 and 192 stipulate EU competences

---

867 European Commission, 'Proposal for a Regulation of the European Parliament and of the Council on the Governance of the Energy Union, Amending Directive 94/22/EC, Directive 98/70/EC, Directive 2009/31/EC, Regulation (EC) No 663/2009, Regulation (EC) No 715/2009, Directive 2009/' (Brussels: European Commission, 2016).

868 European Union, 'Regulation (EU) 2018/1999', *Official Journal of the European Union* (Luxembourg: Publications Office of the European Union, 2018), 1–77.

on climate change, Article 194 affords the EU with a particular set of competences in the energy policy space. To ensure that national energy and climate plans and progress reports of member states are comparable. The regulation would be directly applicable to them. It would further enable national plans to be put in place by 1 January 2021.

The regulation carefully brings together EU energy and climate goals, and caters for the establishment of national and EU inventories on greenhouse gas emissions (GHG) for the post-2020 period. Together with registries measuring member state progress in meeting their national commitments under the United Nations Framework Convention on Climate Change (UNFCCC) 2015 Paris Climate Change Agreement.[869]

The EU energy and climate acquis obligates and requires that planning, reporting and monitoring are currently dispersed in an extensive range of legislation. These numerous legislations were approved at different times in order to meet various objectives. Respectively, each legislation is inclined to have its own set of such obligations and they are not automatically aligned with similar requirements in related legislation. This has resulted in an array of planning and reporting obligations for member states, as well as numerous monitoring obligations for the European Commission.[870] More than a few obligations under present EU legislation are geared towards fulfilling the main targets of the 2020 EU energy and climate package.[871]

This is therefore not directly germane to the 2030 EU energy and climate framework which was approved in October 2014 by the European Council and the EU energy union strategy which was adopted in February 2015 by the EU Commission and endorsed by the European Council on March 2015.[872] Some of the requirements are only operative within the period until 2020 and will cease to be operational from 2021. Under prevailing EU legislation, energy and climate issues are not always fully

869 Alex Benjamin Wilson, 'Governance of the Energy Union [EU Legislation In Progress]' (Strasbourg: EPRS | European Parliamentary Research Service, 2019) <https://epthinktank.eu>.

870 Alex Benjamin Wilson.

871 European Commission, '2020 EU Climate and Energy Package', 2009 <https://ec.europa.eu/clima/policies/strateg,ies/2020_en> [accessed 15 February 2018].

872 European Commission, '2030 EU Climate and Energy Framework', 2014 <https://ec.europa.eu/clima/policies/strateg,ies/2030_en#tab-0-0> [accessed 15 February 2018].; European Commission, 'Energy Union Strategy', 2015 <https://ec.europa.eu/commission/priorities/energy-union-and-climate_en> [accessed 15 February 2018].

coordinated, nonetheless the approach of the EU's energy union strategy is clearly to align them together. Distinct reporting obligations now exist for all key legislation present in the energy and climate acquis.[873]

A release of an annual State of the Energy Union report on 31st October annually by the Commission is obligated under the new energy union regulation. This would regularise a systemic practice, whereby the Commission has set out to deliver such a report approximately on an annual basis with the first presented in November 2015 and the second in February 2017. Another task the regulation would seek to do is to establish an Energy Union committee composed of representatives from member states and chaired by the Commission, to help the latter in its work.

In doing so, the regulation necessitates technical assistance from the European Environmental Agency in the collection of data from member states and performance of quality control and assurance. All in all, the EU energy union regulation provisions would become fully applicable on the 1st of January 2021. Moreover, it would be subject to a formal review on the 28th of February 2026 and thereafter a review will take place every five years. During this period, the Commission could decide to do an earlier review if it is crucial in meeting the necessary energy and climate goals set under the EU energy union strategy.[874]

4.4.3.2 Governance Issues

Experts have advised that the scope of governance issues related to the Energy Union should not be constrained only to the formalized governance mechanisms that are contained in the 2030 framework for energy and climate. Which would be fulfilled in the Energy Union Package but should include informal cooperation between different levels of decision-making processes, specifically at EU-wide, country and sub-national levels.[875]

A challenge of governance arises in the quest to establish and implement the energy union.[876] The breath and role of these different levels of governance is informed by the context of the political economy of the entire

---

873 Alex Benjamin Wilson.

874 Alex Benjamin Wilson.

875 Kacper Szulecki, Andrzej Ancygier, and Karsten Neuhoff, 'Energy Union : From Idea to Reality', in *Conference and Expert Workshop on EU Energy Governance Post-2020* (Berlin, 2015) <www.econstor.eu>.

876 Malcolm Keay and David Buchan, 'Europe's Energy Union : A Problem of Governance', *Oxford Energy Comment* (Oxford, 2015), pp. 1–6.

European energy sector and its impact on industry and society. However, this energy governance challenge arises from the fact that the objectives of the energy union is not just based on a simple rebranding of existing policies. But an attempt to resolve the growing tension that exist between the long-established EU policies of energy market liberalisation and the new obligation to intervene in the energy market to realise climate-linked outcomes such as GHG emission reduction.[877]

One other challenge for the EU as a supranational body is that though it has a common template for market liberalisation, founded on the removal of government intervention in energy as seen in other sectors of the EU single market. A certain form of market intervention is required to meet the target of cutting emissions. Practically, national governments operating their own separate renewable subsidy schemes have mostly taken on this responsibility. A key component of the energy union strategy is an attempt to bring some commonality into the implementation of these renewable schemes. Thus far, it has realised progress based on an *integrationist* process which has not reached the point where member states are ready to solidarize in joint renewable energy subsidy schemes.[878]

To remedy some of these tensions is part of the energy governance challenge that faces the EU under the energy union. Its genesis would be to focus on the current policy that outlines effective energy and climate requirements as well as obligations and seek to steadily harmonise and coordinate regional energy towards a common energy policy.

Buchan and Keay[879] have argued that if the EU energy union really aspires to be a union, EU member states should pool their resources to create a common, EU-wide system not a national feed-in energy planning process for supporting low carbon investment as proposed by the EU Commission and is implementing. However, the counter position to this point would mean a revision of EU treaty articles that safeguard national sovereignty over the composition of national energy mix, such a revamp is not under consideration by the EU Commission.

At first glance, this position levelled by Buchan and Keay would seem to eradicate the governance problem. On the other hand, with imagination and creativity, the challenge could be surmounted as seen in the obliga-

877 Keay and Buchan.

878 Keay and Buchan.

879 David Buchan and Malcolm Keay, *Europe's Long Energy Journey: Towards an Energy Union?*, ed. by David Buchan and Malcolm Keay, 1st edn (Oxford: Oxford University Press, 2016).

tions outlined in the 2018 EU energy union regulation. In spite of existing Treaty constraints, this would offer an opportunity for effecting a Europe-wide approach and at the same time would not hamper the capability of member states to govern their own energy futures.

Furthermore, other stakeholder involvement such as the general EU public, civil society actors, provincial and sub-national authorities, local community opinion leaders among other stakeholders in consultative action and engagement with EU institutions would enrich the energy governance process. However, the Commission in particular has been criticised for the quality of its stakeholder consultative engagement.[880]

Rowe and Frewer further differentiate between the types of stakeholder engagement and how it might help the EU in its future public engagements. They typify stakeholder engagement in three ways namely pure one-way information from decision-makers to the public, one-way information from the public to decision-makers, and finally, two-way dialogue and negotiations between decision-makers and the public. They assert that such two-way dialogue culminates in a profound exchange than the respective one-way dialogues. They explain further that the type of engagement denotes the actual partaking of the public in public engagement activities. In this sense, an emphasis on both the breadth and depth of public engagement action on energy governance can certainly improve the governance process. This will strengthen national support, local communities and civil society actor support to keenly back energy and climate strategies put forward by the EU.

Regional cooperation is also seen as the crucial means to deliver and drive the EU's energy and low-carbon transition. In 2016, the Commission promised an initiative to strengthen regional energy cooperation.[881] Mechanisms for the increased regionalization of the EU electricity markets have so far chalked a number of successes. The process of regionalizing energy infrastructure is reaping benefits because of the presence of these three elements that are in place, that is, a strong political will and leadership which is focused on realizing the objectives of energy co-operation. Moreover, all relevant stakeholders are actively participating. Finally, practical

880 Gene Rowe and Lynn J. Frewer, 'A Typology of Public Engagement Mechanisms', *Science, Technology, & Human Value*, 30.2 (2005), 251–90 <https://doi.org/10.1177/0162243904271724>.

881 Keay and Buchan.

and workable structures are in place that influence the rates of success of achieving the relevant energy goals that have been put in place.[882]

EU institutions have done a remarkable job especially in the bureaucratic space in terms of the energy governance process. Chiefly by taking into consideration the need to use national climate, renewable energy and energy efficiency programmes from 2020 onwards as initial building blocks. This has led for instance, the Commission to support the shaping of national energy planning in this regard. This was done although there was a risk of revolt from two-thirds of EU member states in 2015 especially those who had no medium-term energy plans prepared for 2030 and the small number of nations that had prepared sophisticated energy plans. The perception that this was an unnecessary overreach from Brussels did not suffice and eventually resulted in fruitful bureaucratic processes by EU institutions.

4.5 Institutional Foundations of EU Energy Regionalism

This section explores the institutional foundations that hold EU energy regionalism in place and illustrates the polycentric nature of the interaction that exists between the major players in the regional energy policy process. This includes the state, market and other (non-state and non-market) actors. The section outlines the key actors. Their relations with one another and the importance of the role of their institutions in the regional energy policy process, and lastly the instruments available to them in the governance of regional energy.

Owing to the divergence between Western and Eastern European national interests in energy policy, the prospect to influence the energy decision-making process differs substantially between actors making it difficult to unify positions into an effective common energy governance system. However, energy policies in the EU principally remain in the charge of member states due to the principle of subsidiarity and are essential components of domestic politics because the domestic economy is reliant on affordably priced electricity for commercial and household residential activities.

Private energy purveyors and consumers need affordable energy for business and commercial purposes as well as for residential purposes such as heating together with other energy carrier services such as fuel for their

882 Szulecki, Ancygier, and Neuhoff.

cars among others. Also, private energy purveyors hire domestic lobbying groups that represent their business interests in the energy market to exert pressure as much as possible on governments to ensure that the energy policy actions and decisions being made be it internally or externally reflect and facilitate their commercial interests.

Governments resolve to realize domestic energy interests in international and regional negotiations and in so doing, attempt to mediate between the different political levels. The third actor, transnational or domestic NGOs, prosumers and integrated community energy systems providers, in recent times have influenced the EU energy sector by contributing to resolving energy challenges through advocacy and self-production of energy which in due course has been transformational to the regional energy policy space of the EU. EU energy regionalism is not comprehensible without reference to the various interconnected institutions at EU level and the multi-levels that also provide innovation and entrepreneurship of all sorts in order to find equitable energy solutions for the public.

At EU level, we have general institutions, such as the European Commission, Council of the European Union and Council of Ministers, European Parliament, Court of Justice of the European Union, which influence the entire energy system. Then we have the other energy sector institutions made up of market and state actors (such as ACER, ENSTO-E and ENTSO-G and the proposed EU DSO) as well as non-state and non-market actors.

4.5.1 General Institutions

4.5.1.1 European Commission

The Commission is the backbone for EU energy policy. It benefits from the skilful and targeted transfer of competencies over energy policy decisions from the national to the EU-level.[883] The Commission is noted in its role in energy policy as a supranational policy entrepreneur and collegial body.[884] As a body committed to supranationalism, the Commission, acts independently from the member states in order to represent the interest

883 Per Ove Eikeland, *EU Energy Policy Integration - Stakeholders, Institutions and Issue-Linkages*, *FNI Report*, 2012, 13/2012.

884 Maltby; Vicki L. Birchfield and John S. Duffield, *Toward a Common European Union Energy Policy: Problems, Progress, and Prospects*, ed. by Vicki L. Birchfield and John S. Duffield (Basingstoke, UK: Palgrave Macmillan, 2011).

of the entire EU. It is the only institution that is mandated to initiate Union Law as well as ensure its application by member states. Its executive powers were enhanced with the advent of the Lisbon Treaty especially its daily decision processes such as exercising delegated powers from the Parliament and Council on a case-by-case basis through the adoption of quasi-legislative measures. In simple terms, when the Council and Parliament pass legislation, it is the Commissions responsibility to assess, evaluate and make sure member states effectually apply EU law.

The leadership of the Commission is made up of a president, a number of vice presidents, and a College of Commissioners allocated to different functional units and policy portfolios comparable to national ministerial roles with the total number encompassing twenty-eight. That is, a single representation from each of the member states. The Commission oversees a number of executive divisions known as Directorate-Generals (DG's). Even though the DGs are semi-autonomous, the entire College of Commissioners must agree on their prepared legislative drafts. Consensus is built at the level of the Commissioners because of frequent and regular engagement between the DGs. In the area of EU energy policy, the DGs in the Commission which facilitate energy regionalism are DGs for Energy (ENER), Climate Action (CLIMA), Competition (COMP), Mobility and Transport (MOVE), Enterprise and Industry (ENTR) and Environment (ENV).

As a policy entrepreneur, the Commission functions effectively particularly as its policy ambit has expanded radically from a few limited areas to include almost every imaginable policy field including energy. Maltby[885] has established using Kingdon's[886] ideas that the Commission has effected policy change through: (1) legitimacy by building on pre-existing norms of energy policy-making; (2) expertise and knowledge based authority; (3) continuous advocacy; (4) alliances and interaction with member states and other stakeholders (5) selling solutions during the policy window opened in periods of crisis, and (6) contributing towards the social construction of a narrative that concerns energy problems, and an intersubjective comprehension of a (supranational) remedy.

For instance, the Junker Commission (2014–2019) set about on major restructuring on the Commission's organisation by introducing clusters each headed by one of the vice presidents. In relation to the energy cluster,

885 Maltby.

886 John W. Kingdon, *Agendas, Alternatives, and Public Policies*, ed. by John W. Kingdon, *Agendas, Alternatives, and Public Policies*, 2nd edn (Essex: Pearson, 2014).

dubbed *A Resilient Energy Union with a Forward Looking Climate Change Policy*, headed by Maroš Šefčovič, it was responsible for pooling resources, combining infrastructure, and fusing negotiating power vis-à-vis third party country deals in gas policy relations for instance to ensure security of gas supplies.

Regarding its role on the basis of collegiality, the Secretariat-General (SG) functions as the "clearing house and a nerve centre"[887] by monitoring legislation, convening and chairing meetings of the DGs focused on a particular policy field such as energy and generally facilitating the coordination of the Commission. This is essential for multi-level policy fields like energy and the environment, which requires polycentric approaches to address issues that involve multiple DGs in the formulation of policy proposals. The EU Commission's decisions are arrived at collectively by means of a simple majority and once a common position on a policy is determined, all Commissioners must support the policy irrespective of whose policy portfolio it is and, of course, even if their own national government contests it.

The Commission also invokes its authority in the external dimension of EU energy policy, by directly addressing security of supply issues from external supplier countries on behalf of the EU. It does so by putting into place concrete strategies and proposes organizational reforms when needed in order to ensure diversification and coordination of energy supply. This external aspect of energy policy has historically been the sole prerogative of member states, therefore this gradual institutional and policy transformation, is clear validation and affirmation of the supranational governance authority of the Commission by national governments who are steadily giving up customary energy decision-making authority in certain competencies.[888]

The Commission incorporates all its policy action particularly in energy as in other policy fields within the context of competition in the single market. It does so by emphasizing its regulatory role. DG Competition intervenes in the implementation phase in order to ensure compliance. For instance, during the 1990s, when most of the electricity and natural gas markets at the national level were still under monopolies the Commission

887 Vicki L. Birchfield, 'The Role of EU Institutions in Energy Policy Formation', in *Toward a Common European Union Energy Policy*, ed. by Vicki L. Birchfield and John S. Duffield (London: Palgrave Macmillan, 2011), p. 245 <https://doi.org/10.1007/978-94-009-6092-3_8>.

888 Birchfield.

nudged member states to comply by opening up these energy markets to competition gradually.

It spearheaded this process of deregulation and liberalisation by doing the following: 1) distinguishing clearly between competitive parts of the industry (example, supply to customers) and non-competitive parts (example, operation of the networks); 2) obliging the operators of the non-competitive parts of the industry (example, the networks and other infrastructure) to allow third parties to have access to the infrastructure; 3) freeing up the supply side of the market (example, to remove barriers preventing alternative suppliers from importing or producing energy); 4) removing gradually any restrictions on customers from changing their supplier; and 5) introducing independent regulators to monitor the sector. This culminated in the first, second, third liberalisation directives and its maturation into the energy union.[889]

In his State of the Union letter of intent for 2018 the Commission President Jean-Claude Juncker to the leaders of Council and Parliament, proposed that the Commission intends to develop a new institutional framework for EU energy and climate policy by 2025.[890] This will include possibilities for enhanced qualified majority voting. It also references the possibility for the EU Commission to act in areas of energy policy that are the competence of member states especially in relation to the energy mix and the structure of energy supply. The option for the EU Commission to adopt legislation that affect rights of member state is envisaged in the existing Treaties (Article 192(2) TFEU). Nevertheless, it is applicable only to environmental or climate measures and requires a special legislative procedure involving the Council's unanimity.

4.5.1.2 The European Council and the Council of the European Union

The Council system existent in the EU represents the member states and their interests and facilitates shared decision-making on various policies including energy. Within this context, the member states articulate their

889 DG Competition, 'European Commission - Competition - Energy - Overview', 2012 <http://ec.europa.eu/competition/sectors/energy/overview_en.html> [accessed 17 February 2018].

890 Jean-Claude Juncker and Frans Timmermans, 'State of the Union 2018: Letter of Intent to President Tajani and to Chancellor Sebastian Kurz', *Strasbourg, 13 September* (Strasbourg: European Commission, 2018) <https://ec.europa.eu/commission/sites/beta-political/files/soteu2018-speech_en_0.pdf>.

positions and interests using two official opportunities namely the European Council that brings together the Heads of State and Government and the Council of the European Union (also known as Council of Ministers).

European Council

The European Council's role is two-fold that of giving visibility to the energy policy interests and positions of the entire EU and its elected presidency playing the role of mediator and pooling together the varied national interests as a single agenda.[891] It doubles as a co-legislator with the European Parliament, an innovation which arose because of the ratification of the Treaty of Lisbon. The heads of state and governments that compose of the European Council are represented by permanent representations from each member state, the Coreper I and II. The Working Party (WP) on Energy present in the European Council normally meets on a weekly basis.

Deputy permanent representatives from the member states lead Coreper I meetings, which acts as the main base between the WP and the Council. On the other hand, Coreper II, is led by the ambassadors, and focuses single-handedly on issues related to external and foreign policy, development cooperation and nuclear matters.[892] It is also responsible for setting the EU's overall political direction, and its decision-making processes are always unanimous. The general assumption is members states support the measures adopted facilitating implementation nationally.

Nonetheless, the decisions arrived at are often based on limited consensus because on the issue of energy policy national positions and interests diverge significantly. For instance, on the need to unbundle, vertically integrated energy companies' member states agreed but mechanisms and processes to realise this concretely are mostly bedevilled with highly controversial discussions.[893]

The Energy Union is seen by the European Council as a strategic vision to guarantee energy security and transparency in gas contracts and fully champions its realisation. The European Council has agreed that

---

891 Philipp Thaler, 'The European Commission and the European Council: Coordinated Agenda Setting in European Energy Policy', *Journal of European Integration*, 38.5 (2016), 571–85 <https://doi.org/10.1080/07036337.2016.1178252>.

892 Birchfield.

893 Johannes. Pollak and Samuel. Schubert, *Die Energiepolitik Der EU*, ed. by Johannes. Pollak, Samuel. Schubert, and Peter. Slominski (Wien: facultas wuv UTB, 2010) <https://opac.ub.uni-greifswald.de/DB=1/XMLPRS=N/PPN?PPN=690093802>.

the fruitful implementation of the EU energy union strategy by investing the needed capital required (an estimated 200 billion euros annually in the next decade) necessitates a holistic approach and the consolidation of strategic energy partnerships and energy cooperation with producer and transit third countries.[894]

The Council of the European Union (also known as Council of Ministers)

The second arm of the Council system of the EU is the Council of ministers. It is composed of non-permanent ministerial groupings convened in semi-regular meetings with the delegated Ministers coming from national capitals to deliberate and decide on legislative proposals from the Commission or proposed amendments from the Parliament. On regional energy issues, the Council's grouping on Transport, Telecommunications and Energy (TTE) deals with it. The TTE was established in 2002 and its energy ministers meet approximately in every quarter of the year.

The policy goals it pays attention to are transport, telecommunications and energy policy. The central aim of the TTE Council is to work to establish modern, competitive and efficient markets and infrastructure, and to create trans-European transport, communications and energy networks. As far as energy policy is concerned, the Council focusses on adopting legislation and working with the European Parliament, on dealing with the functioning of energy markets.

It executes this by ensuring energy supplies are secured, while promoting energy efficiency, new and renewable energies, and promoting the interconnection of energy networks.[895] A worthy example is that in October 2014, the European Council endorsed the EU climate and energy framework for 2030 that aims to reduce GHG emission, increase the use of renewable energy, and improve energy efficiency by 2030. The implementation of these targets is now part of the EU contribution to the Paris Agreement on climate change, which concentrates on transitioning to a low-carbon energy system.

894 Climate Policy Observer, 'European Council Endorses the Energy Union', *Climate Policy Observer*, 2015 <http://climateobserver.org/european-council-endorses-energy-union/> [accessed 19 February 2018].

895 Council of the European Union, 'Transport, Telecommunications and Energy Council Configuration (TTE) - Consilium', 2018 <https://www.consilium.europa.eu/en/council-eu/configurations/tte/> [accessed 19 February 2018].

4.5.1.3 European Parliament

The Parliament is composed of directly elected representatives of EU citizens. It plays a crucial role in determining the content of EU energy policies. Since the advent of the Lisbon Treaty (2007), it employs the *ordinary legislative procedure* to exercise its legislative role on EU-wide policy as well as EU energy policy. This enables the co-legislative task it shares with the Council to be done. In view of being compliant with Article 194, which also guarantees security of supply as an explicit EU competence in the energy field, member states reserve the ultimate privilege to determine their choice of energy sources that is their national energy mix, the energy supply structure in the national economy, and the circumstances for extraction and production of energy sources.

In the event that the EU seeks to legislate in a manner, which considerably affects member state interests, then a *special legislative procedure* is triggered which requires an initial decision by unanimity in Council. A similar process is applied to any of the EU energy policies that are oriented to fiscal matters example, energy taxation. Parliament initiates its own resolutions; this includes a broad-ranging resolution on the energy union on December 2015. This assisted members of the European parliament (MEPs) to develop common positions on issues that would later emerge in legislative proposals from the Commission. A significant number of the EU's daily work on energy policy is executed in the standing committees of the European Parliament.

Currently, the specialized parliamentary standing committee responsible for energy is the committee on Industry, Research and Energy (ITRE) formerly christened committee for energy, research and technology (CERT). It is comprised of sixty-six (66) MEPs who are full-time members and sixty-five (65) MEPs who are substitute members. This indicates the breath of its membership.[896]

ITRE's leadership is made up of a chair and four vice-chairpersons with its current chair being the legendary Jerzy Buzek. Other standing committees that deal with energy are the Committee on Foreign Affairs, International Trade and the Committee on Environment, Public Health, and Food Safety. Committees must resolve their differences on a legislation before it is passed whenever that arises. For instance, before the mechanism

896 European Parliament, 'Members and Substitutes of the European Parliament Committee on Industry, Research and Energy' (Strasbourg, 2019), pp. 1–14 <http://www.europarl.europa.eu/committees/en/itre/members.pdf>.

on the reduction of carbon dioxide emissions from an average of 130g/km in 2012 for an automotive was passed as proposed by the Commission the Environment and Industry Committees had to settle their differences.[897]

Energy supply and security were prominent issues during the 2014–2019 parliamentary term with the topmost on the agenda relating to the governance of the energy union. The Parliament's role in policy formulation is affected by its working relationship either in concert or in conflict with its co-legislator the Council. The Treaty of Lisbon requires this co-decision procedure on all policy related matters including energy further guaranteeing veto powers to the Parliament. A proposal dies in its track if a piece of legislation, being considered in a conciliation committee made up of members from the trilogue (which includes the Commission and Council) does not accept the Parliament's amendments. Hence energy policy formulation (and any other policy for that matter) in the EU is fully dependent on this inter-institutional procedure. This fosters an element of rivalry among the institutions in relation to the EU's policymaking process that may include energy issues.[898]

Aside from the formal role of the Parliament its ability to bring on board other views from other actors in the policy arena significantly influences its contributions to the policy/legislative process in the EU.[899] Due to the generalist approach of most MEPs only a few have the technical capabilities to measure up to the technocratic officials of the Commission on an equal footing in defining a given policy area. Thus, the engagement of MEPs with external think tanks, NGOs, the press, and certain national groups exerts a considerable influence in their undertakings.

Overall, the European Parliament has been a solid advocate and champion of the EU energy union in order to secure supply of energy resources whilst at the same time protecting the climate through energy efficiency and reducing GHGs. Moreover, because of its major role in EU energy policy processes it is able to contribute significantly.

4.5.1.4 Court of Justice of the European Union

Simply known as the Court of Justice, it is tasked with the responsibility of interpreting EU law such that it applies uniformly across the member

897 Schubert, Pollack, and Kreutler, pp. 134–35.
898 Birchfield.
899 Matlary.

states. An important dimension in developing the internal market of the European Union. Although the first treaty framework was about energy products, the opening up of the EU energy market was relatively slow in being realised irrespective of its importance.[900] Because, energy was considered a politically and economically sensitive policy area, which had a potential of derailing the European integration agenda. National energy interests were divided as a result European energy markets and their needs were met by nationally owned or controlled monopolies.[901] Eventually, focus on energy became a pressing agenda in EU and further integration discussions. Subsequently, an attempt to deal with it was based on primary provisions on internal market law and competition law.[902]

The European Commission is seen as the key actor in the EU energy market because of the role played by competition law and sector-specific regulation. However, the Court of Justice (hereafter "the Court")[903] has exercised a pivotal role in opening up the energy market. The energy sector is fast-paced; hence, a lot has changed in terms of sector- specific regulation. In these developments, the Court, as one of the principal institutions in the EU and guarantor of the uniform interpretation of EU law has contributed to the process.

In order to form a mental imagery of the nature of the Court's function of opening-up energy markets it is important to understand the institutional role the Court plays in the EU's legal order.

Unlike civil law countries, case law of the Court is of vital significance as a source of law for the EU. It serves as a binding and central source of European law. An all-important aim of this is to ensure uniform application and interpretation of EU law in the 28 member states of the

900 Martha M. Roggenkamp and others, *Energy Law in Europe: National, EU, and International Law and Institutions*, 2nd edn (Oxford: Oxford University Press, 2007).

901 Kim Talus, *EU Energy Law and Policy: A Critical Account*, 1st edn (Oxford: Oxford University Press, 2013).

902 Sirja-Leena Penttinen, 'The Role of the Court of Justice of the European Union in the Energy Market Liberalisation', in *Research Handbook on International Energy Law*, ed. by Kim Talus (Cheltenham, UK: Edward Elgar Publishing, 2014), pp. 241–71.

903 The judicial branch of the EU system is made up of three courts: The Court of Justice, the General Court and the Civil Service Tribunal (which concerns itself with disputes of the European Civil Service). Thus, issues considered here in reference to "the Court "may be applicable to the Court of Justice or the General Court excluding the Tribunal due to its scope of reference on labour disputes.

Union. The differences between the national courts of the member states is compensated for by the general and uniform application of European law irrespective of the situation for which it is being applied.

The Court employs a potent tool, the *preliminary ruling procedure* under Article 267 of the Treaty for the Functioning of the European Union (TFEU), to ensure that EU law is uniformly interpreted. Again, Article 267 of the TFEU allows national courts to make *preliminary references* to the Court on matters of interpretation of EU law and validity of the actions of EU institutions. Rulings by the Court in the use of the preliminary ruling procedure is interlocutory in nature that is, it is not conclusive but constitutes a stage in the proceedings requiring the national court to apply it in the facts of the case which is being considered.[904] Hence, the interaction between the Court and the national courts is referential instead of being appellate in nature.[905]

Aside the function of ensuring uniformity in interpretation the preliminary ruling procedure has been used to promote the political integration of the EU especially laying down the fundamental principles of EU jurisprudence.[906] Because these preliminary rulings are binding, the Court's interpretation of a given case has a binding effect on each party involved in the case. It also serves as a precedent in other words providing a guideline for future cases in national courts or authorities.[907]

It is important to note that the preliminary ruling procedure is not the only means by which the Court is involved in the shaping of EU case law particularly concerning the opening-up of energy markets even though most conversation dwells solely on preliminary rulings. The EU formulates and executes its policies and aims through regulations, directives and decisions, and a mechanism is required to test the legality of such measures. The Court is empowered under Article 263 TFEU to review the legality of the actions of EU institutions and this is especially applicable in the energy field since it is strongly affected by the competition decisions of the Commission, the exercise of Article 263 plays a vital role in limiting the Commission's discretion.[908] Another review function of the Court is exercised in relation to the legality of the actions of the ACER therefore

---

904 Anthony. Arnull, *The European Union and Its Court of Justice*, 2nd edn (Oxford: Oxford University Press, 2006).

905 Paul P. Craig and Gráinne de Búrca, *EU Law : Text, Cases, and Materials*, 5th edn (Oxford: Oxford University Press, 2011), pp. 442–43.

906 Penttinen, p. 246.

907 Craig and de Búrca, p. 453.

908 Penttinen, p. 246.

demarcating the limits of competence of this regulatory agency in the EU energy space.[909]

The Court ensures also that member states fulfil their obligations under the treaties. The Commission can trigger proceedings against member states who fail to comply with requirements set out in the treaties. Because the procedure ensures timely transposition of the energy liberalisation packages that were in the form of Commission issued directives, member states who flout timelines are subjected to proceedings before the Court to ensure compliance under Article 258 of the TFEU. For instance, in 2011 the Commission launched infringement proceedings against 19 member states for non-compliance in transposing the Electricity and Gas Directives of the Third Package. In 2012 and 2013, the Commission sent reasoned opinions to 16 member states, which had not finished the transposition process. By the end of 2012 and the beginning of 2013, a number of member states were referred to the Court.[910]

The Court adopts a teleological approach to the interpretation of EU law. The use of this distinctive method of interpretation means that the Court examines the whole context in which a particular provision is situated and seeks to identify aims and purposes it wants to achieve.[911] Due to the inextricable linkages between energy policy and energy law the political concerns inherent in the energy sector have a marked influence on the interpretation of EU energy law that is mainly dominated by policy-oriented, teleological-purposive interpretation.[912] The teleological method has given rise to a form of judicial activism by the Court, which has been met with some criticism due to its unpredictable dimension in interpretation, and lack of focus on the literal presentation of legal wording in the provisions. However, the Court has made the Treaties and secondary law effective vehicles in the realisation of the single market and has ensured the removal of national trade barriers in moments of stagnation particularly in the use of case law as a tool in the process of opening up the EU energy market.[913]

---

909 Imelda Maher and Oana Stefan, 'Delegation of Powers and the Rule of Law: Energy Justice in EU Energy Regulation', *Energy Policy*, 128.December 2018 (2019), 84–93 <https://doi.org/10.1016/j.enpol.2018.12.046>.

910 European Commission, 'April Infringements Package: Main Decisions; MEMO/13/375' (Brussels: European Commission, 2013).

911 Craig and de Búrca, p. 64.

912 Talus, *EU Energy Law and Policy : A Critical Account*, p. 7.

913 Penttinen, p. 248.

4.5.2 Other Actors

4.5.2.1 Market and State Actors

Market Actors

Private for-profit and business actors play a less formal role in their participation of intergovernmental processes in the energy policy space of the EU. For example, on 16th February 2016 in adopting the legislative proposal for a decision on intergovernmental agreements (IGA)[914] as part of the energy security package, the EU Commission consulted with private commercial actors so as to avoid potential conflicts with EU legislation before the IGA was signed. Notable among such private commercial actors are *BusinessEurope* (that is, the Confederation of European Business), Eurogas (the association representing the European gas industry), the German Association of Energy and Water Industries (BDEW), the Austrian Federal Economic Chamber and many others.[915]

Business actors partake in efforts to address specific energy policy problems by giving inputs to the legislative process. At the EU-wide level, interactions have been endorsed through the granting of voluntary invitations to corporations by EU institutions mainly the Commission and Parliament and their allied agencies as well as member states on issue areas ranging from climate to energy. For instance, *BusinessEurope* and other business actors expressed their reservations on potential problems that could arise if the Commission made ex-ante verification of IGA's mandatory in bilateral energy deals that could disrupt the European energy market.[916] An important attribute of these actors is the transnational and collaborative nature of their contributions on the sector that influence policy makers. In the EU, big, small and medium-sized corporations acquire membership of sectoral, national and European associations in order to monitor progress

914 IGAs are usually bilateral agreements that form the basis of more detailed commercial contracts. Its main purpose is typically to provide legal certainty for the construction of import and export infrastructure, in order to facilitate the purchase of oil and gas or establish a more general framework for energy cooperation.

915 Gregor Erbach, 'Intergovernmental Agreements in the Field of Energy', *EU Legislation in Progress* (Strasbourg: European Parliamentary Research Service (EPRS), 2017) <https://epthinktank.eu/2017/02/03/intergovernmental-agreements-in-the-field-of-energy-eu-Legislation-in-progress/>.

916 BusinessEurope, 'BusinessEurope Position on Intergovernmental Agreements in the Field of Energy' (Brussels, 2015) <https://www.businesseurope.eu>.

of EU legislation that has a potential to affect them and to lobby policy makers to benefit their constituents.

These business actors in addition to their lobbying and consultative roles also serve alongside member states as major investors in the EU energy sector. This may seem obvious; however, due to the huge capital investments and long-term nature of the financing involved in the energy sector, it brings together a panoply of private corporations from various sectors such as finance and banking, engineering, construction, consulting and energy among others. This spans across the business value-chain (upstream, mid-stream and downstream) and across the entire energy value-chain (that is, production, transmission and distribution) to realise long-term investment objectives.

State Actors

The notable state actors in the EU energy scene are National Energy Champions (NECs) and National Regulatory Authorities (NRAs). NECs are corporations that do business in the energy sector with majority shareholding from a particular state or a province or sub-national level in a state. They also include major utility companies in a particular national province or sub-national level within a state. Quite a number of these NECs function multi-sectorally and transnationally across the EU and globally. Some notable names in this group include BP, Royal Dutch Shell, ENI, RWE, and ENGIE among many others.

National regulatory authorities are public bodies that are both independent of both the market and state. They mostly possess statutory authority under domestic and EU law. They are tasked with the responsibility of implementing rules in their respective energy markets in accordance with EU sector-specific regulation. Their input in the network of actors in the EU's internal energy market is vital to say the least. EU law requires member states to establish independent national regulatory bodies in order to ensure fair competition within the single market.[917]

The three legislative energy packages operationalised their role within the EU energy space with subsequent improvements and strengthening of their roles with the commencement of every energy package. The Commission set up the European Regulators' Group for Electricity and Gas (ERGEG,) in 2003 to advise it on internal energy market issues. It was however, succeeded by the Agency for the Cooperation of Energy Regulators (ACER) in 2011 as part of the third internal energy package. ACER

917 Pollak and Schubert.

aims at ensuring and achieving market integration and the harmonisation of regulatory frameworks within the context of the EU's energy policy objectives. They do tout themselves as a central institution in the creation of the internal energy market for the benefit of all EU consumers.[918]

Article 1 (2) of the Third Energy Package (Regulation (EC) No. 713/2009) stipulates that ACER will the assist the national regulatory agencies, "in exercising at Community level, the regulatory tasks performed in the member states and where necessary to coordinate their actions"[919]. Article 4 of the same regulation, draws out its key functions, which include ensuring cooperation among NRAs, the issuance of opinions and recommendations targeted at Transmission System Operators (TSOs), NRAs and general EU level institutions.[920]

ACER also provides assistance in regulatory development decisions. The formal decision-making powers of ACER include the adoption of technical issues under electricity and gas market legislation (Art 7 (1)). In Article 8, on occasions when the NRAs cannot come to an agreement on the terms and conditions regarding interconnectors, ACER can adopt a binding decision. Sometimes the NRAs can make requests in this regard and ACER would have to oblige by issuing a binding decision. Similarly, in situation where NRAs cannot come to a decision on exemptions on Third Party Access (TPA) for new interconnectors the Agency in some cases provide a binding decision.[921]

Finally, ACER has tasks pursuant to other legislation, for instance the REMIT legislation,[922] infrastructure regulation and network codes. Anoth-

918 ACER - Agency for the Cooperation and of the Energy Regulators, 'The Agency', 2017 <http://www.acer.europa.eu/en/The_agency/Pages/default.aspx> [accessed 20 February 2018].

919 European Union, 'Regulation (EC) No 713/2009 Of The European Parliament And Of The Council of 13 July 2009 Establishing an Agency for the Cooperation of Energy Regulators', *Official Journal of the European Union*, L 211. January (2009), 1–14 <https://eur-lex.europa.eu/LexUriServ/LexUriServ.do?uri=OJ:L:2009:211:0001:0014:EN:PDF>.

920 European Union, 'Regulation (EC) No 713/2009 of the European Parliament and of the Council of 13 July 2009 Establishing an Agency for the Cooperation of Energy Regulators', *Official Journal of the European Union*.

921 European Union, 'Regulation (EC) No 713/2009 of the European Parliament and of the Council of 13 July 2009 Establishing an Agency for the Cooperation of Energy Regulators', *Official Journal of the European Union*.

922 REMIT stands for *the Regulation on Wholesale Energy Market Integrity and Transparency*. It is an EU regulation designed to increase the transparency and stability of the European energy markets while combating insider trading and market manipulation. REMIT was adopted in the European Union in 2011.

er body, which shares a similarity with ACER in terms of objectives, functions and structure but whose work does not overlap, is the Council of European Energy Regulators (CEER). The prevailing difference between them is that ACER is a formalised body of the EU energy system and CEER is a voluntary organisation under the patronage of the national regulatory authorities themselves. CEER recognises itself as the mouthpiece of national energy regulators of electricity and gas at the EU and global levels. Their main objective is to facilitate and support the creation of a single, competitive, efficient and sustainable EU internal energy market.[923]

The European Network of Transmission System Operators (ENTSOs) were established by the third energy package. Its essence and purpose is to promote the completion and functioning of the internal energy market and cross-border trade in addition to ensuring the optimal management, coordinated operation and sound technical evolution of the electricity/gas transmission network. That has been stipulated under Article 4 of the third energy package.[924]

Its most important responsibility is to draft network codes and guidelines. In effect, it wields a lot of influence in terms of its importance but it has no legal powers to adopt binding decisions. The ENTSOs simply propose drafts to the EU Commission. Certain non-EU member states participate in the ENTSOs. In the area of electricity, the ENTSO-E has 43 member TSOs from 36 countries including EFTA and some Energy Community states. It includes, for example, STATTNETT from Norway. For gas, the ENTSO-G has 45 member TSOs from 26 countries. Here members from the EFTA and Energy Community States serve as observers. Participation by non-EU membership is less challenging due to its lack of powers to adopt binding decisions.[925]

923 Council of European Energy Regulators, 'ABOUT - Ceer.Eu' <https://www.ceer.eu/eer_about> [accessed 20 February 2018].

924 Henrik Bjørnebye, 'Webinar: Extending the Energy Acquis beyond the EU Institutional Challenges - Florence School of Regulation', 2018 <http://fsr.euthat is,u/event/extending-the-energy-acquis-beyond-the-european-union-institutional-challenges/> [accessed 22 January 2019].

925 Henrik Bjørnebye, 'Webinar: Extending the Energy Acquis beyond the EU Institutional Challenges - Florence School of Regulation'.

The European Union Distribution System Operators (EU DSO) has been proposed in the Recast Electricity Regulation[926], which comes into force in 2020. The Commission seeks to create this new EU-level entity for distribution system operators (DSOs) to enhance cooperation between themselves and with transmission system operators (TSOs) on matters relating to planning and operation of their power networks. This new entity will have a major influence in the deployment and integration of renewable energy systems, which are mainly, distributed energy systems operating on clean energy. Moreover, it would also affect positively or negatively on the growth of demand response, choices on grid tariffs and connection charges for prosumers, and customer data protection and privacy.[927]

4.5.2.2 Non-State and Non-Market Actors

Another set of actors who play a less formal role but pivotal role in developing and implementing EU energy regionalism include transnational non-governmental actors (TNGOs), prosumers and integrated community energy system providers (ICESP).

TNGOs that operate at EU-wide level influence the EU policy process most often through their transnational energy advocacy initiatives that seeks to link energy security concerns with environmental sustainability that is, mitigating climate change. They push for their views to be adopted through joining associations, establishing offices in Brussels and serving as think tanks to influence EU policy making in the area of energy. Some of these TNGOs due to the sources of their funding represent certain corporate interests in the course of their advocacy.

The next group of non-state and non-market participants in the EU energy system are *prosumers*. These are local communities or individuals who are challenging the conventional notion of passive consumers of energy to active producers of energy both for their consumption and for onward transmission.[928] In other words energy prosumers is an overarching term that makes reference to self-generating energy providers, whether

926 Proposal for a Regulation of the European Parliament and of the Council on the internal market for electricity (recast), Brussels 30.11.2016, COM (2016)861 final

927 Josh Roberts, 'The Proposed EU DSO Entity: What Is It and What's at Stake?' (Brussels: ClientEarth, 2016), pp. 1–6 <www.clientearth.org>.

928 Tineke Van Der Schoor and Bert Scholtens, 'Power to the People: Local Community Initiatives and the Transition to Sustainable Energy', *Renewable and*

households or energy communities. These individuals add to the supply of energy in their locality via their own installed energy capacity.

Presently the phenomenon is characterized by power generation using renewables mostly as solar roofing, wind energy or combined heat and power.[929] It is in this function of supply in an integrated manner that links this group of actors (that is, prosumers) to the next group of actors (that is, ICESPs) whom I would discuss later. These new actors are changing the face of the architecture and design of the energy transition in both the emerging and developed economies as already noted in Chapter 3 above.

The role of prosumers currently underpins the decentralized energy system and is literally democratising access to energy and preserving energy security. Among EU member states, a novel energy eco-design and system is evolving, one that progressively harnesses renewable energies through these decentralized providers.[930] In terms of the place for prosumers in the wider governance of the energy union, the legal status of prosumers is one of the issues that has been considered in the newly revised Renewable Energy Directive. The 13 September 2016 resolution *Towards a New Energy Market Design* called for a common understanding of the definition of prosumers at EU level in order to address the main obstacles and barriers to investment in self-generation and self-consumption of renewables.[931]

This feeds into establishing an enabling regulatory framework to facilitate renewable energy communities. It is estimated that electricity, heating and cooling production from bioenergy would ensure a 70 percent reduction in GHG emissions for installations done in 2021 and rising further to 80 percent for those operational by 2026 however, the Commission sets higher targets of 80 percent and 85 percent respectively. This would further on be accomplished with the fulfilment of an EU Commission requirement where a report every two years would be submitted on the

---

Sustainable Energy Reviews, 43 (2015), 666–75 <https://doi.org/10.1016/j.rser.2014.10.089>.

929 Josh Roberts, *Prosumer Rights: Options for an EU Legal Framework Post-2020* (London, 2016) <http://www.greenpeace.org/eu-unit/Global/eu-unit/reports-briefings/2016/ClientEarth Prosumer Rights - options for a legal framework - FINAL 03062016.pdf>.

930 Rafael Leal-Arcas, Feja Lesniewska, and Filippos Proedrou, 'Prosumers: New Actors in EU Energy Security', in *Netherlands Yearbook of International Law*, 2018, XLVIII, 139–72 <https://doi.org/10.1007/978-94-6265-243-9_5>.

931 European Parliament, 'Towards a New Energy Market Design' (European Parliament, 2016).

impacts and benefits of biofuels in the energy union as well as third countries.

Upon conclusive trilogue negotiations and the adoption of the final text by both the Parliament and Council, EU Directive (EU) 2018/2001 was published setting a 32 percent binding target for the share of renewable energy sources (RES) in final energy consumption by 2030 to be delivered through indicative national contributions.[932]

The new roles that have emerged for prosumers under this new framework are energy trading, where they are empowered to trade in energy they have conserved or produced. This facilitates network optimisation and flexibility in addition to raising extra revenue.[933] The use of smart-grids as the technological base to support the prosumer energy economy will eventually spur on the process of digitisation in the EU energy economy. Because most of these prosumers are using decentralised energy systems based on a democratized approach. They assist in establishing a separate type of energy actor or entity known as energy communities or integrated community energy systems.[934]

An integrated community energy system (ICES) is known as the modern development to reorganise local energy systems to integrate distributed energy resources and engage local communities. Moreover, they ensure self-production of energy and provide vital essential system services to the larger traditional energy system.[935] ICESs are defined as a multi- faceted approach for supplying a local community with its energy needs from high-efficiency co-generation or tri-generation as well as from renewable energy technologies coupled with innovative energy storage solutions as well as electric vehicles and demand-side management measures.[936]

---

932 EU, 'Directive (EU) 2018/2001 Of The European Parliament And Of The Council of 11 December 2018 on the Promotion of the Use of Energy from Renewable Sources (Recast)', *Official Journal of the European Union*, 2018 <https://eur-lex.europa.eu/leg,al-content/EN/TXT/PDF/?uri=CELEX:32018L2001&from=EN>.

933 Leal-Arcas, Lesniewska, and Proedrou, XLVIII.

934 Steffen Wirth, 'Communities Matter: Institutional Preconditions for Community Renewable Energy', *Energy Policy*, 70 (2014), 236–46 <https://doi.org/10.1016/j.enpol.2014.03.021>.

935 Binod Prasad Koirala and others, 'Energetic Communities for Community Energy: A Review of Key Issues and Trends Shaping Integrated Community Energy Systems', *Renewable and Sustainable Energy Reviews*, 56. April (2016), 722–44 <https://doi.org/10.1016/j.rser.2015.11.080>.

936 Gonalo Mendes, Christos Ioakimidis, and Paulo Ferrão, 'On the Planning and Analysis of Integrated Community Energy Systems: A Review and Survey of

In deployment, ICESs demonstrate planning, design, implementation and governance of energy systems at the community level to maximize energy performance while cutting costs and reducing environmental impact. Again, in relation to ICESs, they recast EU regulation of renewables, which is to be transposed in national legislations of EU member states, by 30th June 2021. It makes provision for this game-changing development in the architecture of EU energy regionalism.

ICESs play special roles in the new era of EU energy governance. As non-profit entities, they are effective and efficient in the provision of services to local energy customers and because of the direct accountability to the consumer base ICESs are responsive to the concerns and needs of local communities. By doing this they promote self-regulation and polycentric energy governance in action.[937] Since they are connected to the creation of decentralised structures of energy production and supply through novel institutional arrangements using locally owned and collectively owned energy systems, they epitomize energy democracy in action.[938]

In terms of ownership, ICESs represent commons-based energy supply solutions. Using a liberalized market model, it is possible to establish local producer/prosumer – consumer energy commons. It supports co-creation by many actors in establishing a smart local energy system. ICES can be 100 percent community owned or built together with partnerships from the private or public sector under a co-ownership arrangement.[939] In spite of the fact, that many localities are already actively engaged in the ownership and financing of community energy production that is directly fed into the grid. The rollout of ICESs promote a combination of community owned production and consumption of energy.

In considering the literature on the legal and financial ownership models, four ownership arrangements for ICES ownerships are observed name-

---

Available Tools', *Renewable and Sustainable Energy Reviews*, 15.9 (2011), 4836–54 <https://doi.org/10.1016/j.rser.2011.07.067>.

937 Thomas Bauwens, Boris Gotchev, and Lars Holstenkamp, 'What Drives the Development of Community Energy in Europe? The Case of Wind Power Cooperatives', *Energy Research and Social Science*, 13 (2016), 136–47 <https://doi.org/10.1016/j.erss.2015.12.016>; Thomas Bauwens, 'What Roles for Energy Cooperatives in the Diffusion of Distributed Generation Technologies?', *Ssrn*, 7.0 (2014), 1–29 <https://doi.org/10.2139/ssrn.2382596>.

938 Wirth.

939 Gordon Walker, 'What Are the Barriers and Incentives for Community-Owned Means of Energy Production and Use?', *Energy Policy*, 36.12 (2008), 4401–5 <https://doi.org/10.1016/j.enpol.2008.09.032>.

ly co-operatives, community charities, development trusts and co-ownerships (with shares owned by communities).[940] Since majority of the common ownerships in the EU are energy cooperatives, I elaborate further below.

An energy co-operative is an organization owned and run jointly by the group of members who share in the profits or benefits, such as, its employees or customers. In the EU, energy co-operatives have been thriving due to the environmental concerns after the oil crisis in 1973.[941] Examples of these cooperatives are the wind and biogas co-operatives in Denmark and solar photovoltaics co-operatives in Germany[942] in the UK the first cooperatively owned wind farms were set up in 1990[943]. A substantial rise in the number of energy co-operatives was accounted for in Germany between 2007 and 2013 (from 100 to 900). Equally, in the Netherlands, there are close to about 500 active energy co-operatives[944].

Citizen participation in energy co-operatives by means of investments in generation units and energy efficiency measures is a specific way of involving citizens in the diffusion of ICESs. The EU model of co-operatives is well entrenched in the society and part of local culture. This is more suited for the development and proliferation of ICESs. The diffusion of renewable energy sources and other forms of local generation are more suitable for the co-operative approach in light of high initial costs and local availability.[945]

Presently, energy co-operatives in Germany are going through a difficult phase in developing innovative business models this has led to stagnation in their growth.[946] ICESs are fully catered for, endorsed and facilitated by the recast 2018 directive for renewable energy sources and seeks to set out a framework under the fledgling governance agenda for the EU energy union. In conclusion, the activities of prosumers and consumer organisations, energy communities and NGOs cater for other forms of

940 Walker.
941 Koirala and others.
942 Wirth.
943 Walker.
944 Bauwens.
945 Koirala and others.
946 Özgür Yildiz and others, 'Renewable Energy Cooperatives as Gatekeepers or Facilitators? Recent Developments in Germany and a Multidisciplinary Research Agenda', *Energy Research and Social Science*, 6 (2015), 59–73 <https://doi.org/10.1016/j.erss.2014.12.001>.

actor engagement in the strengthening of the energy institutional setup in the EU.

4.6 Recapitulation

The unfolding of the evolution of regionalism and its functioning with energy in the European Union is underpinned by the three conceptual themes of energy, international political economy of energy (IPE of energy), and institutions similar to that of the ECOWAS case discussed in Chapter Three. In this case, I have narrated EU energy regionalism and its governance in a refreshingly new way.

Major issues highlighted in this chapter have been the following:

1. The European Union's energy path-dependence and creation reveal that energy development in the course of European integration has been determined by the adoption of energy technologies at varying times and speeds in the four constitutive sub-regions namely northern, central & eastern, western and southern Europe.
2. To restate the historical narrative of EU regionalism, I have categorised the stages into four under the following headings, first wave: pre-great war years, second wave: mid-war years, third wave: post war years and the fourth wave: founding of the EU. Furthermore, the dual character of EU regionalism in terms of its distinctiveness and cohesiveness was explored.
3. The energy regionalism of the EU can be framed using its past milestones that describe the cooperation towards a common European energy region, present settings that illustrated the integration of the European energy region, and its future prospects that give account of the governance framework that undergird the EU's energy union.
4. To conclude, the institutional foundations serving as a fulcrum on which EU energy regionalism is built has been considered. Thus, outlining the current institutions and actors of EU energy policy which includes the general institutions of the EU Commission, Parliament among others as well as other actors namely market and state along with non-market and non-state actors that deal with energy policy in the EU region.

I have used historical institutionalism to expound on this narrative of EU energy regionalism. Which sums up the proposition that, European nations in spite of their geographical diversities, over the years particularly in the period before the wars, during and after the war years sought to resolve their energy challenges through a new international political economy of energy, always evolving through the organisational and geographical clustering of energy issues at the comparative regionalism level. The EU has done this by developing institutions founded on solid legal norms, general institutions and other actors to combat the regions energy problems.

Chapter 5

Comparative Institutional Analysis of Energy Regimes in ECOWAS and EU: Applying the Combined IAD-SES (CIS) Framework

5.1 Introduction

The Combined IAD-SES (CIS) framework or CIS for short is one of many approaches in conducting institutional analysis of energy systems or regimes. This framework for analysing institutions is a multitier hierarchy of concepts and variables that have been identified through empirical analyses of a number of case studies in the context of fisheries, water, and river-basin common-pool resources.[947]

Features of the CIS framework were borrowed from the SES framework and are the tiers that constitute it. On the first tier, the CIS framework dissects social-ecological systems (SES) and/or social-technical systems (STS) of energy regions (as is the case in this research) into the six concepts of resource system (RS), resource units (RU), governance system (GS), actors (A), interactions (I) and outcomes (O). The lower tiers, that is, second, third, fourth, etc., dissect higher-tier concepts further into more fine-grained variables (see Table 2.3).

To illustrate, RU is decomposed into resource unit mobility, replacement rate, economic value, and size. The variables have been included in the framework because they have been proven useful for explaining outcomes of resource use in empirical analyses. The attributed variables of the RS and RU, to give an example, are suitable for understanding outcomes because the challenges that underlie the biophysical, ecological and/or technical features of the SES/STS represent the nuances inherent in collective action and governance.[948]

---

947 Cole, Mcginnis, and Epstein; Daniel H Cole, Epstein, and McGinnis; Daniel H. Cole, Epstein, and McGinnis; McCord and others; Dustin E Garrick and others, 'Managing the Cascading Risks of Droughts: Institutional Adaptation in Transboundary River Basins', *Earth's Future*, 2018, 809–27 <https://doi.org/10.1002/2018EF000823>.

948 Hinkel and others.

The goal in this section of this research is to use an appropriate approach to analyse energy governance institutions found in a comparative regionalism context but not necessarily to represent the CIS framework as the most appropriate means to undertake such a task. Also, because the CIS framework has been shown to be useful in conducting sophisticated analyses of institutional arrangements present in other settings. It is possible that in the energy policy settings of both ECOWAS and EU it would prove to be useful.

The CIS framework has also been proven to avoid many of the common pitfalls encountered when using the two analytical frameworks that have been combined especially when they are being utilised in isolation. Although at their core, the IAD and SES frameworks are very closely related, similarities inherent in them are countered by certain limitations, which the combined framework attempts to remedy. As espoused by its developers in the Bloomington School of Political Economy[949], the CIS framework does not pretend to offer a completely formed causal theory or model.[950]

The procedure for this analysis would be done iteratively by applying it to the process of energy regionalism in both ECOWAS and the EU. These two cases were chosen because they exhibit a diverse set of attributes in a regional integration setting and in terms of looking into regional energy institutions, they represent attributes of a socio-technical commons (that is, macro energy regions).

The CIS framework emphasizes the careful consideration of the overall policy space(s) where policy actions are taking place, this is termed the

949 Daniel H Cole, Epstein, and McGinnis.

950 In Ostrom's vocabulary, the terms "frameworks," "theories," and "models" are terms of art. As suggested by Ostrom and Cox that "frameworks" may be seen as "metatheoretical conceptual map[s]." Ostrom describes "frameworks" as the "most generalized form of theoretical analysis," providing a general set of variables that comprise a meta-language, which is used for comparative institutional analyses of various "theories" and "models. "Theories" (example, economic theory or game theory) posit assumptions and hypothesized specifications of relevant variables (provided by the framework) deemed sufficient to provide adequate explanations or diagnoses of the policy setting under study. "Models" (example, the rational actor model or game-theory models) use more "precise assumptions about a limited set of variables and parameters to derive precise predictions about the results of combining these variables using a particular theory." See in: Ostrom and Cox, p. 455; Elinor Ostrom, 'Background on the Institutional Analysis and Development Framework', *Policy Studies Journal*, 39.1 (2011), 7–27 (pp. 8–9) <https://doi.org/10.1111/j.1541-0072.2010.00394.x>.

focal action situation. McGinnis[951] denotes a focal action situation as the pattern of policy interactions among resource actors and the particular resources upon which their livelihood relies. Both the social and the ecological/technical components of this focal action situation can be decomposed into smaller components as well as situated within the context of broader aggregations.

The RS, RU, A and GS variables defines what occurs in a focal action situation. In a focal action situation, interactions that occur lead to outcomes. There could be multiple focal action situations in a given policy space that is responsible for different policy decisions in different policy sectors. Thus, a typical policy space comprises of a network of focal action situations geared towards a specific decision-making process. In this particular instance the energy policy decisions with respect to the electricity or power sector has a number of policy actions such as generation, transmission and distribution.

These different policy actions represent different focal action situations and when they all come together, they serve as one particular network of focal action situations in the power sector of a regional energy economy. In the application of the framework, the overall action situation or network of focal action situations in the energy policy space must first be identified. Following that, a careful examination of contextual factors or variables that are composed in the pre-existing conditions. That is, the relevant contextual and explanatory variables located within the four primary categories of the SES (and CIS) framework are considered. However, in this energy policy context, to aid in clarifying, I go further to group the primary categories or first tier in a three set conceptual category, namely, *physical setting*, *attributes of the community* and *existing institutional setting*. This is synonymous to the attributes of the IAD framework.

Furthermore, the next step then draws attention to the full range of selected breakpoints that is, the significant changes or milestones occurring in the contextual factors that lead to a set of specific time references during which a connected group of processes can be identified for further appraisal. This assists in identifying the forces driving changes in the core network of inter-connected action situations during each period. In comparing the values of key contextual factors at different time references, it

951 Michael D. McGinnis, *Updated Guide to IAD and the Language of the Ostrom Workshop: A Simplified Overview of a Complex Framework for the Analysis of Institutions and Their Development*, p. 24.

enables one to trace significant changes and milestones in those and other variables throughout that time period.

As suggested by Cole, Epstein and McGinnis, potential breakpoints or milestones can be selected by identifying times when new rules or laws are passed or new organizations are established. And also by identifying external shocks, such as debuting a new technology, a climate measure, or an external happening that has a significant transformational effect to the setting may also be particularly relevant in some respect. In summary, there can be no clear-cut rules about the selection of breakpoints or milestones in a focal action situation in the application of the CIS framework.[952]

The following subsections illustrates the framework's major elements or variables and how it is used to analyse selected breakpoints in the governance of regional energy in the ECOWAS and EU regions. The first break point is the regionalisation period, when efforts towards energy regionalism was concretely initiated using policy and legal instruments in these two regions. The next major breakpoint comes in the 1970s and 1980s when the global energy crises sought to define a new era of energy politics and set both regions on different but similar paths to deal with energy issues compared to what persisted.

In the 1990s to the year 2000, both regions entered into a new phase of energy reforms, which directly involved deregulating, liberalising, externally cooperating on reducing greenhouse gas emissions and creating energy institutions that would govern the energy space at country levels and region-wide including their respective regional energy markets at varying degrees and depth. My final break point comes within the period after 2000 to 2015 where the formal establishment of a global energy and climate regime concerned with climate change, energy justice and energy security issues within the context of a changing awareness of dealing emphatically with reducing greenhouse gases in the environment was high on the agenda. This has shaped strongly the direction of energy governance in both regions.

The procedure enumerated above is used to demonstrate how the main points of action changes from period to period. Here I focus attention on specific periods when the nature of the relevant regional governance processes altered in a significant manner. Even though the conditions of regional energy governance in both regions continued to change after this periodic time. The following overview of the periods between these

952 Daniel H. Cole, Epstein, and McGinnis.

breakpoints should be sufficient to explain an analysis regarding dynamic institutional processes using the CIS framework.

In the selection of these periodic breakpoints a consideration of the significance of the period is not downplayed. This is because significant changes in energy governance mainly occur due to consequential events that markedly change the evolution of a regional energy sector and its governance system. If I were to attempt a more thorough and complete examination of these empirical cases, I would have needed to also consider other potential types of breakpoints, and further interrogate processes through which those changes were produced.

In Table 5.5, I provide an overview of my understanding of the analysis of these two empirical cases based on the choice of specific breakpoints represented. The top row lists basic conditions of regional energy as a resource unit and the resource system, which they constitute, as well as the nature of the primary actors and the rules that govern these resources. The following second row revises these conditions or introduces new ones in order to reflect the changed conditions observed for subsequent breakpoints. Sandwiched rows between these breakpoint rows summarize the most important patterns of interactions and outcomes observed in the focal action situations of particular significance for that period.

Bold fonts are used to indicate significant changes in the values of key contextual factors at each of the breakpoints. It is important to note with particular attention the changing cast of focal action situations at different times. It is here that the most detailed analysis is focused.

I designate (in bold) those action situations which were newly established by the outcome of the breakpoint which commenced at this period, or earlier important action situations that now operate in a way much different than in the preceding period. After setting the stage by reviewing the conditions of regionalism in the energy sectors of ECOWAS and EU.

I will highlight significant changes in each period in the remainder of this section (as can be seen in Figures 5.1 through to 5.6).

An overview of the case comparisons focuses on four elements that summarise regional energy governance in these two cases namely scale, polycentricism, decentralisation and justice.

5.2 Comparative Regionalism of the Energy Policy Space: Delineating the Network of Focal Action Situations in ECOWAS and EU

The energy policy spaces of both the ECOWAS and EU regions are made up of a network of action situations where strategic decision-making interactions occur to realise certain policy outcomes in relation to the governance of regional energy. At the heart of the institutional analysis, using the CIS framework is to delineate clearly the action situation(s) where policy decisions take place. An action situation is an abstraction of policy environments in which individual and corporate actors interact with one another, making policy choices that jointly determine outcomes of certain aspects of a policy question. Policy choices made by actors and collective outcomes are influenced by the beliefs and incentives of the relevant individuals, as shaped by the responsibilities and social expectations attached to the official positions they may hold, and by the information available to them.[953]

Since the regional energy policy area is a polycentric space it underscores the polycentric and multilevel nature of the decisions to be made in this holistic policy space bringing together a number of action situations in a linked network, put simply in adjacent action situations that are networked or polycentric action situations.[954]

This leads to the development of a coherent energy region with a diverse array of energy policy issues focused on specific energy resources that are tackled in a polycentric governance setting albeit subject to the nuances involved in this complex policy space. To delineate a number of the focal action situations that underpin the regional energy policy space in both geopolitical regions one could enumerate a few which could possibly define the network of focal action situations. These may include but not limited to energy resource appropriation, production, monitoring, technical innovation, technology adoption, financial availability, transportation and distribution, market exchange, ecological change, organizational behaviour, legislative and judicial deliberation, political dynamics and public opinion, or the diffusion of knowledge or cultural norms and other forms of societal change among others. This may relate to a particular energy sector and a group of energy sectors with similar value chains.

953 Daniel H. Cole, Epstein, and McGinnis.

954 Michael D Mcginnis, 'Networks of Adjacent Action Situations in Polycentric Governance', *Policy Journal Studies*, 39.1 (2011), 51–79.

The overall policy area or encompassing action situations stems both from the broad ECOWAS and EU communities of member states and more specifically the energy value chain across each state. The value chains within the ECOWAS and EU states consist of domestic energy producers, external energy suppliers, local power generators, distributors and retailers (most often the same entity), regulators as well as commercial and household consumers. Starting from local networks present in member countries of the two communities to the broader regional energy community. In addition to the rules and policies governing both energy sectors regionally and at national levels.

ECOWAS

The ECOWAS energy region is multi-scalar meaning there are different levels of engagement within the regional community. This includes the local decentralised energy installation in a small village or local district to a provincial energy grid, the entire national grid and the transnational or cross-border power grid or gas pipeline. A growing body of energy law is developing in ECOWAS to deal with the governance of the various aspects of the regional energy sector in the form of decisions, directives, regulations, protocols as well as national laws and policies. All these require a multi-scalar approach to energy governance in the region that spans supranational, national and sub-national structures at the same time considering the strategic interactions of different actors in the delivery of key policy outcomes.

Moreover, it is an energy region with one of the world's major net energy exporters – Nigeria – and a growing profile as a hub for hydrocarbons (oil and gas) based on commercial finds and developments in Ghana, Cote d' Ivoire, Senegal and across the West African Transit Margin in the Gulf of Guinea. It deserves to be mentioned here that the ECOWAS energy space is saddled with severe energy security concerns. This is duly characterised by consumers in the region, although sharing many of the same energy security interests and concerns as any other energy consumer outside the region. The constrains and ability to meet these energy needs have become issues that need to be addressed.

Moreover, the issues energy consumers face in the region are in some situations prompted by foreign energy consumers' escalating demand and investments towards the extraction of West African energy resources for external use. Another factor is the challenge of meeting the increasing local demand of energy through the consumption of petroleum, uranium or other energy resources internally in the region. Further the use and adoption of a variety of other alternative energy strategies and technologies that focus on different other energy resources have not yet been fully explored and exploited.

EU

The EU as an energy region is a net importer of global energy. EU countries produce a sizeable quantity of energy needs along the value-chains inherent in them both nationally and regionally. One significant feature of the holistic action situation in Europe is the specific over-reliance on Russian energy, which is fed into its energy value chains. The acquis or body of rules, which have been developed, governs the EU's regional energy policy. This is made up of directives, regulations, decisions and also national energy laws and policies.

In the same vein, the EU energy sector is multi-scalar, it includes among others local energy communities to provincial energy systems, and extend further to regional energy pipelines for gas transmission and distribution with a special attribute being the several gas corridors that constitute the European gas community. A diverse set of actors participate in the EU regional energy setting. They include foreign energy suppliers, national and municipal power producers and utilities, energy products distributers and retailers, regulators and commercial consumers as well as domestic consumers that may double as prosumers (mainly local energy communities and cooperatives) who produce their own energy with the surplus later fed into the grid.

5.3 Examining the Contextual Setting

The social-technical systems (STS) of the respective ECOWAS and EU energy regions are in many respects similar to social-ecological systems (SES). The ECOWAS energy region and the EU energy region are two different forms of energy regionalism being developed in the context of West African and European regionalisation efforts respectively. They share similar goals of envisioning energy self-sufficiency by reducing energy demand, using alternative, regional or external energy sources and building an interconnected regional energy infrastructure through linking up national infrastructures.[955]

---

955 ECOWAS, *Ecowas Energy Protocol A/P4/1/03*; European Commission Directorate, 'The EU and Energy Union and Climate Action', *Publications Office of*

Energy regionalism in ECOWAS has been in existence since the 1960s whilst in the EU, it emerged since the 1950s and today there are 15 and 28 member states respectively with inhabitants in both regions numbering 350 million and 513 million respectively. As alluded to by Hinkel et.al, although several studies have analysed technical and operational issues of energy production, the relationship between the energy producing system, actors, and the governance system underlying or supporting such processes have hardly been considered.[956] This institutional analysis therefore, compares the development of energy regionalism projects with different contextual conditions and different governance structures. Thereby, the CIS framework is the basis upon which the data of the two regional energy case studies is collected and analysed in a comparative context.

5.3.1 Physical Setting: Comprised of Resource Units (RU) and Resource Systems (RS)

Effectively, the rules governing energy policies in general must be compatible with the underlying physical settings or pre-existing conditions and the nature of the resources in question, that is, the resource units (RU) and resource systems (RS) being governed.[957] In order to observe and govern an energy system, the resource units (RU) that is, the basic components of energy services being delivered, pose a challenge to conceive as discrete units or products thus they are formulated in the mould of a public or common good that is consumed collectively.

Ostrom and McGinnis interpret clearly the resource unit (RU) in a social technical system (STS) as a unit of resource that does not need to "be required to be easily divisible as are most private goods. A public good is by definition, consumed collectively and cannot be divided into discrete subunits. However, if a resource unit is not divisible, then it might be possible to treat it as a single unit."[958] Distinctively, to be able to consider the various resource units in the different energy sectors that constitute an energy system or energy region a consideration of the stock of resource

the European Union, 2017 <https://publications.europa.eu/en/publication-detail/
>.

956 Hinkel and others.

957 Ostrom, Gardner, and Walker, p. 44.

958 Michael Dean McGinnis and Ostrom, p. 8.

units or the energy resource base being governed must be taken into account.

Due to the significant variation in physical settings, resources, and resource governance problems, a search to put in place rules that form the basis of a regional level approach presents a huge institutional challenge. For instance, in terms of physical settings and resource availability for a proposed power generation project, renewable resources such as hydro, wind and solar as well as conventional resources like gas-to-power generation options can be considered as resource units. In addition to the nature of the resource system, a transmission system informs the way the energy resource is deployed and that may determine whether it would be done via a centralised or decentralised grid system. All these issues around the resource type and its deployment require consideration in terms of the resources available in the physical setting of an energy region such as that of ECOWAS and the EU.

5.3.1.1 ECOWAS

In the ECOWAS region, the entire regional energy system is composed of two main sectors namely the power and petroleum sectors. They are made up of various energy resource systems or technical systems constituting their infrastructural setups such as power grid interconnections, gas pipelines, hydropower dams, oil rigs, biomass production facilities as well as renewable energy projects. These resource systems support mostly a particular energy resource unit or type that may include electricity, natural gas, petroleum, solar energy, wind energy or bio-energy.

Again, these particular resource units may come with their attendant peculiar energy governance problems. Hence, a search for the best rule or all-inclusive governance model for all circumstances is likely doomed to failure.[959] For example, a corporate commercial arrangement that is effective in managing extraction (that is, appropriation) of uranium deposits in Niger may not be effective in monitoring the intensity of the utility of sun's rays in the coastal regions of West Africa compared to the Sahel regions for the benefit of solar energy purposes.

959 Ostrom, Gardner, and Walker, p. 237.

Household Energy

Household energy is considered in terms of urban and rural areas and defined by a very high consumption of traditional biomass and insufficient access to modern energy infrastructure. A rural transition from conventional to more modern forms of energy is underway in households, localities, and small as well as cottage industries in the region. With respect to climate change concerns, the phenomenon of deforestation and the changing use of land, is contributing to greenhouse gas emissions and other ecological challenges. Principally, this phenomenon is driven by the urban demand for charcoal and wood fuels for the purposes of food production, other household activities and local economic activities. All these activities explain the pressure on forestry resources.[960]

Policies aimed at a more sustainable household energy supply and also includes the cultivation of forest cover in countries with sufficient rainfall as well as natural forest management is underway. A very cost-effective option, which has led to secure biomass supply particularly in countries with low rainfall like the Sahelian countries, is also underway. Another ongoing policy intervention combined with that of the above is the fuel switching (charcoal to LPG) agenda at country levels across the region particularly in urban areas where purchasing power is much higher, populations are growing and the sources of LPG supply are increasingly becoming available.[961]

On the demand side, decarbonisation of biomass and improved stove technologies remain solid policy interventions. These are being implemented across the region under the support of region-wide and national energy bodies. In summary, the pace of the regional energy transition can be improved by the year 2030 whether or not the region still remains as one of the many world regions with a sizeable number of its population still dependent on traditional biomass as a major fuel source in rural and peri-urban household energy.[962]

---

960 Smail Khennas, 'Understanding the Political Economy and Key Drivers of Energy Access in Addressing National Energy Access Priorities and Policies: African Perspective', *Energy Policy*, 47.SUPPL.1 (2012), 21–26 <https://doi.org/10.1016/j.enpol.2012.04.003>

961 Youba Sokona, Yacob Mulugetta, and Haruna Gujba, 'Widening Energy Access in Africa: Towards Energy Transition', *Energy Policy*, 47.SUPPL.1 (2012), 3–10 <https://doi.org/10.1016/j.enpol.2012.03.040>

962 Abeeku Brew-Hammond, 'Energy Access in Africa: Challenges Ahead', *Energy Policy*, 38.5 (2010), 2291–2301 <https://doi.org/10.1016/j.enpol.2009.12.016>.

Gas and Thermal Energy

Generally, the use of thermal power and gas to power generation is gaining ground as the primary source of energy in the ECOWAS region with almost minor exceptions. The need to diversify energy sources in the regional energy mix at country level has led to the reliance on mega thermal power plants that feed on petroleum and gas. For example, gas to power supply chains in Cote d'Ivoire, Ghana and Nigeria has contributed to energy access and decarbonisation simultaneously. This has led to an increase in natural gas extraction and delivery that is dependent on a set of gas sector infrastructure that feeds into downstream power sector infrastructure.

In Nigeria, the source country for the gas that flows through the West African Gas Pipeline (WAGP), its gas reserves can sustain supply and production for over a century. Nevertheless, its domestic gas infrastructure network is very inadequate and only limited to the Southern coastal federal states that have gained access to the gas. However, in sharp contrast, the commissioning of its main gas export facility that is the Nigerian Liquefied Natural Gas (NLNG) facility in the early 2000s enjoys access to six supply pipelines and did not substantially expand domestic gas usage but rather has guaranteed a reliable supply of gas for export.

This occurrence has been reflective of the perceived economic attractiveness of exports compared to expanding domestic gas consumption. The delivery of gas to WAGP partner countries has been less reliable due to a wave of militant attacks in 2016 on critical oil and gas transmission infrastructure resulting in disruptions in gas-to-power supply chains not only for Nigeria but also region-wide. This has prolonged the pre-existing gas shortage and undermined progress made in generation capacity that was revitalised through privatisation.[963] Since the vision of the ECOWAS community is to ensure energy self-sufficiency by increasing energy supply through diversification in its energy mix. The use of multiple energy resources such as liquefied natural gas (LNG) as well as utilising its vast

963 Donna Peng and Rahmatallah Poudineh, *Gas-to-Power Supply Chains in Developing Countries: Comparative Case Studies of Nigeria and Bangladesh* (Oxford: Oxford Institute for Energy Studies, 2017); Donna Peng and Rahmatallah Poudineh, 'Gas-to-Power Supply Chains in Developing Countries: Comparative Case Studies of Nigeria and Bangladesh', *Energy Insight 6* (Oxford, 2017), pp. 1–19; Donna Peng and Rahmat Poudineh, 'Is Natural Gas a Viable Option to Promote Electrification in Nigeria?', *Economics of Energy & Environmental Policy*, 8.1 (2019) <https://doi.org/10.5547/2160-5890.8.1.dpen>.

renewable resources has created an opportunity to include decentralised energy infrastructure in augmenting the pre-existing centralised infrastructure.

Renewables

Renewable energy deployments have increased at fast pace under regional and national initiatives with the support of external partners. This new-found thrust into exploring the benefits of alternative energy has been also spurred through investments in so-called bankable renewable energy projects across local communities in the region. This has been possible through financing from regional and international development banks.

In addition to that, high on the regional energy agenda in terms of policy and institutional work to resolve energy access and GHG emission problems in the region. National governments have impressed upon themselves to increase their share of energy production from renewables by adding more renewable energy targets to their energy mix advertently contributing to the overall increment in regional energy generation volumes both for household and commercial purposes.

The relative geographic variation between coastal and forested sub-regions as well as the inland and Sahelian sub-regions of ECOWAS and the breadth of its entire geographical region display disparities in terms of the distribution of energy supply, infrastructure, and suitability for certain renewable energy options. However, this geographical situation helps to make local energy production more attractive through the deployment of distributed energy sources such as mini-grids, small-scale hydropower installations among others to make up for the needed energy demand.

An inventory of the renewable energy potential in the ECOWAS region reveal that there is wind energy potential in the coastal zones, prospective hydro schemes in the river basins, abundant solar resources in the northern Sahelian areas and extensive biomass resources everywhere except in Cape Verde and the Sahelian areas. This has the potential of providing added benefits such as newly created jobs, the establishment of new businesses and the springing up of innovations and educational programmes that can raise the awareness and interest of the citizens in the region especially the local rural populace.

A pioneer in prioritising renewable energy in ECOWAS has been the island republic of Cape Verde. It aims for 100 percent electricity generation through renewable energy sources by 2020 and has taken steps towards implementing this vision by using grid-connected wind farms and solar PV plants.[964]

Hydropower

Hydropower is playing a significant role in the ECOWAS energy region with mixed benefits of its potential substitution in the region. It contributes significant volumes of generated commercial energy. This has brought relief from the pressure exerted on the traditional energy sector, but it is still unable to meet total power generation requirements. It has been useful in countering the effect of the commercial energy crisis provoked by the two oil price increases in the 1970s.

Hydropower stations in the region have proved to be a reliable source of supply and in general have a better record in terms of operation and maintenance than previous diesel generators that was used as alternative means of power generation. Due to the poor operation and maintenance of diesel generators, the trend has been shorter project spans than usual for such plants resulting in cost inefficiencies because in a short period it requires replacement.

Hydropower plants are however subject to the vagaries of the hydrological cycle and the severity of drought. It is difficult to overestimate the impact of the series of droughts over the years 1981–1984 as well as 1997–2000 on the energy policy in West Africa. For instance, Ghana had relied on hydropower for most of its independent history with the 1,038 MW Akosombo power station producing most of the power consumed within the country during the 1990s. This allowed the Volta River Authority to export surplus electricity to Cote d'Ivoire and other neighbouring states.

However, the prolonged lack of rainfall resulted in a significant drop in water levels on the giant Lake Volta, occasioning severe power rationing across the region. The water level dropped by 74 meters at one point in 1998, reducing generating capacity by over 600MW to just slightly above 300MW. The regional hydropower capacity is being increased with new constructions and new investments from China in countries that have relied on large-scale hydropower generation for years and new entrants in

964 Anton Eberhard, Orvika Rosnes, and others, *Africa's Power Infrastructure Investment, Integration, Efficiency Infrastructure* (Washington DC: The International Bank for Reconstruction and Development/The World Bank, 2011) <https://library.pppknowledgelab.org/PPIAF/documents/3135>; Vilar and others; Smart Villages, *Energy Situation Report-West Africa* (Abingdon,UK, 2016) <https://e4sv.org/West-Africa-Energy-Report-AW-Draft-3-200516-V3_MT.pdf> [accessed 5 March 2018]; Nordman.

this regard. Typical examples are the Kaleta hydropower station in Guinea on the Konkoure River, the Soubre hydropower station in Cote d'Ivoire on the Naoua Falls and the Bui hydropower station in Ghana on the Black Volta.[965]

A key characteristic of the energy resource system in the region is the predictability of system dynamics (RS7). Almost all 15-member states of the ECOWAS community experience to a certain degree power outage that has led to the rationing of power supplies. This is also in addition to the occasional petroleum supply deficits. Electricity generation is augmented by self-generation of power through the use of petrol and diesel-driven mini generators.

In terms of energy storage (RS8), it is mainly limited to the type of energy resource under consideration and the particular energy sector. To give an instance one can consider the petroleum sector, which has various resource types such as crude oil, LNG, LPG that can be stored and deployed over distances using various mediums like pipelines, storage ships etc. Since the region has been an importer of these energy resources for a long time. It has invested in bulk-oil storage facilities, oil refineries and LPG tank farms. As well as LNG storage facilities that are currently being prioritised because of the growing importance of LNG in thermal power production in the region. This has improved the mission of securing supplies for internal and further cross-border energy trading.

5.3.1.2 EU

There is considerable variation in the physical settings that surround the EU's entire energy resource system. The energy resource type or unit and the resource system as well as the infrastructural set up that underlie it informs the EU energy system. Thus, one discovers energy sectors like coal, petroleum, LNG, nuclear, hydropower among others. The resource system supporting the deployment of these energy units are particularly varied.

965 J.B.C. Lazenby and P.M.S. Jones, 'Hydroelectricity in West Africa: Its Future Role', *Energy Policy*, 15.5 (1987), 441–55 <https://doi.org/10.1016/0301-4215(87)90056-5>; International Water Power and Dam Construction, 'Ghana Balances Hydro and Thermal', 2006 <https://www.waterpowermagazine.com/news/newsghana-balances-hydro-and-thermal> [accessed 19 June 2018]; Deborah Brautigam and Jyhjong Hwang, 'Great Walls over African Rivers: Chinese Engagement in African Hydropower Projects', *Development Policy Review*, 37.3 (2019), 313–30 <https://doi.org/10.1111/dpr.12350>.

The EU is the largest energy importer in the world, importing 53 percent of its energy, at an annual cost of around €400 billion.[966]

Household Energy

Households use energy for multiple purposes like space and water heating, space cooling, cooking, lighting and electrical appliances and other end-uses, which mainly include uses of energy by households outside the dwellings themselves. Household energy in the EU for both rural and urban dwellers has been based on an intense dependence on electricity, which is largely produced by fossil fuels although major improvements have been made to raise the share of renewable energy in the energy mix.

This is due to the growing number of the use of new appliances, IT devices, appliances that are linked to the internet encouraging the growth of the internet of things (IOT), new telecommunication options in addition to the spread of air conditioning. This has taken place mainly due to structural changes occurring in the EU and country level energy policy spaces. An increasing number of dwellings as well as new communities and use of modern appliances contributes to the upward rise of household energy consumption.

Their effect is counter balanced however by improvements in energy efficiency. The main use of energy by households in the EU in 2017 was for home heating accounting for about 64 percent of final energy consumption in the residential sector. Generally speaking, in that same year, household energy accounted for almost 20 percent of gross energy consumption in the whole of the EU. This means the residential sector accounts for only one-fifth of all the energy use in the EU region.

On the whole, EU legislation is a major driver for policies and measures implemented at the national level in the household sector. The price for the consumption of household energy has been fluctuating. This is based on taxes and levies which includes value-added taxes (VAT). To illustrate this phenomenon, electricity prices for households in the EU-28 saw an increase in 2008, became stable in 2009 and then went on an upward trajectory in 2010. Between 2014 and 2015, prices had dropped in 12 EU member states.[967]

---

966 World Nuclear Association., 'Nuclear Power in the European Union', 2018 <https://www.world-nuclear.org/information-library/country-profiles/others/european-union.aspx> [accessed 21 July 2018].

967 Bosseboeuf et al., *Energy Efficiency Trends and Policies in the Household and Tertiary Sectors: An Analysis Based on the ODYSSEE and MURE Databases*, 2015

Hydropower

Hydropower developments in many parts of the EU has passed its peak even though there is extensive activity both in retrofitting and refurbishing old hydropower installations as well as constructing new ones. Notable newly initiated hydropower developments are taking place in Bulgaria, Germany, Greece, Italy, Portugal, Romania, Slovenia, and Spain. For instance, Germany completed the 1060 MW Goldisthal pumped-storage project one of the largest in Europe in the northeast of the country and likely to be the last project on such as scale in the country. In Italy, hydropower played a key role in the development of the energy sector. Since the 1950s virtually all the electricity produced in the country came from hydropower. This means the industrialisation of Italy was mainly dependent on energy from hydropower.

Upgrading existing hydropower infrastructure is the focus of activity in EU countries that heavily rely on hydropower. Retrofitting of hydropower plants with modern equipment to elevate their performance capacities has been the emphasis across a number of western European countries. Whereas in eastern European countries the focus is on rehabilitating very old plants installed during the Soviet period.

In the EU there is significant opposition to the construction of large new dams and reservoirs for the generation of hydropower. However, hydropower would continue to play a critical role in balancing capacities for the European electricity grid, which connects Norway (the non-EU country with the largest dependence on hydropower) and the rest of the EU. The lack of suitable sites remains the main barrier for the further development of hydropower in the EU since most of these sites have already been developed.

Other barriers in hydropower development in the EU include institutional and environmental impact issues. For institutional barriers developments of new projects are hampered by long lead times to obtain or renew concession rights. In addition, holders of concessions actually do not develop the allotted scheme. Another barrier as well is the lack of grid connections. Regarding impact barriers, the deployment of large hydropower plants on the environment is often significant. On the other

---

<https://doi.org/DOI 10.1089/pho.2012.3369>; Eurostat, *Energy Statistics 2017 Edition* (Brussels, 2017) <https://ec.europa.eu/eurostat/documents/4031688/7772824/KS-06-16-230-EN-N.pdf/536884a4-83c5-4640-b87c-a77a160c0910>.

hand, smaller installations involving minimal reservoir and civil construction works causes a relatively low environmental impact.[968]

Renewables

The contribution of renewable energy to the EU's gross final energy consumption has been on the rise reaching 17 percent in 2016. The vision paper Europe 2020 targets a 20 percent share by 2020 and 27 percent share by 2030. For the EU, adoption and use of renewable energy sources is important for the realisation of two purposes, that is, the reduction of its dependence on foreign energy imports, and in meeting targets to combat global warming.

Renewal energy in the region is mainly deployed in three sectors namely electricity, transportation and heating & cooling sectors. With respect to the absolute consumption of renewable energy, the heating and cooling sector has the largest share with a total of 102 Mtoe in 2017, closely followed by renewables generated electricity with a consumption of 86.7 Mtoe, and the transport sector with a consumption of 23.65 Mtoe. In order to realise its ambition to be a global leader in renewable energy the EU has instituted a new revised renewable energy directive, which came into force on December 2018. It establishes a new binding renewable energy target for 2030 that upgrades the intended target of 27 percent to at least 32 percent with a clause for a possible upward revision in by 2023.

Investments in renewable energy in the EU are primarily driven by the market while at the same time share of public subsidies is falling. The most preferred renewable sources are biomass for heating and cooling, hydropower and wind for electricity, and biofuels for transport. Whilst in the electricity sector, a clear paradigm shift is happening towards renewables with the key factors being the decline in the cost of electricity from solar PV and wind power, advances in efficiency and supply chain developments in addition to competitive tendering to support these schemes. From the period between 2015 to 2018, commercial power purchase agree-

968 Alison Bartle, 'Hydropower Potential and Development Activities', *Energy Policy*, 14 (2002), 1231–1239 <https://doi.org/10.1016/S0140-6701(03)83046-1>; SETIS, 'Hydropower' (Brussels: European Commission, 2013), pp. 1–4 <http://setis.ec.europa.eu/technologies/ Hydropower>; Ludovic Gaudard and Franco Romerio, 'The Future of Hydropower in Europe: Interconnecting Climate, Markets and Policies', *Environmental Science and Policy*, 37 (2014), 172–81 <https://doi.org/10.1016/j.envsci.2014.05.005>.

ments (PPAs) for renewable electricity in the EU (including Norway) quadrupled from 506 MW to 1967 MW.[969]

Gas

As an energy resource, natural gas continues to play a vital role in the EU's energy mix. This may surely persist as the status quo may continue way into the future. The EU 2020 strategy document unveiled by the European Commission recognizes the potential of unconventional gas, and advocates for its potential in the region's energy mix: "The potential for further development of EU indigenous fossil fuel resources, including unconventional gas, exists and the role they will play must be assessed in all objectivity"[970].

In its 2011 Energy Roadmap 2050, the European Commission furthermore recognised the potential of unconventional gas for Europe based on the three pillars of EU energy policy (security of supply, competitiveness and a lower carbon economy). The roadmap set out to classify different scenarios required to achieve the 2050 carbon emissions targets for the energy sector. In the context of these scenarios, the Commission notes that "shale gas and other unconventional gas sources have become potential important new sources of supply in or around Europe. Together with internal market integration, these developments could relax concerns on gas import dependency."[971]

The EU's capacity to diversify its natural gas supplies is enabled by its established and growing gas infrastructure. Two major factors are at play namely its vast internal gas distribution infrastructure and the large-capacity of the European gas transportation network. The region's gas distribution infrastructure has over 200,000 kilometres of transmission pipelines, along with distribution pipelines, interconnections and exten-

---

969 Maria da Graça Carvalho, 'EU Energy and Climate Change Strategy', *Energy*, 40.1 (2012), 19–22 <https://doi.org/10.1016/j.energy.2012.01.012>; European Commission, 'Renewable Energy in the EU', *Eurostat* (Brussels, 2018) <http://ec.europa.eu/eurostat/documents/2995521/8612324/8-25012018-AP-EN.pdf/9d28caef-1961-4dd1-a901-af18f121fb2d>; European Commission, *Renewable Energy Progress Report, COM (2019) 225 Final* (Brussels, 2019) <https://ec.europa.eu/commission/sites/beta-political/files/report-progress-renewable-energy-april2019_en.pdf>.

970 European Commission, *Energy 2020 : A Strateg,y for Competitive, Sustainable and Secure Energy COM(2010) 639 Final* (Brussels, 2010), p. 3.

971 European Commission, *Energy Roadmap 2050 COM(2011) 885 Final* (Brussels, 2011), pp. 11–12 <https://eur-lex.europa.eu/leg,al-content/EN/TXT/PDF/?uri=CELEX:52011DC0885&from=EN>.

sions under construction or planned to ensure a reliable security of supply. A transportation network that reaches neighbouring supply regions so that Europe can receive liquefied natural gas (LNG) by tanker is also in place from Russia and Norway.

Gas pipelines transport natural gas from source countries via transit countries through specific gas corridors. For instance, the Southern Gas Corridor, a gas supply route from the Caspian and Middle Eastern regions to Europe, has an ultimate goal of reducing EU dependence on Russian gas and diversifying sources of energy supply. For LNG, gas terminals are the preferred means of infrastructure. Imported LNG in the EU is transported through LNG terminals. These terminals are made up of special tanks, ships, port infrastructure and pipelines. It is essential to note here that LNG is a type of natural gas that is conveyed over long distances mainly from offshore destinations by sea thus require purpose built sea ports exclusively to export and import LNG.

There are two types of LNG terminals present in the EU namely the liquefaction terminals for exporting LNG and the Regasification terminals or receiving terminals for imports. The example of the Klaipeda floating storage and Regasification unit (FSRU) in Lithuania has proven to be a cost-effective solution that has shored up the prospects in the improvements of the security of gas supplies and price competitiveness of energy. These LNG installations are again complemented with total gas storage capacities, which has been growing steadily for a decade in the EU. The Gas Infrastructure Europe (GIE) states that in 2015 Europe had a Regasification capacity of 208 bcm/year but this figure is projected to increase to 400 bcm/year by 2025.[972]

In terms of the impact of thermal energy in reducing global warming, coal-to-gas switching technology has helped to lower greenhouse gas emissions in the EU since the 1990s. Presently, gas-fired power plants in the EU operate at around 33 per cent of their capacity, partly due to gas prices that are about triple the gas prices seen in the U.S. This reversal from gas to coal for power generation has contributed to a rise in emissions in some countries. If EU member states reverse the trend in their power generation fuels from old, high-carbon technologies, such as coal, to newer, lower-carbon and more efficient fossil fuel technologies, such as natural gas, there

972 Austvik; Gas Infrastructure Europe (GIE), 'LNG Map 2015' (Brussels: GIE, 2015) <https://www.gie.eu/download/maps/2015/GIE_LNG_2015_A0_1189x841_FULL_wINFOGRAPHICS_FINAL.pdf>.

could be a major reduction in emissions at relatively low-cost relative to 1990.[973]

Nuclear

The strategic importance of nuclear fission energy in the EU is indicated by the 33 percent share of its contribution to the European energy mix. It represents a critical component in the energy mix of 14 of the 28 EU member states. In the aftermath of the Chernobyl and Fukushima disasters, this form of energy type has become controversial in the region with Italy phasing it out and Germany committed to do same by 2020. This is in addition to the closure of two Belgian reactors after cracks were discovered. Issues such as nuclear safety, radiation protection, transportation of radioactive substances and waste, nuclear waste management, safeguarding nuclear materials. In addition to nuclear research, training activities and information dissemination have become top of the EU nuclear energy agenda.

Nuclear energy provides Europe with a secure and sustainable power supply at a competitive price. Although serving as a proven source of low-carbon, dispatchable electricity and providing around 53 percent of carbon-free electricity production in the EU as well as providing the largest share of energy production in some EU member states such as France, Hungary and Slovakia. Its future within the EU is uncertain due to strong anti-nuclear and populist support for the inclusion of renewables in the electricity sector.

The construction of new nuclear power infrastructure is currently ongoing in only three EU countries that is, Finland, France and Slovakia. However, these projects have all experienced cost overruns and delays. There are also planned new developments likely to come on stream before 2030 in Bulgaria, Czech Republic, Finland, France, Hungary, Lithuania, Poland and the United Kingdom. This has a potential to shape the long-term future of nuclear power in the EU as well as the incremental production of carbon free energy.[974]

---

973 ExxonMobil, 'Natural Gas: Clean and Efficient', 2018 <https://www.exxonmobil.eu/en-eu/policy/natural-gas/clean-and-efficient/clean-and-efficient> [accessed 21 June 2018].

974 Gouardères, 'Nuclear Energy'; O'Connor and Van den Hove; World Nuclear Association., *New Nuclear in Europe : 2030 Outlook.* (London: World Nuclear Association., 2018).

5.3.2 Attributes of the Community: Primary Actors

An inclusive interpretation of primary actors can be denoted as a set of direct participants in processes of resource harvesting/extracting, producing, and consuming. It also includes third party actors who are not direct users or consumers of the extracted resource such as a service or product in the case of energy.[975]

The range of activities in which primary actors are engaged can be distinguished using their group attributes. This is characterised by the number of relevant actors but also includes relevant political, cultural and socioeconomic attributes that they possess. Moreover, it includes their history and past experiences, locations, norms of behaviour and social capital, leadership or entrepreneurship, knowledge of STS/mental models, technologies available to actors and the importance of resource dependence.

The political and cultural attributes often play a role in the choice taken by actors to opt for a particular energy system as well as the use of energy resources and consumption. This is in addition to the influence it presents in the development and administration of rules governing energy policies. For instance, populist support for renewables over nuclear energy in certain parts of the world has shaped policy regarding the energy type that a nation or and energy region would seek to pursue in the future. Again, fuel switching technologies such as charcoal to LPG gas in household cooking requires a policy shift and the political will to ensure its implementation to be successful while in the meantime leading to a paradigmatic shift in the cooking traditions of a local community.

5.3.2.1 ECOWAS

The number of relevant actors (A1) in the ECOWAS energy region can be grouped into a three-level category namely micro level, meso level and macro level actors. At the micro level, actors include individual & household consumers, prosumers and commercial & industrial users. Meso level actors include agents, private contractors, wholesalers, retailers, equipment manufacturers, energy entrepreneurs & energy service companies, non-governmental organisations & energy cooperatives and financial institutions like banks, microfinance firms and savings & loans agencies.

975 Michael Dean McGinnis and Ostrom.

On the third level, macro actors include public utilities (supplying power and other resource services); big energy corporations (that is, multi-national energy companies – MNCs and national energy companies mainly in the oil or gas sectors). Regional and national policy makers and planners are also included at the macro level as actors. Again, macro level actors include regional energy institutions, agencies, directorates and initiatives such as WAPP, WAGP inter alia.

Over the years, energy public utilities in ECOWAS member states have been regulated and owned as monopolies by the state. This trend has been changing since the sector is undergone deregulation and liberalisation since the 1990s. Public electricity boards transmit and distribute electricity in coordination with private and government owned generation companies. Ministries of Power (specific to electricity generation) or a more generalised energy ministry is responsible for oversight in the planning and policy formulation in the power sector as well as the entire energy sectors of member countries of ECOWAS.

In countries with commercial oil and gas endowments such as Nigeria, Ghana and Cote d'Ivoire sector ministries and agencies oversee the entire chain of activities in the petroleum sector which includes exploration and production of crude oil and natural gas. They also oversee energy related activities like refining, distribution and marketing of petroleum products as well as natural gas & LNG production and trade. Their tasks also include exports and imports of needed energy resources.

Generally, when considering the socio-economic attributes of users (A2), the number of people without access to electricity in the region has been on the decline. However, no country in ECOWAS has universal energy access (here I am referring to electricity) as well as clean cooking resources. Although this assertion is generalised, improvements exists in certain countries such as Cape Verde, Ghana and Cote d'Ivoire who have gained impressive metrics on access to electricity through the deployment of decentralised renewable energy systems and extensions to the coverage of the centralised power grid system. This is according to the International Energy Agency's 2017 Energy Access Outlook.[976]

Energy crises that have occurred in West Africa has come with huge social, economic, and human costs over the years. For instance, power outages and blackouts cost the region in excess of two to four percent of GDP annually furthermore undermining job creation and investments. In 2015, eighty percent of primary schools in Burkina Faso and Niger

976 International Energy Agency, 'Energy Access Outlook 2017'.

were without access to electricity. Economic activity was seriously affected again at the height of Ghana's energy crisis in 2006 and again in 2015. Companies reported substantial losses in sales of about fifteen percent. For example, Ghana's labour bureau, the Labour Department conservatively reported thirty-three firms filed for bankruptcy with about two thousand three hundred workers losing jobs at the height of the 2006 energy crisis. This led to unbearable socio-economic consequences for the affected populace.

Affordable and reliable energy underpins every aspect of social and economic life. Nevertheless, in a low-access energy region like ECOWAS with some of the highest cost of power, most consumers are unable to enjoy the needed quality of life. Regions that meet the energy needs of its populace are prosperous, wealthy and more resilient in advancing human development. This singular pathway will remain the ultimate objective to be realised by the ECOWAS region in the coming years.

Culturally, a balanced gender participation is minimal in the energy value chain in the ECOWAS region. This is particularly witnessed at the decision-making levels in government, industry and community levels including at ECOWAS level. Moreover, this contributes to the myopic perspective in terms of region-wide and country-level energy policymaking and problem solving. Women tend to be the most affected in relation to the absence of energy services in households. To remedy this challenge, ECREEE has put forward a policy document on gender mainstreaming in the regional energy sector to influence member states targets. However, intensive gender advocacy is the likely route to alleviate or minimise this cultural challenge.

Regarding the history of energy use and past experiences (A3) in the region it can be assessed as having locked in path dependent dynamics on actors. For instance, hydropower dependent countries in the region for years have been so reliant on hydro resources available to them due to the investments sunk into these projects that have a long-life span. But serve as a detriment to developing other energy resource systems until disasters such as droughts strike thus affecting the functioning of the pre-existing national energy system.

Moreover, it can be said that the experience has and could become path creative. This is because actors in the region have adopted new energy technologies in forms and ways that have led to the provision of energy using novel energy systems that were non-existent before. This is typified by the diffusion of renewable energy systems such mini-grids that power local communities which are far away from the centralised grid system using the form of an energy cooperative model.

Energy actors in ECOWAS as indicated earlier are also located (A4) at various polycentric levels of decision-making that is, from local villages to the regional institutional bodies. Giving rise to a multi-level form of regional energy governance that require synergy, coherence and coordination.

Political leadership (A5) regionally and nationally has been at the forefront of effecting the needed change in the regional energy system through the use of vision, political will and good decision-making mechanisms. It has also encouraged and contributed the needed investments required for small-scale and mega energy projects and infrastructures. Private actors are leveraging on the opportunities for investment both in expertise and in capital in all sectors of the energy region such as petroleum exploration and extraction, power generation and distribution, renewable energy deployments among others. For instance, certain private actors in the region are keen on distributing pay-as-you-go renewable energy systems mainly solar PV installations. At the ECOWAS level leadership has brought together political, private sector and non-governmental actors to pool together resources to initiate major regional energy infrastructures such as a number of energy interconnections to resolve the low-access problem as well as to liberalise the regional energy market.

ECOWAS normativity and social capital (A6) has been seen through its collective action on increasing energy availability as it pools resources and diversifies its entire energy mix through resource extraction primarily for use in the region. This has been realised through its rules and policies as well as the numerous actions of its regional institutions coupled with the actions of national governments.

5.3.2.2 EU

Relevant actors (A1) in the EU energy region can also be categorised into three levels namely micro level, meso level and macro level actors. The micro level involves a wide network of actors. These can be for instance ordinary consumers, prosumers (that may include energy cooperatives, community-based energy projects and energy intermediaries), energy suppliers, multi-national oil and gas firms, utilities, system operators & associations, technology providers, industry associations and environmental NGOs. Some examples of relevant energy actors at the EU-level are in

Table 5.1. To illustrate, meso level actors include eleven agencies in the EU that contribute to energy-related EU governance. These are put forward in Table 5.2.

Table 5. 1 Examples of Relevant EU Energy Actors

Function or Group	*Actors/Stakeholders*
Renewable energy	EREC (European Renewable Energy Council), EWEA (European Wind Energy Association), EPIA (European Photovoltaic Industry Association), etc.
Non-renewable energy	EURACOAL (European Association for Coal and Lignite), EUROGAS (representing the gas industry – wholesale, retail & distribution), etc.
Energy efficiency	ECEEE (European Council for an Energy Efficient Economy), EVIA (European Ventilation Industry Association), HVACR (European air-conditioning, heat pump and refrigeration industry), CENELEC (European Committee for Electro-technical Standardization), BEUC (European Environmental Citizens Organisation for Standardisation), etc.
Energy supply, distribution & networks	Eurelectric (representing the electricity industry in), GEODE (European association of the independent distribution companies of gas and electricity), T&D (European Association of the Electricity Transmission and Distribution Equipment and Services Industry), EASE (European Association for Storage of Energy) etc.
Multi-National Oil and Gas Industry Companies (External and EU)	Lukoil, Rosneft, Gazprom, Statoil, BP, Chevron, ExxonMobil, Total S.A., ENI, ENGIE, Royal Dutch Shell, Sonatrach, Saudi Aramco, Tullow Oil, DEA AG etc.
Utilities	Dong, EDF, Enel, Eon, Iberdrola, RWE, Statkraft, Total
System operators & associations	EDSO, Entso-E, ERDF, Tennet
Technology providers	GE, Alstom

Function or Group	*Actors/Stakeholders*
Citizens' organisations	BEUC (European Consumer Organisation), EEB (European Environmental Bureau), Inforse (International Network for Sustainable Energy), ECF (European Climate Foundation), etc.
Research & Innovation	EUREC (Association of European Renewable Energy Research Centres).

Source[977]

Table 5. 2 Eleven Energy – Related EU Agencies

Actor	*Function*	*Energy Policy Area*
ACER Agency for the Cooperation of Energy Regulators	ACER's coordinates the work of national energy regulators, monitors and aids the development of the single EU energy market for electricity and natural gas and wholesale energy trading.	Energy networks and infrastructure; Internal market
EASME Executive Agency for Small and Medium-Sized Enterprises	EASME manages several EU programmes including: the Energy Efficiency part of the 'Secure, Clean and Efficient Energy'; the legacy of the Intelligent Energy – Europe programme and the Eco-innovation initiative	Energy efficiency; Renewable energy; Climate change

977 Adapted from Stephan Slingerland and others, *EU Energy Governance for the Future* (Brussels, 2015) <http://www.europarl.europa.eu/studies%0A>; Marie Byskov Lindberg, Jochen Markard, and Allan Dahl Andersen, 'Policies, Actors and Sustainability Transition Pathways: A Study of the EU's Energy Policy Mix', *Research Policy*, 2018, 1–15 <https://doi.org/10.1016/j.respol.2018.09.003>. In addition, Author's own inclusions.

Actor	*Function*	*Energy Policy Area*
EEA European Environmental Agency	The EEA provides independent information for the developing, adopting, implementation and evaluation of environmental policy (including the link with some energy policy areas).	Energy efficiency; Renewable energy; Climate change
EIT European Institute of Innovation and Technology	EIT aim is to integrate the three aspects of knowledge – education, research and business, and help bring innovative ideas to the market through Knowledge Innovation Communities (KICs) in areas such as Climate Change and Sustainable Energy.	Energy research and innovation; Energy efficiency; Renewable energy
ENSREG, European Nuclear Safety Regulators Group	ENSREG, aids the establishment of conditions for the improvement and understanding in the areas of nuclear safety and radioactive waste management.	Nuclear energy
ERC / ERCEA European Research Council & the ERC Executive Agency	ERC's aim is to encourage high quality research through competitive funding. It complements national research funding agencies and other EU funding activities. The	Energy research and innovation; Energy efficiency; Renewable energy; Climate change; Security of energy supply

Actor	*Function*	*Energy Policy Area*
	ERCEA manages the ERC operations.	
Euratom Supply Agency	Euratom ensures a secure and equitable supply of nuclear material in the EU – for energy and medical purposes. Its responsibilities include concluding supply contracts for nuclear material for energy and providing expertise on the nuclear market and market trends.	Nuclear energy
F4E Fusion for Energy	F4E is the EU's contribution to ITER6 and the research and development of fusion energy. It was created under the Euratom Treaty and works towards the construction of demonstration fusion reactors.	Nuclear energy
INEA Innovation and Networks Executive Agency	INEA manages several EU programmes including: the Connecting Europe Facility (CEF); the parts of Horizon 2020 on "Smart, green, and integrated transport" and "Secure, clean and efficient energy".	Energy efficiency; Renewable energy; Energy networks and infrastructure; Security of energy supply; Climate change
JRC Joint Research Centre	JRC is the EC's inhouse science service, which aims at aiding	Energy research and innovation; Energy efficiency; Renewable en-

Actor	Function	Energy Policy Area
	the DGs and providing independent, evidence-based scientific and technical support to the policy cycle.	ergy; Nuclear energy; Security of energy supply; Climate change
REA Research Executive Agency	REA is a funding body focused on maximising the efficiency and impact of EU research and innovation programmes. It manages the research proposals and funded projects.	Energy research and innovation; Energy efficiency; Renewable energy; Climate change; Security of energy supply

Source:[978]

Macro actors constitute EU member states and EU institutions like the European Parliament, EU Council, and EU Commission among others at the regional level. These actors play a crucial role in influencing policy and politics around energy thus increasing the complexity involved in actor engagement in EU energy governance.

The socio-economic and political factors (A2) facing actors in the EU region, still a region heavily dependent on fossil-fuel based industries and resource extraction that is, coal and carbon-intensive resources raises numerous global warming problems, a major global collective action problem. Although steps are being taken by the EU and its member states through the clean energy package unveiled in 2019 and ambitious renewable energy targets in various national energy programmes of action to reduce dependence on fossil fuels and push forward decarbonisation efforts. It has been slow in materialising into substantial gains in reversing global warming.

EU energy politics has been challenged in this area by the division between member states requiring adequate sufficient and secure energy provision and those countries pushing to decarbonise energy sources because of intense public opinion on both sides. Economically, developing a

978 Stephan Slingerland, Jessica Yearwood, Mariya Gnacheva and Koen Rademaekers, *EU Energy Governance for the Future* (Brussels, 2015) <http://www.europarl.europa.eu/studies%0A>.

clean energy economy that provides sufficient energy at an affordable price is the current focus of the EU, which is a high access energy region. Efforts are underway through legislation, which will be operational in 2020.

Culturally, local energy activism has played a major role in changing public opinion in the EU, sometimes this has become quite populist in approach. Presently cultural attitudes have led to shifts in certain European countries such as Germany and Denmark to adopt renewable energy at a very rapid pace. Regarding the history of energy use (A3), Europe generally and the EU in particular has been at the forefront of energy path dependence as well as leading novel path creative processes which is defining global energy systems. Pertaining to places where actors are located (A4) polycentric and multi-level interactions ranging from individual households, local communities, national and provincial institutions to regional institutions define the location variable.

Leadership (A5) at EU level has championed interconnectivity, subsidiarity, solidarity and the opening up of the regional energy space including the single energy market. Single member states have played lead roles in pushing for an energy transition Europe-wide and globally. For example, Germany in particular as well as the Nordic countries have led the way in the adoption of renewable energy technology as a viable source of energy supply the instance of the German energy transition labelled *Die Energiewende* irrespective of it not achieving its stated objectives is notable.

The EU's normative behaviour and social capital (A6) has witnessed growing successes. This has been attained by reducing over dependence on Russian energy and becoming a global leader in the transition towards green energy based on the role it played at the Paris climate talks. In addition to this its own efforts to reduce high carbon emissions through the adoption and exercise of transposing EU legislation into national law with concomitant penalties for breaches to national governments has amplified the EU's normative behaviour.

In relation to knowledge of socio-technical systems (A7) the EU and various associations invests heavily in the creation of knowledge and ideas to improve these energy systems and technologies that are used and diffused not only in Europe but around the world through partnerships with China and parts of the developing world. Since the regional energy space in the EU is diverse and mixed in terms of the energy resource dependence (A8) reliance on coal, hydrocarbons, renewables and nuclear has been the main stay of energy activity. This signifies the significant nature of the EU energy region and its dependence on these energy resources making it one of the highest energy access regions in world.

The EU region is at the forefront of innovative research regarding the development, adoption, deployment and global diffusion of energy technologies (A9). This includes renewables, energy efficiency technology, natural gas and LNG, oil exploration among many others. Generally speaking, there is a slight exception to the assertion made above especially in the nuclear technology area which has lagged in terms of innovation for some time in the EU.

5.3.3 Existing Institutional Setting: Governance System

The governance system represents the prevailing set of processes and institutions that have been put in place to issue rules that shape the behaviour of actors thus influencing the existing institutional setting.[979] This literally defines the governance systems tier in the CIS Framework. Institutional organisations and processes that lead to change tend to be incremental meaning in a path dependent and path creative way rather than totally reconstructive or destructive ways.[980]

Since regional energy governance processes are incremental and sequential, early accomplishments are required before participating actors are willing to make further and better commitments such as effort or capital investments. Observed over time, these changes allow participatory actors to improve the capacity of regional energy governance institutions.

Governance processes tends to be path dependent because each institutional change transforms the structure of incentives within which future decisions are made. Moreover, the process also tends to be path creative because new institutions are added to the institutional transformation thus contributing new incentives that were not extant at first. Hence, in dealing with the regional energy governance system it is worthwhile to consider the effect of policy changes in terms of enhancements and constraints towards future policy options. Nevertheless, it must be noted that based on conventional wisdom, the longer a rules-based system stays in place and the more sophisticated and complex it becomes, the more likely it is that

979 E. Ostrom; Elinor Ostrom, 'A General Framework for Analyzing Sustainability of Social-Ecological Systems'; Michael D. McGinnis, 'An Introduction to IAD and the Language of the Ostrom Workshop: A Simple Guide to a Complex Framework'.

980 M.T. Imperial and T. Yandle, 'Taking Institutions Seriously: Using the IAD Framework to Analyze Fisheries Policy', *Society & Natural Resources*, 18.6 (2005), 493–509 <https://doi.org/10.1080/08941920590947922>.

energy policy makers will encounter difficulty when venturing to make changes.

A key rationale behind paying attention to the governance system category is that it explains the capabilities and responsibilities of the actors involved. It takes into consideration the broader repertoire of norms available to actors within the relevant political, social and cultural setting and might best be interpreted as attributes of the whole governance system thus emphasising the structure and agency present in the energy policy area.

Ostrom and Cox[981] emphasize rules, property systems, and network structures as the key characteristics of governance systems. They further include third- tier variables, differentiating rules into operational, collective, and constitutional. This in effect differentiates property-rights systems into private, public, common, and mixed. And further highlights the centrality, modularity, connectivity, and number of levels as the key distinguishing properties of different governance network structures.

McGinnis and Ostrom[982] rearrange the GS variables in their paper hoping for a more productive outcome in terms of analysing different policy areas. This has been adopted in this analysis which is different from what is in the canonical SES framework's original structure. Hence, it begins with GS1 which is a specification of the relevant policy area (in this case regional energy policy area), in a manner analogous to the resource sector (RS) variable that begins the list of regional energy resource system characteristics.

It presents two kinds of scale that need reflection: the geographic range (GS2) as well as the size of the population (GS3) that participates in, or is subject to, this system of energy governance. In certain cases, the population will be members of a jurisdiction defined in geographic terms, but in others, the population may be defined on a functional basis as seen in a special-purpose cross-jurisdictional (that is, Type II) governance organization described by Hooghe and Marks[983].

The regime types (GS4) represents moves to a more macro level by specifying the logic upon which the overarching governance system is organized. The term 'regime' is used in different ways, for distinguishing

981 Ostrom and Cox, p. 458.

982 Michael Dean McGinnis and Ostrom, pp. 8–10.

983 Hooghe and Marks, 'Unraveling the Central States, but How? Types of Multi-Level Governance'.

between democratic and autocratic systems of governance or between monocentric and polycentric systems.[984]

The following factors specify the different types of organizations responsible for crafting and/or implementing different kinds of rules thus delineating the nature of these organisations (GS5) and the nature of the rules generated and /or implemented by the organisations (GS6). GS5 includes the initially specified second-tier factors in the canonical SES framework structure namely governmental and nongovernmental organizations with an expansion to include private corporations, community-based organizations, and hybrid organizational forms that combine aspects of public, private, and voluntary organizations. These rule-making organizations operate at different scales, from local, national, regional to global.

The entire host of organizations can play important roles in shaping the conditions under which rules-in-use are endorsed in increasingly complex systems of governance. GS6 draws on the IAD framework by distinguishing among rules directed at operational decisions, those guiding collective choices, and those relating to constitutional-level questions. Although monitoring and sanctioning rules were initially listed as separate second-tier variables under governance systems.[985] McGinnis and Ostrom further realise monitoring or sanctioning rules can occur in any of the three levels thus the need to treat them as sub-categories of the rules-in-use.[986]

Any of the policy tools or policy instruments that have been used by governmental or other policy agents can be decomposed into constitutional-, collective-, and operational-choice components.[987] To exemplify this a cap-and- trade scheme begins with the constitutional choice of what resources can be legitimately subject to this constructed market. This is followed by the collective choices of the permissible aggregate levels of resource extraction or use and the number and size of tradable units, and finally, the operational-level trades among participating actors as well as the innovative technological responses that such a system is intended to inspire.

---

984 Ostrom, Tiebout, and Warren.

985 E. Ostrom; Elinor Ostrom, 'A General Framework for Analyzing Sustainability of Social-Ecological Systems'.

986 Michael Dean McGinnis and Ostrom.

987 Thomas Sterner, *Instruments for Environmental Policy* (Gothenburg: Sida, 2003); Tanya Heikkila and Krister Andersson, 'Policy Design and the Added-Value of the Institutional Analysis Development Framework', *Policy & Politics*, 46.2 (2018), 309–24 <https://doi.org/10.1332/030557318X15230060131727>.

Rules that relate to ownership of property can also fall within this category. In considering the constitutional level, broad parameters are set concerning what can be considered someone's property, collective-choice decisions include what forms of property can be expropriated for the use of public purposes, and operational-level aspects distinguish among those actors with access, withdrawal, management, exclusion, and alienation. Nevertheless, as underscored by Schlager and Ostrom[988], property-rights systems are not rules. Instead, property-rights systems define relations among people in relation to things, and specify both duties and obligations. This is what is therefore designated as GS7.

GS8 encompasses the entire repertoire of norms or shared strategies that are available for the use of actors engaged in a particular setting as in this case. In effect, the repertoire of norms and strategies reflects the myriad ways in which culture affects decisions regarding socio-technical systems. Network structure (GS9) refers to the linkages among the rule-making organizations and the population subject to these rules. Third-tier variables could for example, include the measures of centrality, modularity, connectivity, and number of levels, as employed by Ostrom and Cox[989].

Historical continuity (GS10), distinguishes between systems of governance that have been in place for long periods of time and those that are more recent in form. All forms of governance have deep roots in historical precedents, but some systems are more inclined toward stasis and others toward more flexible and progressive modes of response.

5.3.3.1 ECOWAS

An all-encompassing policy area (GS1) informing the energy governance system in ECOWAS is comprised of the general energy and climate policy with connected policy and policy initiatives at the regional and national levels in ECOWAS. The policy sub-sectors include the power sector, renewable energy sector, petroleum sector, climate policy, energy efficiency policy, energy and gender policy as well as waste-to-energy sector among others. These policy sectors benefit from country-level and regional level policy making since the competence of energy policy is defined at both the national and regional levels.

---

988 Edella Schlager and Elinor Ostrom, 'Property-Rights Reg,imes and Natural Resources : A Conceptual Analysis', *Land Economics*, 68.3 (1992), 249–62.

989 Ostrom and Cox.

In relation to the geographic scale (GS2), that is, the governance reach of ECOWAS accounts for 5,114,162 square kilometres (that is, 1,974,589 square miles) of land area. Aggregately, all the countries and dependent territories put together as a single territorial unit could be ranked as the seventh largest total area in the world after Australia. Population size (GS3) of the ECOWAS area according to the 2018 United Nations Department for Economic and Social Affairs (UNDESA) estimates 377,436,546 million people with a population density of 73.8 persons to every square kilometre.[990]

The regime type (GS4) based on the typology used by Hettne and Söderbaum[991] would most likely designate ECOWAS as a regional community. They characterise a regional community as a mutually reinforcing relationship between the 'formal' region, defined by the community of states, and the 'real' region, in which a trans-nationalised regional civil society has a role to play. Moreover, the regional civil society may emerge spontaneously from 'below', but is ultimately dependent on that enduring (formal and informal) institutions and 'regimes' that facilitate and promote security, welfare, social communication and convergence of values, norms, identities and actions throughout the region.[992]

In addition, using the dual dimension of governance regimes put in place by Hooghe and Marks[993], ECOWAS generally functions as a Type I governance archetype. With regards to operationalising regional energy policy in this type of a region, ECOWAS uses a polycentric governance approach to attain largely its regional energy goals using both a top-down and bottom-up approach. This satisfies the conditions required to meet the Type II governance regime where various energy sectors overlap in the region requiring a sense of policy coherence.

The energy governance structure in ECOWAS contains different types of organisations responsible for the crafting and implementation of different kind of rules. The nature of these kinds of organisations are typified by the variable that relates to rule-making organisations (GS5). See the Table 5.3 below for organisations that make and influence rules that either govern energy through their normative behaviour or legally require action.

---

990 UNDESA, 'Population of West Africa (2018)'.

991 Björn Hettne and Fredrik Söderbaum, 'Theorising the Rise of Regionness', *New Political Economy*, 5.3 (2000), 457–73 <https://ssrn.com/abstract=2398942>.

992 Hettne and Söderbaum, p. 22.

993 Hooghe and Marks, 'Unraveling the Central States, but How? Types of Multi-Level Governance'.

A typical example is the hybrid energy organizations springing up in Liberia. They are playing an important role in shaping the national energy policy conditions through the creation of community-based electricity cooperatives that utilises renewable sources like solar, biomass, mini-hydro projects, and crude palm oil along-side energy storage technologies to generate and store power for local community use. Between 2015 to 2016 three electricity coops, the Gbarnway Woeyah Electric Cooperative, Kwedin Lorkiah Electric Cooperative and Kpakpormein Electric Cooperative with two others Sorlumba and Totota Electric Cooperatives have been established.

Since the exercise of competencies relating to energy in the ECOWAS region are two-fold namely national and supranational. The nature of the rules-in-use (GS6) that govern institutions at the regional level is supranational in nature meaning it transcends national boundaries and governments. At the ECOWAS level, the rules are in the form of Treaties and Community Acts (that is, supplementary acts, regulations, directives, decisions, and opinions).

To illustrate, the creation of WAPP by Decision A/Dec.5/12/99 at the 22nd Summit of Heads of State and Governments, and furthermore Decision A/Dec.18/01/06 at the 29th Summit of Heads of State and Government adopted the articles of agreement for the organisation of WAPP as well as its functions. Later, in this same summit Decision A/Dec.20 /01/06 raised the status of WAPP as a specialised institution of ECOWAS.[994]

Actual implementation functions at the operational level especially with the inclusion of renewable energy resources is in the programme of action of WAPP with the view of being beneficial in meeting general objectives.[995] Rules related to scale of integration, sanctioning and non-compliance are demarcated at the constitutional level while rules concerning the assignment of monitoring responsibilities and specifications are defined

994 West Africa Power Pool, 'Creation of WAPP', 2017 <http://www.ecowapp.org/en/content/creation-wapp> [accessed 25 June 2018].

995 Omotola Adeoye and Catalina Spataru, 'Sustainable Development of the West African Power Pool: Increasing Solar Energy Integration and Regional Electricity Trade', *Energy for Sustainable Development*, 45 (2018), 124–34 <https://doi.org/10.1016/j.esd.2018.05.007>; Asami Miketa and Bruno Merven, *West African Power Pool: Planning and Prospects for Renewable Energy* (Abu Dhabi, 2013) <www.irena.org>.

at the collective-choice level rules all contained in the decision setting up WAPP.[996]

Table 5. 3 Rule-Making Organisations that Influence Regional Energy in ECOWAS

Type of Rule-making Organisation	*Examples of Organisations*
Regional Organisations (specialised agencies etc.)	Authority of Heads of State and Government, Council of Ministers, Community Parliament, Community Court of Justice, ECOWAS Commission, West Africa Power Pool (WAPP), ECOWAS Regional Electricity Regulatory Authority (ERERA), West African Gas Pipeline (WAGP), West African Gas Pipeline Authority (WAGPA), ECOWAS Centre for Renewable Energy and Energy Efficiency (ECREEE), West African Energy Leaders Group (W-AELG)
Public sector organizations (government agencies, etc.)	Ministries of Energy and Power, Parliaments, Utilities Commissions, Petroleum Commissions, Nuclear Energy Agencies, Environmental Protection Agencies, Investment Promotion Agencies, River Basin Authorities
Private sector organizations (for-profit)	National Energy Companies, Public Utilities, Grid Operators, Energy Suppliers (Gas, Bulk Oil and Power), International Energy Companies, Independent Power Producers
Nongovernmental, non-profit organizations	Consumer Agencies, Energy Think-Tanks, Civil Society Organisations, University Energy Research Departments
Community-based organizations	Chiefs and Youth-based Organisations in energy-rich localities, mass-based social movement organisations, community energy cooperatives

996 West African Power Pool (WAPP), 'Articles of Agreement of the West African Power Pool: Organization and Functions' (Accra: WAPP, 2005), pp. 1–39 <http://www.ecowapp.org/sites/default/files/articles_of_agreement_0.pdf>.

Type of Rule-making Organisation	*Examples of Organisations*
Hybrid organizations	State-owned commercial energy corporations, electricity cooperatives

Source[997]

In terms of the property/ownership rights systems (GS7) prevailing in the ECOWAS energy region. It can be categorised in three perspectives that is, private property, public property and common (or communal) property. According to McGinnis[998], private property are bundles of rights held by and exchanged among individuals or legally recognized corporate entities; typically including full rights of alienation.

Furthermore, he asserts that public properties are bundles of rights held by official agents of some unit of government. Then he concludes that common (or communal) properties are bundles of rights held, defined, and exchanged by some communal entity as a whole. A good example aside the more popular property rights known in the regional energy sector is the diffusion of community-owned energy cooperatives in the region with the Liberian experience a notable mention.

GS8 indicate the repertoire of norms and strategies that underlie the regional energy governance space. This is defined by the myriad of ways in which culture affects energy decisions in ECOWAS. A set of national cultural influences of member states although not fixed tend to represent an interplay of geographic, economic, and political factors that may extend well beyond that individual country.[999] That said, the academic and policy literature does suggest that West Africans emphasise energy access security as a key priority. Evidence for this claim is rooted in two separate sources. One, an academic literature relating to Africa-wide energy access argues that one of the most critical policy concerns facing West Africa in particular and Africa generally is the low energy access rate.[1000]

997 Authors own formulations

998 Michael D. McGinnis, *Updated Guide to IAD and the Language of the Ostrom Workshop: A Simplified Overview of a Complex Framework for the Analysis of Institutions and Their Development*.

999 Ragner E. Löfstedt and David Vogel, 'The Changing Character of Regulation: A Comparison of Europe and the United States', *Risk Analysis*, 21.3 (2001), 399–416.

1000 Brew-Hammond.

Another policy source analyses the overarching principles governing rural energy in West Africa for the past years, and suggests proposals to policymakers on how to prioritise securing affordable and abundant supply of energy and fuels. It prioritises this over other considerations such as environmental protection or the efficient use of energy for the vast mass of people without energy in rural and peri-urban areas.[1001]

Briefly, the linkages that network the governance structure (GS9) involved in the realisation of ECOWAS energy policy goals consists of the main ECOWAS organisations. That is, Parliament, Commission and Council in addition to the fifteen individual member states of ECOWAS. With, five executive and regulatory agencies enabling the realisation of ECOWAS energy policies. The legislative power for energy policies in the ECOWAS lies with the Authority of Heads of State and Governments and the Council of Ministers, with advice on legislation tabled by the Community Parliament and the executive power being the ECOWAS Commission. Member States are represented at every level in the legislative process through the Heads of State and Governments and Council of Ministers. They furthermore transpose these regional legislative instruments in the specific national contexts. Primarily, the existence of differences in the actual roles of each of the main actors depend on their specific energy areas or sectors.

On issues of historical continuity (GS10), regional energy dynamics still suffers from the colonial hangover where attempts to increase consumption of local energy endowments and resources are in contention with external energy importers' efforts to enhance their energy security at the expense of West African energy security. Again, most energy systems and the entire regional energy economy put in place during the colonial era need reinvention in order to design sustainable energy systems that would meet the current regional energy challenges being encountered.

The departure from this past in the post-independent era was either short lived or proceeded at a slow pace. Any major global energy disaster could set the process lagging behind unless an ambitious plan as well as major investments are made towards redefining the ECOWAS energy region according to modern and future energy sufficiency trends. Looking at it from another perspective, this stated status quo has become a blessing in disguise thus accounting for new path creative opportunities to determine an energy future equipped to deal with the pre-existing energy access problems and secure energy needs for the region in the prospective future.

1001 ECOWAS/UEMOA.

5.3.3.2 EU

EU energy policies (GS1) encompass critical public policy decisions over the production, distribution, and consumption of energy. This is in addition to incentives, taxes, and regulations roping in the planning of strategic national security goals. By so doing it unveils various sectors of EU energy policy namely the power sector, renewable energy sector, petroleum sector, climate policy, energy efficiency policy, nuclear energy policy, waste-to-energy sector, transportation & building sector, external energy policy among others. Thus, the various arms of EU energy policy fits together to achieve the ultimate goal of the EU energy union aimed at making energy more secure, affordable and sustainable in the EU. In addition to coupling it with harmonised national energy goals of EU member states since energy is a shared competence.

The geographic scale (GS2) that is, the territorial scope that falls under the EU's governance is about 4,475,757 square kilometres (that is, 1,728,009 square miles). This total area of territories governed by the EU when ranked as a single entity is the eighth largest in the world after ECOWAS. Based on 2018 Eurostat estimates the size of the population (GS3) that participates in or is subject to the EU's system of governance is 512,596,403 million people with a population density of 117.3 persons to every square kilometre.[1002]

Decomposing the regime type (GS4) inherent in the EU, two typologies would help explain it. Using the typology devised by Hettne and Söderbaum the EU can be referred to as a regional state or region state. They characterise its political order as constituting a voluntary evolution of a group of formerly sovereign nations that come together to create a new form of political entity, where sovereignty is pooled (at a deeper level) for the best of all, and which is radically more democratic than other intergovernmental polities.

They further highlight that national interests may prevail but do not necessarily become identical with nation-states. Additionally, the authority, power and decision-making processes are not centralised but layered, decentralised to the local, micro-regional, national and macro-regional/supranational levels.[1003] Again in adopting Hooghe and Marks' two-fold governance regime approach, the EU functions in Type I governance gen-

1002 Eurostat, 'Population Estimates on 1 January 2018', *Eurostat News Release* (Brussels: European Commission, 2018), pp. 1–5.

1003 Hettne and Söderbaum, p. 25.

erally. As well as operationalising regional energy policy, in a multi-level and polycentric governance manner in order to achieve regional energy goals. Therefore, satisfying the requirements to meet a Type II governance regime where various energy actors and sectors overlap, a reason enabling policy coherence in the establishment of the energy union.

A plurality of EU rule-making organisations influence energy policy in the region. The governance structure of the EU consists of a number of organisations responsible for designing and implementing different kinds of rules. A list of an overview of rule-making organisations (GS5) that influence normative behaviour can be seen below in Table 5.4. A good example worth mentioning is the rapid diffusion of renewable energy cooperatives in micro energy regions across the EU, this has pushed the Commission to give new impetus to the new role of energy consumers in EU energy policy as seen in an interim draft report of the working group on consumers as energy market actors[1004]. As the report states, the crucial impact of energy cooperatives in some countries in furtherance of the EU energy transition cannot be understated.

From 2011 to 2012, The Netherlands registered an increase of 300 percent in the creation of RES cooperatives. This figure doubled in the following year presenting an exponential growth in energy consumption, production, retailing, efficiency, etc. In Germany, a significant number of energy cooperatives were founded between 2005 and 2012, delivering energy to about 160,000 households. It reports further that almost fifty per-cent of Germany's renewable capacity comes from citizen-owned projects. The UK presents an equally promising perspective, from 2003 until 2013, community energy capacity has developed almost three times faster than the overall renewable capacity.[1005] Revealing only a small part of what is presently happening in the EU.

Rules-in-use (GS6) that govern energy institutions at EU level are supra-national in nature. The rules are in the form of Treaties and Communi-ty Acts (that is, regulations, directives, decisions recommendations and opinions) in addition to principles laid down in EU case law. Important features of EU energy policies and rules-in-use also include transparency and accountability.

1004 European Commission, *Working Group Report "Consumers as Energy Market Actors"* (Brussels, 2015) <http://www.eesc.europa.eu/resources/docs/draft_wg_report_consumers_market_agents_tc_110315_web_version3.pdf>.

1005 European Commission, *Working Group Report "Consumers as Energy Market Actors"*, p. 26.

Table 5. 4 Rule-Making Organisations that Influence Regional Energy in EU

Type of Rule-making Organisation	*Examples of Organisations*
Regional Organisations (specialised agencies etc.)	European Council, Council of the European Union, European Parliament, Court of Justice of the European Union, European Commission
Public sector organizations (government agencies, executive & regulatory agencies etc.)	National Ministries of Energy and Power, Parliaments, Agency for the Cooperation of Energy Regulators (ACER), Executive Agency for Small and Medium-Sized Enterprises (EASME),European Environmental Agency (EEA), European Institute of Innovation and Technology (EIT), European Nuclear Safety Regulators Group (ENSREG,), European Research Council & the ERC Executive Agency (ERC / ERCEA), Euratom Supply Agency, F4E Fusion for Energy, Innovation and Networks Executive Agency (INEA), Joint Research Centre (JRC), Research Executive Agency (REA)
Private sector organizations (for-profit)	National Energy Companies, Public Utilities, Grid Operators, Energy Suppliers (Gas, LNG, Bulk Oil and Power), International Energy Companies, Independent Power Producers
Nongovernmental, non-profit organizations	Research & Innovation – EUREC (Association of European Renewable Energy Research Centres), Consumer Agencies, Energy think-tanks, Civil Society Organisations, University Energy Research Departments
Community-based organizations	Citizens' organisations – BEUC (European Consumer Organisation), EEB (European Environmental Bureau), Inforse (International Network for Sustainable Energy), ECF (European Climate Foundation), community energy cooperatives, sub-regional energy regions etc.

Type of Rule-making Organisation	*Examples of Organisations*
Hybrid organizations	Prosumers, electricity cooperatives

Source[1006]

A two-fold process define the making of EU energy policy in this respect. Prior to a decision on legislation, stakeholder engagement warrants that all parties potentially interested to give an opinion be given the opportunity to do so. When legislation has been implemented, formal reporting requirements guarantee that monitoring and evaluation of the policies is possible. Moreover, informal consultation between the actors at all stages is a crucial component of the policy process.

Property and ownership rights (GS7) of the EU energy region can be categorised in three ways namely private property, public property and common (or communal) property. The EU's constellation of property/ownership rights has grown into a more complex web of legal, philosophical and regulatory foundations that preserve these rights both at Community and at individual member state level.

The repertoire of norms and strategies (GS8) indicate the underlining socio-cultural factors that shape EU energy governance and its effects on energy decisions at EU level. For instance when considering energy efficiency strategies at EU level, the EU assumes that even though energy efficiency has improved substantially in recent years, it is still technically, economically and feasibly expedient to use in promoting other different strategies across all energy activity sectors in order to register palpable gains.[1007] This approach is exemplified in strategies that include retrofitting walls and roof insulations in residential buildings, improved energy management systems in commercial buildings, equipment replacement in the manufacturing industry and changing modes of transportation.[1008]

1006 Authors own

1007 M. A.R. Lopes, C. H. Antunes, and N. Martins, 'Energy Behaviours as Promoters of Energy Efficiency: A 21st Century Review', *Renewable and Sustainable Energy Reviews*, 16.6 (2012), 4095–4104 <https://doi.org/10.1016/j.rser.2012.03.034>.

1008 European Commission, 'Communication from the Commission - Action Plan for Energy Efficiency: Realising the Potential', *COM(2006) 545 Final*, 2006, p. 25 <http://eur-lex.europa.eu/LexUriServ/LexUriServ.do?uri=CELEX:52006DC0545:EN:NOT>.

In brief, the governance structure involved in the realisation of EU energy policy objectives consists of an interplay of the main EU organisations, which is termed as the network structure (GS 9). They include the Parliament, Commission and Council in addition to the 28 individual member states of the EU. With, 11 executive and regulatory agencies contributing to the execution of EU energy policies. The legislative power for energy policies in the EU lies with the European Parliament (EP) and the Council of Ministers, which co-decide on legislation presented by the executive power, the European Commission (EC).

The Parliament also oversees the work of the EC. The EC, as the executive power, can propose legislation and enforce it. The role of member states in the EU context is to co-decide on European legislation via the Council of Ministers. The transposition process is discharged with member states inculcating and applying legislation in the specific national contexts. Essentially, a large difference in actual roles of each of the main actors depending on their specific energy area exists.

In relation to issues bordering on external EU energy policy the High Representative for Foreign Affairs and Security Policy acts as the *secretary of state* of the EU and together with other Commissioners coordinates actions particularly relevant when relating on policies that deal with external relations that relate to security of energy supply. Although the European Atomic Energy Community (EURATOM) and the EU share the same governance institutions, it maintains a separate Treaty.[1009]

EU energy policy has benefited from an enduring historical continuity (GS10) based on regional energy dynamics that have sought to highlight regional cooperation and innovation. With energy concerns at the heart of the founding antecedents of the EU coupled with a long history of research, innovation and development of novel modern energy technologies prior to and after its formation. The historical continuity of energy in the EU has been both path dependent and path creative playing a critical role in the construction and reconstruction of the region.

5.4 CIS Framework in Motion: Explaining a Dynamic Process of Regional Energy Governance

For this exercise Chapters 3 and 4 respectively provides a good background, especially in the broad historical evaluations of the pivotal

1009 Slingerland and others.

changes that occurred during the major periodic milestones under review. I employ this procedure to demonstrate how the key transition moments in regional energy history occurred from period to period to enable shifts in regional energy governance particularly after new action situations had been put in place or existing ones had started to move in new directions.

Although Chapters 3 and 4 considers several factors in marking important milestones between different periods, I find it useful for the purpose here to demonstrate the virtues of the CIS framework by focusing attention on specific time-periods when the nature of the relevant governance processes changed in a noteworthy manner. Governance of the common regional energy system is of course quite a demanding task, and its analysis and review of efforts expresses immense complexities. The broad degree of aspects, dimensions, dynamics, actors and institutions, at various analytical levels, prompts this challenge. However, I present a brief overview in both cases (ECOWAS and EU) to illustrate the periodic stages or milestones of energy governance in these regions.

5.4.1 Regionalisation efforts towards energy governance in pre-1970s period

Before this analytical process commences it is important to note the historical basis, which informs the selection of these key milestones. Governance structures put in place to focus on energy cooperation within a region building setting in the two cases began in the pre -1970s period. It had a tremendous effect on the pooling of energy resources in the regions and became the foundation upon which regional energy governance evolved over time.

ECOWAS

In ECOWAS, although efforts towards energy regionalism pre-dated its founding in 1975 it is noteworthy to consider that energy cooperation in West Africa formed the basis for any further incremental efforts in this regard after the 1970s because the path dependent dimension in constructing energy systems is definitive in the determination of any future system build-up. In essence, within the framework of ECOWAS energy sector co-operation, the establishment of the West African Grid System (WAGS) became a precursor to the WAPP.

The WAGS purposed to spearhead power interconnections linking Ghana's grid with that of its counterpart nations in neighbouring Togo,

Benin and Cote d'Ivoire by 1969. Negotiations for this power interconnection agreement was under the entrepreneurial leadership of the then Chief Executive of the Volta River Authority, Dr. E. L. Quartey. In the spirit of promoting energy solidarity and economic co-operation in West Africa this move towards regional energy sharing through the linking of national power grids was started. This in effect would form the basis for the creation of regional energy institutions with the ultimate purpose of facilitating energy regionalism within the West African context.

In terms of the regime type (RS 4), the development of the interconnected grid that came into existence and the bilateral energy relations initiated at a very early stage between the partner countries and companies underscored by long-term contracts formed the basis of the type of regime. The cross-border power interconnection linking Ghana and its neighbours were required for the implementation of the circular operation of the grid system.

The details of the basic infrastructures of the WAGS power interconnection meant transmission lines linked the Akosombo supply station in Ghana to the Lome substation in Togo. It was further extended to the Cotonou substation in Benin. The attributes of the interconnection were a double circuit line operating at 161KV with a corresponding total length of the transmission line being 290 kilometres across the three countries. The western end of the power interconnection of WAGS was to link Cote d'Ivoire. The linkage between the two transmission networks intertied the Abobo substation, north of Abidjan in Cote d'Ivoire and the Prestea substation in the western part of the Ghana power grid network.

The operational voltage was 225KV on a single circuit line of 220 kilometres. The attributes of the various national networks, which served as the resource system (RS) and the actors (A) involved in this regard, defined the WAGS energy community. To illustrate, the power interconnection managed by VRA had an installed capacity of about 1072MW derived from two hydro plants at Akosombo and Kpong. Additionally, there was a 30MW diesel plant at Tema. The pre-existing maximum peak load was about 850MW, with an average annual energy consumption of about 6,300GWh of which 2,760 GWh was consumed by an aluminium company, the Volta Aluminium Company (VALCO), located in Tema.

Table 5. 5 Contextual Factors and Focal Action Situations in ECOWAS and EU Energy Regionalism

Overview of key dynamic contextual factors and focal action situations in ECOWAS and EU energy regionalisms

	Resource systems	Resource units and markets	Actors	Governance systems	Focal action situations
Pre-1970s	Energy Infrastructures Nationally concentrated	Defined energy resource sectors Regional use of energy capacity not fully optimised	Households, Colonial Authorities and State Utilities Energy Use, Withdrawal, Trade and Feed-In	Top-down Formal Territorial System Non-Existent to Minimal Regional Connectivity	Appropriation and use, Provisioning and Monitoring Simple Licensing
ECOWAS	• Appropriation and use: energy produced using hydropower, diesel and gas. Unused capacity of energy stock is a challenge to offload to meet energy needs • **Markets:** To trade and share unused electricity stock WAGS is created to serve as a new regional energy market albeit most markets are only national • **From Licensing to Formal Regulation:** Technical committees setup to regulate operations of licenced utilities regarding exchanges on the energy pool, WAGS				
EU	• Appropriation and use: Coal serves as the major fuel source followed by hydropower and thermal. Through the ECSC liberalised coal supply becomes vital for power producers • **Markets:** To trade electricity UCPTE/UCTE is formed to develop a new power pooling market • **From Licensing to Formal Regulation:** Energy pooling through trans-European coordination precede national energy regulation				
1970-1990	Energy Infrastructures **Regional efforts commence** **Promotion of alternative energy sources**	Defined energy resource sectors **Global energy crises and recovery** **Prices and demand fluctuates**	Households, Firms and State Utilities Energy Use, Withdrawal, Trade and Feed-Ins Continues **Regional energy institutions emerge**	Top-down Formal Territorial System **Regional Connectivity improves**	Appropriation and use, Provisioning and Monitoring **Mainly National markets** **Rise of energy diplomacy, diversification and norms**
ECOWAS	• Appropriation: General decline in the supply of petroleoum resources. Resource stocks shrink further affecting consumption and trade between OPEC countries and buyer countries. • Markets: Energy produced from alternative sources were highly prioritised creating new energy markets based on hydropower. • **Complex Governance:** A rise in petro - diplomacy activate concrete collective action in regional energy policy				
EU	• Appropriation: General decline in the supply and demand of petroleoum resources. Resource stocks were further depleted leading to low consumption and trade between OPEC countries and buyer countries • Markets: New energy markets created from alternative energy sources mainly nuclear and an increase in coal use. • **Complex Governance:** A rise in energy diversification and the development of norms to protect the environment				
1990-2000	Energy Infrastructures **Regional efforts commence** **Promotion of alternative energy sources**	Defined energy resource sectors **Deregulation and Liberalisation in markets** **Robust market value**	Households, Firms and State Utilities Energy Use, Withdrawal, Trade and Feed-Ins **Sector, National and Regional regulators**	**Multilevel Formal Territorial System** **Multiple Formal regulations** **Regional Connectivity established**	Appropriation and use, Provisioning and Monitoring **National and Regional markets** **Formal international and regional norms and rules**
ECOWAS	• Appropriation: Incremental regionalism and regionalisation in the multiple energy sectors makes supply and demand of energy resources more available • Markets: West African energy regionalism 2.0 - guaranteeing a liberalised regional energy market starting from national markets under the revised ECOWAS treaty • Governance: Although climate concerns are highlighted, energy access and provision is top of the agenda				
EU	• Appropriation: First energy package guarantees availability, supply and demand of electricity and gas • Markets: Deregulation in national energy markets contribute to a coherent and harmonised EU energy market as part of the Single European Market • Governance: Climate concerns key on the energy agenda this leads to the promotion of norms in the region and globally				
2000-2020	Energy Infrastructures **Advanced Regional efforts** **Focus on Energy Access, Energy Security and Climate Change**	Defined energy resource sectors **Integrated regional energy markets** Robust market value **Reliance on new energy technologies**	Households, Firms and State Utilities Energy Use, Withdrawal, Trade and Feed-Ins Sector, National and Regional regulators	**Co-management regime for clearly defined area** **Deepening energy governance through regionalism** **Pro-energy conservation and climate change norms**	Appropriation and use, Provisioning and Monitoring National and Regional markets **Multiple and complex regulations** **Informal rules and norms**
ECOWAS	• Appropriation and use: Multiple energy sectors provide energy resources for consumption and use • Markets: Expansion in regional and national energy infrastructure with both internal and external financing sources to widen sectoral regional energy market connectivity • **From complex regulation to co-management regime:** Commitments to realise the energy and climate aspects of the SDGs and Paris Agreement whiles aligned to regional energy targets				
EU	• Appropriation and use: Various energy sectors provide energy resources for consumption • Markets: The resolve to create the EU Energy Union to coordinate a coherent energy single market that promotes shared goals and counters external energy security threats while providing affordable and reliable energy • **From complex regulation to co-management regime:** Commitments in the climate and energy framework lead to Energy Union governance regulation specifying the definitive roles for all parties to enable implementation				

The Ivorian power network managed by Cote d'Ivoire Energies (CIE) at the time had an installed capacity of 913MW of which 599MW was generated from five small to medium hydropower plants and 314MW from a number of steam and gas turbine supply stations located on the Vridi Canal which extended to the southern, central and western corners of the country. Cote d' Ivoire had a peak capacity of 365MW and an average annual energy consumption of 2,300 GWh.

Lastly, the Togo-Benin power network comprised of an installed capacity of about 155MW of which 90MW was derived from a gas turbine in Togo and a number of diesel supply stations in Togo and Benin. The remainder was a 65MW supply from a small hydropower plant at Nangbeto in Togo. The peak load was about 120MW with an average annual consumption of 550 GWh. In sum, the minimum generation capacity of the receiver countries of Togo, Benin and Cote d'Ivoire was an imperative for this type of regional power pool with Ghana in order to meet respective national energy demand.

The governance system of the WAGS power pool in terms of operational choice rules (GS6a) and collective choice rules (GS6b) that is, the various types of energy exchanges performed across the WAGS included one-way transfers, two-way sales, network pooling, storage, inadvertent exchanges, emergency supply and guaranteed supply among others. To illustrate how this was done, the one-way sales primarily provided lower cost energy from the hydropower resources of the VRA to Togo and Benin. The two-way exchanges on the other hand provided mutual support and assistance during system disturbances and emergencies.

Alternatively, other practices by the interconnected utilities was the pooling of generation resources of two parties and consequent co-ordination from one central point. Other governance system variables were achieved through separate technical committees formed between VRA and CEB, and also between the VRA and CIE to take decisions on matters concerned with the technical management of each interconnection. These committees approved all operational instructions and technical studies undertaken on the tie-in thus serving as a rule-making organisation (GS5). The committees also prepared protocols for energy exchanges and undertook negotiations on matters related to power sales on behalf of their respective utility management boards. The committees then met at least once a year.

With reference to the Ghana-Cote d'Ivoire interconnection, there was also an operating sub-committee that met quarterly alternating in the two countries. They met to review or initiate power interconnection procedures and rules, operating instructions, balancing energy exchanges and dealing with other issues that affected the regular operation of the network interconnection. This brief review above, that has illustrated the formal and informal multilevel institutional interactions contributed to the remarkable start and progress of the initial process of a polycentric regional energy system in this case the first electricity sharing system in West Africa.[1010]

EU

In the case of the EU, Paul A. Van Baal and Matthias Finger[1011] reveal that the beginnings of regional energy cooperation in the EU that is, the pooling of energy resources across borders with the goal of transnational coordination predated its founding. Its evolution goes as far back as the Union for the Coordination of the Transmission of Electricity in 1951. This historical record on European energy systems, principally concerning power interconnections suggests that transnational governance and cross-border coordination was alongside the formation of the European communities, the antecedents of the EU. Again, it also reveals energy (electricity) pooling through shared governance and trans-European coordination preceded national regulation that is, market liberalisation in the 1990s.[1012] During this period, *coal was king* in Europe, accounting for 70 percent of primary energy within the six members of the Community[1013].

Hydropower still occupied a greater share of the electricity mix than thermal generation in France and Italy (as well as in Austria, Norway, Sweden and Switzerland) but overall coal and lignite were to remain the major fuel sources throughout the 1950s. During persistent shortages, the intended liberalisation of the coal market through the ECSC was undoubtedly of vital importance to the power producers.[1014]

1010 UNECA.

1011 Van Baal and Finger.

1012 Vincent Lagendijk, *Electrifying Europe: The Power of Europe in the Construction of Electricity Networks* (Amsterdam: Aksant, 2008) <https://doi.org/10.6100/IR638264>; Johan Schot and Vincent Lagendijk, 'Technocratic Internationalism in the Interwar Years: Building Europe on Motorways and Electricity Networks', *Journal of Modern European History*, 6.2 (2008), 196–217 <https://doi.org/10.17104/1611-8944_2008_2_196>.

1013 Belgium, the Netherlands, Luxembourg and Italy joining France and Germany to form the Six countries that signed the ECSC Treaty in 1951

1014 Union for the Coordination of Transmission of Electricity (UCTE).

The articles of association (GS6) of the Union for the Coordination of Production and Transmission of Electricity (UCPTE) in accord with the enclosed guidelines and supplementary recommendations were accepted at the inaugural meeting of the UCPTE, on 23rd May 1951 at the headquarters of the OEEC[1015] in Paris. The governance structure made up of founding members were equally listed in the articles of association. Since the tasks and responsibility of this actor, the UCPTE related primarily to operational governance, there was a differentiation between members who had developed the articles and the group of founder members. These articles were amended slightly to ensure that extraordinary members could also be admitted in 1954. Its central function was to add to the development of economic activity through the more effective use of energy resources available due to the interconnection of electricity networks.

In addition, the UCPTE was to ensure the full operation of the national power generation plants. For instance, a surplus of production in nations where generation was based mainly upon hydropower facilities could be used to balance a shortfall in production beyond the frontiers of those nations, thus enabling savings in coal consumption to be attained in the adjoining nations concerned. The prevention of a drop in surplus production of this kind was one of the initial major accomplishments of the UCPTE.

The membership composition of the UCPTE was selected from the management authorities of electricity production and transmission systems in the eight countries. In a way, the UCPTE came out of the process of reconstruction in the immediate post-war years. The electricity grids of the eight founding members: Belgium, Federal Republic of Germany, France, Italy, Luxembourg, the Netherlands, Austria and Switzerland were significantly expanded eastwards and to the west by the grids of Greece and Yugoslavia. The interconnections to Portugal and Spain was done later. Over the period under consideration, the regional interconnection of electricity systems and the pooling of networks was reinforced considerably, in effect increasing the technical interdependence of synced interconnected electricity systems.

The regime type (GS4) that defined the process was mainly based on bilateral energy relations initiated at a very early stage between neighbouring countries and companies and held up through long-term contracts. The regional transnational lines that were required functioned in radial

1015 This will later become the OECD, the Organisation for Economic Cooperation and Development.

operation. By the end of the 1960s, the grid network was interconnected at so many points that rings were created. When the initial 380 KV ring was extended across several countries like France, Italy and Switzerland in 1969, it was followed up with further rings and meshes that were created into the 1970s.

The peak transmission capacity of the regional power interconnections between the eight UCPTE countries in the 1950s had increased more than tenfold by 1974 it amounted to 32,200 MW of baseload. It accounted for about 27 percent of the annual maximum load of all eight UCPTE countries whereas in 1953 the corresponding figure was just 9 percent. By 1974, the electricity exchange across these interconnections was around 38,700 GWh representing roughly 5 percent of the total energy supply in the eight UCPTE countries.

In terms of the network structure (GS9) the UCPTE grid was composed of sub-grids with meshes, this led to a dependence between individual grids of the partner countries. Grid failures or glitches in an individual grid severely affected all the others in the same way, with the closest grids being the most severely affected. It was therefore necessary to employ all possible means of coordination and information (GS8) to achieve the best possible reliability. Because of this, the member partners in terms of collective – choice rules (GS6b) aimed to coordinate the disconnection of major lines. However, in view of the extensive nature of the UCPTE grid, it was not possible to reach the goal of general coordination of all grid lines within the framework of the UCPTE.

In view of these experiences in making the UCPTE grid operational, four definitive rings were created to aid the opening up of a mesh that was beneficial such that without it, major repercussions could occur on a large grid area. This included the Austria-Federal Republic of Germany ring, the France-Italy-Switzerland ring, the Italy-Austria-Yugoslavia ring and lastly the more expansive one, France-Belgium-Netherlands-Federal Republic of Germany-Switzerland ring. This regional power interconnection in the European energy system set in motion a radical cross-border energy coordination contributing to future energy governance particularly in the ensuing years in the aftermath of the global energy crisis.[1016]

A schematic to show the focal action situations in operation to represent this first breakpoint in the two cases of ECOWAS and EU is not included. The institutional response towards regional electricity pooling though new in both cases became a routine and necessary process to meet the basic

1016 Union for the Coordination of Transmission of Electricity (UCTE), p. 29.

need of energy provision in recipient and participating countries. As the power grid interconnections grew in scale in both energy regional cases, it became more diverse in terms of its membership.

In addition, it sought for more favourable conditions to thrive. But a more peculiar feature that is witnessed in both cases is that the regional energy infrastructure system was perceived by all participating countries as a commonly owned property that could be used cooperatively to meet respective national electricity needs. It is the first time the idea of a regional energy commons becomes a reality and a possible tool for analysing energy systems in my informed opinion becomes a reality.

In the West African situation, an interesting observation is made a nucleus of post-independent countries pursue the linking of their respective energy infrastructure in order to maximise energy solidarity and utilise efficiently the excess generated power through cross-border energy sharing and governance. Moreover, this initiates the rise of a set of networked action situations that needed consideration.

As I analyse further, a number of formal and informal institutional changes provide a notable narrative of regional energy governance in both occurrences of energy regionalism.

5.4.2 Phase 1: 1970 --1990

The initial years of this period globally was characterized by a general decline in the size and quantity of petroleum resources and global political economy competition dubbed the 'oil crisis' between OPEC countries and buyer countries mainly in the West. This caused radical changes in the primary energy market of the 1970s.

Figure 5. 1 ECOWAS Energy Regionalism, 1970–1990

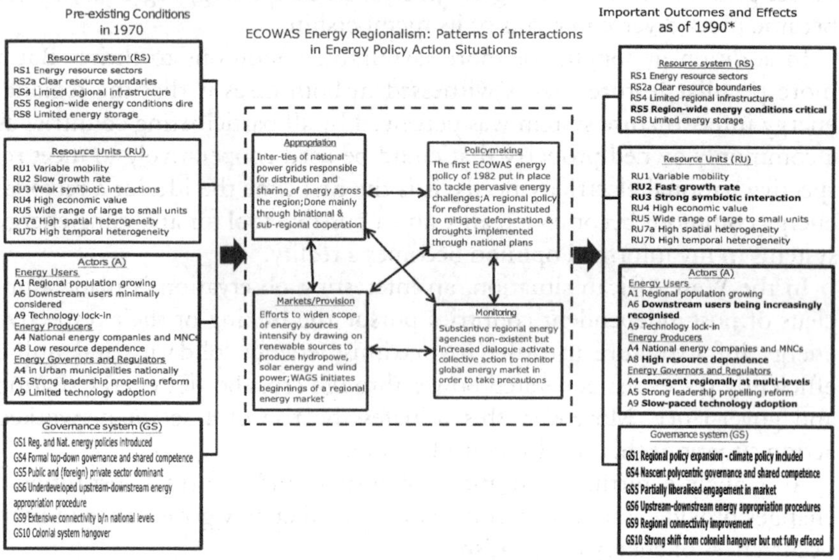

**Note : Significant changes are denoted in bold*

Figure 5. 2 EU Energy Regionalism, 1970–1990

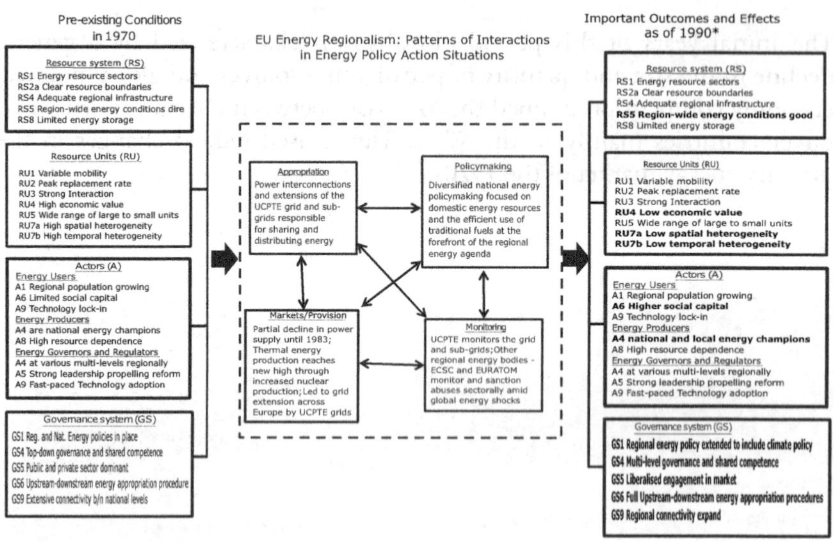

**Note : Significant changes are denoted in bold*

In the power sector, especially pertaining to companies that generated electricity using thermal energy sources it prompted the adaption of their power plants to the new prevailing conditions. It also led to the expansion of nuclear energy use and an increased use of coal in the countries that made up the EU area. Within the same timeframe in the ECOWAS area, a proliferation of small and medium scale hydropower projects were being commissioned across the region.

Additionally, Nigeria sought to use its oil-resource rich advantage to enhance its hegemonic ambitions through skilled petro-diplomacy by signing preferential bilateral oil supply deals with neighbouring states such as Togo, Niger and Benin among other nations in the region which provided the incentive for the founding of ECOWAS.[1017]

By 1980 however, both regions were experiencing varying degrees of economic crises that affected growth rates in energy consumption. This was coupled with the aftershocks of the world energy crises that sent crippling effects particularly in the political economy of the ECOWAS region. The circumstances in ECOWAS prompted the Symposium on Energy for Survival held at Freetown, Sierra Leone, in 1981. A pivotal moment that would activate concrete collective action on regional energy policy under the leadership of ECOWAS.

To be more specific, we witness in this period stronger ECOWAS activism as it sought to devise and chart a more definitive course towards a more strengthened cooperation in developing a regional energy policy that is, the ECOWAS energy policy of 3rd May 1982. The first of its kind to be formulated by a regional energy body in West Africa. This accentuated ECOWAS' readiness and commitment to tackle pervasive regional energy challenges in the region and among member countries.

The Authority of Heads of State and Government codified the regional energy policy by bringing into fruition Article 48 of the ECOWAS Treaty. It formulated this common regional energy policy through the passing of Decision A/DEC.3/5/82. The 1980s was really a dire period in ECOWAS energy regionalism, member states were under immense economic stress and faced the severe droughts particularly in 1983 and 1984. This directly contributed to serious political instability and had the potential of fuelling major social unrest that could lead to political upheavals. Examples of such

1017 Ojo, xxxiv.

happenings were the spate of coups and attempted coups that occurred in Ghana, Liberia, and Nigeria among other places in the region.[1018]

This period also witnessed a surge in ecological awareness and activism. This led to the pursuit in tackling the environmental impact of the droughts that had earlier occurred in the region. A climate decade goal was set to reforest the region. This was dubbed the 'reforestation decade' set between 1983 and 1993. This was declared through a decision by the highest arm of ECOWAS to mitigate the deforestation problem through national work programmes that sought to harmonise these national efforts regionally.

Again, in this period, nine hydropower projects were commissioned in Burkina Faso, Cote d'Ivoire, Ghana, Liberia, Mali, Nigeria and Togo resulting in hydropower generation reaching a new record. This increased energy supply from hydropower sources. The severe deteriorating effects of the regional economy in the early 1980s sparked a move in most of the countries in the region to initiate sectoral reforms in the national power sectors. This was done by designing a dynamic institutional environment in the various national power sectors. However, due to the structural adjustment policies recommended by the Bretton Woods institutions there were extreme difficulties with sourcing traditional financing for most of the planned energy projects. The reasons given by potential financiers were based on the political and economic instabilities found in the ECOWAS region. In addition, energy consumption from wood fuels and charcoal were also gravely impacted due to the dry weather conditions that prevailed in the 1980s.[1019]

To summarise this breakpoint, 1970–1990, in terms of the regional energy trajectory in the ECOWAS region. It was saddled with major internal and external energy problems but it also offered unique opportunities. The lowest points were the global energy crises, droughts and its attendant socio-political upheavals and instability as well as the limited flow of international finance into the regional energy and climate sectors of the region.

But it was mitigated somewhat by the highest point of increased regionalism and regionalisation in the region generally and around energy. This led to the founding of ECOWAS itself where Nigeria used its abundant energy resources as a diplomatic tool to bring the region together. The

1018 Carol Lancaster, 'Africa's Economic Crisis', *Foreign Policy*, 52 (1983), 149–66 <https://www.jstor.org/stable/1148240>.

1019 John K Turkson, *Power Sector Reform in SubSaharan Africa*, ed. by John Turkson (London and New York: Palgrave Macmillan, 2000).

fledgling regionalism was used as a conduit to deepen energy regionalism when energy cooperation took shape through the development of the first regional energy and climate policy to tackle energy provision and deforestation in the ECOWAS region.

In the EU, the economic crisis at the beginning of the 1980s and the exceptional cold spell in January 1985 had resulted in a partial decline in the supply of electricity in Europe. Although by the end of 1983, there was an opposite trend. Adjustments had to be made to the power supply in relation to demand in the various countries by reducing oil dependence. In addition to meeting requirements in the field of environmental protection. This constituted an important breakthrough in the energy and climate fortunes of the EU at the time.

Energy production from hydropower was seriously restricted. Also, production from thermal power plants were maintained with difficulty due to blocked fuel transportation and reductions in gas supplies. Nevertheless, the prevailing conditions boosted energy supply from nuclear energy. eight nuclear energy plants in Belgium, Germany and France were commissioned. This increased thermal production from nuclear energy to an all-time high. Generation from nuclear power increased threefold within this period in the 1980s. It constituted as much as a third of total regional energy production. This contributed to the scaling of the regional power grid in the mid-1980s to third countries such as Albania and Denmark.[1020]

This phase can be characterized as a definitive period in regional energy policy in the ECOWAS region and among its member states. This was due to the fact that this phase intensified region-wide efforts as well as national efforts to tap into a wide variety of energy sources which included rivers and other waterways, solar and wind to consolidate gains in the provision of energy. This was achieved through the generation of hydropower, solar energy and wind power respectively for electricity purposes. At the same time, geological teams intensified their search for coal, oil, gas, uranium, and thorium while forestry experts continued to examine the use of firewood and charcoal alongside their environmental impact. In sum, it heightened interest on energy and climate issues as occasioned by not only the post-independence socio-economic developments that were happening in the ECOWAS region. But also, its effects on energy production, consumption as well as issue of the environment.

With respect to the EU, the phase characterised a need to diversify the use of available energy resources. It also compelled the region to look

1020 Union for the Coordination of Transmission of Electricity (UCTE), p. 30.

increasingly into the use of domestic energy resources and utilise already developed energy technologies such as nuclear energy in a maximised manner. It led the EU to innovate and find ways to use traditional fuels more efficiently and effectively.

In the EU region, energy regionalism, which was already mature with the pooling of power grids, entered into a new maturation phase. This was characterised by the formation of other sectoral energy organisations around oil and gas. This deepened the regionalisation and institutionalisation of regional energy across different energy sectors.

5.4.3 Phase 2: 1990 – 2000

The last decade of the twentieth century marked a unique phase in the review of processes towards energy regionalism in the ECOWAS and EU. This period was characterised by the commencement on an intense global action on climate at the intergovernmental level especially with the follow-up processes of the 1992 United Nations Framework Convention on Climate Change (UNFCCC). It led to the signing of the international treaty, the Kyoto Protocol that was binding on nations to reduce carbon emissions and reverse global warming.

In the ECOWAS region, this phase can be characterised as West Africa's energy regionalism 2.0. Because it set into motion the coming into force of the revised ECOWAS Treaty in 1993, which guaranteed the liberalisation of the regional energy market. It concluded with the process that led to the realisation of the ECOWAS Energy Protocol later in next decade. The energy protocol sought to formalise the building of region-wide energy institutions and enable ongoing national energy reforms. Binational and sub-regional energy cooperation characterised by the exploitation, production and distribution of energy resources was a major component of the energy protocol.

It essentially encouraged the strengthening of connectivity of national energy infrastructures and the sharing of energy resources such as river basins under cross-border and transnational energy agreements. These cross-border agreements and transnational energy cooperation deals proliferated across the ECOWAS energy region leading to bilateral and multilateral cross-border power interconnections, which facilitated the exchange and trade of electricity. It also enabled the facilitation of transnational engagement around energy resources be it natural or constructed. This included engagement around the use and construction of mega regional hydropower dam projects around a common river basin. As well as engagement to construct common gas infrastructure in the region. The revised ECOWAS Treaty invigorated ECOWAS to supervise the coordination and harmonisation of national energy policies and programmes under a common energy policy.

In the EU region, this phase witnessed how deregulation swept through national energy markets and led to the introduction of the Single European Market in 1992. Thereby, initiating the creation of a coherent and harmonised EU internal energy market led by strong institutional assertiveness of the EU Commission unlike no other time witnessed in the energy sector. Again, in this period the first liberalisation package for the EU energy market to facilitate energy exchanges and trade in the electricity and gas markets was unveiled and entered into force. The Trans-European Network for Energy (TEN-E) programme that started in 1995 gave incentive for the development of a common energy infrastructure through priority projects of European interests thus leading to the furtherance of the integration of the EU's energy region.

The ascendency of climate concerns and the role played by the energy sector during this period has tailed off into the first two decades of the 21st century. Incremental regionalisation and regionalism in the energy sectors in ECOWAS and the EU, has encouraged the move to tackle the challenge of a new energy transition that would also guarantee energy provision and energy access.

In conclusion, an important observation to be made here is the willingness of these two energy regions, one an advanced regional economy and the other a developing and emerging regional economy, to the cause of global multilateralism and cooperation on international energy and climate issues

Figure 5. 3 ECOWAS Energy Regionalism, 1990–2000

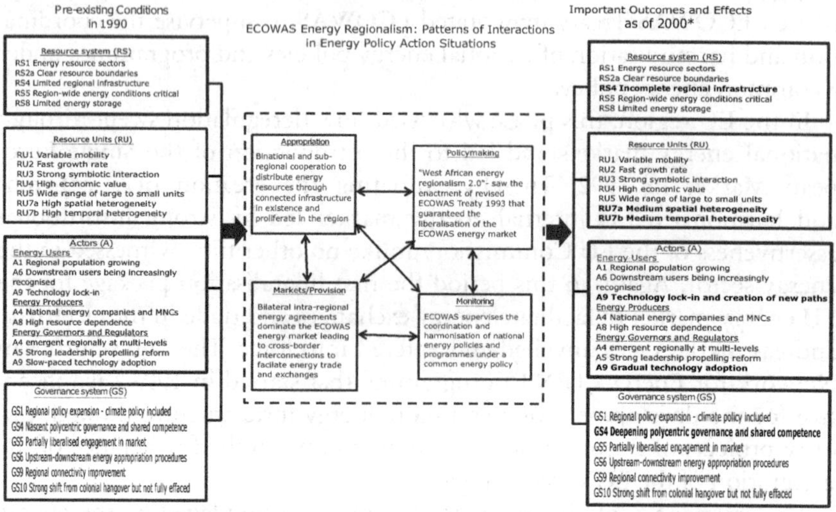

Note : Significant changes are denoted in bold

Figure 5. 4 EU Energy Regionalism, 1990–2000

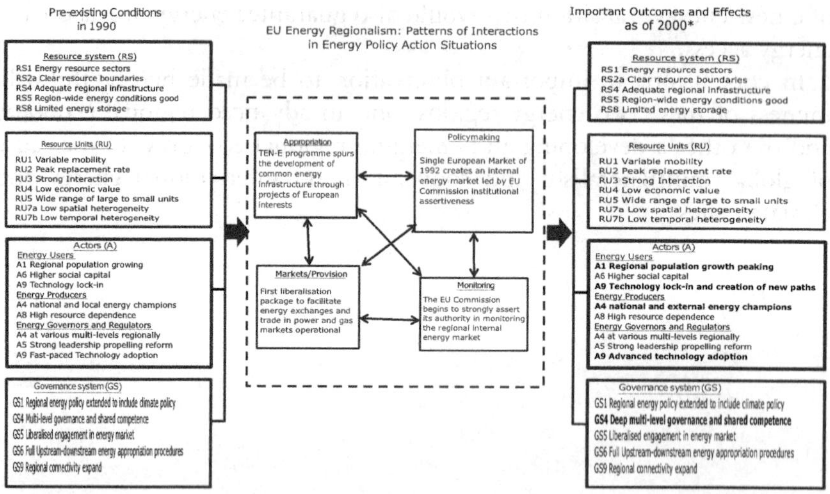

Note : Significant changes are denoted in bold

5.4.4 Phase 3: 2000 – 2020

The year 2000 marked the beginning of fresh mobilisation regarding the future of energy governance in both the ECOWAS and the EU regions. For instance, ECOWAS regional energy institutionalisation was more prominent with the establishment of the regional power pool, the first regional gas pipeline, the regional electricity market regulator and finally the regional body for renewable energy and energy efficiency. On the other hand, the EU energy regionalism dynamic involved the strengthening and consolidation of energy market processes through the passing of the 2003 and 2009 energy market liberalisation packages for gas and electricity. It also witnessed the ambitious objective of finalising the creation of the internal energy market of the EU by 2019.

This periodic phase in the course of ECOWAS energy regionalism witnessed major transitions. The first decade of this period saw the deepening of energy regionalism with the enactment of the ECOWAS Energy Protocol of 2003 that sought to formalise the establishment of specialised regional energy institutions and encourage ongoing national energy reforms that ultimately would consolidate intra-regional energy market processes.

The second decade has been defined by the expansion of energy and climate efforts using new investment sources, a renewed impetus in global collective action and an increase in the role of sustainability issues in regional energy policy formulation. Another interesting phenomenon has been the deepening of regulatory governance in the regional energy sector. This has been characterised by the coordination of national energy regulators in tackling the monitoring, evaluations and sanctioning procedures of the regional energy market. In this regard a lot of activity has been seen in the regional electricity market in the ECOWAS energy region.

In the first place, activities in ECOWAS reveals a renewed stimulus in expanding regional and national energy infrastructure with both internal and external financial investments. With a bulging demographic growth outpacing energy supply, policymakers are saddled with a major hurdle in dealing with the energy deficit and access issues prevailing the regional energy sector. This has steered the implementation of already envisioned and drafted regional energy infrastructure plans such as the construction of transnational hydropower plants, thermal (gas-to-power) energy plants, coal-to-power energy plants, the scaling and extension of the regional energy grid as well as gas pipelines that would supply both national and regional interconnections.

The support for these cross-border and transnational regional energy projects are based on internally financed and external investments from partners such as China, United States (through its Power Africa programme), African Development Bank and the World Bank. However, other external financiers such as the EU and international development agencies of EU member states are more focused on low energy intensity projects and energy efficiency programmes, which are based on renewables especially small to medium scale solar projects among others.

On the other hand, in terms of the exploration and extraction of hydrocarbon reserves such as oil and gas in the Gulf of Guinea, West African Transit Margin and off the coast of Senegal, which are mostly exported to international energy markets. It has attracted major European energy companies such as Shell, Eni, Tullow, Total, BP, Aker among others who have been at the forefront. This is being done alongside other major international energy corporate interests from the USA (such as Chevron and ExxonMobil) and Sinopec from China.

Multilateral energy governance has also influenced the governance of ECOWAS energy regionalism in this period immensely. This is witnessed through the commitment of member states and ECOWAS as a whole in contributing to realise the energy and climate components of the Sustainable Development Goals of the United Nations and the Paris Climate Accord by inculcating energy and climate targets into their respective national and overall regional energy and climate policy strategies. It has led to the expansion of regional energy projects as well as national energy infrastructure.

To aid in the distribution of energy produced in the region, another aspect worth mentioning in the phase has been the proliferation of major intra-regional energy distribution networks. This is coordinated by the activities of WAPP and WAGP in concert with respective national energy management agencies that are responsible for these appropriation processes in the power and gas sectors.

Another feature of this intra-regional distribution network has been the strengthening of national energy regulators and the connectivity to regional energy regulatory bodies. This process of strengthening regulators and their linkages at both country level and regional levels is being done through the monitoring, evaluation and sanctioning procedures that would ensure progress in the gas and power markets in the ECOWAS region.

This period in the EU has been marked by the resolve to complete the creation of the internal energy market of the EU. This will culminate in the establishment of a fully functioning EU energy union. This is a regionally coordinated and coherent energy single market with shared goals and collective commitments in the entire European energy market. It will seek to offset external energy security threats and provide affordable and reliable energy to the people living in the EU. This movement towards the creation of an energy union has been preceded by the incremental role of reliability and sustainability in EU energy policymaking. It has been based on commitments made in the EU climate and energy framework for 2030. It has also been followed through with the energy union's governance regulation thus making the implementation of the energy union more definitive than vague as was the case initially. However, the manner in which the legal instruments will be deployed will depend wholly on the incoming Commission that will take over in December of 2019.[1021]

The trans-European energy infrastructure process (under the TEN-E programme) links the entire energy infrastructure of EU countries. This entails nine priority corridors and three priority thematic areas that include smart grids deployment, electricity highways, and a cross-border carbon dioxide network in the field of electricity, gas and oil infrastructure made possible through the execution of projects of common interests (PCIs).

Another aspect of EU energy regionalism in this period has been the coordination of national energy regulators to monitor progress in gas and power markets, investigate abuses and sanction abusive and dominant behaviour in the energy region. The respective roles of officials in national and regional energy institutions, local energy communities and the role of consumers (especially self-generating energy consumers – prosumers) continues to evolve during this period. This would eventually result in a changing, dynamic and a more sophisticated energy region in the EU. The energy union package has made provision for this sophistication in the governance of the energy region with the introduction of these new energy actors. We are yet to see how it would unfold going forward. In the ECOWAS energy region however, the inclusion of this important innovation in energy governance is non-existent.[1022] Also in this regard we

---

1021 Kacper Szulecki and Dag Herald Claes, 'Towards Decarbonization: Understanding EU Energy Governance', *Politics and Governance*, 7.1 (2019), 1 <https://doi.org/10.17645/pag.v7i1.2029>.

1022 Rafael Leal-Arcas, Feja Lesniewska, and Filippos Proedrou, 'Prosumers as New Energy Actors', in *Africa-EU Renewable Energy Research and Innovation Symposium 2018 (RERIS 2018)*, ed. by M et al. Mpholo (Cham: Springer Proceedings in Energy, 2018), pp. 139–51 <https://doi.org/10.1007/978-3-319-93438-9>.

are yet to see major trends with regards to these new innovators in the regional energy governance architecture in West Africa.

Figure 5. 5 ECOWAS Energy Regionalism, 2000–2020

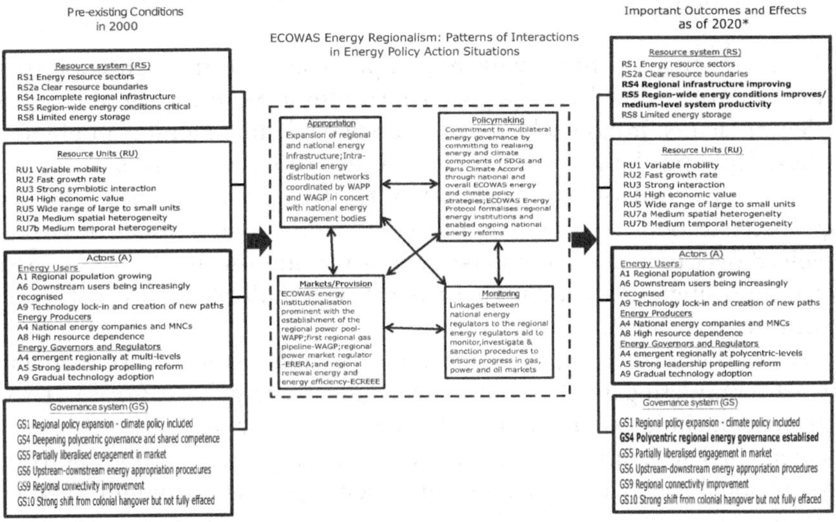

**Note : Significant changes are denoted in bold*

Figure 5. 6 EU Energy Regionalism, 2000–2020

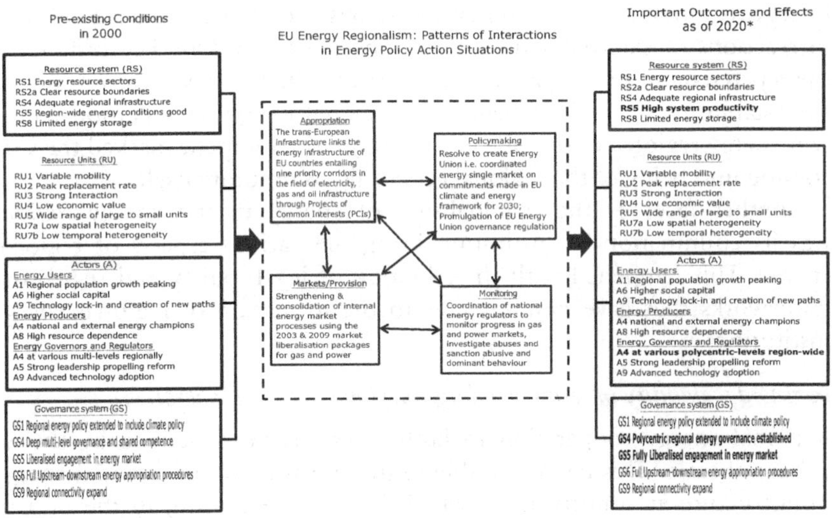

**Note : Significant changes are denoted in bold*

5.5 Overview of Case Comparisons: Some Elements of Regional Energy Governance

The use of the CIS framework has helped condense the rich contextual landscape of regional energy governance into a more manageable set of relevant factors. It has enabled this to done while maintaining a tight analytical focus on the key energy regionalism processes which has occurred over time particularly in the network of focal action situations in the energy spaces of both regions. The reference points or milestones of change evolved over time along both energy histories and this has been interpreted using a single analytical perspective through multiple representations of institutional change.

An overview of comparing the cases presents a number of elements worth considering in the context of regional energy governance. These elements include external factors that necessitated energy regionalism, the incremental scalability of regional energy through cooperation, polycentric regional energy policymaking, multi-level governance and information asymmetry, and the speed of technological change through policy adoption.

External factors initiate and deepen energy regionalism

Energy regionalism in both regions were observed to have taken shape due to reactions to external actions that impacted them. One key instance is the repercussions of the global energy crises, which served as a conduit for the establishment, and deepening of regional energy cooperation in the two energy regions. In the case of ECOWAS, the moment marked the very coming into being of the regional economic community itself.

Another facet of the regionalising of energy in the energy regions was its culmination in institutionalising the various aspects of regional energy. This happened with the adoption of legal, policy and regulatory frameworks that gave new impetus to the formation of regional energy institutions.

Increased scalability in terms of enlarged regional energy cooperation

Regional energy cooperation in both cases has been defined by the attribute of scale. This has arisen due to the construction of essential energy infrastructure at country level, which has been extended, to the idea of regional *energy sharing* through bilateral and multilateral agreements. This is an occurrence mainly seen in the post-independent ECOWAS and post-war EU settings.

Again, scalability improves in regional energy as energy regions seek to establish regional energy markets to facilitate the trade and exchange of energy. This has led to the development of rules, norms and principles that has sought to enable the unhindered trade and exchange of energy in a particular region. A typical observation being the development and progress of a new free movement principle in the EU single market that is literally defining the completion of the created internal energy market that is, the free movement of energy.

Regional energy cooperation in both regions has also been typified by the existence of several regulatory levels and the concern to provide energy services on a very large transnational scale. This has been done with the establishment and governance of regional energy markets. While improving these markets over time by extending energy accessibility through expansive energy infrastructure to accelerate the provision of moderate to high quality energy resources. This has moreover pluralised choices that enable a citizen to attain a sustainable growth in energy consumption.

Scalability in terms of regional energy cooperation has occurred again by incorporating the use of a manifold set of energy resources drawn from the various options of fossil fuels, renewables and nuclear energy inter alia. This has been done with the expectation of accruing benefits such as lowering energy costs, providing abundant and sustainable energy supplies, building political trust through the provision of energy or by stopping the use of a particular energy source, economic growth and development, environmental improvements, and transfer of technology among many others. Likewise, one obvious feature of regional energy cooperation, which has further improved the scalability of regional energy, is its sustenance and security of energy supply across the energy region.

In spite of the benefits seen in the scaling of energy within the context of regional energy cooperation. Various constraints still prevail in terms of the scalability of regional energy systems across both regions. Focusing more on the ECOWAS region the following is observed. The uncompleted nature of the regional energy infrastructure architecture. The weaker linkages inherent in the cross-border cooperation and integration of regional energy systems. The occasionally vague and incomplete legal, institutional and regulatory structures of energy governance at country and region-wide levels.

Another major and substantial feature is the inability to mobilise and attract the much-needed capital investments and financial might to advance the ambitious regional and country level energy plans from internal and external sources. The last factor affecting scalability of regional energy is the lack of confidence among member states in the energy regions in terms of meeting national commitments that result in the fulfilment of overall regional energy objectives. This experience has been responsible for a dearth of mutual trust in region-building in the energy sector.

Polycentric regional energy policymaking tends to design resilient energy systems

The sites for the making of policy and governance of collective regional energy problems has been observed to be generally spread across geographical scales (that is, local, sub-national, regional and even global levels). As well as across different sectors in the energy space namely public, private and commons sectors.

Furthermore, the various bodies at both country and region-wide levels involved with the governance of regional energy often have overlapping institutional mandates, such that multiple regulators address the same energy and climate problems in the very same places. This results in the hierarchies and chains of command extant among the various energy governance bodies region-wide to become ambiguous. Also, the regional energy regulatory arrangement, albeit with a seeming presence of an arbiter, still lacks a final arbiter who maintains the final say due to its trans-scalar, trans-sectoral and variable mode of governance. This multi-level governance of the regional energy policymaking process, in terms of addressing collective energy problems and regulation, defines this polycentric state of affairs.

This polycentricity has also unfolded in both energy regions especially in the area of energy infrastructure governance. It has led to complex governance arrangements which coordinate across local, national and regional scales. The EU exhibited much more evidence of this polycentric nature of energy infrastructure governance especially with its push towards integrating national energy networks through the energy union.

So, this multi-tiered and dispersed approach to governing energy infrastructure and policymaking at the regional level, although messy and seemingly headless, provides a tailored and contextualised set of solutions at country and region-wide levels. In particular, this relates to the processes that lead to setting the regional energy and climate agenda. This has proven beneficial to the design of resilient regional energy systems.

Multi-level governance and Information Asymmetry

In reality, the energy regions, which are multi-level and polycentric in nature, are mainly characterised by blended governance scales that engage multiple stakeholder actors. This allows for the generation and distribution of information in the multiple governance scales. It was observed, that for these energy regions to be able to respond efficiently and robustly to sudden changes and shocks, there needed to be reliance on information sharing across the different governance scales.

In addition, public and private actors in the multiple social sectors also would have to rely on information sharing among them in order that they would also be capable of responding efficiently and robustly to the energy problems that originate in the processes of energy governance at the regional level.

Speed of Technological Change and Policy Adoption

Two key observations in the comparison of both energy regions were the pace at which energy technologies change, and the timeous nature of policy processes that sought to guide and direct these energy technology transitions in the respective energy regions. The power sector in particular highlighted this phenomenon especially with the inclusion of smart meters, distributed generation done mainly through self-generation and feed-ins into the centralised grid as well as energy efficiency technologies in residential energy systems among others.

However, this is not limited only to occurrences in the power sector but is also unfolding in the petroleum sector with technological advancement in the metering of oil and gas pipelines and other distribution networks. The challenge here has been the timeliness of policy to catch up to these technological advancements and guide the transition in the energy regions.

Chapter 6

West African Regional Energy Governance: Potential and Obstacles

6.1 Introduction

The essence of the comparison undertaken in Chapter 5 has laid out from two globally recognised regional perspectives the intricate dimensions and dynamics at play in a functioning energy region, where all or majority of the aspects at play relating to regional energy governance has been considered. An institutional analysis of energy regionalism in West Africa (ECOWAS) and Europe (EU) has been conducted to build on the understanding of the evolutionary nature of regional energy governance over specific periods of time.

Moving forward in this chapter, I consider in the light of the insight gained from this comparative regional analysis, which used the CIS framework, to discuss what the nature of the opportunities and constrains integral in energy regions imply for the development of a more robust, resilient, sustainable and effective energy regionalism in West Africa. An energy regionalism that provides abundant and affordable energy through the means of an efficient regional energy governance process.

West Africa's progressive path towards the provision of abundant energy through the means of energy access and supply sufficiency in its regional energy economy is a matter of interest for the citizens, local communities, businesses, national governments, their international economic partners and regional institutions. This is because of concerns arising from the growing energy access deficit in the region, which is being outpaced by increasing energy demand due to a rapid increase in the region's demography and earning power evidenced through a rapidly growing middle class, under-utilisation of regional energy resources, partial misdirection of national energy policies and global concerns relating to climate change.

The polycentric manner in which the regional energy sector is governed, is one of the foremost elements that will determine the essential qualities and pace for the resolution of this energy access conundrum. Other elements include political determinants, social dynamics, the structure of the regional economy and nature of the financing options available, legal and regulatory systems, technological innovation and bi-regional energy partnerships (here I will place emphasis on the EU).

The scale and significance of the regional energy challenge in West Africa has been clearly recognised by ECOWAS' top leaders who are totally committed to this agenda. Ellen Johnson-Sirleaf, the first female chair of the body between 2016 and 2017, stressed at the launch of the Cote d'Ivoire, Liberia, Sierra Leone and Guinea (CLSG) power interconnection (a priority component of the regional power pool, WAPP) stressed,

> "As ECOWAS proceeds for transformation of our economies, power has been identified as one of our major constraints. Power supports education, security, health, industry, and the comfort of life. The project will enable our nations move at a faster pace in the achievement of our Sustainable Development Goals. We, the Heads of state … commit our full support to its success …".[1023]

Since 1982, ECOWAS leadership has put in place a number of mechanisms to improve both energy access and energy intensity while reducing carbon emissions even though the region is not a net contributor of emissions. Regardless of the minimal success gained from these policies that would ensure energy abundance, the likelihood that the region can sustain or accelerate the pace of ECOWAS' energy self-sufficiency while transitioning in terms of systems towards a low-carbon economy is very ambitious unless there is a quickening in the pace of transformation in the institutions of regional energy governance.

The word 'institution' in this context has been applied here with respect to the Bloomington School of Political Economy and historical institutionalism to mean the rules, norms, and strategies that structure interactions between actors so that there is less uncertainty in these interactions. These institutions engage in normative behaviour by making choices based on values that would characterise the wellbeing of society, the institutional setting (that provides political, economic and social outcomes among others), as well as the specific rules (either in-use or in-form) which govern actor interactions with the pre-existing factors in the policy setting also known as the network of focal action situations.

1023 Samuel Mikenga, 'Liberian President Sirleaf Launches AfDB-Funded Power Grid Project to Supply Electricity to Mano River Union Nations', 2017 <https://www.afdb.org/en/news-and-events/liberian-president-sirleaf-launches-afdb-funded-power-grid-project-to-supply-electricity-to-mano-river-union-nations-17140> [accessed 5 July 2018].

Almost all of the prevailing attributes of energy institutions at all governance scales (including at the region-wide scale) and the overarching regional institutional setting have their roots in West African colonial energy history as well as in the early decades of its post-independence era. The attributes that the ECOWAS energy region exhibits reveals its polycentric nature in the governance of regional energy. Nevertheless, it also assists in the exploration of the implications of potentials and obstacles that underpin the institutional dimensions at play in West African regional energy governance. The institutional dimensions consist of political, social, economic, legal, innovation and bi-regional partnerships. These would be discussed in the ensuing paragraphs.

6.2 Polycentric Nature of Regional Energy in West Africa

As a prelude to the discussions on regional energy policy implications that affect ECOWAS energy regionalism. I consider the polycentric attributes inherent in the West African region's energy system and its potential in further shaping regional energy governance as well as its constraints.

Primarily, the main actor providing governance in the energy sector in the region are national governments. Their form of energy governance presumes that jurisdictions need to be partitioned, mutually exclusive, and non-overlapping while ensuring a hierarchy that is ordered rationally to consolidate authority and exercise power through centralised decision-making.[1024] By implication, one of the tacit assumptions to be made in structuring energy governance is that a dichotomy should be present between public, private and common goods and also between governments, markets and commons as respective forms of organising regional energy.[1025]

1024 Chris Skelcher, 'Jurisdictional Integrity, Polycentrism, and the Design of Democratic Governance', *Governance*, 18.1 (2005), 89–110 <https://doi.org/10.1111/j.1468-0491.2004.00267.x>.

1025 Richard E. Wagner, 'Self-Governance, Polycentrism, and Federalism: Recurring Themes in Vincent Ostrom's Scholarly Oeuvre', *Journal of Economic Behavior and Organization*, 57.2 (2005), 173–88 <https://doi.org/10.1016/j.jebo.2004.06.015>; Roberta Herzberg, 'Commentary on Richard Wagner's "Self-Governance, Polycentrism, and Federalism: Recurring Themes in Vincent Ostrom's Scholarly Oeuvre"', *Journal of Economic Behavior and Organization*, 57.2 (2005), 189–97 <https://doi.org/10.1016/j.jebo.2004.06.016>.

Though most of the literature continues to highlight mainly what these national governments and businesses do, in recent decades scholars are focusing more on governance outside of formal state structures and looking more at scales ranging from communities, regions and intergovernmental organisations.[1026] This then draws the attention of this research to focus on how the West African energy region encapsulates the spread of governing scales based on geography (local, sub-national, national and regional) and across the respective social sectors (public, private, and commons) alongside the often overlapping institutional mandates in the regional energy space. This variable, trans-scalar, trans-sectoral mode of energy governance typifies the polycentricity of energy regionalism in West Africa.

The West African energy sector exhibits polycentrism or polycentric approaches to energy governance. Polycentrism refers to when citizens organize themselves in terms of governance in multiple authorities at many scales simultaneously.[1027] The notion of polycentric regional energy governance refers to how people and institutions make and enforce energy decisions concerning various aspects of energy consumption (electricity supply, petroleum, household and commercial energy etc.) when national jurisdictions and other governance scales overlap at the region-wide level.

Polycentric attributes of regional energy governance involve (1) multiple and overlapping governance scales (local, provincial, national and regional) at the geographical level. Which (2) choose to act by using unique mechanisms (centralised command and control regulations, decentralised and local policies, local communes and self-governance approaches, and the free market). (3) While taking account of the various actors (supranational and intergovernmental institutions, government institutions, corporate and business firms, civil society, communities and communes, individuals and households). Through processes of cooperation, competition, conflict and conflict resolution. These attributes denote the defining characteristics of polycentrism based on Vincent Ostrom et al.[1028] Later on while reflecting on the 1961 seminal paper, Vincent Ostrom wrote:

As formulated by [V. Ostrom et al. (1961)], a polycentric political system would be composed of: (1) many autonomous units formally independent

1026 Benjamin K Sovacool, 'An International Comparison of Four Polycentric Approaches to Climate and Energy Governance', *Energy Policy*, 39.6 (2011), 3832–44 <https://doi.org/10.1016/j.enpol.2011.04.014>.

1027 Elinor Ostrom, 'Polycentric Systems for Coping with Collective Action and Global Environmental Change'; Ostrom, Tiebout, and Warren.

1028 Ostrom, Tiebout, and Warren.

of one another, (2) choosing to act in ways that take account of others, (3) through processes of cooperation, competition, conflict, and conflict resolution.[1029]

The justification for a polycentric regional energy governance approach, reveal that some forms of governance such as top-down centralized control, bottom-up decentralized control, and even free market privatization have unavoidable weaknesses. On the other hand, regional energy governance involving polycentric approaches is not without challenges.[1030]

First, I will deal with the two main attributes inherent in regional energy governance in West Africa before looking at the merits and demerits. To begin with, polycentric attributes of West Africa's (ECOWAS) energy system imply sharing power between multiple and overlapping scales of governance in a nested or polycentric manner. This involves numerous authorities at country level and region-wide level as well as overlapping jurisdictions within these spaces in the confines of the energy region. This reflects the phenomenon described by Andersson and Ostrom regarding multiplicity of authorities and overlapping jurisdictions.[1031]

In turn, the region's energy system has sought to create polycentric institutions that are closely related to the Type II organisations described by Hooghe and Marks[1032], as being functionally defined and not geographically fixed bodies with changeable boundaries and are established to operate at whatever scale deemed best suited to deliver a particular energy service. A typical example in this regard are the trans-scalar and trans-sectoral functions undertaken by regional energy institutions, like WAPP and ECREEE in particular, in the many governance scales in the ECOWAS energy region. They are functionally focused on power generation, renewable energy and energy efficiency across all the constitutive member states.

Another example is WAGPA, whose work is to serve as the regulatory arm concerned with the governance of the regional gas pipeline that transmits gas currently to the four operational countries. These regional energy institutions among other specialised ones have their own scales of governance that serve as policymaking centres where decisions are made relating to their particular energy resource type. These bodies as well have

1029 Vincent Ostrom, *The Meaning of American Federalism* (San Francisco: Institute of Contemporary Studies Press, 1991), p. 225.

1030 Benjamin K Sovacool.

1031 Andersson and Ostrom.

1032 Hooghe and Marks, 'Unraveling the Central States, but How? Types of Multi-Level Governance'.

their domains of decision-making overlapping at multiple scales or simply put their jurisdictions overlap. This occurs when they share certain areas of responsibility literally demonstrating polycentricism.[1033]

To give an instance, a critical function of overlap is seen when energy information flow is disseminated among the specialised regional energy institutions and their respective governance scales. In that, with respect to the energy sectors across ECOWAS, which is a trans-sectoral social setting (public-private partnership, private, public or commons), regional energy institutions operating in this networked space, are enabled to learn based on information flow. This is in spite of whether these institutions are thriving. It literally creates feedback loops for information flow on the governance of that energy resource in the energy region.

Regarding the number of multiple scales inherent in the various institutions, it will be dependent on the contextual factors relating to the energy resource in question and at which level of operation. Again, a need to achieve balance and representation in making decisions is more beneficial than the number of decision-making domains present within a scale of governance.[1034]

As a final point, these multiple and overlapping scales of polycentric regional energy governance reflect a degree of autonomy and independence. This implies that the decision-making domain centres that make up the various regional energy institutions act on their own behalf, with limited or no centralised coordination.[1035] This degree of autonomy emphasise the uncertain and context-specific nature of the needed or appropriate degree of autonomy and independence.[1036] Since institutional energy analysis at the energy region is concerned most with rules-in-use rather than rules-in-form, de facto rather than formal autonomy and independence.[1037]

The West African energy setting reflects this when it is working to achieve regional energy goals. Certain efforts at country level in the energy sector such as rural electrification is devolved to local governance organi-

---

1033 Michael D. McGinnis and Elinor Ostrom, 'Public Administration and the Disciplines Reflections on Vincent Ostrom, Public Administration, and Polycentricity', *Public Administration Review*, 72.1 (2011), 15–25 <https://doi.org/10.111/j.1540-6210.2011.02488.x>.

1034 Carlisle and Gruby.

1035 See: Ostrom, Tiebout, and Warren.

1036 Carlisle and Gruby.

1037 Graham R Marshall, 'Polycentricity and Adaptive Governance', *Working Paper Presented at the 15th Biannual Inter- National Conference of the International Association for the Study of the Commons*, 2015, 1–19.

sations/associations or in some cases sub-national authorities through the formation of local energy communities. In a way, control over outcomes is exerted at the country level using certain means such as financial incentives, compliance requirements and the imposition of burdensome reporting to realise region-wide energy objectives.[1038]

The second attribute implying a polycentric approach in regional energy governance in West Africa emanates from merging the second and third prongs of Vincent Ostrom's[1039] formulation. That is, choosing to act in ways that use mechanisms which take account of other actors through the processes of cooperation, competition, conflict and conflict resolution. This typifies an assemblage of scales of governance operating with a certain degree of autonomy and independence, while at the same time being capable of functioning as a coherent system.[1040]

These governance scales in the regional energy space while implementing fashioned out mechanisms, even though they are formally independent or semi-autonomous of one another, base their decisions partly on the actions and inactions of the other sectors of the regional energy ecosystem. This is due to the fact that, their decision-making processes takes account of each other in the entire energy ecosystem as well as other supporting actors present in the energy ecosystem at the regional level. These are the actors who engage in the interactive processes of cooperation, competition, conflict and conflict resolution that are bound to occur.[1041]

These processes can lead to self-organising possibilities such as the creation of local energy communities. An example is the cooperative processes that are leading to numerous local energy communities in Liberia.[1042] Self-organising governance systems are more capable to persist and adapt without requiring central or external planning or control.[1043] This is

1038 Rebecca L. Gruby and Xavier Basurto, 'Multi-Level Governance for Large Marine Commons: Politics and Polycentricity in Palau's Protected Area Network', *Environmental Science and Policy*, 36 (2013), 48–60 <https://doi.org/10.1016/j.envsci.2013.08.001>; Marshall.

1039 Vincent Ostrom, *The Meaning of American Federalism*.

1040 Carlisle and Gruby.

1041 Ostrom, Tiebout, and Warren.

1042 NRECA International, 'Partnerships Bring Power to Liberia', 2018 <http://www.nrecainternational.coop/where-we-work/liberia/> [accessed 10 July 2018].

1043 See: Louis Lebel and others, 'Governance and the Capacity to Manage Resilience in Regional Social-Ecological Systems', *Ecology and Society*, 11.1 (2006) <https://doi.org/10.5751/ES-01606-110119>.

evidenced once again in the self-organised local energy communities of Liberia.

Reflecting further on the four proclivities fundamental to this second attribute as identified by Vincent Ostrom[1044] namely cooperation, competition, conflict and conflict resolution, and the way it relates to the West African energy governance system. It is understood that through cooperative processes voluntary collective action take place that includes other inclinations such as collaboration and contractual undertakings. With respect to the cooperative tendency, however, they could enhance their collective capacity or subcontract functions to more capable scales of governance or associate actors.[1045]

Since cooperation is a vital ingredient to all human activity. In this specific case of the functioning of an energy region, governance scales perhaps would be unable independently to provide certain energy goods and services as well as address a number of critical energy issues (such as the climate related ones). This idea supports the claim put forward by Vincent Ostrom et al.[1046] that polycentric governance systems with reference to the West African energy governance system, may be capable of performing equally or better than monocentric systems.

The notion advanced in this argument is premised on the fact that an institution which provides a public good or service like energy services to consumers need not be the same institution that produces it, especially when outsourcing it to another body could make it more efficient. The distinction between production and provision elucidates the cooperative tendency better when looking at it from the commons perspective. In the context of the energy commons as is related to the West African energy region, a scale of governance such as WAPP in situations where it lacks the capability to produce energy information that relates to the share of renewable energy in the energy mix. In order to make effective decisions towards its production and distribution can outsource this knowledge or data gathering to a more capable knowledge producer in this area, such as ECREEE.

As typified by McGinnis, "polycentricity allows considerable mixing and matching of consumption, provision, and production units operating

1044 Ostrom, Tiebout, and Warren.
1045 Carlisle and Gruby.
1046 Ostrom, Tiebout, and Warren.

at different scales of aggregation"[1047] The competitive tendency can be reflected through a competition of ideas and methods employed by the various scales of governance. This ideological and methodological competition may serve as a driver for successful self-organisation, particularly in relation to the functioning of a polycentric energy region.[1048]

In West Africa, competition is enabling member states to better address emerging and age-old challenges such as energy access deficits in rural, peri-urban and urban areas. This is in pursuance by these member states to meet their respective energy and climate goals without a centralised direction from ECOWAS energy institutions. It is also important to note that these conditions that foster competition emerge when the country level governance scales in the ECOWAS energy region have access to information about each other's energy objectives and are acquainted with the effects that a successful performance would contribute to overall regional energy goals.

Aside the benefit of this competitive tendency leading to self-organisation, the opposite end of this tendency occurs when it is extreme and intense over distributional issues that ultimately undermine cooperation and impede the governance scales of the energy region's capability for self-organisation.[1049] In order to resolve this constrain, it is important to design the energy institutions in a way to manage or minimise competition over resources while suggesting the need for effective conflict-resolution mechanisms.[1050]

Conflict is nearly inevitable when decisions that pertain to resource allocation and use are being made.[1051] In a situation, relating to the distribution of regional energy resources it is not any different. When conflict is managed properly, it bears fruits of learning, change and growth so long as these conflicts do not escalate and render the energy governance

1047 Michael D. McGinnis, 'Introduction', in *Polycentricity and Local Public Economies: Readings from the Workshop in Political Theory and Policy Analysis*, ed. by Michael D. McGinnis (Ann Arbor, MI: The University of Michigan Press, 1999), pp. 1–27 (p. 4).

1048 Imperial; Folke, Hahn, and others.

1049 Amy R. Poteete and Elinor Ostrom, 'Heterogeneity, Group Size and Collective Action: The Role of Institutions in Forest Management', *Development and Change*, 35.3 (2004), 435–461.

1050 Carlisle and Gruby.

1051 Thomas Dietz, Elinor Ostrom, and Paul C. Stern, 'The Struggle to Govern the Commons', *SCIENCE*, 2003, 1907–12 <https://doi.org/10.1007/978-0-387-73412-5_40>.

in the energy region dysfunctional. The beneficial aspects of measured conflict happen when different interests, philosophies, and perspectives are expressed in the process of deliberation and conflict resolution.[1052]

On the other hand, when the conflicts are too divergent and intractable, they could stymie self-organisation. Thus, the ability to maintain conflict resolution processes and advance such a mechanism in the larger scheme of governance processes could be an important reason for designing energy resource governance institutions as it pertains to the various energy resources in the region bearing in mind trans-sectoral approaches.[1053]

I now turn to the potential disadvantages and advantages inherent in the attributes that pertain to the polycentric nature of energy regionalism in West Africa. In terms of disadvantages as stated by Sovacool,[1054] an amalgam of local, national and international laws and standards in the same spatial context may trigger confusion leading to redundancies and inefficiencies. The divergence of rules can lead to the risk of institutional failure and resource inefficiencies on account of their redundancy. This redundancy of regulation results in confusion in the minds of actors trying to figure out what norms and laws are applicable to them.

Another challenge involved when an energy region exhibits a polycentric approach to energy governance is the time-consuming nature required for policy resolution because parties with imminent concerns could seek redress from the other actors in a polycentric energy governance ecosystem. In some other cases, polycentric energy regions can face functional and systemic challenges such as the difficulty in coordinating fragmented energy networks and agencies that lack centralised points of reference.[1055]

Lastly, to focus on another challenge that needs to be mitigated in the West African polycentric energy space is the presence of complex and ever-changing mechanisms and arrangements that can result in dysfunction and discordance. As mused by Michael D. McGinnis,

"sharing of responsibilities naturally generates contestation, so the system must include mechanisms through which disputes over the consequences of collective decisions can be resolved. It is an extremely complex

1052 Dietz, Ostrom, and Stern.
1053 Dietz, Ostrom, and Stern.
1054 Benjamin K Sovacool.
1055 Julia Black, 'Constructing and Contesting Legitimacy and Accountability in Polycentric Regulatory Regimes', *Regulation & Governance*, 2.2 (2008), 137–64 <https://doi.org/10.1111/j.1748-5991.2008.00034.x>.

system. No single planner would ever design such a mess, nor can any external force impose such complexity on an unsuspecting community."[1056]

This implies that finding the most favourable equilibrium is a major challenge to contend with, since polycentric approaches result in endless processes of renegotiation where new forms of governance emerge and old ones disappear. On top of that, in the process of setting and negotiating new rules on an ad hoc basis, polycentric institutions may find their results and outcomes being contested on the grounds of legitimacy and accountability.[1057]

In spite of these constrains, a polycentric approach of regional energy governance in West Africa could promote adaptive capacity, institutional fit and mitigate the risk of institutional failure of resource losses by ensuring redundancy.[1058] Adaptive capacity is the ability to adapt to actual or anticipated social, ecological and technical change better than more centralised forms of regional energy governance.[1059] This ability includes the design of new institutions that allow for adaptation.[1060]

This adaptive capacity encourages plurality and institutional diversity. That is, a diversity of rules, norms and strategies necessarily emanating from a multiplicity of governance scales or policy making units. Although the presence of the diverse set of semiautonomous governance actors operating in the regional energy space serve as a logical outcome, there is nothing inherent in the polycentric approach that bars these governance units from coalescing around a common policy or approach.[1061]

1056 Michael D. McGinnis, 'Beyond Individualism and Spontaneity: Comments on Peter Boettke and Christopher Coyne', *Journal of Economic Behavior and Organization*, 57.2 (2005), 167–72 <https://doi.org/10.1016/j.jebo.2004.06.014 >.p.168

1057 Skelcher.

1058 Carlisle and Gruby.

1059 R. Patrick Bixler, 'From Community Forest Management to Polycentric Governance: Assessing Evidence from the Bottom Up', *Society & Natural Resources*, 27.2 (2014), 155–69 <https://doi.org/10.1080/08941920.2013.840021>; Marshall; Claudia Pahl-Wostl, 'A Conceptual Framework for Analysing Adaptive Capacity and Multi-Level Learning Processes in Resource Governance Regimes', *Global Environmental Change*, 19.3 (2009), 354–65 <https://doi.org/10.1016/j.gloenvcha.2009.06.001>; Carlisle and Gruby.

1060 Bixler; da Silveira and Richards; Dietz, Ostrom, and Stern; Galaz and others; Pahl-Wostl; Pahl-Wostl and Knieper; Benjamin K Sovacool.

1061 Carlisle and Gruby.

Another enabling condition for this ability to adapt is based on the existence of incentives that boosts productive activity.[1062] The presence of multiple governance actors promises increases in production when they work effectively together in the ecosystem such as in an energy region. This contributes to multiple regulators at numerous energy governance scales. The multiplicity of regulators means that different officials with distinct perspectives interrogate a challenge together bringing to bear diverse perspectives. This produces a broader variety of potential solutions and facilitates experimentation. With multiple interventions undertaken within the regional energy system, opportunities can be created to discuss results and observe experiences, and it may lead to reinforcing this adaptive capacity of the scales of governance in the regional energy system to tackle the energy challenges that arise.[1063]

The other incentive created is the preventative measure. This ensures that socio-energy problems like the lack of rural electrification and energy poverty in peri-urban or rural areas are dealt with using a polycentric approach. For instance, on the occasion where one level of government, industry, or civil society defaults or fails in dealing with a problem, other scales of governance remain available to address the task.[1064]

Another issue is in relation to the institutional fit of agencies in the West African polycentric energy region. Institutional fit in this regard refers to the match or congruence between an institution and the problem or issues that needs to be addressed.[1065] Regional energy bodies in West Africa that exhibit institutional fit may be more robust and effective in accomplishing desired regional energy outcomes as suggested by Folke et al[1066]. In their description of this phenomenon in the case of natural resource systems, the special characteristic exhibited by the polycentric approach is based largely on the fact that they display different levels of political jurisdiction. The different levels of political jurisdiction (local, subnational, national and regional) correspond to multiple spatial levels of

---

1062 Carlisle and Gruby.

1063 William Blomquist, 'Multi-Level Governance and Natural Resource Management: The Challenges of Complexity, Diversity, and Uncertainty', in *Institutions and Sustainability*, ed. by M. Beckmann, V., Padmanabhan (New York: Springer, 2009), pp. 109–126.

1064 Andersson and Ostrom.

1065 See: Lebel and others.

1066 Carl Folke, Lowell Pritchard, and others, 'The Problem of Fit between Ecosystems and Institutions: Ten Years Later', *Ecology and Society*, 12.1 (2007) <https://doi.org/10.5751/ES-02064-120130>.

a resource governance system in this case, the supranational or transnational energy system.

This emphasises that cross-jurisdictional decision-making in a polycentric energy governance system is essentially crucial in dealing with challenges that cascade across levels of governance or jurisdictions.[1067] Additionally, these levels of jurisdiction are coterminous with the boundaries of the problems that are under consideration.[1068]

The final advantage addressed here is that a polycentric West African energy governance system would mitigate the risk of institutional failure and energy resource losses because of redundancy.[1069] Here redundancy occurs when there is a duplication of functions by governance actors within a given sector in the regional energy policy area. It also occurs when there is an existence of diverse institutions that govern a particular energy sector across the energy region.[1070]

Furthermore, this improves accountability, autonomy and participation.[1071] Multiple levels of governance scales in an energy region go on further to mitigate market and regulatory capture by parochial interests than when it is one homogeneous macro governance scale. Additionally, in an energy region like that of West Africa, polycentrism in regional energy governance could lead to a greater sense of trust, legitimacy and a higher level of participation. Since these multiple scales of energy governance in the ECOWAS energy region are closely situated to geographical communities and social sectors, they are more responsive to local energy needs.

6.3 Political Implications of Regional Energy Policy

Geopolitically, there are internal and external implications on regional energy policy in West Africa that affect the region's energy conundrum ad-

1067 Lebel and others.

1068 Folke, Pritchard, and others.

1069 Elinor Ostrom, 'Coping With Tragedies of the Commons'; Carlisle and Gruby.

1070 See: Bobbi Low and others, 'Redundancy and Diversity: Do They Influence Optimal Management?', in *Navigating Social-Ecological Systems: Building Resilience for Complexity and Change*, ed. by Fikret Berkes, Johan Colding, and Carl Folke (Cambridge, UK: Cambridge University Press, 2003), pp. 83–111.

1071 See: Michael D. McGinnis, 'Costs and Challenges of Polycentric Governance', *Workshop on Analyzing Problems of Polycentric Governance in the Growing EU*, 2005, 27 <http://www.indiana.edu/~workshop/papers/mcginnis_berlin.pdf>.

versely. But it also offers opportunities to transform the energy regionalism process in the region. A couple of these external and internal events and their political implications on the ECOWAS energy region will be laid out here in this discussion.

First, let us look at how the external impact of the shale revolution has political implications on the ECOWAS energy region. Shale oil and gas production in the United States has undergone expansive growth literally shifting the balance of power in energy exports. In that, prior to the US shale boom West African oil exports to the USA was substantially huge. The impact of the shale revolution on the West African petroleum sector calls for a new inward-looking approach in terms of intra-West African oil trade. This could be done through competitive energy pricing and long-term energy contracts that would secure supplies in the region. Since the shale trend has come to stay, which has made the USA energy independent and the largest oil producer and net energy exporter by 2022[1072], there would be far-reaching implications for West Africa's energy sector, regional economy and energy governance.

The other global occurrence happening in the petroleum sector is the major influence China has in this space. China's natural gas imports is game-changing the global trend in the sector. The China-effect on the natural gas sector and its implications for West Africa is the increasing demand at highly competitive prices from China and other countries and regions such as Japan, Korea and the European Union on the nascent natural gas and LNG industry in the region. This has disadvantageous effects on energy customers in the ECOWAS energy region who cannot compete with these powerful external energy competitors.

Minimising this adverse competitive effect would require the setting up of bilateral and multilateral regional agreements between producer countries (such as Nigeria, Ghana and Cote d'Ivoire) and buyer countries in the ECOWAS region to secure supplies on preferential terms over their external competitors. This would enhance the transformation of the ECOWAS energy region to become a robust and solid regional energy market that is beneficial to the energy security agenda of ECOWAS and its member states.

1072 U.S. Energy Information Administration (EIA), 'The United States Is Projected to Become a Net Energy Exporter in Most AEO2018 Cases', *Today in Energy* , 2018 <https://www.eia.gov/todayinenergy/detail.php?id=34912> [accessed 10 July 2018].

A constrain with far reaching implications on energy policy in West Africa has to do with the discrepancies that exists in relation to balancing the political interests between national governments and their citizens regarding their national energy sectors.[1073] This disconnect between the interests of some national governments in petroleum producing states and the interests of their respective populations is a major obstacle in increasing petroleum consumption in West Africa.

Despite the fact that the average citizen has a preference to use domestic oil or consume gas, national political elites are more interested in selling these energy resources to the highest external bidder. This is with the aim to maximise revenue and increase financial benefits to the detriment of the citizens domestic energy consumption. The citizenry due to lack of transparency and accountability in international energy deals have limited means to challenge this elite preference and ask for a redistribution of resource revenue.

As noted by Yates[1074], rents obtained from extractives enable leaders to avoid accountability because they are not reliant on national tax revenues. It prevents them from being forthcoming in the delivery of social services such as the provision of energy access and the like. Again, there is minimal incentive for political leaders of rentier states to maintain a national power grid or to construct an oil refining infrastructure due to the lack of any political consequences. This has played a major role in the prevailing energy conundrum in the ECOWAS energy region.

In further consideration of this phenomenon, putting subsides on domestic petroleum consumption is also unappealing since it reduces the revenue that could be accrued through foreign energy resource trade. Consequently, West African citizens located in petroleum-endowed countries like Nigeria are currently no more energy-secure than the populations of countries that lack oil and natural gas reserves.[1075] The continuation of this political behaviour, if not checked, would furthermore prioritise the energy interests of external energy actors towards their maximising of West African energy over that of domestic energy interests. This would disadvantage domestic consumers in the region from benefiting from their own energy resources while external energy consumers rather gain. Politically,

1073 Carbonnier, p. 55.

1074 Douglas A. Yates, *The Rentier State in Africa: Oil Rent Dependency and Neocolonialism in the Republic of Gabon* (Trenton, NJ: Africa World Press, 1996).

1075 International Energy Agency, *World Energy Outlook 2008* (Paris: International Energy Agency, 2008).

this process if it is not discontinued will disempower citizens in the West African energy policy space.

Inherently the provision of energy is connected to politics as implied above. The supply of energy is such a large-scale endeavour which impacts masses of people and their well-being. This association is evidenced in the relationship between electoral politics and the provision of energy. Presently in West Africa, citizens are growing increasingly discontented of being in the dark that is, lacking reliable supply of electricity. This has prompted a growing mantra which is influencing political behaviour among citizens that relates to the provision of energy services and it can be summarised as – "if you want to stay in power then give power"[1076], meaning the staying power of an incumbent government is based on its ability to provide energy access.

It may be that going forward elections are going to be based on the political class' ability to make power and energy available to citizens for their consumption. This would require increased political will on the part of political actors such as elected officials, public servants, political parties among others to deliver and improve energy services to the populace at the local, sub-national, national and regional levels.

One more phenomenon with political implications is the proliferation of the pay-as-you-go (PAYG) renewable energy systems as well as other decentralised energy systems. These systems are enabling onsite generation, particularly at the point of use, for individual energy consumers and in some cases, allow for power feed-in back into the centralised grid for onward transmission. A typical example are the energy communities situated in Liberia which sometimes feed-in power back into the central grid.[1077] This assists these local prosumers to benefit from the excess generation which enables the possibility of shifting energy demand and making available excess energy supplies.

This phenomenon inherently reveals a new power dynamic in the energy sector where these consumers/prosumers are literally capable of controlling their own energy access, availability and consumption at a price convenient for them. The key technologies that are democratising energy access equip prosumers and consumers who produce their own energy to

---

1076 A statement attributable to Akinwumi Ayodeji Adesina, President, African Development Bank (AfDB) at the World Economic Forum 2017 at Davos. See at: World Economic Forum, 'Powering Africa', *Davos 2017*, 2017 <https://www.youtube.com/watch?v=W2fnEYtW-ig> [accessed 10 July 2018].

1077 NRECA International.

become powerful. Thereby having an overall contributory impact on the energy aspects of a nation's political economy.

Politically, the deepening of regional integration implies a potential for stronger regional collective action in the area of energy, that is, it improves energy regionalism. In looking across borders and working with neighbours in order to produce energy, such as jointly generating electricity for productive purposes, requires intense political commitment on the part of the region's leaders towards energy regionalism.

The role of energy in West African regionalism is being prioritised and has also become an exciting and vibrant topical regional issue. In the past, there have been announcements of significant energy investment in the areas of gas-to-power, renewable energy, coal power and even nuclear power in the West African energy region. All this has the intent of collectivising around energy through these energy projects which are mainly regional in nature to help solve the numerous energy challenges in the region.

These regional energy projects accounts for substantial amounts of capital investments that one country cannot pay for, but through the potential that regional integration offers, partnering countries in the energy region can collectively foot the bill for these mega energy projects in the region. Moreover, unlocking this multilateral, multinational mega projects still remain a challenge. Some of these regional energy projects have been conceptualised for many decades and still remain in the planning stage and several others have been stalled for many years on account of numerous financial reasons.

The key obstacles to these stalled regional energy projects that remain on the books include these public policy processes but is not limited to the development of project feasibility, demonstration of project bankability, reassessment of an already approved project by financiers as well as environmental activism that deals with climate change concerns. However, some of the critical success factors already demonstrated include vision, leadership, boldness and commitments on the part of member states and ECOWAS energy institutions in this regard. Increasingly, ECOWAS is playing an influential policymaking role as it shapes the development of energy policies in member states. In addition, ECOWAS as an energy region is becoming more assertive in the regulatory space as it becomes increasingly interdependent energy-wise through regional power interconnections and cross-border energy trade via other critical energy infrastructure.

Finally, implications on strategic energy governance choices made at the ECOWAS level and country level aims at the utilisation of all the available energy resources without reserve in the West African region. They make this consideration devoid of the external political pressures or diplomatic influences that seek to dictate specific terms and preferences towards particular energy resources. This new position is borne out of the failure for so long on being strategic on the question of the reduction of the energy access gap which has resulted in precarious conditions for citizens who have been lacking dignified energy access for so long. This goes a long way to stress the common good principle with respect to energy politics in the regional energy policy process in the West African energy region.

6.4 Social Implications of Regional Energy Policy

Good regional energy policy implies social transformation and advancement where ever it is being applied. Simply put energy has shaped West African contemporary society. Structural energy shifts have always been historically rapid or socially pervasive[1078] as in the case of West Africa. Hence, this makes it crucial to reconfigure regional energy policy as a socio-energy design that requires new strategies for incorporating the human and social dimensions of socio-energy systems into region-wide and country level processes of energy design, planning, and policy-making.[1079]

By so doing, it would require an understanding of the order of the magnitude of the energy conundrum and its impact on any society like that of the West African society. In addition to that, a deep comprehension of the manner in which regional actors' function in the regional energy systems at the various multi-tiered levels particularly the overlapping social sectors (such as public, private, public-private combinations and commons) would enable a viable social benefit for the process of energy policymaking.

The social constrains that pertain to regional energy infrastructures have huge ramifications for societies and livelihoods within the scope of these projects. In order for such regional energy infrastructure projects to be successful, local actors such as communities, households, NGOs among others, must be actively and meaningfully involved in discussions about

1078 IPCC, *Renewable Energy Sources and Climate Change Mitigation: Special Report of the Intergovernmental Panel on Climate Change.* : (Cambridge, UK: Cambridge University Press, 2012).

1079 Clark A. Miller, Jennifer Richter, and Jason O'Leary, 'Socio-Energy Systems Design: A Policy Framework for Energy Transitions', *Energy Research & Social Science*, 6 (2015), 29–40 <https://doi.org/10.1016/j.erss.2014.11.004>.

the nature of these projects with respect to the location, scale and direction of such. These infrastructure projects, which include natural gas pipelines, power grid interconnections and the like, are cross-border and traverse a number of jurisdictions in an energy region. In some parts of West Africa, such as Nigeria, it has been observed that the absence of fruitful public engagements has resulted in the vandalism of critical energy infrastructure such as pipelines and oil storage facilities in places like the Niger Delta.

There is no clear complaints mechanism between communities and energy companies and even the governments that can guide these essential public interactions before and after an energy project has been initiated at the country or regional levels. And even when there is a complaints mechanism it has not been followed to the letter. In cases where there are dispute resolution mechanisms in place between contracting companies and states it does not factor in effective relations with local communities.

To give an example, in the case of cross-border, long-distance gas pipelines that traverse a couple of jurisdictions in the region. They pass through sensitive environmental areas such as farms and fishing areas that are affected both in terms of the livelihoods of local people, communities and local ecosystems. Communities along the reach of such pipeline corridors may be eligible for transit fees, compensations and special rights, or more seriously, may have to be temporarily relocated or permanently resettled if the pipeline goes through their communities.

Corporate mechanisms such as "free prior and informed consent" (a form of community consultation) and "grievance mechanisms" (a way for community members to engage in dialogue with the project sponsor to quickly resolve concerns and injuries) could be lacking. This is in addition to any type of transparency and accountability problems caused by infringements to international human rights standards in the energy region.[1080]

Another social implication on the regional energy sector is the manner in which societal concerns are addressed and how social mobilisation and resistance against certain energy installations are dealt with particularly at the national level. This phenomenon is characterised by the militarisation of energy installations in host local communities revealing the 'us versus them' attitude that defines certain aspects of contested spaces in the regional energy setting. This mostly has to do with the relationships between companies, the state and local communities.

1080 Benjamin K. Sovacool, p. 23-64.

To exemplify this, I again use perspectives from Nigeria's Delta region where some oil and gas companies, such as Shell Nigeria Plc, Total, Eni, Exxon Mobil, and Chevron, employ private security firms (and sometimes with the aid of the Nigerian military) to protect their operations and suppress social dissent. The total neglect and negligence on the part of the Nigerian government and International Oil Companies (IOCs), which are mostly Western companies operating in the area, is a strong repudiation of the social responsibilities of these internal and external actors to the host communities.

This strong repudiation of social responsibilities is manifested in the inequities that prevail in the redistribution of petroleum-generated wealth and its effects on the provision of social amenities and other opportunities for local citizenry. It has also contributed to the deepening of community resentment that has proven to be a perfect recipe for social instability in the West African region especially with reference to acts of maritime criminality and piracy, religious extremism and social unrest in the Gulf of Guinea, Sahel region and petroleum rich communities. This dissatisfaction has given rise to a number of anti-extractive movements and community-based organisations such as the Movement for the Emancipation of the Niger-Delta (MEND) and the Movement for the Survival of the Ogoni People (MOSOP) whose agitation links their goals and interests to long-standing political and social grievances over sovereignty, land rights, climate, water, and environmental justice.[1081]

Another social implication for regional energy policy depends largely on the understanding of the social outcomes that flow from energy policy choices and technology arrangements. Novel methodologies will need to be developed at the regional level, which focus attention on identifying, mapping, and measuring significant social outcomes from the energy choices that are made across a wide range of productive human interactions.

Predictively or even as a general proposition, very little can be said about the social consequences that flow from regional energy infrastructure projects as a tool for human development. For about fifty years, economic

---

1081 Toyin Falola and Jessica Achberger, *The Political Economy of Development and Underdevelopment in Africa*, ed. by Toyin Falola and Jessica Achberger (Oxford and New York: Routledge, 2013), pp. 267–78; Kate J Neville and others, 'Debating Unconventional Energy: Social, Political, and Economic Implications', *Annual Review of Environment and Resources*, 42.241–266 (2017) <https://doi.org/10.1146/annurev-environ>.

theories have emphasised the implication of energy inputs as an essential aspect of human development and transformation. However, we know relatively little about how energy enables specific human transformational outcomes, particularly at the local community level. Additionally, there is limited knowledge about how the design of energy technologies and the kinds of social and economic arrangements we develop around them enable or constrain the ability of local communities to advance different aspects of human development and transformation.[1082] Such insights are crucial if ECOWAS is to make significant progress on developing regional energy systems that deliver high social value and thus contribute to furthering development goals such as the SDGs in the region in a significant way.

A 2014 World Bank report underscores that energy development in regions such as West Africa that do not possess hundred percent electricity coverage, will still remain expensive.[1083] It is even more necessary, therefore, to develop the knowledge base to ensure that investments into regional energy projects contribute to significant improvements in social outcomes such as energy affordability in the ECOWAS energy region.

Perhaps another vital conclusion that can be drawn from the social implications of regional energy policy applicable to West Africa, would border on the need to develop and map out complexities in the socio-economic arrangements that distribute the costs and benefits of regional and national energy production and consumption in varied ways across many social contexts in the region. Such as, in urban, peri-urban and rural communities or other conceptual social settings.

Findings in environmental justice shows that transitions within a large-scale energy setting, such as an energy region on the scale of ECOWAS, calls for appreciating how subtle changes in social meaning, identity, or power relationships, especially in the context of differences in ethnicity, class, race and gender, and how it is influenced by energy systems is extremely essential.[1084]

1082 Practical Action, *Poor People's Energy Outlook 2014: Key Messages on Energy for Poverty Alleviation* (Rugby, UK: Practical Action Publishing, 2014).

1083 Bernard Tenenbaum and others, *From the Bottom Up: How Small Power Producers and Mini-Grids Can Deliver Electrification and Renewable Energy in Africa*, *Directions in Development* (Washington, DC: World Bank, 2014) <https://doi.org/doi: 10.1596/978-1-4648-0093-1>.

1084 David Schlosberg, *Defining Environmental Justice: Theories, Movements, and Nature* (Oxford, New York: Oxford University Press, 2007); Hilda E. Kurtz, 'Acknowledging the Racial State: An Agenda for Environmental Justice Research',

Designing and developing proper energy systems requires focusing on how these social factors are spread across different physical, social, cultural, and economic geographies.[1085] Only through such insight will regional energy policy in the ECOWAS energy region be able to address the forms of energy-related injustices that have led, in recent years, to high profile social resistance in local energy rich communities in the region. It can also improve efforts towards bringing about a socially conscious energy transition in the ECOWAS energy region in other words essentially reversing the access and supply gap inherent in the region.

6.5 Economic and Financing Implications of Regional Energy Policy

According to the Infrastructure Consortium for Africa (ICA), West Africa in terms of energy financing trends was the most popular destination for funding with commitments totalling $8.5 billion, representing 34 percent of the African total.[1086] This indicates that the region is the most attractive destination for Africa-wide energy infrastructure investments. However, a deficit in regional energy provision is a deficit across an energy region in terms of development and transformation. The ability to resolve the energy access deficit by including all measures needed to electrify the region and expand the development base would affect health, education, manufacturing, and a whole range of other areas where the region, has been left behind.

West Africa has been experiencing the most rapid energy demand growth of the Sub-Saharan Africa region because of the rapidly growing population. The Sustainable Energy for All report issued by the IEA and World Bank, estimates that economic growth in West Africa would increase by thirty percent if the energy access gap were closed by 2040.[1087]

Antipode, 41.4 (2009), 684–704 <https://doi.org/10.1111/j.1467-8330.2009.00694.x>; Sarah E. Ryan, 'Rethinking Gender and Identity in Energy Studies', *Energy Research and Social Science*, 1 (2014), 96–105 <https://doi.org/10.1016/j.erss.2014.02.008>.

1085 Miller, Richter, and O'Leary.

1086 The Infrastructure Consortium for Africa, 'Energy Financing Trends - ICA', 2018 <https://www.icafrica.org/en/topics-programmes/energy/energy-financing-trends/> [accessed 10 July 2018].

1087 IEA and World Bank, *Sustainable Energy for All 2015—Progress Toward Sustainable Energy (June)* (Washington DC: World Bank, 2015) <https://doi.org/10.1596/978-1-4648-0690-2>.

Moreover, the potential that the availability of abundant energy has on transforming West African economies and the region-wide economy would result in meaningful economic and industrial growth. This could be accomplished by meeting targets such as, the total provision of electricity services all across the region for every household, an increase in the baseload power in terms of megawatts (MW) at country level, and a thorough roll out of energy infrastructure both small-scale and large-scale at country and regional levels.

The smart execution of this would include actor-partnership interactions between private sector partners and governments, local communities and private sector partners, governments and local communities, private sector working independently as Independent Power Producers (IPPs) and local communities working alone and independently as local energy communities especially in the electricity sector.

An essential implication for the economic and financing dimension of regional energy policy has to do with available energy market information, which facilitates the understanding of regional energy market dynamics for all segments of the regional population. Some of the energy market information that could be gathered to improve energy policy may include: a) what energy services would West Africans pay for? b) At what price point? And c) how many would participate as consumers in a particular energy market? All these would inform regional energy policy choices made at both the national and regional levels.

For instance, market information gathering for renewable energy provision in rural and peri-urban areas of the ECOWAS energy region could be executed when regional energy institutions, such as ECREEE and their international development partners, use a coherent and synergised approach. That is, they committing substantial amounts of grant money to this region-wide market information gathering in all fifteen-member states. By this, they create a platform for regional energy market information that would facilitate market information access and symmetry in the regional energy market particularly for private or community actor participation. Otherwise, any company or local energy community providing off-grid household solutions would have to go to the ground on their own to conduct such market information gathering.

The active and unhindered involvement of the private sector and the third sector that is, local communities in the regional energy space at the national and regional levels would reap immense benefits in resolving the energy access gap in the ECOWAS energy region. However, for that to become possible, it requires vital reforms in the entire regional energy space including the utilities sector. These reforms would enable cost-reflective tariffs to be charged by utilities and energy providers in order to make investments recoupable. It would take ECOWAS institutions, member states, multilateral financing institutions (MFIs) (like the World Bank and the African Development Bank), private sector, local communes, and international development assistance bodies among others to accelerate the actualisation of these reforms across the region.

Leveraging energy regionalism or regional energy integration would fast track the development of regional energy markets (especially in power and gas) through the construction of regional energy mega projects such as pipelines, power grids and hydropower dam projects in transnational river basins such as the OMVS and OMVG. The critical constrain encountered here is that as the energy transmission line be it a grid or pipeline passes through countries, the question to be posed is, who pays for what and how is the financing going to be done. To remedy this challenge the floatation of power purchasing bonds can allow countries, as long as cost-reflective tariffs are devised, to be able to pay for the power (or energy type like gas) passing through these countries. Thus, making these regional projects bankable especially for offtake countries at the receiving end of the transmission line.

Another implication is the opportunity to de-risk private or local community investments in either regional conventional energy projects or renewable energy projects. Regional MFIs and banks like the West African Development Bank, African Development Bank as well as international MFIs like the World Bank could increase their share of regional infrastructure investments particularly in the energy sector and use it to de-risk the financial market in order to leverage investments in the energy sectors of the ECOWAS energy region. This is because it serves as the source of where the private sector goes to seek investment financing.

In being more specific, financing renewable energy projects requires creating access to low-cost local currency financing. In the case of off-grid solutions companies that are breaking through at commercial level and providing off-grid renewable solutions. Such as those connecting thousands of households with solar photovoltaic systems with a pay-as-you-go payment model. It is vital for them to get access to local investment finance because without it their services would literally be unaffordable.[1088] This scenario is

1088 Itamar Orlandi and others, *Off-Grid Solar Market Trends Report 2016* (Bloomberg New Energy Finance and Lighting Global,an innovation of the

also similar to local energy communities that look forward to augment energy supply through off-grid solutions or mini-renewable energy projects.

The financing options available could be provided by detaching the substantial amounts of money sitting in West African banks, which is usually purposed for on-lending to SMEs but has not been moving for different kinds of reasons including risk and high interest rates, to be used in accelerating these local energy initiatives. This means at country level a lot has to be done to reverse the trend of why banks are not lending so that they can take more risk. Other financing options in the energy sector include equity investments in the area of long-term debt. However, they are still expensive.

It is essential for decentralised energy providers to grow in the regional energy space in ECOWAS. Their growth would complement the big utilities and energy providers that are mainly government-owned and big central grid connectors in the ECOWAS energy region. This is because both groups of energy providers need to grow at the same time to alleviate the regional energy challenges faced in the region.

Another aspect to the economic and financing implications is the idea that external finance borrowed on the international lending market is risky. This is due to instability in local currency markets, which are mostly saddled with many currency price fluctuations. This creates challenges for energy investors both at the private and third sector levels when sourcing for external funding or liquidity for energy projects.

Therefore, government intervention especially harmonised at the region-wide level is required to create an enabling monetary and fiscal policy environment. For instance, by making foreign reserves available to support the currency exchange market. This support to the regional energy sector especially in the power and renewable sectors would increase revenues that are accrued in these sectors nationally thus impacting the regional energy market.[1089]

Relating to financing large-scale energy projects in the region. Private sector engagement with government and public sector agencies on an unsolicited basis could result in innovative financing models, through public

World Bank Group Inc, 2016) <https://doi.org/10.1017/CBO9781107415324.004>.

1089 Eberhard, Rosnes, and others.

private partnerships (PPPs).[1090] Currently in Africa, total pension funds amount to one trillion US dollars, sovereign wealth funds are about 350 billion US dollars as reported by the African Development Bank.[1091] All these investments are in the private sector, hence the role of MFIs and others is to de-risk investments into the regional energy sector much more to make sure that when companies are investing, partial risk guarantees and credit enhancement facilities would be provided. This in addition to dealing with the political risks that prevent people from investing in the regional energy sector.[1092]

The discussions in this section implies that the ECOWAS energy region (governments, public sector and regional energy institutions) needs to establish an enabling environment, set up regulatory frameworks and lay down energy pricing mechanisms for financing regional energy projects. And in doing this make sure that it is favourable for the private sector and third sector while ensuring that their investments are de-risked for it to be leveraged for the attainment of transformational energy developments in the regional energy space.

The conclusion to be drawn from the economic and financing implications of regional energy policy requires that West African energy regionalism needs to be done at scale with participation of all actors especially, national governments, companies and local communities. Regional energy projects need to go beyond pilot projects and need to do things at scale with a sense of urgency and speed. Because a large market of millions of unserved and underserved West African energy consumers, who do not just need light or a fan but need enough energy to have productive economic engagement, is a massive opportunity to do things at scale. This would include the construction and roll-out of energy infrastructure as well as the introduction of new energy technologies. And all this can be done with the setting up of a solid financial structure made up of innovative financial models that would de-risk investment finance for private and third sector investors since the costs of their risks are high.

1090 Anton Eberhard and Maria Shkaratan, 'Powering Africa: Meeting the Financing and Reform Challenges', *Energy Policy*, 42 (2012), 9–18 <https://doi.org/10.1016/j.enpol.2011.10.033>.

1091 African Development Bank Group, *African Economic Outlook 2019* (Abidjan, 2019) <www.afdb.org>.

1092 African Development Bank Group, 'Africa Needs Bolder Private Financing Models for Power Transmission Lines - Energy Experts', *Africa Energy Portal*, 2019 <https://africa-energy-portal.org/news/africa-needs-bolder-private-financing-models-power-transmission-lines-energy-experts> [accessed 5 July 2019].

6.6 Legal, Regulatory and Policy Implications of Regional Energy Policy

Robust legal, regulatory and policy frameworks are essential for catalysing and attracting private sector investment as well as involving third sector (that is, local community) participation in promoting West Africa's energy regionalism. This implies making proper regional governance inroads in the petroleum and power sectors, the two main energy providers in the region.

Cooperation and harmonisation of the regional petroleum sector has proven to be a key pillar for the ongoing process of energy regionalism in the SSA region but in this case with particular reference to the ECOWAS energy region.[1093] This is clearly reflected in the ECOWAS Treaty, energy protocol and the WAGP Treaty. Therefore, harmonisation, cooperation and integrative processes in the petroleum sector is in full compliance with the vision, policy and strategies of ECOWAS. Pre-existing legal frameworks are already harmonised to a certain degree evidenced by the existence of the West African Gas Pipeline.

Although the resource potential of ECOWAS member states is varied and may call for different approaches, harmonisation of regulatory and policy processes and practices is in the best interest of the region and its constituent states as well as operating and potential private sector actors. A harmonised framework may provide market information clarity and a de-risking mechanism of investment for potential local and international investors in the regional energy sector.

A number of issues along the regional energy value-chain could benefit from harmonisation that would lead to the development of more petroleum corridors in the region. With respect to the prospecting, exploratory and reconnaissance phases of the energy value chain, fulfilment of terms and conditions are required to enable issuance of licenses in the respective jurisdictions of the energy region. However, through an established harmonised procedure a common regime mutually recognised in the region could be easily set up.

Discrepancies in the energy resource potential may justify different licensing approaches but at the same time, the process could reflect a more transparent and competitive governance regime in circumstances where accountability mechanisms are already established. In that respect, the public

---

1093 African Development Bank Group, *Study Report on Harmonisation of Petroleum Policies, Legal, Regulatory and Institutional Frameworks in the East African Community* (Abidjan, 2018).

can verify and seek information on these deals guided by the principles and mechanisms established to guide the particular regional energy sector.

For the pre-qualification phase, an obvious process for shared standards and simplified regulatory procedures is essential to the process. Therefore, the acceptance of a company's qualifications through a rigorous and robust mutually acceptable procedure should be valid for all ECOWAS countries. However, the qualification criteria should be different with regards to onshore and offshore, operator and participant as well as traditional and potential energy producing countries. Considering, the decommissioning phase a similar general approach with common standards may help the process. In particular, plans for disposal and future use of petroleum facilities could be considered when preparing and designing a development plan.

Increasing regional consumption of petroleum resources within the ECOWAS energy region critically depends on the development of adequate and sufficient infrastructure. Therefore, processes involved with harmonising land acquisition should aim at securing enabling corridors to allow for the development of additional oil and gas pipelines going forward. These corridors would also be vital in securing downstream supply of petroleum products. The current extensions of product lines are facing significant challenges due to excessive costs relating to acquiring a right of way.

Other concerns are in relation to the potential environmental impacts that result from the development of these energy corridors. The establishment of regional environmental institutions that work with national environmental agencies in a well-designed institutional architecture would help in the development of common, mutually acceptable standards in this regard. These standards would go a long way to check any emergent environmental effects in the development of mega regional energy projects.

The downstream sector of the regional petroleum sector is largely deregulated and a well-functioning energy sub-sector with production processes of petroleum products ongoing in the region. Since increased local-content is mainly found in this sector and it is seen as a means to generating employment, ECOWAS members states are developing local-content legislation however the challenge remains in meeting full compliance standards. Another issue in this regard would be the push of the ECOWAS Commission's energy and mines directorate through the support of the African Development Bank to provide technical support in the development of local-content legislation to countries that are prospecting for petroleum resources. Thus, ensuring a set of shared best practices are in place to guide the drafting of policies and legislation in this regard.

In terms of sharing benefits from petroleum production and proceeds, energy producing ECOWAS member states in general use production-sharing agreements to govern the commercial relationships with international oil companies (IOCs). This results in the use of similar key fiscal elements. Nevertheless, there are differences concerning which elements are negotiable. Since international best practice generally recommend that profit from oil be shared based on profitability.

A commonly agreed shift from production-based sharing of profits from oil to a mixed approach that would mutually benefit producer countries and companies could be pushed to the fore. In line with providing legal guarantees for supplying energy to member states on a priority basis. It would go a long way in ensuring security of supply relating to petroleum products in the ECOWAS energy region. Another feature of the legal guarantees would require petroleum-rich countries in the region to consume a flexibly capped quantity of internally produced petroleum resources before considering exports. This would obligate as well as facilitate the development of a thriving regional energy industry in the downstream sector reversing the trending of exporting crude oil and later importing finished products.

Institutional structures for the governance of the petroleum sector in the ECOWAS energy region have remained functionally specialised with responsibilities and established institutions. This includes sector regulators such as the West Africa Gas Pipeline Authority[1094]. This welcomed development is in line with good energy governance principles. In addition, the establishment or reform of national oil companies to become organisations to focus upon the government's commercial interests is also a good indicator of good governance practices. Although there are major variations concerning the national institutional structures and responsibilities, they may not serve as obstacles towards a foreseeable integration and harmonisation process in the region-wide sector.

At member state level, there are differences in the level of independence of the national regulators. Some regulators are independent whereas others are vested in ministries and departments of energy, regional policy harmonisation in this area in favour of a well-resourced independent regulatory agency would be forward looking.

1094 Authority.

Finally, on the petroleum sector harmonisation in terms of a communications and data gathering strategy would inure to the benefit of good regional petroleum governance in West Africa. An internet portal will serve as a good vehicle to disseminate current information and a comprehensive ECOWAS energy portal can be an effective approach to present all actors and stakeholders with updated energy information. This should be coupled with the establishment of a real-time regional and synchronised energy data gathering centre (responsible for all forms of energy data) as part of a regional data and statistics body (or possibly alone from the beginning) to compile energy data that would complement the work of national energy data agencies.

A focus on the power and electricity sector requires consideration of the role of public utilities with respect to their governance and regulation. The majority of utilities in West Africa are vertically integrated and most of them state owned. As we see solar and wind power technologies being adopted into the sector with mostly private investment from independent power producers (IPPs), there is a potential conflict of interest in cases where the state power generator is the single buyer in the many instances where private IPPs are getting involved. Since the incumbent utility can slow these investment processes down. The creation of independent grid and system operators, responsible for contracting new power can accelerate new investments by facilitating unbundling to occur.[1095]

This raises the question of harmonisation in the ECOWAS electricity market and whether this creates a new impetus for ERERA, the regional regulator. This would enable the push towards unbundling in member states, especially in countries, who are yet to fulfil that requirement based on Community law. There are quite a number of regulatory challenges in the ECOWAS power scene. About two-thirds of countries in the region have independent regulators. They face many issues in conventional regulation such as the capacity to do cost of service or rate of return regulation. Many challenges also do occur around this regulatory capability in the area of making consistent and transparent decisions. Also connected to these

1095 Anton Eberhard, Katharine Gratwick, and others, *Independent Power Projects in Sub-Saharan Africa: Lessons from Five Key Countries, Directions in Development - Energy and Mining*, 2016 <https://doi.org/doi:10.1596/978-1-4648-0800-5>.

new regulatory challenges, is how distributed energy resources (DERs) become cost-competitive.[1096]

Regional energy regulators would need to develop appropriate regulatory regimes that encourage the proliferation and diffusion of DERs. This may include differentiating time and location, proper net metering as well as drawing from international best practice and experience.

Energy planning is an often-disregarded approach by market-focused analysts who are of the opinion that everything related to energy should be determined by the market. However, in considering the West African energy space as a tri-partite energy regime, made up of the state (at both supranational and national levels), market and commons moves the lens from only one angle to then encourage energy planning as a vital ingredient for solid regional energy governance.

The introduction and implementation of national electricity laws, by most governments in the ECOWAS energy region, encountered a number of problems chiefly relating to the entry of private sector participation. The responsibility of energy planning then shifted from the incumbent nationalised utility. Previously, the incumbent utility was responsible for everything like planning, procurement, and building of energy plants. But as other actors were introduced the responsibility for planning shifted from the national utility to the government that is, a department or agency responsible for electricity or energy. In these government departments or agencies, expert capacity was most often the urgent need and so they would sometimes outsource this function to consultants who were not usually updated and lacked real-time information.

Principally, the slow pace in linking energy planning to the timely initiation of competitive tenders for the construction of new energy capacity was the main challenge in the regional power sector. Developing a process for good electricity planning which is flexible, timely and dynamic is vital. This process of good energy planning often maps out affordable cost in the provision of energy services going forward and serves as a guide to the competitive procurement process.[1097] This dimension in the West African power sector really needs to be put in place to ensure energy access, security and affordability.

1096 Eric Martinot, 'Grid Integration of Renewable Energy: Flexibility, Innovation, and Experience', *Annual Review of Environment and Resources*, 41 (2016), 223–51 <https://doi.org/10.1146/annurev-environ-110615-085725>.

1097 IRENA, *Insights on Planning for Power System Regulators* (Abu Dhabi: International Renewable Energy Agency, 2018).

Another challenge is that regional public utilities (although aware of the disruptive technologies and emerging local energy communities on the edge of the grid) do not seem to be changing their business models and policy approaches quickly and fully to embrace these innovations. In summary, harmonising regional energy policy and the introduction of local energy communities needs urgent attention going forward. This is in order to attain the needed regional and national energy objective of total energy access and the provision of abundant energy.

6.7 Innovation and Technological Implications of Regional Energy Policy

Renewable energy adoption is growing rapidly in West Africa due to a number of interlinked efforts that have to do with the emergence and popularity of readily accessible technologies in wind and solar energy. Cape Verde, Cote D'Ivoire, Ghana and Nigeria's efforts as well as the adoption of renewable energy policies in almost every ECOWAS country is driving this growth. Nevertheless, the percentage of renewables to the overall electricity growth in the region is barely significant and under five percent.[1098]

To look at this phenomenon sceptically, to think that the deployment of renewables at this rate will solve the decarbonisation and access challenge is extremely optimistic. Since the region falls between a low- and mid-income bracket, incremental power and energy production seeks to shift it towards a high-income bracket. Therefore, the obligation placed on countries in the region not to use carbon intensive energy resources and reserves easily at their disposal to produce electricity and power raises some concern.

To remedy carbon emissions emanating from coal plants like the Sendou coal power station in Senegal would be to use carbon capture and utilisation technology which could play a huge role. Thus, the diffusion of such technology reduces the impact of carbon intensive energy sources from countries using such energy sources.

Technology in the energy space is going through a revolution all by itself. Policy is stuck or nascent and the financial revolution is playing

1098 Ibrahim Kabiru Maji and Chindo Sulaiman, 'Renewable Energy Consumption and Economic Growth Nexus: A Fresh Evidence from West Africa', *Energy Reports*, 5 (2019), 384–92 <https://doi.org/10.1016/j.eg,yr.2019.03.005>.

catch up.[1099] Many of the innovations taking place in the renewable energy sector are generally happening in the African energy crucible. In particular, there are different payment and business models, coupled with the provision of off-the-grid electricity generated through the medium of mini-grids and solar energy systems for the purpose of lightning.[1100] These management and technological innovations are powering West Africa and contributing to reversing climate change.

Granted that there is a push towards renewable energy technologies, a judicious mix of energy sources are to be used with the ultimate idea of moving towards green energy. A key possibility for the ECOWAS region in concert with other regions in Africa would be to take advantage of this lag in the energy race so as to be the first continent to go green by pushing for renewable energy as mooted by the Africa Progress Panel report in 2015.[1101] The deployment of distributed technologies is inevitable however in order to resolve the security and safety issues of the grid such as optimising and rationalising wind and solar power into the grid, it requires essential and significant innovation in this regard.

There are predictions that periphery technologies that enable the decentralisation of energy, are going to make a big difference in the regional energy landscape in West Africa. Some of these technologies include combined heat and power units, solar cooling and heat pumps, combined batteries and batteries for storage and re-optimisation. All these would facilitate an energy demand response that would allow customers in the ECOWAS energy region to virtually become power generators, while reducing dependence on the central grid.[1102] Finally artificial intelligence, would allow for the predictive maintenance on the energy system.

Another group of technologies that are game-changing the energy sector are digitisation technologies. They are mostly big applications that optimise energy systems at varying geographical scales. They include: digital control systems, optimised digital dispatch systems and integrated energy solutions platforms. These big applications allow energy businesses or

---

1099 World Economic Forum, 'Powering Africa'.

1100 SEforALL, 'Integrated Electrification Pathways for Universal Access to Electricity: A Primer' (Vienna and Washington D.C: SEforALL, 2019).

1101 Africa Progress Panel, *Power People Planet Seizing Africa's Energy and Climate Opportunities*.

1102 Rainer Quitzow and others, *Advancing a Global Transition to Clean Energy-the Role of International Cooperation*, Economics Discussion Papers (Kiel, 2019) <http://www.economics-ejournal.org/economics/discussionpapers/2019-37> [accessed 9 June 2019].

local energy communities to optimise the whole energy system under their control throughout the energy value-chain – that is, production, storage, distribution, consumption and demand response.

The other group of technologies are the productivity applications, which optimise productivity of the energy system whether it is centralised or decentralised, that could enhance and modernise the regional energy system at all levels in terms of regional energy productivity.[1103]

The arrival of blockchain on the energy scene provides many prospects with encouraging implications for the governance of regional energy. This could be used in particular when customers themselves produce the energy deployed and transmitted to households in urban or rural areas in the country level. For example, peer-to-peer trading of energy in an automated way at the edge of the grid where consumers, homes and businesses sell to each other with minimal human intervention while at the same time monies being transferred between buyer and seller. This in effect can optimise peak energy especially when it is off the grid. If this is implemented successfully at country level, it can diffuse the learned experiences to other regional countries without reinventing the wheel.

The potential for digitisation is far beyond household or small energy user efficiency. For instance, when digitisation is deployed across the construction phase, transition phase and to the operational phase with suitable applications be it in large-scale military installations, hospitals, universities, communities, and even in buildings. It seeks to obtain energy saving gains through efficiency that accounts for about thirty to forty percent of these installations.

Decentralised energy systems are equipping places in the ECOWAS energy region, which were extremely inaccessible to reach. This includes remote and island areas of the region. It is not limited to a technological challenge but also a socio-economic challenge. What this implies is that these decentralised systems need to be manufactured in the region. And it must be done in concert with the aim of training local people to take care of these decentralised energy systems in the communities where they are installed to create more energy related jobs and services around decentralised energy.

In the scope of scenarios, the worst-case scenario is to import something that has been manufactured externally from a remote place and land it on

1103 Frost & Sullivan, 'Digitization of Energy Transmission & Distribution in Africa', 2018 <http://www.geg,ridsolutions.com/press/gepress/2018/WP-Digitization.pdf>.

a local community with nobody to take care of it. After a couple of months when it stops working, it becomes redundant. But when this is reversed it empowers local communities to become energy communities.

Another inference relating to technology from a resilience standpoint concerns the impact of climatic problems such as droughts, which is putting pressure on regional and national energy systems. This offers a possibility for energy consumers in the any region to equip themselves with decentralised solutions (such as micro-grids) which combine renewables and storage so that the resilience management of the energy system could be possible and effective.[1104] By doing this, customers would be able to manage efficiency of use and cost because in many cases although the initial cost of installation of these technologies are high the spread over time of this technological cost would be competitive enough to bring down costs.

Technologies that enable energy resilience in the face of climate disorders could be deployed in a number of cases. Such as in military installations or an average local community (which inhabit about 115,000 people), hospital facilities that cannot afford to entertain power breakdowns (especially in a surgery room), local communities that are disconnected from the grid, in addition to technology and industrial parks that are at the edge of the grid.

Due to this technological revolution happening in the energy sector, public utilities are undergoing major transformations. Public utilities serve as conductors of the power sector. They play a major role in the sector as middle men who serve as insurers of the system. On the other hand, their role as providers is also undergoing a major reinvention. As a result, utilities are adopting more digital solutions in order to manage fluctuating renewable energy intermittencies and to modulate fluctuating consumption on the part of consumers. This process is becoming more complex than before when power generation and consumption were fixed. This complex technical process of introducing renewable energy intermittencies is influencing the management of public utilities.

Therefore, in West African utilities, there are preparations done by these utilities themselves to transition by using energy planning to move from only a centralised grid to a hybridised grid system that inculcates periphery or on-the-edge energy systems. Most public utilities in ECOWAS member states are not profitable as revealed in the seminal study by Trimble et

---

1104 SEforALL.

al[1105]. But this phenomenon is not only limited to this part of the world. For instance, PG&E – owner of the biggest power utility in the US – filed for bankruptcy in 2019[1106].

So, the key thing being considered in the energy region is to go digital in order to effectively manage the hybrid grid that mixes the central and decentralised grids. This is causing a number of public utilities to reinvent themselves. An implication for this revolution in the energy systems being managed by public utilities in West Africa could be the adoption of micro energy solutions. That is, a combination of distributed energy resources (DER) with natural gas, solar energy or diesel oil in remote places in the region. However, although this transitioning is inevitable, regional utilities are more focused on increasing the power baseload in general. Since in every transition there are risks and opportunities, some utilities are exiting at the end of this transition as winners.

Another concern related to technology and the innovation dimension of already locked-in energy installations in the ECOWAS energy region, is the need to renew, retrofit and repair old power stations. This is to help in surmounting the regional energy challenges. This would contribute to an increased baseload powered by fossil fuels as well as contributions from nuclear energy technology, which is going through a major technological transformation.

The challenge with renewable energy technologies is its low energy intensity. Which means its inability to make up for the power production deficit in West Africa even though it is being adopted at an increasingly fast rate. Therefore, a bold rethink in policy choices, is regional energy technology towards scaling up other alternative energy sources (such as nuclear energy technology) would have a game changing effect on both the access and decarbonisation conundrum faced in the region. Nuclear is already the safest way to make reliable electricity.[1107]

Pushker Kharecha and James Hansen in their study, discovered that nuclear power technology has saved 1.8 million lives to date by preventing

---

1105 Chris Trimble and others, 'Financial Viability of Electricity Sectors in Sub-Saharan Africa. Quasi-Fiscal Deficits and Hidden Costs', *Policy Research Working Paper 7788. World Bank*, 2016 <https://openknowledge.worldbank.org/handle/10986/24869>.

1106 Bradford Cornell, 'Energy and Investing : Financing the Transition to Renewable Energy', 2019 <https://doi.org/http://dx.doi.org/10.2139/ssrn.3343583>.

1107 Anil Markandya and Paul Wilkinson, 'Electricity Generation and Health', *Lancet*, 370.9591 (2007), 979–90 <https://doi.org/10.1016/S0140-6736(07)61253-7>.

the burning of fossil fuels.[1108] Our World in Data, an Oxford University publication, in its elaborate accounting of the safest sources of energy, where they take into consideration all harmful effects and accidents, ranks nuclear energy more safe than any fossil fuels and renewable energy sources combined.[1109] This is contrary to the pervasive public belief regarding the safety of nuclear energy. The evidence then follows that the path of nuclear energy is the way to go in the production of massive amounts of power and in the reduction of global warming substantially for the West African energy region.

However, the challenge pertaining to public perception on nuclear safety and the economics of nuclear energy, concerns over nuclear weapons development and the way forward in dealing with the nuclear waste question. These are all matters still under consideration.

6.8 Implications for Bi-Regional Partnerships on Regional Energy Policy

A reiteration of the fact that West Africa, currently undergoing a hydrocarbons boom in its Gulf of Guinea and Transform Margin, is attracting considerable geopolitical partnerships. This takes the form of investments, technologies and technical expertise in the exploration and development of the sector; and this is noteworthy.

The region is a relatively new petroleum-producing hub, although it inhabits Nigeria which is one of Africa's OPEC members since 1971. The ECOWAS energy region has limited home-grown capital and technical capability to exploit these regional energy resources independently. Many West African governments are willing to accept, in the initial stages, lower royalties and to cede greater control over their petroleum resources than governments in more traditional oil-producing countries.[1110]As a result, these external energy investors be it International Oil Companies (IOCs)

1108 Pushker A. Kharecha and James E. Hansen, 'Prevented Mortality and Greenhouse Gas Emissions from Historical and Projected Nuclear Power', *Environmental Science & Technology*, 47.9 (2013), 4889–95 <https://doi.org/10.1021/es3051197>.

1109 Hannah Ritchie, 'What Are the Safest Sources of Energy?' (Oxford: Oxford University Press, 2020) <https://ourworldindata.org/safest-sources-of-energy>.

1110 Erica S. Downs, 'The Fact and Fiction of Sino-African Energy Relations', *China Security*, 3.3 (2007), 42–68 <https://www.brookings.edu/wp-content/uploads/2016/06/downs20070913.pdf>.

from Europe and the US, or state-owned energy enterprises (SOEs) from China are making high profits from the West African petroleum sector.

High energy-consuming regions and their oil companies also find West Africa attractive because the region facilitates their diversification priorities and interests in relation to possible sources of foreign petroleum supplies. Diversifying places to source external energy reduces concerns about insecurities in terms of security of supply in buyer regions and states and fears of politically motivated field expropriations or supply cut-offs.[1111]

The oil and gas endowments in West Africa are not, for the most part, massive as those found in the Persian Gulf region. However, they possess a number of attractions for external energy consumers. To begin with, West African producer countries consume little oil and gas on their own, although this trend is changing, so most of the production in the past was available for export. Secondly, several of the region's petroleum producing areas are yet to be fully explored which means additional reserves undoubtedly remain undiscovered.

Thirdly, much of the oil being obtained from West Africa is the light sweet variety that is highly fluid with a low sulphur content, highly valued and cherished by European and other refiners.[1112] This has led to multiple bi-regional partnerships between West Africa (at country level and region-wide level) to negotiate partnership deals in the petroleum sector and more generally in other energy sectors of the region.

This section would only consider the bi-regional partnership that exists between the ECOWAS energy region (and its member states) and the EU energy region (and its member states). The main rationale for this consideration is that Europe has a vested interest in Africa because of a number of reasons. Among those reasons are the geographical proximity between both regions, the unsavoury political history that has existed between them, the significant demographic increase in Africa[1113], the emerging security concerns in the Sahel as well as the ungovernable migrant flows which is perceived to be potentially destabilising to European political and social processes.

1111 Carbonnier, pp. 45–49.

1112 Michael T. Klare, *Rising Powers, Shrinking Planet: The New Geopolitics of Energy* (New York: Metropolitan Books, Henry Holt and Company, 2008).

1113 In 1950, European population was twice that of Africa. Today, Africa's population is twice that of Europe. By 2100, Africa's population would be ten times that of Europe. (See: Kishore Mahbubani, Has the West Lost It?: A Provocation, London: Allen Lane, 2019)

Therefore, with this vested interest the EU is intended to commit itself to the sustainable transformation of African economies (with the ECOWAS region serving as a major partner) to accelerate decisive cooperative actions especially in the area of energy to deliver economic prosperity.

King and Marks, in their tracking of the traditional movement of the ECOWAS region's hydrocarbons to Europe, reveals that the structures and agencies inherent in this energy movement are reminiscent of the colonial era.[1114] They describe that raw commodities – crude oil and natural gas – flow from West Africa to Europe, while value-added products – petroleum and its derivatives – make a reverse flow from Europe to West Africa.

It should be emphasised here that the petroleum sector in West Africa had been a mainly European preserve until lately when shifts started to occur with the involvement of other regional players like the US and China. This new shift is happening in the context of new energy supply and demand patterns and are beginning to emerge in the global energy space in terms of commodities being re-aligned, thus causing trade patterns to shift. In the meantime, at country level, West African states are making policy decisions that are changing the status quo, for them to become intense users and consumers of their petroleum commodities across the energy value chain.

With this in mind, the EU being a viable export destination and ECOWAS being a viable resource destination, a new interdependence in the energy space is evolving in this longstanding energy relationship. By implication, European governments and the EU have encouraged their energy extractive companies to invest in West African oil production through financial incentives, increasing diplomatic linkages with the region and supplying the region's petroleum and energy endowed states with military aid among others.[1115]

West African offshore discoveries between 2007 and 2009 bolstered EU and other foreign governments and their companies' interest in the region's oil exploration and extraction.[1116] Estimates of the region's undiscovered reserves are seeing a continuous rise. However, these dramatic increases are not likely to be sustained since regional production is likely

---

1114 Charlotte King and Jon Marks, *European-West African Relations in the Field of Energy – Obstacles to a Sustainable Approach*, WAI-ZEI Paper (Bonn, 2014).

1115 Michael Klare and Daniel Volman, 'The African "Oil Rush" and US National Security', *Third World Quarterly*, 27.4 (2006), 609–28 <https://doi.org/10.1080/01436590600720835>.

1116 Energy Information Administration, *International Energy Outlook* (Washington D.C., 2010).

to stabilise by 2030. Consequently, oil companies and importing countries from the EU have an incentive to engage in West Africa's petroleum sector devoid of any colonial drawbacks, or they would risk losing out to other competitors.

In reaction to this new imperative, external investments have flowed both into the major traditional West African producers such as Nigeria and relative petroleum neophytes such as Ghana, Côte d'Ivoire and Senegal. Also, external capital has also been directed towards countries like Liberia, Sierra Leone and The Gambia where oil exploration is in progress although no substantial commercial finds have been made. In one form or the other external participation especially from European actors in the West African petroleum sector can be seen in the energy rich West African countries.[1117]

Bilateral energy trade relations offer an overwhelming mix of opportunities alongside obstacles. The West African region's rising domestic consumption presents opportunities for European companies operating as well in the downstream sector. Obstacles to a sustainable Europe-West Africa energy relationship are of a commercial and political nature. Relating to the commercial dimension, European companies have been mainly present in the upstream industry sector of West Africa for so long and the relationship had engendered strong social emotions and instigated a lot of political controversy.

By way of illustration, following the 2009 publication of the WikiLeaks US diplomatic cable documents, in which Royal Dutch Shell executive vice president for Africa, Ann Pickard, claimed that the Nigerian government "had forgotten that Shell had seconded people to all relevant ministries and that Shell consequently had access to everything that was being done"[1118] revealed clandestine, corrupt and destabilising political intrusions in Nigeria by a notable European energy MNC. This festered significant mistrust towards Royal Dutch Shell especially in petroleum communities in the Delta Region of Nigeria.

Calls for transparency and good governance among external commercial interests in the West African energy sector are enshrined in global

---

1117 Yinka Omorogbe, 'Regional and National Frameworks for Energy Security in Africa', in *Energy Security: Managing Risk in a Dynamic Legal and Regulatory Environment*, ed. by Barry Barton and others (Oxford: Oxford University Press, 2004).

1118 WikiLeaks, '2008 Leaked US Cable : Ambassador Encourages Oil Companies to Broaden Their Political Base. 09 Lagos155' (WikiLeaks, 2008).

standards such as the Extractive Industries Transparency Initiative (EITI). It provides for a new momentum to ensure accountability, transparency and ethical behavioural efforts on the part of European energy MNCs and the EU as a whole to reset West African and European energy relations. This would make bi-regional relations in the energy space more scrupulous than unscrupulous.

Europe remains one of the significant players shaping West Africa's energy industry and trading relations. European technology, expertise and financial investment is critical in the creation of formidable regional energy industries. Perhaps, the most evident obstacle facing the bi-regional relationship between Europe and West Africa is the failure to reinvent the relationship considering the changing global dynamics.

Energy is one of the eight key strategic partnerships comprising the Africa-EU Joint Strategy that both sides launched in the Africa-EU Energy Partnership (AEEP). The partnership is structured as a long-term framework for political dialogue and cooperation aimed at increasing effectiveness of African and European efforts to secure reliable and sustainable energy services on both continents. This energy partnership seeks to extend access towards modern energy services and expand the use of renewable energy technology especially in Africa.[1119]

However, the urgency on the part of African nations to transform their economies requires a much extensive approach towards energy provision through the use of more energy intensive but cleaner energy technologies and sources such as nuclear energy to drive industrialisation and meet the rapid urbanisation needs of the region. And this is where EU involvement will be much substantial in changing the energy fortunes in Africa more generally and West Africa specifically.

In connection with global energy trade, commercial dynamics are changing and becoming mutually beneficial along this transition. This requires the EU and ECOWAS to work together to extricate themselves completely from this old colonial and neo-colonial attributions as well as the paternalism that has coloured their relationship over the centuries into a new era of a more respectful bi-regional partnership.

On the broader geopolitical African front, other regional organisations, national actors, as well as Africa-wide corporate actors, are changing the manner in which this bi-regional interaction on energy between ECOWAS and the EU is unfolding. Africa has emerged as a distinct player in interna-

---

1119 Africa-EU Energy Partnership, 'Africa-EU Energy Partnership (AEEP)', 2018 <http://www.aeep-forum.org/en/aeep> [accessed 9 July 2018].

tional diplomacy, leaving the balance of interaction between Europe and West Africa through their respective regional bodies to quite vague and ambiguous than it was in the past.[1120]

What is more, the emergence of new energy regions in other parts of Africa, such as the East African energy region, tends to render West Africa's place in the wider Africa energy space weak. This is in connection with West Africa's competitiveness and attractiveness to the EU. It could have an impact on European -West African energy relations even though, in geographical terms, the west coast of Africa is more preferable for Europe in connection to the energy trade.

Another evolving dynamic on both sides of this partnership is the new crop of policy-makers emerging on the scene who comprise internationally conscious, often highly capable young Africans who are not saddled in anyway with a colonial hangover. Likewise, young Europeans who are realistically aware about their place in the new global order, have little to no connection to this imperial past.[1121] This provides a huge opportunity to reset European-West African relations generally and especially in terms of the bi-regional energy partnership.

An alternative feature of the bi-regional energy relations between Europe and West Africa is in the area of fostering electrification and power generation in West Africa. Here the EU's actions are mainly within the scope of international development cooperation and the EU's financial assistance (that is, official development assistance – ODA plus other official flows) to West African governments. They include loans, grants, guarantees, equity, risk sharing mechanisms, technical assistance and interest rate subsidies. These actions seem particularly fragmented. The EU has introduced nineteen ongoing initiatives in the field, emanating from both EU member states and EU institutions.

The multiplicity of these initiatives is understandable, since each country has its own political and commercial interests to promote across the ECOWAS energy region. What lacks clarity is the fragmented initiatives of EU Institutions. Currently, the myriad of fragmented initiatives appears to favour overlaps, inefficiencies and largely higher transaction costs. It is fair to contemplate that European taxpayers would be better off if their contri-

1120 Siphamandla Zondi, Alastair Fraser, Donna Lee, et. al 'Emerging Agents of Change? Africa and International Negotiations' (London: Chatham House, 2011), p. 12 <http://www.chathamhouse.org/sites/default/files/public/Research/Africa/020211summary.pdf>.

1121 King and Marks.

butions are channelled through a unique facility, allowing policy clarity, consistency, removal of overlaps and lowering of transactional costs.[1122] Eventually this would contribute overall to higher efficiency and influence positively the West African electrification agenda particularly in rural areas that cannot access the central grid.

Useful conclusions that could be drawn from making the most out of the bi-regional financing initiatives given its wide and growing landscape would be to focus on what can be done to enhance and scale-up the current EU financing initiatives for West Africa's electrification and power generation. Perhaps this could be modelled after the US 'Power Africa' initiative, a public-private partnership platform which involves US government agencies, African governments, more than hundred private sector partners (for example, energy companies, investment banks, equity funds, institutional investors), and other multilateral partners. This may serve as a panacea in reducing fragmentation in this field.

As hinted in the Africa Progress Panel report of 2015, West Africa's energy needs would not be served by a fragmented system of financial assistance into the regional energy sector.[1123] This fragmentation is happening because available funding often is conveyed through, very bureaucratic delivery structures that fuse high transaction costs with unambitious results, thereby occasioning most of the available finance to be allocated towards small-scale energy projects rather than sizeable and impactful infrastructure projects that could turn around the energy fortunes of the region.[1124]

Table 6. 1 Review of EU and EU Member States Investment Initiatives towards Sub-Saharan African (including West African) Electrification Programs

Name of the initiative	*Responsible institution*	*Aim or activities Funding*
European Institutions		
The European Development Fund (EDF)	Managing: EC and EIB Donors: EU Member States	Funding cooperation activities and promotion of regional cooperation and integration

1122 Tagliapietra and Bazilian.
1123 Africa Progress Panel, *Lights Power Action: Electrifying Africa*.
1124 Tagliapietra, *Electrifying Africa: How to Make Europe's Contribution Count*.

Name of the initiative	*Responsible institution*	*Aim or activities* *Funding*
The ACP Investment Facility (IF)	Managing: EIB Donors: EU Member States (via EDF)	Fostering investment in sustainable infrastructure
ACP-EU Energy Facility(EF)	Managing: EC Donors: EU and Member States (via EDF)	Dialogue facilitation to promote sustainable energy development Dialogue
The EU-Africa Infrastructure Trust Fund (EU-AITF)	Managing: EIB Donors: EC and 12 EU Member States	Support for infrastructure projects in sub-Saharan Africa, namely in the field of energy via loans and grants Promotion
Africa Investment Facility (AfIF)	Managing: EIB Donors: EC and 12 EU Member States	Fostering investment in sustainable infrastructure
Africa Energy Guarantee Fund (AEG,F)	Managing: EIB and EC Donors: EIB (EU-Africa Infrastructure Trust Fund)	Unlocking and leveraging investment in modern electricity solutions in Africa
EU External InvestmentPlan (EIP)	Donors: EU Budget and EDF	Mobilising investments, stepping-up technical assistance and improving business environment in Africa and the Neighbourhood
European Countries		
Proparco	Donor and managing: France (AFD)	Promote private investment in developing countries in general and Africa in particular to boost growth, pro-

Name of the initiative	*Responsible institution*	*Aim or activities Funding*
		mote sustainable development
Sustainable Use of Natural Resources and Energy Finance (Sunref)	Donor and managing: France (AFD)	Support financial institutions in order to boost green finance portfolios in sustainable natural resources management.
Danish Climate Investment Fund (KIF)	Managing: Investment Fund for Developing Countries (IFU) Donors: Denmark	Offers risk capital and advice for climate investments
DEG, – Direct Investments	Germany (KfW)	Loan provided on favourable terms to advance renewables and efficiency projects
Africa's Renewable Energy and Access Program (AFREA)	The Netherlands (Managed: WBG)	Support to widen access to energy services in Sub-Saharan African countries
DFID Impact Fund	Donors: UK (CDC)	Provide finance with focus on off-grid rural electrification
Energy Africa campaign	UK	Focusses on achieving the SDG Goal 7 through market-based delivery of off-grid energy to households.
Energising Development (EnDev)	Donors: The Netherlands, Germany, Norway, UK, Switzerland and Sweden	Development of energy markets to foster the diffusion of renewable energies and efficiency
Renewable Energy Performance Platform (REPP)	Managing: Camco Clean Energy and Green Stream Donors: UK	Supporting the growth of sub-Saharan Africa's renewable energy industry

Name of the initiative	*Responsible institution*	*Aim or activities Funding*
Energy and Environment Partnership South & East Africa (EEP)	Managing: KPMG ECO Donors: Finland, UK, Austria	Multi-donor fund which provides early stage grant and catalytic financing for innovative clean energy projects, technologies and business models
Green Africa Power (GAP)	Donors: UK and Norway	Set up to stimulate private investment in renewable energy in Africa
Nordic Climate Facility (NCF)	Donors: Denmark, Finland, Iceland, Norway, and Sweden	Challenge fund set up to finance early stage climate change projects in developing countries

Source:[1125]

To conclude, the implications for bi-regional energy partnerships between the EU and ECOWAS, within the framework of the Joint Africa-EU Strategy, would reset the energy relationship and make it a win-win. This win-win relationship is required, and can help each party to speed up its internal regional energy transitions. It can also help both sides to tackle their common energy challenges together, thereby achieving shared energy goals and ambitions. It would demand much greater bi-regional efforts and ground-breaking collective initiatives. This should work towards the ultimate aim of expanding affordable, reliable, clean and intensive energy in both regions, but with specific reference to the ECOWAS energy region. Altogether, these would drive regional economic prosperity.

To explore further mutually beneficial ways the two regions can work together effectively on crucial energy sectors, would first require a standing forum of a high-level group of experts and thinkers. Members of this high-level group should be selected from both the EU and ECOWAS to

1125 Adapted from Tagliapietra, *Electrifying Africa: How to Make Europe's Contribution Count*; Tagliapietra and Bazilian. In addition to respective websites of the fund.

deliberate on transforming West Africa's energy future. This high-level dialogue at the regional level should be mediated by external expert energy bodies like the IEA and could serve as a first step in addressing issues concretely.

This high-level dialogue must consist of ample representation from both West African and European stakeholders in the public, private and civil-society sectors. These stakeholders must be able to provide honest and direct views and ideas with no reservations and speak on matters that can shape the energy futures of both regions. This multi-stakeholder dialogue and engagement will definitely promote bi-regional interaction and cooperation on energy at all levels, thereby influencing the crafting of good regional energy policy innovations at all polycentric levels in the ECOWAS and EU regions.

Chapter 7

Conclusion

ECOWAS' headway towards a well-governed energy region is a matter of global interest because of concerns relating to closing the energy deficit gap, angst arising from global climate change coupled with the region's desire to industrialise rapidly as well as dealing with energy resource use and scarcity. The mode of governance of the region's energy space is a major determining factor in resolving the increasing access and consumption, security of supply and sustainability issues that affect West African energy regionalism. Further factors include the structure of the regional economy, financial system, innovation and technological advancement along with the social and demographic dynamics.

The term *institution* as applied here relate to new institutional economics and historical institutionalism, which is underscored by the formal and informal rules that shape how the government, the economy and society interact. These institutions are human-constructed constraints or opportunities within which individual choices take place and which shape the consequences of their choices.[1126] They include long-standing norms and values deeply ingrained into society, including institutional settings that provide the framework for political, economic and social transactions, in addition to specific rules, which govern specific transactions.[1127]

Many of the prevailing characteristics of ECOWAS's national and regional energy institutions and institutional and infrastructural arrangements have their roots in colonial history and the early decades of post-independence history. These attributes occur in a polycentric manner which forms the basis for energy regionalism in West Africa and furthermore informs the governance of the regional energy sector, advertently setting

---

1126 Michael Dean McGinnis, 'An Introduction to IAD and the Language of the Ostrom Workshop: A Simple Guide to a Complex Framework for the Analysis of Institutions and Their Development', *Policy Studies Journal*, 39.1 (2011), 169–83 <https://doi.org/http://dx.doi.org/10.1111/j.1541-0072.2010.00401.x>.

1127 Andrews-Speed, *The Governance of Energy in China: Transition to a Low-Carbon Economy*.

bounds for the capacity of the region to adapt to pre-existing and new energy-related challenges.

The provision and production of energy-related public goods and common-pool resources at the local, national and regional levels require different institutions that include open, competitive markets and highly centralised governmental institutions. In order to solve collective-action problems in West Africa's energy space effectively and efficiently there is a need to rethink the way the region approaches market and governmental institutions. There must be analytical approaches that are consistent with a regional energy sector that encourages human development at multiple levels as suggested by Hans Opschoor when he researched institutional development in the public sector.[1128]

As demonstrated in this study, a fundamental set of problems facing regions in all developed and developing societies are collective-action problems. The scope and confines of these problems however differ dramatically as seen in the European and West African cases as outlined in this work. Polycentricity may help cure defects caused by collective action problems by developing systems of governmental and nongovernmental organisations at multiple scales in relation to resolving governance challenges occurring within the context of West Africa's energy regionalism.

This dissertation's analysis has tried to realise four goals. The first goal was to explore the evolutionary nature of energy regionalism in ECOWAS and EU over time. The second goal was to exhibit that the field of institutionalist studies could clarify the nature of potentials and obstacles facing the governance of energy in a transnational region by identifying, categorising and organising variables and processes for analysis. The third goal was to apply the CIS framework to this approach in a comparative manner to the specific energy regionalism cases of ECOWAS and the EU. This was done to offer an explanation on the polycentric nature of these energy systems and to understand factors associated with failures and successes inherent in their corresponding systems.

On top of that, with respect to the fourth goal, having considered these two separate regional energy spaces, where one is perceived as advanced and the other as developing, Ostrom's design principles is used as a tool to give policy advice on the outlook of the design, reform and transition of a peculiar regional energy governance system. This was to help outline a set

1128 Johannes Baptist Opschoor, 'Knowledge Sharing in Support of Human Development', in *Globalization, Poverty and Conflict: A Critical Development Reader*, ed. by Max Spoor (Dordrecht: Kluwer Academic Press, 2004), pp. 307–22.

of policy principles that may rapidly spearhead the realisation of a good, resilient and robust regional energy system in ECOWAS.

Chapter 2 laid the conceptual and theoretical foundations on which the entire research study has relied, that is, energy, IPE of energy and institutions. Laying out all the notions of energy employed in this work namely energy systems, energy commons and energy policy. It considered IPE of energy from the angle of governing energy at the national, regional and intersectional levels. Furthermore, the third part of the chapter considered the new meta-theoretical framework for institutional analysis (CIS framework) and its elements as well as the theory of Polycentricity in the institutional governance literature.

Chapters 3 and 4 revealed how historical institutionalism can help identify the origins and development of energy regionalism in West Africa and Europe. It assisted in fully understanding the empirical aspects of the two regional energy policy settings. Although portions of the narrative may be open to debate, clarity in relation to its substantive conclusion has been established. Changes across polities, economy, and society has contributed in transitioning over time both polycentric regional energy spaces. Hence, it informs energy governance processes that solve imminent obstacles and challenges or take advantage of the opportunities and concrete potentials inherent in the regional energy sector. This is cognisant of the fact that new energy technologies take some time to be fully embraced by societies because of the structure and nature of prevailing institutions.

Any new approach towards transforming the governance of energy in a transnational region demands a rethink in the general nature of the political and socio-economic order and its readiness to adopt new energy technologies as well as the constrains it faces. The distribution of power in the international political economy setting, the make-up of the policy-making processes, and the systems that implement policy are also crucial determinants.

Moreover, key institutions involved in regional energy policy processes comprise the legal system, the economic markets, civic engagement and the normative spaces prevalent in the region. These aspects of a supranational energy region form the basis for a degree of path-dependency and path creation that typify the nature and development of multilevel energy governance mechanisms, as well as determining the capability of the region to deal with its pre-existing energy challenges. Expressed differently, the bedrock of a supranational region's energy system (that is, energy regionalism) is underpinned by the nature and functioning of its institutions of polycentric governance which would facilitate its progress or regress.

In applying institutionalism comparatively to the energy sectors of ECOWAS and EU (in Chapter 5) I observed a high degree of path-dependency and path creation in its political and economic dimensions as well as a proficiency at developing multiple units nested in their large regional energy systems. The CIS framework leverages the dynamism of the IAD framework, while integrating the details of the SES framework to analyse important and definitive aspects of institutional development and change in the two regional energy spaces over time.

This elaborate process outlined a detailed listing of key characteristics of both regional energy resource systems in different periods namely pre-1970s, 1970–1980s, 1990–2000 and 2000–2020. This highlighted key factors most important in marking the institutional transition from one temporal phase to the next. But before the temporal aspects of the analysis were considered, I focused on the overall configuration of each energy governance system. The implementation of the framework discovered significant institutional and technical changes that define the nature of collective action in energy regionalism such as its dynamism, path dependency, path creativity and its incremental nature.

Moreover, the use of the CIS framework identifies the forces driving these institutional and technical changes present in the networked action situations (that is, the interlinked policy aspects of a given energy sector). They include, energy resource appropriation, production, technical innovation, technology adoption, financial availability, transportation and communication, market exchange, ecological change, organizational behaviour, legislative and judicial deliberation, public opinion, the diffusion of knowledge or norms and other forms of societal change. In considering this broad range of relevant factors relating to their focal action situations, a reliance on the nature of the energy regions within the context of the international political economy of energy supports the analyses to move beyond the parochial use of the framework to a more contextualised occurrence of these (variable and procedural) factors that relate to both regions within a wider geopolitical setting.

Regarding ECOWAS's energy governance, important sources of path dependency and path creation lie in the region's historic political economy, the nature of its structure and its resource endowments. These endowments comprise significant hydropower resources, limited reserves of uranium ore, cheap under-explored coal, conventional reserves of onshore and offshore oil and natural gas, in addition, to underutilised renewable energy resources such as solar, wind and tidal.

Considering the EU's energy governance, it exhibits a similar trajectory of path dependency and path creation which is reliant on its past political economy structure, resource endowments and its access to external energy endowments. These internally and externally derived energy endowments include conventional and unconventional oil and natural gas, cheap coal, limited hydro-electricity resources, abundant nuclear energy sources and limited renewable sources such as wind and solar. For all industrial and industrialising geopolitical regions, the path to an effective and solid energy governance regime is constrained by the nature of the existing infrastructure for energy production, transmission and consumption.

This obstacle is clearly noticeable in ECOWAS and EU. For ECOWAS, the scale of the investment gap in infrastructure over the years has led to an overall vulnerable regional energy system. This was especially so among ECOWAS member states during the early years of the post-independence era. There was little attraction of external funders towards mega-regional energy infrastructure projects during the first two decades of the formation of the regional body's energy infrastructure.

In the case of the EU, the constrain is muted because of the vast scale of investment in infrastructure both from the early years of the century through to the collective action of the regional body in the energy sector. Its major challenges are seen in the area of consistent access to external energy resources and reducing the region's contribution of carbon due to its existing energy infrastructure.

To put aside these perceived constraints, the pace and nature of achieving a more sustainable energy supply regime in a geopolitical region like ECOWAS and EU will also depend on the pace and nature of change occurring in the multiple institutions of governance. These multiple units nested together to make up the institutions of energy governance are an important component of the wider polycentric institutional environment. Given the magnitude of the energy access, supply and carbon emissions challenge facing these geopolitical regions, it can be argued that the need for institutional change is enormous in ECOWAS. In that, it is literally constructing a new energy future from scratch in terms of scale, compared to other geopolitical energy regions.

The conceptual, theoretical and analytical framework used in this dissertation allows one to address five inter-related questions: (1) the interaction of energy and comparative regionalism reveal a number of elements. Describe how these elements come together to inform energy governance in a region? (2) Considering the historical trajectory of energy regionalism and the path taken by institutions of energy governance, what has been the likely evolutionary path taken by ECOWAS and the EU towards a more sustainable energy supply regime using energy, political economy of energy and institutions as the frame? (3) How has the capacity of the interconnected regional energy institutions in the governance of the regional energy been expressed over time to provide energy from a dual perspective? (4) What does this institutional capacity imply for the governance of West Africa's energy regionalism in terms of its potential and obstacles? Finally (5) how does West Africa design a more robust and effective regional energy governance system?

In sum, the principal contribution of the CIS framework to the analysis in this dissertation is the focus it affords in ensuring that institutional analysis in the regional energy sector commences by identifying the full range of variables and dynamic processes needed to be examined. This is in order to understand and execute the task of policy analysis and proffer good policy advice. In addition to ensuring an eventual success when implementing institutional change in the regional energy policy setting in such a case like West Africa's energy space.

Chapter 6 focused solely on discussing the implications concerning the ECOWAS region. It began by discussing the polycentric nature of the governance of West Africa's energy regionalism and the possible implications that may occur as potentials and obstacles inferred from the comparative analysis and how that relates to West Africa's regional energy governance processes in a more specific fashion.

In regard to the political dimension, a shift in the geopolitical export dynamic of petroleum resources while reprioritising energy trade in the regional market either by old and new producers through instruments like preferential energy agreements were observed as potentials among others. In the discussion some political constrains identified included the reversal of the discrepancy of interests that exists between national governments and citizens with regards to the export-consumption dilemma. Also, the snail-paced approach adopted by national governments in making strategic choices in the use of all energy resources available to them in order to aid in the process of closing the energy access and supply gap as well as reducing climate change was discussed.

Socially the implications drawn out from the analysis included the reconfiguration of regional energy policy in West Africa as a socio-energy design, which incorporates human and social dimensions while at the same time developing a knowledge base to make certain regional energy projects contribute to significant social and societal improvements. As a way of constrains, among others, it looked at the lack of active and meaningful local involvement in the planning and implementation stages of large regional energy projects as well as very weak engagement between local communities with energy companies when constructing and running major energy projects.

Economically and financially, the analysis implied an increment in energy infrastructure investment would result in meaningful economic and industrial growth in the West African region. It revealed that, as at 2018, the region is the most attractive destination Africa-wide in energy infrastructure investments. By way of constrains, limited market information such as available information on rural paying power for energy services was found to be lacking in addition to the absence of derisked private and local community investments in national and regional energy projects.

In terms of legal, regulatory and policy implications, the examination revealed regional cooperation and harmonisation in regional energy sectors with particular reference to the petroleum sector. Moreover, deregulation of the downstream petroleum and energy sectors facilitated increased local content involvement. The key obstacles faced in this regard remain the pace at which the development of local-content legislation is executed in both existing and budding energy states. In addition to, the pace at which the uncoupling of vertically integrated utilities in the region is happening even though ERERA has been set up to regulate the entire regional electricity system.

In the area of innovation and technology, the main potentials implied a rapid but reduced-scale rollout of renewable energy technology taking place in the region's energy system. This could lead to the region aspiring to be first in going green in its adoption of renewables as a viable and reliable energy option in terms of its development and use to counteract the energy access and supply lag extant in the region. A good example worthy of mention is the inroads being made by Cape Verde in this regard.

Broadly speaking the main constrain faced is the fast-paced nature of technological innovation in the overall global energy sector and the inability of the region's energy system to play catch-up while at the same time dealing with the immense challenge of renewing, retrofitting and repairing old energy technology such as power stations among others.

Lastly, the implications on bi-regional partnerships were considered. It explored the potential of untapped energy reserves and resources that still exist in relation to West Africa's relationship with Europe, how this partnership has attracted European technology, expertise, financial investment and consumption in effect shaping the region's energy industry.

In dealing with the constrains as it relates to the bi-regional partnerships the implications of attracting lower royalties hence ceding greater control of national energy assets to the benefit of IOCs was highlighted. As well as the commercial and political nature of these partnerships with particular reference to Europe which has engendered strong emotions commercially in addition to instigating political controversy in some cases.

7.1 Outlook for a Robust and Resilient ECOWAS Energy Governance Trajectory

The analysis presented in this dissertation suggests that ECOWAS's energy regionalism pathway towards a robust, resilient, sustainable and effective regional energy governance is possible. In writing these reflections on this possibility, I am concerned that an attribution as based on speculation derived from reading the historical unfolding of the EU case would be drawn. But this is not what I seek to do, rather to consider the historical and empirical basis that has underpinned energy regionalism in West Africa up until now.

To mitigate this perceived bias and help ascertain a robust energy system compared to an ailing system, I employ Elinor Ostrom's set of design principles to give policy advice on the heuristic approaches that underlie the successful functioning of a sustainable and well-governed energy space. Having used Ostrom's design principles repeatedly in the financial services sector, Alexander William Salter and Vlad Tarko concluded that these set of "hands-on" or heuristic devices are actually helpful for understanding and designing a wide variety of governance systems.[1129] This notion serves as a guide with respect to shaping a robust energy governance region in ECOWAS.

In 1990, Elinor Ostrom introduced these eight traits known as *Design Principles* that characterise an effectively governed system and serve as good practices for the sustainable governance of commons.[1130] All of these traits

---

1129 Alexander William Salter and Vlad Tarko, 'Polycentric Banking and Macroeconomic Stability', *Business and Politics*, 19.2 (2017), 365–95 <https://doi.org/10.1017/bap.2016.10>; Alexander William Salter and Vlad Tarko, 'Governing the Banking System: An Assessment of Resilience Based on Elinor Ostrom's Design Principles', *Journal of Institutional Economics*, 15.3 (2019), 505–19 <https://doi.org/10.1017/S1744137418000401>.

1130 Elinor Ostrom, *Governing the Commons - The Evolution of Institutions for Collective Action*, p. 90; Ostrom, CXXXII, p. 259; Elinor Ostrom, *Polycentric Systems as*

do not need to be present but the prospects for an effective and sustainable energy governance system would tend to increase when all or majority of these traits are in place.

The design principles that would ensure success, resilience and robustness in the governance of energy regionalism in ECOWAS are as follows:

(1) *Clearly defined group boundaries.* In the context of ECOWAS energy regionalism, the regional energy regime would work best when it is delineated clearly. This includes clarity relating to the specific types of energy resource systems available in the region. Clearly embedded regional policy, legal and regulatory aspects that secure respective energy resources and rights of all outlined energy actors. Structured regional energy exchanges (at transboundary and local levels) that are scheduled efficiently without or with minimal intermittencies. Effectively communicated and accessible regional energy data. While the multiple and various governance scales of the regional energy regime are set out definitively, recognised and enabled when needed. With all these culminating in the functioning of a bounded regional energy policy framework that facilitates polycentrism but frowns on fragmentation that seek to serve external interests while being detrimental to overall regional and national interests thus alienating the realisation of regional energy visions, goals and objectives in a timely manner. The other dimension has to do with the membership of the energy region-building project. The boundaries between legitimate users and nonusers of the various energy resource sectors being governed under ECOWAS energy regionalism need to be understood clearly to facilitate ownership. Membership of ECOWAS's energy regionalism signals adherence to certain rules (either in-form or in-use) and it is contingent on the regional energy vision, specific energy sector and policy, and information-sharing requirements. Finally, defining clear group boundaries in the regional energy space in West Africa must depend

---

One Approach for Solving Collective - Action Problems; Elinor Ostrom, 'Beyond Markets and States : Polycentric Governance of Complex Economic Systems', *American Economic Review*, 100.June (2010), 408–44 (p. 653) <https://doi.org/10.1080/19186444.2010.11658229>; Elinor Ostrom, 'Do Institutions for Collective Action Evolve?', *Journal of Bioeconomics*, 16.1 (2014), 3–30 <https://doi.org/10.1007/s10818-013-9154-8>; David Sloan Wilson, Elinor Ostrom, and Michael E. Cox, 'Generalizing the Core Design Principles for the Efficacy of Groups', *Journal of Economic Behavior and Organization*, 90 (2013), S21–32 <https://doi.org/10.1016/j.jebo.2012.12.010>.

wholly on integrating and harmonising what the individual member states and their constituent units are working to accomplish.

(2) *Proportional distribution of the benefits and costs of the various actors.* This design principle concerns regional energy governing rules (in-use) that allocate benefits proportional to inputs required from the various actors at the multiple levels of regional energy governance. The rules put in place and utilised is to require actors to contribute their fair share of resource, technical and infrastructural commitments and responsibilities for the wellbeing and proper functioning of the energy region. Elinor Ostrom discovered that a community works best when costs and benefits are distributed fairly. This would not be different in a regional energy community. Subsequently, it ensures equity and proportional equivalence that avoid having some users get all of the benefits at little cost. Moreover, the proportional distribution must take cognisance of the local, national and regional conditions. This mix of consistency between utilisation and community attributes and needs plays an elemental role in effective regional energy governance. The West Africa Gas Pipeline, for example, distributed investment-related program costs among corporate stakeholders and member nations that is, consumers and users so that no single group would bear all the liability and placed in a position to contribute an unfair or asymmetrical amount. Going forward, ensuring this sense of consistency in the proportional distribution of costs and benefits in the implementation of all regional energy projects at all governance scales in ECOWAS would be most beneficial.

(3) *Collective decision making of all the in-group actors*. An effective and resilient regional energy community is in a constant state of inclusive energy policy making that creates space for all the constituent levels of energy governance to partake in decision-making. Although not all members have an equal say in the decision-making processes the communal perception should convey a fair process and a decisive plan of action. This trait reveals one of the main differences between a polycentric regional energy system and a mainly monocentric system governed by top-down regional regulators and regulations. In these collective-choice regional energy arrangements, most of the actors and stakeholders affected by the operational rules can participate in modifying the institutional rules, which may serve as an interesting condition or constraint. A polycentric regional energy system in ECOWAS would be a self-governing system where States and other energy actors and institutions form differentiated energy alliances around particular

energy resources as well as at multiple levels. With such an approach interaction among the states result in win-win energy politics that prevent rent-seeking and regulatory capture behaviour. In sum, collective decision making ensures all national energy interests and challenges are considered in the policymaking processes.

(4) *Monitors and enforcers of rules need to be transparent and accountable in their activities.* Monitoring, transparency and accountability are instrumental ingredients in constructing an effective, resilient and sustainable form of energy regionalism. It requires the keeping track of all the activities present in the constituent members of the regional energy community in order to ensure that all commitments are realised. When monitoring is done openly and transparently, it ensures that all member states fulfil their roles thus enhancing accountability on the part of energy producers and users. This monitoring function in the regional energy community relies on endogenous levels of trust and reciprocity[1131]. To enable it sustain and safeguard a resilient polycentric governance system would mean to create official positions, contribute resources and hire monitors at all levels of energy governance in the region.

(5) *Graduated sanctions for breaking the rules.* Active rule enforcement and requirements that warrant compliance with the possibility of sanctions guarantees an effective ECOWAS energy regionalism project. Energy appropriators who violate operational rules are likely to undergo punitive processes depending on the seriousness and context of the violation. This assessment is closely related to the monitoring function because the monitors would assess and hold culpable appropriators accountable. The graduated sanctions regime in the energy governance system must include anticipated and gradual changes to rules and enforcement when they do occur so that appropriators would change their behaviour when necessary, to avoid costly punitive measures. The emphasis for this design principle relates to its incremental enforcement due to levels of infringement intensity. That is, punishments would be mild through an initial verbal or written reprimand but with the potential to be escalated if needed usually culminating in expulsion from the energy community at whatever level if all else fails. At the macro level of regional governance, the consequence of expulsion could be disastrous for the regional project hence it can

---

1131 Elinor Ostrom, *Polycentric Systems as One Approach for Solving Collective - Action Problems*.

be mitigated by withdrawing certain reliefs that are due all member states as well as the payment of certain financial surcharges that could otherwise be used for investments in the national energy sector.

(6) *Access to low-cost local arenas for conflict resolution providing fast and fair decisions.* Conflict situations are inevitable. In a robust energy governance arrangement where energy exchanges and trade take place, conflicts occur. But an adjudication system that resolves disputes in a low-cost manner especially arbitration and dispute resolutions (ADR) mechanisms inure to the benefit of parties. With devised internal conflict resolution mechanisms, ECOWAS regional energy actors and stakeholders are likely to handle and resolve conflicts and disputes with existing and newly formed designated adjudication entities. The strengthening of these entities by scaling their reach to guarantee access and bolstering institutional capacities with respect to the different energy resources would resolve internal regional conflicts and disputes fairly and quickly.

(7) *Supranational governing authorities recognize, at least to some extent, the right to self-organize.* A huge challenge faced by a polycentric energy system is the top-down interference of government and governing institutions. Especially, when these polities are not fully equipped to regulate the energy sector properly. This is no different in the ECOWAS energy governance system. Thus, their top-down interventions result in destabilising the regional energy system causing a fragile system due to the parochial approach being utilised. This design principle is so vital in the sense that it calls for a radical change in energy public policy in the ECOWAS area by transitioning towards a more polycentric energy system. In this case acknowledging the diverse energy actors' and stakeholders' rights to govern their activities through self-governance and creation of their own tailored institutions without limitations from higher national and supranational levels, in a manner where they all fit together in a solid regional energy space.

(8) *Polycentric Governance* involves an 'appropriation, provision, monitoring, enforcement, conflict resolution, and governance activities ... organized in multiple layers of nested enterprises"[1132]. The ECOWAS energy governance system is an ecosystem with nested energy systems at regional, national, federal, local and sub-local levels. It provides a wide variety of energy services at different scales resulting in major difficulties to maintain top-down energy regulation. The key reason

1132 Ostrom, CXXXII, p. 259.

for this design principle in the context of ECOWAS energy regionalism is to highlight the wide variety of governance activities (namely exploration, production, storage, distribution, processing, refining, monitoring, enforcement, and conflict resolution, trading, sales and marketing) required to be located at governance levels in the region with parallel activities of regulation. In the current system, there is a mismatch between the various energy sectors in their multiple scales of operation and their corresponding energy regulators in addition to how they all fit together at the supranational energy level. This sharing of power between the numerous scales of governance seamlessly connected, would result in a nested polycentric regional energy governance approach that involves multiple authorities and overlapping jurisdictions operating together to ensure collective action that designs effective institutions for the energy system in ECOWAS.

As Elinor Ostrom would assert these *Design Principles* are an effort to identify core principles but not blueprints[1133] suitable for the effective governance of resources. Similarly, in this case of studying the governance of energy resource systems especially at the supranational regional level, I employ this same purpose.

This dissertation is the first academic study that seeks to look into comparative energy regionalism and regional energy governance using the CIS framework at the time of submitting this work. Further research emanating from this could go in different directions. Suggestions for future research following from insights obtained from this study may include a variety of research questions. Even though the research agenda of energy regionalism and regional energy governance is vast and continues to expand, I focus here on three areas, where I think is promising in pursuing further research.

The first set of questions relate to the nature and impact of polycentric energy governance beyond the context of energy regionalism. The assemblage of multiple actors from different branches of society (state, market and common), offers polycentric governance networks a promising conduit to co-ordinate efforts for improving sustainable energy development. An examination of the role of transnational or subnational players in these polycentric energy networks beyond energy regionalism would be helpful.

The second promising area for further enquiry is to analyse global energy politics from the perspective of colonial and post-colonial studies.

1133 Elinor Ostrom, *Polycentric Systems as One Approach for Solving Collective - Action Problems*.

Many if not most studies of energy politics have focused on the split between realist, geopolitical accounts about "energy security", on the one hand, and liberal, institutionalist accounts of "energy governance", on the other. By its focus on the interplay between institutions and markets at the international level, colonial and post-colonial studies has much to offer to study the evolutionary history of energy in colonised parts of the world, relations to the colonising powers and the interplay with current global energy dynamics.

The third set of questions relate to the thematic issue of ECOWAS Energy Governance: Towards a Clean Energy Transition that focuses on broader discussions on ECOWAS' energy policy. With aspects that investigates the current ECOWAS energy cooperation targets, its governance and decarbonisation ambitions through the use of energy resources like nuclear energy. The second looking at overlaps between energy and competition policies particularly for renewable along with conventional energy. Lastly, the third aspect may analyse the energy and climate policy of ECOWAS members and the relationship between ECOWAS and non-members with respect to the energy sector as it relates to prospects from the African Union's Continental Free Trade Area (AfCFTA).

In conclusion, the final point to address in this dissertation relates to the priority that ECOWAS attaches to the rationale for regional energy governance in West Africa. It is straightforward to argue, as I have done, that the pursuit of a robust, resilient and sustainable energy governance system in ECOWAS is consistent with the more pressing needs of regional energy security and justice through the resolution of the imminent challenge of the energy access and supply gap prevalent in the region.

Policies geared towards promoting a regional polycentric approach to energy governance seek to exploit all energy resources available in the region while promoting energy efficiency and renewable energy and serve as a means to minimise the major energy constrains faced in the West African region, which includes the debilitating effects of climate change. Nevertheless, as witnessed in this study, the increasing importance of the partial polycentric energy governance network budding in the region, which are not likely to wither away any time soon, are faced with the complex challenge of how they are to be properly governed.

Periodic calls and proposals have been made in certain quarters to change the meta-governance of multi-stakeholder partnerships in order to increase their effectiveness[1134], I would also include regional agendas in relation to energy and climate particularly in vulnerable energy systems. However, Pattberg and Widerberg[1135] are of the opinion that: 'these calls for more overall synergies can only be realized if the building blocks, that is, the individual governance arrangements, are designed and implemented in ways that enable their success.' This is why the design principles may serve as a means for designing and implementing a resilient and successful energy governance space in West Africa. An energy region that already possesses seeds of polycentric governance.

Based on the proven commitment shown in the ECOWAS region by its leaders and institutions at multiple governance levels of regional energy so far. It further promotes a construction of a strongly interlinked energy policy space that interconnects the political, economic, societal, technological, regulatory and bi- regional dimensions into a complex harmonious energy system that contain large numbers of interacting elements (namely resource systems, resource units, governance systems and actors). This is coupled with their collective interactions producing policy outcomes, feedback loops and intricate networks that enable the realisation of a fully-fledged polycentric energy governance regime in West Africa.

In the final analysis, strengthening regional energy governance in ECOWAS would rapidly promote energy sufficiency, by using all available energy resources and thus enabling a regional energy system transition.

Speedily promoting regional energy self-sufficiency:

Good energy governance would be a means to modernise and industrialise West African societies while remedying the colonial and postcolonial hangover on these predominantly agro-based and overly extractive national economies of the region. By transitioning the region into a modern, self-reliant, and energy-sufficient regional economy it would promote value-added productivity and ultimately foster economic competitiveness. Again, it would lead to the reversal of the growing trend of large areas of the region still suffering from the effects of limited energy access and energy supply deficiencies particularly located in rural and peri-urban areas.

1134 Sander Chan and Pieter Pauw, *Proposal for a Global Framework for Climate Action to Engage Non-State and Subnational Stakeholders in the Future Climate Reg,ime*, Briefing Paper (Bonn, 2014).

1135 Philipp Pattberg and Oscar Widerberg, 'Transnational Multistakeholder Partnerships for Sustainable Development: Conditions for Success', *Ambio*, 45.1 (2016), 42–51 <https://doi.org/10.1007/s13280-015-0684-2>.

Leveraging the use of a diverse range of energy resources available in the region:

Restructuring the entire regional energy space by utilising multiple energy paths will be a solid step towards good regional energy governance. This may be done by taking advantage of all the region's energy resources to address energy challenges effectively in order to resolve the huge energy access deficit bedevilling the region. This must be done irrespective of external geopolitical energy interests that are antithetical to West Africa's energy vision and goals. Concrete ways in doing this will mean increases in the percentages of natural gas consumption via numerous regional pipelines. As well as, a speedy and exponential jump in deploying renewables although challenges associated with solar and wind as intermittent sources may require 24/7 backup support to enable uninterrupted supply of electricity to residential and commercial locations, thus contributing associated costs in relation to the use of these sources. The region's best path to clean, inexpensive and large quantities of energy is nuclear power, a zero-carbon emissions source that could provide a continuous flow of electricity and intensive energy for manufacturing. Utilising major regional collective action approaches at scale could advance efforts in constructing regional nuclear power megaprojects that would serve multiple countries concurrently. The use of internal and external technical expertise while removing paternalistic suspicions and international financing bottlenecks could go a long way in providing access to enormous supplies of sustainable energy to one of the world's most vulnerable energy regions. It is obvious that all energy sources have drawbacks and costs. But I believe that there is an energy and climate emergency in West Africa and it needs every possible means to address it now.

Transition of the entire regional energy system:

The increased attention and momentum in West Africa's energy space calls for a total transition in the overall regional energy system, country by country. Such a transition will deal with the three imminent regional energy challenges. That is, providing abundant access to modern forms of energy to all West Africans, ensuring energy security for all the fifteen member states of ECOWAS and speedily and urgently achieving this new energy vision of a good, resilient and robust regional energy system barely contributing any adverse effects to the global climate. This will require national governments, markets, regional energy institutions and sub-national structures like local communities, provinces and federal regions to think outside the box while being guided by regionally shared energy goals to meet the needed targets. It should also command a long-term commitment, determination, political will, focus and resources to reap the needed successes.

Deeper coordination, harmonisation and integration of national energy policies across governance scales including an intense focus on the supply and demand sides of the national and overall regional energy systems while adopting new energy technologies quickly may achieve the desired result. Moreover, the magnitude of the energy challenges would require a comprehensive involvement of diverse actors and technologies while enabling creativity, flexibility, innovation, openness and variety. West African nations, energy industries and communities will need to devise tailor-made solutions while working in concert with each another and at the same time accommodating less powerful actors.

There is no perfect energy solution on hand today. Therefore, there are no panaceas, irrespective of them being technological or institutional to deal with the energy emergency in the region today. That said, however, a complete transition from a single institutional or policy regime to a polycentric energy governance system perhaps would be successful. Since the elements of such a governance system already exist in the three energy governance challenges inherent in ECOWAS' energy regionalism namely energy security, energy access and climate change. A fully-fledged transition and reform would be needed in the ECOWAS energy space to transform these governance challenges by providing stronger inter-linkages across the diverse regional energy system.

Finally, this research study began with an initial assumption that the process of providing energy in the West African region requires good and proper governance, in order to be effective in realising the energy needs of this fifteen-member-strong, economically, geographically and demographically vast and diverse region.

I reckon that based on the analysis conducted using the methodological processes employed in the research design, to avoid suggesting simplistic policy recommendations in the governance of polycentric and transnational energy regionalism a rigorous consideration of the role of (regionalism and energy) history and an in-depth diagnosis of the regional energy space offers a better understanding of the policy field. The study provides a profound appreciation of this fact and the impact of colonial history, regionalism and governance on current ECOWAS energy policy and a way forward for designing a sustainable energy governance pathway for the region.

Bibliography

Chapter 1

Acharya, Amitav, 'Comparative Regionalism: A Field Whose Time Has Come?', *International Spectator*, 47 (2012), 3–15 <https://doi.org/10.1080/03932729.2012.655004>

African Union, 'Agenda2063: Infrastructure and Energy Initiatives | African Union', 2019 <https://au.int/en/videos/20190301/agenda2063-infrastructure-and-energy-initiatives> [accessed 25 November 2019]

African Union Commission, 'Agenda 2063: The Africa We Want The Voices Of The African People', *Final Edition*, 2015, 1–24 <http://www.un.org/en/africa/osaa/pdf/au/agenda2063.pdf>

Andrews-Speed, Philip, 'Applying Institutional Theory to the Low-Carbon Energy Transition', *Energy Research and Social Science*, 13 (2015), 216–25 <https://doi.org/10.1016/j.erss.2015.12.011>

Bach, Daniel C., 'New Regionalism as an Alias: Regionalisation through Trans-State Networks.', in *The New Regionalism in Africa*, ed. by A. Grant and F. Söderbaum (Aldershot, UK: Ashgate, 2003), pp. 21–30

Bach, Daniel C, *Regionalism in Africa: Genealogies, Institutions and Trans-State Networks*, 1st edn (London: Routledge, 2015) <https://doi.org/10.4324/9781315733180>

Carroll, Toby, and Benjamin Sovacool, 'Pipelines, Crisis and Capital: Understanding the Contested Regionalism of Southeast Asia', *Pacific Review*, 23 (2010), 625–47 <https://doi.org/10.1080/09512748.2010.522248>

Chaplin, Jonathan, 'From Inspiration to Implementation: Laudato Si', Public Theology and the Demands of Energy Policy', in *In Search of Good Energy Policy*, ed. by Marc Ozawa, Jonathan Chaplin, Michael Pollitt, David Reiner, and Paul Warde (Cambridge: Cambridge University Press, 2019), pp. 257–72 <https://doi.org/10.1017/9781108639439.018>

———, 'The Global Greening of Religion', *Palgrave Communications*, 2 (2016) <https://doi.org/10.1057/palcomms.2016.47>

Cherp, Aleh, Jessica Jewell, and Andreas Goldthau, 'Governing Global Energy: Systems, Transitions, Complexity', *Global Policy*, 2 (2011), 75–88 <https://doi.org/10.1111/j.1758-5899.2010.00059.x>

Cole, Daniel H., Graham Epstein, and Michael D. McGinnis, 'Combining the IAD and SES Frameworks', *International Journal of the Commons*, 13 (2019), 244–75 <https://doi.org/10.18352/ijc.777>

Cole, Daniel H, Graham Epstein, and Michael Dean McGinnis, 'Toward a New Institutional Analysis of Social-Ecological Systems (NIASES): Combining Elinor Ostrom's IAD and SES Frameworks', *Maurer School of Law Legal Studies Research Paper Series*, 2014, 1–22 <http://ssrn.com/abstract=2490999>

Dasgupta, Partha, and Veerabhadran Ramanathan, 'Pursuit of the Common Good', *Science* (Washington DC, September 2014), 1457–58 <https://doi.org/10.1126/science.1259406>

Delina, Laurence L., 'The Politics of Energy and Sustainable Development in Sub-Saharan Africa', in *The Oxford Handbook of Energy Politics*, ed. by Kathleen J. Hancock and Juliann Allison (Oxford and New York: Oxford University Press, 2019), pp. 1–26

Dzawu, Moses Mozart, and Andre Janse Van Vuuren, 'Energy Surplus Leaves Ghana Paying for Unneeded Power – Bloomberg', *Bloomberg*, 2019 <https://www.bloomberg.com/news/articles/2019-11-08/how-having-too-much-energy-creates-a-debt-problem-for-ghana> [accessed 25 November 2019]

Edenhofer, Ottmar, Johannes Wallacher, Hermann Lotze-Campen, Michael Reder, Brigitte Knopf, and Johannes Muller, *Climate Change, Justice and Sustainability: Linking Climate and Development Policy* (Dordrecht: Springer, 2012) <https://doi.org/10.1017/CBO9781107415324.004>

Fioretos, Orfeo, 'Historical Institutionalism in International Relations', *International Organization*, 65 (2011), 367–99 <https://doi.org/10.1017/S0020818311000002>

Florini, Ann, and Benjamin K Sovacool, 'Bridging the Gaps in Global Energy Governance', *Global Governance*, 2011, 57–74 <https://doi.org/10.5555/ggov.2011.17.1.57>

———, 'Who Governs Energy? The Challenges Facing Global Energy Governance', *Energy Policy*, 37 (2009), 5239–48 <https://doi.org/10.1016/j.enpol.2009.07.039>

Fuller, Sara, 'The Politics of Energy Justice', in *The Oxford Handbook of Energy Politics*, ed. by Kathleen J. Hancock and Juliann Allison (Oxford and New York: Oxford University Press, 2019)

Fuso Nerini, Francesco, Julia Tomei, Long Seng To, Iwona Bisaga, Priti Parikh, Mairi Black, and others, 'Mapping Synergies and Trade-Offs between Energy and the Sustainable Development Goals', *Nature Energy*, 3 (2018), 10–15 <https://doi.org/10.1038/s41560-017-0036-5>

German Institute for Global Affairs (GIGA), 'Exploring Energy Regionalism', 2015 <https://www.giga-hamburg.de/en/event/exploring-energy-regionalism> [accessed 25 November 2016]

Gerring, John, *Case Study Research: Principles and Practices* (Cambridge: Cambridge University Press, 2007)

———, 'What Is a Case Study and What Is It Good For?', *American Political Science Review*, 98 (2004), 341–54 <https://doi.org/10.1017/S0003055404001182>

Giner-Reichl, Irene, 'Renewable Energy in International and Regional Governance: Propelling Development in Africa', *Energy Research and Social Science*, 5 (2015), 116–19 <https://doi.org/10.1016/j.erss.2014.12.008>

Goldthau, Andreas, and Jan Martin Witte, 'Back to the Future or Forward to the Past? Strengthening Markets and Rules for Effective Global Energy Governance', *International Affairs*, 85 (2009), 373–90 <https://doi.org/10.1111/j.1468-2346.2009.00798.x>

———, *Global Energy Governance: The New Rules of the Game*, ed. by Andreas Goldthau and Jan Martin Witte (Washington, D.C.: Brookings Institution Press, 2010)

Van de Graaf, Thijs, 'Fragmentation in Global Energy Governance: Explaining the Creation of IRENA', *Global Environmental Politics*, 13 (2013), 14–33 <https://doi.org/10.1162/GLEP_a_00181>

Green, Nathaniel, Benjamin K. Sovacool, and Kathleen J. Hancock, 'Grand Designs: Assessing the African Energy Security Implications of the Grand Inga Dam', *African Studies Review*, 58 (2015), 133–58 <https://doi.org/10.1017/asr.2015.7>

Guba, Egon G., and Yvonna S. Lincoln, 'Paradigmatic Controversies, Contradictions, and Emerging Confluences', in *The Sage Handbook of Qualitative Research*, ed. by Norman K. Denzin and Yvonna S. Lincoln, Third (Thousand Oaks, 2005) <https://doi.org/10.1108/17465640610666642>

Gunningham, Neil, 'Confronting the Challenge of Energy Governance', *Transnational Environmental Law*, 1 (2012), 119–35 <https://doi.org/10.1017/S2047102511000124>

Hancock, Kathleen J., 'Comparative Regionalism and Natural Resources: A Focus on Africa', in *International Studies Association Annual Covention*, 2013, pp. 1–24 <https://doi.org/10.1017/CBO9781107415324.004>

———, 'Energy Regionalism: The Intersection of Resources, Regions, and Energy', in *Sustainable Regions* (Centre for the Study of Governance Innovation, University of Pretoria, 2014), pp. 1–5

———, 'Energy Regionalism and Diffusion in Africa: How Political Actors Created the ECOWAS Center for Renewable Energy and Energy Efficiency', *Energy Research and Social Science*, 5 (2015), 105–15 <https://doi.org/10.1016/j.erss.2014.12.022>

———, 'The Expanding Horizon of Renewable Energy in Sub-Saharan Africa: Leading Research in the Social Sciences', *Energy Research and Social Science*, 5 (2015), 1–8 <https://doi.org/10.1016/j.erss.2014.12.021>

Hancock, Kathleen J., and Vlado Vivoda, 'International Political Economy: A Field Born of the OPEC Crisis Returns to Its Energy Roots', *Energy Research and Social Science*, 1 (2014), 206–16 <https://doi.org/10.1016/j.erss.2014.03.017>

Hancock, Kathleen J, and Benjamin K Sovacool, 'International Political Economy and Renewable Energy: Hydroelectric Power and the Resource Curse', *International Studies Review*, 2018, 1–18 <https://doi.org/10.1093/isr/vix058>

Ighobor, Kingsley, 'There Is Energy Momentum in Africa', *Africa Renewal* (New York, April 2014) <https://www.un.org/africarenewal/magazine/april-2014/there-energy-momentum-africa>

Immergut, Ellen M., 'Historical-Institutionalism in Political Science and the Problem of Change', *Constellations of Contingency*, 2002, 237–59 <https://doi.org/10.1177/106591295901200401>

International Energy Agency (IEA), 'Energy Access Outlook 2017' (Paris, 2017) <https://doi.org/10.1787/9789264285569-en>

International Energy Agency (IEA), World Energy Outlook 2019 (Paris: OECD Publishing, 2019) <https://doi.org/https://doi.org/10.1787/d87ceb30-en>

International Energy Agency (IEA), 'Africa Energy Outlook 2019', in World Energy Outlook Special Report (Paris: OECD Publishing, 2019) <https://doi.org/10.1787/g2120ab250-en>.

International Energy Agency (IEA), 'Total Population by Region, China, Africa, India, 2018 and Growth to 2040' (Paris: IEA, 2019) <www.iea.org/data-and-statistics/charts/total-population-by-region-china-africa-india-2018-and-growth-to-2040>.

International Energy Agency (IEA), 'Presentation of the Africa Energy Outlook 2019' (Paris: International Energy Agency, 2019) <https://doi.org/10.1787/g2120ab250-en>.

IPCC, *Climate Change 2007: Impacts, Adaptation and Vulnerability*, ed. by Martin Parry, Osvaldo Canziani, Jean Palutikof, Paul van der Linden, and Clair Hanson, *Contribution of Working Group II to the Fourth Assessment Report of the IPCC* (Cambridge, UK: Cambridge University Press, 2007)

Keho, Yaya, 'What Drives Energy Consumption in Developing Countries? The Experience of Selected African Countries', *Energy Policy*, 91 (2016), 233–46 <https://doi.org/10.1016/j.enpol.2016.01.010>

Koster, Auriane Magdalena, and John Martin Anderies, 'Institutional Factors That Determine Energy Transitions: A Comparative Case Study Approach', in *Lecture Notes in Energy*, ed. by E Michalena and J.M. Hills, 1st edn (London: Springer-Verlag, 2013), XXIII, 33–61 <https://doi.org/10.1007/978-1-4471-5595-9_3>

Mahoney, James, and Dietrich Rueschemeyer, *Comparative Historical Analysis: Achievements and Agendas*, ed. by James Mahoney and Dietrich Rueschemeyer (Cambridge: Cambridge University Press, 2003) <https://doi.org/10.1017/CBO9780511803963.002>

Mahoney, James, and Kathleen Thelen, *Explaining Institutional Change: Ambiguity, Agency, and Power* (Cambridge and New York: Cambridge University Press, 2009)

Marlow, Hilary, 'Theology of Energy / Laudato Si': Pope Francis' Encyclical on the Environment and Human Ecology' (Cambridge, UK: Energy Transitions Research, University of Cambridge, 2016)

Mbachu, Dulue, 'Nigeria Seeks $3 Billion From World Bank to Tackle Power Crisis – Bloomberg', *Bloomberg*, 2019 <https://www.bloomberg.com/news/articles/2019-11-22/nigeria-seeks-3-billion-from-world-bank-to-tackle-power-crisis> [accessed 25 November 2019]

McGinnis, Michael D., *Updated Guide to IAD and the Language of the Ostrom Workshop: A Simplified Overview of a Complex Framework for the Analysis of Institutions and Their Development* (Bloomington, 2016)

Mingers, John, *Realising Systems Thinking: Knowledge and Action in Management Science* (New York: Springer Science + Business Media Inc, 2006)

Moussa P. Blimpo and Malcolm Cosgrove-Davies, *Electricity Access in Sub-Saharan Africa: Uptake, Reliability, and Complementary Factors for Economic Impact*, *Africa Development Forum Series* (Washington, DC: World Bank, 2019) <https://doi.org/10.1596/978-1-4648-1361-0>.

Osae-Brown, Anthony, and Ruth Olurounbi, 'Nigeria Runs on Generators and Nine Hours of Power a Day – Bloomberg', *Bloomberg*, 2019 <https://www.bloomberg.com/news/articles/2019-09-23/nigeria-runs-on-generators-and-nine-hours-of-power-a-day> [accessed 25 November 2019]

Ostrom, Elinor, *Governing the Commons – The Evolution of Institutions for Collective Action* (Cambridge: Cambridge University Press, 1990) <https://doi.org/10.1017/CBO9780511807763>

Ostrom, Elinor, Roy Gardner, and James Walker, *Rules, Games and Common-Pool Resources* (Ann Arbor, MI: The University of Michigan Press, 1994)

Patt, Anthony G., 'Effective Regional Energy Governance-Not Global Environmental Governance-Is What We Need Right Now for Climate Change', *Global Environmental Change*, 20 (2010), 33–35 <https://doi.org/10.1016/j.gloenvcha.2009.09.006>

Pierson, Paul, 'Increasing Returns, Path Dependence, and the Study of Politics', *American Political Science Review*, 94 (2006), 251–67 <https://doi.org/10.2307/2586011>

———, *Politics in Time: History, Institutions, and Social Analysis* (Princeton, NJ: Princeton University Press, 2004) <https://doi.org/10.1515/9781400841080>

Ponzio, Richard, and Arunabha Ghosh, *Human Development and Global Institutions: Evolution, Impact, Reform* (London and New York: Routledge, 2016)

Pope Francis, 'Laudato Si'- On Care for Our Common Home' (Vatican City: Libreria Editrice Vaticana, 2015)

Schneider, Volker, 'Governance and Complexity', in *The Oxford Handbook of Governance*, ed. by David Levi-Faur (Oxford: Oxford University Press, 2012), pp. 129–42 <https://doi.org/10.1093/oxfordhb/9780199560530.013.0009>

Scrase, Ivan, and Gordon MacKerron, *Energy for the Future: A New Agenda* (Basingstoke: Palgrave Macmillan, 2009), LXVI

Shah, Kalim U, and Keron Niles, 'Energy Policy in the Caribbean Green Economy Context and the Institutional Analysis and Design (IAD) Framework as a Proposed Tool for Its Development', *Energy Policy*, 98 (2016), 768–77 <https://doi.org/http://dx.doi.org/10.1016/j.enpol.2016.07.045>

Smil, Vaclav, *Energy and Civilization : A History* (Cambridge, Massachusetts: The MIT Press, 2017)

Sovacool, Benjamin K., Jonn Axsen, and Steve Sorrell, 'Promoting Novelty, Rigor, and Style in Energy Social Science: Towards Codes of Practice for Appropriate Methods and Research Design', *Energy Research and Social Science*, 2018, 12–42 <https://doi.org/10.1016/j.erss.2018.07.007>

Sovacool, Benjamin K., and Thijs Van de Graaf, 'Building or Stumbling Blocks? Assessing the Performance of Polycentric Energy and Climate Governance Networks', *Energy Policy*, 118 (2018), 317–24 <https://doi.org/10.1016/j.enpol.2018.03.047>

Sovacool, Benjamin K, and Ann Florini, 'Examining the Complications of Global Energy Governance', *Journal of Energy and Natural Resource Law*, 30 (2012), 235–64 <https://doi.org/10.1080/02646811.2012.11435295>

Steinmo, Sven, and Kathleen Thelen, 'Historical Institutionalism in Comparative Politics', *Structuring Politics: Historical Institutionalism in Comparative Politics*, 1992, pp. 1–32 <https://doi.org/10.1146/annurev.polisci.2.1.369>

Streeck, Wolfgang, and Kathleen Thelen, *Beyond Continuity: Institutional Change in Advanced Political Economies* (Oxford and New York: Oxford University Press, 2005) <https://doi.org/10.1093/acprof:oso/9780198701309.003.0010>

Thelen, Kathleen, 'Historical Institutionalism in Comparative Politics', *Annual Review of Political Science*, 2 (1999), 369–404 <https://doi.org/10.1017/CBO9780511801938.008>

UNDESA, 'World Population Prospects: The 2015 Revision' (New York: United Nations, Department of Economic and Social Affairs, Population Division, 2015) <http://esa.un.org/ unpd/wpp/dataquery.>;

UNDESA, 'Population of West Africa (2018)' <http://www.worldometers.info/world-population/western-africa-population/>.

Yin, Robert K., *Case Study Research and Applications: Design and Methods*, Sixth Edition (Los Angeles and London: SAGE Publications, 2018)

Chapter 2

Acharya, Amitav, 'Comparative Regionalism: A Field Whose Time Has Come?', *International Spectator*, 47 (2012), 3–15 <https://doi.org/10.1080/03932729.2012.655004>

Africa Progress Panel, *Lights Power Action: Electrifying Africa*, 2015

———, *Power People Planet Seizing Africa's Energy and Climate Opportunities*, *Africa Progress Report* (Geneva, 2015) <http://www.africaprogresspanel.org/>

Agrawal, Arun, 'Sustainable Governance of Common Pool Resources: Context, Methods, and Politics', *Annual Review of Anthropology*, 32 (2003), 243–62 <https://doi.org/10.1146/annurev.anthro.32.061002.093112>

Agrawal, Arun, and Clark C. Gibson, 'Enchantment and Disenchantment: The Role of Community in Natural Resource Conservation', *World Development*, 27 (1999), 629–49 <https://doi.org/10.1016/S0305-750X(98)00161-2>

Aligica, Paul D., and Vlad Tarko, 'Polycentricity: From Polanyi to Ostrom, and Beyond', *Governance*, 25 (2012), 237–62 <https://doi.org/10.1111/j.1468-0491.2011.01550.x>

Aligică, Paul Dragoş., and Peter J. Boettke, *Challenging Institutional Analysis and Development : The Bloomington School* (Routledge, 2009) <https://www.routledge.com/Challenging-Institutional-Analysis-and-Development-The-Bloomington-School/Aligica-Boettke/p/book/9780415778213> [accessed 20 April 2018]

Aligica, Paul Dragos, 'Institutional and Stakeholder Mapping: Frameworks for Policy Analysis and Institutional Change', *Public Organization Review*, 6 (2006), 79–90 <https://doi.org/10.1007/s11115-006-6833-0>

Amorim, Lysianne Reis, 'Institutional Framework and Sustainable Development: A Case from Electricity Generation in Brazil' (Uppsala University, 2013) <http://www.diva-portal.org/smash/get/diva2:606020/FULLTEXT01.pdf> [accessed 26 April 2018]

Anderies, John M., Marco A. Janssen, and Edella Schlager, 'Institutions and the Performance of Coupled Infrastructure Systems', *International Journal of the Commons*, 10 (2016), 495–516 <https://doi.org/10.18352/ijc.651>

Andersson, Krister, 'Understanding Decentralized Forest Governance: An Application of the Institutional Analysis and Development Framework', *Sustainability: Science, Practice and Policy*, 2 (2006), 25–35 <https://doi.org/10.1080/15487733.2006.11907975>

Andersson, Krister P., and Elinor Ostrom, 'Analyzing Decentralized Resource Regimes from a Polycentric Perspective', *Policy Sciences*, 41 (2008), 71–93 <https://doi.org/10.1007/sl>

Andrews-Speed, Philip, *The Governance of Energy in China: Transition to a Low-Carbon Economy*, 1st edn (Basingstoke: Palgrave Macmillan, 2012) <https://doi.org/10.1057/9781137284037>

Araral, Ed; Hartley, Chris, 'Polycentric Governance for a New Environmental Regime : Theoretical Frontiers in Policy Reform and Public Administration', *International Conference on Public Policy, Panel: Polycentric Policy and the Environment*, 2013, 1–31

Archer, Margaret S., *Realist Social Theory: The Morphogenetic Approach* (Cambridge: Cambridge University Press, 1995) <https://doi.org/10.2307/2655684>

———, *Social Morphogenesis*, ed. by Margaret S. Archer (Dordrecht: Springer, 2013)

Bäckman, Anders, 'The Nordic Electricity System as a Common-Pool Resource.', 2011 <http://www.diva-portal.org/smash/record.jsf?pid=diva2:437865>

Basurto, Xavier, Stefan Gelcich, and Elinor Ostrom, 'The Social–Ecological System Framework as a Knowledge Classificatory System for Benthic Small-Scale Fisheries', *Global Environmental Change*, 23 (2013), 1366–80 <https://doi.org/10.1016/J.GLOENVCHA.2013.08.001>

Basurto, Xavier, and Elinor Ostrom, 'Beyond the Tragedy of the Commons', *Economia Delle Fonti Di Energia e Dell'ambiente*, 2009, 35–60 <https://doi.org/10.3280/EFE2009-001004>

Bazilian, Morgan, Smita Nakhooda, and Thijs Van de Graaf, 'Energy Governance and Poverty', *Energy Research & Social Science*, 1 (2014), 217–25 <https://doi.org/10.1016/j.erss.2014.03.006>

Becker, Sören, Matthias Naumann, and Timothy Moss, 'Between Coproduction and Commons: Understanding Initiatives to Reclaim Urban Energy Provision in Berlin and Hamburg', *Urban Research & Practice*, 0 (2016), 1–23 <https://doi.org/10.1080/17535069.2016.1156735>

Benham, Claudia, 'Change, Opportunity and Grief: Understanding the Complex Social-Ecological Impacts of Liquefied Natural Gas Development in the Australian Coastal Zone', *Energy Research and Social Science*, 14 (2016), 61–70 <https://doi.org/10.1016/j.erss.2016.01.006>

Benkler, Yochai, 'The Political Economy of Commons', *UPGRADE*, IV (2003), 1–5

Berkes, Fikret, and Carl Folke, 'Linking Social and Ecological Systems for Resilience and Sustainability', *Linking Social and Ecological Systems*, 1 (1998), 13–20

Bevir, Mark, and Frank Trentmann, *Markets in Historical Contexts: Ideas and Politics in the Modern World*, ed. by Frank Trentmann and Mark Bevir, 1st edn (Cambridge: Cambridge University Press, 2004)

Bixler, Patrick R., J. Dell' Angelo, O. Mfune, and H. Hassan Roba, 'The Political Ecology of Participatory Conservation: Institutions and Discourse', *Journal of Political Ecology*, 22 (2015), 164–82

Blyth, Mark, *Routledge Handbook of International Political Economy (IPE)*, ed. by Mark Blyth, *Routledge Handbook of International Political Economy (IPE): IPE as a Global Conversation*, 1st edn (Abingdon, Oxford: Routledge, 2009) <https://doi.org/10.1355/ae26-3j>

Bollier, David, *Public Assets, Private Profits. Reclaiming the American Commons in an Age of Market Enclosure* (Washington, DC, 2001) <http://www.bollier.org/pdf/PA_Report.pdf>

Bolton, Ronan and Timothy J. Foxon, 'Infrastructure Transformation as a Socio-Technical Process – Implications for the Governance of Energy Distribution Networks in the UK', *Technological Forecasting and Social Change*, 90.PB (2015), 538–50 <https://doi.org/10.1016/j.techfore.2014.02.017>.

Bradshaw, Michael J., *Global Energy Dilemmas: Energy Security, Globalization, and Climate Change* (Cambridge: Polity Press, 2014)

Breslin, Shaun, Richard A Higgott, and Ben Rosamond, *Regions in Comparative Perspective*, *Perspective*, 2002 <https://doi.org/10.4324/9780203361672_chapter_1>

Breslin, Shaun, Christopher W. Hughes, Nicola Phillips, and Ben Rosamond, *New Regionalisms in the Global Political Economy: Theory and Cases*, ed. by Shaun Breslin, Christopher W. Hughes, Nicola Phillips, and Ben Rosamond (London and New York: Routledge, 2002) <https://doi.org/10.4324/9780203361672>

Brown, Marilyn A., 'Market Failures and Barriers as a Basis for Clean Energy Policies', *Energy Policy*, 29 (2001), 1197–1207 <https://doi.org/10.1016/S0301-4215(01)00067-2>

Brown, Marilyn A, and Benjamin K Sovacool, *Climate Change and Global Energy Security-Technology and Policy Options* (Cambridge, Massachusetts: The MIT Press, 2011)

Bryner, Gary C., 'Challenges in Developing a Diverse Domestic Energy Portfolio: IntegratingEnergy and Climate Policy in the Western United States', *New York University Environmental Law Journal*, 15 (2007) <https://heinonline.org/HOL/Page?handle=hein.journals/nyuev15&id=79&div=8&collection=journals> [accessed 26 April 2018]

Buck, Susan J., *The Global Commons: An Introduction* (Washington D.C.: Island Press, 1998) <https://doi.org/10.1016/s0962-6298(00)00042-1>

Carlisle, Keith, and Rebecca L. Gruby, 'Polycentric Systems of Governance: A Theoretical Model for the Commons', *Policy Studies Journal*, 00 (2017) <https://doi.org/10.1111/psj.12212>

Carroll, Toby, and Benjamin Sovacool, 'Pipelines, Crisis and Capital: Understanding the Contested Regionalism of Southeast Asia', *Pacific Review*, 23 (2010), 625–47 <https://doi.org/10.1080/09512748.2010.522248>

Cinner, Joshua E, Tim R McClanahan, M Aaron MacNeil, Nicholas A J Graham, Tim M Daw, Ahmad Mukminin, and others, 'Comanagement of Coral Reef Social-Ecological Systems.', *Proceedings of the National Academy of Sciences of the United States of America*, 109 (2012), 5219–22 <https://doi.org/10.1073/pnas.1121215109>

Cleveland, Cutler J., and Christopher G. Morris, *Dictionary of Energy*, ed. by Cutler J. Cleveland and Christopher G. Morris, 2nd edn (Elsevier Ltd., 2015) <https://doi.org/10.1016/B978-0-08-096811-7.50019-6>

Coelho, Ricardo Lopes, 'On the Concept of Energy: History and Philosophy for Science Teaching', *Procedia – Social and Behavioral Sciences*, 1 (2009), 2648–52 <https://doi.org/10.1016/j.sbspro.2009.01.468>

Cohen, Benjamin J., *Advanced Introduction to International Political Economy, Elgar Advanced Introductions Series*, 1st edn (Massachusetts: Edward Elgar, 2014) <https://doi.org/10.4337/9781783470600.00011>

Cole, Dan, Mike Mcginnis, and Graham Epstein, 'Toward a Combined IAD-SES Framework' (Bloomington,IN, 2013), pp. 1–55 <https://ostromworkshop.indiana.edu/pdf/seriespapers/2013s_c/Cole, McGinnis, Epstein_PowerPoint.pdf>

Cole, Daniel H., 'Laws, Norms, and the Institutional Analysis and Development Framework', *Journal of Institutional Economics*, 2017, 1–19 <https://doi.org/10.1017/S1744137417000030>

Cole, Daniel H., Graham Epstein, and Michael D. McGinnis, 'Combining the IAD and SES Frameworks', *International Journal of the Commons*, 13 (2019), 244–75 <https://doi.org/10.18352/ijc.777>

Cole, Daniel H., and Michael D. McGinnis, *Elinor Ostrom and the Bloomington School of Political Economy: Volume 1, Polycentricity in Public Administration and Political Science*, ed. by Daniel H. Cole and Michael D. McGinnis (Lexington, Lanham, MD, 2015)

Cole, Daniel H, Graham Epstein, and Michael Dean McGinnis, 'Toward a New Institutional Analysis of Social-Ecological Systems (NIASES): Combining Elinor Ostrom's IAD and SES Frameworks', *Maurer School of Law Legal Studies Research Paper Series*, 2014, 1–22 <http://ssrn.com/abstract=2490999>

Cole, Daniel H, and Michael Dean McGinnis, *Elinor Ostrom and the Bloomington School of Political Economy. Volume 2. Resource Governance : Polycentricity in Public Administration and Political Science*, *Books by Maurer Faculty*, 2015 <https://www.repository.law.indiana.edu/facbooks/24> [accessed 20 April 2018]

Cox, Michael, 'Applying a Social-Ecological System Framework to the Study of the Taos Valley Irrigation System', *Human Ecology*, 42 (2014), 311–24 <https://doi.org/10.1007/s10745-014-9651-y>

Crawford, Sue E. S., and Elinor Ostrom, 'A Grammar of Institutions', *The American Political Science Review*, 89 (1995), 582–600

Dafermos, George, Kostas Latoufis, Panos Kotsampopoulos, Ioannis Margaris, Beatriz Rivela, Fausto Paulino Washima, Pere Ariza-Montobbio, and others, 'Transforming The Energy Matrix: Transition Policies For The Development Of The Distributed Energy Model', *Journal of Peer Production*, 2015 <http://peerproduction.net/issues/issue-7-policies-for-the-commons/peer-reviewed-papers/transforming-the-energy-matrix/> [accessed 23 November 2018]

Dangerman, A T C Jérôme, and Hans Joachim Schellnhuber, 'Energy Systems Transformation', *Proceedings of the National Academy of Sciences*, 110 (2013), E549–58 <https://doi.org/10.1073/pnas.1219791110>

Dasgupta, Partha, 'Common Property Resources : Economic Analytics', *Economic and Political Weekly*, 40 (2005), 1610–22 <https://doi.org/10.2307/2404396>

DeCaro, Daniel A, Brian C Chaffin, Edella Schlager, Ahjond S Garmestani, and J B Ruhl, 'Legal and Institutional Foundations of Adaptive Environmental Governance', *Ecology and Society*, 22 (2017) <https://doi.org/10.5751/ES-09036-220132>

Dell'Angelo, Jampel, 'Abusing the Commons? An Integrated Institutional Analysis of Common-Pool Resource Governance in Conflict Situations', *TDX (Tesis Doctorals En Xarxa)* (Universitat Autònoma de Barcelona, 2013) <http://www.tdx.cat/handle/10803/129471> [accessed 25 April 2018]

Dubash, Navroz K., 'From Norm Taker to Norm Maker? Indian Energy Governance in Global Context', *Global Policy*, 2 (2011), 66–79 <https://doi.org/10.1111/j.1758-5899.2011.00123.x>

Dubash, Navroz K., and Ann Florini, 'Mapping Global Energy Governance', *Global Policy*, 2 (2011), 6–18 <https://doi.org/10.1111/j.1758-5899.2011.00119.x>

ECOWAS/UEMOA, *White Paper for a Regional Policy on Access to Energy Services for People In Rural And Peri-Urban Areas* (Niamey, 2005)

Eichenberger, Reiner, and Bruno S. Frey, 'FOCJ: Competitive Governments for Europe', *International Review of Law and Economics*, 16 (1996), 315–27

Elworthy, Charles, 'The Energy Commons: A Governance Framework for Climate Stability and Energy Security', 2011, p. 60 <www.academia.edu>

Epstein, Graham, Jessica M. Vogt, Sarah K. Mincey, Michael Cox, and Burney Fischer, 'Missing Ecology: Integrating Ecological Perspectives with the Social-Ecological System Framework', *International Journal of the Commons*, 7 (2013), 432–53 <https://doi.org/10.18352/ijc.371>

Escribano, Gonzalo, 'Ecuador's Energy Policy Mix: Development versus Conservation and Nationalism with Chinese Loans', *Energy Policy*, 57 (2013), 152–59 <https://doi.org/10.1016/J.ENPOL.2013.01.022>

Farrell, Joseph, and Philip J Weiser, 'Modularity, Vertical Integration, and Open Access Policies: Towards a Convergence of Antitrust and Regulation in the Internet Age', *Harvard Journal of Law & Technology*, 17 (2003), 85 <http://scholar.law.colorado.edu/articleshttp://scholar.law.colorado.edu/articles/539.>

Feeny, David, Fikret Berkes, Bonnie J. McCay, and James M. Acheson, 'The Tragedy of the Commons: Twenty-Two Years Later', *Human Ecology*, 18 (1990), 1–19 <https://doi.org/10.1093/nq/s2-VI.140.189-c>

Feynman, Richard, Robert B. Leighton, and Matthew Sands, *The Feynman Lectures on Physics, Vol. 1: Mainly Mechanics, Radiation, and Heat*, *The Feynman Lectures on Physics*, 1st edn (Reading, Massachusetts; Palo Alto, CA; London, UK: Addisson-Wesley Publishing Company, Inc, 1963), I <https://doi.org/10.1119/1.1972241>

Finger, Matthias, and Rolf W. Künneke, *International Handbook of Network Industries*, 2011

Fleischman, Forrest D., Natalie C. Ban, Louisa S. Evans, Graham Epstein, Sergio Villamayor-Tomas, and Gustavo Garcia-Lopez, 'Governing Large-Scale Social-Ecological Systems: Lessons from Five Cases', *International Journal of the Commons*, 8 (2014), 428–56 <https://doi.org/10.18352/ijc.416>

Fleischman, Forrest D., Kinga Boenning, Gustavo A. Garcia-Lopez, Sarah Mincey, Mikaela Schmitt-Harsh, Katrin Daedlow, and others, 'Disturbance, Response, and Persistence in Self-Organized Forested Communities: Analysis of Robustness and Resilience in Five Communities in Southern Indiana', *Ecology and Society* (Resilience Alliance Inc.) <https://doi.org/10.2307/26268203>

Folke, Carl, Thomas Hahn, Per Olsson, and Jon Norberg, 'Adaptive Governance of Social-Ecological Systems', *Annu. Rev. Environ. Resour.*, 30 (2005), 441–473 <https://doi.org/doi: 10.1146/annurev.energy.30.050504.144511>

Frey, Bruno S., and Reiner. Eichenberger, *The New Democratic Federalism for Europe : Functional, Overlapping, and Competing Jurisdictions* (Edward Elgar, 1999)

Frigo, Giovanni, 'Energy Ethics, Homogenization, and Hegemony: A Reflection on the Traditional Energy Paradigm', *Energy Research and Social Science*, 30 (2017), 7–17 <https://doi.org/10.1016/j.erss.2017.06.030>

Frischmann, Brett, 'Privatization and Commercialization of the Internet Infrastructure', *The Columbia Science and Technology Law Review*, 1 (2001) <http://www.law.columbia.edu/stlr> [accessed 23 November 2018]

Frischmann, Brett M., *Infrastructure : The Social Value of Shared Resources* (New York: Oxford University Press, Inc, 2012)

Frischmann, Brett M, 'An Economic Theory of Infrastructure and Commons Management', *Minesota Law Review*, 89 (2005), 917–1030

Galaz, Victor, Beatrice Crona, Henrik Österblom, Per Olsson, and Carl Folke, 'Polycentric Systems and Interacting Planetary Boundaries – Emerging Governance of Climate Change-Ocean Acidification-Marine Biodiversity', *Ecological Economics*, 81 (2012), 21–32 <https://doi.org/10.1016/j.ecolecon.2011.11.012>

Garner, Bryan A., *Black's Law Dictionary*, ed. by Bryan A. Garner, 8th edn, 2004

GEA, *Global Energy Assessment -Toward a Sustainable Future, Cambridge University Press, Cambridge, UK and New York, NY, USA and the International Institute for Applied Systems Analysis, Laxenburg, Austria.* (New York, 2012) <https://doi.org/10.1017/CBO9780511793677>

Geels, Frank W., *Technological Transitions and System Innovations : A Co-Evolutionary and Socio-Technical Analysis* (Edward Elgar, 2005)

Gilpin, Robert, *The Political Economy of International Relations* (Princeton,NJ: Princeton University Press, 1987)

Global Energy Assessment, *Chapter 1: Energy Primer* (Cambridge: Cambridge University Press, 2012) <https://doi.org/10.1017/CBO9781107415324.004>

Goldthau, Andreas, 'From the State to the Market and Back: Policy Implications of Changing Energy Paradigms', *Global Policy*, 3 (2012), 198–210 <https://doi.org/10.1111/j.1758-5899.2011.00145.x>

———, 'Rethinking the Governance of Energy Infrastructure: Scale, Decentralization and Polycentrism', *Energy Research and Social Science*, 1 (2014), 134–40 <https://doi.org/10.1016/j.erss.2014.02.009>

Goldthau, Andreas, and Nick Sitter, *A Liberal Actor in a Realist World : The European Union Regulatory State and the Global Political Economy of Energy*, 1st edn (Oxford: Oxford University Press, 2015)

Gordillo, Gustavo, and Krister Andersson, 'From Policy Lessons to Policy Actions: Motivation to Take Evaluation Seriously', *Public Administration and Development*, 24 (2004), 305–20 <https://doi.org/10.1002/pad.325>

Gordon, H Scott, 'The Economic Theory of a Common-Property Resource: The Fishery', *The Journal of Political Economy*, 62 (1954), 124–42

Van de Graaf, Thijs, *The Politics and Institutions of Global Energy Governance*, 1st edn (London: Palgrave Macmillan, 2013)

Van De Graaf, Thijs, Benjamin K. Sovacool, Arunabha Ghosh, Florian Kern, and Michael T. Klare, *The Palgrave Handbook of the International Political Economy of Energy*, ed. by Thijs Van De Graaf, Benjamin K. Sovacool, Arunabha Ghosh, Florian Kern, and Michael T. Klare, 1st edn (London: Palgrave Macmillan, 2016) <https://doi.org/10.1057/978-1-137-55631-8_12>

Van De Graaf, Thijs, and Fariborz Zelli, 'Actors, Institutions and Frames in Global Energy Politics.', in *The Palgrave Handbook of the International Political Economy of Energy. Palgrave Handbooks in IPE.*, ed. by Thijs Van De Graaf, Benjamin K. Sovacool, Arunabha Ghosh, Florian Kern, and Michael T. Klare (London: Palgrave Macmillan, 2016), pp. 47–71 <https://doi.org/10.1057/978-1-137-55631-8>

Gutiérrez, Nicolás L., Ray Hilborn, and Omar Defeo, 'Leadership, Social Capital and Incentives Promote Successful Fisheries', *Nature*, 470 (2011), 386–89 <https://doi.org/10.1038/nature09689>

Haas, Reinhard, Nebojsa Nakicenovic, Amela Ajanovic, Thomas Faber, Lukas Kranzl, Andreas Müller, and others, 'Towards Sustainability of Energy Systems: A Primer on How to Apply the Concept of Energy Services to Identify Necessary Trends and Policies', *Energy Policy*, 36 (2008), 4012–21 <https://doi.org/10.1016/j.jpdc.2017.10.001>

Hall, Peter A., and Rosemary C.R. Taylor, 'Political Science and the Three New Institutionalisms', *Political Studies*, 44 (1996), 936–57 <https://doi.org/10.1111/j.1467-9248.1996.tb00343.x>

Hancock, Kathleen J., 'Energy Regionalism : The Intersection of Resources, Regions, and Energy', in *Sustainable Regions* (Centre for the Study of Governance Innovation, University of Pretoria, 2014), pp. 1–5

———, 'Energy Regionalism and Diffusion in Africa: How Political Actors Created the ECOWAS Center for Renewable Energy and Energy Efficiency', *Energy Research and Social Science*, 5 (2015), 105–15 <https://doi.org/10.1016/j.erss.2014.12.022>

———, 'The Expanding Horizon of Renewable Energy in Sub-Saharan Africa: Leading Research in the Social Sciences', *Energy Research and Social Science*, 5 (2015), 1–8 <https://doi.org/10.1016/j.erss.2014.12.021>

Hancock, Kathleen J., and Vlado Vivoda, 'International Political Economy: A Field Born of the OPEC Crisis Returns to Its Energy Roots', *Energy Research and Social Science*, 1 (2014), 206–16 <https://doi.org/10.1016/j.erss.2014.03.017>

Hancock, Kathleen J., 'Comparative Regionalism and Natural Resources: A Focus on Africa.' *Paper presented at the International Studies Association Annual Convention*. (2013)

Hardin, Garrett, 'The Tragedy of the Commons', *Science*, 162 (1968), 1243–48

Hargittai, Istvàn, and Magdolna Hargittai, *In Our Own Image. Personal Symmetry in Discovery*, 2000 <https://doi.org/10.1007/978-1-4615-4179-0>

Helfrich, Silke, and David Bollier, *Commons Als Transformative Kraft*, ed. by Silke Helfrich and Heinrich-Böll-Stiftung, *Commons: Für Eine Neue Politik Jenseits von Markt Und Staat* (Bielefeld,DE: transcript, 2012)

Helm, Dieter, 'Energy Policy: Security of Supply, Sustainability and Competition', *Energy Policy*, 30 (2002), 173–84 <https://doi.org/10.1016/S0301-4215(01)00141-0>

———, 'The Assessment: The New Energy Paradigm', *Oxford Review of Economic Policy*, 21 (2005), 1–18 <https://doi.org/10.1093/oxrep/gri001>

Heverly, Robert A, 'The Information Semicommons', *Berkeley Technology Law Journal*, 18 (2003), 1127–89 <https://doi.org/10.15779/Z38B69G>

Hiller, Janine, Scott Shackelford, and Xiao Ma, *The Firm as Common Pool Resource: Unpacking the Rise of Benefit Corporations*, White Paper Series (Bloomington, 2017)

Hinkel, Jochen, Michael E. Cox, Maja Schlüter, Claudia R. Binder, and Thomas Falk, 'A Diagnostic Procedure for Applying the Social-Ecological Systems Framework in Diverse Cases', *Ecology and Society*, 20 (2015) <http://www.ecologyandsociety.org/vol20/iss1/art32/>

Hodbod, Jennifer, and W. Neil Adger, 'Integrating Social-Ecological Dynamics and Resilience into Energy Systems Research', *Energy Research and Social Science*, 1 (2014), 226–31 <https://doi.org/10.1016/j.erss.2014.03.001>

Hooghe, Liesbet, and Gary Marks, 'Types of Multi-Level Governance', *European Integration Online Papers (EIoP) N°*, 5 (2001) <http://eiop.or.at/eiop/texte/2001-011a.htm>

———, 'Unraveling the Central States, but How? Types of Multi-Level Governance', *The American Political Science Review*, 97 (2003), 233–43 <https://doi.org/10.1017/S0003055403000649>

Hughes, Llewelyn, and Johannes Urpelainen, 'Interests, Institutions, and Climate Policy: Explaining the Choice of Policy Instruments for the Energy Sector', *Environmental Science and Policy*, 54 (2015), 52–63 <https://doi.org/10.1016/j.envsci.2015.06.014>

Hume, David, 'Of the Idea of Necessary Connexion', in *An Enquiry Concerning Human Understanding*, 1748, p. Section VII <https://doi.org/10.4324/9780203802458>

Imperial, Mark T, 'Institutional Analysis and Ecosystem-Based Management: The Institutional Analysis and Development Framework', *Environmental Management*, 24 (1999), 449–65 <https://doi.org/DOI 10.1007/s002679900246>

Inderst, Georg, *Private Infrastructure Finance and Investment in Europe*, EIB Working Papers (Luxembourg, 2013) <http://hdl.handle.net/10419/88101>

Kaffine, Daniel T, and Christopher M Worley, 'The Windy Commons?', *Environmental and Resource Economics*, 47 (2010), 151–72 <https://doi.org/10.1007/s10640-010-9369-2>

Keating, Michael F, Caroline Kuzemko, Andrei V Belyi, and Andreas Goldthau, 'Introduction: Bringing Energy into International Political Economy', in *Dynamics of Energy Governance in Europe and Russia*, ed. by C. Kuzemko, A. Belyi, A. Goldthau, and M. Keating, 1st edn (Palgrave Macmillan UK, 2012), pp. 1–19 <https://doi.org/10.1057/9780230370944_1>

Keohane, Robert O, and Elinor Ostrom, 'Local Commons and Global Interdependence: Heterogeneity and Cooperation in 2 Domains – Introduction', *Journal of Theoretical Politics*, 6 (1994), 403–28

Kong, Bo, 'Governing China's Energy in the Context of Global Governance', *Global Policy*, 2 (2011), 51–65 <https://doi.org/10.1111/j.1758-5899.2011.00124.x>

Koster, Auriane Magdalena, 'An Institutional Approach to Understanding Energy Transitions', *PhD Dissertation* (Arizona State University, 2013) <https://doi.org/10.1017/CBO9781107415324.004>

Koster, Auriane Magdalena, and John Martin Anderies, 'Institutional Factors That Determine Energy Transitions: A Comparative Case Study Approach', in *Lecture Notes in Energy*, ed. by E Michalena and J.M. Hills, 1st edn (London: Springer-Verlag, 2013), xxiii, 33–61 <https://doi.org/10.1007/978-1-4471-5595-9_3>

Künneke, Rolf, and Matthias Finger, 'The Governance of Infrastructures as Common Pool Resources', *Fourth Workshop on the Workshop (WOW4), June 2–7*, 2009, 1–24

Lasswell, Harold D., *Politics: Who Gets What, When, How* (New York: Whittlesey House, 1936)

Lessig, Lawrence, *The Future of Ideas: The Fate of the Commons in a Connected World*, *Duke Law Journal*, 2001, LII <https://doi.org/10.1007/s13398-014-0173-7.2>

Lönnroth, Mans, 'Swedish Energy Policy: Technology in the Political Process', in *The Energy Syndrome: Comparing National Responses to the Energy Crisis*, ed. by LN Lindberg (Lexington: Lexington Books, 1978), pp. 268–69

Madrigal, Róger, Francisco Alpízar, and Achim Schlüter, 'Determinants of Performance of Community-Based Drinking Water Organizations', *World Development*, 39 (2011), 1663–75 <https://doi.org/10.1016/j.worlddev.2011.02.011>

Marquard, Andrew, 'The Origins and Development of South African Energy Policy', 2006, p. 445

Mccay, Bonnie J, and Joan Bennett, 'Elinor Ostrom 1933–2012' (National Academy of Sciences, 2014), p. 9 <http://www.nasonline.org/publications/biographical-memoirs/memoir-pdfs/ostrom-elinor.pdf>

McCord, Paul, Jampel Dell'Angelo, Elizabeth Baldwin, and Tom Evans, 'Polycentric Transformation in Kenyan Water Governance: A Dynamic Analysis of Institutional and Social-Ecological Change', *Policy Studies Journal*, 45 (2017), 633–58 <https://doi.org/10.1111/psj.12168>

McGinnis, Michael D., 'An Introduction to IAD and the Language of the Ostrom Workshop: A Simple Guide to a Complex Framework', *Policy Studies Journal*, 39 (2011), 169–83 <https://doi.org/10.1111/j.1541-0072.2010.00401.x>

———, 'Connecting Commons and the IAD Framework', in *Routledge Handbook of the Study of the Commons*, ed. by Blake Hudson, Jonathan Rosenbloom, and Dan Cole, 1st edn (London and New York: Routledge, 2018)

———, *Updated Guide to IAD and the Language of the Ostrom Workshop: A Simplified Overview of a Complex Framework for the Analysis of Institutions and Their Development* (Bloomington, 2016)

McGinnis, Michael Dean, *Polycentric Governance and Development: Readings from the Workshop in Political Theory and Policy Analysis*, ed. by Michael Dean McGinnis, 4th edn (The University of Michigan Press, 1999) <https://doi.org/10.3998/mpub.16052>

McGinnis, Michael Dean, and Elinor Ostrom, 'Social-Ecological System Framework: Initial Changes and Continuing Challenges', *Ecology and Society*, 19 (2014) <https://doi.org/10.5751/ES-06387-190230>

McGowan, Francis, 'International Regimes for Energy: Finding the Right Level for Policy', in *Energy for the Future*, ed. by I Scarse and K MacKerron (London: Palgrave Macmillan UK, 2009), pp. 20–34 <https://doi.org/10.1057/9780230235441_2>

McKelvey, Vincent E., 'Mineral Resource Estimates and Public Policy', *American Scientist*, 60 (1972), 32–40 <https://doi.org/10.1021/es401221j>

Meadowcroft, James, 'What about the Politics? Sustainable Development, Transition Management, and Long Term Energy Transitions', *Policy Sciences*, 42 (2009), 323–40 <https://doi.org/10.1007/s11077-009-9097-z>

Mitchell, Catherine, *The Political Economy of Sustainable Energy*, 2nd edn (New York: Palgrave Macmillan, 2010) <https://doi.org/10.1057/9780230279452>

Mwangi, Esther N., 'Institutional Change and Politics: The Transformation of Property Rights in Kenya's Maasailand' (Indiana University, 2003) <https://doi.org/10.3102/00346543067001043>

Nordquist, Myron H, John Norton Moore, and Alexander S Skaridov, *International Energy Policy, the Arctic and the Law of the Sea, Center for Oceans Law and Policy* (Leiden/Boston: Martinus Nijhoff Publishers, 2005)

North, Douglass Cecil, *Institutions, Institutional Change and Economic Performance* (Cambridge: Cambridge University Press, 1990)

———, *Understanding the Process of Economic Change* (Princeton, NJ: Princeton University Press, 2005)

Olson, Mancur Jr., *The Logic of Collective Action: Public Goods and the Theory of Groups*, 2nd edn (Cambridge, MA: Harvard University Press, 1965)

Ostrom, E., 'A Diagnostic Approach for Going beyond Panaceas', *Proceedings of the National Academy of Sciences*, 104 (2007), 15181–87 <https://doi.org/10.1073/pnas.0702288104>

Ostrom, E., M. A. Janssen, and J. M. Anderies, 'Going beyond Panaceas', *Proceedings of the National Academy of Sciences*, 104 (2007), 15176–78 <https://doi.org/10.1073/pnas.0701886104>

Ostrom, Elinor, 'A General Framework for Analyzing Sustainability of Social-Ecological Systems', *Science*, 325 (2009), 419–22 <https://doi.org/10.1126/science.1172133>

———, 'A Long Polycentric Journey', *Annual Review of Political Science*, 13 (2010), 1–23 <https://doi.org/10.1146/annurev.polisci.090808.123259>

———, 'Beyond Markets and States: Polycentric Governance of Complex Economic Systems', *American Economic Review*, 100 (2010), 641–72 <https://doi.org/10.1257/aer.100.3.641>

———, 'Common-Pool Resources and Institutions: Toward a Revised Theory', in *Handbook of Agricultural Economics*, ed. by B. Gardner and G. Rausser (Elsevier Science B.V, 2002), II, 1315–39 <https://doi.org/10.1016/S1574-0072(02)10006-5>

———, 'Coping With Tragedies of the Commons', *Annual Review of Political Science*, 2 (1999), 493–535 <https://doi.org/10.1146/annurev.polisci.2.1.493>

———, 'Crossing the Great Divide: Coproduction, Synergy, and Development', *World Development*, 24 (1996), 1073–87 <https://doi.org/10.1016/0305-750X(96)00023-X>

———, *Governing the Commons – The Evolution of Institutions for Collective Action* (Cambridge: Cambridge University Press, 1990) <https://doi.org/10.1017/CBO9780511807763>

———, 'How Types of Goods and Property Rights Jointly Affect Collective Action', *Journal of Theoretical Politics*, 15 (2003), 239–70 <https://doi.org/10.1177/0951692803015003002>

———, *Polycentric Systems as One Approach for Solving Collective – Action Problems*, Working Paper (Bloomington,IN, 2008)

———, 'Polycentric Systems for Coping with Collective Action and Global Environmental Change', *Global Environmental Change*, 2010 <https://doi.org/10.1016/j.gloenvcha.2010.07.004>

———, 'Reflections on "Some Unsettled Problems of Irrigation"', *American Economic Review*, 101 (2011), 49–63 <https://doi.org/10.1257/aer.101.1.49>

———, *Understanding Institutional Diversity*, *Public Choice*, 2005, CXXXII <https://doi.org/10.1007/s11127-007-9157-x>

Ostrom, Elinor, Joanna Burger, Christopher B Field, Richard B Norgaard, and David Policansky, 'Revisiting the Commons: Local Lessons, Global Challenges.', *Science (New York, N.Y.)*, 284 (1999), 278–82 <https://doi.org/10.1126/science.284.5412.278>

———, 'Revisiting the Commons: Local Lessons, Global Challenges Local Lessons, Global Challenges', *Science* (New York, April 1999), 278–82 <https://doi.org/10.1126/science.284.5412.278>

Ostrom, Elinor, and Michael Cox, 'Moving beyond Panaceas: A Multi-Tiered Diagnostic Approach for Social-Ecological Analysis', *Environmental Conservation*, 37 (2010), 451–63 <https://doi.org/10.1017/S0376892910000834>

Ostrom, Vincent, 'Polycentricity', *Annual Meeting of the American Political Science Association, Washington Hilton Hotel, Washington, D.C., September 5–9*, 1972, 47 <http://dlc.dlib.indiana.edu/dlc/handle/10535/3763>

Ostrom, Vincent, Charles M. Tiebout, and Robert Warren, 'The Organization of Government in Metropolitan Areas: A Theoretical Inquiry', *American Political Science Review*, 55 (1961), 831–42 <https://doi.org/10.1017/S0003055400125973>

Pahl-Wostl, Claudia, and Christian Knieper, 'The Capacity of Water Governance to Deal with the Climate Change Adaptation Challenge: Using Fuzzy Set Qualitative Comparative Analysis to Distinguish between Polycentric, Fragmented and Centralized Regimes', *Global Environmental Change*, 29 (2014), 139–54 <https://doi.org/10.1016/j.gloenvcha.2014.09.003>

Pahl-Wostl, Claudia, Louis Lebel, Christian Knieper, and Elena Nikitina, 'From Applying Panaceas to Mastering Complexity: Toward Adaptive Water Governance in River Basins', *Environmental Science and Policy*, 23 (2012), 24–34 <https://doi.org/10.1016/j.envsci.2012.07.014>

Parag, Yael, and Benjamin K. Sovacool, 'Electricity Market Design for the Prosumer Era', *Nature Energy*, 1 (2016), 16032 <https://doi.org/10.1038/nenergy.2016.32>

Pasqualetti, Martin J., and Marilyn A. Brown, 'Ancient Discipline, Modern Concern: Geographers in the Field of Energy and Society', *Energy Research and Social Science*, 1 (2014), 122–33 <https://doi.org/10.1016/j.erss.2014.03.016>

Patt, Anthony G., 'Effective Regional Energy Governance-Not Global Environmental Governance-Is What We Need Right Now for Climate Change', *Global Environmental Change*, 20 (2010), 33–35 <https://doi.org/10.1016/j.gloenvcha.2009.09.006>

Perroux, François, 'Economic Space: Theory and Applications', *The Quarterly Journal of Economics*, 64 (1950), 89–104 <https://doi.org/10.2307/1881960>

Pineau, Pierre Olivier, 'Electricity Sector Integration in West Africa', *Energy Policy*, 36 (2008), 210–23 <https://doi.org/10.1016/j.enpol.2007.09.002>

Polski, Margaret M, *The Invisible Hands of U.S. Commercial Banking Reform: Private Action and Public Guarantees* (Boston, MA: Kluwer, 2003)

Powell, Richard C., 'Configuring an "Arctic Commons"?', *Political Geography*, 27 (2008), 827–32 <https://doi.org/10.1016/j.polgeo.2008.08.008>

Ravenhill, John, 'International Political Economy', in *The Oxford Handbook of International Relations*, ed. by Christian Reus-Smit Duncan Snidal (Oxford: Oxford University Press, 2008), pp. 539–57 <https://doi.org/10.1093/oxfordhb/9780199219322.003.0031>

Ribot, Jesse C., Arun Agrawal, and Anne M. Larson, 'Recentralizing While Decentralizing: How National Governments Reappropriate Forest Resources', *World Development*, 34 (2006), 1864–86 <https://doi.org/10.1016/j.worlddev.2005.11.020>

Ripple, William J, Pete Smith, Helmut Haberl, Stephen A Montzka, Clive Mcalpine, and Douglas H Boucher, 'Ruminants, Climate Change and Climate Policy', *Nature Climate Change*, 4 (2014), 2–5 <https://doi.org/10.1038/nclimate2081>

Roth, Alvin E, 'Marketplaces and Market Design' (London: London School of Economics, 2017)

———, 'The Art of Designing Markets', *Harvard Business Review*, October 2007, pp. 1–8 <www.hbr.org>

———, 'What Have We Learned from Market Design? (Update)', *Economic Journal*, 118 (2008), 285–310

Rudd, Murray A., 'An Institutional Framework for Designing and Monitoring Ecosystem-Based Fisheries Management Policy Experiments', *Ecological Economics*, 48 (2004), 109–24 <https://doi.org/10.1016/j.ecolecon.2003.10.002>

Sabatier, Paul A., *Theories of the Policy Process*, ed. by Paul A. Sabatier (Westview Press, 2007), XLII <https://doi.org/10.1081/E-EPAP2-120041405>

Schaaf, Jeanne, 'Governing a Monopoly Market under Siege: Using Institutional Analysis to Understand Competitive Entry into Telecommunications Markets, 1944–1982' (Indiana University, 1989) <https://ostromworkshop.indiana.edu/resources/publications/dissertations.html> [accessed 25 April 2018]

Shackelford, Scott, Anjanette Raymond, Rakshana Balakrishnan, Prakhar Dixit, Julianna Gjonaj, and Rachith Kavi, 'When Toasters Attack: A Polycentric Approach to Enhancing the Security of Things', *SSRN Electronic Journal*, 2016, 1–54 <https://doi.org/10.2139/ssrn.2715799>

Shah, Kalim U, and Keron Niles, 'Energy Policy in the Caribbean Green Economy Context and the Institutional Analysis and Design (IAD) Framework as a Proposed Tool for Its Development', *Energy Policy*, 98 (2016), 768–77 <https://doi.org/http://dx.doi.org/10.1016/j.enpol.2016.07.045>

da Silveira, André R., and Keith S. Richards, 'The Link Between Polycentrism and Adaptive Capacity in River Basin Governance Systems: Insights from the River Rhine and the Zhujiang (Pearl River) Basin', *Annals of the Association of American Geographers*, 103 (2013), 319–29 <https://doi.org/10.1080/00045608.2013.754687>

Smil, Vaclav, 'Eating Meat: Constants and Changes', *Global Food Security*, 2014, 1–5 <https://doi.org/10.1016/j.gfs.2014.06.001>

———, *Energy: A Beginner's Guide*, 1st edn (Oxford: Oneworld Publications, 2006)

———, *Energy and Civilization : A History* (Cambridge, Massachusetts: The MIT Press, 2017)

———, *Energy at the Crossroads – Global Perspectives and Uncertainties, Global Science Forum Conference on Scientific Challenges for Energy Research* (Cambridge, Massachusetts: The MIT Press, 2003) <https://doi.org/10.1002/joc.1346>

———, 'Energy in the Twentieth Century: Resources, Conversions, Costs, Uses, and Consequences', *Annu. Rev. Energy Environ.*, 2000, 21–51 <https://doi.org/10.1177/000312240507000602>

———, *World History and Energy*, ed. by Cutler J. Cleveland, *Concise Encyclopedia of the History of Energy*, 1st edn (San Diego: Elsevier Inc., 2009), 1 <http://vaclavsmil.com/wp-content/uploads/docs/smil-article-2004world-history-energy.pdf>

Smith, Adrian, and Andy Stirling, 'The Politics of Social-Ecological Resilience and Sustainable Socio – Technical Transitions', *Ecology and Society*, 15 (2010), 11 <https://doi.org/10.5751/ES-03218-150111>

Smith, Roy H, Imad El-Anis, and Christopher Farrands, *International Political Economy in the 21st Century: Contemporary Issues and Analyses*, ed. by Roy H Smith, Imad El-Anis, and Christopher Farrands, 2nd edn (London and New York: Routledge, 2017)

Sovacool, Benjamin K., 'Energy Policy and Cooperation in Southeast Asia: The History, Challenges, and Implications of the Trans-ASEAN Gas Pipeline (TAGP) Network', *Energy Policy*, 37 (2009), 2356–67 <https://doi.org/10.1016/j.enpol.2009.02.014>

Sovacool, Benjamin K., Björn-Ola Linnér, and Michael E. Goodsite, 'The Political Economy of Climate Adaptation', *Nature Climate Change*, 5 (2015), 616–18 <https://doi.org/10.1038/nclimate2665>

Sparrow, Frederick T., William A. Masters and Brian H. Bowen, 'Electricity Trade and Capacity Expansion Options in West Africa', *Purdue University, West Lafayette, IN* (2002).

Spencer, Jennifer W., Thomas P. Murtha, and Stefanie Ann Lenway, 'How Governments Matter to New Industry Creation', *Academy of Management Review*, 30 (2005), 321–37 <https://doi.org/10.5465/AMR.2005.16387889>

Tang, Shui Yan, *Institutions and Collective Action: Self-Governance in Irrigation*, 1992 <http://agris.fao.org/agris-search/search.do?f=1992/US/US92340.xml;US9187212>

Tarko, Vlad, *Elinor Ostrom: An Intellectual Biography* (London, UK and Lanham, Maryland: Rowman & Littlefield International, 2016)

Vatn, Arild, *Institutions and the Environment* (Cheltenham, UK: Edward Elgar)

Verschuere, Bram, Taco Brandsen, and Victor Pestoff, 'Co-Production: The State of the Art in Research and the Future Agenda', *Voluntas*, 23 (2012), 1083–1101 <https://doi.org/10.1007/s11266-012-9307-8>

Villamayor-Tomas, Sergio, Philipp Grundmann, Graham Epstein, Tom Evans, and Christian Kimmich, 'The Water-Energy-Food Security Nexus through the Lenses of the Value Chain and the Institutional Analysis and Development Frameworks', *Water Alternatives*, 8 (2015), 735–55

Vulkan, Nir, Alvin E Roth, and Zvika Neeman, *The Handbook of Market Design*, 2013 <https://doi.org/10.1017/CBO9781107415324.004>

Weimer, David. L, and Aidan. R. Vining, *Policy Analysis : Concepts and Practice*, 5th edn (Upper Saddle River, New Jersey USA: Prentice Hall, 2005)

Wilson, Robert, 'Architecture of Power Markets', *Econometrica*, 70 (2002), 1299–1340 <https://doi.org/10.1111/1468-0262.00334>

Wolsink, Maarten, 'Distributed Generation of Sustainable Energy as a Common Pool Resource: Social Acceptance in Rural Setting of Smart (Micro-)Grid Configurations', *New Rural Spaces : Towards Renewable Energies, Multifunctional Farming, and Sustainable Tourism*, 2014, 36–47

———, 'Non-Hierarchic Polycentric Regimes Facilitating Intelligent Distributed Energy Systems-The CPR Nature of Renewables Conceptualization of Society-Environment Relations View Project Environmental Justice in Environmental Policy Infrastructure View Project N', 2018, p. 6 <https://www.researchgate.net/publication/328916701>

Young, Oran.R., 'Global Commons: The Arctic in World Affairs', *Technology Review*, 93 (1990)

Young, Oran R, 'The Institutional Dimensions of Environmental Change: Fit, Interplay, and Scale', *Organization*, 2002, 221 <https://doi.org/10.1023/A:1024850005580>

Chapter 3

Acemoglu, Daron, Simon Johnson, and James A. Robinson, *The Colonial Origins of Comparative Development: An Empirical Investigation*, NBER Working Paper (Cambridge, MA, 2000)

Adams, William M., *Wasting the Rain: Rivers, People and Planning in Africa* (Minneapolis, MN: University of Minnesota Press, 1992)

Adebajo, Adekeye, 'A Tale of Three Cassandras: Jean Monnet, Raúl Prebisch, and Adebayo Adedeji', in *Region-Building in Africa: Political and Economic Challenges*, ed. by Daniel H. Levine and Dawn Nagar, 1st edn (New York: Palgrave Macmillan, 2016), pp. 53–70

———, 'Two Prophets of Regional Integration : Prebisch and Adedeji', in *International Development: Ideas, Experience, and Prospects*, ed. by Bruce Currie-Alder, Ravi Kanbur, David M. Malone, And Rohinton Medhora, 1st edn (Oxford: Oxford University Press, 2014), pp. 323–38

Adebayo, Akanmu Gafari, 'Of Man and Cattle: A Reconsideration of the Traditions of Origin of Pastoral Fulani of Nigeria', *History of Africa*, 18 (1991), 1–21

Adedeji, Adebayo, 'ECOWAS: A Retrospective Journey', in *West Africa's Security Challenges: Building Peace in a Troubled Region*, ed. by Adekeye Adebajo and Ismail Rashid (Boulder, CO: Lynne Rienner Publishers, 2004), pp. 21–49

Adi, Hakim, *Pan-Africanism : A History* (London: Bloomsbury Academic, 2018)

———, 'Pan-Africanism and West African Nationalism in Britain', *African Studies Review*, 43 (2000), 69–82

Adi, Hakim, and Marika Sherwood, *Pan-African History: Political Figures from Africa and the African Diaspora since 1787* (London and New York: Routledge, 2003)

Adu Boahen, Albert, *General History of Africa. Vol VII: Africa under Colonial Domination 1880–1935*, ed. by A Adu Boahen (Paris: UNESCO Publishing / Heinemann / University of California Press, 2000)

AfDB, 'Launch of the West African Energy Leaders Group Hotel Ivoire, Abidjan, 30 June 2015', 2015, pp. 1–6 <http://www.afdb.org/fileadmin/uploads/afdb/Documents/Generic-Documents/Summary_of_the_launch_event_of_the_WAELG.pdf> [accessed 29 September 2016]

Africa Progress Panel, *Lights Power Action: Electrifying Africa*, 2015

African Union Commission, 'Agenda 2063: The Africa We Want The Voices Of The African People', Final Edition, 2015, 1–24 <http://www.un.org/en/africa/osaa/pdf/au/agenda2063.pdf>

African Development Bank, *The New Deal on Energy for Africa* (Abidjan, 2016)

Ajayi, J.F.A., *General History of Africa, VI: Africa in the Nineteenth Century until the 1880s*, ed. by J.F.A. Ajayi (Paris: UNESCO Publishing / Heinemann / University of California Press, 2000)

Andritz Hydro, 'Hydropower in West Africa', 2016, pp. 24–25 <https://www.andritz.com/hydronews-africa-14-west-africa-data.pdf>

Araújo, Kathleen, 'The Emerging Field of Energy Transitions: Progress, Challenges, and Opportunities', *Energy Research & Social Science*, 1 (2014), 112–21 <https://doi.org/10.1016/j.erss.2014.03.002>

Ardurat, Sophie, 'L'electrification En AOF Avant 1945' (Universite Paris-1, 1999)

Aremu, Johnson Olaosebikan, 'Administration of British West African Colonies and the Furtherance of Nigeria-Gold Coast Relations, 1885–1960', *International Journal of Humanities and Cultural Studies*, 1 (2015), 54–71 <http://ijhcschiefeditor.wix.com/ijhcs>

Asante, Samuel K. B., 'The Neglected Aspects of the Activities of the Gold Coast Aborigines Rights Protection Society', *Phylon (1960-)*, 36 (1975), 32–45 <http://www.jstor.org/stable/274843>

West African Gas Pipeline Authority, 'WAGPA | West African Gas Pipeline Authority', 2018 <http://www.wagpa.org/about-us/> [accessed 10 October 2018]

Bach, Daniel C, *Regionalism in Africa: Genealogies, Institutions and Trans-State Networks*, 1st edn (London: Routledge, 2015) <https://doi.org/10.4324/9781315733180>

Bhatia, Mikul and Niki Angelou, 'Beyond Connections: Energy Access Redefined', *ESMAP Technical Report*, 008/15, (World Bank, Washington, DC: 2015)

Bigman, Laura, *History and Hunger in West Africa: Food Production and Entitlement in Guinea-Bissau and Cape Verde* (Westport, Connecticut: Greenwood Press, 1993)

Bogler, Honoré, 'Overview of Recent Regulatory Developments – ERERA', in *(Fourth High-Level Meeting of Regional Associations of Emerging Markets)* (Milan,Italy: ERERA, 2016)

Brockman, Norbert C., *An African Biographical Dictionary* (Santa Barbara, CA: ABC-CLIO, 1994)

Brownfield, Michael E., and Ronald R. Charpentier, *Assessment of the Undiscovered Oil and Gas of the Senegal Province, Mauritania, Senegal, The Gambia, and Guinea-Bissau, Northwest Africa, U.S. Geological Survey Bulletin 2207–A* (Denver,CO: U.S. Geological Survey, 2003)

Cabral, Amilcar, 'Algumas Consideraçoes Acêrca Das Chuvas (Some Thoughts on the Rains)', *Cabo Verde: Boletim de Propaganda e Informaçao*, 1 (1949), 5–7

———, 'Em Defesa Da Terra (In Defence of the Land), 1949–1950', *Cabo Verde: Boletim de Propaganda e Informaçao*, 1–2 (1950), 15–17,19–22,6–8

Carbonnier, Gilles, *International Development Policy: Energy and Development* (Basingstoke: Palgrave Macmillan, 2011)

Castellano, Antonio, Adam Kendall, Mikhail Nikomarov, and Tarryn Swemmer, 'Brighter Africa', *McKinsey & Company Monthly Journal*, 2015, 4–8 <http://www.mckinsey.com/~/media/mckinsey/dotcom/insights/energy resources materials/powering africa/brighter_africa_the_growth_potential_of_the_sub-saharan_electricity_sector.ashx>

Chafer, Tony, *The End of Empire in French West Africa: France's Successful Decolonization?*, 1st edn (Oxford: Berg, 2002)

Cherp, Aleh, Jessica Jewell, and Andreas Goldthau, 'Governing Global Energy: Systems, Transitions, Complexity', *Global Policy*, 2 (2011), 75–88 <https://doi.org/10.1111/j.1758-5899.2010.00059.x>

Clauson, Gerard. L. M., 'The British Colonial Currency System', *The Economic Journal*, 54 (1944), 1–25 <https://www.jstor.org/stable/216483>

Cleveland, Cutler J., and Christopher G. Morris, *Dictionary of Energy*, ed. by Cutler J. Cleveland and Christopher G. Morris, 2nd edn (Elsevier Ltd., 2015) <https://doi.org/10.1016/B978-0-08-096811-7.50019-6>

Cooper, Frederick, *Decolonization and African Society : The Labor Question in French and British Africa* (Cambridge: University of Cambridge, 1996)

Coquery-Vidrovitch, Catherine, 'Electricity Networks in Africa: A Comparative Study, or How to Write Social History from Economic Sources', in *Sources and Methods in Africa History: Spoken, Written, Unearthed* (Rochester, NY.: University of Rochester Press, 2003), pp. 346–60

Craven, Matthew, 'Between Law and History: The Berlin Conference of 1884–1885 and the Logic of Free Trade', *London Review of International Law*, 3 (2015), 31–59 <https://doi.org/10.1093/lril/lrv002>

Danfak, Papa Waly, 'Equipment Public et Amenagement de La Ville de Dakar, 1930–1957' (Universite Paris-7, 1990)

Daniel Brückenhaus, 'Colonial Suspects: Suspicion, Imperial Rule, and Colonial Society in Interwar French West Africa', *The Journal of Interdisciplinary History*, 49 (2019), 699–700 <https://doi.org/https://doi.org/10.1162/jinh_r_01370>

Deutsche Gesellschaft für Technische Zusammenarbeit – GTZ, *Renewable Energies in West Africa* (Frankfurt /Eschborn, 2009)

Dimier, Véronique, 'Direct or Indirect Rule: Propaganda around a Scientific Controversy', in *Promoting the Colonial Idea : Propaganda and Visions of Empire in France*, ed. by Tony Chafer and Amanda Sackur (London: Palgrave, 2002), pp. 168–83 <https://doi.org/10.1057/9781403919427>

Doortmont, Michel R., 'Producing a Received View of Gold Coast Elite Society? C.F. Hutchison's Pen Pictures of Modern Africans and African Celebrities', *History in Africa: An Annual Journal of Method*, 33 (2006), 473–93 <https://doi.org/10.2307/20065783>

ECOWAS, 'A/DEC.3/5/82 Decision Of The Authority Of Heads Of State And Government Of The Economic Community Of West African States Relating To The Ecowas Energy Policy', *Official Journal of the ECOWAS*, 4 (1982), 46–49

———, 'Economic Community of West African States (ECOWAS): Revised Treaty', *International Legal Materials*, 1996, 660–97 <http://www.jstor.org/stable/20698567>

———, *Ecowas Energy Efficiency Policy* (Praia, Cape Verde, 2015) <http://www.ecreee.org> [accessed 17 August 2016]

———, *Ecowas Energy Protocol A/P4/1/03* (Abuja, 2003) <http://www.ecowapp.org/sites/default/files/eprotocol.pdf> [accessed 17 August 2018]

———, 'History of the Economic Community of West African States (ECOWAS)' <https://www.ecowas.int> [accessed 12 September 2018]

———, 'Treaty of the Economic Community of West African States (ECOWAS)' (Lagos, Nigeria, 1975)

______, 'Adopting Community Competition Rules and the Modalities of their Application within ECOWAS', *Supplementary Act A/SA.1/12/08*, (Abuja, Nigeria, 2008)

______, 'On the Establishment, Functions and Operation of the Regional Competition Authority for ECOWAS', *Supplementary Act A/SA.2/12/08*, (Abuja, Nigeria, 2008)

ECOWAS Centre for Renewable Energy and Energy Efficiency, 'ECOWAS Renewable Energy Policy (EREP)' (Praia, Cape Verde: ECREEE, 2013)

ECOWAS Commission, 'ECOWAS Vision 2020' (Abuja: ECOWAS Commission, 2011) <http://www.spu.ecowas.int/wp-content/uploads/2010/03/ECOWAS-VISION-2020-THEMATICTIC-PAMPHLETS-in-English.pdf>

ECOWAS Community Court of Justice, 'Protocol A/P.L/7/91 On The Community Court Of Justice' (Abuja: ECOWAS, 1991)

———, 'Supplememtary Protocol A/Sp.1/01/05 Amending the Preamble and Articles 1, 2, 9 and 30 of Protocol A/P.1/7/91 Relating to the Community Court Of Justice and Article 4 Paragraph 1 of the English Version of the said Protocol' (Abuja: ECOWAS, 2005)

ECOWAS Parliament, 'Parlement de La CEDEAO / ECOWAS Parliament', *About Us*, 2018 <http://parl.ecowas.int/en/about-us/> [accessed 12 June 2018]

ECOWAS Regional Electricity Regulatory Authority (ERERA), *West African Power Sector Regional Regulation Project. Diagnostic Report on the Institutional and Regulatory Interfaces of the ECOWAS Regional Electricity Regulatory Authority*, 2008 <https://erera.arrec.org/>

ECREEE, 'ROGEP – Regional Off-Grid Electrification Project', 2018 <http://www.ecreee.org/node/87265> [accessed 15 February 2018]

———, 'Supporting Energy Efficiency Access in West Africa (SEEA-WA) Project Funded by the European Union' <http://www.ecreee.org/page/supporting-energy-efficiency-access-west-africa-seea-wa-project-funded-european-union> [accessed 7 June 2018]

Edgerton, David., *Shock of the Old: Technology and Global History Since 1900: Technology in Global History Since 1900* (London: Profile Books, 2008)

Eluwa, Gabriel I. C., 'Background to the Emergence of the National Congress of British West Africa', *African Studies Review*, 14 (1971), 205–218 <https://doi.org/10.2307/523823>

EPRI, *The Integrated Grid: Realizing the Full Value of Central and Distributed Energy Resources* (Palo Alto, CA, 2014) <https://www.epri.com/#/pages/product/3002002733/?lang=en-us>

ERERA, 'The ECOWAS Regional Electricity Regulatory Authority (ERERA)', 2016 <https://erera.arrec.org/en/home> [accessed 10 October 2018]

Francois, Marie-Therese, *La Production de La Force Motrice Aux Colonies, et plus Particulierement En Afrique Francaise* (Paris: Association Colonies-Sciences, 1937)

Fulwood, Mike, 'Opportunities for Gas in Sub-Saharan Africa', *Oxford Energy Insight*, 2019 <https://www.oxfordenergy.org>

Fulwood, Mike, and Thierry Bros, 'Future Prospects for LNG Demand in Ghana', *Oxford Energy Insight*, 2018, 1–15

Garigue, Philip, 'The West African Students' Union. A Study in Culture Contact', *Africa: Journal of the International African Institute*, 23 (1953), 55–69 <http://www.jstor.org/stable/1156033>

Giner-Reichl, Irene, 'Renewable energy in international and regional governance: Propelling development in Africa', *Energy Research & Social Science* 5 (2015), 116–119

Ginio, Ruth, *French Colonialism Unmasked: The Vichy Years in French West Africa* (Lincoln and London: University of Nebraska Press, 2006)

Goldthau, Andreas, 'From the State to the Market and Back: Policy Implications of Changing Energy Paradigms', *Global Policy*, 3 (2012), 198–210 <https://doi.org/10.1111/j.1758-5899.2011.00145.x>

Goldthau, Andreas, and Benjamin K Sovacool, 'The Uniqueness of the Energy Security, Justice, and Governance Problem', *Energy Policy*, 41 (2012), 232–40 <https://doi.org/10.1016/j.enpol.2011.10.042>

Gowon, Yakubu, *The Economic Community of West African States: A Study in Political and Economic Integration* (Warwick, 1984)

Gronenborn, Detlef, 'Kanem-Borno: A Brief Summary of the History and Archeology of an Empire of the Central Bilad Al-Sudan', in *West Africa During the Atlantic Slave Trade: Archaeological Perspectives*, ed. by Christopher DeCorse, 2nd edn (London and New York: Bloomsbury Academic, 2016), pp. 101–30

Guggisberg, Frederick Gordon, The Gold Coast: A Review of the Events of 1920–1926 and The Prospects of 1927–1928 (Accra, 1927)

Haas, Ernst B., *The Uniting of Europe: Political, Social and Economic Forces 1950–1957*, 2nd edn (Stanford, CA: Stanford University Press, 1968)

Hancock, Kathleen J., 'Energy Regionalism and Diffusion in Africa: How Political Actors Created the ECOWAS Center for Renewable Energy and Energy Efficiency', *Energy Research and Social Science*, 5 (2015), 105–15 <https://doi.org/10.1016/j.erss.2014.12.022>

———, 'The Expanding Horizon of Renewable Energy in Sub-Saharan Africa: Leading Research in the Social Sciences', *Energy Research and Social Science*, 5 (2015), 1–8 <https://doi.org/10.1016/j.erss.2014.12.021>

Henriksen, Thomas, 'Portugal in Africa: A Noneconomic Interpretation', *African Studies Review*, 16 (1973), 405–16

Hershey Jr., Robert D., 'How the Oil Glut Is Changing Business', *The New York Times*, 1981 <https://www.nytimes.com/1981/06/21/business/how-the-oil-glut-is-changing-business.html?pagewanted=all> [accessed 9 September 2018]

Hopkins, Antony Gerald, 'The Creation of a Colonial Monetary System : The Origins of the West African Currency Board', *African Historical Studies*, 3 (1970), 101–32 <https://www.jstor.org/stable/216483>

IAEA, 'List of Member States', 2019 <https://www.iaea.org/about/governance/list-of-member-states> [accessed 1 January 2019]

Iliasu, A.A., 'The Origin of the Mossi-Dagomba States', *African Studies Research Review*, 7 (1971), 95–113 <https://doi.org/10.3166/I2M.14.3-4.11-61>

ISSER, *Guide to Electric Power in Ghana* (Accra: Resource Center for Energy Economics and Regulation, Institute of Statistical, Social and Economic Research, University of Ghana, 2005)

Jacobs, Andrew James., 'Collaborative Regionalism and Foreign Direct Investment: The Case of the Southeast Automotive Core and the "New Domestics"', *Economic Development Quarterly*, 26 (2012), 199–219 <https://doi.org/10.1177/0891242412453481>

Johnson, Willard R., and Ernest J. Wilson III, 'The "Oil Crises" and African Economies : Oil Wave on a Tidal Flood of Industrial Price Inflation', *Daedalus*, 111 (1982), 211–41

July, Robert W., *The Origins of Modern African Thought: Its Development in West Africa during the Nineteeth and Twentieth Centuries*, 2004 edn (Trenton, NJ and Asmara, Eritrea: Africa World Press, Inc., 1967)

Karaki, Karim, *Understanding ECOWAS Energy Policy From National Interests to Regional Markets and Wider Energy Access?*, PEDRO (Brussels, 2017) <https://ecdpm.org/wp-content/uploads/ECOWAS-Energy-Background-Paper-PEDRO-Political-Economy-Dynamics-Regional-Organisations-Africa-ECDPM-2017.pdf> [accessed 28 December 2017]

Kerr, Richard A., 'The Sahara Is Not Marching Southward', *Science*, July 1998, 633–34 <https://doi.org/10.1126/science.281.5377.633>

Kitson, Arthur E., *Outline of Mineral and Water-Power Resources of the Gold Coast, British West Africa.*, *Gold Coast Geological Survey Bulletin* (London: C. A. Terry, 1925), I

Kloman Jr., Erasmus H., 'African Unification Movements', *International Organization*, 16 (1962), 387–404

Kohl, Christoph, 'National Integration in Guinea-Bissau since Independence', *Cadernos de Estudos Africanos*, 2011, 85–109 <https://doi.org/10.4000/cea.155>

Kuruk, Paul, 'Performance of Electric Utilities in Developing Countries: The Ghanaian and Nigerian Experience', *Loyola of Los Angeles International and Comparative Law Review*, 11 (1989), 515

Lavrijssen, Saskia, and Arturo Carrilo, *Radical Innovation in the Energy Sector and the Impact on Regulation*, *TILEC Discussion Paper*, TILEC Discussion Paper (Tilburg, 2017) <https://doi.org/10.2139/ssrn.2979206>

Leo, Ben, Jared Kalow, and Todd Moss, 'What Can We Learn about Energy Access and Demand from Mobile-Phone Surveys? Nine Findings from Twelve African Countries', *CGD Policy Paper*, 120 (2018) <https://www.cgdev.org/publication/what-can-we-learn-about-energy-access-and-demand-mobile-phone-surveys>

Levtzion, Nehemia, and Randall L. Pouwels, *The History of Islam in Africa* (Athens, Ohio: Ohio University Press, 2000)

Lindskog, Per A., and Benoit Delaite, 'Degrading Land: An Environmental History Perspective of the Cape Verde Islands', *Environment and History*, 2 (1996), 271–90 <https://doi.org/10.3197/096734096779522266>

Lopes de Lima, José Joaquim, *Ensaios Sobre a Statistica Das Possessoes Portuguezas, Ilhas de Cabo Verde a Suas Dependências.* (Lisbon: Impresa Nacional, 1844), I

Lynch, Hollis R:, *Edward Wilmot Blyden, Pan-Negro Patriot 1832–1912* (London, Ibadan, New York: Oxford University Press, 1967)

Manu River Union, *Mano River Declaration Establishing the Mano River Union*, *United Nations – Treaty Series* (United Nations – Treaty Series, 1973), pp. 266–75 <https://wits.worldbank.org/GPTAD/PDF/archive/MRU.pdf> [accessed 13 August 2018]

Maduekwe, Monica, Ellen Morris, Jennye Greene, and Victoria Healey, 'Gender Equity and Mainstreaming in Renewable Energy Policies—Empowering Women in the Energy Value Chain in the Economic Community of West African States (ECOWAS)', *Current Sustainable/Renewable Energy Reports*, 6 (2019), 13–21 <https://doi.org/10.1007/s40518-019-00127-2>

Manafa, M. N. A., *Electricity Development in Nigeria, 1896–1972* (Yaba, Nigeria: Raheem Publishers, 1979)

Martin, Guy, *African Political Thought* (New York: African Political Thought, 2012)

———, 'Uranium: A Case-Study in Franco- African Relations', *The Journal of Modern African Studies*, 27 (1989), 625–40 <https://www.jstor.org/stable/161112>

McCaskie, Tom C., 'The United States, Ghana and Oil: Global and Local Perspectives', *African Affairs*, 107 (2008), 313–32 <https://doi.org/10.1093/afraf/adn019>

Medinilla, Alfonso, Bruce Byiers, and Karim Karaki, *African Power Pools: Regional Energy, National Power*, Political Economy Dynamics of Regional Organisations in Africa (PEDRO) (Maastricht and Brussels, 2019) <www.ecdpm.org/dp244>

Mendy, Peter Karibe, 'Amilcar Cabral and the Liberation of Guinea-Bissau: Context, Challenges and Lessons for Effective African Leadership', *African Identities*, 4 (2005), 7–21 <https://doi.org/10.1080/14725840500268440>

Miescher, Stephan F., and Dzodzi Tsikata, 'Hydro-Power and the Promise of Modernity and Development in Ghana: Comparing the Akosombo and Bui Dam Projects', *Ghana Studies, V*, 12 (2009), 15–53 <http://www.history.ucsb.edu/wp-content/uploads/1-Miescher_Tsikata.pdf>

Moss, Todd and Morgan Bazilian, 'Signalling, governance, and goals: Reorienting the United States Power Africa initiative', *Energy Research & Social Science*, 39 (2018), 74–77

Mutiso, Rose M., 'How to bring affordable, sustainable electricity to Africa', (July, 2019) [Video file]. Retrieved from https://www.ted.com/talks/rose_m_mutiso_how_to_bring_affordable_sustainable_electricity_to_africa

Nalule, Victoria R., *Energy Poverty and Access Challenges in Sub-Saharan Africa: The Role of Regionalism*, *Energy Poverty and Access Challenges in Sub-Saharan Africa* (Cham: Palgrave Macmillan, 2019) <https://doi.org/10.1007/978-3-319-95402-8>

Ndulu, Benno J., and Stephen A. O'Connell, 'Governance and Growth in Africa', *Journal of Economic Perspectives*, 13 (1999), 41–66

Nordman, Erik, 'Cape Verde's Goal Is 100 % Renewable Energy by 2025. Why It May Just Do It', *The Conversation*, 2017 <https://theconversation.com/cape-verdes-goal-is-100-renewable-energy-by-2025-why-it-may-just-do-it-85759> [accessed 21 June 2018]

Nwauwa, Apollos O, 'The Evolution of the Aro Confederacy in Southeastern Nigeria, 1690–1720. A Theoretical Synthesis of State Formation Process in Africa', *Anthropos*, 90 (1995), 353–64 <http://www.jstor.org/stable/40463184>

Nye, Joseph, *Pan-Africanism and East African Integration* (Cambridge, MA: Harvard University Press, 1966)

Obeng-Odoom, Franklin, 'Oil in the West African Transform Margin: Dangers and Possibilities', *International Critical Thought*, 6 (2016), 101–18 <https://doi.org/10.1080/21598282.2016.1142385>

Obichere, Boniface I., 'Reconstruction in Guinea Bissau: From Revolutionaries and Guerrillas to Bureaucrats and Politicians', *A Current Bibliography on African Affairs*, 8 (1975), 204–19 <https://doi.org/10.1177/001132557500800304>

Ogot, B. A., *General History of Africa, V: Africa from the Sixteenth to Eighteenth Century*, ed. by B.A. Ogot (Berkeley, Carlifornia: University of California Press, 1992)

Oguah, Samuel, and Debabrata Chattopadhyay, 'A Pro-Grid Middle Path for Africa: Sub-Saharan Region Electricity Upgrades', *IEEE Power and Energy Magazine*, 17 (2019), 61–68 <https://doi.org/10.1109/MPE.2018.2884114>

Ogunsola, Olayinka I., 'History of Energy Sources and Their Utilization in Nigeria', *Energy Sources*, 12 (1990), 181–98 <https://doi.org/10.1080/00908319008960198>

Ojo, Olatunde J B, *Nigeria and the Formation of ECOWAS*, *International Organization*, 1980, xxxiv <https://doi.org/10.1017/S0020818300018853>

Olu-Wright, R. J., 'The Physical Growth of Freetown', in *Freetown: A Symposium*, ed. by C. Fyfe and E. Jones (Freetown, Sierra Leone: Sierra Leone University Press, 1968), pp. 24–37

Orano SA, 'Orano Group', 2019 <https://www.orano.group/en> [accessed 1 December 2019]

Osarhieme Benson Osadolor, 'The Evolution of Policy on Security and Defence in ECOWAS, 1978 – 2008', *Journal of the Historical Society of Nigeria* 20 (2011), pp. 87–103. Accessed June 14, 2018. www.jstor.org/stable/41857176.

Oteng Kufuor, Kofi, 'The Origins and Evolution of Regional Integration in West Africa', in *The Institutional Transformation of the Economic Community of West African States* (Oxford and New York: Routledge, 2016)

Pineau, Pierre Olivier, 'Electricity Sector Integration in West Africa', *Energy Policy*, 36 (2008), 210–23 <https://doi.org/10.1016/j.enpol.2007.09.002>

Poindexter, Gregory B., 'Gambia River Basin Organization Seeks to Develop 20-MW Saltinho Hydropower Project in West Africa', *Hydroworld*, 2017 <https://www.hydroworld.com/articles/2017/01/gambia-river-basin-organization-seeks-to-develop-20-mw-saltinho-hydropower-project-in-west-africa.html> [accessed 30 July 2018]

La Porta, Rafael, Florencio Lopez-de-Silanes, Andrei Shleifer, and Robert W. Vishny, 'Law and Finance', *Journal of Political Economy*, 106 (1998), 1113–55

———, 'The Quality of Government', *The Journal of Law, Economics, & Organization*, 15 (1999), 222–79

Ranaboldo, Matteo, Bruno Domenech Leg,a, David Vilar Ferrenbach, Laia Ferrer-Martí, Rafael Pastor Moreno, and Alberto García-Villoria, 'Renewable Energy Projects to Electrify Rural Communities in Cape Verde', *Applied Energy*, 118 (2014), 280–91 <https://doi.org/10.1016/j.apenergy.2013.12.043>

Reiss, Karin, 'Developing Renewable Energy Sectors and Technologies in West Africa', *UN Chronicle* (New York, December 2015) <https://unchronicle.un.org/article/developing-renewable-energy-sectors-and-technologies-west-africa>

Reuters, 'Rebel Attacks Swell Nigeria-to-Ghana Pipeline Cost', *Reuters*, 7 December 2009 <https://af.reuters.com/article/nigeriaNews/idAFGEE5B623520091207>

Robinson, David, 'The Islamic Revolution of Futa Toro', *The International Journal of African Historical Studies*, 8 (1975), 185–221 <https://doi.org/10.2307/216648>

Robson, Peter, 'Regional Integration and the Crisis in Sub-Saharan Africa', *The Journal of Modern African Studies*, 23 (1985), 603–22 <http://www.jstor.org/stable/160681> [accessed 3 July 2018]

Sanders, James, 'The Expansion of the Fante And The Emergence Of Asante In The Eighteenth Century', *The Journal of African History*, 20 (1979), 349–64 <https://doi.org/10.1017/S0021853700017357>

Sanneh, Lamin, *Beyond Jihad: The Pacifist Tradition in West African Islam* (New York: Oxford University Press, 2016)

dos Santos Pereira, M., *Cabo Verde: Duas Tentativas Para a Sua Valorizacao Agropecuária. In Cabo Verde, Guiné, São Tomé e Principe: Curso de Extensao Universitaria Ano Lectivo de 1965–1966* (Lisbon: Instituto Superior de Ciências Sociais e Política Ultramarina. Universidade Técni, 1966)

Sarfoh, Joseph A., *Energy in the Development of West Africa* (Westport, CT: Greenwood Press, 1992)

———, *Hydropower Development in West Africa* (New York: Peter Lang, 1990)

Saupique, Thomas, 'L'electrification de Dakar Depuis 1945' (Universite Paris-7, 2000)

SEFORALL, 'Who we are', 2018 < https://www.seforall.org/who-we-are > [accessed 17 June 2018].

Shaw, Timothy M., J. Andrew Grant, and Scarlett Cornelissen, *The Ashgate Research Companion to Regionalisms*, ed. by Timothy M. Shaw, J. Andrew Grant, and Scarlett Cornelissen, *The Ashgate Research Companion to Regionalisms* (Surrey and Burlington,VT: Ashgate Publishing Limited, 2011) <https://doi.org/10.4324/9781315613499>

Shepperson, George, 'Abolitionism and African Political Thought', *Transition*, 12 (1964), 22–26

Showers, Kate B., 'Congo River's Grand Inga Hydroelectricity Scheme: Linking Environmental History, Policy and Impact', *Water History*, 1 (2009), 31–58 <https://doi.org/10.1007/s12685-009-0001-8>

Showers, Kate B, 'Electrifying Africa: An Environmental History with Policy Implications', *Geografiska Annaler, Series B: Human Geography*, 93 (2011), 193–221 <https://doi.org/10.1111/j.1468-0467.2011.00373.x>

Shumway, Rebecca, 'From Atlantic Creoles to African Nationalists: Reflections on the Historiography of Nineteenth-Century Fanteland', *History in Africa*, 42 (2015), 139–64 <https://muse.jhu.edu/article/583528> [accessed 14 June 2018]

Simpson, E. S., 'Electricity Production in Nigeria', *Economic Geography*, 45 (1969), 239–57 <https://doi.org/10.2307/143093>

Steyn, Phia, 'Oil Exploration in Colonial Nigeria, C.1903 – 1958', *The Journal of Imperial and Commonwealth History*, 37 (2009), 249–74

Surroop, Dinesh, and Pravesh Raghoo, 'Renewable Energy to Improve Energy Situation in African Island States', *Renewable and Sustainable Energy Reviews*, 88 (2018), 176–83 <https://doi.org/10.1016/j.rser.2018.02.024>

Swift, Jeremy, 'Sahelian Pastoralists: Underdevelopment, Desertification, and Famine', *Annual Review of Anthropology*, 6 (1977), 457–78

Tagliapietra, Simone, *Electrifying Africa: How to Make Europe's Contribution Count, Bruegel Policy Contribution*, Bruegel Policy Contribution (Brussels, 2017) <https://ideas.repec.org/p/bre/polcon/20882.html>

———, 'Financing the European Energy Infrastructure of the Future', 2013, 1–13 <www.feem.it> [accessed 11 December 2018]

Tagliapietra, Simone, and Morgan Bazilian, 'The Role of International Institutions in Fostering Sub-Saharan Africa's Electrification', *The Electricity Journal*, 32 (2019), 13–20 <https://doi.org/10.1016/j.tej.2019.01.016>

The Volta River Project, *Appendices to the Report of the Preparatory Commission. Appendix I. White Paper on the Volta River Aluminium Scheme* (London, 1956), Volume II

———, *Engineering Report to the Preparatory Commission* (London, 1956), Volume III

———, *Report of the Preparatory Commission* (London, 1952), Volume I

Thiam, Ibrahima, *Regulatory Issues of the Regional Power Market: West Africa Case* (Abuja,Nigeria, 2011) <https://pubs.naruc.org> [accessed 3 January 2018]

Timilsina, Govinda R., and Kalim U. Shah, 'Filling the Gaps: Policy Supports and Interventions for Scaling up Renewable Energy Development in Small Island Developing States', *Energy Policy*, 98 (2016), 653–62 <https://doi.org/10.1016/j.enpol.2016.02.028>

Ukaigwe, Jerry, *ECOWAS Law*, *ECOWAS Law*, 2016 <https://doi.org/10.1007/978-3-319-26233-8>

UNECA, 'Ghana's Experience in Power Interconnections within the Framework of ECOWAS' (Addis Ababa: UNECA, 1969) <http://repository.uneca.org/bitstream/handle/123456789/17587/Bib-67662.pdf?sequence=1>

UNEP, *Atlas of Africa Energy Resources* (Nairobi: African Development Bank/The Infrastructure Consortium for Africa, 2017)

———, 'Energy Profile of Guinea Bissau', 2015, pp. 182–85

United States Energy Association, 'The West African Energy Sector: Exploring Current Projects Within the Region and Investment Opportunities' <https://www.usea.org> [accessed 26 March 2019]

USAID, 'Examining Energy Efficiency Issues in Sub-Saharan Africa' <https://www.usaid.gov/powerafrica/newsletter/dec2014/smarter-power-in-africa> [accessed 7 June 2018]

———, *Leveraging Partnerships To Increase Access To Power In Sub-Saharan Africa* <www.usaid.gov/powerafrica.>

Vansina, Jan, 'A Comparison of African Kingdoms', *Africa: Journal of the International African Institute*, 32 (1962), 324–35

Vilar, David, Mahama Kappiah, Juan López-Dóriga, Santiago Martínez-Caro, Gonzalo Piernavieja Izquierdo, Brigitte Öppinger-Walchshofer, and others, *Renewable Energy in West Africa: Status, Experiences and Trends* (Praia, Cape Verde: ECREEE and CASA AFRICA, 2012) <http://www.ecreee.org/sites/default/files/renewable_energy_in_west_africa_0.pdf>

WAGP, 'Treaty On The West African Gas Pipeline Project', 1995 <http://www.wagpa.org/Treaty_on_WAGP_Project.pdf> [accessed 10 October 2018]

WAGP, The West African Gas Pipeline, 'Documentation: Documentation Regarding the WAGP Project', Amendments to WAGP Regulations <http://www.wagpa.org/project-documentation/> [accessed 1 February 2018]

Warner, Carolyn M., 'The Rise of the State System in Africa', *Review of International Studies*, 27 (2001), 65–89 <https://doi.org/10.1017/s0260210501008038>

Wendler, Gerd, and Frank Eaton, 'On the Desertification of the Sahel Zone', *Climate Change*, 5 (1983), 365–80

Whitaker, Paul M, 'The Revolutions of "Portuguese" Africa', *The Journal of Modern African Studies*, 8 (1970), 15–35 <https://doi.org/10.1017/S0022278X00019339>

Wilkinson, W.H., E. Gardiner Smith, and Michael F.J. McDonnell. 'West Africa', Journal of Comparative Legislation and International Law, 4, no.3 (1922), 151–57 <https://doi.org/10.1017/CBO9781107415324.004>

Wilson, Charlie, and Arnulf Grubler, 'Lessons from the History of Technological Change for Clean Energy Scenarios and Policies', *Natural Resources Forum*, 35 (2011), 165–84

Wilson, Henry S., *Origins of West African Nationalism* (London: Palgrave Macmillan, 1969)

Wittfogel, Karl A, *Oriental Despotism: A Comparative Study of Total Power* (New Haven, CT: Yale University Press, 1957)

World Bank, *Guinea-Bissau An Introductory Basic Economic Report* (Washington D.C., 1982), I

———, *West African Power Pool (WAPP) – Côte d'Ivoire, Sierra Leone, Liberia, and Guinea Power Interconnection Project WAPP. WAPP Integration and Technical Assistance Project.* (Washington, D.C., 2012) <http://documents.worldbank.org/curated/en/116431468006606003/pdf/672960PAD0P1130Official0Use0Only090.pdf> [accessed 1 May 2018]

World Nuclear Association, 'Uranium in Niger', *Country Profiles – Niger*, 2019 <https://www.world-nuclear.org/information-library/country-profiles/countries-g-n/niger.aspx> [accessed 1 January 2019]

Worrell, Ernst, Lenny Bernstein, Joyashree Roy, Lynn Price, and Jochen Harnisch, 'Industrial Energy Efficiency and Climate Change Mitigation', *Energy Efficiency*, 2 (2009), 109–23 <https://doi.org/10.1007/s12053-008-9032-8>

Worth, David, 'Lighting the Darkness: The Gas Supply Industry in Nineteenth Century Cape Town, and Its Role in the Formation of an Industrial Landscape', in *Proceedings at the Association for Industrial Archaeology Annual Conference, 4–5 September, 1998* (North Abott, Devon, 1998)

Yakohene, Afua Boatemaa, 'Overview of Ghana and Regional Integration: Past, Present and Future', in *Ghana in Search of Regional Integration Agenda*, ed. by LECIAD, 1st edn (Accra: Friedrich-Ebert-Stiftung, 2009), pp. 1–22

Young, Crawford, *The African Colonial State in Comparative Perspective* (New Haven, CT: Yale University Press, 1994)

Chapter 4

ACER - Agency for the Cooperation, and of the Energy Regulators, 'The Agency', 2017 <http://www.acer.europa.eu/en/The_agency/Pages/default.aspx> [accessed 20 February 2018]

Andoura, Sami, Leigh Hancher, and Marc Van der Woude, *Towards a European Energy Community: A Policy Proposal, Notre Europe* (Paris and Berlin, 2010) <http://www.notre-europe.eu>

Araújo, Kathleen, 'The Emerging Field of Energy Transitions: Progress, Challenges, and Opportunities', *Energy Research & Social Science*, 1 (2014), 112–21 <https://doi.org/10.1016/j.erss.2014.03.002>

Arnull, Anthony., *The European Union and Its Court of Justice*, 2nd edn (Oxford: Oxford University Press, 2006)

Arrhenius, Svante, 'On the Influence of Carbonic Acid in the Air upon the Temperature of the Ground', *Philosophical Magazine and Journal of Science*, 41 (1896), 237–76 <https://doi.org/10.1002/cta.4490080404>

Arthur, W Brian, 'Competing Technologies, Increasing Returns, and Lock-In by Historical Events', *The Economic Journal*, 99 (1989), 116–31 <https://doi.org/10.2307/2234208>

———, *Increasing Returns and Path Dependence in the Economy* (University of Michigan Press, 1994)

Austvik, Ole Gunnar, 'The Energy Union and Security-of-Gas Supply', *Energy Policy*, 96 (2016), 372–82 <https://doi.org/10.1016/j.enpol.2016.06.013>

Van Baal, Paul Adrianus, and Matthias Finger, 'The Effect of European Integration on Swiss Energy Policy and Governance', *Politics and Governance*, 7 (2019), 6 <https://doi.org/10.17645/pag.v7i1.1780>

Bartoletto, Silvana, and Maria del Mar Rubio Varas, 'Energy Transition and CO2 Emissions in Southern Europe: Italy and Spain (1861–2000)', *Global Environment*, 2 (2008), 47–81

Bauwens, Thomas, 'What Roles for Energy Cooperatives in the Diffusion of Distributed Generation Technologies?', *SSRN*, 7 (2014), 1–29 <https://doi.org/10.2139/ssrn.2382596>

Bauwens, Thomas, Boris Gotchev, and Lars Holstenkamp, 'What Drives the Development of Community Energy in Europe? The Case of Wind Power Cooperatives', *Energy Research and Social Science*, 13 (2016), 136–47 <https://doi.org/10.1016/j.erss.2015.12.016>

Bellamy, Richard, and Alex Warleigh, 'From an Ethics of Integration to an Ethics of Participation: Citizenship and the Future of the European Union', *Millennium: Journal of International Studies*, 27 (1998), 447–68 <https://doi.org/10.1177/03058298980270030801>

Beloff, Max, 'Churchill and Europe', in *Churchill* (Oxford: Oxford University Press, 1996), pp. 443–56 <https://doi.org/10.1093/acprof:oso/9780198206262.003.0026>

Best, Heinrich, György Lengyel, and Luca Verzichelli, *The Europe of Elites : A Study into the Europeanness of Europe's Political and Economic Elites*, ed. by Heinrich Best, György Lengyel, and Luca Verzichelli, 1st edn (New York: Oxford University Press Inc., 2012)

Birchfield, Vicki L., 'The Role of EU Institutions in Energy Policy Formation', in *Toward a Common European Union Energy Policy*, ed. by Vicki L. Birchfield and John S. Duffield (London: Palgrave Macmillan, 2011) <https://doi.org/10.1007/978-94-009-6092-3_8>

Birchfield, Vicki L., and John S. Duffield, *Toward a Common European Union Energy Policy : Problems, Progress, and Prospects*, ed. by Vicki L. Birchfield and John S. Duffield (Basingstoke, UK: Palgrave Macmillan, 2011)

Bjørnebye, Henrik, 'Webinar: Extending the Energy Acquis beyond the EU Institutional Challenges – Florence School of Regulation', 2018 <http://fsr.euthat is,u/event/extending-the-energy-acquis-beyond-the-european-union-institutional-challenges/> [accessed 22 January 2019]

Borger, Vestert, 'How the Debt Crisis Exposes the Development of Solidarity in the Euro Area', *European Constitutional Law Review*, 9 (2013), 7–36 <https://doi.org/10.1017/S1574019612001022>

Bösch, Frank and Rüdiger Graf, 'Reacting to anticipations: Energy crises and energy policy in the 1970s. An introduction,' *Historical Social Research/Historische Sozialforschung*, (2014): 7–21.

Bouzarovski, Stefan, and Saska Petrova, 'A Global Perspective on Domestic Energy Deprivation: Overcoming the Energy Poverty–Fuel Poverty Binary', *Energy Research & Social Science*, 10 (2015), 31–40 <https://doi.org/10.1016/j.erss.2015.06.007>

Bouzarovski, Stefan, and Neil Simcock, 'Spatializing Energy Justice', *Energy Policy*, 107 (2017), 640–48 <https://doi.org/10.1016/j.enpol.2017.03.064>

Bouzarovski, Stefan, and Sergio Tirado Herrero, 'The Energy Divide: Integrating Energy Transitions, Regional Inequalities and Poverty Trends in the European Union', *European Urban and Regional Studies*, 24 (2017), 69–86 <https://doi.org/10.1177/0969776415596449>

Brondi, Sonia, Alessandra Armenti, Paolo Cottone, Bruno M. Mazzara, and Mauro Sarrica, 'Parliamentary and Press Discourses on Sustainable Energy in Italy: No More Hard Paths, Not yet Soft Paths', *Energy Research and Social Science*, 2 (2014), 38–48 <https://doi.org/10.1016/j.erss.2014.04.011>

Buchan, David, *Energy and Climate Change: Europe at the Crossroads* (Oxford: Oxford University Press, 2009)

———, 'Energy Policy : Sharp Challenges and Rising Ambitions', in *Policy-Making in the European Union*, ed. by Helen Wallace, Mark A. Pollack, and Alasdair R. Young, 7th edn (Oxford: Oxford University Press, 2015), p. 570 <https://doi.org/10.1177/0010414013516917>

Buchan, David, and Malcolm Keay, 'Europe's "Energy Union" Plan: A Reasonable Start to a Long Journey', *OXFORD ENERGY COMMENT*, 2015 <https://www.oxfordenergy.org/wpcms/wp-content/uploads/2015/03/Europes-Energy-Union-plan-a-reasonable-start-to-a-long-journey.pdf> [accessed 30 June 2018]

———, *Europe's Long Energy Journey: Towards an Energy Union?*, ed. by David Buchan and Malcolm Keay, 1st edn (Oxford: Oxford University Press, 2016)

Burgess, Michael, *The British Tradition of Federalism* (London: Leicester University Press, 1995)

Burholt, Vanessa, and Gill Windle, 'Keeping Warm? Self-Reported Housing and Home Energy Efficiency Factors Impacting on Older People Heating Homes in North Wales', *Energy Policy*, 34 (2006), 1198–1208 <https://doi.org/10.1016/j.enpol.2004.09.009>

BusinessEurope, 'BusinessEurope Position on Intergovernmental Agreements in the Field of Energy' (Brussels, 2015) <https://www.businesseurope.eu>

Buzek, Jerzy, and Jacques Delors, *Towards a New European Energy Community* (Brussels, 2010) <http://institutdelors.eu/wp-content/uploads/2018/01/en_buzek-delors_declaration.pdf> [accessed 13 February 2017]

Cameron, Peter, 'Legal Aspects of EU Energy Regulation,' *Implementing the New Directives on Electricity and Gas Across Europe* (2005)

Cavanaugh, Jeffrey, 'FOREX Africa: The CFA Franc aka The African Euro', 2014 <http://afkinsider.com/41946/forex-africa-african-euro/#sthash.bAiuUVxB.dpuf> [accessed 3 February 2019]

Černoch, Filip, 'Natural Gas Market Of the European Union and Its Impact on the Position of Gazprom in Europe', *Energy Security in Central and Eastern Europe and the Operations of Russian State-Owned Energy Enterprises*, (Brno: Masaryk University, 2015) pp. 377–399.

Chalvatzis, Konstantinos J., and Alexis Ioannidis, 'Energy Supply Security in Southern Europe and Ireland', *Energy Procedia*, 105 (2017), 2916–22 <https://doi.org/10.1016/j.eg,ypro.2017.03.660>

Chivvis, Christopher, 'A Liberal History of European Integration', *International Affairs*, 79 (2003), 1065–69

Claude-Henri, Saint-Simon, *De La Réorganisation de La Société Européenne* (Paris: Adrian Égron, 1814)

Climate Policy Observer, 'European Council Endorses the Energy Union', *Climate Policy Observer*, 2015 <http://climateobserver.org/european-council-endorses-energy-union/> [accessed 19 February 2018]

Collier, Ute, 'EU Energy Policy in a Changing Climate', in *Environmental Policy Integration: Greening Sectoral Policies in Europe*, ed. by Andrea Lenschow (London: Earthscan Publications, 2002), pp. 175–92

Council of European Energy Regulators, 'ABOUT – Ceer.Eu' <https://www.ceer.eu/eer_about> [accessed 20 February 2018]

Council of the European Communities, *Resolution Embodying the Opinion of the European Parliament on the Communication from the Commission of the European Communities to the Council on the Energy Objectives of the Community for 1990 and Convergence of Policies of the Member States on Nuclear Energy and Energy Policy*, *Official Journal of the European Communities* (C, 1980), pp. 41–44 <https://eur-lex.europa.eu/> [accessed 20 May 2018]

Council of the European Union, 'Transport, Telecommunications and Energy Council Configuration (TTE) – Consilium', 2018 <https://www.consilium.europa.eu/en/council-eu/configurations/tte/> [accessed 19 February 2018]

Cowan, Robin, 'Nuclear Power Reactors: A Study in Technological Lock-In', *The Journal of Economic History*, 50 (1990), 541–67 <https://doi.org/10.1017/S0022050700037153>

Craig, Paul P., and Gráinne de Búrca, *EU Law : Text, Cases, and Materials*, 5th edn (Oxford: Oxford University Press, 2011)

David, Paul A., 'Clio and the Economics of QWERTY', *American Economic Review*, 75 (1985), 332–37

Dedman, Martin, *The Origins and Development of the European Union 1945–2008: A History of European Integration*, 2nd edn (London and New York: Routledge, 2010)

Delzell, Charles F., 'The European Federalist Movement in Italy: The First Phase, 1918–1947', *The Journal of Modern History*, 23 (1960), 241–50

Deubner, Christian, 'The Expansion of West German Capital and the Founding of Euratom', *International Organization*, 33 (1979), 203–28 <https://doi.org/10.1017/S0020818300032148>

DG Competition, 'European Commission – Competition – Energy – Overview', 2012 <http://ec.europa.eu/competition/sectors/energy/overview_en.html> [accessed 17 February 2018]

Diebold, William, *The Schuman Plan: A Study in Economic Cooperation 1950–1959* (New York : Frederick A. Praeger, 1959)

Dietl, Ralph, 'Suez 1956: A European Intervention?', *Journal of Contemporary History*, 43 (2008), 259–78 <https://doi.org/10.1177/0022009408089032>

Dinan, Desmond, *Europe Recast: A History of European Union*, 2nd edn (Basingstoke, UK: Palgrave Macmillan, 2014)

———, 'European Integration: From the Common Market to the Single Market', in *A Companion to Europe since 1945*, ed. by Klaus Larres, 1st edn (Chichester, West Sussex: Wiley-Blackwell, 2009), pp. 133–50 <https://doi.org/10.1002/9781444308600.ch21>

———, *Ever Closer Union : An Introduction to European Integration*, 4th edn (London: Lynne Rienner Publishers, Inc, 2010)

———, *Origins and Evolution of the European Union*, ed. by Desmond Dinan, 2nd edn (Oxford: Oxford University Press, 2014)

Documents Diplomatiques Français, 'Memorandum of End April/Beginning of May : Document 239', 1955

Eberlein, Burkard, 'The making of the European energy market: The interplay of governance and government,' *Journal of Public Policy* (2008): 73–92.

Eikeland, Per Ove, *EU Energy Policy Integration – Stakeholders, Institutions and Issue-Linkages*, *FNI Report*, 2012, 13/2012

———, 'The Third Internal Energy Market Package: New Power Relations among Member States, EU Institutions and Non-State Actors?', *Journal of Common Market Studies*, 49 (2011), 243–63 <https://doi.org/10.1111/j.1468-5965.2010.02140.x>

Erbach, Gregor, 'Intergovernmental Agreements in the Field of Energy', *EU Legislation in Progress* (Strasbourg: European Parliamentary Research Service (EPRS), 2017) <https://epthinktank.eu/2017/02/03/intergovernmental-agreements-in-the-field-of-energy-eu-legislation-in-progress/>

EU, 'Directive (EU) 2018/2001 of the European Parliament and of the Council of 11 December 2018 on the Promotion of the Use of Energy from Renewable Sources (Recast)', *Official Journal of the European Union*, 2018 <https://eur-lex.europa.eu/legal-content/EN/TXT/PDF/?uri=CELEX:32018L2001&from=EN>

European Commission, '2020 EU Climate and Energy Package', 2009 <https://ec.europa.eu/clima/policies/strategies/2020_en> [accessed 15 February 2018]

———, '2030 EU Climate and Energy Framework', 2014 <https://ec.europa.eu/clima/policies/strategies/2030_en#tab-0-0> [accessed 15 February 2018]

———, 'April Infringements Package: Main Decisions; MEMO/13/375' (Brussels: European Commission, 2013)

———, 'Energy Union Package – A Framework Strategy for a Resilient Energy Union with a Forward-Looking Climate Change Policy COM(2015) 80 Final', 2015, pp. 1–21 <https://doi.org/10.1017/CBO9781107415324.004>

———, 'Energy Union Strategy', 2015 <https://ec.europa.eu/commission/priorities/energy-union-and-climate_en> [accessed 15 February 2018]

———, 'Proposal for a REGULATION OF THE EUROPEAN PARLIAMENT AND OF THE COUNCIL on the Governance of the Energy Union, Amending Directive 94/22/EC, Directive 98/70/EC, Directive 2009/31/EC, Regulation (EC) No 663/2009, Regulation (EC) No 715/2009, Directive 2009/' (Brussels: European Commission, 2016)

European Parliament, 'Members and Substitutes of the European Parliament Committee on Industry, Research and Energy' (Strasbourg, 2019), pp. 1–14 <http://www.europarl.europa.eu/committees/en/itre/members.pdf>

———, 'Towards a New Energy Market Design' (European Parliament, 2016)

European Union, 'Regulation (Ec) No 713/2009 of the European Parliament and of the Council of 13 July 2009 Establishing an Agency for the Cooperation of Energy Regulators', *Official Journal of the European Union*, L 211 (2009), 1–14 <https://eur-lex.europa.eu/LexUriServ/LexUriServ.do?uri=OJ:L:2009:211:0001:0014:EN:PDF>

———, 'Regulation (EU) 2018/1999', *Official Journal of the European Union* (Luxembourg: Publications Office of the European Union, 2018), 1–77

Fresa, Siddharth, 'Multilevel EU Governance in Energy Infrastructure Development: A New Role for ACER,' (DIW Working Paper: 2015). Retrieved from http://www. diw. de/documents/dokumentenarchiv/17/diw_01. c. 508434. de/fresa.

Gales, Ben, Astrid Kander, Paolo Malanima, and Mar Rubio, 'North versus South: Energy Transition and Energy Intensity in Europe over 200 Years', *European Review of Economic History*, 11 (2007), 219–53 <https://doi.org/10.1017/S1361491607001967>

Garavini, Giuliano, *After Empires: European Integration, Decolonization, and the Challenge from the Global South 1957–1986*, 1st edn (Oxford: Oxford University Press, 2012)

Garud, Raghu, and Peter Karnøe, *Path Dependence and Creation.*, ed. by Raghu Garud and Peter Karnøe (Mahwah, New Jersey: Lawrence Erlbaum Associates Inc, Publishers, 2001)

Garud, Raghu, Arun Kumaraswamy, and Peter Karnøe, 'Path Dependence or Path Creation?', *Journal of Management Studies*, 47 (2010), 760–74 <https://doi.org/10.1111/j.1467-6486.2009.00914.x>

Gehler, Michael., *Europa : Ideen – Institutionen – Vereinigung* (Munich: Olzog, 2010)

Gehler, Michael, 'Challenges and Opportunities: Surmounting Integration Crises in Historical Context', in *Crises in European Integration: Challenges and Responses, 1945–2005*, ed. by Ludger Kühnhardt, Challenges and Responses, 1945–2005 (New York and Oxford: Berghahn Books, 2011), pp. 109–30

———, *EUROPA* (Frankfurt am Main: Fischer Taschenbuch Verlag, 2002)

Ghilès, Francis, 'España y El Gas Argelino', *Política Exterior*, 9 (1995), 169–76

Gillingham, John R, 'A Theoretical Vacuum: European Integration and Historical Research Today', *Journal of European Integration History*, 14 (2008), 27–34 <http://www.eu-historians.eu/uploads/Dateien/jeih-27-2008_1.pdf>

———, *Coal, Steel, and the Rebirth of Europe, 1945—1955 : The Germans and French from Ruhr Conflict to Economic Community* (Cambridge,UK: Cambridge University Press, 1991)

———, *European Integration, 1950–2003: Superstate or New Market Economy?* (Cambridge,UK: Cambridge University Press, 2003)

———, 'Jean Monnet and the European Coal and Steel Community: A Preliminary Appraisal', in *Jean Monnet: The Path to European Unity* (New York: St. Martin's Press, 1991), pp. 129–62 <https://doi.org/10.1007/978-1-137-12050-2>

Giuliano, Garavini, 'Western Europe and the Long Energy Crisis of the 1970s,' *Europe in a Globalising World*, (Nomos Verlagsgesellschaft GmbH & Co. KG : 2014)

Godzimirski, Jakub M., and Zuzanna Nowak, 'EU Gas Supply Security: The Power of the Importer', in *Energy Security in Europe* (Cham: Springer International Publishing, 2018), pp. 221–49 <https://doi.org/10.1007/978-3-319-64964-1_9>

Goldstone, Jack A., 'Initial Conditions, General Laws, Path Dependence, and Explanation in Historical Sociology', *American Journal of Sociology*, 104 (2002), 829–45 <https://doi.org/10.1086/210088>

Goldthau, Andreas, and Benjamin K Sovacool, 'The Uniqueness of the Energy Security, Justice, and Governance Problem', *Energy Policy*, 41 (2012), 232–40 <https://doi.org/10.1016/j.enpol.2011.10.042>

Gouardères, Frédéric, *Internal Energy Market* (Strasbourg, 2018) <http://www.europarl.europa.eu/Reg,Data/etudes/fiches_techniques/2017/N54579/en.pdf> [accessed 11 February 2018]

———, 'Nuclear Energy' (Strasbourg: EPRS, 2018)

Grimes, Robin W., and William J. Nuttall, 'Generating the Option of a Two-Stage Nuclear Renaissance', *Science*, 329 (2010), 799–803 <https://doi.org/10.1126/science.1188928>

Grin, Gilles, *Battle Of Single European Market: Achievements and Economics 1945–2000* (New York: Columbia University Press, 2003)

Grubler, Arnulf, 'Transitions in Energy Use', *Encyclopedia of Energy*, 6 (2004), 163–77 <https://doi.org/http://dx.doi.org/10.1016/B0-12-176480-X/00023-1>

Haas, Ernst B., *The Uniting of Europe: Political, Social and Economic Forces 1950–1957*, 2nd edn (Stanford, CA: Stanford University Press, 1968)

von Hagen, Jürgen, 'Through Crises to EMU: Perspectives for Fiscal Union and Political Union', in *Crises in European Integration*, ed. by Ludger Kühnhardt, Challenges and Responses, 1945–2005, NED-New (Berghahn Books, 2009), pp. 61–78 <http://www.jstor.org/stable/j.ctt9qcpnp.8>

Hals, Tom, 'Westinghouse Reaches Deal for $800 Million U.S. Bankruptcy Loan', *Reuters*, 2017 <https://www.reuters.com/article/us-toshiba-accounting-westinghouse/westinghouse-reaches-deal-for-800-million-u-s-bankruptcy-loan-idUSKBN18J2M2> [accessed 12 February 2018]

Hansen, Teis, Antje Klitkou, Mads Borup, Lisa Scordato, and Nina Wessberg, 'Path Creation in Nordic Energy and Road Transport Systems – The Role of Technological Characteristics', *Renewable and Sustainable Energy Reviews*, 70 (2017), 551–62 <https://doi.org/10.1016/j.rser.2016.11.131>

Helm, Dieter, 'European Energy Policy', in *The Oxford Handbook of the European Union*, ed. by Erik Jones, Anand Menon, and Stephen Weatherill, 1st edn (Oxford: Oxford University Press, 2012), pp. 556–69 <https://doi.org/10.1093/oxfordhb/9780199546282.013.0039>

———, 'The European Framework for Energy and Climate Policies', *Energy Policy*, 64 (2014), 29–35 <https://doi.org/10.1016/j.enpol.2013.05.063>

Henriques, Sofia Teives, *Energy Transitions, Economic Growth and Structural Change: Portugal in a Long-Run Comparative Perspective*, *Lund Studies in Economic History 54* (Lund: Lund University Press, 2011)

Hobolt, Sara B., 'The Brexit Vote: A Divided Nation, a Divided Continent', *Journal of European Public Policy*, 23 (2016), 1259–77 <https://doi.org/10.1080/13501763.2016.1225785>

Hobsbawm, Eric J., *Nations and Nationalism since 1780 : Programme, Myth, Reality*, 2nd edn (Cambridge,UK: Cambridge University Press, 1992)

———, *The Age of Extremes : A History of the World, 1914–1991* (London: Vintage Books, 1996)

Howarth, David, and Tal Sadeh, 'The Ever Incomplete Single Market: Differentiation and the Evolving Frontier of Integration', *Journal of European Public Policy*, 17 (2010), 922–35 <https://doi.org/10.1080/13501763.2010.499220>

IAEA, 'The International Chernobyl Project : Technical Report, Assessment of Radiological Consequences and Avaluation of Protective Measures' (Vienna: International Atomic Energy Agency, 1991), p. 640

International Energy Agency and Nordic Energy Research, 'Nordic Energy Technology Perspectives 2013', (Paris: OECD, 2013). Available at www.iea.org/etp/nordic;

International Energy Agency and Nordic Energy Research, 'Nordic Energy Technology Perspectives 2016', (Paris: OECD, 2016). Available at www.iea.org/etp/nordic

Irandoust, Manuchehr, 'The Renewable Energy-Growth Nexus with Carbon Emissions and Technological Innovation: Evidence from the Nordic Countries', *Ecological Indicators*, 69 (2016), 118–25 <https://doi.org/10.1016/j.ecolind.2016.03.051>

Jirušek. Martin et al., ' Energy security in Central and Eastern Europe and the operations of Russian State-Owned Energy Enterprises', (Brno: Masaryk University, 2015).

Juncker, Jean-Claude and Frans Timmermans, 'State of the Union 2018: Letter of Intent to President Tajani and to Chancellor Sebastian Kurz', *Strasbourg, 13 September* (Strasbourg: European Commission, 2018) <https://ec.europa.eu/commission/sites/beta-political/files/soteu2018-speech_en_0.pdf>

Juncker, Jean-Claude, *A New Start for Europe: My Agenda for Jobs, Growth, Fairness and Democratic Change., Political Guidelines for the next European Commission* (Strasbourg, 2014) <https://ec.europa.eu> [accessed 13 February 2018]

———, 'Mission Letter – Vice-President for Energy Union' (Brussels: European Commission, 2014), pp. 1–6 <https://ec.europa.eu/commission/sites/cwt/files/commissioner_mission_letters/sefcovic_en.pdf>

Kander, Astrid, Paolo Malanima, and Paul Warde, *Power to the People: Energy in Europe over the Last Five Centuries*, ed. by Astrid Kander, Paolo Malanima, and Paul Warde, *Power to the People: Energy in Europe over the Last Five Centuries* (Princeton and Oxford: Princeton University Press, 2014) <https://doi.org/10.2307/j.ctt4cgb93>

Kanellakis, M., G. Martinopoulos, and T. Zachariadis, 'European Energy Policy-A Review', *Energy Policy*, 62 (2013), 1020–30 <https://doi.org/10.1016/j.enpol.2013.08.008>

Karnøe, Peter, and Raghu Garud, 'Path Creation : Co-Creation of Heterogeneous Resources in the Emergence of the Danish Wind Turbine Cluster Path Creation : Co-Creation of Heterogeneous Resources in the Emergence of the Danish Wind Turbine Cluster', 4313 (2012) <https://doi.org/10.1080/09654313.2012.667923>

Kay, Adrian, 'A Critique of the Use of Path Dependency in Policy Studies', *Public Administration*, 83 (2005), 553–72

Keay, Malcolm, and David Buchan, 'Europe's Energy Union : A Problem of Governance', *Oxford Energy Comment* (Oxford, 2015), pp. 1–6

Keman, Hans, 'It's a Long Way to Europe : The Post War Process of Integration' (Chengdu, 2007)

Kingdon, John W., *Agendas, Alternatives, and Public Policies*, ed. by John W. Kingdon, *Agendas, Alternatives, and Public Policies*, 2nd edn (Essex: Pearson, 2014)

Klitkou, Antje, Teis Hansen, Nina Wessberg, and Mads Borup, 'Path Creation in Nordic Energy and Road Transport Systems', *Renewable Energy Research Conference (RERC) 2014 Oslo, June 16–18 2014* (Oslo, Norway, 2014), pp. 1–17 <https://doi.org/10.1016/j.rser.2016.11.131>

Koirala, Binod Prasad, Elta Koliou, Jonas Frieg,e, Rudi A. Hakvoort, and Paulien M. Herder, 'Energetic Communities for Community Energy: A Review of Key Issues and Trends Shaping Integrated Community Energy Systems', *Renewable and Sustainable Energy Reviews*, 56 (2016), 722–44 <https://doi.org/10.1016/j.rser.2015.11.080>

Krüger, Peter, *Das Unberechenbare Europa : Epochen Des Integrationsprozesses Vom Späten 18. Jahrhundert Bis Zur Europäischen Union* (Stuttgart: Kohlhammer, 2006)

Kühnhardt, Ludger., *Crises in European Integration : Challenges and Responses, 1945–2005.* (Berghahn Books, Inc, 2008) <http://www.jstor.org/stable/j.ctt9qcpnp> [accessed 15 June 2017]

Kühnhardt, Ludger, *European Union–the Second Founding : The Changing Rationale of European Integration*, 2nd edn (Baden-Baden: Nomos, 2010)

Langsdorf, Susanne, 'EU Energy Policy: From the ECSC to the Energy Roadmap 2050' <https://doi.org/10.1038/179559a0>

Leal-Arcas, Rafael, Feja Lesniewska, and Filippos Proedrou, 'Prosumers: New Actors in EU Energy Security', in *Netherlands Yearbook of International Law*, 2018, XLVIII, 139–72 <https://doi.org/10.1007/978-94-6265-243-9_5>

Leal-Arcas, Rafael, Juan Alemany Rios, and Costantino Grasso, 'The European Union and Its Energy Security Challenges', *Journal of World Energy Law and Business*, 8 (2015), 291–336 <https://doi.org/10.1093/jwelb/jwv020>

Leuffen, Dirk, Berthold Rittberger, and Frank Schimmelfennig, *Differentiated Integration: Explaining Variation in the European Union* (Basingstoke, UK: Palgrave Macmillan, 2013), XII

Lubell, Harold, 'Security of Supply and Energy Policy in Western Europe', *World Politics*, 13 (2006), 400–422 <https://doi.org/10.2307/2009482>

Mahant, Edelgard, and Xavier De Vanssay, 'The Origins of Customs Unions and Free Trade Areas', *Journal of European Integration*, 17 (1994), 181–210 <https://doi.org/10.1080/07036339408429004>

Maher, Imelda, and Oana Stefan, 'Delegation of Powers and the Rule of Law: Energy Justice in EU Energy Regulation', *Energy Policy*, 128 (2019), 84–93 <https://doi.org/10.1016/j.enpol.2018.12.046>

Mahoney, James, 'Path Dependence in Historical Sociology', *Theory and Society*, 29 (2000), 507–48

Mallet, Benjamin, 'France's EDF Throws Areva a Lifeline with Reactor Deal | Reuters', *Reuters*, 2016 <https://www.reuters.com/article/us-france-edf-areva/frances-edf-throws-areva-a-lifeline-with-reactor-deal-idUSKBN13B0TG> [accessed 12 February 2018]

Maltby, Tomas, 'European Union Energy Policy Integration: A Case of European Commission Policy Entrepreneurship and Increasing Supranationalism', *Energy Policy*, 55 (2013), 435–44 <https://doi.org/10.1016/j.enpol.2012.12.031>

Matlary, Haaland Janne, *Energy Policy in the European Union*, 1st edn (London: Macmillan Press Ltd, 1997)

Mayer, Sebastian, 'Path Dependence and Commission Activism in the Evolution of the European Union's External Energy Policy', *Journal of International Relations and Development*, 11 (2008), 251–78 <https://doi.org/10.1057/jird.2008.12>

Mendes, Gonalo, Christos Ioakimidis, and Paulo Ferrão, 'On the Planning and Analysis of Integrated Community Energy Systems: A Review and Survey of Available Tools', *Renewable and Sustainable Energy Reviews*, 15 (2011), 4836–54 <https://doi.org/10.1016/j.rser.2011.07.067>

Meyer, Henry Cord, *Mitteleuropa: In German Thought and Action 1815–1945* (The Hague: Martinus Nijhoff, 1955)

Miller, Vaughne, '"Ever Closer Union" in the EU Treaties and Court of Justice Case Law' (London: House of Commons Library, 2015)

Milward, Alan S., *The European Rescue of the Nation-State*, ed. by Alan S.Milward, George Brennan, and Federico Romero, 2nd edn (London and New York: Routledge, 2000)

Molinari, Guido de, 'L'union Douanière de l'Europe Centrale', *Journal Des Économistes*, 5 (1879), 309–18

Möller, Horst, *Europa Zwischen Den Weltkriegen*, Oldenbourg Grundriss Der Geschichte (München: R. Oldenbourg Verlag, 1998), XXI

Moravscik, Andrew, 'Liberal Intergovernmentalism and Integration: A Rejoinder', *JCMS: Journal of Common Market Studies*, 33 (1995), 611–28 <https://doi.org/10.1111/j.1468-5965.1995.tb00554.x>

Naumann, Friedrich, *Mitteleuropa* (Berlin: Georg Reimer, 1915) <https://archive.org>

Naylor, Phillip C., *France and Algeria: A History of Decolonization and Transformation, Canadian Journal of African Studies / Revue Canadienne Des Études Africaines* (Gainesville: University Press of Florida, 2008), XXXVI <https://doi.org/10.2307/4107416>

Nicolson, Harold, *The Congress of Vienna : A Study in Allied Unity, 1812–1822* (New York: Grove Press, 1946)

Noël, Pierre, 'A Market Between Us: Reducing the Political Cost of Europe's Dependence on Russian Gas,' *Electricity Policy Research Group (EPRG)*, University of Cambridge, EPRG Working Paper 916 (2009);

Novy, Milena, *International Actions to Combat Pollution in the Black Triangle and Katowice Regions*, Working Papers (Laxenburg, Austria, 1996)

O'Connor, Martin, and Sybille Van den Hove, 'Prospects for Public Participation on Nuclear Risks and Policy Options: Innovations in Governance Practices for Sustainable Development in the European Union', *Journal of Hazardous Materials*, 86 (2001), 77–99 <https://doi.org/10.1016/S0304-3894(01)00256-4>

O'Driscoll, Mervyn, 'The Origins and Early History of Euratom, 1955–1968', in *The European Parliament and the Euratom Treaty: Past, Present and Future* (Luxembourg: European Parliament, 2002), pp. 1–44 <http://www.europarl.eu.int/studies.> [accessed 1 March 2018]

Ollila, Jorma and Jens Skov-Spilling, 'Nordic Energy Co-operation: Strong today–Stronger tomorrow', *Nordic Council of Ministers*, Vol. 2017732. (2017); Eirik S. Amundsen and Lars Bergman, 'Why has the Nordic electricity market worked so well?', *Utilities policy,* 14.3 (2006): 148–157.

Padgett, Stephen, 'The Single European Energy Market: The Politics of Realization,' *Journal of Common Market Studies,* 30 (1992) 53.

Pareja-Alcaraz, Pablo, 'Chinese Investments in Southern Europe's Energy Sectors: Similarities and Divergences in China's Strategies in Greece, Italy, Portugal and Spain', *Energy Policy*, 101 (2017), 700–710 <https://doi.org/10.1016/j.enpol.2016.09.034>

Penttinen, Sirja-Leena, 'The Role of the Court of Justice of the European Union in the Energy Market Liberalisation', in *Research Handbook on International Energy Law*, ed. by Kim Talus (Cheltenham, UK: Edward Elgar Publishing, 2014), pp. 241–71

Phinnemore, David, and Alex Warleigh-Lack, *Reflections on European Integration*, ed. by David Phinnemore and Alex Warleigh-Lack, 1st edn (Basingstoke, UK: Palgrave Macmillan, 2009) <https://doi.org/10.1057/9780230232839>

Piebalgs, Andris, *How the European Union Is Preparing the" Third Industrial Revolution" with an Innovative Energy Policy, EUI Working Paper RSCAS*, RSCAS 2009/11 (Florence, 2009), xı <www.euthat is,u>

Pollak, Johannes., and Samuel. Schubert, *Die Energiepolitik Der EU*, ed. by Johannes. Pollak, Samuel. Schubert, and Peter. Slominski (Wien: facultas wuv UTB, 2010) <https://opac.ub.uni-greifswald.de/DB=1/XMLPRS=N/PPN?PPN=690093802>

Prontera, Andrea, 'The New Politics of Energy Security and the Rise of the Catalytic State in Southern Europe', *Journal of Public Policy*, 38 (2018), 511–51 <https://doi.org/10.1017/S0143814X1700006X>

Roberts, Josh, *Prosumer Rights: Options for an EU Legal Framework Post-2020* (London, 2016) <http://www.greenpeace.org/eu-unit/Global/eu-unit/reports-briefings/2016/ClientEarth Prosumer Rights – options for a legal framework – FINAL 03062016.pdf>

———, 'The Proposed EU DSO Entity: What Is It and What's at Stake?' (Brussels: ClientEarth, 2016), pp. 1–6 <www.clientearth.org>

Roggenkamp, Martha M., Anita Roenne, Catherine Redgwell, and Inigo del. Guayo, *Energy Law in Europe : National, EU, and International Law and Institutions*, 2nd edn (Oxford: Oxford University Press, 2007)

Rowe, Gene, and Lynn J. Frewer, 'A Typology of Public Engagement Mechanisms', *Science, Technology, & Human Value*, 30 (2005), 251–90 <https://doi.org/10.1177/0162243904271724>

Sandholtz, Wayne, and Alec Stone Sweet, 'Neo-Functionalism and Supranational Governance', in *The Oxford Handbook of the European Union*, ed. by Erik Jones, Anand Menon, and Stephen Weatherill, 1st edn (Oxford: Oxford University Press, 2012), pp. 18–33

Sandoval, Israel Solorio, and Francesc Morata, 'Introduction: The Re-Evolution of Energy Policy in Europe', in *European Energy Policy: An Environmental Approach*, ed. by Israel Solorio Sandoval and Francesc Morata (Cheltenham: Edward Elgar Publishing, 2012), pp. 1–22 <https://doi.org/10.4337/9780857939203.00008>

Schmalensee, Richard, 'Lecture 5: Path Dependence in Energy Systems' (Cambridge, MA: Sloan School of Management, MIT, 2012) <https://ocw.mit.edu>

Szulecki, Kacper, ed., '*Energy Security in Europe: Divergent Perceptions and Policy Challenges*,' (Springer, 2017)

Van Der Schoor, Tineke, and Bert Scholtens, 'Power to the People: Local Community Initiatives and the Transition to Sustainable Energy', *Renewable and Sustainable Energy Reviews*, 43 (2015), 666–75 <https://doi.org/10.1016/j.rser.2014.10.089>

Schubert, Samuel R., Johannes Pollack, and Maren Kreutler, *Energy Policy of the European Union* (London: Palgrave, 2016)

Schuman, Robert, 'Declaration of 9th May 1950 Delivered by Robert Schuman', *European Issue*, 2011, 1–3

Sereny, Gitta., *Albert Speer : His Battle With Truth* (New York: Vintage Books, 1996)

Simmie, James, 'Path Dependence and New Technological Path Creation in the Danish Wind Power Industry', *European Planning Studies*, 20 (2012), 753–72 <https://doi.org/10.1080/09654313.2012.667924>

Simmie, James, Rolf Sternberg, and Juliet Carpenter, 'New Technological Path Creation: Evidence from the British and German Wind Energy Industries', *Journal of Evolutionary Economics*, 24 (2014), 875–904 <https://doi.org/10.1007/s00191-014-0354-8>

Sjödin, Jörgen and Stefan Grönkvist, 'Emissions Accounting for Use and Supply of Electricity in the Nordic Market,' *Energy policy* 32.13 (2004): 1555–1564.

Sorensen, Bent, 'Can We Learn from History?', *European Review*, 22 (2014), 92–96 <https://doi.org/10.1017/S1062798713000653>

Sovacool, Benjamin K., *Energy & Ethics: Justice and the Global Energy Challenge* (London: Palgrave Macmillan, 2013), xci

Sovacool, Benjamin K., 'Contestation, Contingency, and Justice in the Nordic Low-Carbon Energy Transition,' *Energy Policy*, 102 (2017), 569–582.

Sovacool, Benjamin K., and Michael H. Dworkin, 'Energy Justice: Conceptual Insights and Practical Applications', *Applied Energy*, 142 (2015), 435–44 <https://doi.org/10.1016/j.apenergy.2015.01.002>

Stirk, Peter M.R., *A History of European Integration since 1914*, 2nd edn (London and New York: Continuum, 2001)

Szlavik, Janos, and Maria Csete, 'Climate and Energy Policy in Hungary', *Energies*, 5 (2012), 494–517 <https://doi.org/10.3390/en5020494>

Szulecki, Kacper, *Energy Security in Europe : Divergent Perceptions and Policy Challenges*, ed. by Kacper Szulecki (Cham: Palgrave Macmillan, 2018)

Szulecki, Kacper, Andrzej Ancygier, and Karsten Neuhoff, 'Energy Union : From Idea to Reality', in *Conference and Expert Workshop on EU Energy Governance Post-2020* (Berlin, 2015) <www.econstor.eu>

Szulecki, Kacper, Severin Fischer, Anne Therese Gullberg, and Oliver Sartor, *Giving Shape to the Energy Union: Evolution, National Expectations and Implications for EU Energy and Climate Governance*, *SSRN*, 2015 <https://doi.org/10.2139/ssrn.2623892>

Szulecki, Kacper, and Kirsten Westphal, 'Taking Security Seriously in EU Energy Governance: Crimean Shock and the Energy Union', in *Energy Security in Europe. Energy, Climate and the Environment.*, ed. by Kacper Szulecki (Cham: Springer International Publishing, 2018), pp. 177–202 <https://doi.org/10.1007/978-3-319-64964-1>

Taliotis, Constantinos, Holger Rogner, Stephan Ressl, Mark Howells, and Francesco Gardumi, 'Natural Gas in Cyprus: The Need for Consolidated Planning', *Energy Policy*, 107 (2017), 197–209 <https://doi.org/10.1016/j.enpol.2017.04.047>

Talus, Kim, *EU Energy Law and Policy : A Critical Account*, 1st edn (Oxford: Oxford University Press, 2013)

———, *Introduction to EU Energy Law* (Oxford: Oxford University Press, 2016)

Thaler, Philipp, 'The European Commission and the European Council: Coordinated Agenda Setting in European Energy Policy', *Journal of European Integration*, 38 (2016), 571–85 <https://doi.org/10.1080/07036337.2016.1178252>

Thomson, Harriet, and Carolyn Snell, 'Quantifying the Prevalence of Fuel Poverty across the European Union', *Energy Policy*, 52 (2013), 563–72 <https://doi.org/10.1016/j.enpol.2012.10.009>

Tusk, Donald, 'A United Europe Can End Russia's Energy Stranglehold', *FT.Com* (London, 2014), pp. 4–5 <http://www.ft.com/cms/s/0/91508464-c661-11e3-ba0e-00144feabdc0.html#axzz30viqhrqv> [accessed 13 February 2018]

UK Government, 'DECC Government Major Projects Portfolio Data 2016 – GOV.UK', 2016 <https://www.gov.uk/government/publications/decc-government-major-projects-portfolio-data-2016> [accessed 12 February 2019]

Union for the Coordination of Transmission of Electricity (UCTE), *UCPTE/UCTE: The 50 Year Success Story – Evolution of a European Interconnected Grid* (Brussels: Secretariat of UCTE, 2009)

Unruh, Gregory C., 'Escaping the Carbon Lock-In', *Energy Policy*, 30 (2002), 317–25 <https://doi.org/10.1016/S0301-4215(01)00098-2>

Unruh, Gregory C., 'Understanding Carbon Lock-In', *Energy Policy*, 28 (2000), 817–30

Ürge-Vorsatz, Diana, Gergana Miladinova, and László Paizs, 'Energy in Transition: From the Iron Curtain to the European Union', *Energy Policy*, 34 (2006), 2279–97 <https://doi.org/10.1016/j.enpol.2005.03.007>

Walker, Gordon, 'What Are the Barriers and Incentives for Community-Owned Means of Energy Production and Use?', *Energy Policy*, 36 (2008), 4401–5 <https://doi.org/10.1016/j.enpol.2008.09.032>

Westphal, Kirsten, 'Energy Policy between Multilateral Governance and Geopolitics: Whither Europe?', *Internationale Politik Und Gesellschaft*, 4 (2006), 44–62

Wilson, Alex Benjamin, 'Governance of the Energy Union [EU Legislation In Progress]' (Strasbourg: EPRS | European Parliamentary Research Service, 2019) <https://epthinktank.eu>

Wilson, Alex Benjamin, and Alina Dobreva, 'EU Policies-Delivering for Citizens : Energy Supply and Security' (Strasbourg: EPRS | European Parliamentary Research Service, 2018) <http://www.europarl.europa.eu> [accessed 6 December 2018]

Wirth, Steffen, 'Communities Matter: Institutional Preconditions for Community Renewable Energy', *Energy Policy*, 70 (2014), 236–46 <https://doi.org/10.1016/j.enpol.2014.03.021>

World Economic Forum, 'Fostering Effective Energy Transition. A Fact-Based Framework to Support Decision-Making', *McKinsey & Company*, 2018, p. 40 <http://www3.weforum.org/docs/WEF_Fostering_Effective_Energy_Transition_report_2018.pdf>

World Energy Council, 'Europe : Hydropower', *World Energy Resources*, 2016 <https://www.worldenergy.org/data/resources/region/europe/hydropower/> [accessed 1 March 2019]

Xu, Min, Jeanne M. David, and Suk Hi Kim, 'The Fourth Industrial Revolution: Opportunities and Challenges', *International Journal of Financial Research*, 9 (2018), 90 <https://doi.org/10.5430/ijfr.v9n2p90>

Yildiz, Özgür, Jens Rommel, Sarah Debor, Lars Holstenkamp, Franziska Mey, Jakob R. Müller, and others, 'Renewable Energy Cooperatives as Gatekeepers or Facilitators? Recent Developments in Germany and a Multidisciplinary Research Agenda', *Energy Research and Social Science*, 6 (2015), 59–73 <https://doi.org/10.1016/j.erss.2014.12.001>

Yondorf, Walter, 'Monnet and the Action Committee: The Formative Period of the European Communities', *International Organization*, 19 (1965), 885–912 <https://doi.org/10.1017/S0020818300012650>

Chapter 5

Adeoye, Omotola, and Catalina Spataru, 'Sustainable Development of the West African Power Pool: Increasing Solar Energy Integration and Regional Electricity Trade', *Energy for Sustainable Development*, 45 (2018), 124–34 <https://doi.org/10.1016/j.esd.2018.05.007>

Austvik, Ole Gunnar, 'The Energy Union and Security-of-Gas Supply', *Energy Policy*, 96 (2016), 372–82 <https://doi.org/10.1016/j.enpol.2016.06.013>

Van Baal, Paul Adrianus, and Matthias Finger, 'The Effect of European Integration on Swiss Energy Policy and Governance', *Politics and Governance*, 7 (2019), 6 <https://doi.org/10.17645/pag.v7i1.1780>

Bartle, Alison, 'Hydropower Potential and Development Activities', *Energy Policy*, 14 (2002), 1231–1239 <https://doi.org/10.1016/S0140-6701(03)83046-1>

Bosseboeuf, Didier, Lea Gynther, Bruno Lapillonne, and Karine Pollier, 'Energy Efficiency Trends and Policies in the Household and Tertiary Sectors : An Analysis Based on the ODYSSEE and MURE Databases', 2015 <https://doi.org/DOI 10.1089/pho.2012.3369>

Brautigam, Deborah, and Jyhjong Hwang, 'Great Walls over African Rivers: Chinese Engagement in African Hydropower Projects', *Development Policy Review*, 37 (2019), 313–30 <https://doi.org/10.1111/dpr.12350>

Brew-Hammond, Abeeku, 'Energy Access in Africa: Challenges Ahead', *Energy Policy*, 38 (2010), 2291–2301 <https://doi.org/10.1016/j.enpol.2009.12.016>

Cole, Dan, Mike Mcginnis, and Graham Epstein, 'Toward a Combined IAD-SES Framework' (Bloomington,IN, 2013), pp. 1–55 <https://ostromworkshop.indiana.edu/pdf/seriespapers/2013s_c/Cole, McGinnis, Epstein_PowerPoint.pdf>

Cole, Daniel H., Graham Epstein, and Michael D. McGinnis, 'Combining the IAD and SES Frameworks', *International Journal of the Commons*, 13 (2019), 244–75 <https://doi.org/10.18352/ijc.777>

Cole, Daniel H, Graham Epstein, and Michael Dean McGinnis, 'Toward a New Institutional Analysis of Social-Ecological Systems (NIASES): Combining Elinor Ostrom's IAD and SES Frameworks', *Maurer School of Law Legal Studies Research Paper Series*, 2014, 1–22 <http://ssrn.com/abstract=2490999>

Eberhard, Anton, Orvika Rosnes, Maria Shkaratan, and Haakon Vennemo, *Africa's Power Infrastructure Investment, Integration, Efficiency Infrastructure* (Washington DC: The International Bank for Reconstruction and Development/The World Bank, 2011) <https://library.pppknowledgelab.org/PPIAF/documents/3135>

ECOWAS/UEMOA, *White Paper for a Regional Policy on Access to Energy Services for Populations in Rural and Peri-Urban Areas for Poverty Reduction in line with Achieving the MDGs in Member States.* (Niamey, 2005)

ECOWAS, *Ecowas Energy Protocol A/P4/1/03* (Abuja, 2003) <http://www.ecowapp.org/sites/default/files/eprotocol.pdf> [accessed 17 August 2018]

European Commission, 'Communication from the Commission – Action Plan for Energy Efficiency: Realising the Potential', *COM(2006) 545 Final*, 2006 <http://eur-lex.europa.eu/LexUriServ/LexUriServ.do?uri=CELEX:52006DC0545:EN:NOT >

———, *Energy 2020 : A Strategy for Competitive, Sustainable and Secure Energy COM(2010) 639 Final* (Brussels, 2010)

———, *Energy Roadmap 2050 COM(2011) 885 Final* (Brussels, 2011) <https://eur-lex.europa.eu/legal-content/EN/TXT/PDF/?uri=CELEX:52011DC0885&from=EN>

———, 'Renewable Energy in the EU', *Eurostat* (Brussels, 2018) <http://ec.europa.eu/eurostat/documents/2995521/8612324/8-25012018-AP-EN.pdf/9d28caef-1961-4dd1-a901-af18f121fb2d>

———, *Renewable Energy Progress Report, COM (2019) 225 Final* (Brussels, 2019) <https://ec.europa.eu/commission/sites/beta-political/files/report-progress-renewable-energy-april2019_en.pdf>

———, *Working Group Report "Consumers as Energy Market Actors"* (Brussels, 2015) <http://www.eesc.europa.eu/resources/docs/draft_wg_report_consumers_market_agents_tc_110315_web_version3.pdf>

European Commission Directorate, 'The EU and Energy Union and Climate Action', *Publications Office of the European Union*, 2017 <https://publications.europa.eu/en/publication-detail/>

Eurostat, *Energy Statistics 2017 Edition* (Brussels, 2017) <https://ec.europa.eu/eurostat/documents/4031688/7772824/KS-06-16-230-EN-N.pdf/536884a4-83c5-4640-b87c-a77a160c0910>

———, 'Population Estimates on 1 January 2018', *Eurostat News Release* (Brussels: European Commission, 2018), pp. 1–5

ExxonMobil, 'Natural Gas: Clean and Efficient', 2018 <https://www.exxonmobil.eu/en-eu/policy/natural-gas/clean-and-efficient/clean-and-efficient> [accessed 21 June 2018]

Garrick, Dustin E, Edella Schlager, Lucia De Stefano, and Sergio Villamayor-Tomas, 'Managing the Cascading Risks of Droughts: Institutional Adaptation in Transboundary River Basins', *Earth's Future*, 2018, 809–27 <https://doi.org/10.1002/2018EF000823>

Gas Infrastructure Europe (GIE), 'LNG Map 2015' (Brussels: GIE, 2015) <https://www.gie.eu/download/maps/2015/GIE_LNG_2015_A0_1189x841_FULL_wINFOGRAPHICS_FINAL.pdf>

Gaudard, Ludovic, and Franco Romerio, 'The Future of Hydropower in Europe: Interconnecting Climate, Markets and Policies', *Environmental Science and Policy*, 37 (2014), 172–81 <https://doi.org/10.1016/j.envsci.2014.05.005>

Gouardères, Frédéric, 'Nuclear Energy' (Strasbourg: EPRS, 2018)

Van De Graaf, Thijs, Benjamin K. Sovacool, Arunabha Ghosh, Florian Kern, and Michael T. Klare, *The Palgrave Handbook of the International Political Economy of Energy*, ed. by Thijs Van De Graaf, Benjamin K. Sovacool, Arunabha Ghosh, Florian Kern, and Michael T. Klare, 1st edn (London: Palgrave Macmillan, 2016) <https://doi.org/10.1057/978-1-137-55631-8_12>

da Graça Carvalho, Maria, 'EU Energy and Climate Change Strategy', *Energy*, 40 (2012), 19–22 <https://doi.org/10.1016/j.energy.2012.01.012>

Heikkila, Tanya, and Krister Andersson, 'Policy Design and the Added-Value of the Institutional Analysis Development Framework', *Policy & Politics*, 46 (2018), 309–24 <https://doi.org/10.1332/030557318X15230060131727>

Hettne, Björn, and Fredrik Söderbaum, 'Theorising the Rise of Regionness', *New Political Economy*, 5 (2000), 457–73 <https://ssrn.com/abstract=2398942>

Hinkel, Jochen, Michael E. Cox, Maja Schlüter, Claudia R. Binder, and Thomas Falk, 'A Diagnostic Procedure for Applying the Social-Ecological Systems Framework in Diverse Cases', *Ecology and Society*, 20 (2015) <http://www.ecologyandsociety.org/vol20/iss1/art32/>

Hooghe, Liesbet, and Gary Marks, 'Unraveling the Central States, but How? Types of Multi-Level Governance', *The American Political Science Review*, 97 (2003), 233–43 <https://doi.org/10.1017/S0003055403000649>

Imperial, Mark T., and Tracy Yandle, 'Taking Institutions Seriously: Using the IAD Framework to Analyze Fisheries Policy', *Society & Natural Resources*, 18 (2005), 493–509 <https://doi.org/10.1080/08941920590947922>

International Energy Agency, 'Energy Access Outlook 2017' (Paris, 2017) <https://doi.org/10.1787/9789264285569-en>

International Water Power and Dam Construction, 'Ghana Balances Hydro and Thermal', 2006 <https://www.waterpowermagazine.com/news/newsghana-balances-hydro-and-thermal> [accessed 19 June 2018]

Khennas, Smail, 'Understanding the Political Economy and Key Drivers of Energy Access in Addressing National Energy Access Priorities and Policies: African Perspective', *Energy Policy*, 47 (2012), 21–26 <https://doi.org/10.1016/j.enpol.2012.04.003>

Lagendijk, Vincent, *Electrifying Europe: The Power of Europe in the Construction of Electricity Networks* (Amsterdam: Aksant, 2008) <https://doi.org/10.6100/IR638264>

Lancaster, Carol, 'Africa's Economic Crisis', *Foreign Policy*, 52 (1983), 149–66 <https://www.jstor.org/stable/1148240>

Lazenby, J.B.C., and P.M.S. Jones, 'Hydroelectricity in West Africa: Its Future Role', *Energy Policy*, 15 (1987), 441–55 <https://doi.org/10.1016/0301-4215(87)90056-5>

Leal-Arcas, Rafael, Feja Lesniewska, and Filippos Proedrou, 'Prosumers as New Energy Actors', in *Africa-EU Renewable Energy Research and Innovation Symposium 2018 (RERIS 2018)*, ed. by M. Mpholo et al. (Cham: Springer Proceedings in Energy, 2018), pp. 139–51 <https://doi.org/10.1007/978-3-319-93438-9>

Leo, Ben, Jared Kalow, and Todd Moss, 'What Can We Learn about Energy Access and Demand from Mobile-Phone Surveys? Nine Findings from Twelve African Countries', *CGD Policy Paper*, 120 (2018) <https://www.cgdev.org/publication/what-can-we-learn-about-energy-access-and-demand-mobile-phone-surveys>

Lindberg, Marie Byskov, Jochen Markard, and Allan Dahl Andersen, 'Policies, Actors and Sustainability Transition Pathways: A Study of the EU's Energy Policy Mix', *Research Policy*, 2018, 1–15 <https://doi.org/10.1016/j.respol.2018.09.003>

Löfstedt, Ragner E., and David Vogel, 'The Changing Character of Regulation: A Comparison of Europe and the United States', *Risk Analysis*, 21 (2001), 399–416

Lopes, Marta A.R., Carlos H. Antunes, and Nelson Martins, 'Energy Behaviours as Promoters of Energy Efficiency: A 21st Century Review', *Renewable and Sustainable Energy Reviews*, 16 (2012), 4095–4104 <https://doi.org/10.1016/j.rser.2012.03.034>

McCord, Paul, Jampel Dell'Angelo, Elizabeth Baldwin, and Tom Evans, 'Polycentric Transformation in Kenyan Water Governance: A Dynamic Analysis of Institutional and Social-Ecological Change', *Policy Studies Journal*, 45 (2017), 633–58 <https://doi.org/10.1111/psj.12168>

McGinnis, Michael Dean, 'An Introduction to IAD and the Language of the Ostrom Workshop: A Simple Guide to a Complex Framework', *Policy Studies Journal*, 39 (2011), 169–83 <https://doi.org/10.1111/j.1541-0072.2010.00401.x>

———, *Updated Guide to IAD and the Language of the Ostrom Workshop: A Simplified Overview of a Complex Framework for the Analysis of Institutions and Their Development* (Bloomington, 2016)

McGinnis, Michael Dean, 'Networks of Adjacent Action Situations in Polycentric Governance', *Policy Journal Studies*, 39 (2011), 51–79

McGinnis, Michael Dean, and Elinor Ostrom, 'Social-Ecological System Framework: Initial Changes and Continuing Challenges', *Ecology and Society*, 19 (2014) <https://doi.org/10.5751/ES-06387-190230>

Miketa, Asami, and Bruno Merven, *West African Power Pool: Planning and Prospects for Renewable Energy* (Abu Dhabi, 2013) <www.irena.org>

Nordman, Erik, 'Cape Verde's Goal Is 100 % Renewable Energy by 2025. Why It May Just Do It', *The Conversation*, 2017 <https://theconversation.com/cape-verdes-goal-is-100-renewable-energy-by-2025-why-it-may-just-do-it-85759> [accessed 21 June 2018]

O'Connor, Martin, and Sybille Van den Hove, 'Prospects for Public Participation on Nuclear Risks and Policy Options: Innovations in Governance Practices for Sustainable Development in the European Union', *Journal of Hazardous Materials*, 86 (2001), 77–99 <https://doi.org/10.1016/S0304-3894(01)00256-4>

Oguah, Samuel, and Debabrata Chattopadhyay, 'A Pro-Grid Middle Path for Africa: Sub-Saharan Region Electricity Upgrades', *IEEE Power and Energy Magazine*, 17 (2019), 61–68 <https://doi.org/10.1109/MPE.2018.2884114>

Ojo, Olatunde J B, *Nigeria and the Formation of ECOWAS*, *International Organization*, 1980, xxxiv <https://doi.org/10.1017/S0020818300018853>

Ostrom, E., 'A Diagnostic Approach for Going beyond Panaceas', *Proceedings of the National Academy of Sciences*, 104 (2007), 15181–87 <https://doi.org/10.1073/pnas.0702288104>

Ostrom, Elinor, 'A General Framework for Analyzing Sustainability of Social-Ecological Systems', *Science*, 325 (2009), 419–22 <https://doi.org/10.1126/science.1172133>

———, 'Background on the Institutional Analysis and Development Framework', *Policy Studies Journal*, 39 (2011), 7–27 <https://doi.org/10.1111/j.1541-0072.2010.00394.x>

Ostrom, Elinor, and Michael Cox, 'Moving beyond Panaceas: A Multi-Tiered Diagnostic Approach for Social-Ecological Analysis', *Environmental Conservation*, 37 (2010), 451–63 <https://doi.org/10.1017/S0376892910000834>

Ostrom, Elinor, Roy Gardner, and James Walker, *Rules, Games and Common-Pool Resources* (Ann Arbor, MI: The University of Michigan Press, 1994)

Ostrom, Vincent, Charles M. Tiebout, and Robert Warren, 'The Organization of Government in Metropolitan Areas: A Theoretical Inquiry', *American Political Science Review*, 55 (1961), 831–42 <https://doi.org/10.1017/S0003055400125973>

Peng, Donna, and Rahmat Poudineh, 'Is Natural Gas a Viable Option to Promote Electrification in Nigeria?', *Economics of Energy & Environmental Policy*, 8 (2019) <https://doi.org/10.5547/2160-5890.8.1.dpen>

Peng, Donna, and Rahmatallah Poudineh, *Gas-to-Power Supply Chains in Developing Countries : Comparative Case Studies of Nigeria and Bangladesh* (Oxford: Oxford Institute for Energy Studies, 2017)

———, 'Gas-to-Power Supply Chains in Developing Countries: Comparative Case Studies of Nigeria and Bangladesh', *Energy Insight 6* (Oxford, 2017), pp. 1–19

Schlager, Edella, and Elinor Ostrom, 'Property-Rights Regimes and Natural Resources : A Conceptual Analysis', *Land Economics*, 68 (1992), 249–62

Schot, Johan, and Vincent Lagendijk, 'Technocratic Internationalism in the Interwar Years: Building Europe on Motorways and Electricity Networks', *Journal of Modern European History*, 6 (2008), 196–217 <https://doi.org/10.17104/1611-8944_2008_2_196>

SETIS, 'Hydropower' (Brussels: European Commission, 2013), pp. 1–4 <http://setis.ec.europa.eu/technologies/ Hydropower>

Slingerland, Stephan, Jessica Yearwood, Mariya Gancheva, and Koen Rademaekers, *EU Energy Governance for the Future* (Brussels, 2015) <http://www.europarl.europa.eu/studies%0A>

Smart Villages, *Energy Situation Report-West Africa* (Abingdon,UK, 2016) <https://e4sv.org/West-Africa-Energy-Report-AW-Draft-3-200516-V3_MT.pdf> [accessed 5 March 2018]

Sokona, Youba, Yacob Mulugetta, and Haruna Gujba, 'Widening Energy Access in Africa: Towards Energy Transition', *Energy Policy*, 47 (2012), 3–10 <https://doi.org/10.1016/j.enpol.2012.03.040>

Sterner, Thomas, *Instruments for Environmental Policy* (Gothenburg: Sida, 2003)

Szulecki, Kacper, and Dag Herald Claes, 'Towards Decarbonization: Understanding EU Energy Governance', *Politics and Governance*, 7 (2019), 1 <https://doi.org/10.17645/pag.v7i1.2029>

Turkson, John K, *Power Sector Reform in Sub-Saharan Africa*, ed. by John Turkson (London and New York: Palgrave Macmillan, 2000)

UNDESA, 'Population of West Africa (2018)' <http://www.worldometers.info/world-population/western-africa-population/>

UNECA, 'Ghana's Experience In Power Interconnections Within The Framework Of ECOWAS' (Addis Ababa: UNECA, 1969) <http://repository.uneca.org/bitstream/handle/123456789/17587/Bib-67662.pdf?sequence=1>

Union for the Coordination of Transmission of Electricity (UCTE), *UCPTE/UCTE: The 50 Year Success Story – Evolution of a European Interconnected Grid* (Brussels: Secretariat of UCTE, 2009)

Vilar, David, Mahama Kappiah, Juan López-Dóriga, Santiago Martínez-Caro, Gonzalo Piernavieja Izquierdo, Brigitte Öppinger-Walchshofer, and others, *Renewable Energy in West Africa: Status, Experiences and Trends* (Praia, Cape Verde: ECREEE and CASA AFRICA, 2012) <http://www.ecreee.org/sites/default/files/renewable_energy_in_west_africa_0.pdf>

West Africa Power Pool, 'Creation of WAPP', 2017 <http://www.ecowapp.org/en/content/creation-wapp> [accessed 25 June 2018]

West African Power Pool (WAPP), 'Articles of Agreement of the West African Power Pool: Organization and Functions' (Accra: WAPP, 2005), pp. 1–39 <http://www.ecowapp.org/sites/default/files/articles_of_agreement_0.pdf>

World Nuclear Association., *New Nuclear in Europe : 2030 Outlook.* (London: World Nuclear Association., 2018)

———, 'Nuclear Power in the European Union', 2018 <https://www.world-nuclear.org/information-library/country-profiles/others/european-union.aspx> [accessed 21 July 2018]

Chapter 6

Africa-EU Energy Partnership, 'Africa-EU Energy Partnership (AEEP)', 2018 <http://www.aeep-forum.org/en/aeep> [accessed 9 July 2018]

Africa Progress Panel, *Lights Power Action: Electrifying Africa*, 2015

———, *Power People Planet Seizing Africa's Energy and Climate Opportunities*, *Africa Progress Report* (Geneva, 2015) <http://www.africaprogresspanel.org/>

African Development Bank Group, 'Africa Needs Bolder Private Financing Models for Power Transmission Lines – Energy Experts', *Africa Energy Portal*, 2019 <https://africa-energy-portal.org/news/africa-needs-bolder-private-financing-models-power-transmission-lines-energy-experts> [accessed 5 July 2019]

———, *African Economic Outlook 2019* (Abidjan, 2019) <www.afdb.org>

———, *Study Report on Harmonisation of Petroleum Policies, Legal, Regulatory and Institutional Frameworks in the East African Community* (Abidjan, 2018)

Andersson, Krister P., and Elinor Ostrom, 'Analyzing Decentralized Resource Regimes from a Polycentric Perspective', *Policy Sciences*, 41 (2008), 71–93 <https://doi.org/10.1007/sl>

Bixler, R. Patrick, 'From Community Forest Management to Polycentric Governance: Assessing Evidence from the Bottom Up', *Society & Natural Resources*, 27 (2014), 155–69 <https://doi.org/10.1080/08941920.2013.840021>

Black, Julia, 'Constructing and Contesting Legitimacy and Accountability in Polycentric Regulatory Regimes', *Regulation & Governance*, 2 (2008), 137–64 <https://doi.org/10.1111/j.1748-5991.2008.00034.x>

Blomquist, William, 'Multi-Level Governance and Natural Resource Management: The Challenges of Complexity, Diversity, and Uncertainty', in *Institutions and Sustainability*, ed. by M. Beckmann, V., Padmanabhan (New York: Springer, 2009), pp. 109–126

Carbonnier, Gilles, *International Development Policy: Energy and Development* (Basingstoke: Palgrave Macmillan, 2011)

Carlisle, Keith, and Rebecca L. Gruby, 'Polycentric Systems of Governance: A Theoretical Model for the Commons', *Policy Studies Journal*, 00 (2017) <https://doi.org/10.1111/psj.12212>

Cornell, Bradford, 'Energy and Investing : Financing the Transition to Renewable Energy', 2019 <https://doi.org/http://dx.doi.org/10.2139/ssrn.3343583>

Dietz, Thomas, Elinor Ostrom, and Paul C. Stern, 'The Struggle to Govern the Commons', *SCIENCE*, 2003, 1907–12 <https://doi.org/10.1007/978-0-387-73412-5_40>

Eberhard, Anton, Katharine Gratwick, Elvira Morella, and Pedro Antmann, *Independent Power Projects in Sub-Saharan Africa: Lessons from Five Key Countries, Directions in Development – Energy and Mining*, 2016 <https://doi.org/doi:10.1596/978-1-4648-0800-5>

Eberhard, Anton, Orvika Rosnes, Maria Shkaratan, and Haakon Vennemo, *Africa's Power Infrastructure Investment, Integration, Efficiency Infrastructure* (Washington DC: The International Bank for Reconstruction and Development/The World Bank, 2011) <https://library.pppknowledgelab.org/PPIAF/documents/3135>

Eberhard, Anton, and Maria Shkaratan, 'Powering Africa: Meeting the Financing and Reform Challenges', *Energy Policy*, 42 (2012), 9–18 <https://doi.org/10.1016/j.enpol.2011.10.033>

Energy Information Administration, *International Energy Outlook* (Washington D.C., 2010)

Erica S. Downs, 'The Fact and Fiction of Sino-African Energy Relations', *China Security*, 3 (2007), 42–68 <https://www.brookings.edu/wp-content/uploads/2016/06/downs20070913.pdf>

Falola, Toyin, and Jessica Achberger, *The Political Economy of Development and Underdevelopment in Africa*, ed. by Toyin Falola and Jessica Achberger (Oxford and New York: Routledge, 2013)

Folke, Carl, Thomas Hahn, Per Olsson, and Jon Norberg, 'Adaptive Governance of Social-Ecological Systems', *Annu. Rev. Environ. Resour.*, 30 (2005), 441–473 <https://doi.org/doi: 10.1146/annurev.energy.30.050504.144511>

Folke, Carl, Lowell Pritchard, Fikret Berkes, Johan Colding, and Uno Svedin, 'The Problem of Fit between Ecosystems and Institutions: Ten Years Later', *Ecology and Society*, 12 (2007) <https://doi.org/10.5751/ES-02064-120130>

Frost & Sullivan, 'Digitization of Energy Transmission & Distribution in Africa', 2018 <http://www.geg,ridsolutions.com/press/gepress/2018/WP-Digitization.pdf >

Galaz, Victor, Beatrice Crona, Henrik Österblom, Per Olsson, and Carl Folke, 'Polycentric Systems and Interacting Planetary Boundaries – Emerging Governance of Climate Change-Ocean Acidification-Marine Biodiversity', *Ecological Economics*, 81 (2012), 21–32 <https://doi.org/10.1016/j.ecolecon.2011.11.012>

Gruby, Rebecca L., and Xavier Basurto, 'Multi-Level Governance for Large Marine Commons: Politics and Polycentricity in Palau's Protected Area Network', *Environmental Science and Policy*, 36 (2013), 48–60 <https://doi.org/10.1016/j.envsci.2013.08.001>

Herzberg, Roberta, 'Commentary on Richard Wagner's "Self-Governance, Polycentrism, and Federalism: Recurring Themes in Vincent Ostrom's Scholarly Oeuvre"', *Journal of Economic Behavior and Organization*, 57 (2005), 189–97 <https://doi.org/10.1016/j.jebo.2004.06.016>

Hooghe, Liesbet, and Gary Marks, 'Unraveling the Central States, but How? Types of Multi-Level Governance', *The American Political Science Review*, 97 (2003), 233–43 <https://doi.org/10.1017/S0003055403000649>

IEA, and World Bank, *Sustainable Energy for All 2015—Progress Toward Sustainable Energy (June)* (Washington DC: World Bank, 2015) <https://doi.org/10.1596/978-1-4648-0690-2>

Imperial, Mark T., 'Institutional Analysis and Ecosystem-Based Management: The Institutional Analysis and Development Framework', *Environmental Management*, 24 (1999), 449–65 <https://doi.org/DOI 10.1007/s002679900246>

International Energy Agency, *World Energy Outlook 2008* (Paris: International Energy Agency, 2008)

IPCC, *Renewable Energy Sources and Climate Change Mitigation: Special Report of the Intergovernmental Panel on Climate Change.:* (Cambridge, UK: Cambridge University Press, 2012)

IRENA, *Insights on Planning for Power System Regulators* (Abu Dhabi: International Renewable Energy Agency, 2018)

Kharecha, Pushker A., and James E. Hansen, 'Prevented Mortality and Greenhouse Gas Emissions from Historical and Projected Nuclear Power', *Environmental Science & Technology*, 47 (2013), 4889–95 <https://doi.org/10.1021/es3051197>

King, Charlotte, and Jon Marks, *European-West African Relations in the Field of Energy – Obstacles to a Sustainable Approach*, WAI-ZEI Paper (Bonn, 2014)

Klare, Michael T., *Rising Powers, Shrinking Planet: The New Geopolitics of Energy* (New York: Metropolitan Books, Henry Holt and Company, 2008)

Klare, Michael, and Daniel Volman, 'The African "Oil Rush" and US National Security', *Third World Quarterly*, 27 (2006), 609–28 <https://doi.org/10.1080/01436590600720835>

Kurtz, Hilda E., 'Acknowledging the Racial State: An Agenda for Environmental Justice Research', *Antipode*, 41 (2009), 684–704 <https://doi.org/10.1111/j.1467-8330.2009.00694.x>

Lebel, Louis, John M. Anderies, Bruce Campbell, Carl Folke, Steve Hatfield-Dodds, Terry P. Hughes, and others, 'Governance and the Capacity to Manage Resilience in Regional Social-Ecological Systems', *Ecology and Society*, 11 (2006) <https://doi.org/10.5751/ES-01606-110119>

Low, Bobbi, Elinor Ostrom, Carl Simon, and James Wilson, 'Redundancy and Diversity: Do They Influence Optimal Management?', in *Navigating Social-Ecological Systems: Building Resilience for Complexity and Change*, ed. by Fikret Berkes, Johan Colding, and Carl Folke (Cambridge, UK: Cambridge University Press, 2003), pp. 83–111

Mahbubani, Kishore, 'Has the West Lost It?: A Provocation', London: Allen Lane, 2019

Maji, Ibrahim Kabiru, and Chindo Sulaiman, 'Renewable Energy Consumption and Economic Growth Nexus: A Fresh Evidence from West Africa', *Energy Reports*, 5 (2019), 384–92 <https://doi.org/10.1016/j.eg,yr.2019.03.005>

Markandya, Anil, and Paul Wilkinson, 'Electricity Generation and Health', *Lancet*, 370 (2007), 979–90 <https://doi.org/10.1016/S0140-6736(07)61253-7>

Marshall, Graham R, 'Polycentricity and Adaptive Governance', *Working Paper Presented at the 15th Biannual Inter- National Conference of the International Association for the Study of the Commons*, 2015, 1–19

Martinot, Eric, 'Grid Integration of Renewable Energy: Flexibility, Innovation, and Experience', *Annual Review of Environment and Resources*, 41 (2016), 223–51 <https://doi.org/10.1146/annurev-environ-110615-085725>

McGinnis, Michael D., 'Beyond Individualism and Spontaneity: Comments on Peter Boettke and Christopher Coyne', *Journal of Economic Behavior and Organization*, 57 (2005), 167–72 <https://doi.org/10.1016/j.jebo.2004.06.014>

———, 'Costs and Challenges of Polycentric Governance', *Workshop on Analyzing Problems of Polycentric Governance in the Growing EU*, 2005, 27 <http://www.indiana.edu/~workshop/papers/mcginnis_berlin.pdf>

———, 'Introduction', in *Polycentricity and Local Public Economies: Readings from the Workshop in Political Theory and Policy Analysis*, ed. by Michael D. McGinnis (Ann Arbor, MI: The University of Michigan Press, 1999), pp. 1–27

McGinnis, Michael D., and Elinor Ostrom, 'Public Administration and the Disciplines Reflections on Vincent Ostrom, Public Administration, and Polycentricity', *Public Administration Review*, 72 (2011), 15–25 <https://doi.org/10.111/j.1540-6210.2011.02488.x>

Mikenga, Samuel, 'Liberian President Sirleaf Launches AfDB-Funded Power Grid Project to Supply Electricity to Mano River Union Nations', 2017 <https://www.afdb.org/en/news-and-events/liberian-president-sirleaf-launches-afdb-funded-power-grid-project-to-supply-electricity-to-mano-river-union-nations-17140> [accessed 5 July 2018]

Miller, Clark A., Jennifer Richter, and Jason O'Leary, 'Socio-Energy Systems Design: A Policy Framework for Energy Transitions', *Energy Research & Social Science*, 6 (2015), 29–40 <https://doi.org/10.1016/j.erss.2014.11.004>

Neville, Kate J, Jennifer Baka, Shanti Gamper-Rabindran, Karen Bakker, Stefan Andreasson, Avner Vengosh, and others, 'Debating Unconventional Energy: Social, Political, and Economic Implications', *Annual Review of Environment and Resources*, 42 (2017) <https://doi.org/10.1146/annurev-environ>

NRECA International, 'Partnerships Bring Power to Liberia', 2018 <http://www.nrecainternational.coop/where-we-work/liberia/> [accessed 10 July 2018]

Omorogbe, Yinka, 'Regional and National Frameworks for Energy Security in Africa', in *Energy Security: Managing Risk in a Dynamic Legal and Regulatory Environment*, ed. by Barry Barton, Catherine Redgewell, Anita Rønne, and Donald N. Zillman (Oxford: Oxford University Press, 2004)

Orlandi, Itamar, Nico Tyabji, Jenny Chase, Michael Wilshire, and Ben Vickers, *Off-Grid Solar Market Trends Report 2016* (Bloomberg New Energy Finance and Lighting Global, An innovation of the World Bank Group Inc, 2016) <https://doi.org/10.1017/CBO9781107415324.004>

Ostrom, Elinor, 'Coping With Tragedies of the Commons', *Annual Review of Political Science*, 2 (1999), 493–535 <https://doi.org/10.1146/annurev.polisci.2.1.493>

———, 'Polycentric Systems for Coping with Collective Action and Global Environmental Change', *Global Environmental Change*, 2010 <https://doi.org/10.1016/j.gloenvcha.2010.07.004>

Ostrom, Vincent, *The Meaning of American Federalism* (San Francisco: Institute of Contemporary Studies Press, 1991)

Ostrom, Vincent, Charles M. Tiebout, and Robert Warren, 'The Organization of Government in Metropolitan Areas: A Theoretical Inquiry', *American Political Science Review*, 55 (1961), 831–42 <https://doi.org/10.1017/S0003055400125973>

Pahl-Wostl, Claudia, 'A Conceptual Framework for Analysing Adaptive Capacity and Multi-Level Learning Processes in Resource Governance Regimes', *Global Environmental Change*, 19 (2009), 354–65 <https://doi.org/10.1016/j.gloenvcha.2009.06.001>

Pahl-Wostl, Claudia, and Christian Knieper, 'The Capacity of Water Governance to Deal with the Climate Change Adaptation Challenge: Using Fuzzy Set Qualitative Comparative Analysis to Distinguish between Polycentric, Fragmented and Centralized Regimes', *Global Environmental Change*, 29 (2014), 139–54 <https://doi.org/10.1016/j.gloenvcha.2014.09.003>

Poteete, Amy R., and Elinor Ostrom, 'Heterogeneity, Group Size and Collective Action: The Role of Institutions in Forest Management', *Development and Change*, 35 (2004), 435–461

Practical Action, *Poor People's Energy Outlook 2014: Key Messages on Energy for Poverty Alleviation* (Rugby, UK: Practical Action Publishing, 2014)

Quitzow, Rainer, Sonja Thielges, Andreas Goldthau, Sebastian Helgenberger, and Grace Mbungu, *Advancing a Global Transition to Clean Energy-the Role of International Cooperation*, Economics Discussion Papers (Kiel, 2019) <http://www.economics-ejournal.org/economics/discussionpapers/2019-37> [accessed 9 June 2019]

Ritchie, Hannah, 'What Are the Safest Sources of Energy?' (Oxford: Oxford University Press, 2020) <https://ourworldindata.org/safest-sources-of-energy>

Ryan, Sarah E., 'Rethinking Gender and Identity in Energy Studies', *Energy Research and Social Science*, 1 (2014), 96–105 <https://doi.org/10.1016/j.erss.2014.02.008>

Schlosberg, David, *Defining Environmental Justice: Theories, Movements, and Nature* (Oxford, New York: Oxford University Press, 2007)

SEforALL, 'Integrated Electrification Pathways for Universal Access to Electricity: A Primer' (Vienna and Washington D.C: SEforALL, 2019)

da Silveira, André R., and Keith S. Richards, 'The Link Between Polycentrism and Adaptive Capacity in River Basin Governance Systems: Insights from the River Rhine and the Zhujiang (Pearl River) Basin', *Annals of the Association of American Geographers*, 103 (2013), 319–29 <https://doi.org/10.1080/00045608.2013.754687>

Skelcher, Chris, 'Jurisdictional Integrity, Polycentrism, and the Design of Democratic Governance', *Governance*, 18 (2005), 89–110 <https://doi.org/10.1111/j.1468-0491.2004.00267.x>

Sovacool, Benjamin K., 'Energy Policy and Cooperation in Southeast Asia: The History, Challenges, and Implications of the Trans-ASEAN Gas Pipeline (TAGP) Network', *Energy Policy*, 37 (2009), 2356–67 <https://doi.org/10.1016/j.enpol.2009.02.014>

Sovacool, Benjamin K, 'An International Comparison of Four Polycentric Approaches to Climate and Energy Governance', *Energy Policy*, 39 (2011), 3832–44 <https://doi.org/10.1016/j.enpol.2011.04.014>

Tagliapietra, Simone, *Electrifying Africa: How to Make Europe's Contribution Count*, *Bruegel Policy Contribution*, Bruegel Policy Contribution (Brussels, 2017) <https://ideas.repec.org/p/bre/polcon/20882.html>

Tagliapietra, Simone, and Morgan Bazilian, 'The Role of International Institutions in Fostering Sub-Saharan Africa's Electrification', *The Electricity Journal*, 32 (2019), 13–20 <https://doi.org/10.1016/j.tej.2019.01.016>

Tenenbaum, Bernard, Chris Greacen, Tilak Siyambalapitiya, and James Knuckles, *From the Bottom Up: How Small Power Producers and Mini-Grids Can Deliver Electrification and Renewable Energy in Africa*, *Directions in Development* (Washington, DC: World Bank, 2014) <https://doi.org/doi: 10.1596/978–1–4648–0093–1>

The Infrastructure Consortium for Africa, 'Energy Financing Trends – ICA', 2018 <https://www.icafrica.org/en/topics-programmes/energy/energy-financing-trends/> [accessed 10 July 2018]

Trimble, Chris, Masami Kojima, Ines Perez-Arroyo, and Farah Mohammadzadeh, 'Financial Viability of Electricity Sectors in Sub-Saharan Africa. Quasi-Fiscal Deficits and Hidden Costs', *Policy Research Working Paper 7788. World Bank*, 2016 <https://openknowledge.worldbank.org/handle/10986/24869>

U.S. Energy Information Administration (EIA), 'The United States Is Projected to Become a Net Energy Exporter in Most AEO2018 Cases', *Today in Energy*, 2018 <https://www.eia.gov/todayinenergy/detail.php?id=34912> [accessed 10 July 2018]

Wagner, Richard E., 'Self-Governance, Polycentrism, and Federalism: Recurring Themes in Vincent Ostrom's Scholarly Oeuvre', *Journal of Economic Behavior and Organization*, 57 (2005), 173–88 <https://doi.org/10.1016/j.jebo.2004.06.015>

West African Gas Pipeline Authority, 'WAGPA | West African Gas Pipeline Authority', 2018 <http://www.wagpa.org/about-us/> [accessed 10 October 2018]

WikiLeaks, '2008 Leaked US Cable : Ambassador Encourages Oil Companies to Broaden Their Political Base. 09LAGOS155' (WikiLeaks, 2008)

World Economic Forum, 'Powering Africa', *Davos 2017*, 2017 <https://www.youtube.com/watch?v=W2fnEYtW-ig> [accessed 10 July 2018]

Yates, Douglas A., *The Rentier State in Africa: Oil Rent Dependency and Neocolonialism in the Republic of Gabon* (Trenton, NJ: Africa World Press, 1996)

Zondi, Siphamandla, Alastair Fraser, Donna Lee, Jean-Christophe Hoste, and Hilary Benn, 'Emerging Agents of Change? Africa and International Negotiations' (London: Chatham House, 2011), p. 12 <http://www.chathamhouse.org/sites/default/files/public/Research/Africa/020211summary.pdf>

Chapter 7

Andrews-Speed, Philip, *The Governance of Energy in China: Transition to a Low-Carbon Economy*, 1st edn (Basingstoke: Palgrave Macmillan, 2012) <https://doi.org/10.1057/9781137284037>

Chan, Sander, and Pieter Pauw, *Proposal for a Global Framework for Climate Action to Engage Non-State and Subnational Stakeholders in the Future Climate Regime*, Briefing Paper (Bonn, 2014)

McGinnis, Michael Dean, 'An Introduction to IAD and the Language of the Ostrom Workshop: A Simple Guide to a Complex Framework for the Analysis of Institutions and Their Development', *Policy Studies Journal*, 39 (2011), 169–83 <https://doi.org/http://dx.doi.org/10.1111/j.1541-0072.2010.00401.x>

Opschoor, Johannes Baptist, 'Knowledge Sharing in Support of Human Development', in *Globalization, Poverty and Conflict: A Critical Development Reader*, ed. by Max Spoor (Dordrecht: Kluwer Academic Press, 2004), pp. 307–22

Ostrom, Elinor, 'Beyond Markets and States : Polycentric Governance of Complex Economic Systems', *American Economic Review*, 100 (2010), 408–44 <https://doi.org/10.1080/19186444.2010.11658229>

———, 'Do Institutions for Collective Action Evolve?', *Journal of Bioeconomics*, 16 (2014), 3–30 <https://doi.org/10.1007/s10818-013-9154-8>

———, *Governing the Commons – The Evolution of Institutions for Collective Action* (Cambridge: Cambridge University Press, 1990) <https://doi.org/10.1017/CBO9780511807763>

———, *Polycentric Systems as One Approach for Solving Collective – Action Problems*, Working Paper (Bloomington,IN, 2008)

———, *Understanding Institutional Diversity*, *Public Choice*, 2005, CXXXII <https://doi.org/10.1007/s11127-007-9157-x>

Pattberg, Philipp, and Oscar Widerberg, 'Transnational Multistakeholder Partnerships for Sustainable Development: Conditions for Success', *Ambio*, 45 (2016), 42–51 <https://doi.org/10.1007/s13280-015-0684-2>

Salter, Alexander William, and Vlad Tarko, 'Governing the Banking System: An Assessment of Resilience Based on Elinor Ostrom's Design Principles', *Journal of Institutional Economics*, 15 (2019), 505–19 <https://doi.org/10.1017/S1744137418000401>

———, 'Polycentric Banking and Macroeconomic Stability', *Business and Politics*, 19 (2017), 365–95 <https://doi.org/10.1017/bap.2016.10>

Wilson, David Sloan, Elinor Ostrom, and Michael E. Cox, 'Generalizing the Core Design Principles for the Efficacy of Groups', *Journal of Economic Behavior and Organization*, 90 (2013), S21–32 <https://doi.org/10.1016/j.jebo.2012.12.010>